Objective Biology for NEET

Volume 2

Board of Editors

Universities Press

All rights reserved. No part of this book may be modified, reproduced or utilised in any form, or by any means, electronic or mechanical, including photocopying, recording or by any information storage and retrieval system, in any form of binding or cover other than in which it is published, without permission in writing from the publisher.

OBJECTIVE BIOLOGY FOR NEET, VOLUME 2

UNIVERSITIES PRESS (INDIA) PRIVATE LIMITED

Registered Office
3-6-747/1/A & 3-6-754/1, Himayatnagar, Hyderabad 500 029, Telangana, India
info@universitiespress.com; www.universitiespress.com

Distributed by
Orient Blackswan Private Limited

Registered Office
3-6-752 Himayatnagar, Hyderabad 500 029 Telangana, India

Other Offices
Bengaluru / Chennai / Guwahati / Hyderabad / Kolkata
Lucknow / Mumbai / New Delhi / Noida / Patna / Visakhapatnam

© Universities Press (India) Private Limited 2022
Reprinted 2022

Cover and book design:
© Universities Press (India) Private Limited 2022

ISBN 978-93-89211-71-9

501836

Typeset in Times Ten LT Std 10 points *by*
Cameo Corporate Services Limited, Coimbatore

Printed in India by
Navya Printers, Hyderabad 500 013

Published by
Universities Press (India) Private Limited
3-6-747/1/A & 3-6-754/1, Himayatnagar, Hyderabad 500 029, Telangana, India

Care has been taken to confirm the accuracy of the information presented in this book. The publisher, however, cannot accept any responsibility for errors or omissions or for consequences from the application of the information in this book, and makes no warranty, express or implied, with respect to its contents.

Preface

Objective Biology for NEET, Volumes 1 and 2 are primarily aimed at guiding students who aspire to gain admission to Medical or Dental colleges by boosting their score to a competitive level, thereby enabling them to achieve success in the NEET exam.

The book provides exhaustive coverage of the National Council of Educational Research and Training (NCERT) syllabus using a topic-wise approach. Volume 1 deals with the Class 11 syllabus, while Volume 2 covers the topics studied in Class 12.

More than 5450 exercise questions, comprising multiple choice, true/false, fill in the blank, match the following and diagram-oriented questions, have been presented. About 570 NCERT Exemplar questions have been included for a quick review of concepts. The practice test papers, comprising more than 1750 questions, can be used for self-evaluation and thorough revision. Solutions to all questions have been provided to resolve doubts and improve clarity of understanding in students.

This book has been framed by incorporating the current trends followed in NEET. We hope that students will find the study material useful.

Board of Editors

Contents

Reproduction in Organisms

EXERCISES

Asexual Reproduction

1. Exogenous budding is seen in:
(a) *Hydra* (b) *Obelia*
(c) *Spongilla* (d) Both (a) and (b)

2. Which of the following does not reproduce by multiple fission?
(a) *Amoeba* (b) *Plasmodium*
(c) *Monocystis* (d) *Paramecium*

3. Asexual reproduction is not seen in:
(a) *Planaria* (b) *Sycon*
(c) *Hydra* (d) *Pheretima*

4. Which of the following is a disadvantage of asexual methods of reproduction?
(a) It is a rapid mode of reproduction
(b) It helps in retaining the characters
(c) It is uniparental
(d) It has no role in evolution

5. In response to unfavourable living conditions, *Amoeba:*
(a) Divides by binary fission
(b) Reproduces by budding
(c) Withdraws pseudopodia and creates a three-layered cyst around itself
(d) Breaks into fragments

6. Find the odd one out with respect to functions of reproduction:
(a) It replaces members of the population that die due to ageing
(b) It maintains continuity of species
(c) It introduces variation
(d) It makes the individuals immortal

7. Select the incorrect statement:
(a) The average lifespan refers to the average number of years survived or age reached by the members of a population
(b) Asexual reproduction is also called agamogony
(c) In rotifers and rock lizard, only females are produced by parthenogenesis
(d) The maximum lifespan of a crow is 60 years

8. The end of the juvenile phase marks the beginning of:
(a) Senescence
(b) Ageing
(c) Reproductive phase
(d) Vegetative phase

9. ______ organisms reproduce only once in their lifetime:
(a) Semelparous (b) Iteroparous
(c) Perennial (d) Both (b) and (c)

10. Transverse binary fission is seen in:
(a) *Paramecium* (b) *Planaria*
(c) Diatoms (d) All of the above

11. The type of parthenogenesis in which only males are produced from unfertilised eggs is called:
(a) Arrhenotoky (b) Thelytoky
(c) Amphitoky (d) Sporogony

12. Select the incorrect statement:
(a) Exogenous budding is seen in certain annelids (*Syllis*) and urochordates
(b) Fragmentation is seen in sponges and some coelenterates
(c) Regeneration ability is marked in *Hydra* and *Planaria*
(d) Sexual reproduction can occur without the involvement of gamete fusion

13. Which of the following is incorrect with respect to multiple fission?
(a) It produces a number of daughter individuals
(b) It is seen in *Plasmodium* under favourable conditions and in *Amoeba* in unfavourable conditions

(c) The nucleus of the parent organism divides only once
(d) None of the above

14. The lifespan of parrot is:
(a) 25 years (b) 50 years
(c) 140 years (d) 7–8 years

15. Meiosis takes place in:
(a) Gemmule (b) Conidia
(c) Megaspore (d) Meiocyte

16. The type of asexual reproduction seen in:
(a) *Planaria* is binary fission
(b) *Hydra* is budding
(c) *Monocystis* is multiple fission
(d) All are correct

17. External syngamy occurs in the case of:
(a) Snakes (b) Birds
(c) Frog (d) Shark

18. Oestrous cycle consists of cyclic changes in the female reproductive system of:
(a) Monkeys (b) Apes
(c) Humans (d) Dogs

19. Which of the following is an incorrect statement?
(a) Animals performing external fertilisation produce large number of gametes
(b) Clones are genetically identical individuals obtained from asexual reproduction
(c) Most bisexual animals reproduce by cross-fertilisation
(d) Oviparous animals always lay fertilised eggs covered by hard calcareous shell

20. Mark the odd one out with respect to the disadvantages of external fertilisation:
(a) It occurs only in aquatic medium
(b) There is no protection to young ones
(c) A change factor is involved requiring synchronous release of gametes nearby and absence of turbulence of water
(d) The gametes and young ones are not vulnerable to predators

21. Sexual mode of reproduction is better than asexual methods because:
(a) It causes genetic variation
(b) It causes evolution
(c) It yields characters that are useful for survival under unfavourable conditions
(d) All of the above

22. An example of unicellular organism showing isogamy is:
(a) *Amoeba* (b) *Plasmodium*
(c) *Monocystis* (d) *Paramecium*

23. ________ is the phase of ageing when an organism loses its capacity of reproduction:
(a) Juvenile (b) Reproductive
(c) Senescent (d) Growth

24. The asexual method of reproduction in which division occurs in a multinucleate parent into many multinucleate daughter individuals without division of nuclei, is called:
(a) Multiple fission (b) Plasmotomy
(c) Binary fission (d) Budding

25. Select the incorrect statement:
(a) Oestrous cycle is characteristic of mammalian females other than primates
(b) Reproduction introduces variations essential for adaptability and struggle for existence
(c) Gemmule formation takes place only in marine sponges
(d) If a female gamete develops into a complete individual without fertilisation, it is called parthenogenesis

Introduction, Lifespan, Basic Features of Reproduction

26. The period from birth to the natural death of an organism represents its:
(a) Lifespan (b) Life cycle
(c) Life expectancy (d) All of the above

27. The lifespan of an organism:
(a) May be too short
(b) Is not a specific trait
(c) Usually depends upon its body size
(d) Both (a) and (b)

28. Select the incorrect match with respect to lifespan:

Organism	Lifespan
(a) Crow	15 years
(b) Parrot	140 years
(c) Butterfly	1–2 months
(d) Tortoise	100–150 years

29. Reproduction is defined as a:
(a) Biological process
(b) Cellular process
(c) Physiological process
(d) All of the above

30. There is great diversity in the mode of reproduction. This diverse mode of reproduction depends upon:
A. Internal physiology
B. Habitat

C. External factors
(a) Only A (b) Only C
(c) Only B and C (d) A, B and C

31. Read the following statements and select the correct option:
A. A mango tree has a longer lifespan as compared to the peepal tree
B. No individual is immortal, except single-celled organisms
C. Reproduction enables continuity of the species, generation after generation
(a) A and B are correct
(b) B and C are correct
(c) A and C are correct
(d) A, B and C are correct

32. In asexual reproduction:
(a) There is no need to search for a mate
(b) Offspring are produced by a single parent of any sex
(c) Genetically identical population is produced
(d) All of the above

33. Select the incorrect statement for asexual reproduction:
(a) Offspring are likely to be genetically identical
(b) It is common among unicellular organisms
(c) Never involves gamete formation and fusion
(d) New individuals are formed even from vegetative cells

34. Asexual reproduction is seen in:
(a) Single-celled organisms
(b) Multicellular organisms
(c) Organisms having simple organisation
(d) All of the above

35. Match the columns and select the correct option:

Column I	Column II
A. Rhizome	(i) Potato
B. Tuber	(ii) Ginger
C. Corm	(iii) Onion
D. Bulb	(iv) *Colocasia*

(a) A – (ii), B – (iv), C – (i), D – (iii)
(b) A – (ii), B – (i), C – (iv), D – (iii)
(c) A – (iii), B – (iv), C – (i), D – (ii)
(d) A – (ii), B – (iii), C – (iv), D – (i)

36. Cell division is itself a mode of reproduction in:
(a) *Chlamydomonas*, *Penicillium*
(b) *Amoeba*, *Drosophila*
(c) *Neurospora*, *Drosophila*
(d) *Amoeba*, *Paramecium*

37. A population of genetically identical individuals obtained from asexual reproduction is called:
(a) Clone (b) Deme
(c) Callus (d) Aggregate

38. Cell division is itself a mode of reproduction in members of:
(a) Social insects
(b) Fungi
(c) Monera and Protista
(d) Monera only

39. Asexual reproduction:
(a) Has evolutionary significance
(b) Can never be observed in multicellular individuals
(c) Is a simple and quick method of multiplication
(d) All of the above

40. Identify the method of asexual reproduction shown in the diagram below:

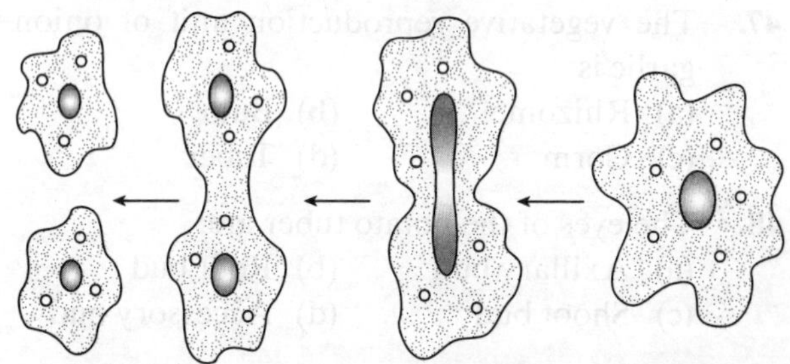

(a) Fragmentation (b) Binary fission
(c) Budding (d) Gemmule formation

41. The phenomenon in which *Amoeba* forms a cyst around itself in unfavourable conditions is called:
(a) Sporulation
(b) Encystation
(c) Gemmule formation
(d) Both (a) and (c)

42. Identify the type of asexual reproduction shown in the diagram below:

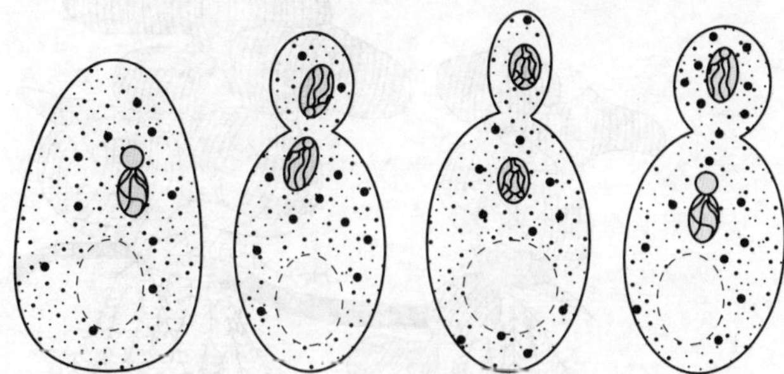

(a) Binary fission (b) Budding
(c) Regeneration (d) Fragmentation

43. The most common asexual reproduction structure of algae and fungi are, respectively:
(a) Zoospores and conidia

(b) Conidia and zoospores
(c) Akinetes and chlamydospores
(d) Aplanospores and zoospores

44. Asexual spore structure in *Penicillium* is:
(a) Zoospores (b) Gemmules
(c) Conidia (d) Buds

45. In *Penicillium*, conidia production is:
(a) Acropetal and Endogenous
(b) Basipetal and Exogenous
(c) Acropetal and Exogenous
(d) Basipetal and Endogenous

46. Complete the given analogy:
Budding: Yeast :: __________ : *Chlamydomonas*
(a) Zoospores (b) Conidia
(c) Buds (d) Gemmae

47. The vegetative reproduction unit of onion and garlic is:
(a) Rhizome (b) Bulb
(c) Corm (d) Tuber

48. The eyes of the potato tuber are:
(a) Axillary bud (b) Root bud
(c) Shoot bud (d) Accessory bud

49. In *Marchantia*, vegetative propagation occurs through:
(a) Rhizome (b) Gemmae
(c) Bulbil (d) Turions

50. Foliar buds can give rise to new plants in:
(a) *Bryophyllum* (b) *Kalanchoe*
(c) *Agave* (d) Both (a) and (b)

51. The given vegetative propagate marked by A and B is:

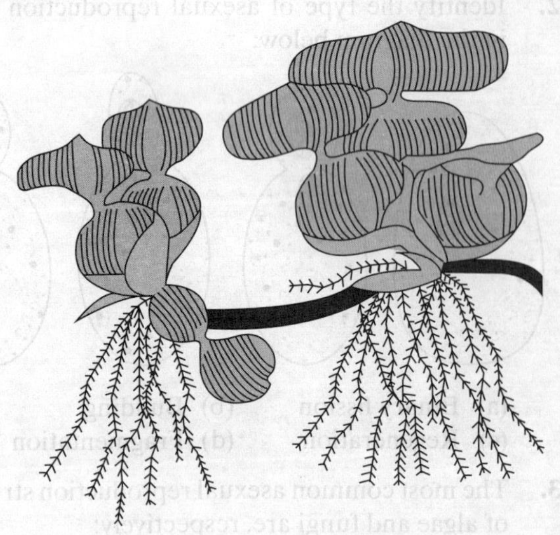
A

B

	A	B
(a)	Offset	Bubil
(b)	Bulbil	Offset
(c)	Offset	Bulb
(d)	Offset	Sucker

52. Select the mismatched pair:
(a) Terror of Bengal - *Eichhornia*
(b) Sucker - Pineapple
(c) Bulbil - *Agave*
(d) Stolen - Banana

53. *Eichhornia* is also known as Terror of Bengal because it:
(a) Drains oxygen from stagnant water bodies
(b) Releases toxins
(c) Leads to death of fishes
(d) All of the above

54. Transverse binary fission has been observed in all of the following, except:
(a) Bacteria (b) *Paramecium*
(c) Diatoms (d) *Euglena*

55. Which of the following is not a vegetative propagate?
(a) Bud (b) Bulbil
(c) Gemmule (d) Nucule

56. In the life cycle of any organism, there is a cycle of:
(a) Birth, growth and death
(b) Birth reproduction and senescence
(c) Juvenile, reproduction and senescence
(d) Pre-fertilisation, fertilisation and post-fertilisation

57. In the given diagrams of potato and *Bryophyllum* leaf, identify the correct labels:

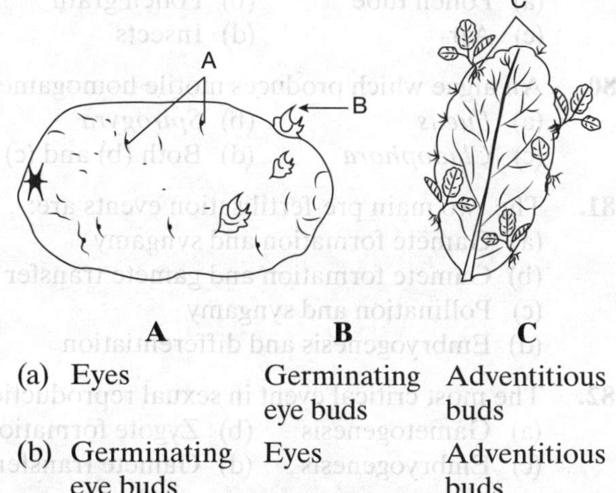

	A	B	C
(a)	Eyes	Germinating eye buds	Adventitious buds
(b)	Germinating eye buds	Eyes	Adventitious buds
(c)	Eyes	Shoot buds	Foliar buds
(d)	Eyes	Accessory buds	Axillary buds

58. Vegetative propagation is a type of asexual reproduction commonly seen in:
(a) Protist (b) Animals
(c) Monerans (d) Plants

59. Encystation is:
(a) Formation of hard covering around itself in *Amoeba*
(b) Formation of special kind of spores in fungi
(c) Formation of spores in *Marchantia*
(d) A method of sexual reproduction in *Amoeba*

60. *Chlamydomonas* shows asexual method of reproduction in favourable conditions by:
(a) Conidia (b) Aplanospore
(c) Zoospores (d) Binary fission

Sexual Reproduction (Phases in Life Cycle, Events in Sexual Reproduction, Pre-fertilisation Events, Gametogenesis and Gamete Transfer)

61. Read the following statements with respect to sexual reproduction:
A. It involves formation and fusion of male and female gametes
B. It results in offspring that are not identical to parents
(a) Only A is correct
(b) Only B and C are correct
(c) Only A and B are correct
(d) A, B and C are correct

62. Which of the following creates new genetic combinations leading to variation?
(a) Vegetative propagation
(b) Sexual reproduction
(c) Tissue culture
(d) Parthenogenesis

63. As compared to asexual reproduction, sexual reproduction is:
(a) Complex, elaborate and slow process
(b) Simple and quick
(c) Simple, elaborate and fast process
(d) Complex, elaborate and fast process

64. Sexual reproduction is different from asexual reproduction in having:
(a) Only one parent
(b) Quick method of multiplication
(c) Gametogenesis
(d) Introduction of genetic variation in a population

65. Interaction of which of the following factors regulates the reproductive process and the associated behavioural expression of the organism?
A. PGR
B. Environmental factors
C. Photosynthetic efficiency
D. Morphology of organism
(a) Only A (b) A, B and C
(c) A and B (d) A, B, C and D

66. Before all organisms can reproduce sexually, they have to reach a stage of growth and maturity. This period of growth is called:
(a) Juvenile phase
(b) Vegetative phase
(c) Reproduction phase
(d) Both (a) and (b)

67. Sexual reproduction is favoured under adverse conditions in:
(a) Higher animals (b) Algae and fungi
(c) Higher plants (d) Flowering plants

68. Clear-cut distinction between all the three phases of the life cycle is absent in:
(a) Annuals
(b) Biennials
(c) Monocarpic plants
(d) Polycarpic plants

69. Which pair of terms means the same?
(a) Homothallic and Monoecious
(b) Heterothallic and Monoecious
(c) Homothallic and Dioecious
(d) Heterothallic and Bisexual

70. Find the odd one out with respect to sexuality:
(a) Cucurbits (b) Date palm
(c) Coconut (d) Maize

71. A perennial plant which bears flowers throughout the year is:
(a) Apple (b) China rose
(c) Mango (d) Orange

72. Complete the given analogy:
Dioecious plant: Date palm :: Monoecious plant: ________
(a) Mulberry (b) Papaya
(c) *Cucurbita* (d) Both (a) and (b)

73. Read the following events:
A. Bringing of male and female gametes together
B. Gametogenesis
C. Formation of seed and fruit
D. Syngamy
Arrange the given events according to their sequence during sexual reproduction:
(a) A, B, D, C (b) B, A, C, D
(c) A, B, C, D (d) B, A, D, C

74. Papaya and date palm belong to which of the following categories?
(a) Monocarpic and perennial
(b) Polycarpic and monoecious
(c) Polycarpic and dioecious
(d) Monocarpic and monoecious

75. Inter-flowering period of polycarpic plants is:
(a) Juvenile phase
(b) Recovery phase as a part of juvenile phase
(c) Recovery phase as a part of maturity phase
(d) Vegetative phase

76. In plants, transition between juvenile, mature and senescent phases is carried out by:
(a) Light (b) Minerals
(c) Temperature (d) Plant hormones

77. The chromosome number in meiocyte is 12. The organism could be:
(a) Housefly (b) Butterfly
(c) Fruit fly (d) Mayfly

78. Consider the following statements and select the option that correctly fills in the blank:
(i) A diploid parent produces ____**A**____ gametes by ____**B**____ division
(ii) A haploid parent produces ____**C**____ gametes by ____**D**____ division

	A	B	C	D
(a)	Haploid	Meiotic	Haploid	Mitotic
(b)	Diploid	Mitotic	Haploid	Meiotic
(c)	Haploid	Mitotic	Haploid	Mitotic
(d)	Diploid	Meiotic	Diploid	Mitotic

79. In seeded plants, ________ are the carrier of male gametes, at the time of pollination:
(a) Pollen tube (b) Pollen grain
(c) Air (d) Insects

80. An algae which produces motile homogametes is:
(a) *Fucus* (b) *Spirogyra*
(c) *Cladophora* (d) Both (b) and (c)

81. The two main pre-fertilisation events are:
(a) Gamete formation and syngamy
(b) Gamete formation and gamete transfer
(c) Pollination and syngamy
(d) Embryogenesis and differentiation

82. The most critical event in sexual reproduction is:
(a) Gametogenesis (b) Zygote formation
(c) Embryogenesis (d) Gamete transfer

83. Match Column I and Column II and choose the correct option:

Column I (Organism)	Column II (Chromosome in gamete)
A. Potato	(i) 8
B. Onion	(ii) 630
C. Rice	(iii) 24
D. *Ophioglossum*	(iv) 12

(a) A – (iii), B – (a), C – (iv), D – (ii)
(b) A – (ii), B – (iii), C – (iv), D – (i)
(c) A – (i), B – (ii), C – (iii), D – (iv)
(d) A – (iv), B – (iii), C – (iv), D – (ii)

84. In a majority of organisms:
(a) Male gamete is motile and female gamete is non-motile
(b) Male gamete is non-motile and female gamete is motile
(c) Both male and female gametes are non-motile
(d) Both male and female gametes are motile

85. Select the odd one out with respect to plant groups that use water as a medium for male gamete transfer:
(a) Algae (b) Bryophytes
(c) Pteridophytes (d) Spermatophytes

86. Consider the following statements and select the option that correctly fills in the blanks:
A. China rose plant bears ____**A**____ flowers
B. *Marchantia* is a ____**B**____ bryophyte
C. *Chara* is a ____**C**____ green algae

	A	B	C
(a)	Bisexual	Dioecious	Monoecious
(b)	Bisexual	Monoecious	Dioecious
(c)	Unisexual	Monoecious	Dioecious
(d)	Unisexual	Dioecious	Monoecious

87. Number of chromosomes in meiocyte of maize and rice, respectively:

(a) 20, 34 (b) 40, 48
(c) 20, 24 (d) 24, 20

88. Meiocytes are:
(a) Mostly haploid cells
(b) Result of meiotic cell division during gametogenesis
(c) Cells which show equational division during gamete formation
(d) Cells which undergo meiotic division during gamete formation

89. Read the following statements with respect to the given diagram:

(a) Member of class Chlorophyceae
(b) Monoecious plant body
(c) Sex organs are multicellular and jacketed
(d) Nucule occupies upper position relative to the globule
(e) Produce both motile male and female gametes
(f) Show external fertilisation
How many of the above statements are true?
(a) Three (b) Four
(c) Five (d) Two

90. When did *Strobilanthus kunthiana* flower the last time?
(a) Sep–Oct 2008 (b) Sep–Oct 2006
(c) Sep–Oct 2018 (d) Sep–Oct 2012

91. Select the correct statements with respect to monocarpic plants:
(a) These plants produce single fruit every year
(b) Recovery phase is prominent in these plants
(c) There is no clear-cut distinction of vegetative reproduction and senescent phase
(d) These plants flower only once in their life

92. Unisexual flower having only male part is called:
(a) Pistillate (b) Pedicellate
(c) Staminate (d) Homothallic

93. Male gamete requires water to reach the female gamete in:
(a) Algae (b) Bryophytes
(c) Pteridophytes (d) All of the above

94. Male and female sex organs are present on separate plant bodies in all, except:
(a) Papaya (b) Date palm
(c) *Chara* (d) *Marchantia*

95. The male and female sex organs of *Chara* are, respectively:
(a) Globule and nucule
(b) Nucule and globule
(c) Globule and archegonium
(d) Nucule and oogonium

96. Transfer of pollen grains to stigma is called:
(a) Translocation (b) Dispersal
(c) Fertilisation (d) Pollination

97. The perennial plant that flowers only once in its lifetime is:
(a) Bamboo (b) Maize
(c) Coconut (d) Apple

98. In how many of these flowering plants is the inter-flowering period present?
Apple, Wheat, Marigold, Mango, Rice, Jackfruit
(a) Three (b) Two
(c) One (d) Four

Fertilisation, Post-fertilisation Events, Zygote, Embryogenesis

99. Formation of the ________ is universal in all sexually reproducing organisms:
(a) Zygote (b) Embryo
(c) Seed (d) All of the above

100. Select the odd one out with respect to external fertilisation:
(a) Requires great synchrony between sexes
(b) Large number of gametes are released in a medium
(c) Offspring are safer
(d) Offspring are extremely vulnerable to predators

101. Identify the following statements as true (T) or false (F) and choose the option accordingly:
A. Zygote is always a diploid structure
B. Zygote is a vital link between two successive generations
C. In all the sexually reproducing organisms, zygote is the first cell of the new generation

	A	B	C
(a)	T	T	T
(b)	T	F	T
(c)	T	T	F
(d)	F	T	T

102. Choose the odd one out with respect to post-fertilisation events in the life cycle of a plant:
(a) Pollination (b) Embryogeny
(c) Fruit formation (d) Seed formation

103. In the majority of algae, syngamy takes place in:
(a) Water (b) Oogonium
(c) Archegonium (d) Soil

104. External fertilisation does not take place in:
(a) Fishes (b) Amphibians
(c) Bryophytes (d) Both (a) and (b)

105. Formation of zygote in angiosperms is the result of:
(a) Syngamy
(b) Gametogenesis
(c) Pseudo fertilisation
(d) Fusion of two haploid polar nuclei

106. In organisms with diplontic life cycle:
(a) Zygote divides by meiosis
(b) Gamete divides by meiosis
(c) Meiosis occurs before gamete formation
(d) Zygote act as meiocyte

107. First cell of sporophytic generation is:
(a) Gamete (b) Spore
(c) Zygote (d) Embryo

108. Which of the following is not a post-fertilisation event?
(a) Embryogenesis (b) Seed formation
(c) Gametogenesis (d) Fruit formation

109. Every sexually reproducing organism begins life as a:
(a) Embryo (b) Zygote
(c) Gamete (d) Spore

110. In organisms having haplontic life cycle, zygote divides by ___A___ to form ___B___ spores that grow into ___C___ individuals:

	A	B	C
(a)	Meiosis	Haploid	Haploid
(b)	Meiosis	Haploid	Diploid
(c)	Mitosis	Diploid	Diploid
(d)	Mitosis	Diploid	Haploid

111. During embryogenesis, zygote undergoes:
(a) Mitosis (b) Cell differentiation
(c) Meiosis (d) All except (c)

112. Read the following statements and select the correct option:
A. In algae and fungi, zygote develops a thick wall that is resistant to desiccation and damage
B. Inside the mature seed, the embryo is the progenitor of the next generation
(a) Only (A) is correct
(b) Only (B) is correct
(c) Both (A) and (B) are correct
(d) Both (A) and (B) are incorrect

113. Embryogenesis is absent in:
A. Algae
B. Bryophytes
C. Gymnosperms
D. Angiosperms
(a) Only (A) (b) Both (A) and (B)
(c) Only (B) (d) (A), (B) and (C)

114. Which floral part forms the pericarp after fertilisation?
(a) Outer integument (b) Inner integument
(c) Ovary wall (d) Testa

NCERT EXEMPLAR QUESTIONS

1. A few statements describing certain features of reproduction are given below:
   (i) Gametic fusion takes place
   (ii) Transfer of genetic material takes place
   (iii) Reduction division takes place
   (iv) Progeny have some resemblance to parents

   Select the options that are true for both asexual and sexual reproduction from the options given below:
   (a) (i) and (ii)
   (b) (ii) and (iii)
   (c) (ii) and (iv)
   (d) (i) and (iii)

2. The term 'clone' cannot be applied to offspring formed by sexual reproduction because:
   (a) Offspring do not possess exact copies of parental DNA
   (b) DNA of only one parent is copied and passed on to the offspring
   (c) Offspring are formed at different times
   (d) DNA of parent and offspring are completely different

3. Asexual method of reproduction by binary fission is common to which of the following?
   (i) Some eukaryotes
   (ii) All eukaryotes
   (iii) Some prokaryotes
   (iv) All prokaryotes

   Choose the correct option from the following:
   (a) (i) and (ii)
   (b) (ii) and (iii)
   (c) (i) and (iv)
   (d) (iii) and (iv)

4. A few statements with regard to sexual reproduction are given below:
   (i) Sexual reproduction does not always require two individuals
   (ii) Sexual reproduction generally involves gametic fusion
   (iii) Meiosis never occurs during sexual reproduction
   (iv) External fertilisation is a rule during sexual reproduction

   Choose the correct statements from the options below:
   (a) (i) and (iv)
   (b) (i) and (ii)
   (c) (ii) and (iii)
   (d) (i) and (iv)

5. A multicellular, filamentous alga exhibits a type of sexual life cycle in which meiotic division occurs after the formation of the zygote. The adult filament of this alga has:
   (a) Haploid vegetative cells and diploid gametangia
   (b) Diploid vegetative cells and diploid gametangia
   (c) Diploid vegetative cells and haploid gametangia
   (d) Haploid vegetative cells and haploid gametangia

6. The male gametes of the rice plant have 12 chromosomes in their nucleus. The chromosome number in the female gamete, zygote and cells of the seedling will be, respectively:
   (a) 12, 24, 12
   (b) 24, 12, 12
   (c) 12, 24, 24
   (d) 24, 12, 24

7. Given below are a few statements related to external fertilisation. Choose the correct statements:
   (i) The male and female gametes are formed and released simultaneously
   (ii) Only a few gametes are released into the medium
   (iii) Water is the medium in the majority of organisms exhibiting external fertilisation
   (iv) Offspring formed as a result of external fertilisation have better chance of survival than those formed inside an organism

   (a) (iii) and (iv)
   (b) (i) and (iii)
   (c) (ii) and (iv)
   (d) (i) and (iv)

8. The statements given below describe certain features that are observed in the pistil of flowers.
(i) Pistil may produce more than one seed
(ii) Each carpel may have more than one ovule
(iii) Each carpel has only one ovule
(iv) Pistil have only one carpel
Choose the statements that are true from the options below:
(a) (i) and (ii)
(b) (i) and (iii)
(c) (ii) and (iv)
(d) (iii) and (iv)

9. Which of the following situations correctly describe the similarity between an angiosperm egg and a human egg?
(i) Eggs of both are formed only once in a lifetime
(ii) Both the angiosperm egg and human egg are stationary
(iii) Both the angiosperm egg and human egg are mobile
(iv) Syngamy in both results in the formation of zygote
Choose the correct answer from the options given below:
(a) (ii) and (iv)
(b) (iv) only
(c) (iii) and (iv)
(d) (i) and (iv)

10. Appearance of vegetative propagules from the nodes of plants such as sugarcane and ginger is mainly because:
(a) Nodes are shorter than internodes
(b) Nodes have meristematic cells
(c) Nodes are located near the soil
(d) Nodes have non-photosynthetic cells

11. Which of the following statements support the view that elaborate sexual reproductive process appeared much later in organic evolution?
(i) Lower groups of organisms have simpler body design
(ii) Asexual reproduction is common in lower groups
(iii) Asexual reproduction is common in higher groups of organisms
(iv) The high incidence of sexual reproduction in angiosperms and vertebrates
Choose the correct answer from the options given below:
(a) (i), (ii) and (iii)
(b) (i), (iii) and (iv)
(c) (i), (ii) and (iv)
(d) (ii), (iii) and (iv)

12. Offspring formed by sexual reproduction exhibit more variation than those formed by asexual reproduction because:
(a) Sexual reproduction is a lengthy process
(b) Gametes of parents have qualitatively different genetic composition
(c) Genetic material comes from parents of two different species
(d) Greater amount of DNA is involved in sexual reproduction

13. Choose the correct statement from amongst the following:
(a) Dioecious (hermaphrodite) organisms are seen only in animals
(b) Dioecious organisms are seen only in plants
(c) Dioecious organisms are seen in both plants and animals
(d) Dioecious organisms are seen only in vertebrates

14. There is no natural death in single-celled organisms like *Amoeba* and bacteria because:
(a) They cannot reproduce sexually
(b) They reproduce by binary fission
(c) Parental body is distributed among the offspring
(d) They are microscopic

15. There are various types of reproduction. The type of reproduction adopted by an organism depends on:
(a) The habitat and morphology of the organism
(b) Morphology of the organism
(c) Morphology and physiology of the organism
(d) The organism's habitat, physiology and genetic makeup

16. Identify the incorrect statement:
(a) In asexual reproduction, the offspring produced are morphologically and genetically identical to the parent
(b) Zoospores are sexual reproductive structures

(c) In asexual reproduction, a single parent produces offspring with or without the formation of gametes
(d) Conidia are asexual structures in *Penicillium*

17. Which of the following is a post-fertilisation event in flowering plants?
(a) Transfer of pollen grains
(b) Embryo development
(c) Formation of flower
(d) Formation of pollen grains

18. The number of chromosomes in the shoot tip cells of a maize plant is 20. The number of chromosomes in the microspore mother cells of the same plant shall be:
(a) 20 (b) 10
(c) 40 (d) 15

PRACTICE TEST PAPER

1. Select the incorrect match:
(a) Sponge - Gemmule
(b) *Hydra* - Bud
(c) *Penicillium* - Endospore
(d) *Chlamydomonas* - Zoospore

2. Choose the odd one out with respect to monoecius plants:
(a) Cucumber (b) Maize
(c) Date palm (d) *Chara*

3. Which of the following can propagate by foliar bud:
(a) *Bryophyllum* (b) Water hyacinth
(c) *Agave* (d) *Dahlia*

4. Water hyacinth:
A. Is a fast growing aquatic weed
B. Is known as Terror of Bengal
C. Was introduced in India because of its beautiful flowers and shape of leaves
(a) Only (A)
(b) Only (A) and (B)
(c) Only (B) and (C)
(d) (A), (B) and (C)

5. What is the number of chromosomes in the meiocyte of rice, maize and onion, respectively:
(a) 24, 20, 16 (b) 48, 40, 32
(c) 12, 10, 8 (d) 20, 16, 24

6. Select the odd one out with respect to external fertilisation:
(a) Amphibians (b) Fishes
(c) Majority of algae (d) *Spirogyra*

7. Which of the following is a post-fertilisation event in plants:
(a) Transfer of pollen grain
(b) Pollen tube growth
(c) Embryo sac development
(d) Embryo development

8. Identify the vegetative propagate shown in the figure:

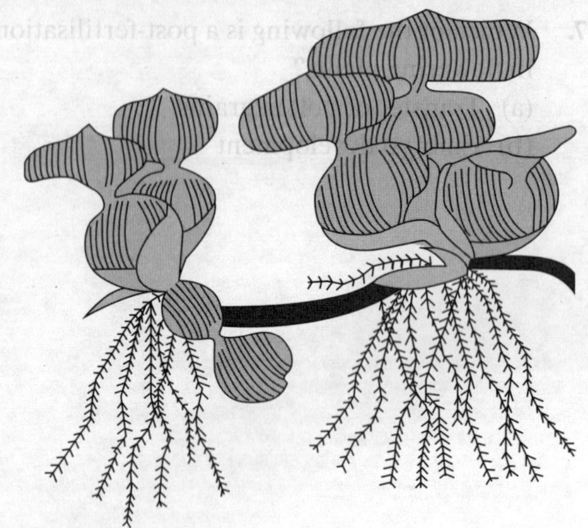

(a) Bulbil of *Agave*
(b) Offset of water hyacinth
(c) Rhizome of ginger
(d) Bulb of onion

9. Select the incorrect statement with respect to asexual reproduction:
(a) It is uniparental
(b) Individuals produced are genetically identical
(c) It is a complex and slow method of multiplication
(d) It can occur with or without gamete formation

10. In some organisms, the body breaks into distinct pieces and each piece grows into an adult capable of producing offspring. In which of the following organisms is such a phenomenon shown?
(a) *Paramecium* (b) *Hydra*
(c) *Chlamydomonas* (d) *Euglena*

11. Water hyacinth:
(a) Is an invasive aquatic weed
(b) Increases the amount of oxygen in water
(c) Grows in running water
(d) All except (c)

12. Isogametes are found in:
(a) *Fucus* (b) *Chara*
(c) *Cladophora* (d) *Marchantia*

13. After fertilisation, ovules develop into:
(a) Fruits (b) Seeds
(c) Embryos (d) Zygotes

14. All of the given plants are polycarpic, except:
(a) Apple (b) Mango
(c) Jackfruit (d) *Strobilanthes*

15. Asexual reproduction by means of conidia occurs in:
(a) *Hydra* (b) *Amoeba*
(c) *Chamydomonas* (d) *Penicillium*

16. Among the following, which organism is said to be immortal?
(a) Banyan tree (b) *Drosophila*
(c) Parrot (d) *Amoeba*

17. Identify the mismatched pair:

Organism	**Vegetative propagate**
(a) *Eichhornia*	Offset
(b) *Agave*	Bulbil
(c) Potato	Bulb
(d) Banana	Rhizome

18. Organisms exhibiting external fertilisation:
(a) Are mostly terrestrial plants
(b) Show synchrony in release of gametes
(c) Produce a small number of non-motile male gametes
(d) Both (b) and (c)

19. Select the incorrect match from the following:
(a) Antherozoid - Male gamete
(b) Monoecious plant - Unisexual flower
(c) Staminate - Sterile stamen
(d) Hetero gametes - Dissimilar in morphology

20. The perennial plant that flowers only once in its life time is:
(a) Maize (b) Bamboo
(c) Coconut (d) Apple

21. Curcubits and maize belong to which of the following categories?
(a) Monocarpic and annual
(b) Perennial and dioecious
(c) Monocarpic and perennial
(d) Polycarpic and monoecious

22. A group of morphologically and genetically similar individuals is called:
(a) Twins (b) Hybrid
(c) Clones (d) Ramet

23. Among the following
A. Gametogenesis
B. Gamete transfer
C. Growth of pollen tube
D. Syngamy
E. Embryogenesis
Select the correct option for pre-fertilisation events:
(a) (C), (D) and (E) (b) (A), (B), (C)
(c) (B), (C) and (D) (d) (A), (B) and (E)

24. In seeded plants, the non-motile male gametes are carried to the female gametes by:
(a) Pollen tubes (b) Water
(c) Air (d) All of the above

25. Inside the mature seed, the progenitor of the next generation is:
(a) Endosperm (b) Embryo sac
(c) Nucleus (d) Embryo

26. In unfavourable conditions, the encysted amoeba divides by multiple fission and produces pseudo-podiospores. The phenomenon is known as:
(a) Budding (b) Sporulation
(c) Fragmentation (d) Regeneration

27. Transverse binary fission occurs in:
(a) *Euglena* (b) *Amoeba*
(c) *Hydra* (d) *Paramecium*

28. Natural parthenogenesis occurs in:
(a) *Drosophila* (b) Housefly
(c) Honey bee (d) All of the above

29. Gametogenesis refers to the process of:
(a) Fusion of two gametes
(b) Formation of embryo
(c) Formation of two types of gametes
(d) Formation of male gametes only

30. Lifespan of crow is:
(a) 15 years (b) 50 years
(c) 25 years (d) 140 years

31. *Planaria* possesses high capacity for:
(a) Regeneration
(b) Metamorphosis
(c) Bioluminescence
(d) Alternation of generations

32. Identify the incorrect statement:
(a) Oestrous cycle is characteristic of mammalian females other than in primates
(b) Longitudinal binary fission is seen in *Euglena* and *Vorticella*
(c) External budding is seen in freshwater sponges like *Spongilla*
(d) *Amoeba* develops a tri-layered cyst wall during unfavourable conditions

33. Which of the following is the correct statement?
(a) Sexual reproduction in comparison to asexual method is a quick method of multiplication
(b) Asexual method produces genetic variability
(c) Sexual methods are always uniparental
(d) Sexual reproduction involves formation and fusion of gametes

34. Read the following statements:
(i) The daughter cells produced as a result of mitosis are clones
(ii) Clones are morphologically similar but genetically dissimilar
(iii) Asexual methods of reproduction are seen in animals, plants and prokaryotes
(iv) *Amoeba* reproduces by binary fission during unfavourable conditions
Which of the above statements are correct?
(a) (i) and (ii) (b) (ii) and (iii)
(c) (iii) and (iv) (d) (i) and (iii)

35. The plane of division during asexual method of reproduction is oblique in:
(a) *Plasmodium* (b) *Planaria*
(c) *Ceratium* (d) *Amoeba*

36. Which of the following is a pair of words with the same meaning?
(a) Bisexual, dioecious
(b) Dioecious, hermaphrodite
(c) Monoecious, unisexual
(d) Monoecious, hermaphrodite

37. The formation of organisms by asexual methods like budding or fragmentation is called:
(a) Fission (b) Blastogenesis
(c) Morphallaxis (d) Epimorphosis

38. Sexual method is the preferred method of reproduction in higher animals because:
(a) It is mostly biparental
(b) It does not create variation
(c) It enables continuity of species
(d) Genetic recombination takes place

39. The type of parthenogenesis in which females are formed from an unfertilised egg is called:
(a) Amphitoky (b) Thelytoky
(c) Arrhenotoky (d) Metagenesis

40. Sexual methods of reproduction are mostly biparental, but may be uniparental as is observed in:
(a) Roundworm (b) Tapeworm
(c) Housefly (d) Frog

41. Walking fern reproduces vegetatively in nature by:
(a) Axillary bud (b) Leaf bud
(c) Marginal bud (d) Shoot tip bud

42. In organisms with haplontic life cycle:
(a) Zygote divides by meiosis
(b) Gametes are formed by reductional division
(c) Zygote divides by mitosis
(d) Shows embryogeny

43. The terms homothallic and monoecious are used to denote:
(a) Bisexual condition
(b) Unisexual condition
(c) Staminate flowers
(d) Pistillate flowers

44. The technique of obtaining a large number of plants by tissue culture method is called:
(a) Macropropagation
(b) Somatic hybridisation
(c) Plantlet culture
(d) Micropropagation

45. Seeds are called products of sexual reproduction because they:
(a) Are formed by fusion of gametes
(b) Give rise to new plants
(c) Can be stored for a long time
(d) All of the above

ANSWER KEYS

Exercises

1. (d) **2.** (d) **3.** (d) **4.** (d) **5.** (c) **6.** (d) **7.** (d) **8.** (c) **9.** (a) **10.** (d)

11. (a) **12.** (d) **13.** (c) **14.** (c) **15.** (d) **16.** (d) **17.** (c) **18.** (d) **19.** (d) **20.** (d)

21. (d) **22.** (c) **23.** (c) **24.** (b) **25.** (c) **26.** (a) **27.** (a) **28.** (c) **29.** (d) **30.** (d)

31. (b) **32.** (d) **33.** (c) **34.** (d) **35.** (b) **36.** (d) **37.** (a) **38.** (c) **39.** (c) **40.** (b)

41. (b) **42.** (b) **43.** (a) **44.** (c) **45.** (b) **46.** (a) **47.** (b) **48.** (a) **49.** (b) **50.** (d)

51. (a) **52.** (d) **53.** (d) **54.** (d) **55.** (d) **56.** (a) **57.** (a) **58.** (d) **59.** (a) **60.** (c)

61. (c) **62.** (b) **63.** (a) **64.** (d) **65.** (c) **66.** (d) **67.** (b) **68.** (d) **69.** (a) **70.** (b)

71. (b) **72.** (c) **73.** (d) **74.** (c) **75.** (c) **76.** (d) **77.** (a) **78.** (a) **79.** (b) **80.** (c)

81. (b) **82.** (b) **83.** (a) **84.** (a) **85.** (d) **86.** (a) **87.** (c) **88.** (d) **89.** (b) **90.** (c)

91. (d) **92.** (c) **93.** (d) **94.** (c) **95.** (a) **96.** (d) **97.** (a) **98.** (a) **99.** (a) **100.** (c)

101. (a) **102.** (a) **103.** (a) **104.** (c) **105.** (a) **106.** (c) **107.** (c) **108.** (c) **109.** (b) **110.** (a)

111. (d) **112.** (c) **113.** (a) **114.** (c)

NCERT Exemplar Questions

1. (c) **2.** (a) **3.** (c) **4.** (b) **5.** (d) **6.** (c) **7.** (b) **8.** (a) **9.** (a) **10.** (b)

11. (c) **12.** (b) **13.** (c) **14.** (c) **15.** (d) **16.** (b) **17.** (b) **18.** (a)

Practice Test Paper

1. (c) **2.** (c) **3.** (a) **4.** (d) **5.** (a) **6.** (d) **7.** (d) **8.** (b) **9.** (c) **10.** (b)

11. (a) **12.** (c) **13.** (b) **14.** (d) **15.** (d) **16.** (d) **17.** (c) **18.** (b) **19.** (c) **20.** (b)

21. (a) **22.** (c) **23.** (b) **24.** (a) **25.** (d) **26.** (b) **27.** (d) **28.** (c) **29.** (c) **30.** (a)

31. (a) **32.** (c) **33.** (d) **34.** (d) **35.** (c) **36.** (d) **37.** (b) **38.** (d) **39.** (b) **40.** (b)

41. (b) **42.** (a) **43.** (b) **44.** (d) **45.** (a)

SOLUTIONS

Asexual Reproduction

1. Exogenous budding is observed in *Hydra* and *Obelia*. Internal budding is seen in freshwater sponges like *Spongilla*.
2. Multiple fission is seen in *Amoeba*, *Plasmodium* and *Monocystis*. Binary fission is seen in *Paramecium*.
3. *Pheretima* does not reproduce by asexual methods.
4. Asexual methods of reproduction do not involve meiotic divisions and hence do not generate variation. Thus, they have no role in evolution.
5. In response to unfavourable living conditions, *Amoeba* withdraws pseudopodia and secretes a three-layered cyst wall around itself. It then multiples by multiple fission.
6. Reproduction does not make individuals immortal.
7. The lifespan of crow is around 15 years.
8. The end of the juvenile phase marks the beginning of the reproductive phase.
9. Semelparous organisms have a single reproductive episode before death. In truly semelparous species, death after reproduction is part of an overall strategy that includes all available resources into maximising reproduction. For example, annual plants complete their life cycle in a single season, and are therefore semelparous.
10. Transverse binary fission is seen in *Paramecium* and *Planaria*.
11. In arrhenotokous parthenogenesis, only males are produced from unfertilised eggs.
12. Sexual reproduction involves formation and fusion of gametes.
13. Multiple fission occurs in many protists, (sporozoans). The nucleus of the parent cell divides several times by amitosis, producing several nuclei. The cytoplasm then separates, creating multiple daughter cells.
14. The lifespan of parrot is 140 years.
15. A meiocyte is a type of cell that differentiates into a gamete through the process of meiosis. Through meiosis, the diploid meiocyte divides into four genetically different haploid gametes.
16. Option (d) is correct.
17. External syngamy is seen in frog. Both male and female frogs release their gametes into water, where fertilisation takes place.
18. Oestrous cycle is observed in non-primate mammals like dogs.
19. Oviparous animals may lay either fertilised or unfertilised eggs.
20. The disadvantage of external-fertilisation is that the gametes and young ones are vulnerable to predators.
21. Option (d) is correct.
22. *Monocystis* is an example of unicellular organism showing isogamy.
23. During senescent phase of ageing, the organism loses its capacity of reproduction.
24. Plasmotomy is the asexual method of reproduction in which a multinucleate parent divides into many multinucleate daughter individuals without division of nuclei.
25. Gemmule formation is seen in freshwater sponges like *Spongilla*.

Introduction, Lifespan, Basic Features of Reproduction

26. Each and every organism can live only for a certain period of time. The period from birth to the natural death of an organism represents its lifespan.

27. Lifespan varies from a few days to several thousand years. Lifespan is not necessarily correlated to size or complexity of organisms. It is the specific trait of each organism.

28. Butterfly has a lifespan of 1–2 weeks.

29. Option (d) is correct.

30. Habitat, internal physiology of the organism and several other factors are collectively responsible for how the organism reproduces.

31. Mango tree lives for 200 years while peepal tree has a lifespan of about 2500 years.

32. Option (d) is correct.

33. Asexual reproduction can occur with or without the formation of gametes but gametic fusion is absent.

34. Option (d) is correct.

35. Rhizome – Ginger, Tuber – Potato, Corm – *Colocasia*, Bulb – Onion

36. Cell division is itself a mode of reproduction in unicellular organisms belonging to kingdoms Monera and Protista.

37. Option (a) is correct.

38. Option (c) is correct.

39. Asexual reproduction is a simple and quick method of multiplication.

40. Option (b) is correct.

41. Under unfavourable conditions, *Amoeba* withdraws its pseudopodia and secretes a three-layered hard covering or cyst around itself. This phenomenon is termed encystation. When favourable conditions return, the encyst amoeba divides by multiple fission and produces many minute amoeba or pseudopodiospores. The cyst wall bursts open and the spores are liberated in the surrounding medium to grow into many amoeba.

42. Option (b) is correct.

43. The most commonly produced spores are zoospores and conidia in algae and fungi, respectively.

44. Asexual spores in *Penicillium* is conidia. Conidia are non-motile spores produced by special hyphae called conidiophore. In *Penicillium,* the conidiophore may show branching, and over these branches a flask-shaped structure called sterigmata is formed. Each sterigmata produces a chain of conidia.

45. Conidia are non-motile spores, which are exogenous in origin, and the arrangement of conidia is basipetal.

46. *Chlamydomonas*

47. A bulb is an underground reduced disc-shaped stem. Terminal bud is surrounded by several leaves, for example, onion and garlic.

48. The eyes of the potato tuber are modified axillary buds.

49. Gemmae formation

50. Leaves of *Bryophyllum*, *Kalanchoe* have adventitious buds that help in vegetative reproduction.

51. A – Offset, B – Bulbil

52. Stolen – mint, jasmine

53. Water hyacinth or Terror of Bengal was introduced in Bengal because of its beautiful flowers and shape of leaves. However, it turned out to be a highly invasive aquatic weed that not only spread to all the water bodies of Bengal but also throughout India. It drains oxygen from water, which leads to the death of fish and other animals.

54. *Euglena* reproduce by longitudinal binary fission.

55. Nucule is not a vegetative propagule; it is the female sex organ of *Chara*.

56. In the life cycle of any organism, there is a cycle of birth, growth and death.

57. A – Eyes, B – Germinating eye buds, C – Adventitious buds

58. In plants, during asexual reproduction, new plants are produced from the vegetative part; hence called vegetative propagation.

59. Encystation is the formation of a hard covering around itself in *Amoeba* during unfavourable conditions.

60. In *Chlamydomonas*, the protoplast of the cell divides to form 8–16 zoospores. They are pyramid-shaped and anteriorly flagellated. The parent cell wall breaks and the zoospores are liberated in water. They enlarge and behave as adult individuals.

Sexual Reproduction (Phases in Life Cycle, Events in Sexual Reproduction, Pre-fertilisation Events, Gametogenesis and Gamete Transfer)

61. Only (A) and (B) are correct. Sexual reproduction can be uniparental or biparental (mostly).

62. Sexual reproduction creates new genetic combinations, so it produces genetic variation.

63. Sexual reproduction is a slow, elaborate and complex process, so multiplication is not rapid. While asexual reproduction is a simple and quick method of multiplication.

64. Introduction of genetic variation

65. Interaction between hormones and certain environmental factors regulates the reproductive processes and the associated behavioural expression of organisms.

66. During the vegetative or juvenile phase, organisms will slow growth so that they can attain certain maturity to perform sexual reproduction.

67. Algae and fungi reproduce asexually under favourable conditions.

68. Polycarpic plants are perennial plants which, after reaching maturity, flower repeatedly at intervals.

69. When the gametes belong to the same parent, such organisms are called homothallic, and when male flowers (staminate) and female flowers (pistillate) are present on the same plant body, such plants are called monoecious.

70. Cucurbits, coconut and maize plants are monoecious while date palm is a dioecious plant.

71. China rose is a perennial plant which bears flowers throughout the year.

72. *Cucurbita* is a monoecious plant.

73. The correct sequence of events during sexual reproduction is (i) Gametogenesis, (ii) Bringing of male and female gametes together, (iii) Syngamy, (iv) Formation of seeds and fruits.

74. Papaya and date palm are polycarpic and dioecious. Polycarpic plants are those that flower and set seeds many times during its lifetime. Dioecious plants are those that bear male and female flowers on different plants.

75. The inter-flowering period is used for building up resources and is therefore the recovery phase. It is not the juvenile phase but a part of the mature phase.

76. Plant hormones are responsible for the transition between the juvenile, vegetative and senescent phases.

77.

Name of organism	Chromosome number in meiocyte (2N)
Housefly	12
Butterfly	380
Fruit fly	8

78. A – Haploid, B – Meiotic, C – Haploid, D – Mitotic

Gametes are always haploid, so in a haploid parent, gametes are produced by mitotic division, while diploid organisms produce gametes by meiotic division.

79. In seeded plants, during pollination, pollen grains are the carrier of male gametes.

80. When the fusing gametes are morphological identical, they are called homogametes or isogametes. For example, *Cladophora*.

81. Pre-fertilisation events include gametogenesis and gamete transfer.

82. Gamete transfer

83.

Name of organism	Chromosome number in gametes
(i) Potato	24
(ii) Onion	16
(iii) Rice	12
(iv) *Ophioglossum*	630

84. In a few fungi and algae, both types of gametes are motile, but in the majority of organisms, the male gamete is motile and the female gamete is non-motile.

85. In algae, bryophytes and pteridophytes, water is the medium for transfer of gametes.

86. A – Bisexual, B – Dioecious, C – Monoecious

87. 20, 24

88. The cells that undergo meiosis are called meiocytes.

89. Four statements (a, b, c and d) are correct. *Chara* produces motile male gametes and shows internal fertilisation.

90. *Strobilanthes kunthiana* (Neelakurinji) flowers once in 12 years. The last time it flowered was in September–October 2018.

91. Monocarpic plants are those which produce flowers only once in their life; after flowering, they produce fruits and die. All annual, biennial and a few perennial plants (bamboo species) are monocarpic.

92. Staminate flowers

93. In algae, bryophytes and pteridophytes, water is the medium for male gamete transfer.

94. *Chara* is a monecious, green algae.

95. In *Chara*, the sex organs are highly specialised; they are multicellular and jacketed. Male and female sex organs are called globule (antheridium) and nucule (oogonium). The nucule occupies the upper position compared to that of the globule.

96. Pollen grains are transferred to the stigma of the carpel through the process of pollination.

97. A few perennial plants are also monocarpic. Certain bamboo species (*Bambusa tulda*) live vegetatively for 50–100 years, flower and fruit abundantly and then die.

98. Option (a) is correct.

Fertilisation, Post-fertilisation Events, Zygote, Embryogenesis

99. The most vital event of sexual reproduction is the fusion of gametes. This process is called syngamy and it results in the formation of the zygote. Formation of zygote is universal in all sexually reproducing organisms.

100. A major disadvantage of external fertilisation is that the offspring are extreme vulnerable to predators, threatening their survival up to adulthood.

101. (A), (B) and (C) are true.

102. Pollination is the pre-fertilisation event.

103. In the majority of algae, syngamy takes place in water.

104. Fertilisation is external in the majority of aquatic organisms like most algae, fishes and amphibians. Internal fertilisation is seen in the majority of plants like bryophytes, pteridophytes, gymnosperms and angiosperms.

105. Syngamy

106. Organisms exhibiting diplontic lifecycle pattern are diploid and produce gametes by meiotic division.

107. Zygote is the first cell of the sporophytic generation.

108. Gametogenesis is a pre-fertilisation event.

109. Zygote

110. A – Meiosis, B – Haploid, C – Haploid

111. In embryogenesis, the zygote undergoes repeated cell division. Through mitosis, the cells undergo differentiation, attaining specific shape, size and function.

112. Both (A) and (B) are correct.

113. Embryo formation occurs in all plants, except algae.

114. The wall of the ovary proliferates and produces the pericarp.

Sexual Reproduction in Flowering Plants

EXERCISES

Flower, Pre-fertilisation Structure and Events, Stamen, Microsporangium and Pollen Grain

1. Essential whorls of a flower are:
A. Calyx
B. Corolla
C. Androecium
D. Gynoecium
(a) (A) and (B) (b) (A) and (D)
(c) (C) and (D) (d) (B) and (C)

2. Stamen is technically equivalent to:
(a) Microsporangium (b) Microsporophyll
(c) Male gametophyte (d) Megasporophyll

3. Pollen sac develops from:
(a) Microspore
(b) Microspore mother cell
(c) Megasporangium
(d) Microsporangium

4. The important unit of male and female reproductive organs in flowering plants, respectively:
(a) Stamen and carpel
(b) Androecium and gynoecium
(c) Carpel and anther
(d) Megasporophyll and microsporophyll

5. A typical anther is:
A. Dithecous and bisporangiate
B. Tetragonal
C. Bilobed
D. Tetrasporangiate
(a) (A) and (C) are correct
(b) (A) and (B) are correct
(c) (B), (C) and (D) are correct
(d) (A), (B) and (C) are correct

6. During formation of pollen grains, a microspore mother cell undergoes:
(a) One meiotic division
(b) One mitotic division
(c) One meiotic and one mitotic division
(d) One meiotic and two mitotic divisions

7. In a flowering plant, the largest number of haploid cells occur in:
(a) Ovule (b) Microsporangia
(c) Root tip (d) Stele

8. Identify A to D in the male reproductive parts of the angiosperm:

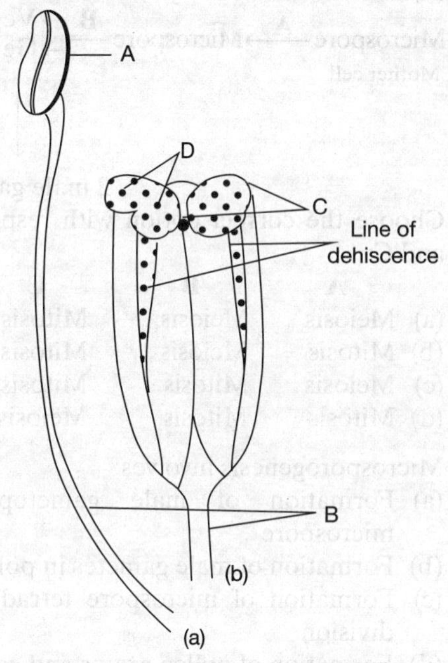

	A	B	C	D
(a)	Anther	Filament	Pollen sac	Pollen grains
(b)	Anther	Petiole	Microsporangia	Microspores
(c)	Pollen sac	Filament	Megasporangia	Pollen grains
(d)	Pollen sac	Pedicel	Microsporangia	Microspores

9. *a*-cellulosic fibrous thickening is present in:
(a) Walls of tapetum
(b) Middle layers
(c) Walls of endothecium
(d) Epidermis of anther

10. Which of the following cells of the anther wall contains dense cytoplasm and more than one nucleus?
(a) Tapetum (b) Endothecium
(c) Middle layers (d) Epidermis

11. Pollen kit, sporopollenin and incompatibility proteins are synthesized by ________ of anther wall:
(a) Endothecium (b) Tapetum
(c) Middle layers (d) Epidermis

12. Microsporangium is surrounded by four wall layers: the epidermis, endothecium, middle layers and tapetum. Which layers perform the function of protection and help in dehiscence of anther to release the pollen?
(a) Epidermis only
(b) Epidermis and endothecium
(c) Outer three wall layers
(d) Inner three wall layers

13. Microspore Mother cell $\xrightarrow{A}$ Microspore $\xrightarrow{B}$ → Vegetative cell / → Generative cell $\xrightarrow{C}$ 2 male gametes

Choose the correct option with respect to A, B and C:

	A	B	C
(a)	Meiosis	Meiosis	Mitosis
(b)	Mitosis	Meiosis	Mitosis
(c)	Meiosis	Mitosis	Mitosis
(d)	Mitosis	Mitosis	Meiosis

14. Microsporogenesis involves:
(a) Formation of male gametophyte from microspore
(b) Formation of male gametes in pollen grains
(c) Formation of microspore tetrad by meiotic division
(d) Formation of pollen grains and gametes

15. In angiosperms, meiosis occurs in which of the following structures?
(a) Microspore (b) Root tip
(c) Pollen grain (d) Anther

16. Pollen grains:
A. Shed at three-celled stage in 60% of angiosperms
B. Of many species cause severe allergies and bronchial afflictions
C. Remain viable for several months in some members of Rosaceae, Leguminosae and Solanaceae
D. Have no taxonomical significance
The correct statements are:
(a) (A) and (B) (b) (B) and (C)
(c) (A) and (D) (d) (B) and (D)

17. In angiosperms, all the four microspores of tetrad are covered by a layer formed by:
(a) Pectocellulose (b) Sporopollenin
(c) Cellulose (d) Callose

18. Ubish bodies are secreted by:
(a) Tapetum (b) Sporogenous tissue
(c) Endothecium (d) Epidermal cells

19. Sporopollenin is present in:
(a) Exine (b) Intine
(c) Endothecium (d) Tapetum

20. Sporopollenin:
A. Cannot be degraded by enzymes
B. Can withstand high temperature, strong acid and alkali
C. Helps in fossilisation of pollen grains
D. Is the major component of exine and intine
The correct statements are:
(a) Only (A)
(b) Only (B) and (C)
(c) Only (A), (B) and (C)
(d) (A), (B), (C) and (D)

21. Germ pore on the pollen grain is the area where sporopollenin is:
(a) Thick (b) Thin
(c) Uniform (d) Absent

22. Pollen grains are generally ___**A**___, measuring about ___**B**___ μm in diameter:

	A	B
(a)	Spherical	25–50
(b)	Elongated	20–50
(c)	Elongated	100–200
(d)	Spherical	100–200

23. Pollen grains lose viability within 30 minutes of their release in:
(a) Rice and wheat
(b) Leguminous plants
(c) Grasses and rose
(d) Members of Rosaceae, Solanaceae, Leguminosae

24. Pollen banks:
(a) Store pollen grain in liquid nitrogen at −196°C
(b) Are a source of germplasm
(c) Source of pollen grains for various artificial plant breeding programmes
(d) More than one option is correct

25. Pollen grains in most angiosperms are shed at:
(a) Three-celled stage
(b) Two-celled stage
(c) One-celled stage
(d) Four-celled stage

26. In an angiosperm, the number of microspore mother cells involved in the production of 120 male gametes is:
(a) 30 (b) 60
(c) 15 (d) 40

27. How many haploid nuclei are present in a mature pollen grain?
(a) One (b) Two
(c) Three (d) Four

28. How many pollen mother cells are required to produce 1000 pollen grains?
(a) 200 (b) 500
(c) 100 (d) 250

29. Generative cell in a pollen grain:
(a) Is small and spindle shaped
(b) Has dense cytoplasm and irregularly shaped nucleus
(c) Has abundant food reserves
(d) Is small and has a spindle-shaped nucleus

30. Vegetative cell in pollen grain:
A. Is bigger in size
B. Has abundant food reserves
C. Is spindle shaped with dense cytoplasm and nucleus
D. Floats in the cytoplasm of the generative cell
(a) (A) and (C) (b) (B) and (D)
(c) (A) and (B) (d) (C) and (D)

31. Which of the following came into India as a contaminant of imported wheat and has become ubiquitous in occurrence and causes pollen allergy?
(a) *Parthenium* (b) *Chenopodium*
(c) *Amaranthus* (d) All of the above

32. The period for which pollen grains remain viable is called pollen viability. It is highly variable and to some extent depends on:
(a) Thickness of sporopollenin
(b) Number of germ pores
(c) Prevailing temperature and humidity
(d) Amount of cytoplasm

33. Viability period of pollen grains for several months is observed in:
(a) Some cereals
(b) Members of Poaceae
(c) Some members of family Solanaceae
(d) Both (a) and (b)

34. In angiosperms, how many meiotic and mitotic divisions are required for the formation of a mature male gametophyte from a microspore mother cell?
(a) One meiotic, two mitotic
(b) One meiotic, three mitotic
(c) Zero meiotic, two mitotic
(d) Zero meiotic, three mitotic

35. Anther wall layer which degenerates in the early development phase is:
(a) Epidermis (b) Tapetum
(c) Middle layers (d) Endothecium

36. The cytoplasm of pollen grain is surrounded by:
(a) Exine (b) Intine
(c) Sporoderm (d) Plasma membrane

37. In over 60% of angiosperms, the generative cell divides mitotically to give rise to two male gametes:
(a) Before pollen grains are shed
(b) After transfer of pollen grain directly on ovule
(c) Before pollination
(d) After transfer of pollen grains to stigma

Pistil, Megasporangium (Ovule) and Embryo Sac

38. The pistil (**A**) and ovule (**B**) in an angiosperm are technically equivalent to:

	A	B
(a)	Megasporangium	Megasporophyll
(b)	Megasporophyll	Megasporangium
(c)	Megasporangium	Female gametophyte
(d)	Megasporophyll	Female gametophyte

39. A multicarpellary, syncarpous gynoecium occurs in:

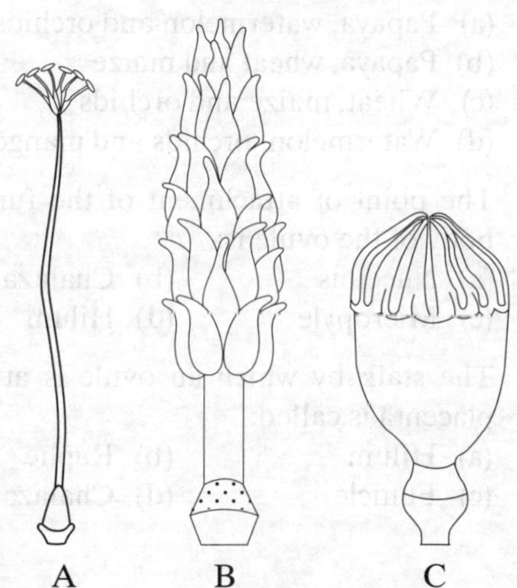

(a) Only B (b) Only A
(c) A and B (d) A and C

40. In angiosperm, the landing platform for the pollen grains after their pollination is:
(a) Ovule (b) Stigma
(c) Thalamus (d) Style

41. A multicarpellary, apocarpous gynoecium occurs in:
(a) *Hibiscus* (b) *Papaver*
(c) *Cocos* (d) *Michelia*

42. Identify the type of gynoecium in the given figure:

(a) Multicarpellary syncarpous
(b) Multicarpellary apocarpous
(c) Monocarpellary apocarpous
(d) Monocarpellary superior

43. In *Michelia*, pistil is:
(a) Multicarpellary apocarpous
(b) Multicarpellary syncarpous
(c) Monocarpellary apocarpous
(d) Monocarpellary syncarpous

44. Which of the following is not a structural feature of pistil?
(a) Stigma (b) Ovary
(c) Filament (d) Style

45. The number of ovules in an ovary are many in:
(a) Papaya, watermelon and orchids
(b) Papaya, wheat and maize
(c) Wheat, maize and orchids
(d) Watermelon, orchids and mango

46. The point of attachment of the funicle with the body of the ovule is:
(a) Nucellus (b) Chalaza
(c) Micropyle (d) Hilum

47. The stalk by which an ovule is attached to the placenta is called:
(a) Hilum (b) Raphe
(c) Funicle (d) Chalaza

48. Which of the following pairs is not correctly matched?
(a) Ovule – Megasporophyll
(b) Filiform apparatus – Synergids
(c) Largest cell of embryo sac – Central cell
(d) Chalaza – Base of ovule

49. Formation of embryo sac from a single megaspore nuclei is ________ development:
(a) Monosporic (b) Bisporic
(c) Tetrasporic (d) Polysporic

50. Tetrad of megaspore is generally:
(a) Tetrahedral (b) Linear
(c) Decussate (d) Isobilateral

51. Formation of embryo sac is:
(a) Megasporogenesis
(b) Megagametogenesis
(c) Microsporogenesis
(d) Microgametogenesis

52. During formation of embryo sac, a functional megaspore undergoes:
(a) One mitotic division
(b) One meiotic and two mitotic divisions
(c) One meiotic and three mitotic divisions
(d) Three mitotic divisions

53. An ovule generally has ________ embryo sac(s):
(a) Four (b) Three
(c) Two (d) One

54. Polygonum type of embryo sac comprises:
(a) 7 cells and 7 nuclei
(b) 7 cells and 7 nuclei
(c) 8 cells and 7 nuclei
(d) 7 cells and 8 nuclei

55. Synergids are two in number in polygonum type of embryo sac and:
(a) Have special cellular thickening at the micropylar tip
(b) Present at micropylar end of embryo sac
(c) Are haploid
(d) All of the above

56. In a fully organised polygonum type embryo sac, what is the ratio of haploid, diploid and triploid cells?
(a) 6 : 1 : 0 (b) 6 : 1 : 1
(c) 6 : 2 : 1 (d) 3 : 2 : 0

57. Select the odd one out with respect to the female reproductive structure of a flower:
(a) Micropyle (b) Embryo sac
(c) Nucellus (d) Germ pore

58. The parenchymatous mass of tissue enclosed within the integuments and which forms the body of ovule is:
(a) Nucellus (b) Haploid
(c) Embryo sac (d) Future sporophyte

59. Most common type of ovule present in angiosperms is:
(a) Anatropous (b) Orthotropous
(c) Hemianatropous (d) Amphitropous

60. The ploidy level of egg apparatus is:
(a) (2n + n) (b) (n + n + n)
(c) (2n + n + n) (d) (3n + 2n + 3n)

61. Filiform apparatus is a characteristic feature of:
(a) Zygote (b) Egg cell
(c) Antipodals (d) Synergid

62. First cell of female gametophyte is:
(a) Microspore (b) Megaspore
(c) Megaspore mother cell (d) Central cell

63. 250 megaspore mother cells will give rise to ______ megaspores:
(a) 250 (b) 500
(c) 500 (d) 1000

64. How many megaspore nuclei take part in the development of polygonum type embryo sac?
(a) Two (b) Three
(c) Four (d) One

65. In the nucellus, megaspore mother cell:
(a) Generally differentiates at micropylar end
(b) Possesses dense cytoplasm and inconspicuous nuclei
(c) Divides by free nuclear division to form embryo sac
(d) Is small in size but possesses prominent haploid nucleus

66. The method of polygonum type embryo sac development that is used in most flowering plants is:
(a) Monosporic
(b) Bisporic
(c) Tetrasporic
(d) More than one options is correct

67. Function of filiform apparatus is to:
(a) Recognise suitable pollen at stigma
(b) Stimulate division of generative cell
(c) Produce nectar
(d) Guide entry of pollen tube

68. Identify the parts labelled A, B, C and D:

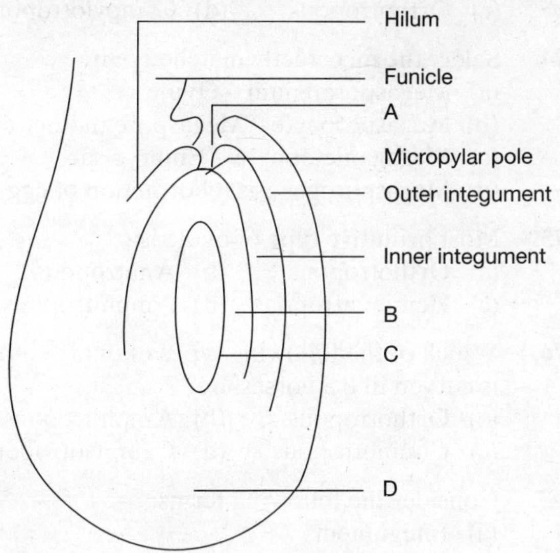

	A	B	C	D
(a)	Micropyle	Nucellus	Embryo sac	Chalaza
(b)	Micropyle	Perisperm	Embryo sac	Integument
(c)	Germpore	Nucellus	Female gametophyte	Chalaza
(d)	Germpore	Endosperm	Female gametophyte	Chalaza

69. In 82% of angiosperm families, the ovule is:
(a) Anatropous (b) Orthotropous
(c) Amphitropous (d) Circinotropous

70. In the majority of flowering plants, the functional megaspore is:
(a) First from micropyle
(b) Fourth from micropyle
(c) Second from micropyle
(d) Second from chalaza

71. In the majority of flowering plants, the embryo sac develops from:
(a) Single micropylar functional megaspore
(b) Single chalazal functional megaspsore
(c) Two functional megaspore of chalazal end
(d) Coenomegaspore

72. The ploidy of the cells of the nucellus, megaspore mother cell and embryo sac are, respectively:
(a) 2N, 2N and 2N (b) 2N, N and 2N
(c) N, 2N and N (d) 2N, 2N and N

73. When an ovule is inverted such that the body is parallel to the funicle and the micropyle is near the hilum, it is called:

(a) Anatropus (b) Amphitropous
(c) Orthotropous (d) Campylotropous

74. Select the incorrectly matched pair:
(a) Megasporangium – Ovule
(b) Megasporocyte – Megaspore mother cell
(c) Megagametophyte – Embryo sac
(d) Megasporogenesis – Formation of egg

75. Most primitive type of ovule is:
(a) Orthotropous (b) Anatropous
(c) Hemianatropous (d) Amphitropous

76. Which of the following types of ovule embryo sac is curved like a horseshoe?
(a) Orthotropous (b) Amphitropous
(c) Circinotropous (d) Campylotropous

77. Consider the following terms:
(a) Integument
(b) Nucellus
(c) Antipodals
(d) Polar nuclei
(e) Chalaza
(f) Funicle
(g) Synergid
(h) Egg cell
How many of the above structures are gametophytic in origin?
(a) Five (b) Three
(c) Six (d) Four

Pollination and Outbreeding Devices

78. Pollination is:
(a) Shedding of pollen grains from anther
(b) Transfer of pollen grains from anther to stigma
(c) Dispersal of pollen
(d) Transfer of pollen from female flower to male flower

79. The pollination of two flowers on different plants is known as:
(a) Xenogamy (b) Cleistogamy
(c) Dichogamy (d) Autogamy

80. Read the following statements with respect to autogamy and select the correct option:
A. Pollination achieved within the same flower
B. Rare in those flowers which do not open
C. Need synchrony in pollen release and stigma, respectively
D. Male and female sex organs of the same flower should be close to each other
(a) (A), (B), (C) are correct
(b) (B) and (C) are incorrect
(c) (A), (C) and (D) are correct
(d) (A), (B), (C) and (D) are correct

81. Functionally similar to cross-pollination but genetically similar to autogamy is:
(a) Geitonogamy (b) Homogamy
(c) Chasmogamy (d) Xenogamy

82. Pollination by wind is a hit or miss affair. What does the plant do to compensate for these uncertainties?
(a) Produce large number of ovules
(b) Produce large number of pollen grains
(c) Produce copious nectar
(d) Produce only single ovule in a flower

83. Cleistogamous flower can be traced in:
(a) *Oxalis* (b) *Commelina*
(c) *Viola* (d) All of the above

84. In cleistogamous flower:
(a) Fruit formation never occurs
(b) No seed formation
(c) Chance of cross-pollination is absent
(d) Geitonogamy occurs

85. *Viola*, *Oxalis* and *Commelina* possess:
(a) Unisexual cleistogamous flowers
(b) Chasmogamous flowers only
(c) Both cleistogamous and chasmogamous flowers
(d) Cleistogamous flowers only

86. In *Zea mays*, male and female inflorescence is called, respectively:
(a) Cob, tassel (b) Tassel, cob
(c) Cob, pod (d) Pod, cob

87. Majority of plants use ________ agents for pollination:
(a) Abiotic (b) Biotic
(c) Air (d) Water

88. Pollination can be classified on the basis of:
(a) Source of pollen
(b) Type of pollen
(c) Agency of pollination
(d) Environmental condition

89. Which larger animals have not been reported as pollinators in plants?
(a) Lemurs
(b) Tree dwelling rodents
(c) Garden lizards and gecko lizard
(d) Shrews

90. Water pollination requires that the pollen grains are:
(a) Light, unwettable
(b) Light and sticky

(c) Heavy and unwettable
(d) Heavy with high specific gravity

91. Wind pollination is quite common in:
(a) Grasses (b) Orchids
(c) Lilies (d) All of these

92. *Zostera* (Sea grass):
A. Pollen grains are long and ribbon shaped
B. Pollen grains are carried passively in water
C. Shows epihydrophily
(a) Only (A) (b) Only (A) and (B)
(c) Only (C) (d) (A), (B) and (C)

93. Which one of the following contrivances ensures cent per cent autogamy?
(a) Monocliny (b) Dicliny
(c) Cleistogany (d) Homogamy

94. Identify the incorrect match with respect to pollination:
(a) Anemophily - Dusty pollen
(b) Hydrophily - Unwettable pollen grain
(c) Entomophily - Non-stick pollen grain
(d) Ornithophily - Pollination by birds

95. Pollination in water hyacinth and water lily is brought about by the agency of:
(a) Bats (b) Water
(c) Insects or wind (d) Birds

96. Flowers which have a single ovule in the ovary and are packed into inflorescence are usually pollinated by:
(a) Water (b) Bee
(c) Wind (d) Bat

97. Pollen grains are protected by a mucilaginous covering and have a specific gravity. This is a characteristic of which type of pollination?
(a) Anemophily (b) Entomophily
(c) Hydrophily (d) Zoophily

98. Anemophily is associated with reduction in:
(a) Ovule number (b) Size of pollen grain
(c) Stamen number (d) Both (a) and (b)

99. Water pollination is commonly seen in some genera of:
(a) Dicots (b) Monocots
(c) Gymnosperms (d) Pteridophytes

100. Which of the following is incorrectly matched?
(a) Long feathery stigma - Hydrophily
(b) Sticky pollen grains - Entomophily
(c) Pollen allergies - Hay fever
(d) Pollen tablets - Food supplement

101. Condition which prevents both autogamy and geitonogamy:
(a) Bud pollination (b) Cleistogamy
(c) Dioecy (d) Homogamy

102. The flower height in *Amorphophalus* is:
(a) 8 feet (b) 3 metres
(c) 6 feet (d) 12 feet

103. *Pronuba* moth has its larval stage in the plant pollinated by it. The plant is:
(a) *Ficus* (b) *Tagetes*
(c) *Yucca* (d) *Cosmos*

104. In papaya:
(a) Both male and female flowers are present on the same plant
(b) Flowers are bisexual
(c) Both autogamy and geitonogamy are prevented
(d) Allogamy is prevented

105. Read the following statements and state whether they are true (T) or false (F):
A. Wind pollination is quite common in grasses
B. Hydrophily is limited to about 30 genera, mostly monocots
C. Both wind- and water-pollinated flowers are rarely colourful and do not produce nectar
D. Plants provide no advantage to insects in terms of reward

	A	B	C	D
(a)	F	T	T	T
(b)	T	T	T	F
(c)	F	T	T	F
(d)	T	F	F	T

106. Chief pollinators of agricultural crops are:
(a) Butterflies (b) Bees
(c) Moths (d) Beetles

107. When a flower is brightly coloured, scented and secretes nectar, it is probably:
(a) Pollinated by wind
(b) Pollinated by insects
(c) Pollinated by water
(d) Pollinated by larger animals

108. "Biological arms race" is concerned with:
(a) Defense mechanism
(b) Adaptation for feeding
(c) Co-evolution for flowers and pollinators
(d) Adaptation for megasporogenesis

109. The given plant shows all adaptations for pollination, except:

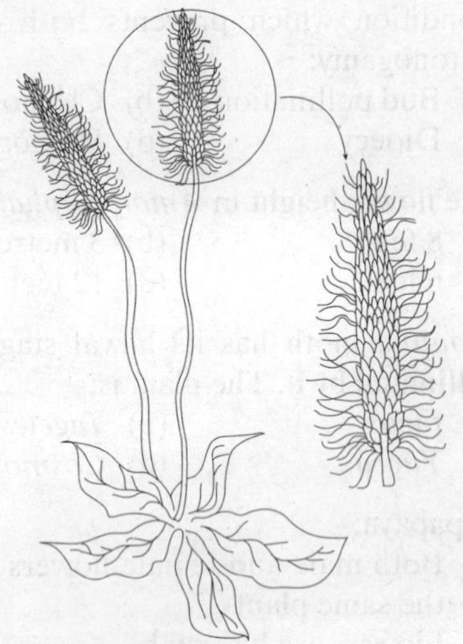

(a) Compact inflorescence
(b) Well-exposed stamens
(c) Large often feathery stigma
(d) Safe place to lay eggs

110. The pedicel of the female flower coils after pollination in:
(a) *Vallisneria* (b) Waterlily
(c) Water hyacinth (d) Both (b) and (c)

111. Pollen prepotency is defined as:
(a) Bud pollination
(b) Autogamy
(c) Preference for foreign pollen
(d) All of the above

112. Pollination by water is seen in:
(a) *Vallisneria* (b) *Zostera*
(c) Waterlily (d) All except (c)

113. A floral visitor that consumes pollen or nectar without performing pollination is:
(a) Pollen robber (b) *Colpa*
(c) *Bombus affinis* (d) Both (a) and (c)

114. Read the following statements:
(a) Flowers are small and are often packed in inflorescence
(b) Flowers are colourless, odourless, and nectarless
(c) Flowers often have a single ovule in each ovary
The above contrivances favour:
(a) Autogamy (b) Anemophily
(c) Entomophily (d) Ornithophily

115. In *Kigellia pinnata*/sausage tree, pollination is performed by:
(a) Bats (b) Birds
(c) Insects (d) Wind

116. Consider the following statements about plants pollinated by insects:
(a) Pollination by flies and beetles occurs in foul-odoured flowers
(b) Bees are the most common insect pollinating agent
(c) Flowers have colourful appearance
Which of the above statements is/are correct?
(a) Only (a) (b) Only (b) and (c)
(c) Both (a) and (b) (d) (a), (b) and (c)

117. Which of the following cannot be a floral reward provided by plants to pollinators?
(a) Pollens
(b) Nectar
(c) Fragrance
(d) Providing safe place to lay eggs

118. A plant species which provides a safe place to lay eggs as pollination reward is:
(a) *Salvia* (b) *Commelina*
(c) *Calotropis* (d) *Amorphophallus*

119. If both male and female flowers are present on the same plant, such as castor and maize:
(a) It prevents autogamy but not geitonogamy
(b) It prevents geitonogamy but not autogamy
(c) It allows both autogamy and geitonogamy
(d) It allow xenogamy but not geitonogamy

120. An advantage of cleistogamy is:
(a) It leads to greater genetic diversity
(b) Seed dispersal is more efficient
(c) Each visit of the pollinator brings hundreds of pollen grains
(d) Seed set is not dependent on the pollinator

121. Self-incompatibility or self-sterility is:
(a) The production of unisexual flowers
(b) A genetically controlled mechanism which prevents self pollen from fertilising the ovules
(c) An ecologically controlled mechanism which prevents self pollen from fertilising the ovules
(d) Production of male and female flowers on the same plant

122. In *Vallisneria*:
A. The female flower has a very long pedicel; therefore, it reaches the surface of the water
B. The male flower floats on the surface of the water
C. Pollen grains are carried passively on water currents
D. Epihydrophily occurs
(a) Only (A) and (D)
(b) Only (B), (C) and (D)
(c) Only (A) and (C)
(d) (A), (B), (C) and (D)

123. Both autogamy and geitonogamy are prevented in:
(a) Monoecious plants
(b) Chasmagamous flowers
(c) Mulberry, date palm, papaya
(d) Plants bearing bisexual flowers

124. Which of the following aquatic plants are not pollinated by water?
(a) Water hyacinth and *Hydrilla*
(b) *Vallisneria* and *Hydrilla*
(c) Water hyacinth and water lily
(d) Water lily and *Vallisneria*

125. Select the incorrect option with respect to out-breeding devices:
(a) Prevent inbreeding depression
(b) Encourage cross-pollination
(c) Involve self-incompatibility
(d) Involve the production of cleistogamous flower

126. Presence of anther and stigma at different levels in the same flower:
(a) Prevents allogamy
(b) Is a contrivance for autogamy
(c) Is an outbreeding device
(d) All except (c)

127. Type of pollination that brings genetically different types of pollen grains to the stigma of a plant is:
(a) Xenogamy (b) Geitonogamy
(c) Chasmogamy (d) Autogamy

Pollen–Pistil Interaction, Double Fertilisation

128. Pollination does not guarantee the transfer of the right type of pollen (compatible pollen). If the pollen is of the wrong type, the pistil rejects the pollen by preventing:
(a) Pollen germination on the stigma
(b) Pollen tube growth in style
(c) Double fertilisation
(d) Both (a) and (b)

129. Stigma provides to pollen grains:
(a) Boron, sugars and amino acids
(b) Malice acid and sugar
(c) Malice acid and citric acid
(d) Citric acid and amino acids

130. The pollen tubes grow through the solid style by separating their cells through the secretion of:
(a) Protease (b) Lipase
(c) Pectinase (d) Amylase

131. Germination of pollen grain on the stigma is:
(a) Autogamy
(b) In-situ germination
(c) In-vivo germination
(d) In-vitro germination

132. Generative cell was destroyed by laser, but a normal pollen tube was still formed because:
(a) Vegetative cell is not damaged
(b) Contents of killed generative cell stimulate pollen growth
(c) Laser beam stimulates growth of pollen tube
(d) The region of emergence of pollen tube is not harmed

133. In the majority of flowering plants, entry of pollen tube in ovule is:
(a) Porogamy (b) Mesogamy
(c) Chalazogamy (d) Basogamy

134. Fertilisation involving carrying of male gametes by pollen tube is:
(a) Porogamy (b) Siphonogamy
(c) Chalazogamy (d) Mesogamy

135. Pollen tube discharges its male gametes into:
(a) Central cell
(b) Cytoplasm of the synergids
(c) Egg cell
(d) Antipodals

136. Double fertilisation is unique in angiosperms. It was discovered by:
(a) Nawaschin in *Lilium* and *Fritillaria*
(b) Strasburger in *Lilium* and *Fritillaria*
(c) Nawaschin in *Polygonum*
(d) Amici in *Portulaca*

137. Pollen tube up to 4.5 cm long is observed in:
(a) *Malva* (b) *Datura*
(c) Maize (d) China rose

138. The generative cell nucleus divides mitotically to form two male gametes, which are:
(a) Small and flagellated
(b) Diploid and non-flagellated
(c) Always produced before pollination
(d) Slightly unequal in size

139. During triple fusion, male gametes fuse with:
(a) Egg ell
(b) Nucleus of antipodal cell
(c) Nucleus of one polar nuclei
(d) Secondary nucleus

140. The nutritive tissue formed in the fertilised embryo sac is the result of:
(a) Syngamy (b) Triple fusion
(c) Free fertilisation (d) Amphimixis

141. Total number of gametes involved in triple fusion is:
(a) One (b) Two
(c) Three (d) Zero

142. After double fertilisation, a mature ovule has:
(a) One diploid and one haploid cell
(b) One diploid and one triploid cell
(c) Two haploid cells and one triploid cell
(d) One diploid and three haploid cells

143. In angiosperm, endosperm is produced after fertilisation of a male gamete with:
(a) Antipodals (b) Egg cell
(c) Two synergids (d) Secondary nucleus

144. Pollen tube shows:
(a) Phototropic movement
(b) Geotropic movement
(c) Chemotropic movement
(d) Chemotactic movement

145. If, in a flowering plant, male gametes are 2N and female gametes are N, the ploidy level in the embryo and endosperm will be:
(a) 5 N, 2 N (b) 8 N, 5 N
(c) 6 N, 10 N (d) 3 N, 4 N

146. In a fertilised ovule n, 2n and 3n conditions occur in:
(a) Egg, secondary nucleus, endosperm
(b) Antipodal, zygote, endosperm
(c) Egg, nucleus, endosperm
(d) Synergid, endosperm, perisperm

147. A characteristic feature exclusive to angiosperms is:
(a) Formation of non-motile gametes
(b) Double fertilisation
(c) Siphonogamous fertilisation
(d) Formation of seed

148. How many gametes take part in double fertilisation?
(a) 3 (b) 2
(c) 4 (d) 5

149. A chemical dialogue between pollen grains and the pistil provides the pistil the ability:
(a) To reject the pollen
(b) To modify pollen
(c) To accept pollen
(d) To recognise the pollen grains

150. What is meant by emasculation?
(a) Pollination between flowers of the same plant
(b) Artificial pollination
(c) Removal of anthers in bud condition
(d) Covering of stigma with butter paper to prevent contamination

151. Removal of anther from the floral bud is called:
(a) Anthesis (b) Bagging
(c) Emasculation (d) Anthectomy

152. Artificial hybridisation is one of the major approaches of the crop improvement programme. For a bisexual flower, it includes the following steps in correct sequence:
(a) Bagging, pollination, rebagging
(b) Pollination, bagging, rebagging
(c) Emasculation, bagging, pollination, rebagging
(d) Bagging, emasculation, pollination, rebagging

153. In the study of pollen germination, some pollen from flowers such as pea, chickpea, *Crotalaria* and balsam is collected and dusted on a glass slide containing a drop of ___A___ in a solution of about ___B___ percentage:

	A	B
(a)	Saline	5
(b)	Sugar	5
(c)	Saline	10
(d)	Sugar	10

154. Which of the following elements is essential for in-vitro pollen germination?
(a) Boron (b) Manganese
(c) Iron (d) Copper

155. Which is the site of double fertilisation?
(a) Endosperm (b) Embryo sac
(c) Embryo (d) Perisperm

156. Read the following statements and select the correct option:
A. There is no need of emasculation if the female parent bears unisexual flowers
B. Bagging is necessary for both emasculated and non-emasculated flowers
(a) Only (A) is correct
(b) Only (B) is correct
(c) Both (A) and (B) are correct
(d) Both (A) and (B) are incorrect

157. Pollen germination in angiosperms:
(a) Starts even before its release from the anther
(b) Cannot occur in nutrient medium containing sugar solution and minerals
(c) Occurs in stigma when the pollen is compatible
(d) More than one option is correct

158. Pollen pistil interaction is a ____A____ process involving pollen recognition followed by ____B____ of pollen tube growth:

	A	B
(a)	Static	Promotion
(b)	Dynamic	Promotion or inhibition
(c)	Static	Inhibition
(d)	Dynamic	Only rejection

159. Artificial hybridisation does not include or cause:
(a) Crop improvement
(b) Inbreeding depression
(c) Emasculation
(d) Bagging

Post-fertilisation Structure and Events, Endosperm, Embryo, Fruit and Seeds

160. Endosperm development precedes embryo development because:
(a) Its ploidy level is 3N
(b) It is larger than the embryo
(c) It provides nutrition to the embryo
(d) All of the above

161. The coconut water from tender coconut is:
(a) Free nuclear endosperm
(b) Cellular endosperm
(c) Made up of thousands of cells
(d) Both (a) and (c)

162. White kernel in coconut is:
(a) Cellular endosperm
(b) Mesocarp
(c) Cotyledons
(d) Helobial endosperm

163. The outermost layer of the endosperm of maize grain:
A. Is proteinaceous in nature
B. Is diploid
C. Is called aleuron layer
(a) Only (A)
(b) (A) and (C)
(c) (A) and (B)
(d) (A), (B) and (C)

164. Double endosperm is present in:
(a) Coconut (b) *Capsella*
(c) Cotton (d) Maize

165. Free nuclear division occurs in:
(a) Flower (b) Gametes
(c) Fruit (d) Endosperm

166. In angiosperms, endosperm is generally formed before:
(a) Pollination (b) Gametogenesis
(c) Embryogenesis (d) Syngamy

167. The part that separates the embryo region from the endosperm region in the seed of maize is the:
(a) Scutellum (b) Husk
(c) Hilum (d) Testa

168. A single large shield-shaped cotyledon seen in grass embryo is:
(a) Suspensor (b) Scutellum
(c) Epiblast (d) Coleoptile

169. Development of embryo in angiosperm is meroblastic because:
(a) Embryo develops from a part of the zygote only
(b) Suspensor is nutritive tissue
(c) Embryo development occurs after endosperm development
(d) All of the above

170. What stage of endosperm development will you examine to find out whether it is a nuclear type or cellular type of endosperm?
(a) Just after the division of the primary endosperm nucleus
(b) Mature stage of endosperm
(c) When the embryo has started dividing
(d) The stage of the endosperm when the embryo is heart-shaped

171. How many of the labelled structures are triploid in ploidy with respect to the following diagram?

(a) Four (b) Three
(c) One (d) Two

172. Select the incorrect match:
(a) Perispermic seed - Black pepper
(b) False fruit - Unfertilised ovary

(c) Parthenocarpic fruits - Seedless
(d) Non-endosperm seed - Orchid

173. Perisperm is:
(a) Diploid sporophytic tissue
(b) The future sporophytic generation
(c) The result of triple fusion
(d) More than one option is correct

174. Find the odd one out with respect to endospermic seeds:
(a) Coconut (b) Pea
(c) Castor (d) Maize

175. The thalamus also contributes to fruit formation in:
(a) Strawberry and cashew nut
(b) Apple and orange
(c) Tomato and banana
(d) Guava and mango

176. In date palm, the size of fruits and maturity time depends upon:
(a) Foreign pollens (b) Size of ovary
(c) Placental tissue (d) Size ovules

177. Which of the following is incorrect with respect to seed development?
(a) Water content is reduced
(b) Metabolic activities of the embryo decrease
(c) The micropyle remains as a small pore in the pericarp
(d) Integument of the ovules hardens and develops into protective seed coat

178. Plant part having many generations, one within the other, is:
(a) Embryo
(b) Seed
(c) Germinated pollen grain
(d) Unfertilised ovule

179. Endosperm formation is absent in:
(a) Orchids (b) Pea
(c) Maize (d) Date palm

180. As the seed matures, its water content decreases and is reduced to ________% moisture by mass:
(a) 10–15 (b) 15–25
(c) 25–30 (d) 1–5

181. Very old and viable seeds are recorded in:
(a) *Phoenix dactylifera*
(b) *Lupinus arcticus*
(c) *Oxalis*
(d) Orchid

182. The diploid number of chromosomes is 32 in a plant of an angiosperm. What will be the number of chromosomes in its endosperm?
(a) 32 (b) 16
(c) 64 (d) 48

183. Number of meiotic divisions required to produced 100 seeds of pea would be:
(a) 125 (b) 200
(c) 150 (d) 50

184. Fill in the blanks and choose the correct the option:
(i) The portion of the embryonal axis above the level of the cotyledons is the ____**A**____ which terminates with ____**B**____
(ii) The cylindrical portion below the level of cotyledons is ____**C**____ that terminates in the radicle ____**D**____

	A	B	C	D
(a)	Epicotyl	Radicle	Hypocotyl	Plumule
(b)	Epicotyl	Plumule	Hypocotyl	Radicle
(c)	Plumule	Coleoptile	Radicle	Coleoptile
(d)	Plumule	Epicotyl	Radicle	Hypocotyl

185. Albuminous seeds are all of the following, except:
(a) Sunflower (b) Castor
(c) Maize (d) Bean

186. In which of the following is there no sense of parthenocarpy?
(a) Banana (b) Orange
(c) Pomegranate (d) Lemon

187. Aleurone layer occurs in the peripheral region of:
(a) Cotyledon (b) Endosperm
(c) Coleoptile (d) Coleorhiza

188. During unfavourable climatic conditions:
(a) Seeds become dormant
(b) Plant develops healthy seeds
(c) Embryo becomes more active
(d) Seeds germinate more quickly

189. Identify A, B, C and D in the given figure of false fruit of apple:

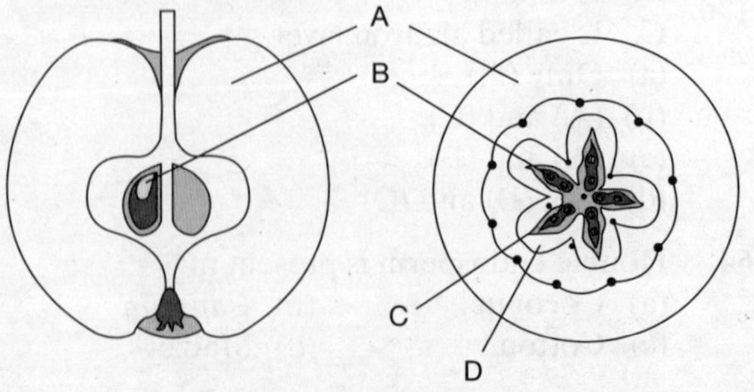

	A	B	C	D
(a)	Mesoarp	Endocarp	Seed	Thalamus
(b)	Seed	Thalamus	Mesocarp	Endocarp
(c)	Thalamus	Seed	Endocarp	Mesocarp
(d)	Mesocarp	Endocarp	Seed	Thalamus

190. In the seeds of some grasses, there are remains of the second cotyledon. It is called:
(a) Coleorhiza (b) Epiblast
(c) Coleoptile (d) Radicle

191. Function of suspensor of embryo is:
(a) Push the embryo into nutritive endosperm region
(b) Provide nutrition
(c) Formation of secondary embryos
(d) All of the above

192. Read the following statements with respect to embryogeny and select the correct option:
A. Most zygotes divide only after a certain amount of endosperm is formed
B. Early stages of embryo development greatly differ in both monocotyledons and dicotyledons
C. The zygote gives rise to the pro embryo and subsequently to the heart-shaped, globular and mature embryo
(a) Only (A) is correct
(b) Only (A) and (C) are correct
(c) Only (B) and (C) are correct
(d) (A), (B) and (C) are correct

193. Aleurone layer has the same ploidy as that of:
(a) Zygote (b) Pericarp
(c) Endosperm (d) Testa and tegmen

194. In non-albuminous seeds:
(a) Endosperm is not formed
(b) Endosperm is proteinaceous
(c) Endosperm is haploid
(d) Endosperm is completely consumed by developing embryo

195. Monocot embryo does not have:
(a) Scutellum (b) Epiblast
(c) Coleoptile (d) Hilum

196. Which of the following structures are not associated with dicot embryo?
(a) Plumule and radicle
(b) Coleoptile and coleorhiza
(c) Embryonic leaves
(d) Epicotyl and hypocotyl

197. Viable seeds of lupines that are thousands of years old have been discovered in:
(a) Arctic tundra
(b) Kind Herod's palace near Dead Sea
(c) Rohtang pass near Manali
(d) Tropical Pacific island

198. Seeds in angiospermic plants:
A. Provide protection to young embryo
B. Have sufficient food reserves
C. Are the product of sexual reproduction
(a) Only (A) is correct
(b) Only (B) and (C) are correct
(c) Only (C) is correct
(d) (A), (B), (C) are correct

199. The diagram given below shows the stages in embryogenesis in a typical dicot plant. Identify the structures A to D and select the correct option:

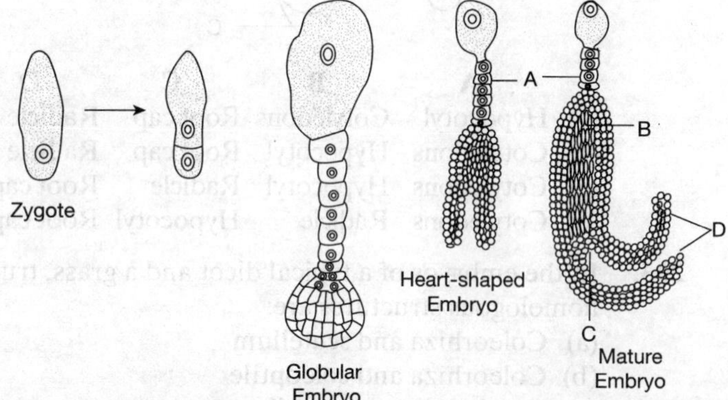

	A	B	C	D
(a)	Suspensor	Radicle	Plumule	Cotyledons
(b)	Hypophysis	Radicle	Plumule	Epiphysis
(c)	Suspensor	Plumule	Radicle	Cotyledons
(d)	Epiphysis	Plumule	Radicle	Hypophysis

200. Match the columns and select the correct option:

Column I	Column II
A. Ovary	(i) Pericarp
B. Ovary well	(ii) Perisperm
C. Ovule	(iii) Fruit
D. Nucleus	(iv) Seed

(a) A – (iii), B – (i), C – (iv), D – (ii)
(b) A – (iii), B – (iv), C – (i), D – (ii)
(c) A – (ii), B – (i), C – (iv), D – (iii)
(d) A – (ii), B – (iii), C – (iv), D – (i)

201. Choose the correct statement(s) with respect to parthenocarpic fruits:
(a) These fruits generally develop from the thalamus
(b) These can be produced through application of auxin hormone
(c) These are seedless fruits
(d) Both (b) and (c)

202. Identify the parts labelled A, B, C and D in the given figure and mark the correct option:

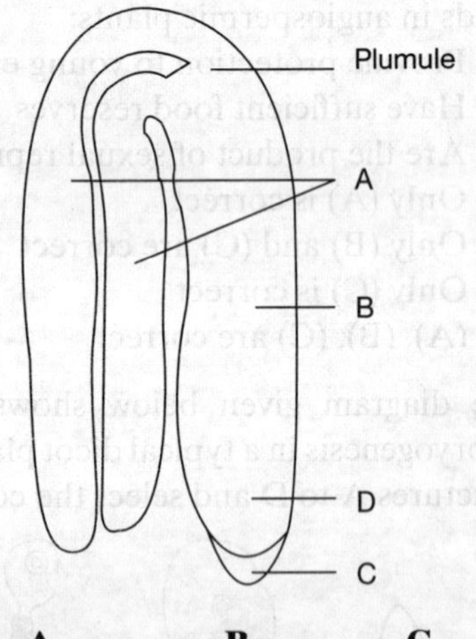

	A	B	C	D
(a)	Hypocotyl	Cotyledons	Root cap	Radicle
(b)	Cotyledons	Hypocotyl	Root cap	Radicle
(c)	Cotyledons	Hypocotyl	Radicle	Root cap
(d)	Cotyledons	Radicle	Hypocotyl	Root cap

203. In the embryos of a typical dicot and a grass, true homologous structures are:
(a) Coleorhiza and scutellum
(b) Coleorhiza and coleoptile
(c) Cotyledons and scutellum
(d) Hypocotyl and radicle

204. Non-albuminous seeds store their reserve food mainly in:
(a) Perisperm (b) Endosperm
(c) Chalazosperm (d) Cotyledons

205. The given figure shows the LS of a monocot embryo. Choose the correct labelling for A, B, C and D marked in the figure from the options given below:

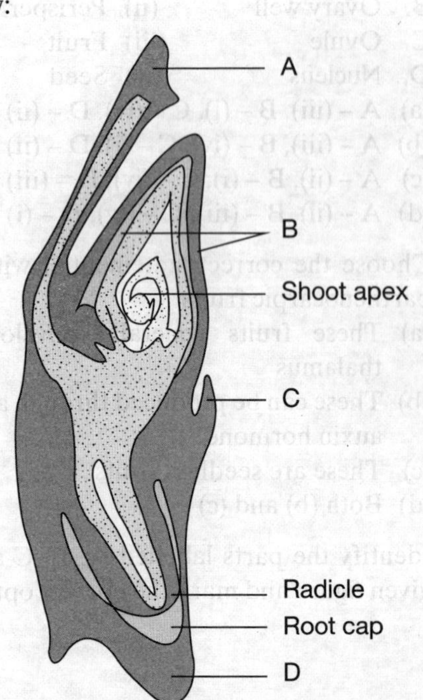

	A	B	C	D
(a)	Coleoptile	Scutellum	Epiblast	Coleorhiza
(b)	Scutellum	Coleoptile	Coleorhiza	Epiblast
(c)	Scutellum	Epiblast	Coleoptile	Coleorhiza
(d)	Scutellum	Coleoptile	Epiblast	Coleorhiza

206. Formation of embryo from zygote includes all, except:
(a) Mitosis
(b) Cell differentiation
(c) Reduction division
(d) Equational division

207. Seeds of legumes have no residual endosperm:
(a) They do not show triple fusion
(b) It is consumed partially by young plantlets
(c) It is completely consumed during embryo development
(d) They produce albuminous seeds

208. The seeds germinated and flowered after an estimated record of 2000 years of dormancy in:
(a) *Phoenix dactylifera*
(b) *Trifolium*
(c) *Lupinus arcticus*
(d) *Nelumbo*

209. Find the parasitic plants containing thousands of tiny seeds in each fruit:
(a) Orchids, *Ficus*
(b) *Ficus, Striga*
(c) *Zea mays, Orobanche*
(d) *Orobanche, Striga*

Apomixis and Polyembryony

210. Read the following statements with respect to hybrid seeds:
A. Progeny segregate and do not maintain hybrid character
B. Production of hybrid seed is costly
C. Hybrid seeds have to be produced every year correct
The correct statement(s) is/are:
(a) Only (A) (b) Only (A) and (B)
(c) Only (B) and (C) (d) (A), (B) and (C)

211. Select the odd one out with respect to apomixis:
(a) It mimics sexual reproduction
(b) It creates genetic variability
(c) Common in Asteraceae and grasses
(d) Retains hybrid characters indefinitely

212. Apomictic seeds are of great importance in agriculture because:
(a) They are better in quality than their parents
(b) Their useful characters are environmentally induced

(c) They increase pressure for hybrid seed production
(d) There is no segregation of characters

213. Which of the following types of embryos are apomictic?
(a) Nucellar (b) Zygotic
(c) Integumentary (d) Both (a) and (c)

214. Which of the following biological phenomena help to save the time of plant breeders?
(a) Fertilisation (b) Apomixis
(c) Emasculation (d) Hybridisation

215. Parthenocarpy and apomixes are similar in:
(a) Absence of fertilisation
(b) Absence of embryo formation
(c) Absence of seed formation
(d) Absence of fruit formation

216. A cross is made between male 4 N and female 4 N plants. Plants obtained by this cross-reproduce apomictically. What would be the ploidy level in the subsequent progeny?
(a) 4 N (b) 6 N
(c) 5 N (d) 8 N

217. Seed formation without fertilisation is called:
(a) Double fertilisation (b) Parthenocarpy
(c) Apomixis (d) Syngamy

218. In adventive embryony:
(a) Embryo develops from zygote
(b) Embryo arises from diploid sporophytic tissue such as nucellus or integument
(c) Diploid embryo sac is formed from megaspore mother cell
(d) Haploid embryo is formed from any of the haploid cells of the embryo sac

219. Polyembryony was first reported by ____A____ in ____B____:

	A	B
(a)	Leeuwenhoek	*Citrus*
(b)	Leeuwenhoek	Mango
(c)	Hofmeister	*Citrus*
(d)	Pasteur	Tomato

220. Polyembryony is:
(a) One embryo in one seed
(b) More than one embryo in a seed
(c) More seeds in one fruit
(d) Seed development before fertilisation

221. More than one embryo in a seed is formed due to:
A. Cleavage of zygote
B. Fertilisation of nucellar cell
C. Formation of more than one embryo sac
(a) Only A (b) Only C
(c) (A) and (C) only (d) (A), (B) and (C)

NCERT EXEMPLAR QUESTIONS

1. Among the terms listed below, those that are not technically correct names for a floral whorl are:
(i) Androecium
(ii) Carpel
(iii) Corolla
(iv) Sepal
(a) (i) and (iv) (b) (iii) and (iv)
(c) (ii) and (iv) (d) (i) and (ii)

2. Embryo sac is to ovule as ________ is to anther.
(a) Stamen (b) Filament
(c) Pollen grain (d) Androecium

3. In a typical complete, bisexual and hypogynous flower, the arrangement of floral whorls on the thalamus from the outermost to the innermost is:
(a) Calyx, corolla, androecium and gynoecium
(b) Calyx, corolla, gynoecium and androecium
(c) Gynoecium, androecium, corolla and calyx
(d) Androecium, gynoecium, corolla and calyx

4. A dicotyledonous plant bears flowers but never produces fruits and seeds. The most probable cause for the above situation is:
(a) Plant is dioecious and bears only pistillate flowers
(b) Plant is dioecious and bears both pistillate and staminate flowers
(c) Plant is monoecious
(d) Plant is dioecious and bears only staminate flowers

5. The outermost and innermost wall layers of microsporangium in anther are, respectively:
(a) Endothecium and tapetum
(b) Epidermis and endodermis
(c) Epidermis and middle layer
(d) Epidermis and tapetum

6. During microsporogenesis, meiosis occurs in:
(a) Endothecium
(b) Microspore mother cells

(c) Microspore tetrads
(d) Pollen grains

7. From among the terms given below, identify those that are associated with the gynoecium:
(a) Stigma, ovule, embryo sac, placenta
(b) Thalamus, pistil, style, ovule
(c) Ovule, ovary, embryo sac, tapetum
(d) Ovule, stamen, ovary, embryo sac

8. Starting from the innermost part, the correct sequence of parts in an ovule are:
(a) Egg, nucellus, embryo sac, integument
(b) Egg, embryo sac, nucellus, integument
(c) Embryo sac, nucellus, integument, egg
(d) Egg, integument, embryo sac, nucellus

9. From the statements given below, choose the option that is true for a typical female gametophyte of a flowering plant:
(i) It is 8-nucleate and 7-celled at maturity
(ii) It is free-nuclear during the development
(iii) It is situated inside the integument but outside the nucellus
(iv) It has an egg apparatus situated at the chalazal end
(a) (i) and (iv) (b) (ii) and (iii)
(c) (i) and (ii) (d) (ii) and (iv)

10. Autogamy can occur in a chasmogamous flower if:
(a) Pollen matures before ovule
(b) Ovules mature before pollen
(c) Both pollen and ovules mature simultaneously
(d) Both anther and stigma are of equal length

11. Choose the correct statement from the following:
(a) Cleistogamous flowers always exhibit autogamy
(b) Chasmogamous flowers always exhibit geitonogamy
(c) Cleistogamous flowers exhibit both autogamy and geitonogamy
(d) Chasmogamous flowers never exhibit autogamy

12. A particular species of plant produces light, non-sticky pollen in large numbers and its stigmas are long and feathery. These modifications facilitate pollination by:
(a) Insects (b) Water
(c) Wind (d) Animals

13. From among the situations given below, choose the one that prevents both autogamy and geitonogamy:
(a) Monoecious plant bearing unisexual flowers
(b) Dioecious plant bearing only male or female flowers
(c) Monoecious plant with bisexual flowers
(d) Dioecious plant with bisexual flowers

14. In a fertilised embryo sac, the haploid, diploid and triploid structures are:
(a) Synergid, zygote and primary endosperm nucleus
(b) Synergid, antipodal and polar nuclei
(c) Antipodal, synergid and primary endosperm nucleus
(d) Synergid, polar nuclei and zygote

15. In an embryo sac, the cells that degenerate after fertilisation are:
(a) Synergids and primary endosperm cell
(b) Synergids and antipodals
(c) Antipodals and primary endosperm cell
(d) Egg and antipodals

16. While planning for an artificial hybridisation programme involving dioecious plants, which of the following steps would not be relevant:
(a) Bagging of female flower
(b) Dusting of pollen on stigma
(c) Emasculation
(d) Collection of pollen

17. In the embryos of a typical dicot and a grass, true homologous structures are:
(a) Coleorhiza and coleoptile
(b) Coleoptile and scutellum
(c) Cotyledons and scutellum
(d) Hypocotyl and radicle

18. The phenomenon observed in some plants wherein parts of the sexual apparatus are used for forming embryos without fertilisation is called:
(a) Parthenocarpy
(b) Apomixis
(c) Vegetative propagation
(d) Sexual reproduction

19. In a flower, if the megaspore mother cell forms megaspores without undergoing meiosis and if one of the megaspores develops into an embryo sac, its nuclei would be:
(a) Haploid
(b) Diploid
(c) A few haploid and a few diploid
(d) With varying ploidy

20. The phenomenon wherein the ovary develops into a fruit without fertilisation is called:
(a) Parthenocarpy
(b) Apomixis
(c) Asexual reproduction
(d) Sexual reproduction

PRACTICE TEST PAPER

1. All of the following plants have flowers producing assured seed set even in the absence of pollinators, except:
(a) *Yucca* (b) *Oxalis*
(c) *Viola* (d) *Commelina*

2. The number of nuclei taking part in double fertilisation:
(a) 5 (b) 3
(c) 4 (d) 1

3. One advantage of cleistogamy is:
(a) It leads to greater genetic diversity
(b) Seed dispersal is more efficient and widespread
(c) Seed set is not dependent on pollinators
(d) Each visit of a pollinator results in transfer of hundreds

4. Mark the correct statement with respect to the structure of the anther:
(a) Only epidermis performs the function of protection
(b) Endothecium is the innermost layer of the anther wall
(c) Cells of tapetum have dense cytoplasm and generally have more than one nucleus
(d) Anther consists of four microsporangia in each lobe

5. In flowering plants, endosperm is generally formed before:
(a) Pollination (b) Embryo development
(c) Sporogenesis (d) Fertilisation

6. Egg apparatus in embryo sac consists of:
(a) Two polar nuclei + one egg cell
(b) Two synergids + one egg cell
(c) Central cell + egg cell
(d) Antipodals + egg cell + synergids

7. The form of asexual reproduction that mimics sexual reproduction:
A. Is known as apomixes
B. Occurs in some members of grasses and Asteraceae
C. Produces seed without fertilisation
(a) Only (A) is correct
(b) Only (A) and (B) are correct
(c) Only (C) is correct
(d) (A), (B) and (C) are correct

8. Endosperm is completely consumed by the developing embryo in the seeds of:
(a) Rice and wheat (b) Maize and castor
(c) Pea and bean (d) Castor and groundnut

9. Which of the following plants possess both cleistogamous and chasmogamous flowers:
(a) *Commelina* (b) Maize
(c) *Ficus* (d) *Amorphophallus*

10. How many pollen mother cells should undergo meiotic division to produce 100 pollen grains?
(a) 100 (b) 50
(c) 25 (d) 75

11. An obligate relationship between a plant and insect where both cannot complete their life cycles without each other is shown by:
(a) *Pronuba* moth and *Yucca*
(b) Honey bee and *Salvia*
(c) Butterfly and sunflower
(d) Honey bee and rose

12. Select the incorrect statement with respect to pollen grains:
(a) It represents the male gametophyte
(b) It is always oval in shape
(c) Germ pore of pollen lack sporopollenin
(d) In the majority of flowering plants, pollen grains shed at the two-celled stage

13. How many of the following possess a single ovule in each ovary?
Papaya, Watermelon, Wheat, Rice, Mango, Orchid
(a) Five (b) Four
(c) Two (d) Three

14. The ploidy of secondary nucleus, nucellus, endosperm antipodals and pollen grains in flowering plants is, respectively:
(a) 2n, n, 3n, n, n (b) 2n, 2n, 3n, n, 2n
(c) 2n, 2n, 3n, n, n (d) n, n, 3n, n, 2n

15. Multicarpellary apocarpus pistil is found in:
(a) *Michelia* (b) *Papaver*
(c) *Hibiscus* (d) All except (a)

16. The plant part that consists of two generations, one within the other, is:
(a) Germinated pollen grain
(b) Seed
(c) Embryo sac
(d) Both (a) and (c)

17. How many of the following features is/are associated with wind-pollinated plants?
(i) Flowers packed into inflorescence

(ii) Large and feathery stigma
(iii) Flowers are nectarless and colourless
(iv) Non-sticky pollen grains
(a) Four (b) Three
(c) Two (d) One

18. Endosperm persists in the mature seeds of:
(a) Pea (b) Bean
(c) Gram (d) Wheat

19. Aleurone layer is a part of:
(a) Endosperm (b) Embryo
(c) Embryo sac (d) Perisperm

20. In cereals like rice and wheat, pollen viability is up to:
(a) 30 minutes (b) 30 seconds
(c) 30 hours (d) Several months

21. In pollen banks, pollen grains are stored at:
(a) 0°C of liquid nitrogen
(b) –196°C of liquid N_2
(c) 40°C of liquid N_2
(d) –96°C of liquid N_2

22. Largest cell of a typical embryo sac is:
(a) Antipodal cell (b) Synergids
(c) Egg cell (d) Central cell

23. Of the following, how many characters are usually associated with entomophilous flowers?
Large feathery stigma, fragrant flowers, sticky pollen grains, rich in nectar, mucilage-covered pollen grains, pollen kit, cleistogamous flowers
(a) Two (b) Three
(c) Four (d) Five

24. The marine plant in which female flowers remain submerged in water and pollination occurs in water is:
(a) *Vallisneria* (b) *Zostera*
(c) Coconut (d) Tape grass

25. In the majority of angiosperms, shedding of pollen grains occurs at:
(a) Two-celled stage (b) Three-celled stage
(c) Four-celled stage (d) Five-celled stage

26. In grass family, remains of second cotyledon is called:
(a) Coleoptile (b) Coleorhiza
(c) Scutellum (d) Epiblast

27. Which among the following features/conditions in plants can prevent autogamy but not geitonogamy?
(a) Cleistogamy (b) Dioecy
(c) Dichogamy (d) Monoecy

28. How many chromosomes will be present in the endosperm cell of a flowering plant if the root tip cell of the same plant has 24 chromosomes?
(a) 24 (b) 12
(c) 36 (d) 48

29. Select the incorrect match:
(a) Apomictic embryo - Nucellar embryo
(b) False fruit - Unfertilised ovary
(c) Perispermic seed - Black paper
(d) Polyembryony - *Citrus*

30. Majority of insect-pollinated flowers are:
(a) Nectarless, odourless and coloured
(b) Colourful, fragrant and nectar-rich
(c) Coloured, fragrant and nectarless
(d) Coated by waxy layer

31. Effect of foreign pollen on endosperm is called:
(a) Xenia
(b) Metaxenia
(c) Nemec phenomenon
(d) Apomixis

32. The female gametophyte in the angiosperm is/has:
(a) Seven-celled and eight-nucleated
(b) Produced by one meiosis and three successive generations of mitosis
(c) Called embryo sac
(d) All of the above

33. Egg apparatus is homologous to:
(a) Megasporangium (b) Female gametophyte
(c) Archegonium (d) Female gamete

34. Which of the following biological phenomena help to save the time of plant breeders?
(a) Emasculation (b) in breeding
(c) Hybridisation (d) Apomixis

35. How many meiotic divisions are usually required for the formation of 200 seeds in flowering plants?
(a) 100 (b) 250
(c) 400 (d) 200

36. Endothecium in anther helps in:
(a) Nutrition
(b) Dehiscence of anther
(c) Formation of ubisch bodies
(d) Germination of pollen

37. The viability of seeds of *Lupines arcticus* is:
(a) 500 years (b) 2000 years
(c) 10000 years (d) 1,00,000 years

38. The thalamus also contributes to fruit formation in:

(a) Orange and mango
(b) Strawberry and cashew net
(c) Tomato and brinjal
(d) Coconut and almond

39. Which one of the following is resistant to enzyme action?
(a) Leaf cuticle (b) Cork
(c) Wood fibre (d) Pollen exine

40. The majority of angiosperms:
(a) Have monosporic embryo sac
(b) Show pollen dispersal of three-celled stage
(c) Show hydrophily
(d) Show apomixes

41. The scutellum observed in a grain of wheat or maize is comparable to which part of the seed in other monocotyledons?
(a) Plumule (b) Cotyledon
(c) Endosperm (d) Aleurone layer

42. Polypoid cells are seen in ________ layer of anther wall:
(a) Epidermis (b) Endothecium
(c) Middle layers (d) Tapetum

43. Ovary may have many ovules in:
(a) Wheat (b) Rice
(c) Orchids (d) Mango

44. Parthenocarpic fruits are found in:
(a) Apple (b) Castor
(c) Wheat (d) Banana

45. In some seeds, remnants of the nucellus are also persistent. This residual persistent nucellus is called:
(a) Perisperm (b) Pericarp
(c) Mesoderm (d) Endosperm

ANSWER KEYS

Exercises

1. (c) **2.** (b) **3.** (d) **4.** (a) **5.** (c) **6.** (c) **7.** (b) **8.** (a) **9.** (c) **10.** (a)
11. (b) **12.** (c) **13.** (c) **14.** (c) **15.** (d) **16.** (b) **17.** (d) **18.** (a) **19.** (a) **20.** (c)
21. (d) **22.** (a) **23.** (a) **24.** (d) **25.** (b) **26.** (c) **27.** (b) **28.** (d) **29.** (a) **30.** (c)
31. (a) **32.** (c) **33.** (c) **34.** (a) **35.** (c) **36.** (d) **37.** (d) **38.** (b) **39.** (d) **40.** (b)
41. (d) **42.** (a) **43.** (a) **44.** (c) **45.** (a) **46.** (d) **47.** (c) **48.** (a) **49.** (a) **50.** (b)
51. (b) **52.** (d) **53.** (d) **54.** (d) **55.** (d) **56.** (a) **57.** (d) **58.** (a) **59.** (a) **60.** (b)
61. (d) **62.** (b) **63.** (a) **64.** (d) **65.** (a) **66.** (a) **67.** (d) **68.** (a) **69.** (a) **70.** (b)
71. (b) **72.** (d) **73.** (a) **74.** (d) **75.** (a) **76.** (b) **77.** (d) **78.** (b) **79.** (a) **80.** (c)
81. (a) **82.** (b) **83.** (d) **84.** (c) **85.** (c) **86.** (b) **87.** (b) **88.** (a) **89.** (d) **90.** (a)
91. (a) **92.** (b) **93.** (c) **94.** (c) **95.** (c) **96.** (c) **97.** (c) **98.** (d) **99.** (b) **100.** (a)
101. (c) **102.** (c) **103.** (c) **104.** (c) **105.** (b) **106.** (b) **107.** (b) **108.** (c) **109.** (d) **110.** (a)
111. (c) **112.** (d) **113.** (d) **114.** (b) **115.** (a) **116.** (d) **117.** (c) **118.** (d) **119.** (a) **120.** (d)
121. (b) **122.** (d) **123.** (c) **124.** (c) **125.** (d) **126.** (c) **127.** (a) **128.** (d) **129.** (a) **130.** (c)
131. (c) **132.** (d) **133.** (a) **134.** (b) **135.** (b) **136.** (a) **137.** (c) **138.** (d) **139.** (d) **140.** (b)
141. (a) **142.** (b) **143.** (d) **144.** (c) **145.** (d) **146.** (b) **147.** (b) **148.** (a) **149.** (d) **150.** (c)
151. (c) **152.** (c) **153.** (d) **154.** (a) **155.** (b) **156.** (c) **157.** (c) **158.** (b) **159.** (b) **160.** (c)
161. (a) **162.** (a) **163.** (b) **164.** (a) **165.** (d) **166.** (c) **167.** (a) **168.** (b) **169.** (a) **170.** (a)
171. (d) **172.** (b) **173.** (a) **174.** (b) **175.** (a) **176.** (a) **177.** (c) **178.** (b) **179.** (a) **180.** (a)
181. (b) **182.** (d) **183.** (a) **184.** (b) **185.** (d) **186.** (c) **187.** (b) **188.** (a) **189.** (c) **190.** (b)
191. (a) **192.** (a) **193.** (c) **194.** (d) **195.** (d) **196.** (b) **197.** (a) **198.** (d) **199.** (a) **200.** (a)
201. (d) **202.** (b) **203.** (c) **204.** (d) **205.** (d) **206.** (c) **207.** (c) **208.** (a) **209.** (d) **210.** (d)
211. (b) **212.** (d) **213.** (d) **214.** (b) **215.** (a) **216.** (a) **217.** (c) **218.** (b) **219.** (a) **220.** (b)
221. (c)

NCERT Exemplar Questions

1. (c) **2.** (c) **3.** (a) **4.** (d) **5.** (d) **6.** (b) **7.** (a) **8.** (b) **9.** (c) **10.** (c)
11. (a) **12.** (c) **13.** (b) **14.** (a) **15.** (b) **16.** (c) **17.** (c) **18.** (b) **19.** (b) **20.** (a)

Practice Test Paper

1. (a) **2.** (a) **3.** (c) **4.** (c) **5.** (b) **6.** (b) **7.** (d) **8.** (c) **9.** (a) **10.** (c)
11. (a) **12.** (b) **13.** (d) **14.** (c) **15.** (a) **16.** (b) **17.** (a) **10.** (d) **13.** (a) **20.** (a)
21. (b) **22.** (d) **23.** (c) **24.** (b) **25.** (a) **26.** (d) **27.** (d) **28.** (c) **29.** (b) **30.** (b)
31. (a) **32.** (d) **33.** (c) **34.** (d) **35.** (b) **36.** (b) **37.** (c) **38.** (b) **39.** (d) **40.** (a)
41. (b) **42.** (d) **43.** (c) **44.** (d) **45.** (a)

SOLUTIONS

Flower, Pre-fertilisation Structure and Events, Stamen, Microsporangium and Pollen Grain

1. A typical angiospermic flower consists of four whorls. Two non-essential whorls – calyx and corolla, and two essential whorls – androecium and gynoecium.

2. Stamen is technically equivalent to microsporophyll. A typical stamen consists of two parts: the anther (terminal bilobed structure) and the filament (long slender stalk).

3. Each anther is a tetragonal structure consisting of four microsporangia located at the corners, two in each lobe. The microsporangia form the pollen sac which, on maturity, becomes filled with pollen grains.

4. Stamen and carpel

5. A typical anther is a bilobed, tetragonal, tetrasporangiate structure.

6. Microspore mother cells undergo meiotic division to form microspore tetrads. As the anther matures and dehydrates, the microspores dissociate from each other and develop into pollen grains. During the formation of pollen grains, the microspore divides mitotically into two cells: vegetative and generative.

7. In a flowering plant, the largest number of haploid cells (pollen grains) is present in the microsporangia.

8. A – Anther, B – Filament, C – Pollen sac, D – Pollen grains

9. The inner and radial walls of the endothecium become thick due to thickening of a-cellulose fibres. The endothecium becomes hydroscopic due to the presence of fibrous thickening; so it helps in dehiscence of the anther.

10. Tapetum is the innermost layer of the anther wall which surrounds the sporogenous tissue. Cells of tapetum possess dense cytoplasm and more than one nucleus, so they are polypoid. The tapetal cells show an increase in DNA content.

11. Tapetum

12. The outer three wall layers (epidermis, endothecium and middle layers) perform the function of protection and help in dehiscence of the anther to release the pollen.

13. A – Meiosis, B – Mitosis, C – Mitosis

14. The formation of haploid microspores from the microspore mother cell (2n) inside the microsporangium by meiotic division is called microsporogenesis.

15. Anther

16. (B) and (C) are correct. In the majority of flowering plants (60%), pollination occurs at the two-celled stage (vegetative and generative cells). Pollen exine exhibits a fascinating array of patterns and designs which is of taxonomic significance.

17. At the initial stage, all four microspores are attached together with the help of the callose layer.

18. Ubisch bodies are spherical bodies that are formed inside the tapetal cells before their disintegration. An Ubisch body is made up of a complex substance called sporopollenin.

19. Pollen exine is made up of sporopollenin. It is the most resistant organic material known.

20. (A), (B) and (C) are correct. Sporopollenin can withstand high temperature, acid and alkali. No enzyme that degrades that sporopollenin is so far known. Pollen grains are well preserved as fossils because of the presence of sporopollenin.

21. Pollen exine has prominent apertures called germ pores where sporopollenin is absent.

22. A – spherical, B – 25–50 μm

23. Pollen viability is highly variable and depends on the prevailing temperature and humidity.

It is 30 minutes in cereals (rice and wheat); in some members of Rosaceae, Solanaceae and Leguminosae, pollen viability may be several months.

24. Pollen grains can be stored as pollen banks, similar to seed banks in plant breeding programmes. Pollen grains are stored in liquid nitrogen at −196°C.

25. Two-celled stage

26. One microspore produces two male gametes and one microspore mother cell produces four microspores. Thus, for production of 120 male gametes, 15 microspore mother cells are required.

27. When the pollen grain is mature, it contains two haploid cells, vegetative and generative.

28. 250

29. The generative cell in a pollen grain is small and floats in the cytoplasm of the vegetative cell. It is spindle-shaped with dense cytoplasm and a nucleus.

30. The vegetative cell is bigger in size, having abundant food reserves and a large irregularly shaped nucleus.

31. Parthenium or carrot grass

32. Prevailing temperature and humidity

33. Please refers to answer (23)

34. For formation of mature male gametophyte from microspore mother cell, 1 meiotic and 2 mitotic divisions are required (pollen grain is best regarded as a partially developed male gametophyte).

35. Middle layers

36. Cytoplasm of pollen grain is surrounded by plasma membrane.

37. In the majority of following plants, the generative cell of the pollen grain divides and forms two non-motile male gametes during the growth of the pollen tube at the stigma, as the pollen grains are shed at the two-celled stage. If the pollen grains are shed at the three-celled stage, they would carry two male gametes from the beginning.

Pistil, Megasporangium (Ovule) and Embryo Sac

38. A – Megasporophyll, B – Megasporangium

39. Figures (A) and (C) represent the multicarpellary syncarpous gynoecium of *Hibiscus* and *Papaver.* Figure (B) shows the multicarpellary apocarpous gynoecium of *Michelia.*

40. Stigma

41. *Michelia*

42. Multicarpellary syncarpous

43. Multicarpellary apocarpous

44. Filament is a long and slender stalk of stamen.

45. Many ovules are present in the ovary of papaya, watermelon and orchid.

46. Hilum is the junction between the ovule and funicle (stalk of ovule).

47. Funicle is the stalk of the ovule by which it remains attached to the placenta.

48. Ovule is technically known as megasporium.

49. The process of embryo sac development from a single megaspore is called monosporic development. In the majority of flowering plants, one of the megaspores functions while the other three generate.

50. Megaspores are arranged in a linear tetrad of four megaspores.

51. Megagametogenesis

52. During formation of the embryo sac, a functional megaspore undergoes three mitotic divisions. After rearrangement of nuclei, a seven-celled, eight-nucleated embryo sac is formed.

53. An ovule generally has one embryo sac, which is a 7-celled, 8-nucleated structure.

54. Polygonum type of embryo sac is monosporic and comprises 7-celled 8-nucleated structure. Three of the nuclei are organised as cells at the micropylar end, forming the egg apparatus (egg cell + two synergids).Three nuclei are organised as antipodal cells at the chalazal end while two nuclei in the centre are called polar nuclei.

55. Synergids are haploid cells present at the micropylar end. They are characterised by the presence of a filiform apparatus (in the form of finger-like projections) at the micropylar end, which play an important role in guiding the pollen tubes into the synergids.

56. Haploid cells – 6 (three antipodals cells + one egg cell + two synergids); Diploid cells – 1 (central cell possess two polar nuclei)

57. Germ pores are present on the exine of the pollen grain.

58. Nucellus is a parenchymatous mass of tissue enclosed within the integuments and which forms the body of the ovule.

59. The most common type of ovule present in an angiosperm is anatropous. In this type, the ovule completely is turned at 180° due to unilateral growth of the funicle, so it is also called inverted ovule.

60. The three haploid cells (egg cell and two synergids) at the micropylar end are collectively known as the egg apparatus.

61. Synergid

62. Megaspore mother cell divides meiotically to form a linear tetrad of megaspores. Megaspore acts as the first cell of the female gametophyte.

63. Generally, the lowermost or chalazal megaspore is functional of the tetrad of megaspores, while the other three that lie towards the micropyle degenerate. So, for the formation of 250 functional megaspores, 250 megaspore mother cells are required.

64. Polygonum type embryo sac shows monosporic development.

65. Ovules generally differentiate a single megaspore mother cell in the micropylar region of the nucellus. It is a large cell containing dense cytoplasm and prominent nucleus.

66. Monosporic development

67. Function of filiform apparatus is to guide the path of the pollen tube into the synergids.

68. A – Micropyle, B – Nucellus, C – Embryo sac, D – Chalaza

69. Anatropous ovule

70. Fourth from the micropyle

71. Single chalazal functional megaspore

72. Nucellus – 2n, Megaspore mother cell – 2n, Embryo sac – n

73. Anatropous ovule

74. Formation of egg is called megagametogenesis.

75. Most primitive type of ovule is orthotropous. The body of the ovule is upright in position. The micropyle, chalaza and helium lie on one straight line, so that the ovule is called straight or upright ovule.

76. In amphitropous ovule, the curvature is more effective in the nucellus and due to this effect, the embryo sac becomes horseshoe-shaped.

77. Four structures (antipodals, polar nuclei, synergid and egg cell) are gametophytic in origin. They are part of the embryo sac or female gametophyte.

Pollination and Outbreeding Devices

78. Pollination is defined as the process of transfer of pollen grains from the anther to the stigma of the same flower or of different flowers of the same species.

79. Xenogamy is the transfer of pollen grains from the anther to the stigma of other flowers of the same species.

80. (A), (C) and (D) are correct. Cleistogamy is a condition in which the flower does not open. Cleistogamous flowers are invariably autogamous as there is no chance of cross-pollination.

81. Geitonogamy is the transfer of pollen grains from the anther to the stigma of another flower of the same plant. From the genetic point of view, geitonogamy is self-pollination because all the flowers of the same plant are genetically similar, but ecologically it is considered as cross-pollination.

82. Flowers should produce a large number of pollen grains.

83. Cleistogamous flowers are bisexual flowers that never open. For example, *Commelina*, *Viola*, *Oxalis*.

84. Cleistogamous flowers never open, so only self-pollination takes place in these plants. It ensures seed formation even in the absence of any pollinating agent.

85. Some plants like *Viola* (pansy), *Oxalis* and *Commelina* produce both types of flowers, that is, open flowers (chasmogamous) and closed flowers (cleistogamous).

86. In maize, the male and female inflorescence is called tassel and cob, respectively. Tassel are borne terminally and cobs are borne laterally at lower levels.

87. The majority of flowering plants use a range of animals as pollinating agents.

88. Pollination can be classified on the basis of agency of pollination.

89. Shrews

90. Water-pollinated plants are characterised by the presence of light, unwettable pollen grains and generally surrounded by nucilogenous covering.

91. Wind pollination is quite common in grasses.

92. In *Zostera*, hypohydrophily occurs. The female flowers remain submerged in water and pollen grains are long, ribbon-like structures carried passively inside the water. Some of them reach the stigma and achieve pollination.

93. Cleistogamy

94. Entomophilous flowers are characterised by the presence of sticky pollen grains.

95. In water hyacinth and water lily, the flowers emerge above the level of water and are pollinated by insects or wind.

96. Wind

97. Hydrophily

98. Anemophily is associated with reduction in ovule number and size of the pollen grain. Pollen grains are light in weight and very small and the pistil commonly possesses a single ovule.

99. Pollination by water is very rare in flowering plants and is limited to about 30 genera, mostly monocots.

100. The presence of long feathery stigma is characteristic of wind-pollinated flowers.

101. In several species such as papaya, the male and female flowers are present on different plants, that is, each plant is either male or female (dioecy). This condition prevents both autogamy and geitonogamy.

102. The flower height in *Amorphophallus* is 6 feet.

103. *Pronuba* moth lays its eggs in the ovary of the *Yucca* plant and its flowers are pollinated by the moth.

104. In papaya, male and female flowers are present on different plants. It prevents autogamy and geitonogamy.

105. D is false. To sustain animal visits, flowers have to provide rewards to the animals. Nectar and pollen grains are the usual floral rewards.

106. Bees are the most common insects which act as pollinating agents in agricultural fields.

107. Pollinated by insects

108. "Biological arms race" is concerned with coevolution of flowers and pollinators.

109. The given diagram is a wind-pollinated plant showing compact inflorescence and well-exposed stamens.

110. In *Vallisneria*, epihydrophily occurs. *Vallisneria* is a submerged dioecious plant. The female flower has a very long pedicel, therefore it reaches the surface of the water.

111. Preference for foreign pollen grains

112. *Vallisneria* and *Zostera* are water-pollinated plants.

113. Pollen robbers are insects that consume pollen or nectar without bringing about pollination. Queens of *Bombus affinis* perforate *Aquilegia* spurs and steal nectar.

114. Anemophily

115. Bats (chiropterophily)

116. (A), (B) and (C) are correct.

117. Pollen grains, nectar and providing a safe place to lay eggs are common floral rewards.

118. *Amorphophallus*

119. Monoecious plants like maize and castor have male and female flowers that are produced on the same plant. This prevents autogamy but not geitonogamy.

120. An advantage of cleistogamy is that the seed set is not dependent on pollinators because cleistogamous flowers are invariably autogamous.

121. Self-sterility is a condition of pollen grains of flowers that cannot germinate on the stigma of the same flower. This is characteristic feature which is controlled by genes.

122. All the statements are correct.

123. Dioecious plants like mulberry, date palm and papaya prevent both autogamy and geitonogamy.

124. Water hyacinth and water lily

125. Cleistogamy is a contrivance for self-pollination.

126. Presence of anther and stigma at different levels in the same flower is an out breeding device; it prevents autogamy and encourages cross-pollination.

127. Xenogamy (cross-pollination)

Pollen–Pistil Interaction, Double Fertilisation

128. If the pollen grain is of the wrong type, the pistil rejects the pollen by preventing pollen germination on the stigma. The ability of the pistil to recognise the pollen followed by its acceptance or rejection is the result of a chemical dialogue between the pollen grain and the pistil.

129. After pollination, the pollen grains germinate on the stigma. They absorb moisture, sugar, boron and amino acids from the stigma and swell up.

130. Pollen tube secretes enzymes like pectinases and cellulases.

131. In-vivo germination

132. The region of emergence of the pollen tube is not damaged.

133. In the majority of flowering plants. the entry of the pollen tube in the ovule is porogamy, that is, the pollen tube enters through the micropyle. In chalazogamy, the pollen tube enters through the chalaza and in misogamy, the pollen tube enters through the integuments.

134. Siphonogamy is a condition in plants in which the pollen tubes are developed for the transfer of male gametes to the egg cells.

135. After entering one of the synergids, the pollen tube releases two male gametes to the cytoplasm of the synergid.

136. Double fertilisation was discovered by SG Nawaschin in *Lilium* and *Fritillaria*.

137. Maize

138. The generative cell of the pollen grain divides mitotically to form two non-motile male gametes, which are slightly unequal in size.

139. Triple fusion involves fusion of male gamete with secondary nucleus to form a triploid primary endosperm nucleus (PEN).

140. Endosperm is nutritive tissue which develops from the primary endosperm nucleus. It is utilised by the embryo during early development and at the time of seed germination, the endosperm is the result of triple fusion.

141. Only one male gamete is involved in triple fusion.

142. After double fertilisation, a mature ovule has one diploid cell (zygote) and one triploid cell (endosperm). Synergids and antipodal cells are degenerated.

143. Secondary nucleus

144. The filiform apparatus of synergids release chemicals that offer chemotropic stimulus to the pollen tube.

145. Ploidy level of zygote = Ploidy level of male gamete + Ploidy level of female gamete
= 2 N + N = 3 N

Ploidy level of endosperm = Ploidy level of male gamete + Ploidy of secondary nucleus
= 2 N + 2 N = 4 N

146. Antipodals (n), Zygote (2n), Endosperm (3n)

147. Double fertilisation is a unique feature of angiosperms.

148. Three gametes (two male gametes + one female gamete) takes part in double fertilisation.

149. To recognise the pollen grain, whether it is the right type or wrong type

150. Emasculation is the removal of the anther from the female parent floral beads before the anther dehisces.

151. Emasculation

152. Emasculation, bagging, pollination, rebagging

153. A – Sugar solution, B – 10%

154. In-vitro pollen germination of pollen grains requires 10% sugar solution with boric acid, Ca, Mg and K salts.

155. Embryo sac is the site of double fertilisation.

156. Both (A) and (B) are correct.

157. Pollen germination occurs on the stigma when pollen is compatible.

158. A – Dynamic process, B – Promotion or inhibition

159. Inbreeding depression is the reduction in fertility or vigour due to continuous selfing.

Post-fertilisation Structure and Events, Endosperm, Embryo, Fruit and Seeds

160. Endosperm development precedes embryo development because its cells contain reserve food material that are used by the developing embryo.

161. Free nuclear endosperm

162. White kernel in coconut is cellular endosperm, while the coconut water is liquid endosperm.

163. The outermost layer of the endosperm of maize grain is called the aleurone layer. It is made up of protein and is triploid in nature.

164. Double endosperm is found in coconut (*Cocos nucifera*).

165. Free nuclear division occurs in the endosperm. In the most common type of endosperm development, PEN undergoes successive nuclear division to give rise to free nuclei.

166. Endosperm is generally formed before embryo development because endosperm provides nutrition to the developing embryo.

167. Scutellum is situated on the one side of the embryonal axis which separates the embryo region from the endosperm.

168. Scutellum is a single, shield-shaped cotyledon seen in the grass embryo.

169. When a part of the zygote is involved in the development of the embryo, this type of embryo development is called meroblastic development.

170. Just after the first division of primary endosperm nucleus

171. Two structures (endosperm and aleurone layer) are triploid in nature.

172. False fruit or pseudocarpic fruits from other parts of the flower such as the thalamus.

173. Perisperm is derived from the nucellus, which surrounds the embryo sac within the ovule. It represents the remains of the nucellus in the seed, so it is a diploid and of sporophytic tissue and represents the parental sporophytic generation in the seed.

174. Pea is a non-endospermic seed.

175. In a few species such as apple, strawberry and cashew, the thalamus also contributes to fruit formation. Such fruits are called false fruit.

176. In date palm, the size and maturity time depends on foreign pollen grains. It is called metaxenia.

177. The micropyle remains as a small pore in the seed coat. This facilitates entry of O_2 and water into the seed at the time of germination.

178. Seed is the final product of sexual reproduction. Seed is a mature integumented megasporangium (parental sporophyte) which consists of the embryo (future sporophytic generation).

179. Members of families such as Trapaceae, Orchidaceae and Podostemonaceae do not contain endosperms.

180. As the seed matures, its water content is reduced and seeds become relatively dry (10–15% moisture by mass).

181. Very old and viable seeds are recorded in lupines (*Lupines arcticus*) excavated from the Arctic tundra. The seeds germinated and flowered after an estimated record of 10,000 years of dormancy.

182. Endosperm is generally triploid.
Diploid number of chromosome is (2n) = 32
n = 16, 3n = 48.

183. Number of meiotic divisions required to produce

$$\text{n number of seeds} = \left(n + \frac{n}{4}\right)$$

$$n = 100$$

$$= 100 + \frac{100}{4} = 125$$

184. A – Epicotyl, B – Plumule, C – Hypocotyl D – Radicle

185. Albuminous seeds are endospermic seeds. Pea is a non-albuminous or non-endospermic seed.

186. Parthenocarpic fruits are seedless, so in pomegranate, there is no sense of parthenocarpy.

187. Endosperm

188. If favourable conditions are not available, the embryo may enter a state of inactivity called dormancy. The general metabolic activities of the embryo slow down in the dormant seed.

189. A – Thalamus, B – Seed, C – Endocarp, D – Mesocarp

190. In the seed of grasses, the remains of the second cotyledon are called epiblast.

191. Suspensor pushes the growing embryo deep inside the nutritive endosperm within the embryo sac.

192. Only (A) is correct. Early stages of embryo development are similar in both monocots and dicots. The zygote gives rise to the pre-embryo and subsequently to the globular embryo, heart shaped-embryo and mature embryo.

193. Endosperm (3n)

194. Non-endospermic seeds have no residual endosperm as they are completely consumed during embryo development.

195. Hilum

196. Coleoptile and coleorhiza are the covering of the plumule and radicle in monocotyledonous seeds.

197. Arctic tundra

198. (A), (B) and (C) are correct.

199. A – Suspensor, B – Radicle, C – Plumule, D – Cotyledons

200. (A) Ovary – Fruit, (B) Ovary wall – Pericarp, (C) Ovule – Seed, (D) Nucellus – Perisperm

201. Parthenocarpic fruits are seedless and parthenocarpy can be induced by the application of growth regulators like auxin.

202. A – Cotyledons, B – Hypocotyl, C – Root cap, D – Radicle

203. Cotyledons and scutellum

204. In non-endospermic seeds, cotyledons store food.

205. (A) – Scutellum, (B) – Coleoptile, (C) – Epiblast, (D) – Coleorhiza

206. Reduction division

207. In legume seeds, there is no endosperm; it is completely consumed during embryo development.

208. *Phoenix dactylifera*

209. Parasitic species like *Orobanche* and *Striga* contain thousands of tiny seeds.

Apomixis and Polyembryony

210. (A), (B) and (C) are correct.

211. Apomixis is a kind of asexual reproduction, so it cannot create genetic variability.

212. Embryo in apomictic seeds often develops from diploid cells. Segregation of traits will not occur and new seeds contain all the traits of the hybrid variety.

213. Nucellar and integumentary

214. Apomixis. If the hybrid seeds are converted into apomicts, farmers will not have to worry about losing the desirable characters as these will not segregate. Hence, hybrid seeds will not be required every year.

215. Parthenocarpy and apomixes are similar in the absence of fertilisation.

216. Ploidy level of embryo = $\frac{1}{2}$ ploidy of male plant + $\frac{1}{2}$ ploidy of female plant

$\therefore 2n + 2n = 4n$

217. Apomixis

218. In adventive embryony, the embryo arises from diploid sporophytic tissues such as nucellus or integument.

219. A – Leeuwenhoek, B – Citrus

220. Polyembryony is the formation of more than one embryo in a seed.

221. (A) and (C) are correct.

3 Human Reproduction

EXERCISES

Male Reproductive System

1. Each seminiferous tubule is lined on its inside by two types of cells called:
   (a) Leydig cells and Sertoli cells
   (b) Sertoli cells and spermatogonial cells
   (c) Leydig cells and spermatogonial cells
   (d) Interstitial cells and spermatogonial cells

2. Select the incorrect statement:
   (a) The testes are situated outside the abdominal cavity within a pouch called the scrotum
   (b) The scrotum helps in maintaining the low temperature of the testes
   (c) In adults, the testes is oval in shape with a length of 4–5 cm and a width of 2–3 cm
   (d) Each testis has about 500 compartments called testicular lobules

3. The testicular hormones called androgens are secreted by:
   (a) Nurse cells
   (b) Spermatogonial cells
   (c) Leydig cells
   (d) Spermatozoa

4. _________ cells provide nutrition to germ cells:
   (a) Interstitial cells
   (b) Sertoli cells
   (c) Leydig cells
   (d) Immunologically competent cells

5. The regions outside the seminiferous tubules, called interstitial spaces, contain ____I____ and ____II____. Fill in the blanks with the correct options:

	I	II
(a)	Leydig cells	Sertoli cells
(b)	Small blood vessels	Sertoli cells
(c)	Small blood vessels	Leydig cells
(d)	Sertoli cells	Immunologically competent cells

6. The seminiferous tubules of the testes open into the ____X____ through ____Y____. Fill in the blanks with the correct options for 'X' and 'Y':
   (a) Vasa efferentia, vas deferens
   (b) Vasa efferentia, rete testis
   (c) Rete testis, vasa efferentia
   (d) Vas deferens, ejaculatory duct

7. The male sex accessory ducts include:
   (a) Epididymis and vas deferens only
   (b) Urethra and ejaculatory duct
   (c) Ureter and urethra
   (d) Retes testis, vasa efferentia, epididymis and vas deferens

8. The vasa efferentia leaves the testes and opens into ____I____ located along the ____II____ surface. Fill in the blanks with the correct option:

	I	II
(a)	Seminal vesicle	Posterior
(b)	Epididymis	Posterior
(c)	Rete testis	Anterior
(d)	Epididymis	Anterior

9. The unpaired gland in the male reproductive system is:
   (a) Prostate gland
   (b) Seminal vesicle
   (c) Bulbourethral gland
   (d) Cowper's gland

10. _________ is the male external genitalia:
    (a) Epididymis (b) Penis
    (c) Vasa efferentia (d) Vas deferens

11. The scrotum is connected to the abdominal cavity by the:
    (a) Inguinal canal (b) Femoral canal
    (c) Haversian canal (d) Spermatic canal

12. _________ is also called uterus masculinus:
    (a) Prostate gland
    (b) Seminal vesicle

(c) Seminiferous tubule
(d) Bulbourethral gland

13. Which of the following is an incorrect statement?
(a) Bulbourethral glands are also called Cowper's gland
(b) The male primary sex organ is the penis
(c) Testes are formed in the abdominal cavity in foetal life
(d) The hormone responsible for the descent of the testes into the scrotal sac is testosterone

14. Sugars that sperm use for energy is secreted by:
(a) Prostate gland (b) Seminal vesicle
(c) Epididymis (d) Vasa efferentia

15. The percentage of seminal plasma contributed by the seminal vesicles is:
(a) 30% (b) 70%
(c) 50% (d) 90%

16. Sperms are stored and nourished inside:
(a) Seminal vesicle
(b) Prostate gland
(c) Epididymis
(d) Bulbourethral gland

17. Vas deferens unites with the duct of the seminal vesicle to form:
(a) Vasa efferentia
(b) Epididymis
(c) Ejaculatory duct
(d) Urethral meatus

18. Sertoli cells are also called:
(a) Nurse cells
(b) Sustentacular cells
(c) Sustentocytes
(d) All of the above

19. A condition in which one or both of the testes fail to descend from the abdomen into the scrotum is called:
(a) Impotency
(b) Cryptorchidism
(c) Inguinal hernia
(d) Klinefelter syndrome

20. The surgical removal of foreskin/prepuce is called:
(a) Castration (b) Cryptorchidism
(c) Circumcision (d) Orchidectomy

21. The secretions of the seminal plasma are:
(a) Rich in fructose and calcium but do not have enzymes
(b) Rich in fructose, but do not have calcium
(c) Rich in fructose, calcium and certain enzymes
(d) Rich in glucose and calcium

22. Which of the following is an incorrect statement?
(a) Seminal plasma is not contributed by Bartholin's glands
(b) Hydrocele refers to a swelling in the scrotum due to collection of fluid in the tunica vaginalis surrounding the testes
(c) If the vas deferens of both the sides are cut, then there is no desire for sexual intercourse
(d) Impotency is a condition where a man cannot get or keep an erection firm enough for sexual intercourse

23. Identify the correct set of animals having intra-abdominal testes:
(a) Dog, wolf and whale
(b) Whale, elephant and platypus
(c) Dolphin, cat and kangaroo
(d) Kangaroo, sea cow and platypus

24. Scrotum provides the necessary temperature in the testes:
(a) 2–2.5°C lower than normal body temperature
(b) 2–2.5°F lower than normal body temperature
(c) 2–2.5°C more than normal body temperature
(d) 2–2.5°F more than normal body temperature

25. Which among the following releases secretions that help in lubrication of the penis?

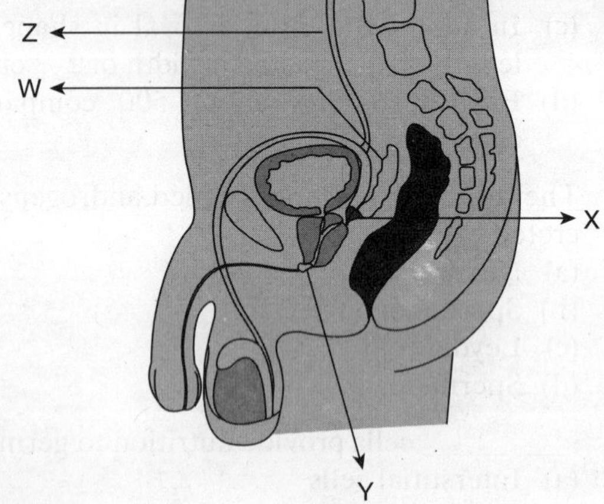

(a) X (b) W
(c) Z (d) Y

26. Tubuli recti connect:
(a) Rete testis and epididymis
(b) Seminiferous tubule and rete testis
(c) Epididymis and vas deferens
(d) Two seminiferous tubules

27. A diagram of the sectional view of a seminiferous tubule is shown below. Choose the correct option which includes all the diploid cells:

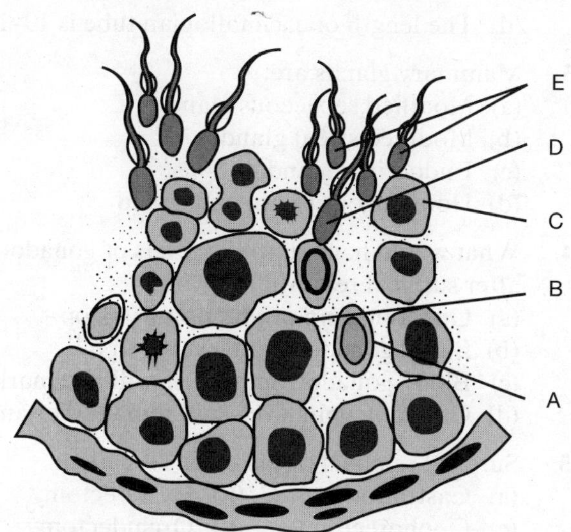

(a) A, B (b) C, E
(c) A, D, C (d) A, E

28. Which of the following is the correct labelling of the sectional view of the male reproductive system?

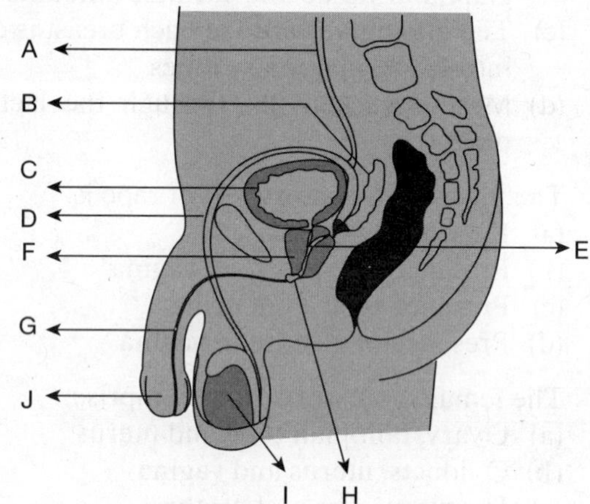

(a) Endocrine structure → B, E
(b) Primary sex organ → J
(c) Accessory glands → B, F, H
(d) Ejaculatory duct → A

29. Which of the following functions of the Sertoli cell mediates a negative feedback control of follicle stimulating hormone (FSH) secretions?
(a) Formation of testosterone
(b) Formation of anti-Mullerian factor
(c) Formation of blood–testis barrier
(d) Synthesis of inhibin

30. A diagrammatic view of the male reproductive system is shown below. Which among the following labels represents the gland that provides maximum contribution to seminal plasma and secretes fructose?

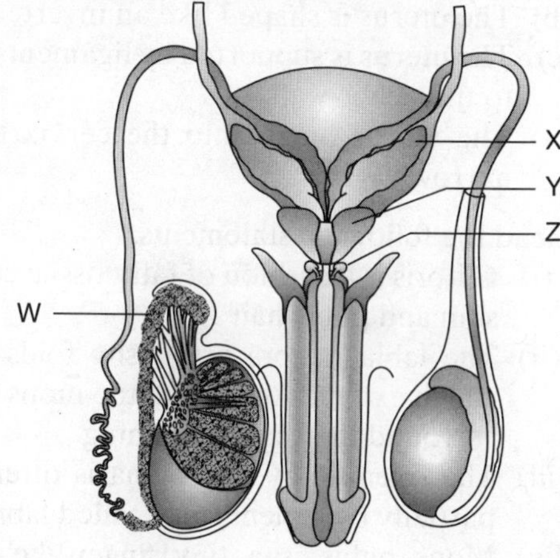

(a) X (b) Z
(c) Y (d) W

31. Which of the following is the correct sequence related to the contribution of the following glands to seminal plasma in descending order?
(a) Seminal vesicle > Prostate gland > Bulbourethral
(b) Prostate > Seminal vesicle > Bulbourethral
(c) Bulbourethral > Prostate > Seminal vesicle
(d) Seminal vesicle > Bulbourethral > Prostate

32. The male accessory glands whose secretions help in lubrication of the penis are:
(a) Bartholin's glands
(b) Bulbourethral glands
(c) Greater vestibular glands
(d) Seminal vesicle

Female Reproductive System

33. The part of the fallopian tube that is closer to the ovary is:
(a) Isthmus (b) Infundibulum
(c) Cervix (d) Ampulla

34. ________ and ________ together form the birth canal:
(a) Uterus, cervix
(b) Uterus, vagina
(c) Cervical canal, vagina
(d) Fallopian tube, uterus

35. Mark the odd one out with respect to the parts of the female external genitalia:
(a) Mons pubis (b) Labia majora
(c) Clitoris (d) Vagina

36. Select the incorrect statement:
(a) The uterus is single and it is also called the womb

(b) The uterus is shaped like an inverted pear
(c) The uterus is supported by ligaments attached to the pelvic wall
(d) The uterus opens into the cervix through a narrow vagina

37. Read the following statements:
(i) Clitoris is a cushion of fatty tissue covered by skin and pubic hair
(ii) The labia majora are fleshy folds of tissue, which extend down from the mons pubis and surround the vaginal opening
(iii) The opening of the vagina is often covered partially by a membrane called labia minora
(iv) Mons pubis is a tiny finger-like structure, which lies at the upper junction of the two labia minora and below the urethral opening

Which of the statements given above is/are correct?
(a) (ii) and (iii) (b) (iii) and (iv)
(c) Only (ii) (d) (ii) and (iv)

38. The wall of the uterus has three layers of tissue: an external thin membranous ___I___, middle thick layer of smooth muscle called ___II___ and inner glandular layer called ___III___. Fill in the blanks with the correct options:

	I	II	III
(a)	Perimetrium	Myometrium	Endometrium
(b)	Myometrium	Perimetrium	Endometrium
(c)	Endometrium	Perimetrium	Myometrium
(d)	Endometrium	Myometrium	Perimetrium

39. In the fallopian tube, the edges of the infundibulum possess finger-like projections called:
(a) Isthmus (b) Fimbriae
(c) Ampulla (d) Clitoris

40. The hymen:
(a) Is never torn during coitus
(b) Can be broken by a sudden fall or jolt
(c) Can sometimes persist after coitus
(d) More than one option is correct

41. In females, an erectile body homologous with the penis of males is:
(a) Prepuce (b) Uterus
(c) Clitoris (d) Hymen

42. Select the incorrect statement:
(a) Vagina is rich in glands that produce acidic secretions
(b) The narrow end of the fallopian tube that joins the uterus is the isthmus
(c) The greater vestibular glands are also called Bartholin's glands
(d) The length of each fallopian tube is 10–12 cm

43. Mammary glands are:
(a) Modified sebaceous gland
(b) Modified sweat gland
(c) Endocrinal gland
(d) Homologous to prostate gland

44. What would happen to the levels of gonadotropin after surgical removal of ovaries?
(a) Gonadotropin production will stop
(b) Blood gonadotropin levels will fall
(c) Blood gonadotropin levels will rise markedly
(d) Gonadotropin levels will remain the same

45. Surgical removal of the uterus is called:
(a) Castration (b) Hysterectomy
(c) Oophorectomy (d) Orchidectomy

46. Select the incorrect statement with respect to the mammary glands:
(a) A functional mammary gland is characteristic of all female vertebrates
(b) They are paired structures that contain glandular tissue and variable amounts of fat
(c) The glandular tissue of each breast is divided into 15–20 mammary lobes
(d) Milk is sucked out through the lactiferous duct

47. The most confirmatory test of rape is:
(a) Presence of hymen
(b) Presence of fructose in vagina
(c) Presence of hCG in urine
(d) Presence of glucose in vagina

48. The female accessory ducts comprise:
(a) Ovary, fallopian tube and uterus
(b) Oviducts, uterus and vagina
(c) Uterus, vagina and urethra
(d) Ovary, vagina and urethra

49. Which of the following is an incorrect statement with respect to the ovary?
(a) It is the primary sex organ in females
(b) It produces the female gamete (ovum) and several steroid hormones
(c) Each ovary is about 2–4 cm in length and connected to the pelvic wall and uterus by ligaments
(d) The ovarian stroma is divided into two zones: peripheral medulla and inner cortex

50. Select the option that gives the correct identification of the labelled parts A and B along with functional characteristics, in the given sectional view of the female reproductive system:

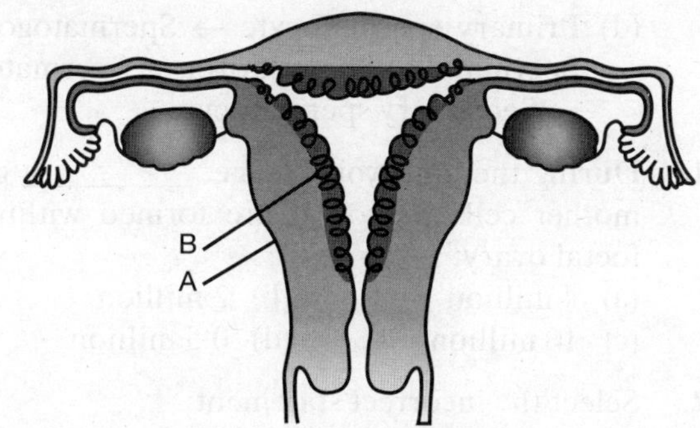

(a) A – Perimetrium, composed of ciliated cuboidal epithelium
(b) B – Myometrium, which undergoes strong uterine contraction at the time of child birth
(c) B – Endometrium, which is the inner glandular lining formed of columnar epithelium
(d) A – Myometrium, which is made of smooth muscles

51. Fertilisation of the sperm and ovum takes place in the ________ of the fallopian tube:
(a) Infundibulum (b) Isthmus
(c) Ampulla (d) Fimbriae

52. Find the incorrect statement:
(a) Clitoris is homologous to penis
(b) Bartholin's glands are homologous to prostate glands
(c) Labia majora is homologous to scrotum
(d) Labia minora is homologous to penile urethra

53. The lower narrow end of the uterus is called:
(a) Cervix (b) Urethra
(c) Oviduct (d) Fimbriae

54. Which of the following is the correct statement?
(a) The internal genitalia of females is called vulva
(b) The endometrium of the uterus has smooth muscles and exhibits strong contractions during delivery of the baby
(c) Each ovary is covered by a thin epithelium which encloses the ovarian stroma
(d) The length of the fallopian tube is 18–20 cm

55. Which of the following is the correct pathway of milk flow in the mammary glands?
I. Alveoli
II. Mammary duct
III. Lactiferous duct
IV. Mammary ampulla
V. Mammary tubules
(a) I → II→ IV→ III→ V
(b) I→ V→ IV→ II→ III
(c) II→ III→ IV→ I→ II
(d) I→ V→ II→ IV→ III

Gametogenesis

56. Which of the following cells undergo second meiotic division?
(a) Spermatids
(b) Spermatogonia
(c) Secondary oocyte
(d) Ovum

57. The acrosomal cap of the sperm is derived from:
(a) Mitochondria (b) Golgi bodies
(c) Centriole (d) Nucleus

58. During oogenesis, meiosis II is completed in the:
(a) Secondary follicle (b) Tertiary follicle
(c) Fallopian tube (d) Uterus

59. Select the incorrect statement:
(a) Each primary spermatocyte gives rise to 4 sperms
(b) Middle piece of sperm provides energy for sperm motility
(c) Ovum moves with the help of cilia lining oviducts
(d) During oogenesis, meiosis I is completed in the secondary follicle, resulting in the formation of secondary oocyte and first polar body

60. The enzyme released by acrosomes for digesting the zona pellucida surrounding the ovum is:
(a) Zona lysine (b) Acrosin
(c) Hyaluronidase (d) Both (a) and (b)

61. ________ are the immediate predecessors of spermatids:
(a) Spermatogonia
(b) Primary spermatocyte
(c) Secondary spermatocyte
(d) Spermatozoa

62. At puberty, only ________ primary follicles are left in each ovary:
(a) 20,000–30,000 (b) 60,000–80,000
(c) 1.2–1.4 lakhs (d) 400–420

63. Which of the following undergoes the first meiotic division, leading to the formation of two equal haploid cells with 23 chromosomes?
(a) Spermatogonia
(b) Primary oocyte
(c) Primary spermatocyte
(d) Secondary oocyte

64. Which of the following is an incorrect statement?
(a) Formation of secondary oocyte is the result of unequal meiotic division

(b) The sperm head contains mitochondria, the anterior portion of which is covered by a cap-like structure called the acrosome
(c) The human male ejaculates about 200 to 300 million sperms during a coitus
(d) No polar bodies are formed in males during gametogenesis

65. "9 + 0" arrangement of microtubules is seen in ________ of sperms:
(a) Head (b) Neck
(c) Middle piece (d) Tail

66. After spermiogenesis, the sperm head becomes embedded in the Sertoli cells, and are finally released from the seminiferous tubules by a process called:
(a) Spermatogenesis
(b) Spermateliosis
(c) Spermatocytogenesis
(d) Spermiation

67. Identify the stage at which the female gamete is released from the ovary:
(a) In the primary oocyte stage
(b) Before meiosis I
(c) After completing meiosis II
(d) In the secondary oocyte stage, after completing meiosis I

68. Identify the haploid stages seen during spermatogenesis:
(a) Spermatogonia and spermatozoa
(b) Primary spermatocyte and spermatids
(c) Secondary spermatocyte and spermatozoa
(d) Spermatogonia and primary spermatocyte

69. ________ acts on Sertoli cells and stimulates the secretion of some factors which help in the process of spermiogenesis:
(a) Luteinising hormone
(b) Gonadotropin releasing hormone
(c) Follicle stimulating hormone
(d) Testosterone

70. Identify the correct sequence in the process of spermatogenesis:
(a) Spermatogonia → Spermatids → Spermatozoa → Primary spermatocyte → Secondary spermatocyte
(b) Spermatogonia → Primary spermatocyte → Secondary spermatocyte → Spermatid → Spermatozoa
(c) Spermatozoa → Spermatid → Primary spermatocyte → Secondary Spermatocyte → Spermatogonia
(d) Primary spermatocyte → Spermatogonia → Spermatid → Spermatozoa → Spermatogonia → Secondary spermatocyte

71. During the embryonic stage, ________ gamete mother cells (oogonia) are formed within each foetal ovary:
(a) 4 million (b) 2 million
(c) 10 million (d) 0.5 million

72. Select the incorrect statement:
(a) Oogenesis is initiated during the embryonic stage
(b) Oogonial cells are formed and keep multiplying after birth
(c) Theca layer is first seen in the secondary follicle stage
(d) The secondary oocyte retains the bulk of the nutrient-rich cytoplasm of the primary oocyte

73. ________ follicle is characterised by a fluid-filled cavity called antrum:
(a) Primary (b) Secondary
(c) Tertiary (d) Both (b) and (c)

74. Which of the following statements is incorrect with respect to the tertiary follicle stage?
(a) Primary oocyte within the tertiary follicle grows in size and completes the first meiotic division
(b) The theca layer is organised into theca interna and theca externa
(c) The first polar body is formed in the tertiary follicle stage
(d) The tertiary follicle has a single layer of granulosa cells surrounding the primary oocyte

75. Nebenkern in human sperm refers to:
(a) Nucleus (b) Mitochondria
(c) Tail (d) Centriole

76. Which of the following layers in the antral follicle is acellular?
(a) Zona pellucida (b) Theca interna
(c) Granulosa (d) Cumulus oophorus

77. The second meiotic division of the mammalian ovum occurs:
(a) In the Graafian follicle
(b) During foetal life
(c) Shortly after ovulation, before the ovum enters the fallopian tube
(d) In the fallopian tube, as the ovum is penetrated by the sperm

78. Identify the incorrect statement with respect to the primary spermatocyte:
(a) It is diploid in nature
(b) It is formed from spermatogonial cells by undergoing meiosis
(c) It gives rise to four haploid gametes by undergoing meiotic division
(d) Both (a) and (c)

79. Identify the correct difference between oogenesis and spermatogenesis:
(a) Oogenesis begins at puberty while spermatogenesis begins during the embryonic stages
(b) Cytoplasmic division is unequal in oogenesis and equal in spermatogenesis
(c) Primary spermatocyte forms a single haploid sperm while primary oocyte forms four haploid ova
(d) Oogenesis is completed in the ovary while spermatogenesis is completed only during fertilisation in the fallopian tube

80. If the proximal centriole is removed from the sperm, which of the following shall not occur?
(a) Acrosomal reaction
(b) Movement of sperm
(c) First cleavage of zygote
(d) Amphimixis

81. Spermiogenesis is also called:
(a) Spermatogenesis
(b) Spermatocytogenesis
(c) Spermateliosis
(d) Spermiation

82. Sperm releases sperm lysins to:
(a) Enhance the movement of the tail
(b) Delay fertilisation
(c) Locate the female gamete using chemotaxis
(d) Dissolve the layers overlying the female gamete, facilitating fertilisation

83. For normal fertility:
(a) At least 40% of sperms must have normal shape and size and at least 60% of them must show vigorous motility
(b) All the sperms must have normal shape, size and vigorous motility
(c) At least 60% of sperms must have normal shape and size, and at least 40% of them must show vigorous motility
(d) At least 20% of sperms must have normal shape and size, and at least 60% of them must show vigorous motility

84. ________ follicle ruptures to release the secondary oocyte (ovum) from the ovary by the process called ovulation:
(a) Primary (b) Secondary
(c) Tertiary (d) Graafian

85. Which of the following is an incorrect statement?
(a) Sperms released from the seminiferous tubules are transported by the accessory ducts
(b) Secretions of the epididymis, vas deferens, seminal vesicle and prostate are essential for maturation and motility of sperms
(c) The seminal plasma, along with the sperms, constitutes the semen
(d) The functions of the male sex accessory ducts and glands are maintained by the pituitary hormones (gonadotropins)

86. The term for reduced sperm motility is:
(a) Oligospermia (b) Asthenozoospermia
(c) Azoospermia (d) Teratozoospermia

87. Oogenesis is initiated during the embryonic stage when the primary oocyte starts dividing by undergoing meiosis but is temporarily arrested at:
(a) Metaphase II (b) Prophase I
(c) Prophase II (d) Metaphase I

88. There are millions of follicles in the foetal ovary and these follicles:
(a) Multiply and increase in number from birth to puberty
(b) Degenerate during the phase from birth to puberty
(c) Maintain their number constantly during the phase from birth to puberty
(d) Turn into the Graafian follicle during the phase from birth to puberty

89. Choose the incorrect statement:
(a) Oogenesis is initiated by puberty
(b) Gamete mother cells are formed in females only after birth
(c) The first meiotic division is equal in terms of cytoplasmic distribution between secondary oocyte and first polar body
(d) All of the above

90. The maturation and motility of sperms is governed by:
(a) Epididymis only
(b) Vas deferens only
(c) Prostate only
(d) Prostate, epididymis, vas deferens and seminal vesicle

91. Identify the correct option with respect to the labelling of the diagram given below:

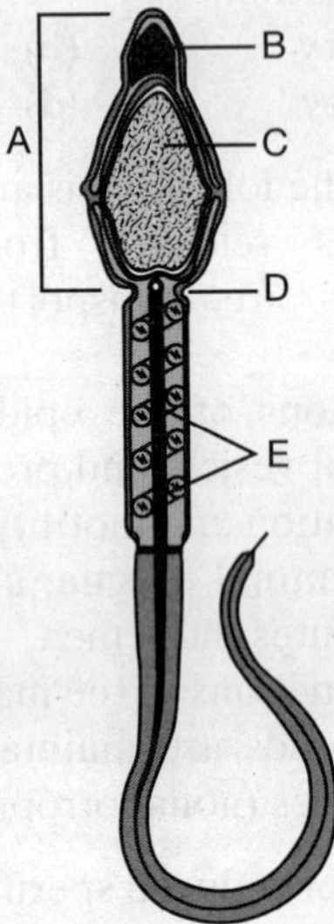

(a) A-Head, B-Nucleus
(b) C-Nucleus, D-Neck
(c) A-Nucleus, C-Acrosome
(d) B-Acrosome, C-Mitochondria

Menstrual Cycle

92. Read the following statements. Which of them are correct?
(i) The follicular phase of the menstrual cycle is also called proliferative phase
(ii) The duration of the follicular phase is 3–5 days
(iii) The levels of progesterone are very high and peak during the proliferative phase
(iv) The natural cessation or stopping of a woman's menstrual cycle at around the age of 50 years is called menopause
(a) (i) and (ii) (b) (ii) and (iii)
(c) (iii) and (iv) (d) (i) and (iv)

93. Select the incorrect statement:
(a) The reproductive cycle of female primates (monkeys, apes and human beings) is called menstrual cycle
(b) The first menstrual cycle begins at puberty and is called menarche
(c) In human females, menstruation is repeated at an average interval of about 28/29 days
(d) One ovum is released (ovulation) at the beginning of each menstrual cycle

94. In human females, the corpus luteum secretes:
(a) Progesterone mainly
(b) Oestrogen mainly
(c) Luteinising hormone
(d) Follicle stimulating hormone

95. The hormone whose levels rise and appears in urine after menopause is:
(a) Progesterone
(b) Follicle stimulating hormone (FSH)
(c) Oestrogen
(d) Androgen

96. If the duration of a menstrual cycle is 32 days in a woman, ovulation occurs on:
(a) 11th day (b) 14th day
(c) 18th day (d) 25th day

97. The zona pellucida, a specialised extracellular matrix made of glycoproteins surrounding the developing oocyte (ovum) within each follicle, is secreted by:
(a) Corona radiata (b) Theca interna
(c) Theca externa (d) Secondary oocyte

98. Corpus luteum develops from:
(a) Ovum
(b) Ovarian stroma
(c) Primary follicle
(d) Left-over Graafian follicle after release of ovum

99. Menstruation only occurs when:
(a) The released ovum is fertilised
(b) The released ovum is not fertilised
(c) The levels of progesterone remain high
(d) The levels of prostaglandins fall

100. Which of the following does not occur during the follicular phase of the menstrual cycle?
(a) The primary follicles in the ovary grow to become fully mature Graafian follicles
(b) The endometrium of the uterus regenerates through proliferation
(c) The changes in the ovary and uterus are induced by changes in the levels of pituitary and ovarian hormones
(d) The secretion of gonadotropins (LH and FSH) decreases gradually during the follicular phase

101. If a woman wishes to postpone menstrual bleeding for few days, it may be done by giving ________ 3–4 days before the expected date:
(a) Gonadotropin releasing hormone

(b) Luteinising hormone (LH)
(c) Follicle stimulating hormone (FSH)
(d) Progesterone

102. Lack of menstruation may be indicative of:
(a) Pregnancy (b) Poor health
(c) Stress (d) All of the above

103. Menstruation occurs with an abrupt decrease in the levels of:
(a) Progesterone (b) Oestrogen
(c) LH (d) FSH

104. Which of the following is the correct sequence of hormones from the beginning of the menstrual cycle?
(a) FSH, progesterone, LH, oestrogen
(b) LH, progesterone, FSH, oestrogen
(c) FSH, oestrogen, LH, progesterone
(d) FSH, progesterone, oestrogen, LH

105. Select the incorrect statement:
(a) Corpus luteum is also called yellow body
(b) Around 40–50 ml of blood loss takes place during a menstrual cycle
(c) Menses takes place for 3–5 days
(d) Menstrual blood clots very easily

106. The hormone essential for maintenance of the endometrium during the luteal phase is:
(a) FSH (b) Inhibin
(c) Oestrogen (d) Progesterone

107. A diagram of the sectional view of the ovary is given below. The labelled structure that secretes a large amount of progesterone is:

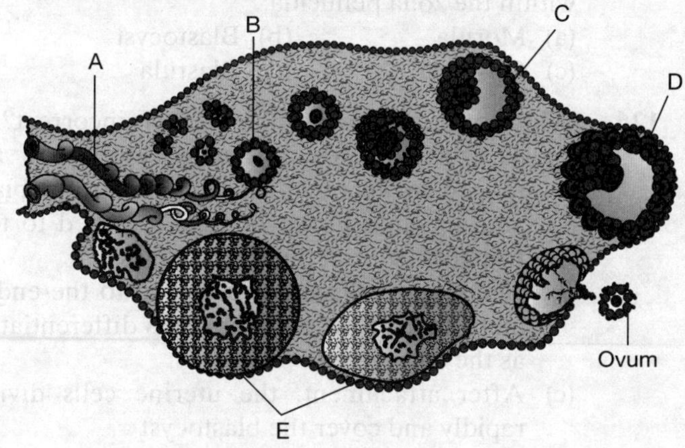

(a) B (b) C
(c) D (d) E

108. If the ovum fails to be fertilised, the corpus luteum degenerates into a white scar in the ovary called:
(a) Corpus albicans (b) Corpus callosum
(c) Corpus striatum (d) Corpus spongiosum

109. Painful menstruation is called:
(a) Menorrhagia
(b) Dysmenorrhoea
(c) Amenorrhoea
(d) Hypomenorrhoea

110. If the ovum does not get fertilised, fall in the level of ________ causes regression of the corpus luteum:
(a) Progesterone
(b) Oestrogen
(c) Follicle stimulating hormone
(d) Luteinising hormone

111. Identify the incorrect statement:
(a) Thermogenic effect is associated with progesterone
(b) During the menstrual cycle, uterine changes are induced by hormones secreted by the adenohypophysis
(c) During ovulation, peak of LH is higher than FSH
(d) Corona radiata is a cellular covering around the ovum in the Graafian follicle

112. Which of the following is not secreted by the corpus luteum?
(a) Progesterone (b) Oestrogen
(c) LH (d) Inhibin

113. Which of the following is incorrect with respect to the estrous cycle?
(a) There is no endometrial shedding in the estrous cycle
(b) There is a strong urge for sexual intercourse and is called period of heat
(c) These are reproductive cycles observed in non-primate females
(d) The level of oestrogen falls when the female observes these cycles

114. Menstruation usually occurs in about ________ days after ovulation:
(a) 7–8 (b) 14
(c) 22 (d) 3–5

115. ________ is the stage formed just after the release of the secondary oocyte (ovulation) due to rupturing of the Graafian follicle:
(a) Corpus albicans
(b) Corpus haemorrhagicum
(c) Corpus callosum
(d) Corpus cardiaca

Fertilisation and Implantation

116. All copulations do not lead to fertilisation and pregnancy because:
(a) Ovulation does not occur in each menstrual cycle
(b) Sperm count may not be adequate in ejaculates at times
(c) Most of the sperms are not always transported simultaneously to the site of fertilisation
(d) Ovum and sperms are not always transported simultaneously to the site of fertilisation

117. If implantation occurs at a site other than the uterus, it is called:
(a) Pseudo pregnancy
(b) Ectopic pregnancy
(c) Improper pregnancy
(d) Retrogressive pregnancy

118. Select the correct sequence of layers around the ovum from inside to outside:
(a) Corona radiata → Zona pellucida → Plasma membrane
(b) Plasma membrane → Zona pellucida → Corona radiata
(c) Zone pellucida → Plasma membrane → Corona radiata
(d) Plasma membrane → Corona radiata → Zona pellucida

119. Read the following statements and choose the correct option:
I: Only one sperm can fertilise an ovum
II: During fertilisation, a sperm comes in contact with the zona pellucida and induces changes in the membrane that block the entry of additional sperms
(a) Both statements are incorrect
(b) Only Statement I is correct
(c) Both statements are correct and Statement II is the correct explanation of Statement I
(d) Both statements are correct and Statement II is not the correct explanation of Statement I

120. Select the correct statement:
(a) Zona pellucida is a cellular envelope surrounding the ovum
(b) Both male and female gametes are motile and swim rapidly
(c) The secretions of the acrosome help the sperm enter the cytoplasm of the ovum through the zona pellucida and plasma membrane
(d) Corona radiata is a non-cellular glycoprotein covering secreted by the female gamete

121. Fertilisation induces the completion of:
(a) First meiotic division resulting in the formation of ovum and second polar body
(b) Second meiotic division resulting in the formation of ovum and second polar body
(c) Second meiotic division resulting in the formation of secondary oocyte and first polar body
(d) First meiotic division resulting in the formation of secondary oocyte and first polar body

122. Capacitation is the penultimate step in the maturation of mammalian spermatozoa and is required to render them competent to fertilise an oocyte. It occurs in:
(a) Epididymis (b) Vas deferens
(c) Ejaculatory duct (d) Uterus

123. Polyspermy is prevented by:
(a) Fast block reaction
(b) Depolarisation reaction
(c) Slow block reaction
(d) All of the above

124. Capacitation of the sperm occurs in the female genital tract due to:
(a) Destabilisation of the acrosomal sperm head membrane
(b) Removal of sterols and non-covalently bound epididymal/seminal glycoproteins
(c) Increased permeability to Ca^{2+}
(d) All of the above

125. ________ is an early stage embryo consisting of 16 cells/blastomeres in a solid ball contained within the zona pellucida:
(a) Morula (b) Blastocyst
(c) Gastrula (d) Blastula

126. Which of the following statements is incorrect?
(a) The blastomeres in the blastocyst are arranged in an outer layer called trophoblast and an inner group of cells attached to the trophoblast, called inner cell mass
(b) The inner cell mass is attached to the endometrium and the trophoblast is differentiated as the embryo
(c) After attachment, the uterine cells divide rapidly and cover the blastocyst
(d) The blastocyst becomes embedded in the uterus by a process called implantation, leading to pregnancy

127. The fast block to check polyspermy during fertilisation develops due to:
(a) Acrosomal reaction

(b) Opening of Na^+ channels to cause depolarisation of the egg membrane
(c) Influx of Ca^{2+} causing release of cortical granules outside the ovum
(d) Influx of Na^+ causing exocytosis of the cortical granules

128. Which of the following is/are sperm lysins released by the acrosome to facilitate fertilisation?
(a) Zona lysine
(b) Hyaluronidase
(c) Corona penetrating enzyme
(d) All of the above

129. Where does formation of the second polar body occur in the female genital tract?
(a) In the uterus
(b) In the ovary
(c) In the fallopian tube after contact of the sperm with the zona pellucida and before completion of fertilisation
(d) In the fallopian tube after entry of the sperm into the cytoplasm of the ovum and before completion of fertilisation

130. The gravindex test is performed on a urine sample to detect pregnancy and is based on the detection of:
(a) Human placental lactogen (hPL)
(b) Human chorionic gonadotropin (hCG)
(c) Oestrogens
(d) Progestogens

131. Identify the incorrect statement:
(a) Sperm lysin called acrosin helps in dissolving the corona radiata
(b) Secretions of the corpus luteum prepare the endometrium for implantation
(c) Implantation takes place one week after fertilisation
(d) Morula continues to divide and transforms into the blastocyst

132. Fertilisation occurs in:
(a) Ovary
(b) Uterus
(c) Isthmic region of oviduct
(d) Ampullary region of oviduct

133. Which of the following is the correct statement?
(a) Clcavagc starts when the zygote reaches the uterus
(b) Zona pellucida dissolves after the first cleavage division
(c) With each cleavage division, the nuclear to cytoplasmic ratio increases in blastomeres
(d) The sex of the baby is determined by the mother

134. Identify A, B and C in the diagram given below:

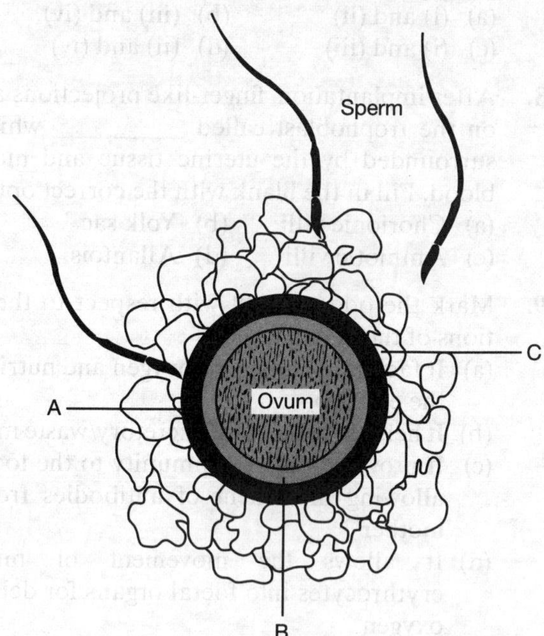

	A	B	C
(a)	Zona pellucida	Perivitelline space	Corona radiata
(b)	Perivitelline space	Zona pellucida	Corona radiata
(c)	Corona radiata	Zona pellucida	Perivitelline space
(d)	Corona radiata	Perivitelline space	Zona pellucida

Pregnancy and Embryonic Development

135. Temporary endocrine gland in the human reproductive system is/are:
(a) Bartholin's gland (b) Mammary glands
(c) Placenta (d) Both (a) and (b)

136. Which of the following is the correct sequence of embryonic development stages?
(a) Gastrula → Zygote→ Blastocyst→ Morula
(b) Zygote→ Morula→ Blastocyst→ Gastrula
(c) Zygote→ Blastocyst → Morula→ Gastrula
(d) Morula→ Blastocyst→ Gastrula→ Zygote

137. Placenta produces several hormones during gestation. Select the correct option with respect to placental hormones:
(i) Human chorionic gonadotropin (hCG) and progestogens
(ii) Oxytocin and pitressin
(iii) Oestrogens and human placental lactogen (hPL)

(iv) Relaxin and anti-diuretic hormone (ADH)
(a) (i) and (ii) (b) (iii) and (iv)
(c) (i) and (iii) (d) (ii) and (iv)

138. After implantation, finger-like projections appear on the trophoblast called ________ which are surrounded by the uterine tissue and maternal blood. Fill in the blank with the correct option:
(a) Chorionic villi (b) Yolk sac
(c) Amniotic villi (d) Allantois

139. Mark the odd one out with respect to the functions of the placenta:
(a) It facilitates supply of oxygen and nutrients to the embryo
(b) It helps in removal of excretory/waste material
(c) It provides passive immunity to the foetus by allowing movement of antibodies from the mother
(d) It allows the movement of maternal erythrocytes into foetal organs for delivering oxygen

140. Identify the correct set of hormones that are produced in women only during pregnancy:
(a) Oestrogen, progesterone and relaxin
(b) Relaxin, oxytocin and human chorionic gonadotropin (hCG)
(c) Human chorionic gonadotropin (hCG), human placental lactogen and relaxin (hPL)
(d) Oestrogen, human chorionic gonadotropin (hCG) and progesterone

141. The first movements of the foetus and appearance of hair on the head are usually observed during:
(a) Third month (b) Fifth month
(c) Second month (d) First month

142. Select the incorrect statement:
(a) The placenta is connected to the embryo by an umbilical cord
(b) In the early stages of pregnancy (first trimester), a hormone called relaxin is secreted by the ovary to keep uterine muscles relaxed
(c) During pregnancy, the levels of other hormones like oestrogens, progestogens, cortisol, prolactin, and thyroxine are increased several-fold in maternal blood
(d) Increased production of hormones in the maternal body supports foetal growth, metabolic changes in the mother and maintenance of pregnancy

143. ________ refers to the formation of three germinal layers:
(a) Notogenesis (b) Embryogenesis
(c) Gastrulation (d) Blastogenesis

144. Immediately after implantation, the ________ differentiates into an outer layer called ectoderm and an inner layer called endoderm:
(a) Trophoblast (b) Inner cell mass
(c) Trophoectoderm (d) Chorionic villi

145. The first sign of the growing foetus may be noticed by:
(a) Experiencing foetal movements
(b) Observing eyelids and eyelashes
(c) Both (a) and (b)
(d) Listening to the heart sound carefully through the stethoscope

146. The morula stage does not show increase in size because:
(a) Zona pellucida dissolves
(b) Zona pellucida is intact
(c) Blastomeres divide rapidly
(d) Corona radiata is intact

147. The cleavage divisions in humans are:
(a) Fast and synchronous
(b) Slow and synchronous
(c) Slow and asynchronous
(d) Fast and asynchronous

148. Select the incorrect statement:
(a) By the end of the first month of pregnancy, the foetus develops limbs and digits
(b) By the end of 12 weeks, most of the major organ systems are formed; for example, the limbs and external genital organs are well developed
(c) By the end of 24 weeks, the body is covered with fine hair, eyelids separate and eyelashes are formed
(d) By the end of nine months of pregnancy, the foetus is fully developed and is ready for delivery

149. The blood flowing through the umbilical cord is:
(a) Only foetal
(b) Only maternal
(c) Both foetal and maternal
(d) None of the above

150. The umbilical cord has:
(a) Two arteries and two veins
(b) Two arteries and one vein
(c) One artery and two veins
(d) One artery and one vein

151. The human egg has:
(a) Large amount of yolk
(b) No yolk
(c) Yolk at the centre
(d) Yolk at animal pole

152. Termination of gastrulation is indicated by:
(a) Obliteration of blastocoel
(b) Obliteration of archenteron
(c) Formation of neural tube
(d) Closure of blastopore

153. Which of the following is/are correct with respect to cleavage divisions in early embryonic development?
(a) Rapid DNA replication
(b) No growth during interphase
(c) Size of blastomeres becomes smaller
(d) All of the above

154. Phocomelia is a rare congenital deformity in which the hands or feet are attached close to the trunk, the limbs being grossly underdeveloped or absent. This condition was a side effect of ________ taken during early pregnancy:
(a) Alcohol (b) Drug thalidomide
(c) Drug tetracycline (d) X-ray exposure

Parturition and Lactation

155. Foetal ejection reflex in a pregnant woman is induced by:
(a) Release of oxytocin from pituitary gland
(b) Release of cortisol from adrenal gland
(c) Fully developed foetus only
(d) Fully developed foetus and placenta

156. Vigorous contraction of the uterus at the end of pregnancy causes expulsion/delivery of the foetus by process called:
(a) Braxton Hicks contractions
(b) Parturition
(c) Gestation
(d) Gastrulation

157. The hormone injected to begin or improve uterine contractions during labor is:
(a) Vasopressin (b) Cortisol
(c) Oxytocin (d) Angiotensin

158. The antibodies present in the colostrum are:
(a) IgG (b) IgA
(c) IgM (d) IgD

159. ________ is called the milk ejecting hormone:
(a) Prolactin (b) Oxytocin
(c) Oestrogen (d) Progesterone

160. ________ is the first form of milk produced by the mammary glands of mammals immediately following delivery of the newborn:
(a) Sebum (b) Cerumen
(c) Colostrum (d) Serum

161. Foetal ejection reflex triggers:
(a) Release of corticotropin releasing hormone (CRH)
(b) Release of oxytocin from maternal pituitary
(c) Release of oxytocin from foetal pituitary
(d) Release of cortisol

162. The hormone responsible for switch-over in respiratory and circulatory system as soon as the umbilical cord is cut is:
(a) Oestrogen (b) Relaxin
(c) Progesterone (d) Nitric oxide

163. The hormone produced by the ovary during pregnancy for preparation of child birth by relaxing the ligaments in the pelvis and softening the cervix is:
(a) Progesterone (b) Relaxin
(c) Inhibin (d) Cortisol

164. Which of the following is incorrect with respect to the umbilical cord?
(a) It has only foetal blood
(b) It helps in transport of substances to and from the embryo
(c) It secretes hormones like hCG and hPL
(d) It connects the placenta to the embryo

165. Humans have haemochorial placenta in which:
(a) Maternal blood is in contact with foetal blood
(b) Maternal blood is in direct contact with chorionic villi
(c) No antibodies can cross over the placenta
(d) Antigens of the mother and foetus can mix with each other

166. Identify the labels A and B in the diagram given below:

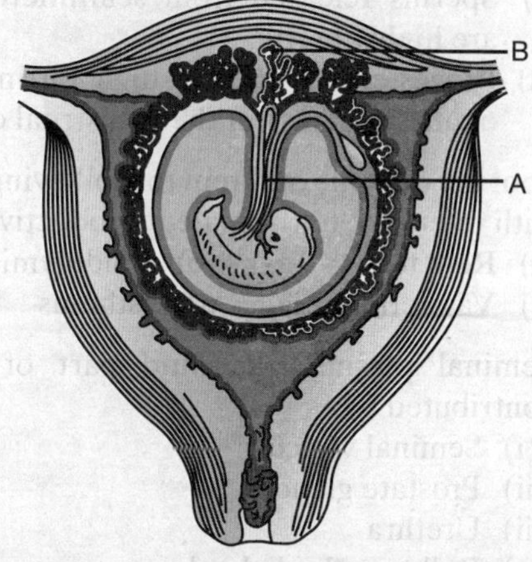

(a) A-Chorionic villi, B-Umbilical chord
(b) A-Umbilical chord, B-Placental villi
(c) A-Amniotic sac, B-Umbilical cord
(d) A-Umbilical cord, B-Amniotic sac

167. Which of the following is the correct statement with respect to the umbilical cord?
(a) It comprises two veins and one artery
(b) It carries both maternal and foetal blood
(c) It carries only oxygenated blood
(d) It carries both oxygenated and deoxygenated blood

168. Parturition is a:
(a) Neural mechanism only
(b) Endocrine mechanism only
(c) Neurosensory mechanism
(d) Neuroendocrine mechanism

169. Which of these is not an important component of initiation of parturition in humans?
(a) Release of oxytocin
(b) Synthesis of prostaglandins
(c) Release of prolactin
(d) Increase in oestrogen to progesterone ratio

170. Select the incorrect statement:
(a) In humans, yolk sac functions as the region of formation of blood cells up to the sixth week of development when the liver of the foetus takes up this function
(b) Allantois helps in the formation of umbilical vessels
(c) In humans, the placenta is expelled out of the birth canal after child birth
(d) Human placenta is metadiscoidal since the chorion of the foetus will float in the blood pools of the mother's uterus

NCERT EXEMPLAR QUESTIONS

1. Choose the incorrect statement from the following:
(a) In birds and mammals, internal fertilisation takes place
(b) Colostrum contains antibodies and nutrients
(c) Polyspermy in mammals is prevented by the chemical changes in the egg surface
(d) In the human female, implantation occurs almost seven days after fertilisation

2. Identify the correct statement from the following:
(a) High levels of oestrogen trigger the ovulatory surge
(b) Oogonial cells start to proliferate and give rise to functional ova in regular cycles from puberty onwards
(c) Sperms released from seminiferous tubules are highly motile
(d) Progesterone level is high during the post ovulatory phase of the menstrual cycle

3. Spot the odd one out from the following structures with reference to the male reproductive system:
(a) Rete testis (b) Epididymis
(c) Vasa efferentia (d) Isthmus

4. Seminal plasma, the fluid part of semen, is contributed by.
(i) Seminal vesicle
(ii) Prostate gland
(iii) Urethra
(iv) Bulbourethral gland
(a) (i) and (ii) (b) (i), (ii) and (iv)
(c) (ii), (iii) and (iv) (d) (i) and (iv)

5. Spermiation is the process of the release of sperms from:
(a) Seminiferous tubules
(b) Vas deferens
(c) Epididymis
(d) Prostate gland

6. Mature Graafian follicle is generally present in the ovary of a healthy human female around:
(a) 5–8 day of menstrual cycle
(b) 11–17 day of menstrual cycle
(c) 18–23 day of menstrual cycle
(d) 24–28 day of menstrual cycle

7. Acrosomal reaction of the sperm occurs due to:
(a) Its contact with zona pellucida of the ova
(b) Reactions within the uterine environment of the female
(c) Reactions within the epididymal environment of the male
(d) Androgens produced in the uterus

8. Which one of the following is not a male accessory gland?
(a) Seminal vesicle (b) Ampulla
(c) Prostate (d) Bulbourethral gland

9. The spermatogonia undergo division to produce sperms by the process of spermatogenesis. Choose the correct one with reference to the above:
(a) Spermatogonia have 46 chromosomes and always undergo meiotic cell division
(b) Primary spermatocytes divide by mitotic cell division
(c) Secondary spermatocytes have 23 chromosomes and undergo second meiotic division
(d) Spermatozoa are transformed into spermatids

10. Match between the following columns representing parts of the sperm and their functions and choose the correct option:

Column I	Column II
A. Head	(i) Enzymes
B. Middle piece	(ii) Sperm motility
C. Acrosome	(iii) Energy
D. Tail	(iv) Genetic material

(a) A – (ii), B – (iv), C – (i), D – (iii)
(b) A – (iv), B – (iii), C – (i), D – (ii)
(c) A – (iv), B – (i), C – (ii), D – (iii)
(d) A – (ii), B – (i), C – (iii), D – (iv)

11. Which among the following has 23 chromosomes?
(a) Spermatogonia (b) Zygote
(c) Secondary oocyte (d) Oogonia

12. Match the following and choose the correct options:

Column I	Column II
A. Trophoblast	(i) Embedding of blastocyst in the endometrium
B. Cleavage	(ii) Group of cells that would differentiate as embryo
C. Inner cell mass	(iii) Outer layer of blastocyst attached to the endometrium
D. Implantation	(iv) Mitotic division of zygote

(a) A – (ii), B – (i), C – (iii), D – (iv)
(b) A – (iii), B – (iv), C – (ii), D – (i)
(c) A – (iii), B – (i), C – (ii), D – (iv)
(d) A – (ii), B – (iv), C – (iii), D – (i)

13. Which of the following hormones is not secreted by human placenta?
(a) hCG (b) Oestrogen
(c) Progesterone (d) LH

14. The vas deferens receives a duct from the seminal vesicle and opens into urethra as:
(a) Epididymis (b) Ejaculatory duct
(c) Efferent ductule (d) Ureter

15. Urethral meatus refers to the:
(a) Urinogenital duct
(b) Opening of vas deferens into urethra
(c) External opening of the urinogenital duct
(d) Muscles surrounding the urinogenial duct

16. Morula is a developmental stage:
(a) Between the zygote and blastocyst
(b) Between the blastocyst and gastrula
(c) After implantation
(d) Between implantation and parturition

17. The cellular covering of the ovum at ovulation is:
(a) Corona radiata (b) Zona radiata
(c) Zona pellucida (d) Chorion

18. Identify the odd out from the following:
(a) Labia minora (b) Fimbriae
(c) Infundibulum (d) Isthmus

PRACTICE TEST PAPER

1. In humans, at the end of the first meiotic division, the male germ cells differentiate into the:
(a) Spermatids
(b) Primary spermatocyte
(c) Secondary spermatocyte
(d) Spermatogonia

2. In females, menstruation can be deferred by the administration of:
(a) Gonadotrophin releasing hormone (GRH)
(b) Follicle stimulating hormone (FSH)
(c) Luteinising hormone (LH)
(d) Combination of oestrogen and progesterone

3. Identify the odd one out with respect to the function of Sertoli cells:
(a) Supply nutrients to sperms
(b) Release factors that promote spermiogenesis
(c) Secrete androgens
(d) Secrete inhibin to cause inhibition of FSH

4. Vasa efferentia are the ductules leading from:
(a) Vas deferens to epididymis
(b) Rete testis to epididymis
(c) Seminal vesicles to urethra
(d) Testicular lobules to rete testis

5. The part of the fallopian tube closest to the ovary is:
(a) Isthmus (b) Ampulla
(c) Infundibulum (d) Cervix

6. Seminal plasma in human males is rich in:
(a) Glucose and calcium
(b) Sodium and ribose
(c) Fructose and calcium
(d) Testosterone and glucose

7. Select the incorrect statement:
(a) Sertoli cells are regulated by FSH secreted by pituitary
(b) Morula has an outer trophoblast and an inner cell mass
(c) Implantation occurs at blastocyst stage
(d) Acrosome of sperm is derived from Golgi bodies

8. Foetal ejection reflex in human females is induced by:
(a) Release of oxytocin from the pituitary gland
(b) Pressure exerted by amniotic fluid
(c) Fully developed foetus and placenta
(d) Release of prolactin by the pituitary gland

9. ________ is devoid of glands:
(a) Uterus (b) Vagina
(c) Vulva (d) Oviduct

10. Bartholin's glands are also called:
(a) Gland of Skene
(b) Bulbourethral glands
(c) Greater vestibular gland
(d) Paraurethral glands

11. The head of sperm contains:
(a) Mitochondria
(b) Nucleus
(c) Proximal centriole
(d) Distal centriole

12. Corpus luteum releases:
(a) Oxytocin (b) Oestrogen
(c) Progesterone (d) Both (b) and (c)

13. In a 32-day menstrual cycle, the duration of the luteal phase is:
(a) 14 days (b) 18 days
(c) 20 days (d) 10 days

14. Which of the following is correct with respect to cleavage divisions?
(a) These divisions begin in the uterus
(b) These divisions begin in the fallopian tube
(c) They are unequal and meroblastic
(d) They are a type of meiotic division

15. Which of the following accessory sex glands secrete fructose and contribute 60–70% of seminal plasma?
(a) Prostate gland
(b) Seminal vesicle
(c) Bulbourethral gland
(d) Gland of Tyson

16. The ejaculatory duct in the male reproductive system is formed by the union of:
(a) Vasa efferentia and epididymis
(b) Vas deferens and duct of seminal vesicle
(c) Vas deferens and urethra
(d) Vas deferens and epididymis

17. During oogenesis in human females, the first meiotic division is completed in the ________ follicle, resulting in the formation of secondary oocyte and tiny first polar body:
(a) Primary (b) Secondary
(c) Tertiary (d) Graafian

18. Primary spermatocyte differs from spermatogium in:
(a) DNA content
(b) Size and volume
(c) Number of chromosomes
(d) Size of chromosomes

19. Select the incorrect statement:
(a) Middle piece of sperm contains mitochondria
(b) In humans, ovum is macrolecithal
(c) Vaginal orifice is partially covered by a membrane called hymen
(d) The shared terminal duct of the reproductive and urinary systems in the human male is the urethra

20. The number of autosomes in the human primary oocyte is:
(a) 46 (b) 44
(c) 23 (d) 22

21. Home-use kits for determining a woman's fertile period is based on the detection of ________ in urine:
(a) Progesterone
(b) GnRH
(c) Luteinising hormone
(d) Oestrogen

22. ________ is termed the milk ejecting hormone:
(a) Oxytocin (b) Prolactin
(c) Estradiol (d) Progesterone

23. What will happen when one ovary of a female is removed?
(a) Ovulation will not take place at all
(b) Ovulation will take place every month from the remaining ovary
(c) Menopause will occur immediately
(d) Ovulation will take place in alternate months

24. Which of the following enzymes present in the acrosome help to penetrate the zona pellucida?
(a) Corona penetrating enzyme
(b) Acrosin
(c) Hyaluronidase
(d) Elastase

25. Surgical removal of the uterus is called:
(a) Oophorectomy (b) Castration
(c) Hysterectomy (d) Salpingectomy

26. Which term represents the condition of failure of descent of the testis into the scrotum?
(a) Cryptorchidism (b) Vasectomy
(c) Oligospermia (d) Castration

27. __________ present in the neck of the spermatozoa helps in first cleavage division:
(a) Proximal centriole (b) Distal centriole
(c) Ring centriole (d) Mitochondria

28. Completion of the second meiotic division is induced by:
(a) Rupture of Graafian follicle
(b) Contact of the sperm with the zona pellucida layer of the ovum
(c) The entry of the sperm into the cytoplasm of the ovum through the zona pellucida and the plasma membrane
(d) Copulation

29. In human females, a tiny finger-like structure called __________ lies at the upper junction of the two labia minora above the urethral opening:
(a) Mons pubis (b) Clitoris
(c) Hymen (d) Vulva

30. In the menstrual cycle, maximum progesterone levels are observed in:
(a) Proliferative phase
(b) Follicular phase
(c) Luteal phase
(d) More than one option is correct

31. The birth canal in females is formed by:
(a) Vagina only
(b) Cervical canal and uterus
(c) Vagina and cervical canal
(d) Uterus only

32. During parturition, strong contractions of __________ are observed under the influence of __________:
(a) Endometrium, oxytocin
(b) Myometrium, prolactin
(c) Endometrium, prolactin
(d) Myometrium, oxytocin

33. Which of the following is an incorrect statement?
(a) Uterus is also called womb
(b) Spermiogenesis is a process in which spermatids are transformed into spermatozoa
(c) Spermatogonial cells are also called Sertoli cells
(d) The solid mass of cells produced by cleavage is morula

34. Which of the following is an incorrect statement?
(a) The site of fertilisation is the ampulla
(b) Parturition is induced by a complex neuroendocrine mechanism
(c) The cells produced by cleavage are called blastomeres
(d) The cyclical changes in the uterus during a menstrual cycle are induced by changes in the levels of pituitary hormones only

35. Bulbourethral glands of males are homologous with:
(a) Paraurethral glands
(b) Glands of Skene
(c) Prostate gland
(d) Bartholin's gland

36. In human females, the blastocyst:
(a) Transforms into morula
(b) Is implanted into the endometrium a week after fertilisation
(c) Is a solid ball of blastomeres
(d) Has three germinal layers

37. Identify the incorrect statement:
(a) The first menstruation at puberty is called menarche
(b) Lack of menstruation may occur due to factors like stress and poor health
(c) Corpus luteum secretes progesterone which is responsible for maintenance of endometrium
(d) In the absence of fertilisation, the corpus luteum degenerates due to fall in levels of FSH

38. Which of the following groups of hormones are produced in women only during pregnancy?
(a) Cortisol, prolactin, relaxin
(b) Oxytocin, thyroxine, relaxin
(c) hCG, hPL, relaxin
(d) hCG, prolactin, oxytocin

39. Which of the following is an unpaired accessory gland in males?
(a) Seminal vesicle
(b) Prostate gland
(c) Bulbourethral gland
(d) Cowper's gland

40. If fertilisation does not occur, the corpus luteum degenerates to form:
(a) Corpus callosum
(b) Corpus albicans
(c) Corpus haemorrhagicum
(d) Corpora quadrigemina

41. Identify the diploid stages during spermatogenesis:
(a) Spermatogonia and sperms
(b) Primary spermatocyte and spermatogonia
(c) Spermatid and primary spermatocyte
(d) Secondary spermatocyte and spermatogonia

42. Which of the following sets represent the external genitalia of human females?
(a) Labia majora, labia minora, cervix
(b) Labia majora, mons pubis, clitoris
(c) Labia minora, vagina, clitoris
(d) Mons pubis, hymen, cervix

43. Transformation of spermatid into sperm is termed:
(a) Spermatocytogenesis
(b) Spermiogenesis
(c) Spermatogenesis
(d) Spermiation

44. A non-cellular covering around the secondary oocyte in the Graafian follicle is:
(a) Corona radiata (b) Theca interna
(c) Zona pellucida (d) Granulosa

45. Which of the following is an incorrect statement?
(a) Menstruation usually occurs about 14 days after ovulation
(b) Menstrual blood can easily clot as it is rich in fibrin
(c) Mid-cycle LH surge induces rupture of Graafian follicle during ovulation
(d) In human females, the menstrual cycle ceases around 50 years of age and is called menopause

ANSWER KEYS

Exercises

1. (b) **2.** (d) **3.** (c) **4.** (b) **5.** (c) **6.** (b) **7.** (d) **8.** (b) **9.** (a) **10.** (b)
11. (a) **12.** (b) **13.** (b) **14.** (b) **15.** (b) **16.** (c) **17.** (c) **18.** (d) **19.** (b) **20.** (c)
21. (c) **22.** (c) **23.** (b) **24.** (a) **25.** (d) **26.** (b) **27.** (a) **28.** (c) **29.** (d) **30.** (a)
31. (a) **32.** (b) **33.** (b) **34.** (c) **35.** (d) **36.** (d) **37.** (c) **38.** (a) **39.** (b) **40.** (d)
41. (c) **42.** (a) **43.** (b) **44.** (c) **45.** (b) **46.** (a) **47.** (b) **48.** (b) **49.** (d) **50.** (c)
51. (c) **52.** (b) **53.** (a) **54.** (c) **55.** (d) **56.** (c) **57.** (b) **58.** (c) **59.** (d) **60.** (d)
61. (c) **62.** (b) **63.** (c) **64.** (b) **65.** (b) **66.** (d) **67.** (d) **68.** (c) **69.** (c) **70.** (b)
71. (b) **72.** (b) **73.** (c) **74.** (d) **75.** (b) **76.** (a) **77.** (d) **78.** (b) **79.** (b) **80.** (c)
81. (c) **82.** (d) **83.** (c) **84.** (d) **85.** (d) **86.** (b) **87.** (b) **88.** (b) **89.** (d) **90.** (d)
91. (b) **92.** (d) **93.** (d) **94.** (a) **95.** (b) **96.** (c) **97.** (d) **98.** (d) **99.** (b) **100.** (d)
101. (d) **102.** (d) **103.** (a) **104.** (c) **105.** (d) **106.** (d) **107.** (d) **108.** (a) **109.** (b) **110.** (d)
111. (b) **112.** (c) **113.** (d) **114.** (d) **115.** (b) **116.** (d) **117.** (b) **118.** (b) **119.** (c) **120.** (c)
121. (b) **122.** (d) **123.** (d) **124.** (d) **125.** (a) **126.** (b) **127.** (b) **128.** (d) **129.** (d) **130.** (b)
131. (a) **132.** (d) **133.** (c) **134.** (a) **135.** (c) **136.** (b) **137.** (c) **138.** (a) **139.** (d) **140.** (c)
141. (b) **142.** (b) **143.** (c) **144.** (b) **145.** (d) **146.** (b) **147.** (c) **148.** (a) **149.** (a) **150.** (b)
151. (b) **152.** (a) **153.** (d) **154.** (b) **155.** (d) **156.** (b) **157.** (c) **158.** (b) **159.** (b) **160.** (c)
161. (b) **162.** (d) **163.** (b) **164.** (c) **165.** (b) **166.** (b) **167.** (d) **168.** (d) **169.** (c) **170.** (d)

NCERT Exemplar Questions

1. (c) **2.** (d) **3.** (d) **4.** (b) **5.** (a) **6.** (b) **7.** (a) **8.** (b) **9.** (c) **10.** (b)
11. (c) **12.** (b) **13.** (d) **14.** (b) **15.** (c) **16.** (a) **17.** (a) **18.** (a)

Practice Test Paper

1. (c) **2.** (d) **3.** (c) **4.** (b) **5.** (c) **6.** (c) **7.** (b) **8.** (c) **9.** (b) **10.** (c)
11. (b) **12.** (d) **13.** (a) **14.** (b) **15.** (b) **16.** (b) **17.** (c) **18.** (b) **19.** (b) **20.** (b)
21. (c) **22.** (a) **23.** (b) **24.** (b) **25.** (c) **26.** (a) **27.** (a) **28.** (c) **29.** (b) **30.** (c)
31. (c) **32.** (d) **33.** (c) **34.** (d) **35.** (d) **36.** (b) **37.** (d) **38.** (c) **39.** (b) **40.** (b)
41. (b) **42.** (b) **43.** (b) **44.** (c) **45.** (b)

SOLUTIONS

Male Reproductive System

1. Each testicular lobule contains one to three highly coiled seminiferous tubules in which sperms are produced. Each seminiferous tubule is lined on its inside by two types of cells called male germ cells (spermatogonia) and Sertoli cells.

2. Each testis has about 250 compartments called testicular lobules.

3. The regions outside the seminiferous tubules, called interstitial spaces, contain blood vessels and interstitial cells or Leydig cells. Leydig cells synthesise and secrete testicular hormones called androgens.

4. Sertoli cells provide nutrition to the germ cells. Thus, they keep the germ cells healthy and nourished. They also function at the end of spermatogenesis by absorbing extra cytoplasm from the newly created spermatozoa, just prior to their release into the lumen of the seminiferous tubule.

5. The regions outside the seminiferous tubules, called interstitial spaces, contain small blood vessels and Leydig cells.

6. The seminiferous tubules of the testes open into the vasa efferentia through rete testis.

7. The male sex accessory ducts include rete testis, vasa efferentia, epididymis and vas deferens.

8. The vasa efferentia leave the testes and open into the epididymis located along the posterior surface of each testis.

9. The prostate gland is an unpaired, walnut-sized gland located between the bladder and the penis. The prostate lies just in front of the rectum. The urethra runs through the centre of the prostate, from the bladder to the penis, letting urine flow out of the body. The prostate secretes fluid that nourishes and protects sperm.

10. The penis is the male external genitalia. In addition to it sexual function, the penis acts as a conduit for urine to leave the body.

11. The inguinal canal links the abdominal cavity to the scrotum. It conveys the spermatic cord, which contains the vas deferens, vessels, nerves and cremaster muscles.

12. The seminal vesicles are also called uterus masculinus and are located in the pelvis. They are positioned below the urinary bladder and are lateral to the vas deferens.

13. Testis is the male primary sex organ. Its function is to produce both sperm and androgens, primarily testosterone.

14. The secretions of the seminal vesicle contain fructose that provide nutrient energy for the spermatozoa.

15. The seminal vesicles secrete a significant proportion of the fluid that ultimately becomes semen. About 70% of the seminal fluid in humans originates from the seminal vesicles. The duct of each seminal gland opens into the corresponding vas deferens as it enters the prostate gland. Seminal vesicle fluid is alkaline, resulting in human semen having mildly alkaline pH.

16. Spermatozoa formed in the testes enter the caput epididymis, progress to the corpus and finally reach the cauda region, where they are stored. The sperms entering the caput epididymis are immature. They lack the ability to swim forward (motility) and to fertilise the egg. Epididymal transit takes about 2.5 months in humans, but sperms can be stored in the cauda for 2–3 days. During their transit in the epididymis, sperms undergo the maturation process necessary for them to acquire motility and fertility.

17. The duct of each seminal vesicle unites with the corresponding vas deferens to form the ejaculatory duct, which passes through the substance of the prostate gland and opens into the prostatic urethra.

18. Sertoli cells are also called sustentacular cells or nurse cells as they supply nutrients to sperms.

19. Cryptorchidism is a condition of the undescended testis; when one or both the male testes have not passed into the scrotal sac.

20. Circumcision is the removal of the foreskin from the human penis.

21. Seminal vesicles release up to 60–70% of the fluid found in semen. Its secretions contain fructose, calcium and certain enzymes. Fructose provides energy for swimming sperm cells.

22. Vasectomy is a surgical procedure for male sterilisation or permanent contraception. During the procedure, the male vas deferens are cut and tied or sealed so as to prevent sperms from entering into the urethra, thereby preventing fertilisation of a female through sexual intercourse. However, this procedure does not interfere with the desire for sexual intercourse or libido.

23. Scrotum is absent in whale, elephant and platypus. Therefore, they have intra-abdominal testis.

24. The scrotum helps in maintaining the low temperature of the testes (2–2.5°C lower than the normal internal body temperature) necessary for spermatogenesis.

25. The label 'Y' represents the bulbourethral glands or Cowper's glands, whose secretions help in the lubrication of the penis. When sexually aroused, the glands produce a mucous-like fluid called pre-ejaculate that neutralises any residual acidity in the urethra.

26. Tubuli recti are structures in the testicle connecting the convoluted region of the seminiferous tubules to the rete testis.

27. The labels A and B represent Sertoli cells and primary spermatocyte, respectively, both of which are diploid. The labels C, D and E represent secondary spermatocyte, spermatid and spermatozoa, respectively, which are all haploid.

28. The label B represents a seminal vesicle and F represents the prostate gland, while H represents the bulbourethral gland.

29. The Sertoli cells produce the hormone inhibin, which is released into the blood when the sperm count is too high. This inhibits the release of FSH, which will cause spermatogenesis to slow down.

30. The label X represents the seminal vesicle, which secretes around 60–70% of seminal plasma, rich in fructose.

31. Maximum seminal plasma is contributed by the seminal vesicle (60–70%), followed by prostate gland (20–30%) and the least by the bulbourethral glands.

32. Bulbourethral gland, also called Cowper's gland, is one of two pea-shaped glands in the male, located beneath the prostate gland at the beginning of the internal portion of the penis. It produces secretions that lubricate the penis during coitus. Their secretions also neutralise the acidity in the urethra.

Female Reproductive System

33. The infundibulum is a funnel-shaped dilation covering the ovulation fossa that transports the oocyte from the ovary to the ampullary region of the oviduct where fertilisation occurs.

34. Birth canal is the channel formed by the cervical canal along with the vagina. The foetus passes through this canal during parturition.

35. The female external genitalia is called vulva and comprises the labia majora, labia minora, clitoris, mons pubis and hymen.

36. The uterus opens into the vagina through a cylinder-shaped neck of tissue called the cervix. Located at the lowermost portion of the uterus, the cervix is composed primarily of fibromuscular tissue.

37. Mons pubis is a cushion of fatty tissue covered by skin and pubic hair. The opening of the vagina is often covered partially by a membrane called the hymen. Clitoris is a tiny finger-like structure which is at the upper junction of the two labia minora and above the urethral opening.

38. The wall of the uterus has three layers of tissue: an external thin membranous perimetrium, middle thick layer of smooth muscle called myometrium, and an inner glandular layer called endometrium.

39. In the fallopian tube, the edges of the infundibulum possess finger-like projections called fimbriae.

40. The opening of the vagina is often covered partially by a membrane called the hymen. It may be torn during coitus. It may be broken by a sudden fall or jolt.

41. In females, the clitoris is an erectile body homologous with the penis of males.

42. Vagina is devoid of glands and the bacteria present there produce acidic secretions.

43. Mammary glands are modified sweat glands and are a characteristic feature of all mammals.

44. The surgical removal of ovaries will result in fall in levels of hormones like oestrogen and progesterone, due to which feedback inhibition of gonadotropins does not occur. So, the levels of gonadotropins markedly increase in blood.

45. Hysterectomy is the process of surgical removal of a woman's uterus. Castration (also known as orchiectomy) is any action, surgical, chemical, or otherwise, by which an individual loses the use of the testicles: the male gonad. Surgical castration is bilateral orchidectomy (excision of both testes). Oophorectomy or ovariectomy is the surgical removal of one or both ovaries.

46. A functional mammary gland is characteristic of all female mammals.

47. Presence of fructose in the vagina is used as forensic evidence in cases of rape, since it is present in seminal plasma.

48. The oviducts (fallopian tubes), uterus and vagina constitute the female accessory ducts.

48. The ovarian stroma is divided into two zones: peripheral cortex and inner medulla.

50. Option (c) is correct.

51. Fertilisation of the sperm and ovum takes place in the ampullary region of the fallopian tube.

52. Bartholin's glands are homologous to the bulbourethral glands of males. The lesser vestibular glands or paraurethral glands are homologous to the prostate gland of males.

53. Cervix is the lowermost portion of the uterus and is composed primarily of fibromuscular tissue. It connects the uterus with the vagina.

54. The external genitalia of the female is called vulva. The myometrium of the uterus has smooth muscles and exhibits strong contractions during delivery of the baby.

55. Option (d) is correct.

Gametogenesis

56. The second meiotic division occurs in the secondary oocyte, resulting in the formation of ovum and second polar body.

57. The acrosomal cap of sperms contains enzymes called sperm lysins. It is derived from Golgi bodies.

58. During oogenesis, meiosis II is completed in the fallopian tube. The secretions of the acrosome help the sperm enter the cytoplasm of the ovum through the zona pellucida and plasma membrane, inducing completion of the meiotic division of the secondary oocyte. The second meiotic division is unequal and results in the formation of a second polar body and haploid ovum. Soon, the haploid nucleus of the sperm and that of the ovum fuse together to form a diploid zygote.

59. During oogenesis, meiosis I is completed in the tertiary follicle. The primary oocyte grows in size and completes its first meiotic division. It is an unequal division resulting in the formation of a large haploid secondary oocyte and tiny first polar body. The secondary oocyte retains the bulk of the nutrient-rich cytoplasm of the primary oocyte.

60. The acrosomal cap of the sperm releases zona lysine or acrosin to digest the zona pellucida surrounding the ovum.

61. The secondary spermatocytes undergo the second meiotic division to produce four equal haploid spermatids.

62. During foetal life, each primary oocyte is surrounded by a layer of granulosa cells and then called primary follicle. A large number of these follicles degenerate during the phase from birth to puberty. Therefore, at puberty only 60,000–80,000 primary follicles are left in each ovary.

63. A primary spermatocyte completes the first meiotic division (reduction division) leading to the formation of two equal, haploid cells called secondary spermatocytes, which have only 23 chromosomes each.

64. The sperm head contains an elongated haploid nucleus, the anterior portion of which is covered by a cap-like structure called the acrosome.

65. "9 + 0" arrangement of microtubules is seen in the centrioles present in the neck of sperms.

66. After spermiogenesis, the sperm head become embedded in the Sertoli cells and are finally released from the seminiferous tubules by a process called spermiation.

67. The Graafian follicle ruptures to release the secondary oocyte (ovum) from the ovary by a process called ovulation.

68. Secondary spermatocytes and spermatozoa are haploid stages formed during spermatogenesis. Spermatogonia and primary spermatocytes are diploid stages.

69. Follicle stimulating hormone (FSH) acts on Sertoli cells and stimulates secretion of some factors which help in the process of spermiogenesis.

70. Option (b) is correct.

71. Oogenesis is initiated during the embryonic development stage when a couple of million gamete mother cells (oogonia) are formed in each foetal ovary; no more oogonia are formed and added after birth.

72. Oogonial cells are formed only during foetal life. No more oogonial cells are formed and added after birth.

73. The tertiary follicle is characterised by a fluid-filled cavity called antrum.

74. A primary follicle has a primary oocyte surrounded by a single layer of granulosa cells. The primary follicles are surrounded by more layers of granulosa cells and a new theca layer and called secondary follicle. The secondary follicle soon transforms into a tertiary follicle which is characterised by a fluid-filled cavity called antrum.

75. Nebenkern is the double-stranded helical structure in the sperm derived from mitochondria.

76. Zona pellucida is a glycoprotein, non-cellular covering surrounding the female gamete in the Graafian follicle.

77. The secretions of the acrosome help the sperm enter the cytoplasm of the ovum through the zona pellucida and plasma membrane, including completion of the second meiotic division to form haploid ovum and second polar body.

78. The spermatogonia present on the inside wall of the seminiferous tubules multiply by mitotic division and increase in number. Each spermatogonium is diploid and contains 46 chromosomes. Some of the spermatogonia, called primary spermatocytes, periodically undergo meiosis.

79. The cytoplasmic division is equal during spermatogenesis, since one primary spermatocyte forms four equal haploid sperms.

80. The proximal centriole present in the neck of the sperm is responsible for the first cleavage division of the zygote, while the distal centriole gives rise to the axial filament.

81. Spermiogenesis, also referred to as spermateliosis, is the formation of spermatozoa from spermatids. The Golgi apparatus surrounds the condensed nucleus, becoming the acrosomal cap. The mitochondria gather in the middle piece and the distal centriole begins to form an axoneme. The excess cytoplasm is shed and a tail is formed that provides motility to sperm.

82. The acrosomal cap of the sperm bursts to release enzymes called sperm lysins, which dissolve the outer layers of the ovum like corona radiata and zona pellucida in order to fuse with it, resulting in the formation of the zygote.

83. The human male ejaculates about 200 to 300 million sperm during a coitus of which, for normal fertility, at least 60 percent must have normal shape and size and at least 40 percent must show vigorous motility.

84. The Graafian follicle ruptures to release the secondary oocyte (ovum) from the ovary by a process called ovulation.

85. The functions of the male sex accessory ducts and glands are maintained by the testicular hormones (androgens).

86. Asthenospermia refers to reduced sperm motility.

87. Oogenesis is initiated during the embryonic stages, when the primary oocyte begins undergoing meiosis I and is temporarily arrested in prophase I.

88. The ovarian follicles degenerate during the phase from birth to puberty, and continually occur throughout life. Follicular atresia refers to the breakdown of these ovarian follicles.

89. Oogenesis is initiated during the embryonic development stage, when a couple of million gamete mother cells (oogonia) are formed within each foetal ovary; no more oogonia are formed and added after birth. The first meiotic division is unequal, resulting in the formation of a large haploid secondary oocyte and a tiny first polar body.

90. Secretions of the epididymis, vas deferens, seminal vesicle and prostate are essential for maturation and motility of sperms.

Menstrual Cycle

91. Option (b) is correct.

92. The duration of the follicular phase of the menstrual cycle is 7–8 days. The levels of progesterone peak during the luteal phase.

93. Ovulation occurs in the middle of the menstrual cycle (about the 14th day).

94. In human females, the corpus luteum secretes mainly progesterone, which is essential for maintenance of the endometrium.

95. The levels of FSH rise and appear in urine after menopause.

96. The day of ovulation = Duration of menstrual cycle − 14. Thus, in a 32-day cycle, ovulation occurs on the 18th day.

97. Zona pellucida is a non-cellular layer of carbohydrates and proteins located between the surface of the oocyte and the granulosa cells. This layer is secreted by the secondary oocyte.

98. Corpus luteum is a yellow-hormone secreting body in the female reproductive system. It is formed from the remaining follicle after ovulation.

99. During pregnancy, all events of the menstrual cycle stop and there is no menstruation. In the absence of fertilisation, the corpus luteum degenerates. This causes disintegration of the endometrium leading to menstruation, marking a new cycle.

100. The secretion of gonadotropins (LH and FSH) increases gradually during the follicular phase, and stimulates follicular development as well as secretion of oestrogens by the growing follicles. Both LH and FSH attain peak level in the middle of the cycle.

101. Menstruation can be postponed by giving progesterone pills 3–4 days before the expected date of menses.

102. Lack of menstruation may be indicative of pregnancy. However, it may also be caused due to some other underlying causes like stress, poor health, etc.

103. Menstruation occurs with an abrupt decrease in the levels of progesterone, due to degeneration of the corpus luteum in the absence of fertilisation.

104. Option (c) is correct.

105. Menstrual blood does not clot since it has a protein plasmin/fibrinolysin.

106. The corpus luteum secretes large amounts of progesterone, which is essential for maintenance of the endometrium.

107. Option (d) is correct.

108. If fertilisation does not occur, the corpus luteum involutes to form the corpus albicans that is filled with fibrous tissue.

109. Dysmenorrhoea refers to painful menstruation, typically involving abdominal cramps.

110. If the ovum fails to become fertilised, fall in the levels of the luteinising hormone (LH) causes regression of the corpus luteum.

111. During the menstrual cycle, the uterine changes are induced by oestrogen and progesterone secreted by the ovary.

112. LH is secreted by adenohypophysis.

113. The levels of oestrogen are very high in the oestrous phase.

114. Menstruation usually occurs about 14 days after ovulation.

115. The corpus haemorrhagicum is a temporary structure formed immediately after ovulation from the ovarian follicle as it collapses and is filled with blood that quickly clots.

Fertilisation and Implantation

116. Fertilisation can occur only if the ovum and sperms are transported simultaneously to the ampullary region of the fallopian tube. This is why not all copulations lead to fertilisation and pregnancy.

117. An ectopic pregnancy occurs when an implantation occurs outside the uterus. The embryo, however, cannot survive outside the uterus. If left to grow, it may damage nearby organs and cause life-threatening loss of blood. The most common site of implantation outside the uterus is the fallopian tube and is called tubal pregnancy.

118. Option (b) is correct.

119. The process of fusion of a sperm with an ovum is called fertilisation. During fertilisation, a sperm comes in contact with the zona pellucida layer of the ovum and induces changes in the membrane that blocks the entry of additional sperms. Thus, it ensures that only one sperm can fertilise an ovum.

120. Zona pellucida is a non-cellular glycoprotein covering surrounding the ovum. Sperms are motile and swim using their tail. Ovum is immotile and moves in the oviduct due to ciliary movement of the ciliated epithelium lining it. Corona radiata is formed from granulosa cells and is present outside the zona pellucida. The acrosome contains digestive enzymes (including hyaluronidase and acrosin) which break down the outer membrane of the ovum, called the zona pellucida, allowing the haploid nucleus in the sperm cell to join with the haploid nucleus in the ovum.

121. Fertilisation induces completion of the meiotic division of the secondary oocyte. The second meiotic division is unequal and results in the formation of a second polar body and a haploid ovum. Soon the haploid nucleus of the sperm and that of the ovum fuse together to form a diploid zygote.

122. Capacitation occurs after ejaculation, when the spermatozoa leave the vagina and enter the uterus. The uterus aids in the steps of capacitation by secreting sterol-binding albumin, lipoproteins, and proteolytic and glycosidasic enzymes. Capacitation has two effects: destabilisation of the acrosomal sperm head membrane which allows it to penetrate the outer layer of the egg and chemical changes in the tail that allow greater mobility in the sperm.

123. The fast block to polyspermy involves the opening of Na^+ channels in the egg plasma membrane. Na^+ flows into the egg cell, depolarising the membrane. This prevents additional sperm from fusing with the egg plasma membrane. The slow block to polyspermy occurs when excess calcium is released from the endoplasmic reticulum resulting in fusion of the cortical vesicles with the egg plasma membrane, releasing their contents into the space surrounding the egg, called the perivitelline space. This raises the vitelline membrane and inactivates receptors on the vitelline membrane. Thus, any additional sperms are released from the vitelline membrane and no more bind.

124. Capacitation has two effects: destabilisation of the acrosomal membrane and inducing chemical changes in the tail to allow greater mobility of sperm. The changes are facilitated by the removal of sterols and non-covalently bound epididymal/seminal glycoproteins. The result is a more fluid membrane with increased permeability to calcium. An influx of calcium produces increased intracellular cAMP levels, and thus, an increase in motility.

125. A morula is an early-stage embryo consisting of 16 cells (called blastomere) in a solid ball contained within the zona pellucida.

126. The blastomeres in the blastocyst are arranged into an outer layer called trophoblast and an inner group of cells attached to the trophoblast called the inner cell mass. The trophoblast layer then becomes attached to the endometrium and the inner cell mass is differentiated as the embryo.

127. The fast block to polyspermy involves the opening of Na^+ channels in the egg plasma membrane. Na^+ flows into the egg cell, depolarising the membrane. This prevents additional sperm from fusing with the egg plasma membrane.

128. The acrosomal cap of sperm has enzymes that help the sperm to get through the egg's protective coat to allow the plasma membranes of the sperm and egg to fuse. These enzymes are hyaluronidase, zona lysine/acrosin and corona penetrating enzyme.

129. The second polar body is formed in the fallopian tube by completion of second meiotic division of the secondary oocyte. The second meiotic division is also unequal and results in the formation of second polar body and a haploid ovum.

130. The gravindex test is performed on a urine sample to detect pregnancy. The test detects the presence of human chorionic gonadotropin (hCG) in the urine of pregnant women.

131. Acrosin is a protease (digestive enzyme) released from the acrosome of spermatozoa as a consequence of the acrosomal reaction. It aids in the penetration of the zona pellucida.

132. Fertilisation is the process of fusion of sperm and ovum in the ampullary region of the fallopian tube.

133. Cleavage divisions begin in the fallopian tube. Zona pellucida persists until the embryo reaches the uterine cavity. The sex of the baby is determined by the father. The mother produces gametes with only X chromosome while father produces 50 per cent of sperms carry the X chromosome while the other 50 per cent carry the Y chromosome.

134. Option (a) is correct.

Pregnancy and Embryonic Development

135. Placenta acts as an endocrine tissue and produces several hormones like human chorionic gonadotropin (hCG), human placental lactogen (hPL), oestrogens, progestogens, etc.

136. The zygote undergoes cleavage division and forms the morula stage consisting of 16 cells in a solid ball. Morula turns into blastocyst, in which blastomeres are arranged into an outer layer called trophoblast and an inner group of cells called inner cell mass, Gastrula stage, which is characterised by the presence of three germinal layers: endoderm, ectoderm and mesoderm.

137. Option (c) is correct.

138. After implantation, finger-like projections appear on the trophoblast called chorionic villi which are surrounded by uterine tissue and maternal blood.

139. The placenta does not allow the passage of maternal RBCs into foetal blood. Oxygen diffuses across the placenta from maternal to foetal blood.

140. The hormones hCG, hPL and relaxin are produced in women only during pregnancy.

141. The first movements of the foetus and appearance of hair on foetal head are usually observed during the fifth month.

142. In the later phase of pregnancy, a hormone called relaxin is secreted by the ovary. It relaxes the ligaments of the pubic symphysis and softens the cervix to assist in parturition.

143. Gastrulation is a phase in early embryonic development during which the single-layered blastula is reorganised into a multilayered structure known as gastrula. During gastrulation, the blastula folds in on itself to form three germ layers: the ectoderm, mesoderm and endoderm.

144. Immediately after implantation, the inner cell mass (embryo) differentiates into an outer layer called ectoderm and an inner layer called endoderm. A mesoderm soon appears between the ectoderm and endoderm. These three layers give rise to all tissues (organs) in adults.

145. In human beings, after one month of pregnancy, the embryo's heart is formed. The first sign of a growing foetus may be noticed by listening to the heart sound carefully through the stethoscope.

146. The morula stage does not increase in size due to the presence of the intact zona pellucida.

147. The cleavage divisions in humans are slow and asynchronous.

148. By the end of the second month of pregnancy, the foetus develops limbs and digits.

149. The umbilical cord links the foetus to the placenta. Only foetal blood is present in the umbilical vessels.

150. Umbilical cord has two umbilical arteries and one umbilical vein. Umbilical artery, one of a pair of blood vessels, supplies deoxygenated blood from within the foetus to the placenta. Umbilical vein is the blood vessel that carries oxygenated blood from the placenta into the foetus.

151. The human egg is alecithal; that is, it lacks yolk.

152. During gastrulation, the blastocyst stage transforms into a gastrula characterised by three germinal layers. The blastocoel cavity of the blastocyst is obliterated during gastrulation.

153. Cleavage divisions are very rapid and involve very fast DNA replication. There is no growth during the interphase. The size of the blastomeres progressively decreases and the nuclear to cytoplasmic ratio increases.

154. Thalidomide was consumed to prevent vomiting and nausea in pregnant women. However, this drug was found to have a teratogenic effect as it caused a congenital deformity called phocomelia. In these patients, the hands and feet were attached close to the trunk and limbs were grossly underdeveloped or absent.

Parturition and Lactation

155. The signals for parturition originate from the fully developed foetus and placenta, which induce mild uterine contractions called foetal ejection reflex.

156. Vigorous contractions of the uterus at the end of pregnancy cause expulsion/delivery of the foetus, and the process is called parturition.

157. The hormone oxytocin is injected to begin or improve uterine contractions during labour.

158. The antibodies present in the colostrum are IgA and provide natural passive immunity to the newborn.

159. Oxytocin is the hormone responsible for milk ejection or let-down reflex. Oxytocin stimulates contraction of the myoepithelial cells that surround the alveoli, causing the milk to be ejected into the ducts leading to the nipple.

160. Colostrum is the first form of milk produced by the mammary glands of mammals immediately following delivery of the newborn.

161. The foetal ejection reflex triggers the release of oxytocin from the maternal pituitary. Oxytocin acts on the uterine contractions, which in turn stimulate further secretion of oxytocin. The stimulatory reflex between uterine contraction and oxytocin secretion continues, resulting in expulsion of the baby from the uterus through the birth canal – parturition.

162. Nitric oxide is the hormone responsible for the switch-over in respiratory and circulatory system as soon as umbilical cord is cut.

163. The hormone relaxin is secreted by the ovary towards the end of pregnancy for preparation of parturition by relaxing the ligaments of the pelvis and softening the cervix.

164. Hormones like hCG and hPL are secreted by the placenta.

165. The haemochorial placenta is a type of placenta in which maternal blood is in direct contact with the chorionic villi which are covered by maternal blood, and exchange of gases and nutrients from the mother's blood and the foetus takes place.

166. Option (d) is correct.

167. Umbilical vessels carry both oxygenated and deoxygenated blood. The umbilical arteries carry deoxygenated blood from the foetus to the placenta while umbilical veins carry oxygenated blood from the placenta to the foetus.

168. Parturition is induced by a complex neuroendocrine mechanism. The signals for parturition originate from the fully developed foetus and placenta, which induce mild uterine contractions called foetus ejection reflex. This triggers release of oxytocin from the maternal pituitary.

169. Prostaglandins play an important role during parturition and are synthesized within the human foetal membranes (amnion and chorion) and decidua and act to ripen the cervix, change membrane structure and contract the myometrium. Oxytocin is released during parturition and helps in contraction of muscles of the uterus. The oestrogen to progesterone ratio rises at the time of parturition. Oestrogen promotes parturition by inducing changes in the uterus and cervix required for labour and delivery.

170. Human placenta is haemochorial since the chorion of the foetus will float in the blood pools of the mother's uterus. It is termed meta discoidal because the chorionic villi are initially distributed all over the surface of the placenta, but are later confined to the disc-like region.

4 Reproductive Health

EXERCISES

Human Population Growth, Methods of Birth Control, Medical Termination of Pregnancy

1. Which of the following is an incorrect match with respect to the function of the given contraceptive method?
   (a) Multiload 375 – Suppresses sperm motility
   (b) Cervical cap – Blocks entry of sperms through the cervix
   (c) Norplant – Kills sperms in cervix by releasing boric acid
   (d) Progestasert – Makes the uterus unsuitable for implantation
2. Which among the following contraceptive methods has minimum failure rate?
   (a) Barrier method (b) Coitus interruptus
   (c) Vasectomy (d) Periodic abstinence
3. There is no menstruation and ovulation during intense lactation following parturition. This can be effective only up to a maximum period of:
   (a) 12 months (b) 6 months
   (c) 3 months (d) 4 months
4. Which of the following is a reusable contraceptive device made of soft rubber?
   (a) Progestasert (b) Diaphragm
   (c) Condom (d) Implant
5. Which of the following is correct with respect to copper releasing IUD?
   (a) They can be inserted into the uterus by the user herself
   (b) Once inserted, they need not be replaced throughout life
   (c) They suppress sperm motility
   (d) They suppress oogenesis
6. The legally permissible use of the technique of amniocentesis is for:
   (a) Detecting sex of the foetus
   (b) Deciding on foeticide after undergoing sex determination through amniocentesis
   (c) Detecting genetic abnormalities in the foetus
   (d) MTPs which are performed beyond the 25th week of pregnancy
7. Intensely lactating mothers do not generally conceive, which is a natural method of contraception. It is due to:
   (a) Suppression of ciliary motility in oviducts
   (b) Hypersecretion of oxytocin
   (c) Suppression of release of gonadotropins by high level of prolactin
   (d) Retardation of sperm movement through cervix
8. When did the Medical Termination of Pregnancy Act in India come into existence?
   (a) 1987 (b) 2004
   (c) 1994 (d) 1971
9. The technique called tubectomy in a female:
   (a) Prevents ovulation
   (b) Makes the cervix hostile to sperms
   (c) Involves removal of the uterus
   (d) Is a terminal method of contraception
10. Select the correct statement with respect to Saheli?
    (a) It is often called "once a day" pill
    (b) It was developed by Indian Council of Medical Research (ICMR), Lucknow
    (c) It prevents ovulation
    (d) Ormeloxifene present in it is effective as selective estrogen receptor modulator (SERM)
11. Steroidal contraceptives or hormonal contraceptives can be given as:
    (a) Oral pills (b) Implants
    (c) Injectable preparation (d) All of the above
12. Read the following statements and choose the correct option:

(a) 'Nirodh' is a popular brand of female condoms
(b) Permissible use of the technique of amniocentesis in India is for detecting the sex of the unborn foetus
(c) Lactational amenorrhoea is a natural contraceptive method effective up to 2 years
(d) Diaphragm and cervical cap are examples of reusable barrier contraceptives

13. Multiload 375:
(a) Is the most widely accepted method of contraception in the world
(b) Is a hormonal IUD that makes the uterus unsuitable for implantation
(c) Works by suppressing sperm motility and reducing the fertilising capacity
(d) Is an example of non-medicated IUD

14. Identify the contraceptive method among the following that protects against sexually transmitted infections:
(a) LNG-20 (b) Cu-7
(c) Sponge (d) Condom

15. Which of the following is effective as emergency contraceptive and can be used within 72 hours of coitus to avoid unwanted pregnancy due to rape or causal unprotected intercourse?
(a) Administration of progestogens
(b) Insertion of IUDs
(c) Both (a) and (b)
(d) Tubectomy

16. Select the hormone releasing IUDs:
(a) Lippes loop, Cu-T
(b) Multiload 375, Cu-7
(c) Progestasert, LNG-20
(d) Diaphragm, LNG-20

17. Identify the correct statement:
(a) IUDs can be inserted by the user themselves
(b) IUDs suppress gametogenesis
(c) IUDs are effective only up to 3 months
(d) IUDs increase phagocytosis of sperms in the uterus

18. Which of the following is correct with respect to Saheli?
(a) It is an IUD
(b) It is only used as a post-coital contraceptive
(c) It increases the concentration of oestrogen and prevents ovulation
(d) It blocks oestrogen receptors in the uterus and prevents implantation

19. Which of the following is incorrect regarding vasectomy?
(a) It is a terminal method and blocks gamete transport
(b) Small part of the vas deferens is removed or tied up through a small incision on the scrotum
(c) The technique is highly effective but has poor reversibility
(d) No sperms occurs in epididymis

20. Select the correct statement:
(a) Tubectomy is a method of sterilisation in which ovaries are removed surgically
(b) Amniocentesis can be used for detection of cleft palate
(c) Lactational amenorrhoea is a natural method of contraception due to high level of prolactin
(d) MTPs are used as a contraceptive method

21. ________ is one of the most widely accepted methods of contraception in India:
(a) Condom (b) Intrauterine device (IUD)
(c) Oral pill (d) Vault

22. Which of the following is incorrect with respect to the oral contraceptive pill with a small dose of either progestogens or progestogen-oestrogen combination?
(a) It is a contraceptive method used either by males or females
(b) Pills have to be taken daily for a period of 21 days starting within the first five days of the menstrual cycle
(c) They inhibit ovulation and implantation
(d) They alter the quality of the cervical mucus to prevent/retard entry of sperms

23. In which of the following contraceptive methods are the ovum and sperm prevented from physically meeting with the help of barriers?
(a) Saheli and vaults
(b) Cervical caps and diaphragm
(c) Condom and LNG-20
(d) Progestasert and vaults

24. Read the following statement and choose the correct option:
I: Surgical method of contraception is terminal method to prevent any more pregnancies
II: Surgical methods, also called sterilisation, prevent gamete formation
(a) Both statements are correct
(b) Only Statement I is correct
(c) Only Statement II is correct
(d) Both statements are incorrect

25. Population of India crossed ________ in May 2011:
(a) 1.7 billion (b) 350 million
(c) 125 million (d) 1.2 billion

26. Chances of failure are very high in which of the following contraceptive methods?

(a) Oral pills (b) Progestasert
(c) Coitus interruptus (d) Tubectomy

27. According to the 2011 census report, the population growth rate was around:
(a) 15/1000/year (b) 20/1000/year
(c) 25/1000/year (d) 17/1000/year

28. Which of the following is not a reason for population explosion in India?
(a) Decline in maternal mortality rate (MMR)
(b) Decline in infant mortality rate (IMR)
(c) Increase in number of people in reproducible age
(d) A rapid increase in death rate

29. Which of the following is a correct statement?
(a) Hysterectomy is a useful contraceptive method
(b) Saheli is a non-steroidal preparation
(c) By the year 2000, world population rocketed to 2000 million
(d) Barrier methods work on the principle of preventing ovum and sperm from meeting

30. Which of the following contraceptive methods involves hormones?
(a) Cu-T, barrier methods
(b) Lactational amenorrhoea, oral pills
(c) Saheli, Cu-7
(d) Coitus interruptus, Lippes loop

31. Select the incorrect statement:
(a) IUDs increase phagocytosis of sperms
(b) Spermicidal creams, jellies, foams are usually used along with barrier devices to increase their contraceptive efficiency
(c) IUDs are inserted by doctors or expert nurses in the uterus through the vagina
(d) Diaphragm and vaults cover the cervix and vagina in the female during coitus

32. Coitus interruptus is also called:
(a) Rhythm method
(b) Withdrawal method
(c) Periodic abstinence
(d) Lactational amenorrhoea

33. Read the following statements and choose the correct option:
I: Castration can be considered as an effective contraceptive method
II: Contraceptive method should in no way interfere with the sexual drive or desire for the sexual act of the user
(a) Both statements are correct
(b) Both statements are incorrect
(c) Statement I is incorrect
(d) Statement II is incorrect

34. Identify the contraceptive and the corresponding category to which it belongs in the given diagram:

(a) Condom for female: Barrier contraceptive
(b) Condom for male: Barrier contraceptive
(c) Norplant: Hormonal implant
(d) Cervical cap: Barrier contraceptive

35. Fill in the blanks by selecting the correct option:
A. ___I___ methods work on the principle of avoiding chances of ovum and sperm meeting
B. ___II___ is a contraceptive method in which the male partner withdraws his penis from the vagina just before ejaculation to avoid insemination
C. ___III___ is a contraceptive method in which the couples avoid or abstain from coitus from days 10 to 17 of the menstrual cycle

	I	II	III
(a)	Artificial	Coitus interruptus	Withdrawal
(b)	Natural	Coitus interruptus	Periodic abstinence
(c)	Artificial	Withdrawal	Lactational amenorrhoea
(d)	Natural	Periodic abstinence	Withdrawal

36. Identify the contraceptives given in the diagrams labelled A and B:

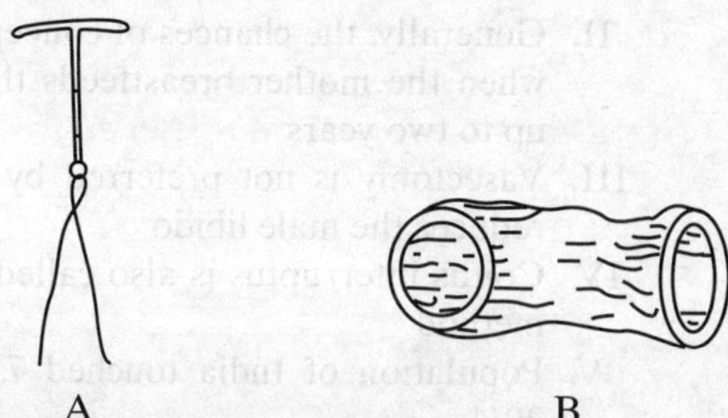

(a) A: IUD, B: Male condom
(b) A: Implant, B: Female condom
(c) A: IUD, B: Female condom
(d) A: Vault, B: Implant

37. Identify the contraceptive method in the diagram given below:

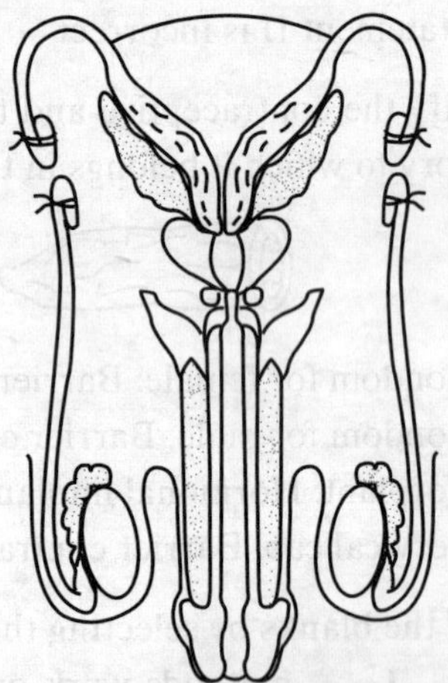

(a) Tubectomy (b) Castration
(c) Hysterectomy (d) Vasectomy

38. Identify the contraceptive procedure/method in the diagrams illustrated below:

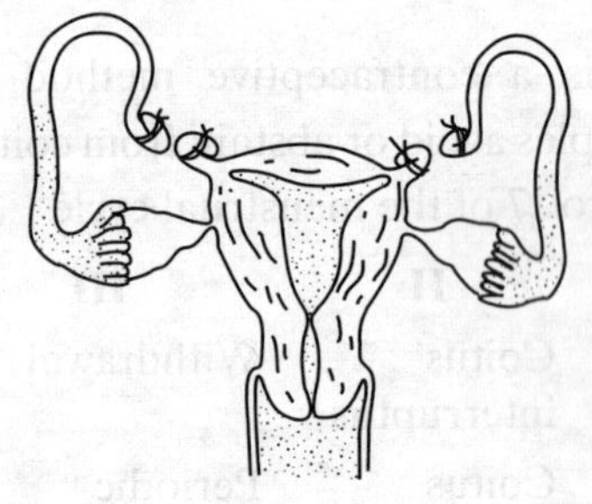

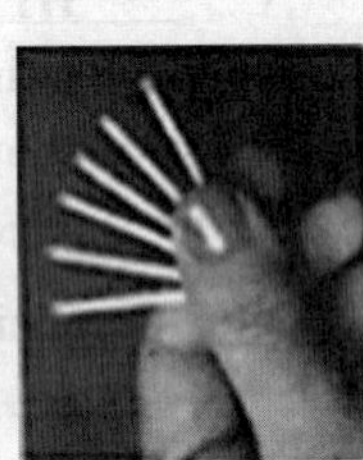

I II

(a) I-Vasectomy, II-Implant
(b) I-IUD, II-Condom
(c) I-Tubectomy, II-Implant
(d) I-Tubectomy, II-Copper T

39. Identify the correct statements:

I. Contraceptive pills may be taken up to one week after coitus to prevent coitus
II. Generally, the chances of conception are nil when the mother breastfeeds the infant for up to two years
III. Vasectomy is not preferred by males as it reduces the male libido
IV. Coitus interruptus is also called withdrawal method
V. Population of India touched 7.2 billion by 2011

(a) I and III (b) II, III and V
(c) III, IV and V (d) Only IV

40. Match the options given in Column I with Column II and choose the correct option:

Column I	Column II
A. Condom	(i) Semen contains no sperms
B. Vasectomy	(ii) Prevents ovulation
C. Cu-T	(iii) Prevents sperms from reaching the cervix
D. Pills	(iv) Suppresses sperm motility

(a) A – (ii), B –(i), C – (iii), D – (iv)
(b) A – (i), B –(iv), C – (iii), D – (ii)
(c) A – (iii), B –(i), C – (ii), D – (iv)
(d) A – (iii), B –(i), C – (iv), D – (ii)

41. Which of the following is/are correct statement(s) with respect to IUDs:

(a) IUDs are made of plastic or metal which are inserted in the uterus through the vagina by doctors or expert nurses
(b) IUDs are presently available as non-medicated IUDs, copper releasing IUDs and hormone releasing IUDs
(c) IUDs are ideal contraceptives for females who want to delay pregnancy and/or space children
(d) All of the above

42. Which of the following is a correct statement?

(a) The purpose of tubectomy is to prevent egg formation
(b) Surgical methods of contraception have good reversibility
(c) Saheli has very few side effects and high contraceptive value
(d) Chances of failure of natural methods of contraception are almost nil

Sexually Transmitted Infections, Infertility

43. Which of the following is a correct match with respect to sexually transmitted infection and its causative agent?

	STI	Causative agent
(a)	Gonorrhoea	*Chlamydia trachomatis*
(b)	Syphilis	*Treponema pallidum*
(c)	Chancroid	Human papilloma virus
(d)	Genital herpes	*Haemophilus ducrei*

44. Which of the following sexually transmitted infections (STI) caused by bacteria can be transmitted to the foetus from an infected mother through the placenta?

(a) AIDS
(b) Syphilis
(c) Gonorrhoea
(d) More than one option is correct

45. Which of the following sexually transmitted infections do not specifically affect the reproductive organs?

(a) Syphilis and Hepatitis B
(b) Genital warts and chlamydiasis
(c) AIDS and Hepatitis B
(d) Syphilis and AIDS

46. Which of the following sexually transmitted infections can be treated and cured if detected at an early stage?
(a) HIV infection (b) Genital herpes
(c) Syphilis (d) Hepatitis B

47. In case of couples where the male has a very low sperm count, which technique will be suitable for fertilisation?
(a) Intracytoplasmic sperm injection
(b) Intrauterine transfer
(c) Artificial insemination
(d) Gamete intra-fallopian transfer

48. In assisted reproductive technologies, in vitro fertilisation (IVF) involves the transfer of:
(a) Zygote into the fallopian tube
(b) Zygote into the uterus
(c) Ovum into the fallopian tube
(d) Embryo with 16 blastomeres into the fallopian tube

49. Which of the following techniques is used in the test tube baby programme?
(a) Artificial insemination (AI)
(b) Intrauterine insemination (IUI)
(c) Gamete intra-fallopian transfer (GIFT)
(d) Zygote intra-fallopian transfer (ZIFT)

50. The technique called GIFT is recommended for those females:
(a) Whose husbands have low sperm count
(b) Who cannot provide a suitable environment for fertilisation
(c) Who cannot produce an ovum
(d) Whose cervical canal is too narrow to allow passage of sperms

51. Read the following statements and choose the correct option:
I: Inability to conceive or produce children even after 2 years of unprotected sexual cohabitation is called infertility
II: All cases of infertility are treated with in vitro fertilisation
(a) Both statements are correct
(b) Both statements are incorrect
(c) Only Statement I is correct
(d) Only Statement II is correct

52. Sexually transmitted infections (STIs), if not properly treated, may lead to all of the following, except:
(a) Still birth (b) Pelvic inflammatory diseases
(c) Abortion (d) Pregnancy

53. Which of the following sexually transmitted infections can be transmitted by sharing infected needles, syringes and blood?
(a) Hepatitis B and trichomoniasis
(b) Syphilis and genital herpes
(c) HIV and Hepatitis B
(d) Genital warts and syphilis

54. Artificial insemination means:
(a) Transfer of sperms directly into the ovary
(b) Transfer of sperms into a test tube containing the ovum
(c) Transfer of ovum into the fallopian tube
(d) Transfer of sperms of healthy donor into the vagina

55. Chancroid is caused by a bacterium:
(a) *Treponema pallidum*
(b) *Haemophilus ducrei*
(c) *Neisseria gonorrhoeae*
(d) *Chlamydia trachomatis*

56. Which of the following venereal diseases is caused by a protozoan?
(a) Gonorrhoea (b) Syphilis
(c) Trichomoniasis (d) Chlamydiasis

57. Absence of sperms in semen is called:
(a) Teratozoospermia (b) Asthenozoospermia
(c) Azoospermia (d) Normozoospermia

58. Infertility may occur in males due to:
(a) Cryptorchidism
(b) Orchitis due to mumps
(c) Dilation of testicular veins or varicocele
(d) All of the above

59. Antibiotics are not used for the treatment of:
(a) Chlamydiasis (b) Gonorrhoea
(c) Chancroid (d) Genital herpes

60. Select the incorrect statement:
(a) Incidence of venereal disease is high among persons in the age group of 15–24
(b) Early symptoms of sexually transmitted infections are itching, fluid discharge, slight pain and swelling in the genital region
(c) Gonorrhoea and syphilis are infections caused by viruses
(d) Oligospermia refers to very low sperm count in semen

61. The procedure used for treatment of infertility, in which a sperm is directly injected into the ovum, is called:
(a) Intrauterine insemination (IUI)
(b) In vitro fertilisation (IVF)

(c) Gamete intra-fallopian transfer (GIFT)
(d) Intracytoplasmic sperm injection (ICSI)

62. Identify the incorrect statement:
(a) Infertility can be caused by congenital diseases, drugs or immunological diseases
(b) In India, often the male is blamed for the couple being childless, but more often than not, the problem lies in the female partner
(c) Infertile couples could be assisted to have children through special techniques called assisted reproductive technologies (ART)
(d) In vitro fertilisation refers to fertilisation outside the body in almost similar conditions to that in the body

63. Which of the following sexually transmitted diseases is characterised by the development of a painless ulcer called chancre on the genital organs?
(a) Chancroid (b) Gonorrhoea
(c) Syphilis (d) Genital herpes

64. Which of the following statements is correct regarding sexually transmitted infections?
(a) Hemophilia is an example of a venereal disease
(b) Genital herpes and sickle cell anaemia are both sexually transmitted infections
(c) The chances of a 5-year-old boy contracting a venereal disease are very little
(d) A person may contract syphilis by sharing utensils with an infected person

65. Match the options given in Column I with those in Column II:

Column I	Column II
A. AIDS	(i) *Treponema*
B. Genital warts	(ii) *Neisseria*
C. Gonorrhoea	(iii) Human papilloma virus
D. Syphilis	(iv) HIV

(a) A – (i), B – (iv), C – (iii), D – (ii)
(b) A – (iv), B – (iii), C – (ii), D – (i)
(c) A – (iv), B – (ii), C – (iii), D – (i)
(d) A – (iii), B – (iv), C – (ii), D – (i)

66. In which of the following sexually transmitted infections does the patient experience pain in the genital region, burning sensation while urination and pus-containing discharge?
(a) Hepatitis B (b) AIDS
(c) Gonorrhoea (d) Genital warts

67. Which of the following is/are preventive measures for avoiding sexually transmitted infections (STIs)?
(a) Avoiding sex with unknown partners/multiple partners
(b) Avoiding use of condoms during coitus
(c) To consult a qualified doctor for early detection and to get treatment
(d) Both (a) and (c)

NCERT EXEMPLAR QUESTIONS

1. The method of directly injecting a sperm into ovum in Assisted Reproductive Technology is called:
(a) GIFT (b) ZIFT
(c) ICSI (d) ET

2. Increased IMR and decreased MMR in a population will:
(a) Cause rapid increase in growth rate
(b) Result in decline in growth rate
(c) Not cause significant change in growth rate
(d) Result in an explosive population

3. Intensely lactating mothers do not generally conceive due to the:
(a) Suppression of gonadotropins
(b) Hyper secretion of gonadotropins
(c) Suppression of gametic transport
(d) Suppression of fertilisation

4. Sterilisation techniques are generally fool proof methods of contraception with least side effects. Yet, this is the last option for the couples because:
(i) It is almost irreversible
(ii) Of the misconception that it will reduce sexual urge
(iii) It is a surgical procedure
(iv) Of lack of sufficient facilities in many parts of the country

Choose the correct option:
(a) (i) and (iii) (b) (ii) and (iii)
(c) (ii) and (iv) (d) (i), (ii), (iii) and (iv)

5. A national level approach to build up a reproductively healthy society was taken up in our country in:
(a) 1950s (b) 1960s
(c) 1980s (d) 1990s

6. Emergency contraceptives are effective if used within:
(a) 72 hrs of coitus
(b) 72 hrs of ovulation

(c) 72 hrs of menstruation
(d) 72 hrs of implantation

7. Choose the right one among the statements given below:
(a) IUDs are generally inserted by the user herself
(b) IUDs increase phagocytosis reaction in the uterus
(c) IUDs suppress gametogenesis
(d) IUDs once inserted need not be replaced

8. The following are statements about MTP:
(i) MTPs are generally advised during first trimester
(ii) MTPs are used as a contraceptive method
(iii) MTPs are always surgical
(iv) MTPs require the assistance of qualified medical personnel

Choose the correct options given below:
(a) (ii) and (iii) (b) (ii) and (iii)
(c) (i) and (iv) (d) (i) and (ii)

9. From the sexually transmitted diseases mentioned below, identify the one which does not specifically affect the sex organs:
(a) Syphilis (b) AIDS
(c) Gonorrhea (d) Genital warts

10. Condoms are one of the most popular contraceptives becuase of the following reasons:
(a) These are effective barriers for insemination
(b) They do not interfere with coital act
(c) These help in reducing the risk of STDs
(d) All of the above

11. Choose the correct statement regarding the ZIFT procedure:
(a) Ova collected from a female donor are transferred to the fallopian tube to facilitate zygote formation
(b) Zygote is collected from a female donor and transferred to the fallopian tube
(c) Zygote is collected from a female donor and transferred to the uterus
(d) Ova collected from a female donor and transferrerd to the uterus

12. The correct surgical procedure as a contraceptive method is:
(a) Ovariectomy (b) Hysterectomy
(c) Vasectomy (d) Castration

13. Diaphragms are contraceptive devices used by the females. Choose the correct option from the statements given below:
(i) They are introduced into the uterus
(ii) They are placed to cover the cervical region
(iii) They act as physical barriers for sperm entry
(iv) They act as spermicidal agents
(a) (i) and (ii) (b) (i) and (iii)
(c) (ii) and (iii) (d) (iii) and (iv)

PRACTICE TEST PAPER

1. Medical termination of pregnancy is considered safe up to how many weeks of pregnancy?
(a) 4 weeks (b) 12 weeks
(c) 20 weeks (d) 24 weeks

2. Which of the following sexually transmitted infections (STIs) cannot be treated with antibiotics?
(a) Syphilis (b) Gonorrhoea
(c) Chlamydia (d) Genital herpes

3. Which of the following is incorrect with respect to "Saheli"?
(a) It was developed at the Central Drug Research Institute (CDRI) in Lucknow
(b) It is a "once a week" pill
(c) It is an oral contraceptive pill containing steroids
(d) It prevents implantation

4. Infertility cases either due to inability of the male partner to inseminate the female, or due to very low sperm count in ejaculates, could be corrected by:
(a) Gamete intra-fallopian transfer (GIFT)
(b) Artificial insemination (AI)
(c) Intrauterine insemination (IUI)
(d) Both (b) and (c)

5. Which of the following is a copper releasing IUD?
(a) LNG-20 (b) Progestasert
(c) Lippes loop (d) Mulitload 375

6. Which of the following is incorrectly matched?
(a) Non-mediated IUDs → Lippes loop
(b) Oral contraceptive pill → Mala D
(c) Hormone releasing IUDs → LNG-20
(d) Barrier contraceptive → Cu-7

7. Oral contraceptive pills are very effective and very well accepted by females. They work by:
(a) Altering the quality of the cervical mucus to prevent/retard the entry of sperms

(b) Preventing ovulation
(c) Preventing implantation
(d) All of the above

8. All of the following sexually transmitted infections (STIs) are curable if detected early and treated properly, except:
(a) Chancroid (b) Chlamydia
(c) Genital herpes (d) Syphilis

9. Which of the following is a natural method of contraception?
(a) Condoms (b) Saheli
(c) Lactational amenorrhoea (d) Diaphragm

10. Which one of the following techniques is used during the test tube baby programme?
(a) Gamete intra-fallopian transfer (GIFT)
(b) Artificial insemination (AI)
(c) Zygote intra-fallopian transfer (ZIFT)
(d) More than one option is correct

11. Which of the following is an incorrect statement?
(a) Amniocentesis is misused for sex determination
(b) Involuntary termination of pregnancy is called MTP
(c) Nearly 45 to 50 million MTPs are performed in a year all over the world
(d) Castration cannot be taken as a contraceptive method

12. Which of the following is incorrect with respect to oral contraceptive pills (OCPs)?
(a) They inhibit ovulation and make the uterus unsuitable for implantation
(b) They have to be taken orally for a period of 21 days, starting preferably within the first five days of the menstrual cycle
(c) Ovum and sperms are prevented from physically meeting with the help of barriers
(d) They contain progestogens or oestrogen-progesterone combination

13. The copper releasing IUDs act by:
(a) Inhibiting ovulation
(b) Making the uterus unsuitable for implantation
(c) Suppressing sperm motility and reducing the fertilising capacity
(d) Making the cervix hostile for sperms

14. Natural methods of contraception act by:
(a) Inhibiting ovulation
(b) Inhibiting implantation
(c) Avoiding chances of ovum and sperm meeting
(d) Reducing sperm motility

15. In India, the population increased to 1.2 billion by 2011. The probable reason for this is increase in:
(a) Maternal mortality rate (MMR)
(b) Infant mortality rate (IMR)
(c) Death rate
(d) Number of people in reproducible age

16. In test tube baby programme:
(a) Fertilisation occurs due to artificial insemination
(b) Ovum is released in the fallopian tube
(c) Ovum from wife/donor and sperm from husband/donor are fused to form a zygote in a laboratory
(d) A surrogate mother is always involved

17. In India, "Family Planning" programmes were launched in:
(a) 1941 (b) 1951
(c) 1971 (d) 1984

18. In 1900, the population of the world was around:
(a) 2 billion (b) 6 billion
(c) 4 billion (d) 7.2 billion

19. Which of the following is not a natural method of contraception?
(a) Coitus interruptus
(b) Diaphragm
(c) Periodic abstinence
(d) Lactational amenorrhoea

20. The consequences of population explosion are:
(a) Unemployment (b) Poverty
(c) Housing problem (d) All of the above

21. Which of the following contraceptive methods has minimum failure rate?
(a) Coitus interruptus (b) Vasectomy
(c) Oral contraceptive pill (d) Cervical cap

22. Which of the following barrier methods of contraception protect against sexually transmitted infections (STIs)?
(a) Diaphragm (b) Vaginal vault
(c) Cervical cap (d) Condom

23. Which of the following are ideal contraceptives for females who want to delay pregnancy or space children?
(a) Oral contraceptive pills
(b) Intrauterine devices (IUDs)
(c) Hormonal implant
(d) Nirodh

24. If a couple avoids sexual intercourse from days 10 to 17 of each menstrual cycle, to avoid pregnancy, then it is called:
(a) Lactational amenorrhoea
(b) Withdrawal method
(c) Coitus interruptus
(d) Periodic abstinence

25. Which of the following contraceptive methods has the highest failure rate?

(a) Barrier methods (b) Hormonal implants
(c) Oral contraceptives (d) Natural methods

26. All of the following are reusable barrier devices of contraception, except:
(a) Diaphragm (b) Vaginal vault
(c) Cervical cap (d) Condom

27. Which of the following methods of contraception have the least side effects?
(a) Oral pills (b) Hormonal implants
(c) IUD (d) Coitus interruptus

28. The sterilisation procedure in males is called:
(a) Tubectomy (b) Vasectomy
(c) IUD (d) Vault

29. In which of the following methods of contraception does the male partner withdraw the penis from the vagina before ejaculation to avoid insemination?
(a) Lactational amenorrhoea
(b) Coitus interruptus
(c) Withdrawal method
(d) Both (b) and (c)

30. Oral contraceptive pills are aimed at lowering the levels of:
(a) Prolactin
(b) Follicle stimulating hormone (FSH)
(c) Luteinising hormone (LH)
(d) Both (b) and (c)

31. All of the following are copper releasing IUDs, except:
(a) Cu-7 (b) Cu-T
(c) Multiload 375 (d) Progestasert

32. An intrauterine device (IUD) can be made of:
(a) Steel (b) Copper
(c) Plastic only (d) Any of the above

33. The transfer of zygote or embryo with up to eight blastomeres into the fallopian tube is called:
(a) Intrauterine transfer (IUT)
(b) Gamete intra-fallopian transfer (GIFT)
(c) Zygote intra-fallopian transfer (ZIFT)
(d) Intrauterine insemination (IUI)

34. The term venereal disease refers to diseases spread by:
(a) Contaminated food (b) Air
(c) Blood (d) Sexual contact

35. Which of the following sexually transmitted infections (STIs) is caused by a protozoan?
(a) Syphilis (b) Trichomoniasis
(c) Genital warts (d) Hepatitis B

36. Which of the following can be used for emergency contraception?
(a) Intrauterine device (IUD)
(b) Oestrogen-progesterone combination
(c) Progestogens
(d) All of these

37. Sexually transmitted infections can cause complications like:
(a) Abortions
(b) Ectopic pregnancy
(c) Pelvic inflammatory diseases
(d) All of the above

38. Which of the following sexually transmitted infections can spread through contaminated blood as well?
(a) Genital herpes and gonorrhea
(b) Genital warts and syphilis
(c) Chlamydiasis and trichomoniasis
(d) HIV and Hepatitis B

39. Which of the following is a subcutaneous hormonal implant that offers contraception for nearly 5 years?
(a) Mala D (b) Norplant
(c) Depo provera (d) Saheli

40. The technique in which a single spermatozoa is injected directly into the cytoplasm of an ovum by microneedle is:
(a) Gamete intra-fallopian transfer (GIFT)
(b) Zygote intra-fallopian transfer (ZIFT)
(c) Intracytoplasmic sperm injection (ICSI)
(d) Testicular sperm extraction (TESE)

41. MTPs carried out in a year all over the world are:
(a) 45 to 50 billion
(b) About 20% of the total number of pregnancies conceived
(c) Safe up to 30 weeks of pregnancy
(d) More than one option is correct

42. All of the following are causes of infertility in males, except:
(a) Impotency (b) Alcoholism
(c) Cryptorchidism (d) Circumcision

43. Which of the following cannot be a strategy for obtaining a reproductively healthy society?
(a) Family planning programme
(b) Sex education in schools
(c) Awareness in fertile couples about available birth control devices
(d) Early marriage of children as soon as they attain puberty

44. Sterilisation procedures are very effective in preventing pregnancy as they:
(a) Prevent ovulation

(b) Block gamete transport and hence prevent fertilisation
(c) Have good reversibility
(d) Prevent release of gonadotropic hormones

45. Which of the following techniques involves in vivo fertilisation?
(i) GIFT
(ii) IUI
(iii) ICSI
(iv) IVF
(a) Only (ii) (b) (i) and (ii)
(c) (i) and (iii) (d) (ii) and (iii)

ANSWER KEYS

EXERCISES

1. (c)	**2.** (c)	**3.** (b)	**4.** (b)	**5.** (c)	**6.** (c)	**7.** (c)	**8.** (d)	**9.** (d)	**10.** (d)
11. (d)	**12.** (d)	**13.** (c)	**14.** (d)	**15.** (c)	**16.** (c)	**17.** (d)	**18.** (d)	**19.** (d)	**20.** (c)
21. (b)	**22.** (a)	**23.** (b)	**24.** (b)	**25.** (d)	**26.** (c)	**27.** (b)	**28.** (d)	**29.** (b)	**30.** (b)
31. (d)	**32.** (b)	**33.** (c)	**34.** (b)	**35.** (b)	**36.** (c)	**37.** (d)	**38.** (c)	**39.** (d)	**40.** (d)
41. (d)	**42.** (c)	**43.** (b)	**44.** (b)	**45.** (c)	**46.** (c)	**47.** (c)	**48.** (a)	**49.** (d)	**50.** (c)
51. (c)	**52.** (d)	**53.** (c)	**54.** (d)	**55.** (b)	**56.** (c)	**57.** (c)	**58.** (d)	**59.** (d)	**60.** (c)
61. (d)	**62.** (b)	**63.** (c)	**64.** (c)	**65.** (b)	**66.** (c)	**67.** (d)			

NCERT Exemplar Questions

1. (c)	**2.** (c)	**3.** (a)	**4.** (d)	**5.** (a)	**6.** (a)	**7.** (b)	**8.** (c)	**9.** (b)	**10.** (d)
11. (b)	**12.** (c)	**13.** (c)							

Practice Test Paper

1. (b)	**2.** (d)	**3.** (c)	**4.** (d)	**5.** (d)	**6.** (d)	**7.** (d)	**8.** (c)	**9.** (c)	**10.** (c)
11. (b)	**12.** (c)	**13.** (c)	**14.** (c)	**15.** (d)	**16.** (c)	**17.** (b)	**18.** (a)	**19.** (b)	**20.** (d)
21. (b)	**22.** (d)	**23.** (b)	**24.** (d)	**25.** (d)	**26.** (d)	**27.** (d)	**28.** (b)	**29.** (d)	**30.** (d)
31. (d)	**32.** (d)	**33.** (c)	**34.** (d)	**35.** (b)	**36.** (d)	**37.** (d)	**38.** (d)	**39.** (b)	**40.** (c)
41. (b)	**42.** (d)	**43.** (d)	**44.** (b)	**45.** (b)					

SOLUTIONS

1. Norplant is a hormonal implant and a contraceptive consisting of small rods implanted under the skin which gradually release the hormone levonorgestrel over a number of years.

2. Vasectomy is a surgical method of contraception and thus has minimum failure rate.

3. Lactational amenorrhea is a natural method of contraception where no menstruation and ovulation occurs during intense lactation following parturition. However, this method is effective up to a maximum period of six months.

4. Diaphragms, cervical caps and vaults are barrier contraceptives made of rubber that are inserted into the female reproductive tract to cover the cervix during coitus. This prevents conception by blocking the entry of sperms through the cervix. They are reusable.

5. Copper ions released from IUDs suppress sperm motility and the fertilising capacity of sperms.

6. The legally permissible use of the technique amniocentesis is for the detection of genetic abnormalities in the foetus.

7. Lactational amenorrhoea is a natural method of contraception due to suppression of the release of gonadotropins by high level of prolactin.

8. Government of India legalised MTP in 1971 with some restrictions to avoid its misuse.
9. In tubectomy, a small part of the fallopian tube is removed or tied through a small incision in the abdomen or through the vagina.
10. Saheli is a "once a week pill" containing centchroman or ormeloxifene and is effective as selective estrogen receptor modulator (SERM) and prevents implantation.
11. Steroidal or hormonal contraceptives can be given as oral pills, implants or injectable preparations.
12. "Nirodh" is a popular brand of male condoms. In India, prenatal determination of sex using amniocentesis is prohibited. Lactational amenorrhoea is a natural contraceptive method effective for up to 6 months.
13. Mulitload 375 is a copper releasing IUD that works by suppressing sperm motility and reducing the fertilising capacity.
14. Condoms can protect against sexually transmitted infections.
15. Progestogens alone or in combination with oestrogen or IUDs within 72 hours of coitus have been found to be very effective as emergency contraceptive as they could be used to avoid possible pregnancy due to rape or casual unprotected intercourse.
16. Progestasert and LNG-20 are hormone releasing IUDs.
17. IUDs are inserted by doctors or trained health workers. They are effective for 3–5 years. IUDs increase phagocytosis of sperms within the uterus and the copper ions released suppress sperm motility and the fertilising capacity of sperms.
18. Saheli, the new oral contraceptive for females, contains a non-steroidal preparation. It is a 'once a week' pill with very few side effects and high contraceptive value. It blocks oestrogen receptors in the uterus and prevents implantation.
19. Sterilisation procedure in males is called vasectomy, in which part of the vas deferens is removed or tied through a small incision in the scrotum. Thus, sperms are present in the epididymis, but fail to reach the urethra. In such patients, the semen is without sperms.
20. Tubectomy is a sterilisation procedure in females in which a part of the fallopian tube is removed or tied. Amniocentesis is used for detecting genetic and chromosomal diseases. MTP has a significant role in decreasing the population size, but it is not a contraceptive method.
21. IUDs are one of the most widely accepted methods of contraception in India.
22. Oral contraceptive pills with a small dose of either progestogens or progestogen-oestrogen combination can be used only by females.
23. Cervical caps and diaphragm are barrier devices and prevent the physical meeting of sperms and egg.
24. Surgical methods, also called sterilisation, block gamete transport and thereby prevent conception.
25. Population of Indian crossed 1.2 billion in May 2011.
26. Chances of failure are very high in natural methods of contraception like coitus interruptus.
27. According to the 2011 census, the population growth rate was around 20/1000/years.
28. A rapid decline in death rate, maternal mortality rate (MMR) and infant mortality rate (IMR) as well as increase in the number of people in the reproducible age group are reasons for population explosion in India.
29. Hysterectomy is not a contraceptive method. Saheli is a non-steroidal preparation. By the year 2000, world population rocketed to 6 billion. Natural methods work on the principle of avoiding ovum and sperm meeting.
30. Lactational amenorrhoea and oral pills are contraceptive methods that involve hormones.
31. Diaphragm and vaults cover the cervix in the female during coitus.
32. Withdrawal or coitus interruptus is a natural method of contraception in which the male partner withdraws his penis from the vagina just before ejaculation to avoid insemination.
33. Castration refers to the removal of the testes and thus cannot be used as a contraceptive method. Removal of testes would lower testosterone levels and therefore cause impotency.
34. Option (b) is correct.
35. Option (b) is correct.
36. Option (c) is correct.
37. Option (d) is correct.
38. Option (c) is correct.

39. Chances of conception are nil if the mother breastfeeds the infant for up to 6 months. Contraceptive pills may be given up to 72 hours after coitus. Diaphragms and vaults cover the cervix during coitus. Population of India reached 1.2 billion in 2011.

40. Option (d) is correct.

41. Option (d) is correct.

42. The purpose of tubectomy is to block gamete transport. Surgical methods of contraception have poor reversibility. Natural methods of contraception have high failure rates.

43. Gonorrhoea is a bacterial disease caused by *Neisseria gonorrhoea*. Chancroid is caused by *Haemophilus ducrei*. Genital herpes is a viral disease caused by herpes simplex virus.

44. Syphilis is a bacterial sexually transmitted infection caused by *Treponema pallidum* and can be transmitted to the foetus from the infected mother through the placenta.

45. AIDS and Hepatitis B are sexually transmitted infections that do not specifically affect the reproductive organs.

46. Except for Hepatitis B, genital herpes and HIV infections, other sexually transmitted infections are completely curable if detected early and treated properly.

47. Infertility due to inability of the male partner to inseminate the female or due to low sperm counts in the ejaculates could be corrected by artificial insemination.

48. In vitro fertilisation is followed by transfer of the zygote or early embryos (with up to 8 blastomeres) into the fallopian tube.

49. Zygote intra-fallopian transfer (ZIFT) is a technique used in test-tube baby programme.

50. Transfer of ovum collected from a donor into the fallopian tube is called gamete intra-fallopian transfer (GIFT). This ovum is transferred into the fallopian tube of another female who cannot produce one, but can provide a suitable environment for fertilisation and further development.

51. Several assisted reproductive technologies including in vitro fertilisation are used for treating infertility.

52. Sexually transmitted infections can cause complications like pelvic inflammatory diseases (PID), abortions, stillbirths, ectopic pregnancies, infertility or even cancer of the reproductive tract.

53. Sexually transmitted infections like HIV and Hepatitis B can be transmitted by sharing infected needles, syringes and blood.

54. Artificial insemination (AI) is a procedure in which the semen collected either from the husband or a healthy donor is artificially introduced into the vagina or uterus.

55. Chancroid is caused by a bacterium *Haemophilus ducrei*. It is a venereal infection causing ulceration of the lymph nodes in the groin.

56. Trichomoniasis is a venereal infection caused by a flagellate protozoan *Trichomonas vaginalis*.

57. Azoospermia refers to complete absence of sperms in semen.

58. Infertility in males could be caused by cryptorchidism, orchitis due to mumps or due to dilation of the testicular veins (varicocele).

59. Genital herpes is a viral infection and thus antibiotics cannot be used for its treatment.

60. Gonorrhoea and syphilis are venereal infections caused by bacteria.

61. Intracytoplasmic sperm injection is a specialised procedure to form an embryo in a laboratory in which the sperm is directly injected into the ovum.

62. In India, often the female is blamed for the couple being childless.

63. Syphilis a bacterial venereal infection caused by *Treponema pallidum* in which patients have painless ulcer called chancre on the genital organs.

64. Haemophilia is a genetic disease that impairs the body's ability to make blood clots, a process required to stop bleeding. Sickle cell anemia is an inherited disorder in which red blood cells are sickle shaped and break down easily. Syphilis is another venereal infection.

65. Option (b) is correct.

66. Gonorrhoea is a sexually transmitted infection in which the patient experiences pain in the genital region, burning sensation while urination and pus-containing discharge.

67. Sexually transmitted infections can be avoided by avoiding sexual intercourse with multiple partners. Use of condoms during coitus is also useful for preventing these infections. In case of doubt, the patient should go to qualified doctors for early treatment and detection.

Principles of Inheritance and Variation

EXERCISES

Introduction, Inheritance of One Gene, Mendel's Law of Inheritance – Dominance, Segregation

1. Genetics deals with:
(a) Inheritance only
(b) Variation of characters only
(c) Artificial hybridisation only
(d) Both inheritance and variation of character

2. Transmission of genetic characters from parents to offspring is called:
(a) Variation (b) Germplasm
(c) Heredity (d) Blending

3. Who performed hybridisation experiments on the tobacco plant before Mendel?
(a) Kolreuter (b) Darwin
(c) Hugo de Vries (d) Correns

4. Mendel selected:
(a) 7 tree breeding sweet pea plant varieties
(b) 7 tree breeding garden pea plant varieties
(c) 14 tree breeding sweet pea plant varieties
(d) 14 tree breeding garden pea plant varieties

5. Mendel conducted hybridisation experiments on the garden pea for:
(a) Five years (1856–1860)
(b) Seven years (1856–1863)
(c) Five years (1860–1865)
(d) Seven years (1860–1867)

6. Mendel published the results of his experiments in the year:
(a) 1568 (b) 1773
(c) 1873 (d) 1866

7. The degree by which progeny differ from their parents is:
(a) Basis of heredity
(b) Known as variation
(c) One of the causes hidden in asexual reproduction
(d) Also known as inheritance

8. Mendel conducted hybridisation experiments on:
(a) *Pisum sativum* (b) Cow pea
(c) Sweet pea (d) Wild pea

9. An allele is a:
(a) Slightly different form of a gene
(b) Haploid set of chromosomes
(c) Total number of genes on a chromosome
(d) Total number of chromosomes in a cell

10. Alleles of a gene are found on:
(a) Same chromosome
(b) Any chromosome
(c) Non-homologous chromosomes
(d) Homologous chromosomes

11. When only one allele of a pair is present, the condition is called:
(a) Homozygous (b) Heterozygous
(c) Hemizygous (d) Monohybrid

12. All alleles originate from:
(a) Crossing over (b) Gene flow
(c) Non-disjunction (d) Mutation

13. Sum total of genes with all the alleles at any time in a unit of evolution is called:
(a) Genotype (b) Genome
(c) Gene library (d) Gene pool

14. Monohybrid cross involves:
(a) Individuals of two different parents
(b) Individuals different in one trait
(c) Individuals different in two traits
(d) Individuals of one species

15. Genome represents:
(a) Haploid set of chromosomes
(b) Diploid set of chromosomes
(c) Complete chromosome set
(d) All the genes present in the population

16. Primary source of allelic variation is:
(a) Independent assortment
(b) Mutation
(c) Recombination
(d) Polyploidy

17. The offspring of two pure strains are called:
(a) Mutants (b) Hybrids
(c) F_2 generation (d) Recombinant

18. A character that is expressed in a hybrid is called:
(a) Dominant (b) Recessive
(c) Epistatic (d) Codominant

19. To see the effect of sex on inheritance, Mendel performed:
(a) Test cross (b) Back cross
(c) Reciprocal cross (d) Monohybrid cross

20. In a cross, 45 tall plants and 14 dwarf plants were obtained. The genotype of the parents was:
(a) TT X TT (b) Tt X tt
(c) Tt X Tt (d) TT X tt

21. Find the incorrect match:
(a) Allele: Alternate form of a gene
(b) Pure line: True breeding line
(c) Gene: Unit factor
(d) Homozygous: Always dominant

22. Mendel selected the pea plant for hybridisation experiments because of:
(a) Clear contrasting characters
(b) Short lifespan
(c) It is easy to artificially cross-pollinate the pea flower, and the hybrids thus produced were fertile
(d) All of the above

23. Mendel's experimental plant was *Pisum sativum*; he failed to find similar results with the:
(a) Sweet pea (b) *Hieracium*
(c) *Lablab* (d) All except (a)

24. Law of dominance explains:
(a) Characters are not controlled by factors
(b) Factors never occur in pairs
(c) Expression of only one of the parental characters in the F_1 generation of a monohybrid cross
(d) Gamete receives only one of the two factors

25. Select the correct match with respect to the number of alleles of a gene:
(a) Gamete: TT
(b) Zygote: T
(c) Diploid organism: TT
(d) Haploid organism: TTT

26. Read the given statement carefully:
Though the parents contain two alleles, during gamete formation, the alleles of a pair segregate from each other such that a gamete receives only one of the two factors.
This statement is related to:
(a) Law of dominance
(b) Law of purity of gametes
(c) Law of segregation
(d) More than one option is correct

27. Heterozygous term is not applicable for:
(a) Dominant (b) Recessive
(c) Gamete (d) Hybrid

28. Number of phenotypes possible from a cross AaBbCc X AaBbCc is:
(a) 16 (b) 12
(c) 4 (d) 8

29. $\frac{1}{4}TT \cdot \frac{1}{2}Tt, \frac{T}{4}tt$ is the binomial expression of:
(a) $\left(\frac{1}{2}T+\frac{1}{2}t\right)^2$ (b) $\left(\frac{1}{4}T+\frac{1}{4}t\right)^2$
(c) $\left(\frac{1}{4}T+\frac{1}{2}t\right)^2$ (d) $\left(\frac{1}{2}T+\frac{1}{4}t\right)^2$

30. Which law of Mendelian genetics can be considered universal?
(a) Law of dominance
(b) Law of segregation
(c) Law of independent assortment
(d) Both (a) and (b)

31. Among seven pairs of traits studied by Mendel, the number of traits related to flower, pod and seed are:
(a) 2, 2, 2 (b) 2, 2, 2
(c) 1, 2, 2 (d) 1, 1, 2

32. Biometric genetics is connected with:
(a) Effect of radiation on living organisms
(b) Biochemical explanation of genetic phenomenon
(c) Effect of environment on genetic set-up of organisms
(d) Inheritance of quantitative traits

33. Marriage between close relatives should be avoided because it induces more:
(a) Recessive alleles to come together
(b) Multiple births
(c) Mutations
(d) Blood group abnormalities

34. How many gametes will have the recessive alleles only if the genotype of an individual is AabbCcdd?
(a) 100% (b) 50%
(c) 75% (d) 25%

35. Which one of the Mendelian traits can be expressed in the presence of its identical alleles only?
(a) Violet flower colour
(b) Round seed
(c) Constricted pod
(d) Yellow seed

36. Find the correctly matched pair with respect to contrasting traits studied by Mendel:
(a) Stem height – Dwarf (Dominant)
(b) Flower colour – White (Dominant)
(c) Seed colour – Green (Recessive)
(d) Pod shape – Inflated (Recessive)

37. Different investigations by Blixt on the pea plant led to the identification of the location of Mendel's 7 selected characters on chromosome numbers ________:
(a) 1, 2, 4 and 7 (b) 1, 4, 5 and 7
(c) 1, 3, 5 and 7 (d) 1, 4, 6 and 7

38. Mendel studied 7 characters which were located on 4 different chromosomes. Maximum 3 characters are located on:
(a) Chromosome 1 (b) Chromosome 4
(c) Chromosome 5 (d) Chromosome 7

39. Mendel published his research under the title:
(a) Law of Heredity
(b) Experiment on Plant Hybridisation
(c) Hybridisation Experiments on Pea
(d My Experiments on Particulate Inheritance

40. In *Pisum sativum*, the gene for pod shape and seed colour is present on ________ and ________ chromosomes, respectively.
(a) 1, 4 (b) 4, 1
(c) 5, 7 (d) 4, 5

41. What is a tree breeding line?
(a) Having undergone continuous cross-pollination
(b) Shows the stable inheritance of traits
(c) Shows heterozygosity only
(d) Exhibits expression of traits for one generation only

42. Which of the following genotypes represents a pure line?
(a) AAbbCc (b) aabbCC
(c) aaBBCc (d) AaBBCc

43. Which of the following truly represents a heterozygous organism?
(a) aaBB (b) AABb
(c) AAbb (d) AaBb

44. A dihybrid condition is:
(a) ttRr (b) TtRR
(c) TtRr (d) All of the above

45. Which of the following genotypes will produce eight different types of gametes?
(a) AaBBcc (b) AaBbCc
(c) aaBbCc (d) AaBBCC

46. Gregor Johann Mendel, the Father of Genetics, was a/an:
(a) Austrian monk (b) British monk
(c) Italian monk (d) German scientist

47. Which of the following represents the composition of gametes?
(a) Ggl (b) HLl
(c) GgLl (d) gHl

48. A scientist, who is one of the rediscoverers of Mendel's work, is
(a) Darwin (b) Morgan
(c) Correns (d) Bateson

49. How many gametes will have recessive alleles only if the genotype of an individual is AabbCc?
(a) 50% (b) 25%
(c) 75% (d) 100%

50. In Mendel's monohybrid cross on pea plants, the proportion of dwarf plants in the F_2 generation was found to be:
(a) $\frac{1}{2}$ (b) $\frac{2}{3}$
(c) $\frac{1}{4}$ (d) $\frac{3}{4}$

51. How many types of gametes will be produced by an organism with genotype AabbCcDDee?
(a) Two (b) Four
(c) Sixteen (d) Thirty-two

52. Fill in the blanks and select the correct option:
(i) ____**A**____ are the unit of inheritance
(ii) Alleles are similar as in the case of ____**B**____
(iii) The morphological expression of a character is called ____**C**____
(iv) XY condition in human males is called ____**D**____

	A	B	C	D
(a)	Genes	Homozygous	Phenotype	Hemizygous
(b)	Genes	Homozygous	Phenotype	Heterozygous
(c)	Factors	Heterozygous	Genotype	Homozygous
(d)	Factors	Heterozygous	Genotype	Heterozygous

53. Which of the following scientists is not a rediscoverer of principles which were already worked out by Mendel?
(a) Carl Correns (b) de Vries
(c) Charles Darwin (d) Tschermak

54. A pair of dominant traits in the garden pea are:
(a) Axial flower position, green pod colour
(b) Violet flower colour, terminal flower position
(c) Round seed shape, yellow pod colour
(d) Constricted pod shape, wrinkled seed shape

55. Mendelian observations were converted into laws by:
(a) Hugo de Vries (b) Carl Correns
(c) Bateson (d) Tschermak

56. Which of the following Mendel's laws of inheritance has no exception?
(a) Law of dominance
(b) Law of segregation
(c) Law of paired factors
(d) Law of independent assortment

57. One of the following is an exception to Mendel's laws:
(a) Purity of gametes
(b) Dominance
(c) Independent assortment
(d) Codominance

58. Mendel's factor is now called:
(a) Gene (b) DNA
(c) Introns (d) Chromosome

59. How many given characters of *Pisum sativum* are expressed when the factors are homozygous only? Terminal flower, Green seed, Yellow pod, Constructed pod, Violet petals, Dwarf stem, Round seed
(a) Four (b) Five
(c) Six (d) One

60. The statement "The factors or alleles of a pair dissociate from each other such that a gamete receives only one of the two factors" is:
(a) Law of dominance
(b) Law of segregation
(c) Law of independent assortment
(d) Law of paired factors

61. Punnett square was developed by:
(a) GJ Mendel (b) Bateson
(c) Morgan (d) RC Punnett

62. Which of the following is incorrect with respect to the law of dominance?
(a) Factors occur in pairs
(b) In a dissimilar pair of factors, one member of the pair dominates the other
(c) Based upon the observation of Mendel on dihybrid cross
(d) Explains the proportion of 3:1 in the F_2 generation

63. How many types of zygotes will be formed in a cross of AaBB X AaBB?
(a) 2 (b) 4
(c) 8 (d) 16

64. What was the reason for Mendel's success?
(a) He applied statistical analysis
(b) He eliminated all those varieties which showed any inconsistency
(c) Maintenance of accurate records of results obtained
(d) All of these are correct

65. One of the reasons why Mendel selected the garden pea as his experimental organism:
(a) It required large space for cultivation
(b) Intervarietal crossing produced fertile offspring
(c) It reproduces in a particular season
(d) It had a long lifespan

66. The procedure adopted by Mendel which was different from his predecessors was:
(a) Keeping breeding records
(b) Employing many traits at one time
(c) Differentiating inherited traits
(d) Quantitative analysis of data

67. During Mendel's investigations into inheritance pattern, it was for the first time that ______ were applied to problems in biology:
(a) Hybridisation experiment on plants
(b) Contrasting traits of *Pisum sativum*
(c) Statistical analysis and mathematical logic
(d) More than one option is correct

68. Mendel's work remained unappreciated for several years due to all of the following reasons, except:
(a) Could not provide physical proof for the existence of factors
(b) Limited circulation of the journal in which he published his work

(c) Use of statistical analysis
(d) Worked on continuous traits

69. Select the correct statements:
(i) Dominance is an autonomous feature of a gene
(ii) Dominance depends on the gene product
(iii) Product of a single gene always produce only one effect
(a) Only (ii) (b) (ii) and (iii)
(c) (i) and (iii) (d) (i) and (ii)

70. Which contributed to the success of Mendel?
(a) Qualitative analysis of data
(b) Observation of distinct inherited traits
(c) His knowledge of biology
(d) Consideration of one character at one time

71. Allelomorphic pair implies:
(a) A pair of contrasting traits
(b) A pair of non-contrasting traits
(c) Any two traits
(d) Sex-linked traits

72. The graphical representation to calculate the probability of all the possible genotypes of offspring in a genetic cross is called:
(a) Pedigree analysis (b) Punnett square
(c) Karyotype (d) Genotype ratio

73. Choose the odd one out with respect to the characters of pea plants used by Mendel for his experiments:
(a) Flower position (b) Seed shape
(c) Pod colour (d) Pod symmetry

74. Choose the genotype which does not represent a true breeding/pure line:
(a) aabb (b) AABB
(c) AABb (d) AAbb

Explanation of Concept of Dominance, Incomplete and Codominance, Multiple Alleles, Pleiotropy, Test Cross, Lethal Gene, Inheritance of Two Genes, Law of Independent Assortment

75. Incomplete dominance is a case where:
(a) Recessive allele also expresses itself
(b) Dominant allele produces non-functional enzyme
(c) Intermediate phenotype appears
(d) Both the alleles express themselves independently

76. Starch synthesis in pea seeds shows:
(a) Complete dominance
(b) Codominance
(c) Incomplete dominance
(d) Multiple illusion

77. If F_1 phenotype resembles both parents, then it is an exception to:
(a) Law of dominance
(b) Law of segregation
(c) Law of independent assortment
(d) Incomplete dominance

78. Both the alleles express themselves equally in the F_1 generation, except in:
(a) Snapdragon (b) Sickle cell anaemia
(c) Roan cattle (d) AB blood group

79. The phenotype ratio in the F_2 generation of an incompletely dominant gene is:
(a) 3:1 (b) 9:3:3:1
(c) 1:2:1 (d) 2:1:2

80. Modified alleles are equivalent to unmodified alleles when they:
(a) Produce normal enzymes
(b) Produce non-efficient enzymes
(c) Produce non-functional enzymes
(d) Produce no enzyme at all

81. Dominant allele is:
(a) Unmodified allele
(b) Modified allele which produces non-functional enzyme
(c) Modified allele which produce no enzyme at all
(d) Both (b) and (c)

82. Read the following statements and state whether true (T) or false (F):
A. Recessive allele is a modified allele
B. Recessive allele is expressed in heterozygous condition
C. Recessive allele may produce non-functional or no enzyme
D. Dominant allele produces normal functional enzyme

	A	B	C	D
(a)	T	F	F	T
(b)	F	T	T	F
(c)	T	F	T	T
(d)	T	T	F	F

83. Find the odd one out with respect to codominance:
(a) ABO blood group
(b) Heterozygous sickle cell individual
(c) Coat colour in cattle
(d) Flower colour in snapdragon

84. Blood group ABO produces:
(i) Four phenotypes
(ii) Three genotypes

(iii) Six genotypes
(iv) Three phenotypes
(a) Only (i) (b) Both (i) and (ii)
(c) (iii) and (iv) (d) (i) and (iii)

85. A gene with five different alleles can form ________ different genotypic combinations in a population:
(a) Fifteen (b) Six
(c) Thirteen (d) Seven

86. Human blood grouping is a common example of:
(a) Quantitative inheritance and multiple allelism
(b) Codominance and incomplete dominance
(c) Multiple allelism and codominance
(d) Multiple allelism and incomplete dominance

87. A couple with blood group AB and B cannot have a child with blood group________:
(a) AB (b) B
(c) A (d) O

88. Similar phenotypic and genotypic ratios are obtained in the F_2 generation, in the case of:
(a) Incomplete dominance
(b) Codominance
(c) Both (a) and (b)
(d) Duplicate genes

89. In snapdragon, a cross yielded pink and white flowered plants in the ratio 1:1. The cross was made between ______ and ______ flower plants:
(a) Pink, pink (b) Red, white
(c) Pink, white (d) Red, pink

90. Multiple characters are affected by:
(a) Polygenes (b) Pleiotropic gene
(c) Multiple alleles (d) Polygenes

91. The phenomenon of incomplete dominance was observed by:
(a) Hugo de Vries (b) Morgan
(c) Carl Correns (d) Tschermak

92. In which of the following conditions does the F_1 phenotype not resemble either of the parents but rather represents a blending of parental traits?
(a) Complete dominance
(b) Incomplete dominance
(c) Codominance
(d) Multiple allelism

93. Both the alleles are equally expressed in the condition of:
(a) Codominance
(b) Complete dominance
(c) Incomplete dominance
(d) Both (a) and (c)

94. Mendel's law of independent assortment can be demonstrated by:
(a) Test cross (b) Back cross
(c) Monohybrid cross (d) Dihybrid cross

95. When a hybrid is crossed with a dominant parent, it is called:
(a) Reciprocal cross (b) Back cross
(c) Test cross (d) Out cross

96. How many true breeding plant varieties are required to perform a dihybrid cross?
(a) One (b) Two
(c) Three (d) Four

97. Law of independent assortment:
(a) Can be observed for genes present on some chromosomes
(b) Applies only when genes are present on non-homologous chromosomes
(c) Is a universal phenomenon
(d) Results in parental phenotypes only

98. A cross made between a dominant phenotype and the recessive parent in order to check its genotype is called:
(a) Test cross (b) Monohybrid cross
(c) Reciprocal cross (d) Out cross

99. A pea plant with red flowers was test crossed, resulting in progeny in the ratio of plants with red flowers and white flowers as 1:1. What is the genotype of the parent plant with red flowers?
(a) Heterozygous Rr (b) Homozygous Rr
(c) Hemizygous (d) Cannot be predicted

100. In the F_2 generation of a Mendelian dihybrid cross, find the ratio of seeds having dwarf plant with violet flower characters?
(a) 2/16 (b) 3/16
(c) 4/16 (d) 9/16

101. The per cent of seeds with double heterozygous characters in the F_2 generation of a Mendelian cross when the total number of seeds collected is 640 is:
(a) 60 (b) 80
(c) 120 (d) 160

102. A heterozygous tall and violet flowered plant (TtWw) was selfed, and a total of 2000 seeds were collected. The number of seeds with ttWw genotype is:
(a) 250 (b) 125
(c) 500 (d) 750

103. Select the incorrectly matched pair:
(a) Flower colour in snapdragon – Incomplete dominance

(b) Starch grain size in pea plant – Codominance
(c) ABO blood group in human beings – Multiple allelism
(d) Law of purity of gametes – Basis of law of segregation

104. The genotype of a person with blood group AB is:
(a) I^aI^a (b) I^aI^o
(c) I^aI^b (d) I^oI^o

105. The F_2 phenotypic ratio of a Mendelian dihybrid cross is:
(a) 9:3:3:1 (b) 1:2:2:2
(c) 9:1 (d) 1:2:1:2:4:2:1:2:1

106. A child of blood group O cannot have parents of blood group:
(a) O and O (b) A and B
(c) AB and O (d) B and O

107. Human erythrocyte on its surface contains two types of sugars with respect to the blood group:
(a) B (b) A
(c) O (d) AB

108. Choose the correct option with respect to the ABO blood group:

	Gene	Alleles	Phonotypes	Genotypes
(a)	2	3	4	6
(b)	1	3	4	6
(c)	1	3	6	4
(d)	2	4	4	4

109. In a dihybrid cross, if the first gene shows a dominant recessive interaction and the second gene shows incomplete dominance, the F_2 generation ratio will be:
(a) 9:3:3:1 (b) 9:3:4
(c) 3:6:3:1:2:1 (d) 1:4:6:4:1

110. The proportion of homozygous dominant progeny in the F_2 generation of a dihybrid cross is:
(a) $\frac{1}{16}$ (b) $\frac{3}{16}$
(c) $\frac{9}{16}$ (d) $\frac{1}{3}$

111. Source of Mendelian recombination is:
(a) Linkage
(b) Independent assortment
(c) Mutations
(d) Dominant traits

112. The first child of a couple has AB blood group. Which of the following types of parental cross is possible for it?
(a) I^AI^A X I^OI^O (b) I^AI^O X I^AI^A
(c) I^BI^O X I^BI^B (d) I^AI^O X I^BI^B

113. Find out the feature which does not hold true for multiple alleles:
(a) All alleles occur on the same locus of the same chromosome
(b) A gamete receives only one allele of the group
(c) Controls multiple characters in an individual
(d) All the alleles can be detected in a population only

114. What is the ratio of homozygous and heterozygous traits of snapdragon in the F_2 generation of a cross between red and white flowered plants?
(a) 1:2:1 (b) 1:2
(c) 2:1 (d) 1:1

115. Find the odd one out with respect to one gene interaction:
(a) Incomplete dominance
(b) Codominance
(c) Duplicate gene
(d) Multiple allelism

116. The recessive trait is due to:
A. Normal enzyme
B. Less efficient enzyme
C. Non-functional enzyme
D. No enzyme
(a) Only (A)
(b) Both (B) and (C)
(c) Both (C) and (D)
(d) Only (B)

117. How many types of gametes, phenotypes and genotypes would be expected on the selfing of AABbCc plants, respectively?
(a) 8, 16, 64 (b) 4, 9, 4
(c) 4, 8, 16 (d) 4, 4, 9

118. What is the proportion of F_2 progeny with parental combination of characters in a dihybrid cross?
(a) 10/16 (b) 9/16
(c) 6/16 (d) 5/16

119. During a dihybrid test cross, the number of phenotypes and genotypes in the F_2 generation is, respectively:
(a) 4, 4 (b) 2, 4
(c) 1, 4 (d) 4, 9

120. Law of independent assortment:
(a) Can be observed for genes present on the same chromosome
(b) Occurs only when genes are present on non-homozygous chromosomes

(c) Is a universal phenomenon
(d) Results in new linkage groups

121. A heterozygous individual (Tt) produces two kinds of gametes, each having one allele with equal proportion:
A. Shows phenotype ratio of 1:1 in test cross
B. Shows phenotype ratio of 3 :1 on selfing
C. Shows 100% progeny with dominant phenotype in out cross
(a) Only (A) is correct
(b) Only (A) and (C) are correct
(c) Only (B) and (C) are correct
(d) (A), (B) and (C)are correct

122. In a cross between round yellow and wrinkled green plants, a total of 16 seeds was obtained in the F_2 generation. The probability of RrYY, RrYy and rrYy genotype is, respectively:
(a) $\frac{2}{16}, \frac{4}{16}, \frac{2}{16}$ (b) $\frac{4}{16}, \frac{2}{16}, \frac{2}{16}$
(c) $\frac{4}{16}, \frac{4}{16} \times \frac{2}{16}$ (d) $\frac{2}{16}, \frac{4}{16}, \frac{4}{16}$

123. Blood group 'O' carries:
(a) A antigen (b) B antigen
(c) AB antigen (d) No antigen

124. How many single heterozygotes will be produced in the F_2 generation of a dihybrid cross of Mendel?
(a) $\frac{8}{16}$ (b) $\frac{2}{16}$
(c) $\frac{1}{16}$ (d) $\frac{4}{16}$

125. What percentage of gametes will have all dominant alleles if the genotype of the plant is AaBbCc?
(a) 12.5% (b) 25%
(c) 50% (d) 100%

126. The probability of the plant being heterozygous for both characters in a dihybrid cross of Mendel is:
(a) $\frac{5}{16}$ (b) $\frac{6}{16}$
(c) $\frac{4}{16}$ (d) $\frac{8}{16}$

127. Starch synthesis in the garden pea is controlled by a gene which has two alleles 'B' and 'b'. Choose the incorrect option with respect to starch synthesis:
(a) Starch synthesis is efficient in seeds with genotype BB
(b) Seeds with genotype Bb show incomplete dominance
(c) In bb homozygotes, starch syntheses is less efficient
(d) Seeds with bb genotype produce large-sized starch grains

128. Nine pairs of chromosomes can assort in how many ways during gamete formation in any organism?
(a) 9^2 (b) 2^2
(c) 9×2 (d) 2^9

129. Pleiotropic characters are controlled by:
(a) Polygenes (b) Single gene
(c) Multiple alleles (d) Linked genes

130. Lethal genes were first discovered by:
(a) Cuenot in rats
(b) Ehle in wheat
(c) Punnett in snapdragon
(d) Cuenot in *Drosophila*

131. What is the genotype ratio of Mendel's dihybrid cross?
(a) 12:2:4:1:2:1:2:1 (b) 1:1:1:1
(c) 1:1:2:2:4:2:2:1 (d) 1:2:1:2:4:2:1:2:1

132. Select the incorrect statement with respect to pleiotropy:
(a) Alternation of multiple distinct traits of an organism by a mutation in a single gene
(b) White eye mutation in *Drosophila* leads to depigmentation of body parts
(c) Basis is inter-relationship between the metabolic pathways
(d) Gene controlling starch synthesis in sweet pea

133. Find the incorrect statement with respect to pleiotropic expression:
(a) A gene product may produce more than one phenotype
(b) Can be exemplified by phenylketonuria
(c) A gene can be responsible for complete dominance as well as incomplete dominance
(d) Can be studied in dihybrid or polyhybrid cross but not in monohybrid cross

134. If a modified allele is equivalent to the unmodified allele, then:
(a) It will not produce any phenotype
(b) It will result in transformation of substrate
(c) The phenotype is changed
(d) No enzyme is produced

135. In *Drosophila,* the gene for white eye mutation is also responsible for depigmentation of body parts. Thus, the gene that controls several phenotypes is called:
(a) Oncogene (b) Epistatic gene
(c) Homeotic gene (d) Pleiotropic gene

Complementary Genes, Duplicate Genes, Epistasis, Polygenic Inheritance

136. Which of the following F_2 phenotype ratios represents complementary gene interaction?
(a) 9:3:3:1 (b) 1:1:1:1
(c) 9:7 (d) 9:3:4

137. The gene that masks the phenotypic expression of another non-allelic gene is said to be:
(a) Hypostatic (b) Epistatic
(c) Duplicate gene (d) Complementary gene

138. Concept of complementary genes was given by:
(a) Mendel (b) Morgan
(c) Bateson (d) Sutton

139. Many traits which are not so distinct in their occurrence and are spread across a gradient is due to:
(a) Dominance
(b) Pleiotropy
(c) Quantitative inheritance
(d) Qualitative inheritance

140. Epistasis is due to:
(a) Interaction of two alleles of the same gene
(b) Interaction of two separate genes
(c) Polygenes
(d) Multiple alleles

141. Which of the following exemplifies recessive epistasis?
(a) Fruit colour in summer squash
(b) Fruit shape in *Capsella*
(c) Fruit shape in *Cucurbita pepo*
(d) Coat colour in mice

142. Dominant alleles of two non-allelic genes produce the same phenotype, whether inherited together or separately; such genes are called:
(a) Complementary genes
(b) Duplicate genes
(c) Epistatic genes
(d) Polygenes

143. A type of gene interaction where the recessive alleles in homozygous condition mask the expression of the dominant allele of the other gene is called:
(a) Dominant epistasis
(b) Recessive epistasis
(c) Codominance
(d) Incomplete dominance

144. *Lathyrus odoratus* having CcPp and ccpp genotypes were crossed. What percentage of their progeny will have purple flowers?
(a) 25% (b) 50%
(c) 75% (d) 100%

145. An example of dominant epistasis is:
(a) Kernel colour in wheat
(b) Flower colour of sweet potato
(c) Fruit colour of summer squash
(d) Fruit shape of *Capsella*

146. If a heterozygous plant on selfing produces coloured flowered and white flowered plants in the ration of 9:7, it is case of ________ inheritance:
(a) Complementary gene
(b) Dominant epitasis
(c) Supplementary gene
(d) Duplicate gene

147. Calculate the sum total of phenotypes and genotypes in the F_2 generation of a character controlled by 3 pair of polygenes:
(a) 7 (b) 27
(c) 34 (d) 35

148. Kernel colour of wheat is controlled by how many pairs of polygenes?
(a) 3 (b) 2
(c) 4 (d) 5

149. Which of the following genotypes will show the darkest skin colour in humans?
(a) AaBbCc (b) AABbCc
(c) AABbCC (d) AABBCC

150. What is the probability of getting very light skin colour in progeny if both the parents have AaBbCc type of genotype?
(a) $\frac{20}{64}$ (b) $\frac{1}{64}$
(c) $\frac{6}{64}$ (d) $\frac{15}{64}$

151. Read the following statements with respect to quantitative inheritance:
(a) A single dominant allele is responsible for all the extreme phenotypes
(b) The character is always regulated by a pair of alleles only
(c) Intermediate phenotypes are more frequent than the extreme phenotypes
(d) F_1 individuals are phenotypically similar to one of their extreme-phenotype-showing parents

How many of these statements are correct?
(a) Two (b) Three
(c) Four (d) One

152. What will be the total number of genotypes if any character is controlled by 5 pairs of polygenes?
(a) 25 (b) 11
(c) 243 (d) 9

153. Polygenic inheritance is characterised by all of these, except:
(a) Bell-shaped histogram
(b) Such traits are discontinuous
(c) More than one locus is involved
(d) Each dominant gene has additive effect on phenotype

154. Match Column I and Column II:

	Column I	Column II
A.	Complementary gene	(i) 15:1
B.	Duplicate gene	(ii) 9:3:4
C.	Dominant epistasis	(iii) 9:7
D.	Recessive epistasis	(iv) 12:3:1

(a) A – (iv), B – (i), C – (iii), D – (ii)
(b) A – (iii), B – (i), C – (iv), D – (ii)
(c) A – (iii), B – (iv), C – (i), D – (ii)
(d) A – (iii), B – (i), C – (ii), D – (iv)

155. Find the odd one out with respect to non-allelic gene interaction:
(a) Flower colour in *Lathyrus odoratus*
(b) Fruit colour in summer squash
(c) Flower colour in *Mirabilis jalapa*
(d) Coat colour in mice

156. Which of the following genotypes will have very dark and intermediate skin colour in humans?
(a) AABBCC, aabbcc
(b) AaBbCc, aabbcc
(c) AABBCC, AaBbCc
(d) AaBBCc, aaBBcc

157. Coat colour in mice is the result of interaction between two genes A and C. Both A and C are:
(a) Supplementary genes
(b) Show dominant epistasis
(c) Complementary genes
(d) Show recessive epistasis

158. Height of humans shows a lot of variation. It is an example of:
(a) Multiple alleles
(b) Pleiotropy
(c) Polygenic inheritance
(d) Pseudo alleles

159. Human skin colour is controlled by:
(a) Two alleles (b) Three alleles
(c) Three genes (d) Six genes

160. What will be the phenotypes of the given genotypes for flower colour in sweet pea with respect to complementary genes?
A. CCpp
B. CcPP
C. ccPP

	A	B	C
(a)	White	Purple	White
(b)	White	Purple	Purple
(c)	Purple	White	White
(d)	Purple	White	Purple

161. Which of the given characters is controlled by two pairs of genes?
(a) Human skin colour
(b) Flower colour in *Mirabilis*
(c) Kernel colour in wheat
(d) Height in human beings

162. When a wheat variety of red kernels is crossed with white-kernelled wheat, the F_2 ratio would be (it is a polygenic trait and controlled by 2 pairs of polygenes):
(a) 9:7 (b) 1:10:4:1
(c) 1:6:15:20:15:6:1 (d) 1:4:6:4:1

163. If a mulatto man marries an African woman, what proportion of progeny can be very dark?
(a) $\frac{1}{4}$ (b) $\frac{1}{8}$
(c) $\frac{3}{14}$ (d) $\frac{1}{2}$

164. The phenotype ratio of individuals if a character is controlled by 3 pairs of polygenes is:
(a) 9:3:3:1 (b) 1:4:6:4:1
(c) 1:6:15:20:15:6:1 (d) 9:4:3

165. If a very light-skinned woman marries an African man, the probability of having mulatto children is:
(a) 25% (b) 50%
(c) 75% (d) 100%

166. There are seven phenotypes of skin colour in humans. Which phenotype is more frequent than others?
(a) Fairly dark (b) Albino
(c) Mulatto (d) Lighter than mulatto

167. Human skin pigmentation is controlled by three pairs of polygenes. The number of different phenotypes and genotypes is:

(a) Six, twenty-seven (b) Seven, twenty-seven
(c) Seven, nine (d) Six, nine

168. Phenotype of an organism is the result of:
(a) Mutations and linkage
(b) Cytoplasmic effects and nutrition
(c) Environmental changes and sexual dimorphism
(d) Genotype and environmental interaction

169. Which of the following genotypes of humans will have a very light skin colour?
(a) AABBCC (b) aaBbCc
(c) aabbcc (d) AaBbCc

170. The maximum height of a plant is 24 feet and the minimum is 12 feet. What is the height of the plant with genotype AaBbCc if height is controlled by quantitative inheritance?
(a) 16 feet (b) 18 feet
(c) 20 feet (d) 14 feet

171. Two white-flowered sweet pea plants (Ccpp X ccPb) were crossed. Find the probability of coloured to colourless flowered plants in their progeny:
(a) 9:7 (b) 1:4
(c) 1:3 (d) 1:15

172. In *Lathyrus odoratus*, genes C and P are required to produced purple colour in petals. The flowers are white in the absence of either or both of the genes. The ratio of coloured and white flowers in the offspring of the cross ccPP X CcPp is:
(a) 2:1 (b) 1:1
(c) 4:0 (d) 3:1

173. If the cob length of maize is due to two forms of genes, how many offspring of the F_2 generation will have an intermediate size?
(a) $\frac{1}{16}$ (b) $\frac{14}{16}$
(c) $\frac{6}{64}$ (d) $\frac{20}{64}$

174. A character in the tobacco plant is determined by three pairs of polygenes. A cross between AABBCC X aabbcc will produce progeny in F_2 in what proportion that is likely to resemble either parent?
(a) 10% (b) 50%
(c) Less than 5% (d) 100%

Chromosomal Theory of Inheritance, Linkage, Recombination, Sex Determination

175. Parallelism between chromosome and behaviour of gene was established by:
(a) Hugo de Vries, Correns and Tschermak
(b) Sutton and Boveri
(c) Bateson and Punnett
(d) Landsteiner and de Castello

176. Select the incorrect statement with respect to chromosomal theory of inheritance:
(a) Hereditary traits always retain their number and structure through the life of an organism
(b) Chromosomes occur in pairs in haploid cells
(c) Chromosomes segregate at the time of gamete formation
(d) Paired condition of Mendelian factor is restored during fertilisation

177. Chromosomal theory of inheritance was proposed independently by:
(a) Sutton
(b) Sutton and Boveri
(c) Bateson and Punnett
(d) TH Morgan

178. The relationship between the behaviour of chromosomes and Mendel's factors was established by Sutton and Boveri in the year:
(a) 1900 (b) 1902
(c) 1924 (d) 1910

179. Father of experimental genetics is:
(a) TH Morgan (b) Mendel
(c) Garrod (d) Beadle and Tatum

180. Experimental verification of chromosomal theory of inheritance was carried out by:
(a) Sutton and Boveri (b) Bateson and Punnett
(c) Carl Correns (d) Thomas Hunt Morgan

181. *Drosophila*:
(a) Has a life cycle of about 2 weeks
(b) Does not grow on simple synthetic medium
(c) Females are very similar to males
(d) Has a total of four morphologically district chromosomes in its somatic cell

182. Read the following statements and select the correct option:

A. Meiosis results in 4 haploid daughter cells from one diploid parent cell
B. Sutton and Boveri found the similarity between transmission of hereditary traits and behaviour of chromosomes
(a) Both statements are correct
(b) Both statements are incorrect
(c) Only (A) is correct
(d) Only (B) is correct

183. Movement of chromosomes at meiosis can be used to explain:
(a) Law of dominance
(b) Law of segregation
(c) Law of independent assortment
(d) More than one option is correct

184. Who gave the term linkage?
(a) Sutton and Boveri (b) Johanssen
(c) Morgan (d) Bateson and Punnett

185. Total number of chromosomes in a somatic cell of *Drosophila* is:
(a) 4 (b) 6
(c) 2 (d) 8

186. State true (T) or false (F) for the following statements with respect to linkage and select the correct option:
A. Genes present on the same chromosome may or may not assort independently during gametogenesis
B. Number of offspring having recombinants is higher than parental phenotypes
C. Frequency of crossing over is not correlated to the distance between genes

	A	B	C
(a)	T	F	F
(b)	T	T	T
(c)	T	F	T
(d)	F	F	T

187. During meiosis, in which of the following stages does segregation of Mendelian factors occur?
(a) Metaphase I (b) Metaphase II
(c) Anaphase I (d) Anaphase II

188. Find the incorrect statement with respect to genes:
(a) Occur in pairs
(b) Segregate at gamete formation and only one of each pair is transmitted to a gamete
(c) Independent pairs segregate independently of each other
(d) Both (b) and (c)

189. If two non-allelic genes present on the same chromosome have 3 map unit distance between them, the maximum percentage of gametes having parental combination of those genes can be:
(a) 5% (b) 2.5%
(c) 97% (d) 47.5%

190. In a test cross between AaBb X aabb, if 10% of the progeny have non-parental phenotype and genes A and B are present on same chromosome, what will be the distance between these genes?
(a) 50 cm (b) 20 cm
(c) 10 cm (d) 5 cm

191. Select the correct statement with respect to linkage.
(a) Linked genes are present on different chromosomes
(b) Linked genes always assort independently during gametogenesis
(c) Completely linked genes are present far away on the same chromosome
(d) No crossing over is observed between two completely linked genes

192. Out of 400 progeny of *Drosophila,* only 350 show the parental type of combination for two of three characters. Considering that the genes regulating those characters are present on the same chromosome, what is the recombination frequency between the genes?
(a) 87.5% (b) 12.5%
(c) 14.2% (d) 50%

193. Which of the following are mechanisms of genetic variation in the population of a sexually reproducing organism?
(a) Transduction
(b) Chromosomal aberrations
(c) Genetic drift
(d) Recombination

194. In a test cross between AaBb X aabb, if 20% of the progeny have non-parental phenotype and genes A and B are present on the same chromosome, what will be the distance between these genes?
(a) 50 cm (b) 20 cm
(c) 10 cm (d) 5 cm

195. Morgan found that when genes were grouped on the same chromosome, some genes were ____A____ linked as they show ____B____ recombination:

	A	B
(a)	Tightly	Very low
(b)	Tightly	High
(c)	Loosely	Very low
(d)	Loosely	Low

196. In a cross made between two individuals who have genotypes ab/ab and ++/++, the following offspring were obtained. Find out the distance between genes a and b:

ab	-	1420
+a	-	120
+b	-	80
++	-	380

(a) 10 cm (b) 40 cm
(c) 20 cm (d) 18 cm

197. Recombination frequency is:
(a) Always < 50% (b) Always > 50%
(c) 100% (d) ≤ 50%

198. A set of genes will be in a complete linkage when the progeny phenotype for parental (P) and recombinant (R) types are:
(a) P = 0 % R = 100 %
(b) P = 100 % R = 0 %
(c) P = 50 % R = 50 %
(d) P = 75 % R = 25 %

199. Select the odd one out with respect to linkage:
(a) Physical association of genes
(b) Formation of more proportion of non-parental type
(c) Decreases crossing over frequency
(d) Complete linkage is found in male *Drosophila* and female *Bombyx mori*

200. A cross is made between AaBb X AaBb and 77.6% of the progeny was found to be of parental type. This shows:
(a) Genes are completely linked
(b) Genes are incompletely linked
(c) No chances of getting recombinants
(d) Completely independent assortment of genes

201. Red eye colour of *Drosophila* is:
(a) A recessive trait
(b) Regulated by a gene present on the Y chromosome
(c) A sex-linked trait
(d) Seen in females only

202. Out of 500 progeny of *Drosophila*, only 450 show the parental type of combination for two of their characters. Considering that the genes regulating those characters are present on the same chromosome, what is the recombinant frequency between the genes?
(a) 10% (b) 25%
(c) 14.2% (d) 87.5%

203. In a dihybrid cross conducted by Morgan (given below) the percentage of parental type of progeny in F_2 generation was

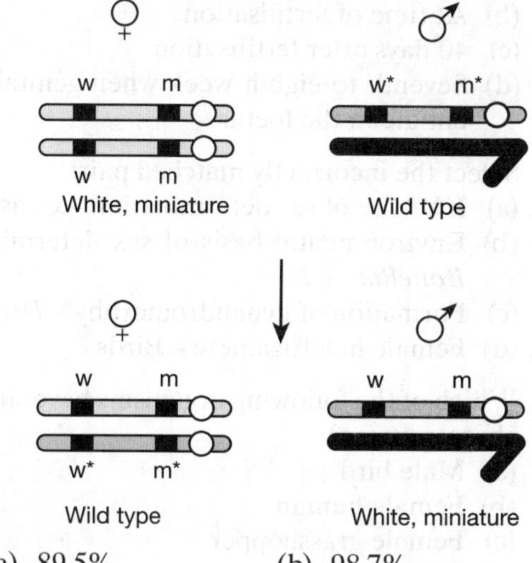

(a) 89.5% (b) 98.7%
(c) 62.8% (d) 96.4%

204. Which of the following is a non parental type of progeny obtained by Morgan while carrying out dihybrid cross

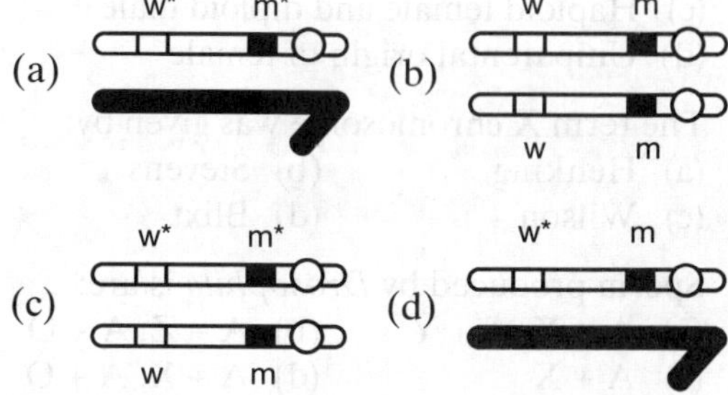

205. Male is heterogametic in all of the following, except:
(a) Humans (b) *Drosophila*
(c) Grasshopper (d) Butterfly

206. In birds:
(a) Female organism is homogametic
(b) Organism having ZZ chromosome is male
(c) Organism having ZO chromosome is male
(d) 50% of female gametes do not have any sex chromosome

207. Drones of honeybee:
(a) Are diploid
(b) Are developed by unfertilised eggs
(c) Produce gametes by meiosis
(d) Do not have father but can have sons

208. In insects like grasshopper, 50% of their sperms lack:
(a) Sex chromosome (b) All chromosome
(c) Autosomes (d) Nucleus

209. Sex is determined in human beings:
(a) By ovum

(b) At time of fertilisation
(c) 40 days after fertilisation
(d) Seventh to eighth week when genitals differentiate in the foetus

210. Select the incorrectly matched pair:
(a) XY type of sex determination – Grasshopper
(b) Environmental basis of sex determination – *Bonellia*
(c) Formation of gynandromorphy – *Drosophila*
(d) Female heterogamete – Birds

211. Which of the following organisms have similar sex chromosomes?
(a) Male bird
(b) Female human
(c) Female grasshopper
(d) All of the above

212. Mechanism of sex determination in the honeybee shows:
(a) Haploid male and diploid female
(b) Male and female with same ploidy level
(c) Haploid female and diploid male
(d) Uniparental origin of female

213. The term X chromosome was given by:
(a) Henking (b) Stevens
(c) Wilson (d) Blixt

214. Sperm produced by *Drosophila* is/are:
(a) A + X, A + Y (b) A + Z, A + O
(c) A + X (d) A + X, A + O

215. Organisms having homomorphic sex chromosome:
(a) Female *Drosophila* (b) Female grasshopper
(c) Male bird (d) All of the above

216. Eggs decide the sex of the offspring in:
(a) Humans (b) *Drosophila*
(c) *Dioscorea* (d) Butterflies

217. Which of the following represents the genetic make-up of female grasshoppers?
(a) AA + XY (b) AA + XO
(c) AA + XX (d) AA + XY

218. Number of chromosomes is different in male and female individuals in:
(a) Grasshopper (b) Humans
(c) *Drosophila* (d) Birds

219. Which of the given statements is not correct with respect to human gametes?
(a) 50% of sperms contain X chromosomes
(b) 50% of sperms contain Y chromosomes
(c) 100% of eggs contain X chromosomes
(d) Only 50% of eggs contain X chromosomes

220. In honey bee, the male produce gametes by ___A___ and they have ___B___ chromosomes:

	A	B
(a)	Mitosis	32
(b)	Mitosis	16
(c)	Meiosis	32
(d)	Meiosis	16

221. Probability of three sons to a couple is:
(a) $\frac{1}{2}$ (b) $\frac{1}{4}$
(c) $\frac{1}{8}$ (d) $\frac{1}{16}$

222. Choose the correct statement with respect to the given organism:

(a) The genotype of the sex chromosome is represented by ZO
(b) It produces a single type of gamete
(c) It is responsible for sex determination
(d) It is heterogametic

223. Henking first observed the sex chromosome in the form of:
(a) Barr body (b) Y chromosome
(c) X body (d) Z chromosome

224. In the XX-XO type of sex determination:
(a) Female individuals are heterogametic
(b) Male individuals have two types of sex chromosomes
(c) Male individuals produce some gametes without sex chromosomes
(d) Female individuals have two types of sex chromosomes

225. Select the incorrect statement:
(a) Y chromosome of human beings is shorter than X chromosome
(b) Genes of Y chromosomes show holandric traits
(c) Inactivation of Y chromosomes from Barr bodies
(d) Genes for hypertrichosis is found on Y chromosomes

226. Concept of gene mapping was first suggested by:
(a) Morgan (b) Bridge
(c) Avery (d) Sturtevant

227. The number of linkage groups present in *Escherichia coli*:
(a) One (b) Two
(c) Four (d) Seven

228. Distance between the genes and percentage of recombination shows:
(a) A direct relationship
(b) Parallel relationship
(c) An inverse relationship
(d) No relationship

229. The frequency of crossing over occurring between two genes present on the same chromosome depends on:
(a) Length of chromosome
(b) Position of centromere
(c) Distance between two genes
(d) Activities of two genes

230. Which of the following is the most relevant conclusion for the figure given below?

Meiosis I - anaphase

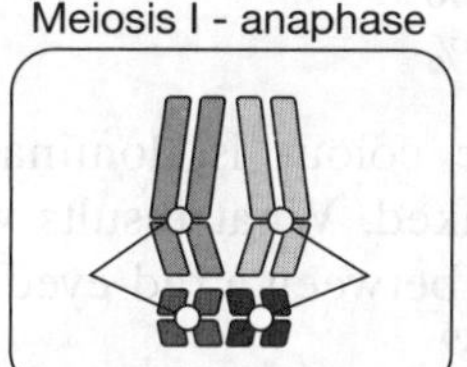

Meiosis I - anaphase

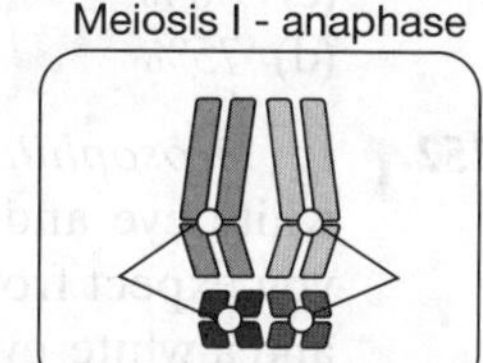

Meiosis II - anaphase

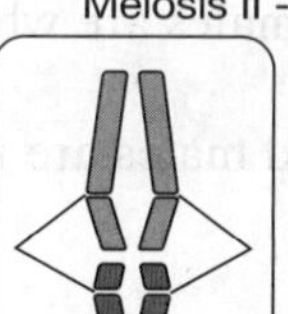

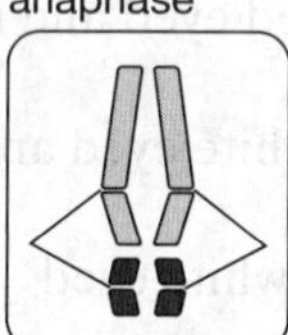

Meiosis II - anaphase

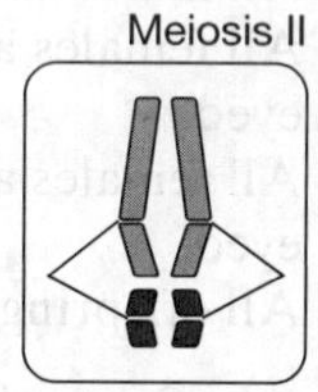

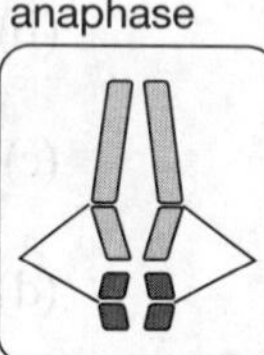

Germ cells

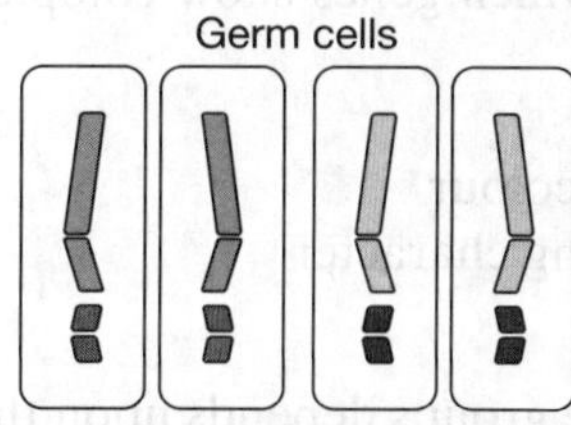

Germ cells

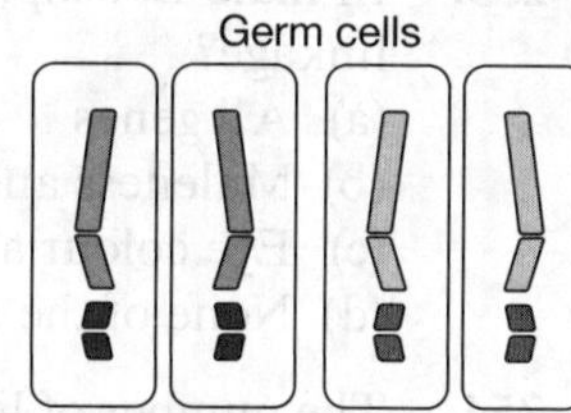

(a) Alignment of chromosome pairs at metaphase phase of meiosis I is not universal
(b) Reduction division occurs in meiosis I
(c) Gamete receives one-fourth of the DNA of a meiocyte
(d) Nothing is different in meiosis II and mitosis

231. Which Mendelian law may not be applicable for linked genes of the same chromosomes?
(a) Law of dominance
(b) Law of segregation
(c) Law of independent assortment
(d) Both (b) and (c)

232. The fruit fly, *Drosophila melanogaster,* was found to be very suitable for experimental verification of chromosomal theory of inheritance by Morgan and his coworkers because:
(a) Completes its life cycle in about 2 weeks
(b) Single mating could produce large number of progeny flies
(c) Has many hereditary variations that can be seen under high-power microscope
(d) All of the above

233. Mendel did not observe linkage due to:
(a) Mutation
(b) Synapsis
(c) Crossing over
(d) Independent assortment

234. Separation of linked genes is called:
(a) Genetic mutation (b) Polyploidy
(c) Crossing over (d) Linkage

235. If two genes of a chromosome lie at adjacent gene locii, they show/are:
(a) Maximum recombination
(b) Highly linked
(c) No crossing over
(d) All except (a)

236. Red eye colour of *Drosophila* is:
(a) A dominant trait
(b) Regulated by a gene present on the X chromosome
(c) A sex-linked strait
(d) All of the above

237. TH Morgan found *Drosophila* with eye trait due to a mutant gene on:
(a) Non-sex chromosome
(b) Y chromosome
(c) Autosome
(d) Allosome

238. A dihybrid test cross ratio for two completely linked genes will be:
(a) 1:1:1:1 (b) 1:1
(c) 1:7:7:1 (d) 7:1:1:7

239. An individual with cd/cd genes was crossed with wild type ++/++. On test crossing F_1, the progeny was +c 105, +d 115, cd 880 and ++900. Distance between the c and d genes is
(a) 11 map units (b) 5.5 map units
(c) 44 map units (d) 88 map units

240. Select the correct statement(s) with respect to linked genes:
A. They are present on the same chromosomes
B. They do not show independent assortment
C. Strength of linkage is directly proportional to the distance between them
(a) Only (B) (b) (B) and (C)
(c) Only (A) (d) (A), (B) and (C)

241. Traits that are coded for in autosomes but expressed only in one sex due to effect of sex chromosomes are:
(a) Sex linked (b) Sex limited
(c) Sex influenced (d) Both (b) and (c)

242. How many genomes are present in the skin cell of humans?
(a) Two (b) Four
(c) One (d) Forty-six

243. Genetic map is one that:
(a) Establishes sites of the genes on a chromosome
(b) Establishes the various stages in gene evolution
(c) Shows the stages during cell division
(d) Shows distribution of various species in a region

244. How many linkage groups are present in human male and female, respectively:
(a) 23, 23 (b) 23, 24
(c) 24, 23 (d) 46, 46

245. The expression of genes for the production of milk in females is:
(a) Sex-linked trait (b) Y-linked trait
(c) Sex-limited trait (d) Sex-influenced trait

246. A recessive gene is expressed only in the homozygous condition. Sometimes, a single recessive gene can express itself when it is:
(a) Autosomal gene
(b) Located on the X chromosome of female
(c) Located on the X chromosome of male
(d) All of the above

247. Traits that are coded for in autosomes but appear more frequently in one of the sexes are ________ traits:
(a) Sex-dominant traits
(b) Sex-influenced traits
(c) Sex-limited traits
(d) Sex-linked traits

248. Mark the incorrect pair:
(a) Beard in man – Sex-limited trait
(b) Pattern baldness – Sex-influenced trait
(c) Haemophilia – Sex-linked trait
(d) Hypertrichosis – Criss-cross inheritance

249. A holandric gene in man causes hypertrichosis. When a man with a hairy ears marries a normal woman:
(a) The percentage of their sons would be 100% to have hairy ears
(b) Half the daughters will have this trait
(c) Ratio of hairy ears and normal child will be 1:2
(d) All are correct

250. In *Drosophila*, genes for y (yellow body), w (white eye) and m (miniature wing) do not show:
(a) Very tight linkage (b) Loose linkage
(c) Complete linkage (d) Recombination

251. The results of the F_2 generations of four dihybrid test crosses are given below. Which demonstrate the principle of independent assortment?

	Parental	**Recombinants**
(a)	50%	50%
(b)	60%	40%
(c)	80%	20%
(d)	75%	25%

252. In *Drosophila*, red eye colour is dominant to white eye and is sex linked. What results would you expect from a cross between a red-eyed male and a white-eyed female?
(a) All males and females are red eyed
(b) All females are red eyed and males are white eyed
(c) All females are white eyed and males are red eyed
(d) All offspring are white eyed

253. In male *Drosophila*, which genes show complete linkage?
(a) All genes
(b) Maleness and eye colour
(c) Eye colour and wing character
(d) None of the above

254. The number of linkage groups depends upon the:
(a) Length of chromosomes
(b) Diploid number of chromosomes
(c) Total number of chromosomes
(d) Haploid number of chromosomes

255. Crossing over occurs at:
(a) Two-strand stage of chromosome during prophase I

(b) Four-strand stage of pachytene
(c) Zygotene of meiosis I
(d) All except (c)

256. A drone (male honey bee) cannot be a:
(a) Grandson (b) Maternal grandfather
(c) Father (d) All of the above

257. Which of the following cannot be a reason for use of *Drosophila* as ideal material for genetic studies?
(a) Can grow in simple synthetic medium
(b) Male is larger than female
(c) Easily observable hereditary variations
(d) Single mating produces large number of progeny

258. Mendelian 'factors' were later called genes by:
(a) Bateson (b) Johannsen
(c) Knight (d) Kolreuter

259. Law of segregation and law of independent assortment can be explained by ________ movement of chromosome:
(a) Metaphase (b) Anaphase I
(c) Anaphase II (d) Crossing over

260. Identify A, B and C in the following diagram with respect to segregation of chromosomes during germ cell formation:

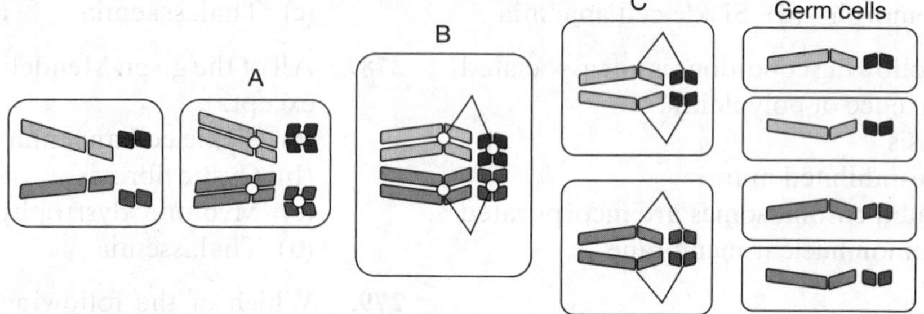

	A	B	C
(a)	G_2 phase	Anaphase I	Anaphase II
(b)	S phase	Metaphase I	Anaphase I
(c)	G_1 phase	G_2 phase	Anaphase II
(d)	G_2 phase	Metaphase II	Anaphase II

Gene Mutation, Chromosomal Aberration, Genomatic Mutation, Pedigree Analysis, Genetic Disorders, Mendelian and Chromosomal Disorders, Cytoplasmic Inheritance

261. Mutation:
(a) Does not change metabolism
(b) Creates continuous variation
(c) Changes phenotype but not genotype
(d) Results in alteration of genetic architecture

262. Select the incorrect statement:
(a) Mutation provides variation upon which artificial selection can act
(b) The vast majority of mutations produce alleles which are dominant
(c) Mutations arise spontaneously, infrequently and randomly
(d) Mutation rates can be increased by artificial means

263. Mutation which alters the chromosome structure is called:
(a) Genomatic mutation
(b) Chromosomal aberration
(c) Polyploidy
(d) Euploidy

264. Which of the following conditions is present in cancer cells?
(a) Point mutation
(b) Frame shift mutation
(c) Genomatic mutation
(d) Chromosomal aberrations

265. Point mutation is a change in:
(a) A single base pair of DNA
(b) Entire sequence of base pairs in mRNA
(c) Three base pairs of DNA due to deletion
(d) Two base pairs of DNA due to addition

266. Gene mutation occurs by all of the following methods, except:
(a) Deletion of one nucleotide
(b) Insertion of one nucleotide

(c) Substitution of one nucleotide by another nucleotide
(d) Substitution of a small part of a chromosome by a part of a different chromosome

267. Transition mutation occurs when there is:
(a) Substitution of purine base with a pyrimidine base
(b) Substitution of purine base with a purine base
(c) Substitution of pyrimidine base with a purine base
(d) Insertion of one or more bases in the nucleotide chain

268. Which one is due to point mutation?
(a) Intersex (b) Downs syndrome
(c) Gynandromorph (d) Sickle cell anaemia

269. Which of the following conditions is not associated with the occurrence of polyploidy?
(a) Endomitosis
(b) Colchicine-inhibited mitosis
(c) Reduplicated chromosomes are incorporated into a common nuclear membrane
(d) Polyteny

270. Which of the following represents a substitution mutation?
(a) Frameshift (b) Transition
(c) Translocation (d) Duplication

271. Removal of one or two bases from the nucleotide chain can lead to:
(a) Frameshift mutation
(b) Transition
(c) Sickle cell anaemia
(d) Both (b) and (c)

272. Transversion is:
(a) Substitution of a purine base with a pyrimidine base
(b) Replacement of a purine base with another purine base
(c) Deletion of one base from the nucleotide chain
(d) Deletion of a segment of the chromosome

273. When purine is replaced by another purine, it is called:
(a) Deletion (b) Addition
(c) Insertion (d) Transition

274. Loss or gain of chromosomes occurs due to:
(a) Abnormal meiosis
(b) Non-disjunction
(c) Polyploidy
(d) More than one option is correct

275. Identify the given mutation:
–AGGCCTACCAAT–
↓
–AGGCCTACCCCT–
(a) Transition (b) Transversion
(c) Substitution (d) Both (b) and (c)

276. The chromosomal constitution (2n - 2) of an organism represents:
(a) Triploidy (b) Double monosomy
(c) Monosomy (d) Nullisomy

277. Which condition is caused by mutations that involve the entire chromosome rather than a single gene?
(a) Haemophilia (b) Sickle all anaemia
(c) Thalassaemia (d) Down's syndrome

278. All of the given Mendelian disorders are recessive, except:
(a) Sickle cell anaemia
(b) Cystic fibrosis
(c) Myotonic dystrophy
(d) Thalassemia

279. Which of the following mutations is responsible for chronic myelogenous leukemia?
(a) Deletion (b) Duplication
(c) Inversion (d) Translocation

280. Major mutagenic effect of UV rays is:
(a) Causes breaks in chromosomes
(b) Induces frameshift mutation
(c) Formation of thymine dimers
(d) Causes agglutination of chromosomes

281. Y rays:
(a) Are ionizing radiation
(b) Can cause breaks in the chromosome
(c) Have longer wavelength
(d) Both (a) and (b)

282. Identify the incorrect statement with respect to sickle cell anaemia:
(a) An autosomal recessive trait
(b) Caused by substitution of glutamic acid with valine
(c) Heterozygous individuals appear apparently unaffected
(d) Mutant alpha haemoglobin chain forms biconcave-shaped RBC

283. If a normal man marries a colour-blind woman, what are the chances of their children being colour-blind?
(a) 25% (b) 50%
(c) 75% (d) 100%

284. Trisomic condition:
(a) Is due to aneuploidy
(b) Is a type of hyperploidy condition
(c) Results in (2n+1) condition
(d) All of the above

285. How many trisomes are possible if an organism has 14 chromosome in its gamete?
(a) 14 (b) 28
(c) 42 (d) 7

286. Chromosome number of Down's syndrome and Turner's syndrome is:
(a) 47, 48 (b) 47, 45
(c) 45, 47 (d) 43, 45

287. A disorder due to trisomy of autosome is:
(a) Down's syndrome (b) Edward syndrome
(c) Patau syndrome (d) All of the above

288. Condition of sex chromosome in a male child of Down's syndrome will be:
(a) XXY (b) XY
(c) XO (d) XYY

289. In an organism, 4N = 100. The haploid and monoploid number of chromosomes in this organism will be:
(a) 25, 25 (b) 25, 50
(c) 50, 25 (d) 50, 50

290. Sickle cell anaemia is an example of:
(a) Point mutation
(b) Transversion mutation
(c) Mis-sense mutation
(d) All of the above

291. Match the following and select the correct option:

Column I	Column II
A. Trisomy	(i) (2n+2)
B. Tetrasomy	(ii) (2n – 1)
C. Monosomy	(iii) (2n + 1 + 1)
D. Double trisomy	(iv) (2n + 1)

(a) A – (iv), B – (i), C – (ii), D – (iii)
(b) A – (iv), B – (ii), C – (i), D – (iii)
(c) A – (iii), B – (i), C – (ii), D – (iv)
(d) A – (ii), B – (iii), C – (iv), D – (i)

292. Number of Barr bodies in Klinefelter syndrome is:
(a) 0 (b) 1
(c) 2 (d) 3

293. If the mother is heterozygous for haemophilia and the father suffers from the disease, what would be the probability of their son being haemophiliac?
(a) 0% (b) 25%
(c) 50% (d) 75%

294. The symbols A, B, C and D indicate (respectively):

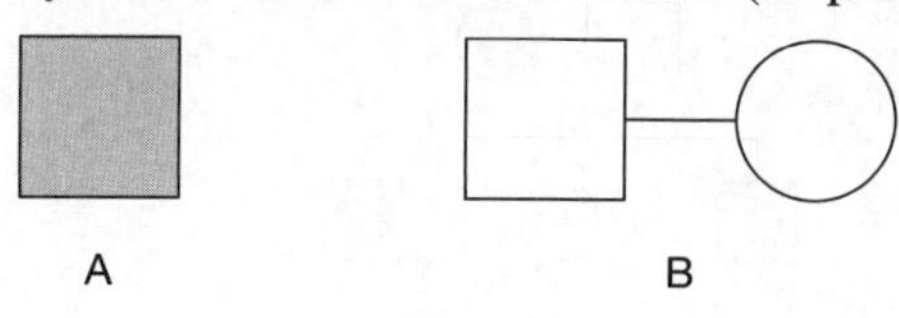

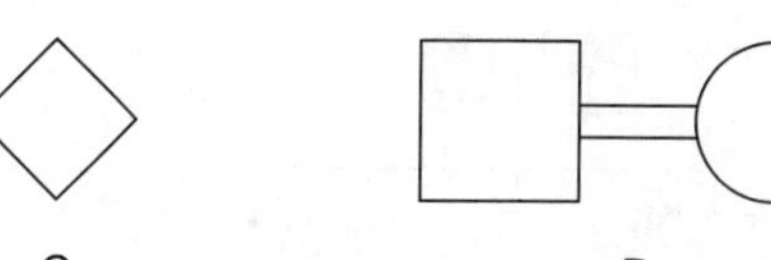

	A	B	C	D
(a)	Affected male	Mating	Sex unspecified	Consanguineous mating
(b)	Affected male	Mating	Unaffected male	Consanguineous mating
(c)	Affected female	Consanguineous mating	Sex unspecified	Mating
(d)	Affected female	Mating	unaffected female	Consanguineous mating

295. If the base number of chromosome in *Triticum aestivum* is 7, give the total number of chromosomes present in a somatic cell:
(a) 7 (b) 14
(c) 21 (d) 42

296. Which of the following most appropriately describes haemophilia?
(a) Chromosomal disorder
(b) Autosomal dominant disorder
(c) X-linked recessive disorder
(d) X-linked dominant disorder

297. Which of the pedigree charts represents the inheritance of autosomal recessive disorders?
(a)

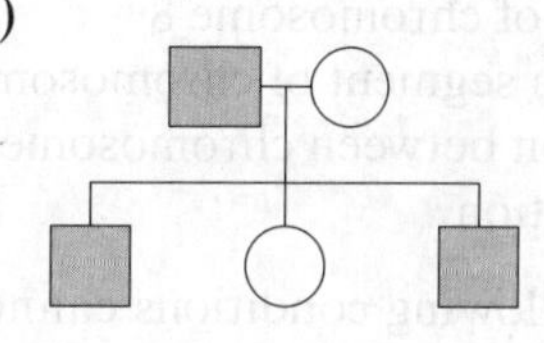

(b)

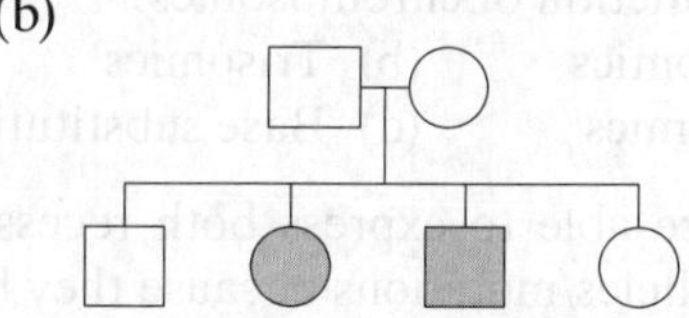

(c)

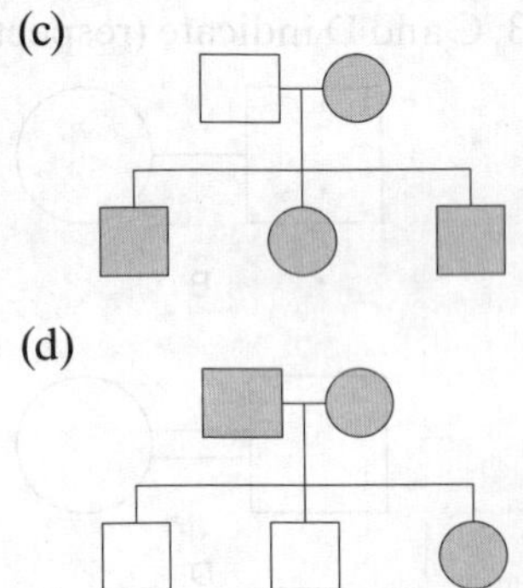

(d)

298. In pedigree analysis, the symbol represents:
(a) Consanguineous marriage
(b) Sex unspecified
(c) Monozygotic twins
(d) Dizygotic twins

299. Reciprocal translocation involving chromosome 9 and chromosome 22 results in:
(a) Chronic myelogenous leukemia
(b) Bar eye
(c) Nullisomies
(d) Polyploidy

300. Polyploidy develops as a result of:
(a) Failure of cytokinesis after telophase stage
(b) Non-disjunction of two homologous chromosomes
(c) Duplication of a segment of a chromosome
(d) Loss of a part of a chromosome

301. A woman whose father was a haemophilic marries a man whose father was also a haemophilic. The probability of a haemophilic son would be:
(a) 100% (b) 50%
(c) 0% (d) 25%

302. Christmas disease occurs due to absence of:
(a) Rh-antigen
(b) Factor IX
(c) Antihemophilic globulin
(d) Factor XI

303. In humans, Burkitt lymphoma disease is due to:
(a) Duplication of chromosome 8
(b) Deletion of a segment of chromosome 14
(c) Translocation between chromosome 14 and 8
(d) Non-disjunction

304. Which of the following conditions cannot be due to non-disjunction of chromosomes?
(a) Monosomics (b) Trisomics
(c) Tetrasomics (d) Base substitution

305. Haploids are able to express both recessive and dominant alleles/mutations because they have:
(a) Many alleles for each gene
(b) Two alleles for each gene
(c) Only one allele for each gene
(d) Only one allele in a chromosome

306. The given pedigree can best explain:

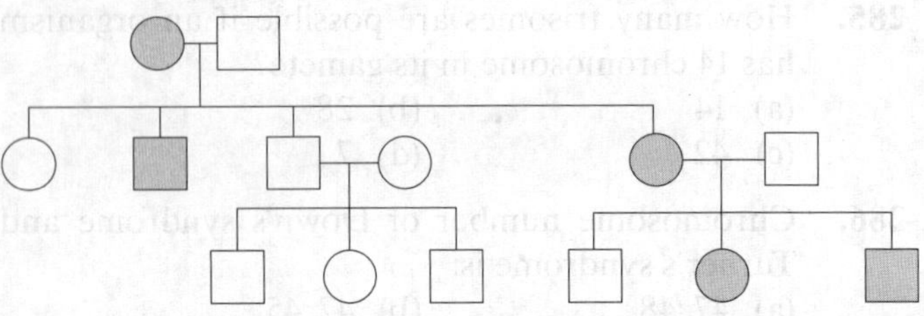

(a) Haemophilia
(b) Turner's syndrome
(c) Myotonic dystrophy
(d) Hypertrichosis

307. Cytoplasmic male sterility in maize is due to defective:
(a) Plastid (b) Mitochondria
(c) Nucleus (d) Both (b) and (c)

308. If a colour-blind man marries a normal woman, what will be probability of having colour-blind sons?
(a) Nil (b) 25%
(c) 50% (d) 100%

309. Both husband and wife have normal vision, though their fathers were colour-blind. The probability of their daughters becoming colour-blind is:
(a) 0% (b) 20%
(c) 50% (d) 75%

310. In a population, about ______ of male and ______ of females are colour-blind:
(a) 80%, 4% (b) 8%, 0.4%
(c) 8%, 4% (d) 0.8%, 0.4%

311. What is true for thalassaemia?
(a) Nutritional disorder leading to anaemia
(b) Autosomal recessive disorder leading to clotting abnormalities
(c) X-linked recessive disorder leading to reduced haemoglobin synthesis
(d) Autosomal recessive disorder leading to reduced haemoglobin synthesis

312. The genetic disorder that occurs due to additional copy of X chromosome in the human male shows:
(a) Congenital heart disease
(b) Gynaecomastia
(c) Physical, psychomotor and mental development is retarded
(d) All of the above

313. A haemophilic daughter is born when:
(a) Father is haemophilic and mother is normal
(b) Father is normal and mother is carrier
(c) Father is haemophilic and mother is carrier
(d) Father is normal and mother is haemophilic

314. Unaffected parents can have affected children (skip generations) during inheritance of:
(a) Hypertrichosis
(b) Albinism
(c) Myotonic dystrophy
(d) Morphan's syndrome

315. Phenylketonuria is a genetic disorder caused by a defect in the metabolism of:
(a) Fatty acids (b) Polysaccharides
(c) Vitamins (d) Amino acids

316. Which of the given disordesr is an inborn error of metabolism?
(a) Sickle cell anemia
(b) PKU
(c) Down's syndrome
(d) Turner's syndrome

317. The presence of an extra X chromosome in the genome of a human male indicates:
(a) Down's syndrome
(b) Klinefelter syndrome
(c) Turner's syndrome
(d) Edward syndrome

318. A. Exchange of genes between different linkage group is ___A___
B. Exchange of genes with in linkage group is ___B___

	A	B
(a)	Translocation	Crossing over
(b)	Translocation	Duplication
(c)	Duplication	Inversion
(d)	Duplication	Recombination

319. X-linked recessive disorder shows transmission from male to:
(a) Male progeny only
(b) Female progeny only
(c) Both male and female progeny in equal proportion
(d) Both male and female progeny in unequal proportion

320. Which is the example of a chromosomal disorder?
A. Haemophilia
B. Down's syndrome
C. Klinefelter syndrome
D. Turner's syndrome
E. Colour blindness
F. Cystic fibrosis
(a) (D), (E), (F) (b) (A) and (E)
(c) (B), (C) and (D) (d) All of the above

321. Individuals inflicted with Klinefelter syndrome:
(a) Have 47; XXY type of chromosome complement
(b) Show trisomy of autosomes
(c) Are fertile male with gynaecomastia
(d) All of the above

322. Phenylketonuria is associated with:
(a) Elevated level of tyrosine
(b) Mental retardation due to lipid accumulation in the brain
(c) Autosomal recessive inheritance
(d) More than one option is correct

323. Which of the following pedigrees represents X-linked recessive disorder?
(a)
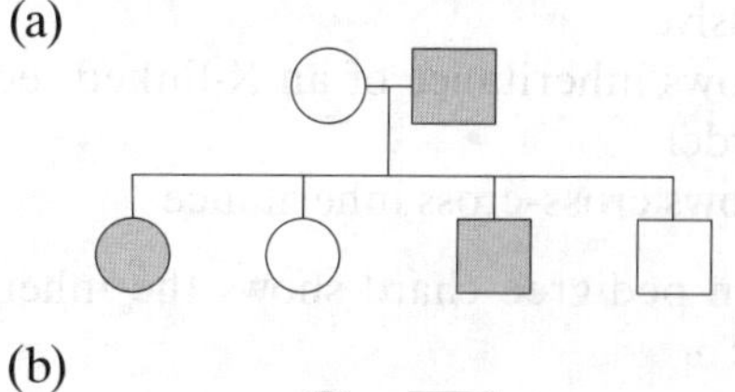
(b)
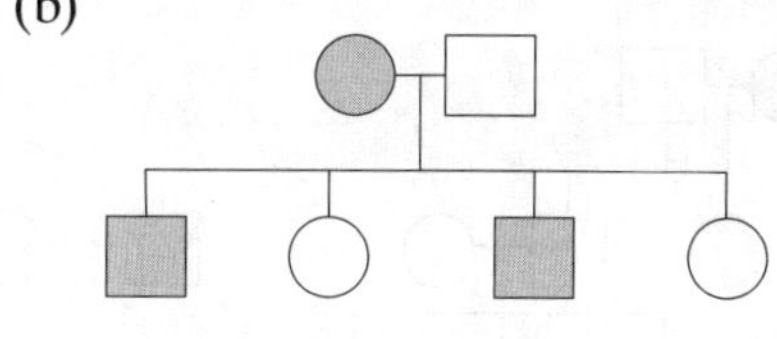
(c)
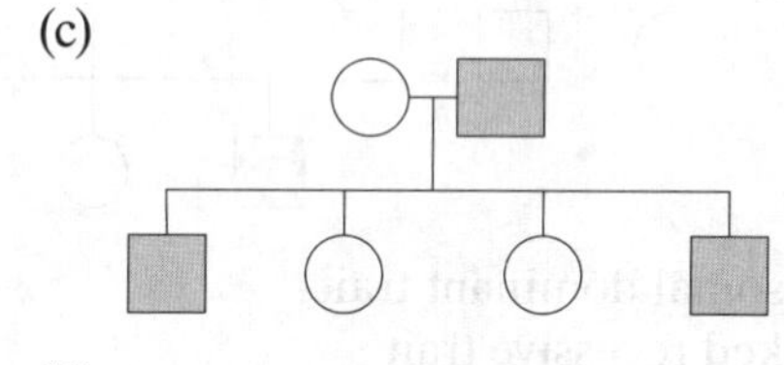
(d)
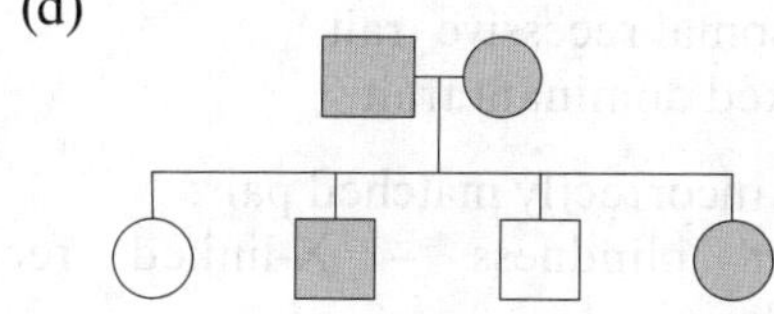

324. Results of reciprocal cross is different in the case of:
(a) Cytoplasmic inheritance
(b) Sex-linked inheritance
(c) Nuclear gene inheritance
(d) All except (a)

325. A colour-blind man marries a woman whose father was haemophilic. Choose the correct option regarding their offspring:
A. 50% of daughters will be colour-blind
B. 50% of sons will be haemophilic

C. Daughters will neither be haemophilic nor colour-blind
D. All daughters will be carriers for haemophilia
(a) (A) and (B) (b) (B) and (D)
(c) (B) and (C) (d) (B), (C) and (D)

326. Study the pedigree chart given below. What does it represent?

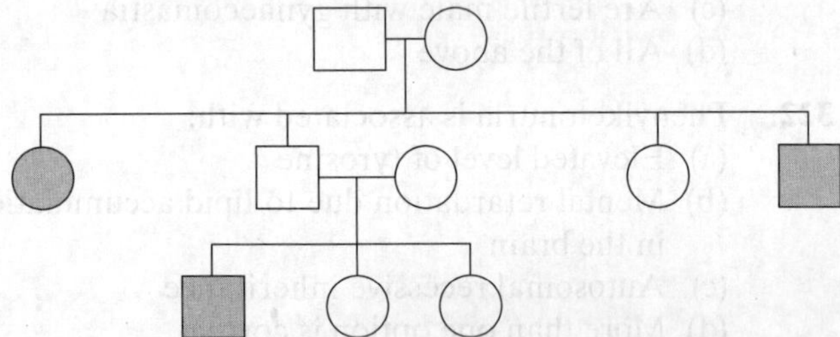

(a) Both the parents are homozygous for the trait
(b) The trait under study could be autosomal recessive
(c) It shows inheritance of an X-linked recessive disorder
(d) It shows cross-cross inheritance

327. The given pedigree chard shows the inheritance of a trait:

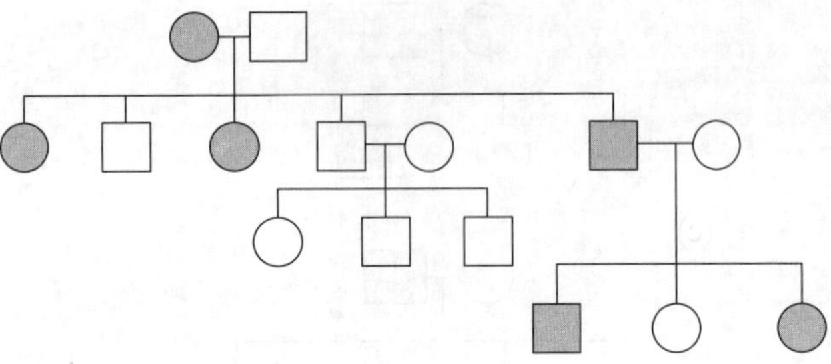

(a) Autosomal dominant trait
(b) X-linked recessive trait
(c) Autosomal recessive trait
(d) X-linked dominant trait

328. Select the incorrectly matched pair:
(a) Colour blindness – X-linked recessive disorder
(b) Haemophilia – Bleeders disease
(c) Philadelphia chromosome – Chromosome 22
(d) Phenylketonuria – Chromosomal aberration

329. The abnormality which arises due to decrease in chromosome number is:
(a) Myotonic dystrophy
(b) Down's syndrome
(c) Turner's syndrome
(d) All except (a)

330. Which of the following is not related to Klinefelter syndrome?
(a) Karyotype 47; XXY
(b) Sterility
(c) Gynaecomastia
(d) Overall masculine development in females

331. How many of the given disorders can be studied by a pedigree chart?
Thalassemia, Klinefelter syndrome, Down's syndrome, Colour-blindness, Haemophilia, Myotonic dystrophy, Cystic fibrosis, Turner's syndrome
(a) Five (b) Four
(c) Six (d) Seven

332. In thalassaemia, the affected chromosome may be:
(a) 16th and 11th (b) 16th and 17th
(c) 16th and 19th (d) 11th and 17th

333. A Klinefelter individual is different from an individual with Turner's syndrome in:
(a) Short stature
(b) Having Barr body
(c) Not having feminine voice
(d) Rudimentary ovaries

334. The total hereditary material outside the chromosome is called:
(a) Genome (b) Cytosol
(c) Kinetosome (d) Plasmon

335. Extrachromosomal bodies in *Paramecium* are:
(a) Plasmids (b) Episome
(c) Kappa particle (d) Lambda particle

336. Heterochromatisation of X-chromosome in human females forms:
(a) Barr body (b) Nu body
(c) Y spot (d) Yellow spots

337. Which amino acid is substituted in sickle all anaemia?
(a) Glutamic acid replaced by valine in α-chain
(b) Glutamic acid replaced by valine in β– chain
(c) Valine replaced by glutamic acid in α -chain
(d) Valine replaced by glutamic acid in β-chain

338. Study the given pedigree chart and find the genotype of the father and mother:

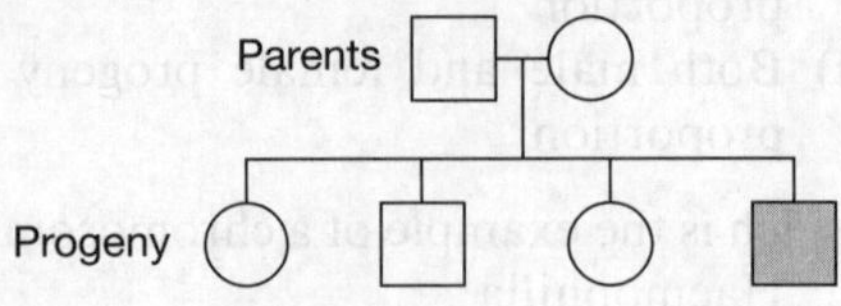

	Father	**Mother**
(a)	AA	aa
(b)	aa	aa
(c)	Aa	Aa
(d)	AA	Aa

339. How many of the given statements are correct for the disorder associated with quantitative problems of haemoglobin?
(i) Autosomal recessive disorder
(ii) Possibility of affected female is rare
(iii) Substitution of glutamic acid with valine
(iv) Reduced synthesis of β-chain of haemoglobin
(a) Three (b) One
(c) Four (d) Two

340. Gene for haemophilia is located on:
(a) Y chromosome (b) 13th chromosome
(c) X chromosome (d) 21st chromosome

341. Failure of segregation of chromatids during cell division cycle:
A. Results in gain or loss of chromosomes
B. It is known as aneuploidy
C. Causes syndrome which can be studied by pedigree chart
(a) (A) and (B) are correct
(b) (A) and (C) are correct
(c) (B) and (C) are correct
(d) All are correct

342. The given pedigree represents the inheritance of:

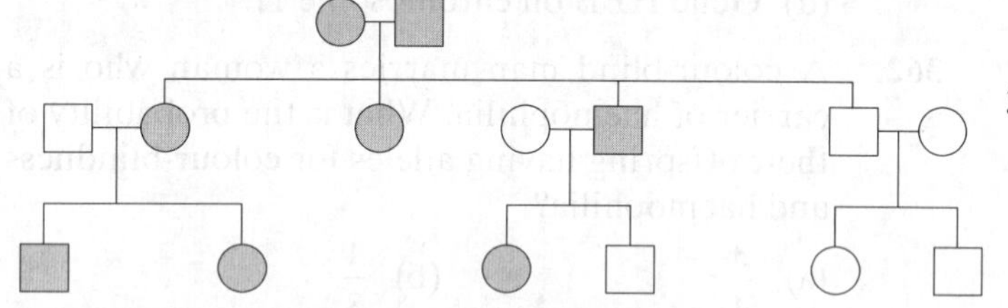

(a) Autosomal recessive disorder
(b) Y-linked disorder
(c) X-linked dominant disorder
(d) X-linked recessive disorder

343. If enzymes phenylalanine is absent, then:
A. Phenylalanine and its derivatives are excreted through urine due to poor absorption by kidneys
B. Phenyl pyruvic acid and other derivatives accumulate in the brain causing mental retardation
C. Amino acid phenylalanine is converted into tyrosine
(a) (A) and (B) are correct
(b) Only (A) is correct
(c) Only (C) is correct
(d) (B) and (C) are correct

344. Choose the incorrect statement with respect to the figure given below:

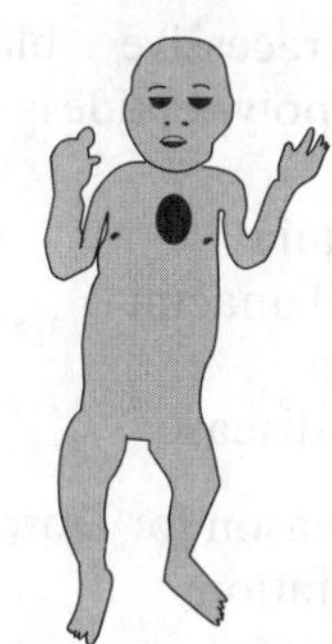

(a) It is a Mendelian disorder
(b) The affected individual is short-statured with a small head
(c) Palm is broad with characteristic palm crease
(d) Physical, psychomotor and mental development is retarded

345. A human male is heterozygous for two autosomal genes A and B and homozygous dominant for a third autosomal gene C. An individual has the sry gene (S) on his/her Y chromosome. What will be the probability that the sperm carries the abcs condition?
(a) $\frac{1}{4}$ (b) $\frac{1}{8}$
(c) 0 (d) $\frac{1}{16}$

346. Which of the following is not associated with haemophilia?
(a) X-linked recessive trait
(b) Shows cross-cross inheritance
(c) Mendelian disorder
(d) Transmitted from female carrier to female progeny

347. Haploid number of chromosomes in an organism is 10. What would be the number of chromosomes in monosomic, trisomic and tetrasomic conditions, respectively?
(a) 19, 21, 22 (b) 9, 11, 12
(c) 20, 21, 24 (d) 18, 20, 22

348. ________ provides a strong tool, which is utilised to trace the inheritance of a specific trait, abnormality or disease in human genetics:
(a) Controlled cross (b) Pedigree chart
(c) Punnett square (d) All of the above

349. Colour-blindness appears more in males than in females because:
(a) Males are hemizygous
(b) Males have more cones and rods in the retina
(c) It is a Y-linked disorder
(d) Females develop immunity to disease

350. Autosomal recessive blood disease where haemoglobin polypeptide is affected quantitatively is:
(a) Thalassemia
(b) Sickle cell anaemia
(c) Leukemia
(d) Bleeders disease

351. What is the reason for Down's syndrome
(a) Point mutation
(b) 21st monosomy
(c) Trisomy of allosome
(d) 21st trisomy

352. Karyotype of individual with Turner's syndrome is:
(a) 44 + XX (b) 45 + XO
(c) 45; XO (d) 44 + XXY

353. A women has an X-linked condition on one of her X chromosomes. This chromosome can be inherited by:
(a) Only grand children
(b) Only sons
(c) Only daughters
(d) Both sons and daughters

354. Barr body is present in:
(a) Sperm
(b) Ovum
(c) Somatic cell of female
(d) Somatic cell of male

355. It is well known that Queen Victoria of England was a carrier for haemophilia. Since it is an X-linked disease, it can be predicted that:
(a) All her sons would have had the disease
(b) All her daughters would have been carriers
(c) Her father must definitely have had haemophilia
(d) Haemophilia would have occurred in more of her male than her female descendants

356. Persons who are colour-blind cannot distinguish between:
(a) Black and white (b) Yellow and white
(c) Orange and red (d) Red and green

357. In the hexaploid wheat plant, the haploid (n) and basic (x) number of chromosome are:
(a) n = 21, X = 14 (b) n =21, X = 7
(c) n = 7, X = 21 (d) n = 21, X = 21

358. A couple, both carriers for the gene for sickle cell anaemia, are planning to get married and want to know the chances of having a sickle cell anaemic progeny:
(a) 100% (b) 75%
(c) 50% (d) 25%

359. Albinism is known to be due to an autosomal recessive disorder. The first child of a couple with normal skin pigments was albino. What is the probability of their second child being an albino as well?
(a) 25% (b) 50%
(c) 75% (d) 100%

360. Select the incorrectly matched pair:
(a) Sickle cell anemia – GAG is replaced by GUG
(b) Thalassemia – Qualitative problem of synthesizing an incorrectly functioning globin
(c) Cri du Chat syndrome – Deletion of short arm of 5th chromosome
(d) Cystic fibrosis – Autosomal recessive disorder

361. Beta thalassemia is due to mutation in the:
(a) Genes HBA 1 and HBA 2 on chromosome 11
(b) Genes HBA 1 and HBA 2 on chromosome 16
(c) Gene HBB on chromosome 16
(d) Gene HBB on chromosome 11

362. A colour-blind man marries a woman who is a carrier of haemophilia. What is the probability of their offspring having alleles for colour-blindness and haemophilia?
(a) $\frac{3}{4}$ (b) $\frac{1}{8}$
(c) $\frac{1}{2}$ (d) $\frac{1}{4}$

363. Which of the following is an autosomal dominant disorder?
(a) Myotonic dystrophy (b) Cystic fibrosis
(c) Thalassemia (d) Phenylketonuria

364. Alpha thalassemia is controlled by two genes HBA1 and HBA2 which are located on chromosome number:
(a) 11 (b) 16
(c) 18 (d) 21

NCERT EXEMPLAR QUESTIONS

1. All genes located on the same chromosome:
   (a) Form different groups depending upon their relative distance
   (b) Form one linkage group
   (c) Will not from any linkage groups
   (d) Form interactive groups that affect the phenotype

2. Conditions of a karyotype 2n +1, 2n –1 and 2n + 2, 2n – 2 are called:
   (a) Aneuploidy (b) Polyploidy
   (c) Allopolyploidy (d) Monosomy

3. Distance between the genes and percentage of recombination shows:
   (a) A direct relationship
   (b) An inverse relationship
   (c) A parallel relationship
   (d) No relationship

4. If a genetic disease is transferred from a phenotypically normal but carrier female to only some of the male progeny, the disease is:
   (a) Autosomal dominant
   (b) Autosomal recessive
   (c) Sex-linked dominant
   (d) Sex-linked recessive

5. In sickle cell anaemia, glutamic acid is replaced by valine. Which one of the following triplets codes for valine?
   (a) G G G (b) A A G
   (c) G A A (d) G U G

6. Person having genotype I^A I^B would show the blood group as AB. This is because of:
   (a) Pleiotropy
   (b) Codominance
   (c) Segregation
   (d) Incomplete dominance

7. Z Z / ZW type of sex determination is seen in:
   (a) Platypus (b) Snails
   (c) Cockroach (d) Peacock

8. A cross between two tall plants resulted in offspring having few dwarf plants. What would be the genotypes of both the parents?
   (a) TT and Tt (b) Tt and Tt
   (c) TT and TT (d) Tt and tt

9. In a dihybrid cross, if you get the ratio 9:3:3:1, it denotes that:
   (a) The alleles of two genes are interacting with each other
   (b) It is multigenic inheritance
   (c) It is a case of multiple allelism
   (d) The alleles of two genes are segregating independently

10. Which of the following will not result in variations among siblings?
    (a) Independent assortment of genes
    (b) Crossing over
    (c) Linkage
    (d) Mutation

11. Mendel's law of independent assortment holds good for genes situated on:
    (a) Non-homologous chromosomes
    (b) Homologous chromosomes
    (c) Extra nuclear genetic element
    (d) Same chromosome

12. Occasionally, a single gene may express more than one effect. The phenomenon is called:
    (a) Multiple allelism (b) Mosaicism
    (c) Pleiotropy (d) Polygeny

13. In a certain taxon of insects, some have 17 chromosomes while others have 18 chromosomes. The 17 and 18 chromosome bearing organisms are:
    (a) Males and females, respectively
    (b) Females and males, respectively
    (c) All males
    (d) All females

14. The inheritance pattern of a gene over generations among humans is studied by pedigree analysis. The character studied in pedigree analysis is equivalent to:
    (a) Quantitative trait (b) Mendelian trait
    (c) Polygenic trait (d) Maternal trait

15. It is said that Mendel proposed that the factor controlling any character is discrete and independent. His proposition was based on the:
    (a) Results of F_3 generation of a cross
    (b) Observations that the offspring of a cross between plants having two contrasting characters show only one character without any blending
    (c) Self-pollination of F_1 offspring
    (d) Cross-pollination of F_1 generation with the recessive parent

16. In the F_2 generation of a Mendelian dihybrid cross, the number of phenotypes and genotypes are:

(a) Phenotypes - 4; genotypes - 16
(b) Phenotypes - 9; genotypes - 4
(c) Phenotypes - 4; genotypes - 8
(d) Phenotypes - 4; genotypes - 9

17. The mother and father of a person with 'O' blood group have 'A' and 'B' blood groups, respectively. What would be the genotype of the mother and father?

(a) Mother is homozygous for 'A' blood group and father is heterozygous for 'B'
(b) Mother is heterozygous for 'A' blood group and father is homozygous for 'B'
(c) Both mother and father are heterozygous for 'A' and 'B' blood groups, respectively
(d) Both mother and father are homozygous for 'A' and 'B' blood groups, respectively

PRACTICE TEST PAPER

1. How many types of gametes can be produced by a plant having genotype AaBbccDDEe?
(a) 16 (b) 8
(c) 32 (d) 4

2. Which of the following traits shows expression in homozygous condition only?
(a) Violet flower
(b) Axial position of flower
(c) Constricted pod
(d) Yellow-colour seed

3. When a single allele exhibits multiple phenotypic expression, it is known as:
(a) Multiple allelism
(b) Pleiotropy
(c) Polygenic inheritance
(d) Polymorphism

4. Law of independent assortment can be explained with the help of:
(a) Test cross
(b) Out cross
(c) Monohybrid cross
(d) Dihybrid cross

5. In a population of 800 individuals in the F_2 generation of a cross between yellow round and green wrinkled pea seeds plants, what would be the number of yellow and wrinkled seeds?
(a) 400 (b) 80
(c) 150 (d) 200

6. Which law of Mendel does not have any exceptions?
(a) Law of independent assortment
(b) Law of dominance
(c) Law of segregation
(d) Both (a) and (b)

7. In the case where a modified allele is equivalent to the unmodified allele:
(a) It will produce the same phenotype
(b) It will produce a non-functional enzyme
(c) It will produce a changed phenotype
(d) It will transform the product instead of the substrate

8. In a dihybrid cross AABB X aabb, F_2 progeny of AABB, aaBB, AAbb, aabb occurs in the ratio of:
(a) 9:3:3:1 (b) 1:2:2:1
(c) 1:1:1:1 (d) 1:2:2:4

9. How many types of gametes are produced by a diploid organism that is heterozygous for 2 loci and homozygous for 3 loci?
(a) 8 (b) 4
(c) 16 (d) 32

10. Read the following statements:
(i) When two dominant, independently assorting non-allelic genes interact with each other, it is called complementary behaviour.
(ii) The phenomenon of an allele of a gene suppressing the activity of the allele of another gene is called epistasis.
(iii) The process of mating between closely related individuals is called inbreeding.
(iv) An allele, if dominant, is expressed only in the homozygous condition.
How many of these statements are correct?
(a) Two (b) Three
(c) Four (d) One

11. How many possible genotypes can be observed in a human population for the ABA blood group system?
(a) 12 (b) 10
(c) 6 (d) 3

12. To determine the genotype of a tall plant of the F_2 generation, which of the following crosses can be performed?
(a) Test cross (b) Back cross
(c) Reciprocal cross (d) Out cross

13. Select the incorrect statement with respect to polygenic inheritance:
(a) Human skin colour is an example of polygenic inheritance
(b) Dominant phenotypes are more frequent
(c) Dominant alleles show cumulative effect
(d) Also called quantitative inheritance

14. Mark the incorrect match:

	Interaction	Example
(a)	Dominant epistasis	Fruit colour in summer squash
(b)	Recessive epistasis	Coat colour in mice
(c)	Complementary gene	Flower colour in sweet pea
(d)	Duplicate gene	Coat colour in shorthorn cattle

15. Which of the following phenotypic ratios can explain the law of independent assortment?
(a) 3:1 (b) 1:2:1
(c) 9:3:3:1 (d) 1:1

16. The progeny of a dihybrid cross has four possible phenotypes in equal proportion. The genotypes of the parents would be:
(a) RRYY X rryy
(b) Rryy X rrYy
(c) Rryy X Rryy
(d) RrYY X rrYy

17. Read the following statements:
A. A gamete carries only one factor of a character
B. F_1 individual always resembles either of the two parents
C. Hybrid containing alleles which express contrasting traits are called heterozygous
D. Punnett square is a graphical representation to calculate the probability of all possible genotypes of offspring in a genetic cross
The correct statement(s) is/are:
(a) Only (B)
(b) Only (A) and (C)
(c) (A), (C) and (D)
(d) (A), (B) and (D)

18. Which of the following is an example of incomplete dominance?
A. Flower colour in snapdragon
B. Starch grain size in garden pea
C. Flower colour in *Mirabilis jalapa*
(a) Only (A)
(b) Only (C)
(c) Only (A) and (B)
(d) (A), (B) and (C)

19. Both the characters in a monohybrid cross are recovered as such in the F_2 generation. The interpretation is based on the:
(a) Law of dominance
(b) Law of segregation
(c) Law of incomplete dominance
(d) Law of independent assortment

20. For a polygenic trait controlled by three genes, what percentage of the F_2 generation would have parental genotype?
(a) 36.8% (b) 3.2%
(c) 31.25% (d) 68.75%

21. Which one of the following conditions correctly describes the manner of determining the sex in a given example?
(a) Homozygous sex chromosomes (ZZ) determine female sex in birds
(b) XO type of sex chromosomes determine male sex in grasshopper
(c) XO condition in humans, as found in Turner's syndrome, determines male sex
(d) Homozygous sex chromosomes (XX) produce males in *Drosophila*

22. Mark the odd one out:
(a) Sickle-cell anaemia
(b) Phenylketonuria
(c) Colour blindness
(d) Thalassemia

23. A man whose father was colour-blind marries a woman who had a colour-blind mother and normal father. What percentage of children of the couple can be colour-blind?
(a) 0% (b) 25%
(c) 50% (d) 100%

24. Eye colour in *Drosophila* shows which phenomenon?
(a) Pleiotropism
(b) Codominance
(c) Multiple alleles
(d) Polygenic inheritance

25. Genes for which of the following characters in *Drosophila* were found by Morgan to be very closely linked?
(a) Eye colour and wing size
(b) Body colour and wing size
(c) Wing size and eye colour
(d) Body colour and eye colour

26. One of the examples of polygenic inheritance is:
(a) Size of starch grains in pea seeds
(b) Pattern baldness
(c) Human skin colour
(d) Sickle-cell anaemia

27. In which of the following insects does the male progeny not receive any set of chromosomes from the male parent?
(a) Grasshopper
(b) Honey bee
(c) *Drosophila*
(d) Butterfly

28. Read the following statements:
A. Simply looking at the phenotype of a dominant trait, it is impossible to known the genotypic composition
B. To determine the genotype of a tall plant of F_2, Mendel crossed the tall plant from F_2 with a dwarf plant

C. On the basis of monohybrid crosses, Mendel proposed only two general rules
(a) (A) and (B) are correct
(b) (A) is incorrect
(c) Only (A) is correct
(d) (A), (B) and (C) are correct

29. Turner's syndrome is related with all, except:
(a) Karyotype 45; XO
(b) A chromosomal disorder
(c) Monosomy of the sex chromosome
(d) Sterile males

30. Sickle-cell anaemia is an example of ____**A**____, which occurs due to ____**B**____:

	A	B
(a)	Silent mutation	Deletion of gene
(b)	Point mutation	Transversion
(c)	Non-sense mutation	Substitution reaction
(d)	Mis-sense mutation	Transition

31. Which of the following pairs represents an autosomal recessive disorder?
(a) Colour blindness, Haemophilia
(b) Turner's syndrome, Klinefelter syndrome
(c) Muscular dystrophy, Cystic fibrosis
(d) Sickle-cell anaemia, Thalassemia

32. Which of the following statement is incorrect with respect to phenylketonuria?
(a) Inborn errors of metabolism
(b) Sex-linked recessive trait
(c) Affected individual lacks phenylalanine hydroxidase enzyme
(d) Phenylalanine is accumulated and converted into phenylpyruvic acid and other derivatives

33. The given pedigree chart shows the inheritance of:

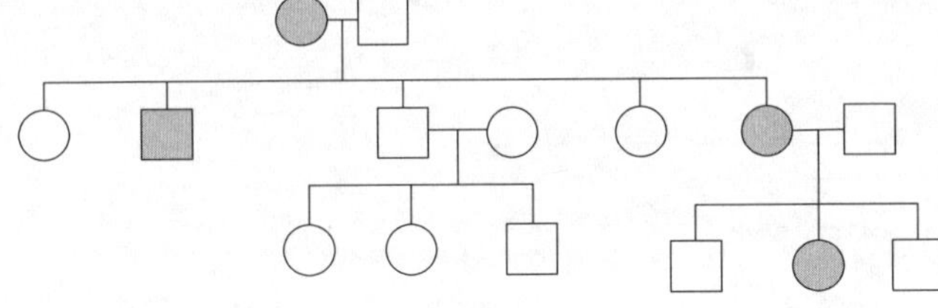

(a) Chromosomal disorder
(b) X-linked recessive disorder
(c) Autosomal recessive disorder
(d) Autosomal dominant disorder

34. When a single gene product produces more than one effect, the phenomenon is called:
(a) Multiple allelism
(b) Pleiotropy
(c) Polyploidy
(d) Epistasis

35. Cross between AaBB and aaBB will form:
(a) 1 AaBB : 1 aaBB
(b) All AaBB
(c) 3AaBB : 1 aaBB
(d) 1 AaBB : 3 aaBB

36. Find the odd one out with respect to a Mendelian disorder?
(a) Sickle-cell anaemia
(b) Haemophilia
(c) Cystic fibrosis
(d) Chronic myelogenous leukemia

37. The genotypic and phenotypic ratio is the same in the case of:
(a) Recessive epistasis
(b) Multiple alleles
(c) Incomplete dominance
(d) Dominant epistasis

38. If substrate S is transformed into product p with the help of enzyme E, then E is the product of wild allele A^+. After mutation, A^+ changes into multiple modified forms:

$A^+ \xrightarrow{\text{Mutation}} A$, A produces normal enzyme

$A \xrightarrow{\text{Mutation}} A^a$, A^a produces less efficient enzyme

$A^a \xrightarrow{\text{Mutation}} A^\beta$, A^β produces non-functional enzyme

$A^\beta \xrightarrow{\text{Mutation}} A^\gamma$, A^γ produces no enzyme

After considering the above findings, which of the following allele pairs will produce recessive phenotype?
(a) A, A^a
(b) A^β, A
(c) A^+, A
(d) A^β, A^γ

39. Human skin pigmentation is controlled by a pair of polygenes. The number of different phenotypes is:
(a) Six
(b) Seven
(c) Five
(d) Four

40. Which of the following phenomena cannot be observed in male *Drosophila*?
(a) Linkage
(b) Crossing over
(c) Law of segregation
(d) Independent assortment of autosomal genes

41. Thymine dimer formation is due to:
(a) Acridine dyes
(b) X-rays
(c) UV rays
(d) Base analogues

42. All characters are controlled by nuclear genes, except:
(a) Plant height in pea
(b) Male sterility in maize
(c) Kernel colour in wheat
(d) Seed colour in pea

43. Which of the following diseases is due to deletion of chromosome?
(a) Cat cry syndrome
(b) Patau's syndrome
(c) Edward's syndrome
(d) Down's syndrome

44. A holandric gene in humans causes hypertrichosis. When such a male marries a normal woman, the percentage of their sons expected to have hairy pinnae is equal to:
(a) 50% (b) 25%
(c) 100% (d) 0%

45. Continuous variation is attributed to:
(a) Mutation
(b) Crossing over
(c) Chromosomal aberration
(d) Polyploidy

ANSWER KEYS

Exercises

1. (d)	**2.** (c)	**3.** (a)	**4.** (d)	**5.** (b)	**6.** (d)	**7.** (b)	**8.** (a)	**9.** (a)	**10.** (d)
11. (c)	**12.** (d)	**13.** (d)	**14.** (b)	**15.** (a)	**16.** (c)	**17.** (b)	**18.** (a)	**19.** (c)	**20.** (c)
21. (d)	**22.** (d)	**23.** (d)	**24.** (c)	**25.** (c)	**26.** (d)	**27.** (c)	**28.** (d)	**29.** (a)	**30.** (b)
31. (a)	**32.** (c)	**33.** (a)	**34.** (d)	**35.** (c)	**36.** (c)	**37.** (b)	**38.** (b)	**39.** (b)	**40.** (d)
41. (b)	**42.** (b)	**43.** (d)	**44.** (c)	**45.** (b)	**46.** (a)	**47.** (d)	**48.** (c)	**49.** (b)	**50.** (c)
51. (b)	**52.** (a)	**53.** (c)	**54.** (a)	**55.** (b)	**56.** (b)	**57.** (d)	**58.** (a)	**59.** (b)	**60.** (b)
61. (d)	**62.** (c)	**63.** (b)	**64.** (d)	**65.** (b)	**66.** (d)	**67.** (c)	**68.** (d)	**69.** (a)	**70.** (d)
71. (a)	**72.** (b)	**73.** (d)	**74.** (c)	**75.** (c)	**76.** (c)	**77.** (a)	**78.** (a)	**79.** (c)	**80.** (a)
81. (a)	**82.** (c)	**83.** (d)	**84.** (d)	**85.** (a)	**86.** (c)	**87.** (d)	**88.** (c)	**89.** (c)	**90.** (b)
91. (c)	**92.** (b)	**93.** (a)	**94.** (d)	**95.** (d)	**96.** (b)	**97.** (b)	**98.** (a)	**99.** (a)	**100.** (b)
101. (d)	**102.** (a)	**103.** (b)	**104.** (b)	**105.** (a)	**106.** (c)	**107.** (d)	**108.** (b)	**109.** (c)	**110.** (a)
111. (b)	**112.** (d)	**113.** (c)	**114.** (d)	**115.** (c)	**116.** (c)	**117.** (d)	**118.** (a)	**119.** (a)	**120.** (b)
121. (d)	**122.** (a)	**123.** (d)	**124.** (a)	**125.** (a)	**126.** (c)	**127.** (d)	**128.** (d)	**129.** (b)	**130.** (a)
131. (d)	**132.** (d)	**133.** (d)	**134.** (b)	**135.** (d)	**136.** (c)	**137.** (b)	**138.** (c)	**139.** (c)	**140.** (b)
141. (d)	**142.** (b)	**143.** (b)	**144.** (a)	**145.** (c)	**146.** (a)	**147.** (c)	**148.** (b)	**149.** (c)	**150.** (b)
151. (d)	**152.** (c)	**153.** (b)	**154.** (b)	**155.** (c)	**156.** (c)	**157.** (d)	**158.** (c)	**159.** (c)	**160.** (a)
161. (c)	**162.** (d)	**163.** (b)	**164.** (c)	**165.** (d)	**166.** (c)	**167.** (b)	**168.** (d)	**169.** (c)	**170.** (a)
171. (c)	**172.** (b)	**173.** (b)	**174.** (c)	**175.** (b)	**176.** (b)	**177.** (b)	**178.** (b)	**179.** (a)	**180.** (d)
181. (a)	**182.** (a)	**183.** (d)	**184.** (c)	**185.** (d)	**186.** (a)	**187.** (c)	**188.** (c)	**189.** (c)	**190.** (c)
191. (d)	**192.** (b)	**193.** (d)	**194.** (b)	**195.** (a)	**196.** (a)	**197.** (d)	**198.** (b)	**199.** (b)	**200.** (b)
201. (c)	**202.** (a)	**203.** (c)	**204.** (d)	**205.** (d)	**206.** (b)	**207.** (b)	**208.** (a)	**209.** (b)	**210.** (a)
211. (d)	**212.** (a)	**213.** (c)	**214.** (a)	**215.** (d)	**216.** (d)	**217.** (c)	**218.** (a)	**219.** (d)	**220.** (b)
221. (c)	**222.** (b)	**223.** (c)	**224.** (c)	**225.** (c)	**226.** (d)	**227.** (a)	**228.** (c)	**229.** (c)	**230.** (a)
231. (c)	**232.** (d)	**233.** (d)	**234.** (c)	**235.** (d)	**236.** (d)	**237.** (d)	**238.** (b)	**239.** (a)	**240.** (c)
241. (c)	**242.** (a)	**243.** (a)	**244.** (c)	**245.** (a)	**246.** (c)	**247.** (c)	**248.** (d)	**249.** (a)	**250.** (c)
251. (a)	**252.** (b)	**253.** (d)	**254.** (d)	**255.** (b)	**256.** (c)	**257.** (b)	**258.** (b)	**259.** (b)	**260.** (a)
261. (d)	**262.** (b)	**263.** (b)	**264.** (d)	**265.** (a)	**266.** (d)	**267.** (b)	**268.** (d)	**269.** (c)	**270.** (b)
271. (a)	**272.** (a)	**273.** (d)	**274.** (d)	**275.** (d)	**276.** (d)	**277.** (d)	**278.** (c)	**279.** (d)	**280.** (c)
281. (d)	**282.** (d)	**283.** (b)	**284.** (d)	**285.** (a)	**286.** (b)	**287.** (d)	**288.** (b)	**289.** (c)	**290.** (d)
291. (a)	**292.** (b)	**293.** (c)	**294.** (a)	**295.** (d)	**296.** (c)	**297.** (b)	**298.** (c)	**299.** (a)	**300.** (a)
301. (b)	**302.** (b)	**303.** (c)	**304.** (d)	**305.** (c)	**306.** (c)	**307.** (b)	**308.** (a)	**309.** (a)	**310.** (b)
311. (d)	**312.** (b)	**313.** (c)	**314.** (b)	**315.** (d)	**316.** (b)	**317.** (b)	**318.** (a)	**319.** (b)	**320.** (c)
321. (a)	**322.** (c)	**323.** (b)	**324.** (a)	**325.** (c)	**326.** (b)	**327.** (a)	**328.** (d)	**329.** (c)	**330.** (d)
331. (a)	**332.** (a)	**333.** (b)	**334.** (d)	**335.** (c)	**336.** (d)	**337.** (b)	**338.** (c)	**339.** (d)	**340.** (c)
341. (a)	**342.** (c)	**343.** (a)	**344.** (a)	**345.** (b)	**346.** (d)	**347.** (a)	**348.** (b)	**349.** (a)	**350.** (a)
351. (d)	**352.** (c)	**353.** (d)	**354.** (d)	**355.** (d)	**356.** (d)	**357.** (b)	**358.** (d)	**359.** (b)	**360.** (b)
361. (d)	**362.** (d)	**363.** (a)	**364.** (b)						

NCERT Exemplar Questions

1. (b)	**2.** (a)	**3.** (a)	**4.** (d)	**5.** (d)	**6.** (b)	**7.** (d)	**8.** (b)	**9.** (d)	**10.** (c)
11. (a)	**12.** (c)	**13.** (a)	**14.** (b)	**15.** (b)	**16.** (d)	**17.** (c)			

Practice Test Paper

1. (b) **2.** (c) **3.** (b) **4.** (d) **5.** (c) **6.** (c) **7.** (a) **8.** (c) **9.** (b) **10.** (b)
11. (c) **12.** (a) **13.** (b) **14.** (d) **15.** (c) **16.** (b) **17.** (d) **18.** (d) **19.** (b) **20.** (b)
21. (b) **22.** (c) **23.** (b) **24.** (c) **25.** (d) **26.** (c) **27.** (b) **28.** (a) **29.** (d) **30.** (b)
31. (d) **32.** (b) **33.** (d) **34.** (b) **35.** (a) **36.** (d) **37.** (c) **38.** (d) **35.** (b) **40.** (b)
41. (c) **42.** (b) **43.** (a) **44.** (c) **45.** (b)

SOLUTIONS

Introduction, Inheritance of One Gene, Mendel's Law of Inheritance – Dominance, Segregation

1. Genetics is the branch of biology that deals with the study of heredity and variation.
2. Transmission of genetic characters from parents to offspring from generation to generation is called heredity.
3. Before Mendel, J Kolreuter had conducted hybridisation experiments on the tobacco plant. He reported that the progeny may resemble any one of the parents or may be intermediate between them.
4. Mendel selected 14 tree breeding pea plant varieties for his hybridisation experiment.
5. Mendel conducted hybridisation experiments on the garden pea for seven years (1856–1863) and proposed the law of inheritance.
6. Mendel published the results of his experiments in the year 1866, in the fourth volume of the proceedings of the Natural Science Society of Brunn.
7. Variations are differences like morphological, cytological, physiological or behavioural amongst individuals of the same species and offspring of the same parent.
8. *Pisum sativum*
9. An allele is a slightly different form or alternate form of a gene, which is present on the same locus on a homologous chromosome.
10. All the alleles of a gene are present on the same locus of a homologous chromosome. Each chromosome carries only one allele of a gene.
11. When only one allele of a pair is present, the condition is called hemizygous. For example, XY condition in human males.
12. All alleles originate from mutation.
13. All the genotypes of all organisms in a population are from a gene pool.
14. When we consider the inheritance of one character at a time by a cross, it is called monohybrid cross.
15. Total set of genes in a haploid set of chromosomes is called genome.
16. Primary source of allelic variations is recombination.
17. When a cross is made between two pure-line (homozygous) individuals considering contrasting traits of a simple character, the offspring produced in the F_1 generation are called hybrids.
18. A character which is expressed in a hybrid is called dominant character and the other is called recessive trait.
19. To observe the effect of sex on inheritance, Mendel performed reciprocal cross.

Reciprocal cross

20. Tt X Tt. Cross produces tall and dwarf plants in the ratio of 3:1.
21. When two alleles of a gene are similar, they are said to be in homozygous condition. For example, TT or tt.
22. All of these.
23. Mendel could not convince himself about his conclusion being universal as he failed to reproduce the results on hawk weed (*Hieracium*) and bean (*Lablab*).
24. The law of dominance explains that when two alternative forms of a trait are present in a hybrid, only one trait expresses itself in the F_1 progeny and is called dominant, while the other that remains masked is called recessive.
25. Correct expressions are as follows: Gamete – T, Zygote – TT, Diploid organism – TT, Haploid organism – T.
26. Law of segregation (Law of purity of gametes)

27. A gamete receives only one factor or gene of a trait.

28. Number of phenotypes = 2^n
n = 3 (n = no of heterozygous)

29. $\left(\frac{1}{2}T+\frac{1}{2}t\right)^2$

30. Law of segregation is universally applicable.

31. Number of characters related to
(i) Flower – 2 (flower colour, flower position)
(ii) Pod – 2 (pod colour, pod shape)
(iii) Seed – 2 (seed shape, seed colour)

32. Effect of environment on the genetic set-up of organisms.

33. Children are at increased risk of autosomal recessive genetic disorders.

34. Gametes with recessive alleles only:
$$abcd = \frac{1}{2}\times 1\times \frac{1}{2}\times 1 = \frac{1}{4} = 25\%$$

35. Constricted pod. Recessive characters express only in homozygous condition.

36. Stem height – Dwarf (Recessive), Flower colour – White (Recessive), Seed colour – Green (Recessive), Pod shape – Inflated (Dominant)

37. Detailed investigation by S Blixt on the pea plant led to identification of the location of Mendel's seven characters on four different chromosomes: 1, 4, 5 and 7.
Chromosome 1 – Flower colour, seed colour
Chromosome 4 – Flower position, pod shape, plant height
Chromosome 5 – Pod colour
Chromosome 7 – Seed shape

38. Chromosome 4

39. Experiment on plant hybridisation

40. Chromosome numbers 4 and 5

41. True breeding lines produce only one trait generation after generation on being self-pollinated or cross-pollinated among themselves.

42. Generations of homozygous genotypes are called pure lines (aabbcc).

43. AaBb

44. Dihybrid condition is TtRr.

45. If an organism produces 8 different types of gametes, its genotype should be heterozygous for 3 genes (AaBbCc).
No of gametes = 2^n
$8 = 2^n$
n = 3

46. Gregor Johann Mendel was an Austrian monk.

47. Gamete receives only one factor or gene of a trait (gHI).

48. In 1900, three scientists, Hugo de Vries, Carl Correns and Von Tschermak independently rediscovered the principles of inheritance stated by Mendel.

49. Genotype of an individual is AabbCc gametes with recessive alleles only.
$$abc = \frac{1}{2}\times 1\times \frac{1}{2} = \frac{1}{4} = 25\%$$

50. $\frac{1}{4}$ (Ratio of tall and dwarf plants is 3:1).

51. Genotype of organism is AabbCcDDee.
No of gametes = 2^n (Heterozygous for 2 characters A and C)
n = No of heterozygous gametes
n = 2
No of gametes = $2^2 = 4$

52. A – Genes, B – Homozygous, C – Phenotype, D – Hemizygous

53. Charles Darwin

54. Axial flower position and green pod colour

55. Carl Correns converted Mendel's observations into laws.

56. Law of segregation

57. Codominance

58. Gene

59. Recessive characters are expressed only in homozygous condition. Among the given traits, five are recessive: terminal flower, green seed, yellow pod, constricted pod and dwarf stem.

60. Law of segregation

61. Punnett square was developed by the British geneticist, Reginald C Punnett. It is a graphical representation to calculate the probability of all possible genotypes of offspring in a genetic cross.

62. Law of dominance was based on monohybrid cross.

63. Type of zygotes = $(\text{gametes})^2$
No of gametes = 2^n, n = 1
= $2^1 = 2$
Type of zygotes = $(2)^2 = 4$

64. All of the given statements are correct

65. Option (b) is correct.

66. Quantitative analysis of data

67. Mendel was the first to apply statistical analysis and mathematical logic.

68. Option (d) is correct.

69. Only (ii) is correct. Dominance is not an autonomous feature of a gene or the product that it has information for. It depends as much on the gene product and the production of a particular phenotype from this product as it does on the particular phenotype that we choose to examine, in case more than one phonotype is influenced by the same gene.

70. Option (d) is correct.

71. Allelomorphic pair implies a part of contrasting traits.

72. Punnett square

73. Pod symmetry

74. AABb genotype is heterozygous.

Explanation of Concept of Dominance, Incomplete and Codominance, Multiple Alleles, Pleiotropy, Test Cross, Lethal Gene, Inheritance of Two Genes, Law of Independent Assortment

75. In incomplete dominance, none of the contrasting alleles of the same gene is dominant. It means that the two alleles of a pair are not related as dominant and recessive. But both the alleles in a heterozygous condition have reduced expression, so that each of them expresses itself partially.

76. Starch synthesis is pea seeds shows incomplete dominance. The gene for starch synthesis has two alleles, B and b. Starch synthesis in BB (homozygous) is efficient and therefore large starch grains are produced. bb (homozygous) starch synthesis is less efficient, so that it produces small starch grains. In Bb (heterozygous) condition, the starch grains are of intermediate size.

77. If F_1 phenotype resembles both parents, it is an exception to the law of dominance.

78. Flower colour in snapdragon shows incomplete dominance, in which the F_1 individuals do not resemble either of their parents.

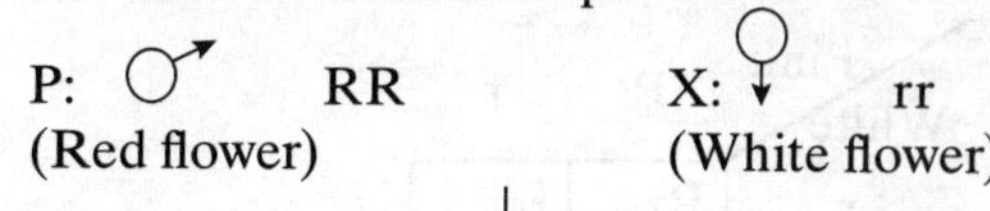

P: ♂ RR X: ♀ rr
(Red flower) (White flower)

↓

F_1: Rr
(pink flower)

F_2:

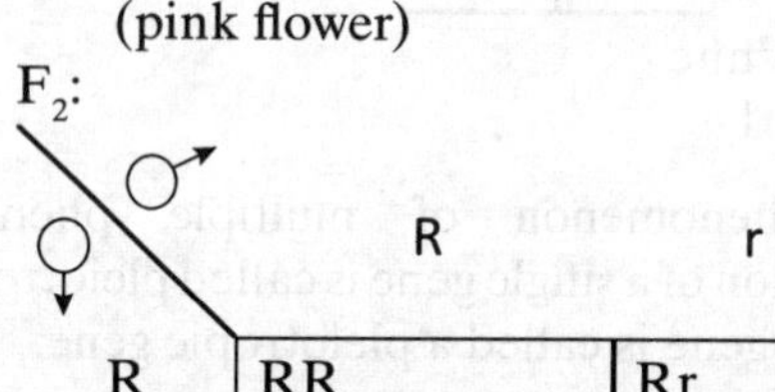

	R	r
R	RR (Red)	Rr (Pink)
r	Rr (Pink)	rr (White)

Phenotypic ratio	Red:	Pink:	White
	1:	2:	1
Genotypic ratio:	RR	Rr	rr
	1:	2:	1

79. 1:2:1

80. The modified allele is equivalent to the unmodified allele when it produces a normal enzyme; it will produce the same phenotype/trait and result in the transformation of substrate S.

81. The unmodified allele (functioning allele), which represents the original phenotype, is the dominant allele and the modified allele is generally recessive.

82. (B) is false. Recessive alleles express themselves only in heterozygous condition.

83. Flower colour in snapdragon shows incomplete dominance.

84. ABO blood group produces:
- Four phenotypes (A, B, AB, O)
- Six genotypes (I^aI^a, I^aI^o, I^bI^b, I^bI^o, I^aI^b, I^oI^o)

85. No. of genotypes $= \frac{n}{2}(n+1)$

n = No. of multiple alleles
n = 5 (given)
No. of genotypes $= \frac{5}{2}(5+1) = 15$

86. Multiple allelism and codominance

87. O blood group

88. Similar phenotype and genotype ratios are obtained in the F_2 generation in the case of incomplete dominance and codominance.

89.

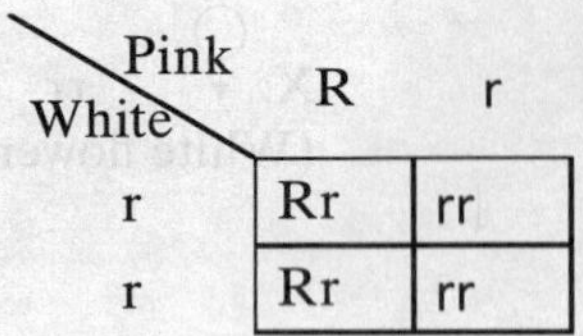

Pink : White
1 : 1

90. The phenomenon of multiple phenotype expression of a single gene is called pleiotropism, and the gene is called a pleiotropic gene.

91. Carl Correns reported incomplete dominance in the case of the 4 o'clock plant (*Mirabilis jalapa*).

92. Incomplete dominance

93. Both the alleles express equally in the case of codominance. The alleles for blood group A (I^a) and B (I^b) are codominant when they come together in an individual. They express and produce blood group AB.

94. Dihybrid cross

95. Out cross (Aa X AA)

96. Two true breeding (homozygous) plant varieties

97. Option (b) is correct.

98. Test cross (Tt X tt) helps to find out the genotype of a dominant individual, whether it is homozygous or heterozygous for that character.

99.

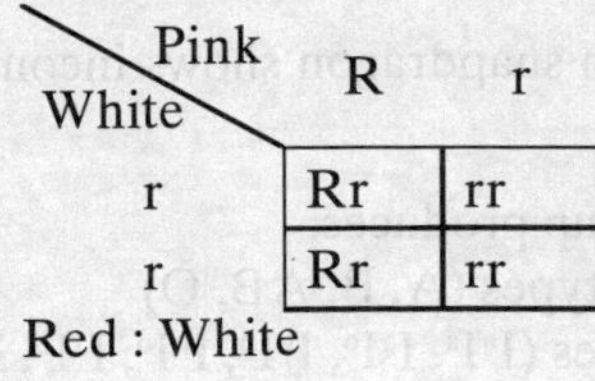

Red : White
1 : 1

100. In the given cross TtRr X TtRr, probability of dwarf plant with violet flowers $= \frac{1}{4} \times \frac{3}{4} = \frac{3}{16}$.

101. In a typical dihybrid cross, the probability of getting seeds with double heterozygous character is:

$$AaBb = \frac{1}{4} \times \frac{1}{4} = \frac{2}{16}$$

Total number of seeds = 640

Seeds with genotype AaBb $= \frac{2}{16} \times 640 = 80$

102. Total number of seeds = 2000

Plants with genotype ttWw $= \frac{1}{4} \times \frac{2}{4} = \frac{2}{16}$
$= \frac{2}{16} \times 2000$
$= 250$

103. Option (b) is correct.

104. The genotype of blood group AB is I^aI^b.

105. Phenotypic ratio of Mendelian dihybrid cross is 9:3:3:1.

106. AB and O

107. When I^a and I^b are present together, they both express their own types of sugars. This is because of codominance.

108. For ABO blood group, Gene = 1, Allele = 3, Phenotype = 4 and Genotype = 6.

109. Phenotypic ratio in F_2 generation: $3:1 \times 1:2:1 = 3:6:3:1:2:1$.

110. In a typical dihybrid cross, the proportion of homozygous dominant progeny (AABB) $= \frac{1}{16}$

111. Independent assortment

112. $I^aI^o \times I^bI^b$

113. All are correct except (C).

114. In the case of flower colour in snapdragon

For F_2
Rr × Rr

Pink \ Pink	R	r
R	RR	Rr
r	Rr	rr

Homozygous = 2

Heterozygous = 2
Ratio = 1 : 1

115. Duplicate gene

116. Recessive trait is seen due to non-functional enzyme, or no enzyme is produced.

117. Given genotype AABbc
No of heterozygous (n) = 2
Type of gametes = $2^n = 2^2 = 4$
Types of phenotypes = $2^n = 2^2 = 4$
Type of genotypes = $3^n = 3^2 = 9$

118. Parental combination of characters $\frac{10}{16}$

119. In test cross, number of possible genotype or phenotypes = 2^n
For dihybrid cross, n = 2
No of genotypes/phenotypes = $2^2 = 4$

120. Option (b) is correct.

121. (a), (b) and (c) are correct.

122. Probability of getting

$$RrYY = \frac{2}{4}\times\frac{1}{4}=\frac{2}{16}$$

$$RrYy = \frac{2}{4}\times\frac{2}{4}=\frac{4}{16}$$

$$rrYy = \frac{1}{4}\times\frac{2}{4}=\frac{2}{16}$$

123. Blood group 'O' has no antigen, but anti-A and anti-B antibodies are present in plasma.

124. Single heterozygous are Aabb, AaBB, aaBb, AABb

$$Aabb = \frac{2}{4}\times\frac{1}{4}=\frac{2}{16}$$

$$AaBB = \frac{2}{4}\times\frac{1}{4}=\frac{2}{16}$$

$$aaBb = \frac{1}{4}\times\frac{2}{4}=\frac{2}{16}$$

$$AABb = \frac{1}{4}\times\frac{2}{4}=\frac{2}{16}$$

$$Total = \frac{8}{16}$$

125. Given genotype AaBbCc
Probability of gametes having all the dominant alleles, ABC $=\frac{1}{2}\times\frac{1}{2}\times\frac{1}{2}=\frac{1}{8}=12.5\%$.

126. $AaBb = \frac{2}{4}\times\frac{2}{2}=\frac{4}{16}$

127. 4th statement is incorrect.

128. 2^9 ways

129. The ability of a single gene to have multiple phenotypic effect is called pleiotropy.

130. All the genes present in an organis are not useful, but some of them show harmful effects and some may cause death or lethality. Lethal genes were first reported by L Cuenot in rats.

131. Genotypic ratio of dihybrid cross is 1:2:1:2:4:2:1:2:1.

132. Gene controlling starch synthesis in garden pea shows incomplete dominance and pleiotropy.

133. Option (d) is correct.

134. If a modified allele is equivalent to an unmodified allele, it will result in transformation of the substrate (s). So, it will produce the same phenotype or trait.

135. Pleiotropic gene

Complementary Genes, Duplicate Genes, Epistasis, Polygenic Inheritance

136. Complementary genes are two non-allelic, dominant genes which independently show a similar effect, but when they are present together, a new trait is obtained. Here, the 9:3:3:1 ratio is modified into a 9:7 ratio.

137. Epistatic gene

138. Bateson and Punnett observed that in the sweet pea, the purple colour of flowers developed as a result of interaction of two dominant, non-allelic genes, C and P.

139. Quantitative inheritance

140. Epistasis is due to interaction of two non-allelic genes.

141. In recessive epistasis, the recessive allele in the homozygous condition suppress the expression of the dominant allele at another locus. For example, coat colour in mice.

142. Duplicate genes

143. Recessive epistasis

144. CcPp x ccpp
Purple colour

$$C\_P\_ = \frac{1}{2} \times \frac{1}{2} = \frac{1}{4} = 25\%$$

145. Fruit colour in summer squash shows dominant epistasis.

146. Complementary genes

147. In the case of polygenic inheritance
No of phenotypes = (2n + 1) = $(2\times3+1) = 7$
No of genotypes = $3^n = 3^3 = 27$
(n = 3)
Total = 7 + 27 = 34

148. Kernel colour of wheat is controlled by two pairs of polygenes.

149. In the case of polygenic inheritance, the dominant alleles have a cumulative effect of a functional polypeptide, and a full trait is shown when all the dominant alleles are present (AABBCC).

150. $\frac{1}{64}$

151. Only one statement (iii) is correct. In the F_1 generation, pure breeding parents do not produce the dominant trait of one parent, instead an intermediate trait is obtained. So, polygenic inheritance is also called blending inheritance.

152. Number of genotypes = 3^n
$\therefore 3^5 = 3\times3\times3\times3\times3$
$= 243$

153. Polygenic traits are continuous.

154. Complementary genes: 9 : 7, Duplicate genes: 15 : 1, Dominant epistasis: 12:3:1, Recessive epistasis: 9:3:4.

155. Option (c) is correct.

156. Very dark skin colour AABBCC, Intermediate skin colour AaBbCc

157. Recessive epistasis

158. Polygenic inheritance

159. Human skin colour is determined by three pairs of genes.

160. CCpp – white, CcPP – purple, ccPP – white

161. Kernel colour in wheat is determined by two pairs of genes.

162. 1:4:6:4:1

163. Mulatto man × African woman
AaBbCc AABBCC
F_1

	ABC	ABc	AbC	Abc	aBC	aBc	abC	abc
ABC	AABBCC	AABBCc	AABbCC	AABbCc	AaBBCC	AaBBCc	AaBbCC	AaBbCc

Very dark (AABBCC) = $\frac{1}{8}$

164. 1:6:15:20:15:6:1

165. The F_1 progeny between an albino and an African individual, called mulatto, produces intermediate skin colour.

166. Mulatto (20/64)

167. For human skin colour (determined by three pairs of genes), number of phonotypes = 7 and number of genotypes = 27.

168. Phenotype of an organism is the result of genotype and environmental interaction.

169. aabbcc

170. Height due to a dominant polygene (A/B/C)

$$= \frac{\text{Maximum given height}}{\text{Total number of polygenes}} = \frac{24}{6}$$
$$= 4 \text{ feet}$$

Height due to a recessive polygene (a/b/c)

$$= \frac{\text{Minimum given height}}{\text{Total number of polygenes}} = \frac{12}{6} = 2 \text{ feet}$$

Height of the plant with the genotype

$$\text{AaBbcc} = 4+2+4+2+2+2$$
$$= 16 \text{ feet}$$

171. Ccpp × ccPp

	Cp	cp
cP	CcPp	ccPp
cp	Ccpp	ccpp

Coloured : Colourless
1 : 3

172. 1 : 1

173. No. of polygenes = 2
Phenotypic ratio = 1:4:6:4:1
Intermediates $= \frac{14}{16}$

174. No. of polygenes = 3
Phenotypic ratio = 1:6:15:20:15:6:1
Parental types $= \frac{2}{64} \approx$ less than 5%

Chromosomal Theory of Inheritance, Linkage, Recombination, Sex Determination

175. Sutton and Boveri

176. Both chromosomes and genes occur in pairs in somatic or diploid cells.

177. Sutton and Boveri

178. 1902

179. TH Morgan is popularly known as the Father of Experimental Genetics.

180. Option (d) is correct.

181. *Drosophila* could be grown on simple synthetic medium in the laboratory, females are easily distinguishable from males by larger body size and it has four pairs of morphologically distinct chromosomes.

182. Both statements are correct.

183. Law of segregation and law of independent assortment

184. Morgan

185. *Drosophila* has four pairs of morphologically distinct chromosomes.

186. (B) and (C) are false. Distance between the two genes is directly proportional to crossing over.

187. Anaphase I

188. For genes, one pair segregates independently of another pair.

189. The distance between two linked genes is 3 map units. ∴ Frequency of crossing over is 3%. ∴ Parental combinations = 97%.

190. Frequency of crossing over is 10%. ∴ The distance between gene A and gene B is 10 cm.

191. Linked genes are present on the same chromosome in linear sequence and the strength of linkage between two genes is inversely proportional to the distance between them. Linked genes cannot assort independently, rather they tends to be inherited together.

192. Recombination frequency
$$= \frac{\text{Total no of recombinations}}{\text{Total progeny}} \times 100$$

193. Recombination

194. Option (b) is correct.

195. A – tightly B – very few

196. Frequency of crossing over
$$= \frac{\text{Total no of recombinants}}{\text{Total progeny}} \times 100$$
∴ Distance between gene a and b is 10 cm.

197. Recombination frequency is always ≤ 50%.

198. Complete linked genes are present very close together on the chromosome. Crossing over is absent, so they always show parental combination. They never form new combinations. Complete linkage is very rare in nature. For example, male *Drosophila*, female silk moth.

199. Option (b) is correct.

200. Genes are incompletely linked because completely linked genes always show parental combination.

201. In *Drosophila*, the gene for eye colour is located on the X chromosome. So it is a sex-linked trait.

202. Recombination frequency $= \frac{50}{500} \times 100$

203. Genes for white eye and miniature wings are loosely linked as they showed 37.2% recombination. Hence, 62.8% of parental type of progeny were obtained the in F_2 generation.

204. Option (d) is correct.

205. Butterflies shows ZO-ZZ type sex determination, where O determines femaleness.

206. In birds (ZZ-ZW type), females are heterogametic and produce two types of gametes, (A + Z) and (A + W), while males produce only one type of gamete, (A + Z).

207. In the honeybee, an unfertilised egg develops as a male (drone) by means of parthenogenesis.

208. In the grasshopper, the number of chromosomes is different in male and female individuals. All eggs bear an additional X chromosome, besides the autosomes, while 50% of sperms bear an X chromosome.

209. In human beings, sex is determined at the time of fertilisation.

210. Grasshopper shows XX-XO type of sex determination.

211. Option (d) is correct.

212. In the honeybee, female flies are diploid while male flies are haploid. This mechanism of sex determination is called arrhenotoky or haploid-diploid mechanism.

213. The term X chromosome was given by Wilson.

214. In *Drosophila*, the male contains two heteromorphic sex chromosomes, X and Y.

215. Option (d) is correct.

216. Butterflies shows ZZ-ZO type of sex determination, where O determines femaleness. The females are heterogametic, they produce two types of eggs, (A + Z) and (A + O). Males are homogametic and form a similar type of sperm, (A + Z).

217. (AA + XX)

218. Grasshopper

219. In human beings, all the ova formed by females are similar in their chromosome type (22 + X).

220. A – Mitosis; B – 16

221. Probability of three sons to a couple is $=\frac{1}{2}\times\frac{1}{2}\times\frac{1}{2}=\frac{1}{8}$

222. The given diagram is of a male bird which has a homomorphic sex chromosome (AA + ZZ).

223. Henking first observed the sex chromosome in the form of the X body.

224. Option (c) is correct.

225. Inactivation of one X chromosome in a human female forms the Barr body. Lyon suggested that one X chromosome from the maternal side becomes coiled, inert and heteropycnotic and forms a Barr body.

226. Sturtevant

227. In prokaryotes, only one linkage group is present.

228. Option (c) is correct.

229. Option (c) is correct.

230. Option (a) is correct.

231. Linkages are exceptions to Mendel's independent law of assortment.

232. All the given statements are correct.

233. Option (d) is correct.

234. Crossing over

235. Option (d) is correct.

236. Red eye colour of *Drosophila* is a dominant trait and the determining gene is present on the X chromosome.

237. Allosome

238. Completely linked genes do not show independent assortment. Their dihybrid test cross ratio is 1 : 1.

239. Frequency of crossing over $=\frac{220}{2000}\times 100=11\%$.

$\therefore$ Distance between c and d is 11 map units.

240. Only (A) is correct. Strength of linkage is inversely proportional to the distance between linked genes.

241. Sex-influence traits are autosomal and influenced by the sex of the bearer. These traits appear more frequently in one sex than in the other. For example, pattern boaldness (affected by male sex hormone/testosterone).

242. Haploid set of chromosomes is called genome. Thus, our genome is made up of 23 chromosomes.

243. Option (c) is correct.

244. Linkage group in human male = 24 (XY chromosome), human female = 23.

245. Sex-linked traits are autosomal and found in both sexes, but expressed in one sex only.

246. Hemizygous condition (XY) in human male

247. Sex-limited traits.

248. Hypertrichosis is a Y-linked trait and inherited from male to male only. Haemophilia and colour blindness show criss-cross inheritance.

249. Refer answer to Q248.

250. Genes for white eye and yellow body are very tightly linked and produce 1.3% recombinant types.

251. Dihybrid test cross ratio is 1:1:1:1 (50% parental and 50% recombinant)

252. Option (b) is correct.

253. Option (c) is correct.

254. Number of linkage groups in an organism = Haploid number of chromosomes.

255. Crossing over occurs at tetrad stage of Pachytene in Prophase I.

256. In *Drosophila*, males do not have a father and thus cannot have sons, but they have grandfathers and can have grandsons.

257. In *Drosophila*, females are larger than males.

258. Johannsen coined the term gene for Mendelian factor.

259. Anaphase I

260. A – G_2 phase, B – Anaphase, C – Anaphase II

Gene Mutation, Chromosomal Aberration, Genomatic Mutation, Pedigree Analysis, Genetic Disorders, Mendelian and Chromosomal Disorders, Cytoplasmic Inheritance

261. Sudden heritable change in the genetic material of an organism is called mutation. Mutations are a discontinuous source of variations.

262. Option (b) is correct.

263. The change in chromosome morphology is called chromosomal aberration.

264. Chromosomal aberrations are observed in cancer cells.

265. If gene mutations arise due to change in a single base pair of DNA, it is called point mutation.

266. Substitution of a small part of a chromosome by a part of a different chromosome is called translocation (chromosomal aberration).

267. Transition mutation occurs when a purine base (A or G) is replaced by another purine base or a pyrimidine base (T or C) is substituted by another pyrimidine base.

268. A classical example of point mutation is sickle-cell anaemia.

269. Option (c) is correct.

270. Transition mutation

271. Removal of one or more bases from a nucleotide chain results in frame shift mutation.

272. Transversion mutation is substitution of a purine base with a pyrimidine base, or vice versa.

273. Transition mutation

274. Option (d) is correct.

275. Transversion (substitution of purine by pyrimide)

276. Nullisomy

277. Down's syndrome develops due to trisomy of chromosome 21.

278. Myotonic dystrophy is an autosomal dominant genetic disorder.

279. CML occurs due to translocation of a segment of the long arm from chromosome 22 to chromosome 9.

280. Thymine dimer formation is a major mutagenic effect of UV rays that disturbs the DNA double-helix, and thus, DNA replication.

281. Ionizing radiation (X-rays, γ rays, α-rays, β rays) cause breaks in the chromosome.

282. Mutant β haemoglobin chain forms sickle-cell shaped RBCs.

283.

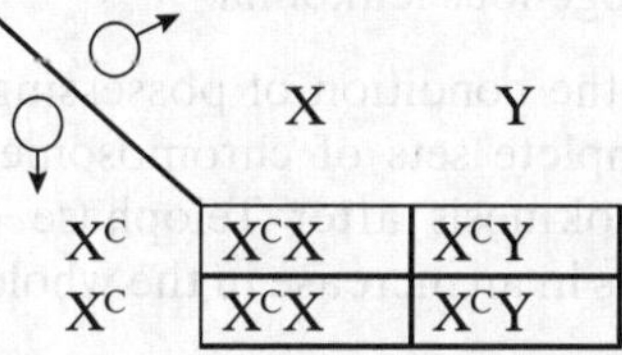

Colour-blind children $\frac{2}{4}$. 50% chances of their children being colour-blind.

284. All statements are correct.

285. Number of possible trisomics in an organism = Haploid number of chromosomes.

286. Down's syndrome (2n + 1) = 47; Turner's syndrome (2n - 1) = 45

287. In human beings, Down's syndrome is due to trisomy of chromosome 21, Edward's syndrome is due to trisomy of chromosome 18 and Patau's syndrome is due to trisomy of chromosome 14.

288. XY

289. Chromosomes in haploid set = 50, Chromosomes in monoploid set = 25

290. Option (d) is correct.

291. Trisomy = (2n + 1), Tetrasomy = (2n + 2), Monosomy = (2n – 1), Double trisomy = (2n + 1 + 1)

292. Karyotype of Klinefelter individuals represents 47; XXY
No. of Barr bodies = Total chromosomes = 1 = (2 – 1) = 1

293.

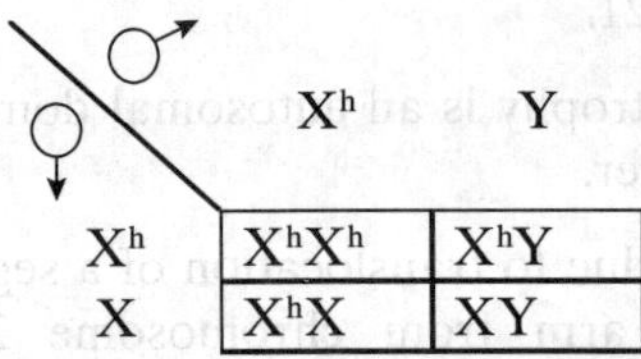

50% of sons will be haemophilic.

294. Option (a) is correct.

295. Wheat plant (*Triticum aestivum*) is hexaploid (6N = 42).

296. Haemophilia is an X-linked recessive disorder.

297. Option (b) is correct.

298. Monozygotic twins

299. Chronic myelogenous leukemia

300. Polyploidy is the condition of possessing more than two complete sets of chromosomes. The failure of cytokinesis after Telophase of cell division results in an increase in the whole set of chromosomes.

301. A women whose father was haemophilic means she is a carrier. A man whose father was haemophilic means he is normal, because haemophilia is an X-linked recessive disorder.

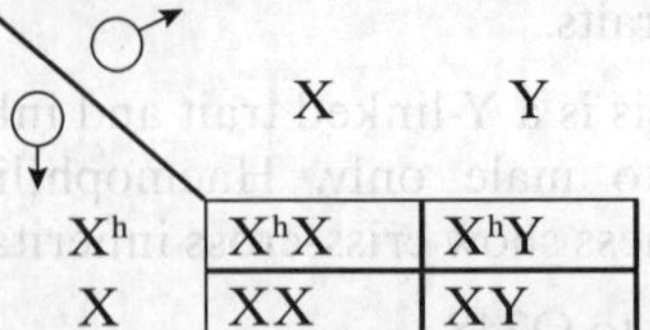

The probability of haemophilic son would be 50%.

302. Factor IX (plasma thromboplastin)

303. Burkitt lymphoma occurs due to translocation between chromosomes 14 and 8.

304. Base substitution

305. Only one allele for each gene

306. Myotonic dystrophy

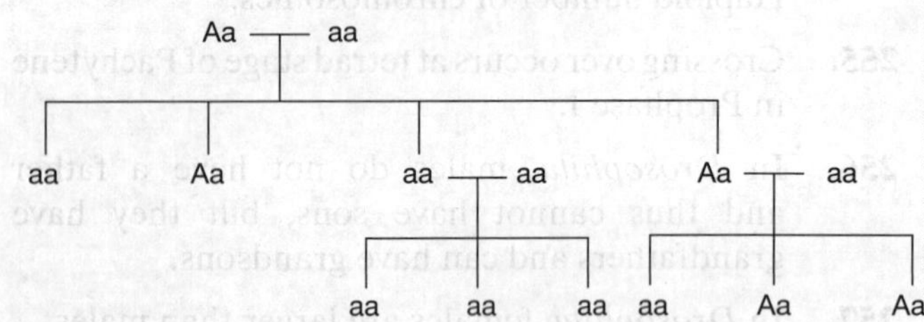

307. Cytoplasmic male sterility in maize is due to defective mitochondria.

308.

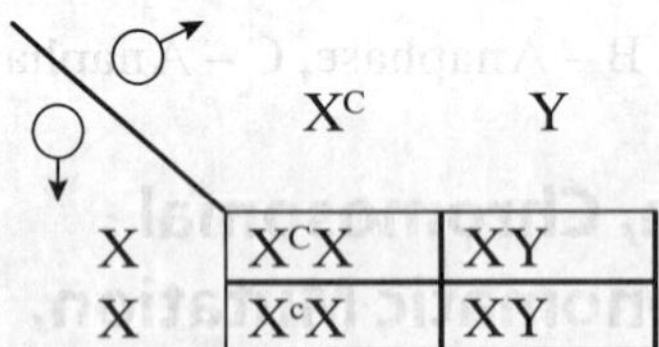

Probability of getting colour-blind sons = 0

309. Option (a) is correct.

310. In a population, about 8% of males and 0.4% of females are colour-blind.

311. Thalassemia is a recessive autosomal disorder caused by defects in the synthesis of globin polypeptide in RBC that makes up haemoglobin.

312. Gynaecomastia (breast development in male)

313. Option (c) is correct.

314. Albinism (autosomal recessive disorder)

315. Phenylketonuria is an inborn error of metabolism and is inherited as an autosomal recessive trait. The affected individual lacks an enzyme called phenylalanine hydroxylase that converts the amino acid phenylalanine into tyrosine in the liver.

316. PKU

317. Klinefelter syndrome

318. A – Translocation, B – Crossing over

319. X-linked recessive disorders show transmission from male to female progeny only.

320. (b), (c) and (d) are correct.

321. For Klinefelter syndrome, only (a) is correct.

322. Autosomal recessive trait

323.

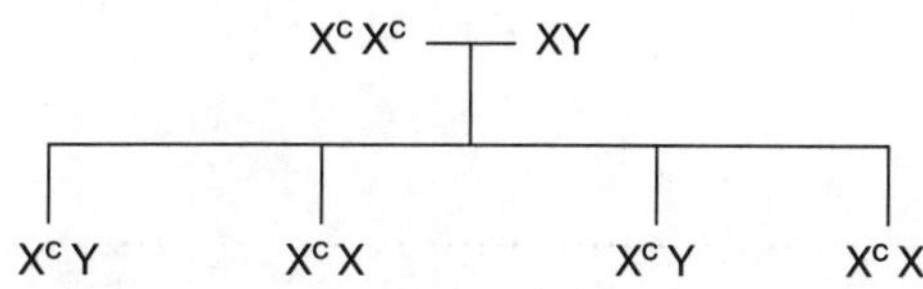

324. Cytoplasmic inheritance

325.

	X^c	Y
X^h	X^cX^h	X^hY
X	X^cX	XY

(b) and (c) are correct.

326. Autosomal recessive trait

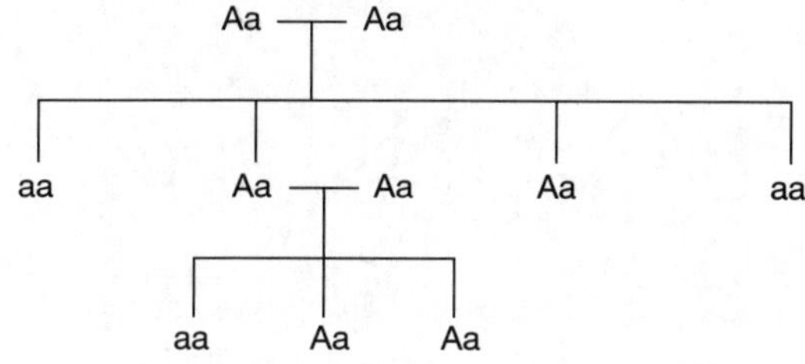

327. Autosomal dominant disorder because it displays vertical pattern in pedigree chart.

328. Phenylketonuria is a gene-related disorder.

329. Turner's syndrome occurs due to monosomy of the X-chromosome in human females.

330. Sex of the individual is masculine but possesses feminine characters.

331. Gene-related disorders (thalassemia, colour blindness, haemophilia, myotonic dystrophy, cystic fibrosis) can be studied by pedigree chart.

332. In thalassemia, the affected chromosome may be 16 (in α thalassemia) or 11 (in β thalassemia).

333. Klinefelter syndrome is characterised by the presence of Barr body in human males.

334. Plasmon

335. Kappa particles

336. Barr body

337. In sickle-cell anaemia, the 6th amino acid of the β chain of haemoglobin, glutamic acid, is replaced by valine.

338. Both mother and father are heterozygous (Aa).

339. Two statements (i, iv) are correct about thalassemia (quantitative problem of haemoglobin).

340. Haemophilia is an X-linked recessive genetic disorder.

341. Only (A) and (B) are correct.

342. X-linked dominant disorder

343. (a) and (b) are correct.

344. (a) is not true for Down's syndrome.

345. Probability of sperm to carry abcs condition $= \frac{1}{2} \times \frac{1}{2} \times 1 \times \frac{1}{2} = \frac{1}{8}$.

346. Option (d) is correct.

347. 19, 21, 22

348. Pedigree chart

349. Colour blindness appears more in males than in females because males are hemizygous (XY).

350. Thalassemia is a quantitative problem of synthesizing too few globin molecules.

351. Option (d) is correct.

352. Turner's syndrome is caused due to absence of one of the X chromosomes, 45; XO.

353. Option (d) is correct.

354. Barr bodies are present in somatic cells of females.

355. Option (d) is correct.

356. Colour blindness results in defect in either red or/and green cone of the eye, leading to failure to discriminate between red and green colours.

357. n =21, x = 7

358. 25% risk of inheriting the genetic disorder

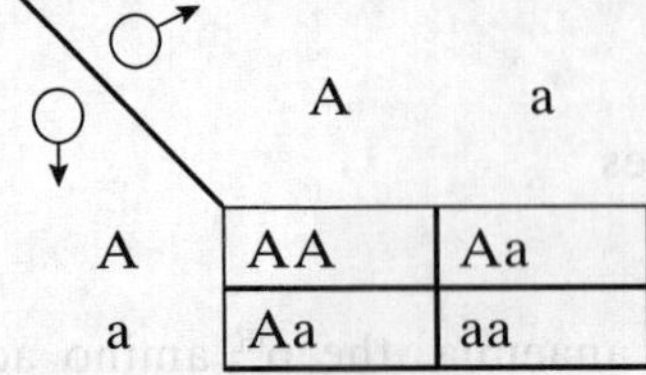

359. Both parents are heterozygous for albinism.

360. Option (b) is correct.

361. β thalassemia is controlled by a single gene, HBB, on chromosome 11 of each parent and occurs due to mutation of one or both the genes.

362.

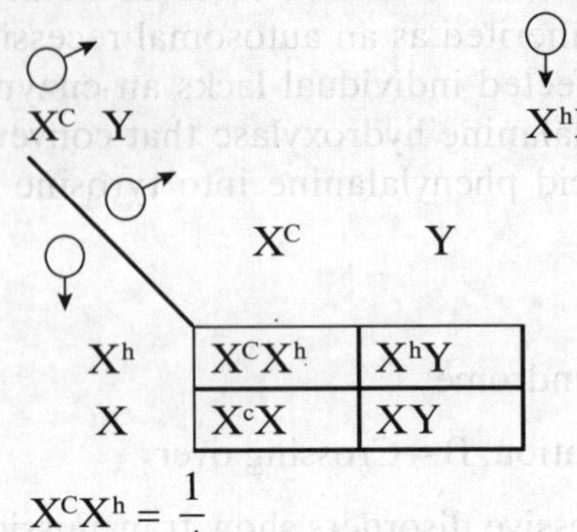

$X^CX^h = \dfrac{1}{4}$

363. Myotonic dystrophy is an autosomal dominant disorder.

364. Alpha thalassemia is controlled by two genes, HBA 1 and HBA 2, located on chromosome 16.

Molecular Basis of Inheritance

EXERCISES

DNA, Structure of Polynucleotide Chain, Packaging of DNA Helix

1. Select the mismatched pair:
(a) ϕX174 bacteriophage – 5386 bases
(b) λ phase – 48502 bp
(c) *E. coli* – 4.6×10^6 bp
(d) Human genome – 6.6×10^9 bp

2. DNA as an acidic substance present in the nucleus was first identified by:
(a) Crick (b) Friedrich Miescher
(c) Watson (d) Both (a) and (c)

3. In 1868, DNA was discovered by the Swedish biochemist:
(a) R Feulgen (b) H Mosely
(c) Miescher (d) Watson and Crick

4. Length of DNA usually depends on:
(a) Position of nucleotides
(b) Number of nucleotides
(c) Orientation of nucleotides
(d) All of the above

5. Who gave the concept that for a double-stranded DNA, the ratios between A = T and C = G are equal and constant?
(a) Chargaff (b) Watson and Crick
(c) Wilkins (d) Franklin

6. Which of the given propositions based on the observation of Ervin Chargaff is correct for a double-stranded DNA?
(a) $A+G=T+C$ (b) $\frac{A+T}{G+C}=1$
(c) $\frac{A+C}{G+T}=>1$ (d) $A=C$

7. Number of thymine bases in DNA is equal to:
(a) Guanine (b) Cytosine
(c) Uracil (d) Adenine

8. In the ribose of RNA, unlike DNA, every nucleotide residue has an additional:
(a) Uracil in the 5th position
(b) OH group at the 5th position
(c) OH group at the 2nd position
(d) COOH group at the 2nd position

9. Two nucleotides in a polynucleotide chain are linked by:
(a) Hydrogen bonds
(b) Glyosidic bonds
(c) Phosphodiester bonds
(d) Peptide bonds

10. In a DNA sample, cytosine was found to be 18%. What would be the percentage of the other bases in the sample?

	G	T	A
(a)	18%	32%	32%
(b)	18%	18%	32%
(c)	32%	18%	32%
(d)	32%	32%	18%

11. A nitrogenous base is linked to a pentose sugar through:
(a) N-glycosidic linkage
(b) Hydrogen bond
(c) Peptide bond
(d) Phosphodiester linkage

12. The 5′ end of a polynucleotide chain contains:
(a) Hydroxyl group (b) Methyl group
(c) Carboxyl group (d) Phosphate group

13. The two strands of DNA are held together by:
(a) Peptide bond (b) Sulphide bond
(c) Hydrogen bond (d) Phosphodiester bond

14. DNA is acidic due to:
(a) Sugar (b) Purine
(c) Pyrimidine (d) Phosphoric acid

15. Variable part of DNA molecule is:
(a) Phosphate (b) Sugar
(c) Nitrogen base (d) All of the above

16. A genophore is made up of:
(a) Single ds-circular DNA + Histone protein
(b) Single ds-linear DNA + Non-histone proteins
(c) Single ds circular DNA only
(d) Single ds circular DNA + Non-histone proteins

17. Which is not a part of the histone core in the nucleosome?
(a) H_1 (b) H_2A
(c) H_2B (d) H_4

18. The figure represents the DNA double-helix model proposed by Watson and Crick. Select the option that represents the correct measurement of A, B and C marked in the figure:

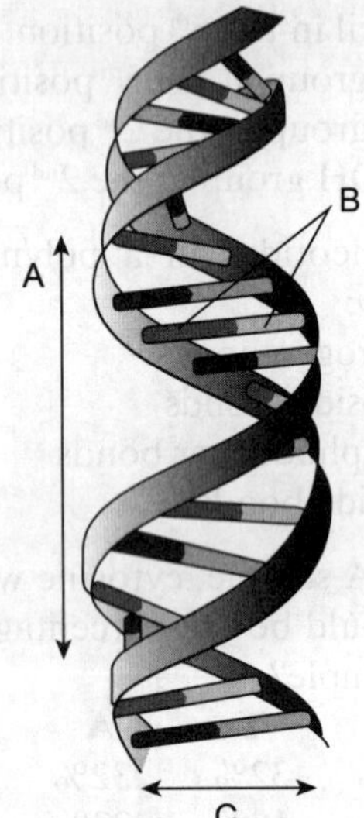

	A	B	C
(a)	3.4 nm	0.34 nm	2 nm
(b)	34 nm	3.4 nm	20 nm
(c)	3.4 Å	0.34 Å	2 Å
(d)	3.4 Å	0.34 Å	20 Å

19. Which of the following is not uniform in all DNA molecules?
(a) The pairing of adenine with thymine and cytosine with guanine
(b) The arrangement of the sugar phosphate group
(c) The sequence of nitrogenous base on a strand of DNA
(d) The pattern of the helix structure

20. How many phosphodiester bonds are present in a polynucleotide chain having 100 nucleotides?
(a) 100 (b) 99
(c) 50 (d) 48

21. In bacteria, DNA in the nucleoid is organised in large loops by:
(a) Acidic proteins
(b) Histone proteins
(c) Negative charged proteins
(d) Positive charged proteins

22. In the structure of a nucleosome given below, what does A, B and C represent, respectively?

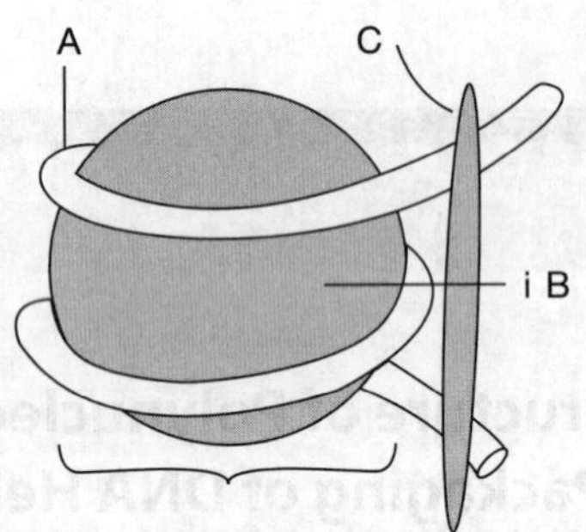

	A	B	C
(a)	DNA	Histone octamer	H_1 histone
(b)	DNA	Histone octamer	Linker DNA
(c)	Linker DNA	Nu-body	RNA
(d)	RNA	H_1 histone protein	DNA

23. Negatively charged DNA is wrapped around the positively charged histone octamer in all, except:
(a) *Drosophila* (b) Yeast
(c) *Pneumococcus* (d) *Pisum*

24. Which of the following structures is present in the core portion of the nucleosome?
(a) Octamer of histone protein
(b) H_1 histone protein
(c) Linker DNA
(d) All of the above

25. How many phosphodiester bonds and N-glycosidic linkages are present in a DNA molecule if one strand has 50 nucleotides?
(a) 98, 98 (b) 98, 100
(c) 49, 49 (d) 49, 50

26. Length of DNA with 23 base pairs is:
(a) 78.4 Å (b) 78.2 Å
(c) 78 Å (d) 74.8 Å

27. Eleven base pairs per turn are generally present in ______ DNA:
(a) B-DNA (b) C-DNA
(c) Z-DNA (d) A-DNA

28. If a DNA molecule is 200 bp long, how many phosphate molecules and N-glycosidic linkages are present?
(a) 400, 400 (b) 200, 200
(c) 200, 400 (d) 400, 200

29. Which of the following confers a very stable property to the DNA?
(a) Base pairing
(b) Glycosidic bonds
(c) Acidic nature
(d) Phosphodiester linkage

30. How many nucleotides are found in a typical nucleosome?
(a) 80 (b) 160
(c) 400 (d) 200

31. The packaging of chromatin at higher level requires an additional set of proteins that collectively are referred to as:
(a) Polyamines
(b) Non-histone proteins
(c) Non-histone chromosomal proteins
(d) Histone chromosomal protein

32. Heterochromatin:
A. Is densely packed
B. Is lightly stained
C. Is transcriptionally inactive
D. Is loosely packed
(a) (A) and (B) (b) (A) and (C)
(c) (C) and (D) (d) (B) and (C)

33. If the length of DNA is 2.2 in a human diploid cell, calculate the number of bp in the DNA:
(a) 6.6×10^9 (b) 4.6×10^6
(c) 46×10^6 (d) 3.3×10^9

34. Fill in the blanks with the correct answer and select the option accordingly:
A. Histones are organised to form a unit of eight molecules called ________.
B. ________ constitute the repeating unit of a structure in the nucleus called chromatin.
C. The chromatin that is loosely packed and stains light is called ________.

	A	B	C
(a)	Nucleosome	Nucleoid	Euchromatin
(b)	Histone octamer	Nucleoid	Heterochromatin
(c)	Histone octamer	Nucleosome	Euchromatin
(d)	Nu body	Nucleosome	Heterochromatin

35. The DNA in the nucleoid:
(a) Is organised into large loops held by proteins
(b) Has a positive charge
(c) Has an abundance of basic histone proteins
(d) Shows a beads-on-string structure

36. A typical nucleosome contains ________ of DNA helix:
(a) 200 bases (b) 200 bp
(c) 200 nucelotides (d) 80 bp

37. The two other investigators associated with James D Watson and Francis Crick, who performed X-ray crystallography of DNA, were:
(a) Chargaff and Lever
(b) Avery and Macleod
(c) Wilkins and Franklin
(d) Meselson and Stahl

38. The DNA double-helix model proposed by Watson and Crick was published in the journal *Nature* in the year:
(a) 1963 (b) 1953
(c) 1968 (d) 1853

39. For their work on the DNA structure, Watson and Crick, along with ________, received the Nobel Prize (Medicine and Physiology) in 1962:
(a) Wilkins (b) Rosalind E Franklin
(c) Erwin Chargaff (d) Levin

40. In a given polynucleotide chain:

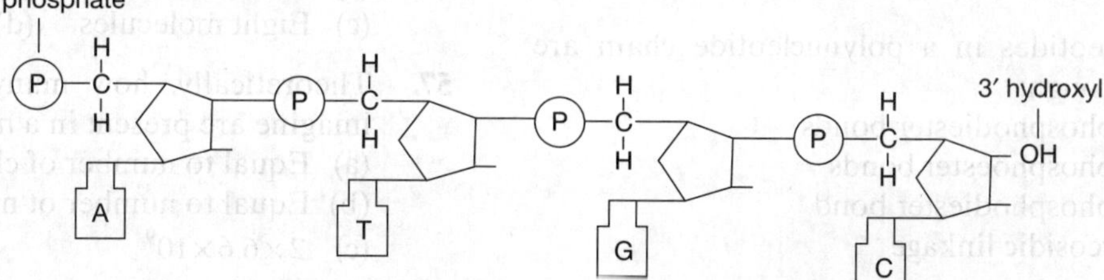

A. The backbone is constituted of sugar phosphate and the base project outside
B. A free phosphate moiety at the 5′ end of sugar
C. Pentose sugar has a free 3′-OH
D. Purine and pyrimidines nucleosides have 1′-1 glycosidic linkage

(a) (B) and (C) only
(b) (A), (B) and (C) only
(c) (B), (C) and (D) only
(d) (A), (B), (C) and (D)

41. Which one of the following DNA molecules will melt at the lowest temperature?
(a) 5′ TGCAGCGGCGATTAG 3′ 3′ ACGTCGCCGCTATTC 5′
(b) 5′ CGCTAGTATTAGGTA 3′3′ GCGATCATAATCCAT 5′
(c) 5′ ATGTAATTGTGATAT 3′ 3′ TAGATTAACACTATA 5′
(d) 5′ ATGCTCGATGCAGCT 3 3′ TACGAGCTACGTCGA 5′

42. Denaturation of DNA after heating can be studied by comparing:
(a) Number of nucleotides
(b) A:T ratio
(c) CG Ratio
(d) Sugar phosphate ratio

43. Melting of DNA at elevated temperature is primarily due to breakdown of:
(a) Phosphodiester bond
(b) Glycosidic bonds
(c) Disulphide
(d) Hydrogen bonds

44. C-value paradox is:
(a) Diploid DNA content
(b) Variation in C-value
(c) Haploid DNA content
(d) Constancy of C-value

45. Maximum number of bonds present in a double-stranded DNA molecule is made up of:
(a) Glycosidic bonds (b) Phosphoester bonds
(c) Hydrogen bonds (d) N-glycosidic linkage

46. In a double-helix structure of DNA:
(a) Backbone is constituted of sugar and phosphate
(b) The pitch of the helix is 34 Å
(c) Approximately uniform distance exists between the two strands
(d) All of the above

47. Two nucleotides in a polynucleotide chain are linked through:
(a) 5′-3′ phosphodiester bonds
(b) 3′-5′ phosphoester bonds
(c) 3′-5′ phosphodiester bond
(d) N-glycosidic linkage

48. Stability of DNA double-helix is due to:
(a) Numerous H bonds present
(b) Plane of one base pair stacking over another
(c) Both (a) and (b)
(d) N-glycosidic linkage

49. The genetic information of DNA is encoded in:
(a) The major grooves
(b) The backbone
(c) N-glycosidic linkage
(d) Sequence of nitrogenous bases

50. In a nucleoside, the nitrogenous base is attached to __________ carbon atoms of ribose sugar:
(a) 2nd (b) 3rd
(c) 5th (d) 1st

51. DNA is a double-helix and:
(a) Complementary and parallel
(b) Complementary and antiparallel
(c) Always circular
(d) Without supercoils

52. The beads-on-string structure seen in a chromosome under the electron microscope are:
(a) Histone octamer (b) Nucleosome
(c) Chromatin (d) Nucleoid

53. Nucleosome contains:
(a) Only DNA
(b) Only histone protein
(c) Double-stranded circular DNA + Histone proteins
(d) Histone octamer + Approximately two rounds of linear DNA

54. Histones are sets of:
(a) Positively charged, acidic proteins
(b) Negatively charged, acidic proteins
(c) Positively charged, basic proteins
(d) Negatively charged, basic proteins

55. Histone proteins are rich in the basic amino acid residues:
(a) Lysines and arginines
(b) Lysine and tryptophan
(c) Tyrosine and tryptophan
(d) Leucine and arginines

56. Histones are organised to form a unit of:
(a) Four molecules (b) Two molecules
(c) Eight molecules (d) Five molecules

57. Theoretically, how many nucleosomes do you imagine are present in a mammalian cell?
(a) Equal to number of chromosomes
(b) Equal to number of nucleotides
(c) $2 \times 6.6 \times 10^9$
(d) Equal to number of base pairs divided by 200

58. Two complementary chains of DNA are:
(a) Parallel
(b) Anti-parallel
(c) At right angles to each other
(d) Turned around forming a left-handed spiral

59. The double-helix of DNA is made up of polynucleotide chains, where the backbone is constituted of sugar phosphate and bases are projected:
(a) Inside
(b) Outside
(c) One base inside and other outside
(d) Bases remain in line of sugar phosphate

60. A stretch of DNA consisting of 10–20 bases is most approximately called:
(a) Nucleotides (b) Nucleosides
(c) Polynucleotides (d) Oligonucleotides

61. Adenylic acid is a/an:
(a) Nucleoside (b) Nucleotide
(c) Amino acid (d) Nitrogen base

62. In DNA, the phosphate group forms a bridge between:
(a) –OH groups of two adjacent sugars
(b) –OH groups of two adjacent bases
(c) –OH group of sugars and base
(d) More than one option is correct

63. DNA duplex shows:
(a) Right-handed coiling and parallel
(b) Right-handed coiling and anti-parallel
(c) Left-handed coiling and anti-parallel
(d) Left-handed coiling and parallel

The Search for Genetic Material (Transforming Principle, The Genetic Material is DNA, Properties of Genetic Material, RNA World)

64. Transformation experiments in bacteria were first performed by:
(a) C Macleod
(b) F Griffith
(c) Meselson and Stahl
(d) Lederberg and Zinder

65. First transformation experiment on bacteria was performed on:
(a) *Escherichia coli*
(b) *Salmonella typhimurium*
(c) *Pasteurella pestis*
(d) *Diplococcus pneumoniae*

66. The biochemical nature of transforming principle was defined by:
(a) Griffith
(b) Miescher
(c) Avery, Macleod, McCarty
(d) Hershey and Chase

67. Avery et al. inhibited bacterial transformation by using the enzyme:
(a) RNase (b) Ligase
(c) DNase (d) Polymerase

68. Prior to the work of Avery, Macleod and McCarty, the genetic material was thought to be a:
(a) Protein (b) DNA
(c) RNA (d) Sugars

69. The debate between proteins versus DNA as the genetic material was resolved from the experiment of:
(a) Frederick Griffith (b) Hershey and Chase
(c) Watson and Crick (d) Meselson and Stahl

70. The unequivocal proof that DNA is genetic material came from the experiment of _________:
(a) Miescher
(b) Hershey and Chase
(c) Griffith
(d) Avery, Macleod, McCarty

71. What was the finding of Hershey and Chase?
(a) The viral inflecting agent is protein
(b) The T_2 bacteriophage has RNA as its genetic material
(c) DNA acts as genetic material
(d) DNA replication is semiconservative

72. Which of the following correctly represents the sequence of events during the Hershey-Chase experiment?
(a) Infection → Blending → Centrifugation
(b) Blending → Infection → Centrifugation
(c) Infection → Centrifugation → Blending
(d) Blending → Centrifugation → Infection

73. Isotopes used in proving that DNA is the genetic material were:
(a) $N^{14}N^{15}$ (b) $S^{35}P^{32}$
(c) $C^{14}O^{18}$ (d) $S^{32}P^{35}$

74. Central Dogma of molecular biology is:
(a) DNA → RNA → Protein
(b) DNA → Protein → RNA
(c) RNA ←DNA → Protein
(d) RNA → DNA → RNA → Protein

75. RNA, being a catalyst, is more reactive and hence unstable because of:
(a) Mutation at faster rate
(b) Presence of 2′ OH of ribose
(c) Presence of uracil
(d) All of the above

76. Which of the following pyrimidine bases confers additional stability to DNA over RNA?

(a) Thymine (b) Uracil
(c) 5-Methyl uracil (d) All except (b)

77. RNA, a polymer of ribonucleotides:
A. Acts as genetic material in plant viruses like TMV
B. May function as catalyst
C. Functions as adapter molecule
D. Is directly involved in protein synthesis
(a) Only (A) and (D)
(b) Only (A) and (B)
(c) (A), (B), (C) and (D)
(d) All except (C)

78. The pyrimidine base that confers additional stability of DNA over RNA is:
(a) Uracil (b) Adenine
(c) Thiamine (d) 5-methyl uracil

79. DNA and RNA differ by:
(a) Nitrogen bases and sugars
(b) Nitrogen bases and phosphate groups
(c) Number of C-atoms in sugars
(d) Sugar and number of phosphate group

80. RNA is genetic material in:
(a) QB bacteriophage (b) ϕX174
(c) Herpes virus (d) M-13 phage

81. The unidirectional flow of information described as "central dogma" of molecular biology was proposed by:
(a) Beadle and Tatum (b) Garrod
(c) FHC Crick (d) Temin and Baltimore

82. DNA acts as a template for the synthesis of:
(a) DNA (b) RNA
(c) Both DNA and RNA(d) Protein

83. Which of the following acts as catalyst in a prokaryotic cell?
(a) Sn RNA (b) 23 S-r RNA
(c) 28SrRNA (d) Both (a) and (b)

84. Read the following statements with respect to the RNA world:
A. DNA is dependent on RNA for synthesis of proteins
B. RNA can easily express characters
(a) Only (A) is correct
(b) Only (B) is correct
(c) Both (A) and (B) are incorrect
(d) Both (A) and (B) are correct

85. Of the following, which sequence is present in retroviruses?
(a) DNA → RNA → Protein
(b) DNA → DNA → Protein
(c) DNA → RNA → DNA → Protein
(d) RNA → DNA → RNA → Protein

86. In eukaryotes, the dominance of RNA world is represented by/at:
(a) Transcriptional level
(b) Process of splicing
(c) Transport of mRNA
(d) Translational level

87. Reverse transcriptase enzyme is found in:
(a) Retrovirus
(b) HIV
(c) Rous sarcoma virus
(d) All of the above

88. A molecule that can act as genetic material must fulfill the following criteria, except:
(a) It should be able to generate its replica
(b) It should chemically and structurally be stable
(c) It should provide scope for rapid change required for evolution
(d) It should be able to express itself in the form of Mendelian characters

89. Reverse transcription was discovered by:
(a) Beadle and Tatum
(b) Temin and Baltimore
(c) Watson and Crick
(d) H Khorana

90. Autocatalytic function is shown by:
(a) RNA (b) DNA
(c) Enzymes (d) Hormone

91. Which is not a ribozyme?
(a) SnRNA
(b) Amino-acyl t RNA synthetase
(c) Peptidyl transferase
(d) Ribonuclease P

92. Which of the following enzymes helps in the process of formation of phosphodiester bond during reverse transcription?
(a) RNA-dependent RNA polymerase
(b) RNA-dependent DNA polymerase
(c) DNA-dependent DNA polymerase
(d) DNA-dependent RNA polymerase

93. (i) Protein synthesizing machinery has evolved around ___A___
(ii) ___B___ is best for the transmission of genetic information.
Choose the correct option for A and B:

	A	B
(a)	RNA	RNA
(b)	RNA	DNA
(c)	DNA	RNA
(d)	DNA	DNA

94. DNA acts as genetic material in organisms because of:
A. Presence of 2′–OH in pentose sugar
B. Chemically less reactive nature
C. Structurally more stable structure
D. Slow rate of mutation
(a) Only (A) and (B)
(b) Only (B) and (D)
(c) Only (B), (C) and (D)
(d) (A), (B), (C) and (D)

95. C-DNA is:
(a) Cytoplasmic DNA of mitochondria
(b) Complementary DNA produced from template DNA
(c) Complementary SS DNA produced from mRNA template
(d) Short segment of DNA present in bacterial cytoplasm

Replication (The Experimental Proof, The Machinery and the Enzyme)

96. Synthesis of new DNA strand over DNA template is called:
(a) Replication (b) Transcription
(c) Translation (d) Transfection

97. The one which is capable of self-replication is:
(a) DNA (b) RNA
(c) Enzyme (d) Protein

98. Watson and Crick suggested that during DNA replication, the daughter DNA contains ______:
(a) Both the strands newly synthesized
(b) Both parental strands
(c) One strand is parental and other is newly synthesized
(d) One strand from each of parent

99. Who proposed the semiconservative mode of replication in DNA?
(a) Meselson and Stahl
(b) Watson and Crick
(c) Cair N
(d) Taylor

100. Meselson and Stahl used an isotope to demonstrate the semiconservative nature of DNA duplication. Which isotope did they use?
(a) C^{12} (b) H^3
(c) P^{32} (d) N^{15}

101. *Escherichia coli* labelled with N^{15} is allowed to grow in N^{14} medium. The two strands of the DNA molecule of first-generation bacteria have:
(a) Different density and do not resemble parent DNA
(b) Different density but resemble parent DNA
(c) Same density but resemble parent DNA
(d) Same density but do not resemble parent DNA

102. DNA replication is:
(a) Autocatalytic function of DNA
(b) Semiconservative process
(c) Semidiscontinuous process
(d) All of the above

103. Read the following statements and select the correct option:
A. Prokaryotes have single origin of replication which is called ori-C in *E. coli*
B. Replication begins in a particular region of DNA which is called the origin of replication
(a) Only (A) is correct
(b) Only (B) is correct
(c) Both (A) and (B) are correct
(d) Both (A) and (B) are incorrect

104. After completion, in which mode of replication would each DNA molecule have one parental and one newly synthesized strand?
(a) Conservative mode
(b) Semiconservative mode
(c) Dispersive mode
(d) Disruptive mode

105. Taylor conducted an experiment to prove the semiconservative mode of chromosome replication on:
(a) *E. coli*
(b) *Streptococcus pneumonia*
(c) *Vinca rosea*
(d) *Vicia faba*

106. During Meselson and Stahl's experiments, heavy DNA was distinguished from normal DNA by centrifugation in:
(a) $^{15}NH_4Cl$ (b) $^{14}NH_4Cl$
(c) CsOH gradient (d) CsCl gradient

107. Replication is discontinuous on the template strand with polarity ___A___ and the DNA polymerase catatyse polymerization in ___B___:

	A	B
(a)	5′ → 3′	5′ → 3′
(b)	3′ → 5′	5′ → 3′
(c)	5′ → 3′	3′ → 5′
(d)	3′ → 5′	3′ → 5′

108. Kornberg enzyme is:
(a) DNA polymerase I
(b) DNA polymerase II

(c) DNA polymerase III
(d) RNA polymerase

109. Read the following statements with respect to DNA polymerase and select the correct option:
A. It cannot initiate replication of DNA
B. Direction of polymerisation is $5' \rightarrow 3'$
C. In bacteria, main polymerising enzyme is DNA polymerase II
(a) Only (A) and (B) (b) Only (B) and (C)
(c) Only (B) (d) (A), (B) and (C)

110. DNA replication in eukaryotes is:
(a) Unidirectional with many ori
(b) Bidirectional with single ori
(c) Unidirectional with single ori
(d) Bidirectional with many ori

111. DNA replication is semiconservative was proved in Eukaryotes by:
(a) Meselson and Stahl
(b) Avery
(c) Taylor
(d) F Crick

112. During DNA replication, Okazaki fragments are formed in the direction of:
(a) $3' \rightarrow 5'$ (b) $5' \rightarrow 3'$
(c) $3' \rightarrow 3'$ (d) $5' \rightarrow 5'$

113. In DNA replication, the strand which supports the continuous DNA nucleotide is the ________ strand and the one which is replicated in short stretches is called the ________ strand:
(a) Leading, lagging
(b) Lagging, leading
(c) Discontinuous, continuous
(d) Template, non-template

114. Uncoiling of the supercoils of the double helix is done by:
(a) Topoisomerase
(b) Helicase
(c) Single-strand binding protein
(d) DNA polymerase

115. The replication of DNA is a multistep process. One of them is separation of two strands by breaking the hydrogen bonds between the base pairs. This is done by the enzyme:
(a) Helicase (b) Ligase
(c) Primarase (d) Gyrase

116. DNA gyrase is a type of:
(a) Topoisomerase
(b) Polymerase
(c) Reverse transcriptase
(d) Sugar

117. The ligase enzyme is required for:
(a) Breaking of DNA
(b) Joining DNA bits
(c) Renaturation of DNA
(d) Proof reading

118. Read the following statements with respect to the given figure and select the correct option:

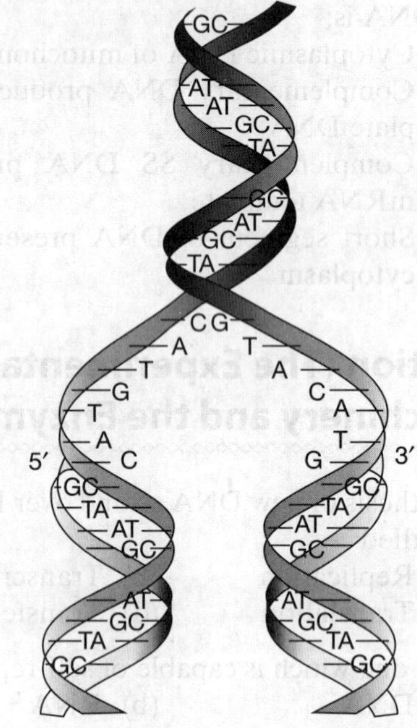

A. Structure exhibits semiconservative mode of replication
B. The replication of DNA takes place at the S-phase of the cell cycle in both prokaryote and eukaryote cells
C. Any mistake during replication would result in mutation
(a) Only (A) is correct
(b) Only (A) and (B) are correct
(c) Only (B) is incorrect
(d) (A), (B) and (C) are correct

119. Assuming that 50 heavy (containing N^{15}) DNA molecules are replicated twice in a medium containing N^{14}, we expect:
(a) 100 hybrid and 150 light DNA molecules
(b) 100 hybrid and 100 light DNA molecules
(c) 50 heavy and 150 hybrid DNA molecules
(d) 50 heavy, 50 hybrid and 100 light DNA molecules

120. If a nucleotide lacking a hydroxyl group at the 3′ end is added to a PCR, the result would be:

(a) No additional nucleotides would be added to a growing strand containing that nucleotide
(b) Strand elongation would proceed normallly
(c) Nucleotides would only be added at the 5′ end
(d) Taq polymerase would be denatured

121. Energetically, DNA replication is a very expensive process. The energy during polymerisation was provided by:
(a) ATP
(b) Ribozyme
(c) Deoxyribonucleoside triphosphate
(d) GTP

122. The average rate of polymerisation by DNA polymerase in bacteria is approximately:
(a) 200 bp/sec (b) 2000 bp/second
(c) 2000 bp/minute (d) 200 bp/minute

123. Okazaki fragments give rise to:
(a) Master strand (b) Sense strand
(c) Lagging strand (d) Leading strand

124. Which involved in DNA repair?
(a) Ligase
(b) Primase
(c) DNA polymerase III
(d) DNA polymerase I

Transcription (Transcription Unit and the Gene, Types of RNA, The Process of Transcription)

125. The process of synthesis of messenger RNA on the DNA template is called:
(a) Replication (b) Transcription
(c) Translation (d) Reverse transcription

126. In the given transcription unit, what do A, B and C represent, respectively?

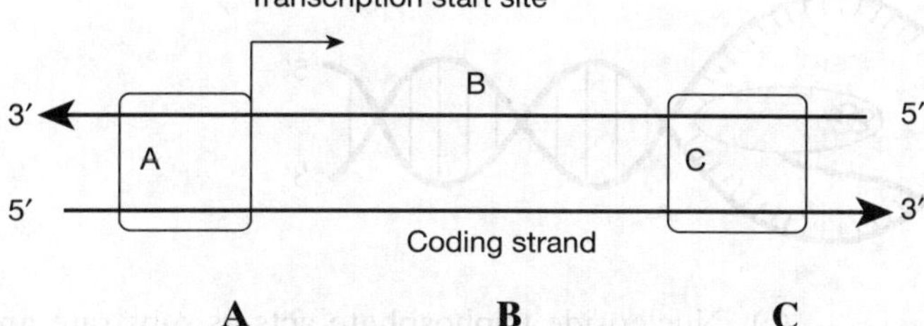

	A	B	C
(a)	Promoter	Template strand	Terminator
(b)	Terminator	Template strand	Promoter
(c)	Promoter	Coding strand	Operator
(d)	Operator	Non-template strand	Terminator

127. Select the correct statement about transcription:
A. In transcription, only a segment of DNA and one of the strands is copied into RNA
B. Terminator is located downstream of the structural gene
C. Intervening sequences do appear in processed RNA
D. In bacteria, translation can begin much before transcription starts
(a) (A) and (B) (b) (A) and (D)
(c) (B) and (C) (d) (A) and (C)

128. For attachment of RNA polymerase enzyme at the correct location on the promoter region, which of the following factors is required?
(a) Pho factor (b) F factor
(c) Sigma factor (d) RNA primer

129. The transcription of any gene is an indication of its:
(a) Activity (b) Induction
(c) Stimulation (d) Hypersensitivity

130. Which genes flank the structural gene in a transcription unit?
(a) Operator and promoter
(b) Promoter and regulator
(c) Promoter and operator
(d) Promoter and terminator

131. Which one of the following is not a part of the transcription unit in DNA?
(a) The inducer (b) A promoter
(c) A terminator (d) The structural gene

132. Read the following statements:
A. m-RNA does not require any processing to become active
B. Transcription and translation take place in the same compartment
The inputs given above are correct for:
(a) *Saccharomyces* (b) *E. coli*
(c) *Neurospora* (d) *Drosophila*

133. ____A____ is the initiation factor and ____B____ is the termination factor during the process of transcription in bacteria:

	A	B
(a)	σ	ρ
(b)	ρ	σ
(c)	ρ	γ
(d)	σ	γ

134. RNA polymerase enzyme binds to ________ and starts the transcription process:
(a) Promoter (b) Operator
(c) Regulator (d) Terminator

135. UTRs are required for efficient translation process, and are present on:
(a) 3′ mRNA (b) 5′ mRNA
(c) Both (a) and (b) (d) 3′ t RNA

136. Read the following statements with respect to RNA polymerase:
A. Binds to promoter
B. Catalyses polymerisation in the 5′ → 3′ direction
C. Helps in opening the DNA helix
D. Needs RNA primer to initiate transcription
E. Three different types of RNA polymerase are seen in Eukaryotes
How many of the given statements are correct?
(a) Two (b) Four
(c) Five (d) Three

137. The longest RNA in a eukaryotic cell is:
(a) rRNA (b) mRNA
(c) tRNA (d) ScRNA

138. Absence of which of the following enzymes shall affect the formation of 16 S rRNA in *E. coli*?
(a) Replicase (b) RNA polymerase III
(c) RNA polymerase (d) RNA polymerase I

139. The precursor of eukaryotic mRNA is:
(a) hnRNA (b) SnRNA
(c) ScRNA (d) rRNA

140. In eukaryotes, RNA polymerase II transcribes:
(a) t-RNA (b) 18S-rRNA
(c) hn-RNA (d) 5S-rRNA

141. Removal of RNA polymerase III from the nucleoplasm will affect the synthesis of:
(a) mRNA (b) hnRNA
(c) 18S rRNA (d) tRNA

142. Methyl guanosine triphosphate is added at the 5′ end of hn-RNA in a process of:
(a) Tailing (b) Capping
(c) Splicing (d) Tailoring

143. If all the RNA is transcribed by DNA in the nucleus, mRNA accounts for:
(a) 15% (b) 5%
(c) 25% (d) 40%

144. In the split gene arrangement of eukaryotes, the expressible part of the genes, called exons, expresses to form:
(a) Carbohydrates (b) Fatty acids
(c) Proteins (d) All except (c)

145. Portion of DNA which is transcribed but not translated is:
(a) Intron (b) Codon
(c) Exon (d) Cistron

146. Maximum RNA synthesis occurs in:
(a) Cytoplasm (b) Nucleoplasm
(c) Ribosome (d) Nucleolus

147. Gene and cistron are sometimes used as synonyms because:
(a) One gene contains one cistron
(b) One gene contains many cistron
(c) One gene contains no cistron
(d) One cistron contains many genes

148. An mRNA template is:
(a) Transcribed from protein
(b) Transcribed into protein
(c) Translated into DNA
(d) Transcribed from DNA

149. The transcription unit in DNA is defined primarily by which of the following regions in the DNA?
(a) Promoter (b) Structural gene
(c) Terminator (d) All of the above

150. Three RNA types can be differentiated on the basis of their:
(a) Size
(b) Sedimentation behaviour
(c) Genetic function
(d) All of the above

151. Select the incorrect statement with respect to the given figure:

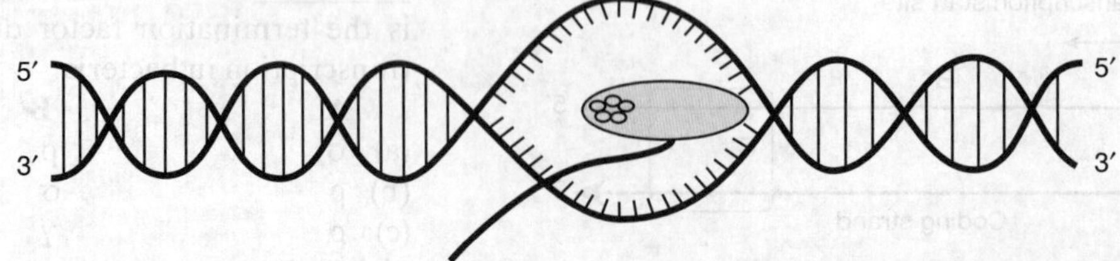

(a) The principle of complementarity governs this process
(b) Adenosine does not form a base pair with thymine
(c) Nucleoside triphosphate acts as substrate and polymerase in a template-independent manner
(d) The DNA-dependent RNA polymerase catalyses polymerisation on the strand that has the polarity 3′ → 5′.

152. Prokaryotic mRNA begins translation much before mRNA is fully transcribed and its nature is:
(a) Polycistronic (b) Monocistronic
(c) HnRNA (d) Monogenic

153. The mRNA of eukaryotes is:
(a) Formed by splicing of hnRNA
(b) Carrier information of many proteins
(c) Monocistronic
(d) All except (b)

154. State true (T) or false (F) for the following statements and select the correct option:
A. In capping, methyl guanosine triphosphate is added to the 3′ end of the primary transcript
B. In tailing, adenylate residues are added in a template-independent manner
C. Introns are removed by splicing and the exon sequences are ligated together

	A	B	C
(a)	F	T	T
(b)	F	F	T
(c)	T	T	T
(d)	T	T	F

155. Product of one gene required to activate another gene is called:
(a) Catalase (b) Coenzyme
(c) Episome (d) Transcription factor

156. Split genes are made up of:
(a) Cistron and intron (b) Exon and intron
(c) Exon and cistron (d) Recon and muton

157. The processing of hnRNA:
(a) Occurs in cytoplasm
(b) Occurs in nucleus
(c) Is about in bacteria
(d) More than one option is correct

158. In the process of transcription in eukaryotes, identify A, B, C and D:

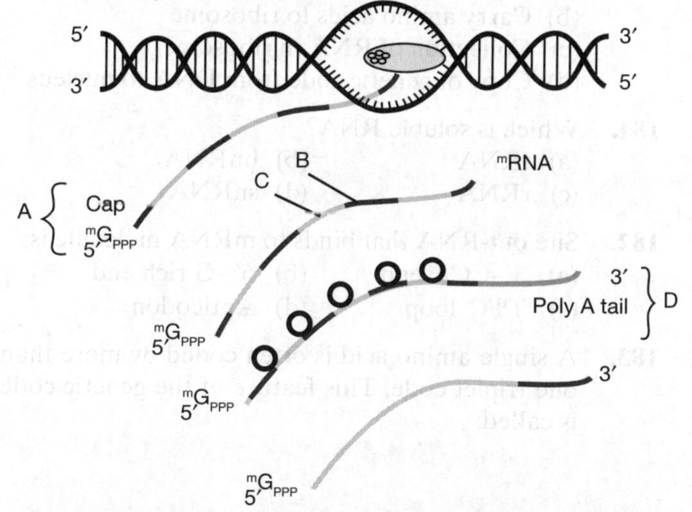

	A	B	C	D
(a)	Capping	Introns	Exons	Polyadenylation
(b)	Capping	Exons	Introns	Polyadenylation
(c)	Polyadenylation	Introns	Exons	Capping
(d)	Polyadenylation	Exons	Introns	Capping

Genetic Code (Mutations and Genetic Code, t-RNA, The Adapter Molecule)

159. Genetic code determines:
(a) Structural pattern of organisms
(b) The sequence of amino acids in a protein
(c) The number of variations in offspring
(d) Constancy or morphological traits

160. The term genetic code was given by:
(a) Watson and Crick
(b) Gamow
(c) Beadle and Tatum
(d) Hoagland

161. Which of the following finally helped the genetic code to be deciphered:
(a) Marshall Nirenberg's cell-free system of protein synthesis
(b) Method developed by Frederick Sanger
(c) R-DNA technology
(d) DNA polymorphism

162. Genetic code translates the language of:
(a) Amino acid into that of RNA
(b) RNA into that of protein
(c) Protein that into DNA
(d) RNA into that of DNA

163. Triplet nature of genetic code was proposed by:
(a) Nirenberg (b) Hoagland
(c) FHC Crick (d) Khorana

164. To decipher which genic code was ochoa enzyme used for?
(a) Polymerasing RNA in template-dependent manner
(b) Polymerasing DNA
(c) DNA-dependent RNA synthesis
(d) Template-independent RNA synthesis

165. Genetic code is degenerate, which means:
(a) One codon codes for only one amino acid
(b) Codon is read on mRNA in a contiguous fashion

(c) Three codons do not code for any amino acid
(d) Some amino acids are coded by more than one codon

166. The number of triplet codons having all the three bases the same in 64 triplet codons is:
(a) 2 (b) 4
(c) 6 (d) 8

167. What will be the codons in mRNA if the DNA codes are ATG-CAG?
(a) TAC-GTC (b) UAC-GUC
(c) UGA-TUA (d) TCA-GTC

168. Khorana et al. synthesized RNA with copolymer of UGUGUGUGUG. It produces a peptide with alternate cysteine and valine. The codons for the two are:
(a) UGU and GUG (b) UUG and GGU
(c) GUG and UGU (d) UGG and GUU

169. Who was awarded the Nobel Prize for in-vitro synthesis of polyribonucleotides:
(a) Kornberg (b) Tatum
(c) Ochoa (d) Khorana

170. Which of the following mutations forms the genetic basis of proof that codon is a triplet and it is read in a contiguous manner?
(a) Point insertion mutation only
(b) Point deletion mutation only
(c) Substitution of one or more nucleotides
(d) Frameshift mutation

171. Wobble hypothesis was proposed by:
(a) FHC Crick (b) Khorana
(c) Nirenberg (d) Holley

172. Wobble hypothesis establishes:
(a) Peptide chain formation
(b) Initiation of peptide chain
(c) Economy of t-RNA molecules
(d) Termination of peptide chain

173. Out of 64 codons, 61 code for 20 types of amino acids. It is due to:
(a) Overlapping genes
(b) Degeneracy of genetic code
(c) Wobbling of codons
(d) Unambiguous nature

174. How many triplet codons are possible after full probability base substitution in one triplet?
(a) 3 (b) 6
(c) 9 (d) 27

175. Which of the following amino acids has only one codon?
(a) Isoleucine (b) Tryptophan
(c) Tyrosine (d) Valine

176. Which codon is not an indicator of completion of protein synthesis?
(a) UAA (b) UGA
(c) AUG (d) UAG

177. Amino acid binding site of t-RNA is:
(a) 5′ end (b) 3′ end
(c) TΨC loop (d) DHU loop

178. In a three-dimensional view, the molecule of t-RNA is:
(a) L-shaped (b) S-shaped
(c) J-shaped (d) V-shaped

179. Clover leaf model of t-RNA shows ________ structure:
(a) 2-dimensional (b) 3-dimensional
(c) 4-dimentional (d) 5-dimentional

180. With respect to the given figure, which of the following is correct?

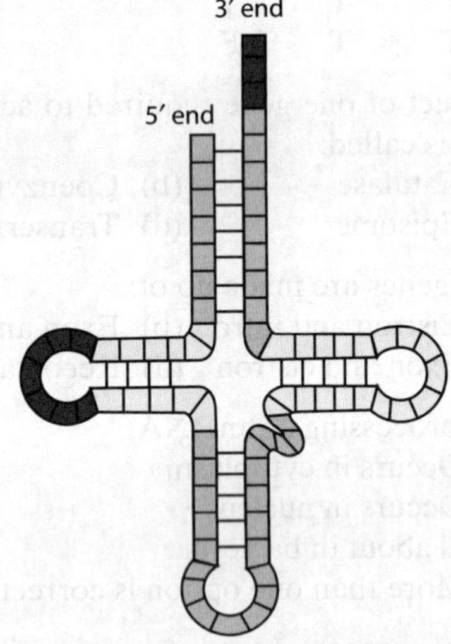

(a) Transfer of genetic code of cytoplasm
(b) Carry amino acids to ribosome
(c) Collection of RNA in ribosome
(d) Copy of genetic code from DNA to nucleus

181. Which is soluble RNA?
(a) tRNA (b) hnRNA
(c) rRNA (d) snRNA

182. Site of t-RNA that binds to mRNA molecule is:
(a) 3′-CCA end (b) 5′-G rich end
(c) TΨC loop (d) Anticodon

183. A single amino acid is often coded by more than one triplet code. This feature of the genetic code is called:

(a) Universality (b) Degeneracy
(c) Non-ambiguity (d) Non-overlapping

184. Experimental evidence supporting concept of triplet genetic code was first provided by:
(a) Beadle and Tatum
(b) Watson
(c) Crick
(d) Michaelis and Menten

185. Genetic codes are:
A. Triplet
B. Universal
C. Ambiguous
D. Degenerate
(a) (A), (B) and (C) only
(b) (A) and (B) only
(c) (A), (B) and (D) only
(d) (A), (B), (C) and (D)

186. How many of the following statements are correct with respect to genetic code?
A. The codon is read in mRNA in a contiguous fashion
B. 61 codons out of 64 are code for amino acid
C. The codons are read in $3' \rightarrow 5'$ direction
D. AUG has dual function
E. Due to degeneracy, production of mRNA is not accurate
(a) Three (b) Four
(c) Five (d) Three

187. Seth Wright observed gene mutation for the first time in:
(a) *Drosophila* (b) Maize
(c) Ancon sheep (d) Evening primrose

188. A mutation at one base of the first codon of a gene that forms a non-functional protein is:
(a) Non-sense mutation
(b) Reverse mutation
(c) Frameshift mutation
(d) Mis-sense mutation

189. Frameshift mutation occur when:
(a) Anticodons are absent on t RNA
(b) Bases are substituted
(c) Base is deleted or added
(d) All of the above

190. A gene coding for polypeptide of 50 amino acids is mutated at 25 codon UAU, becoming UAG. The result would be:
(a) Polypeptide of 24 amino acid
(b) Two polypeptides: one with 24 amino acids and the other with 25 amino acids
(c) A polypeptide with 49 amino acids
(d) A polypeptide of 25 amino acids

191. A point mutation that changes a codon specifying an amino acid into a stop codon is called:
(a) Nonsense mutation
(b) Same sense mutation
(c) Frameshift mutation
(d) Mis-sense mutation

192. Silent mutations in DNA are not expressed due to:
(a) Universality of genetic material
(b) Non-ambiguous nature of genetic code
(c) Degeneracy of genetic code
(d) DNA is linear

193. The adapter molecule is:
(a) t-RNA (b) m-RNA
(c) r-RNA (d) hn-RNA

194. Codons are unambiguous in nature, but ambiguous codon is:
(a) AUG (b) GUG
(c) UAG (d) UGA

195. Consider the given diagram and select the correct option with respect to amino acids:

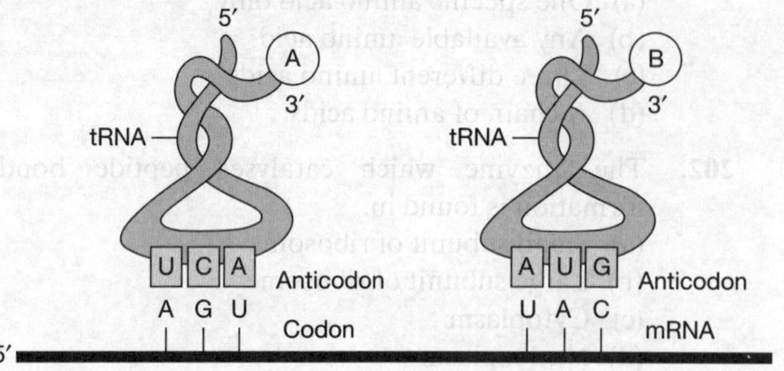

	A	B
(a)	Ser	Leu
(b)	Tyr	Ser
(c)	Ser	Tyr
(d)	Tyr	Glu

Translation

196. The process by which genetic information is transferred from a polymer of nucleotides to a polymer of amino acids is called:
(a) Transcription (b) Transformation
(c) Translation (d) Transduction

197. The cellular factory responsible for synthesizing protein is:

(a) ER (b) Ribosomes
(c) Nucleus (d) Golgi bodies

198. A translational unit in mRNA is flanked by:
(a) The start codon at the 5′ end and the stop codon at the 3′ end
(b) The start codon at the 3′ end and the stop codon at the 5′ end
(c) Cap at the 3′ end and tail at the 5′ end
(d) Promoter at the 5′ end and terminator at the 3′ end

199. The order and sequence of amino acids for a polypeptide are defined by:
(a) Charging and discharging of t RNA
(b) Presence and absence of anticodon in t RNA
(c) Sequence of codons in the mRNA
(d) Sequence of bases in the rRNA, mRNA and tRNA

200. There are two sites in a ribosome where tRNA binds to it. These two sites are called:
(a) A-site and B-site (b) P-site and Q-site
(c) A-site and P-site (d) M-site and N-site

201. A free tRNA molecule can combine with:
(a) One specific amino acid only
(b) Any available amino acid
(c) Three different amino acids
(d) A chain of amino acids

202. The enzyme which catalyses peptide bond formation is found in:
(a) Small subunit of ribosome
(b) Large subunit of ribosome
(c) Cytoplasm
(d) Nucleoplasm

203. Which RNA picks up specific amino acids from the amino acid pool in the cytoplasm to the ribosome during protein synthesis?
(a) tRNA (b) mRNA
(c) snRNA (d) rRNA

204. In *E. coli*:
A. Transcription and translation both occur in the cytoplasm
B. There is only one RNA polymerase enzyme
C. mRNA does not require any processing to become active
D. Transcription and translation can be coupled
Select the correct option:
(a) Only (A) and (B)
(b) Only (C) and (D)
(c) (A), (B), (C) and (D)
(d) Only (C) and (D)

205. In translation, amino acyl t-RNA synthetase recognises the correct amino acids on the basis of:
(a) –COO group (b) R-group
(c) Hat ion (d) NH_3 group

206. How many amino acids can be translated from the given structure of nucleotides in mRNA of the 9th nucleotide undergoing deletion?
AUGUUUUGCACUAUAGCGUAA
(a) Two (b) Three
(c) Four (d) Five

207. During the translation process, the ribosome moves along the ________ in the ________ direction:
(a) mRNA, 3′ to 5′ (b) mRNA 5′ to 3′
(c) tRNA 5′ to 3′ (d) tRNA 3′ to 5′

208. Termination of polypeptide chain is brought about by:
(a) UUG, UAG, UCG
(b) UAA, UAG, UGA
(c) UUG, UGC, UCA
(d) UCG, GUC, ACC

209. Correct sequence of code transfer during polypeptide formation is:
(a) DNA, mRNA, tRNA and amino acids
(b) DNA, tRNA, rRNA and mRNA
(c) mRNA, tRNA, DNA, amino acids
(d) rRNA, DNA, mRNA and tRNA

210. The amino acylation in tRNA occurs at its:
(a) 5′ end having bases CCA
(b) 3′ end having bases CCA
(c) Anticodon site
(d) DHU loop

211. If an mRNA consists of 50 codons and its 23rd base undergoes a deletion, how many amino acids remain unchanged in the formed polypeptide chain?
(a) 8 (b) 7
(c) 15 (d) 22

212. During translation, AUG functions as the initiator codon in mRNA. What should be the anticodon on the t-RNA molecule that picks up and brings the amino acid specified by the codon?
(a) UAC (b) TAC
(c) CAU (d) GUA

213. During translation, at the initiation step, mRNA first binds to:
(a) The smaller ribosomal subunit
(b) The larger ribosomal subunit
(c) The whole ribosome
(d) No such specificity exists

214. Read the following statements with respect to the given figure and select the correct option:

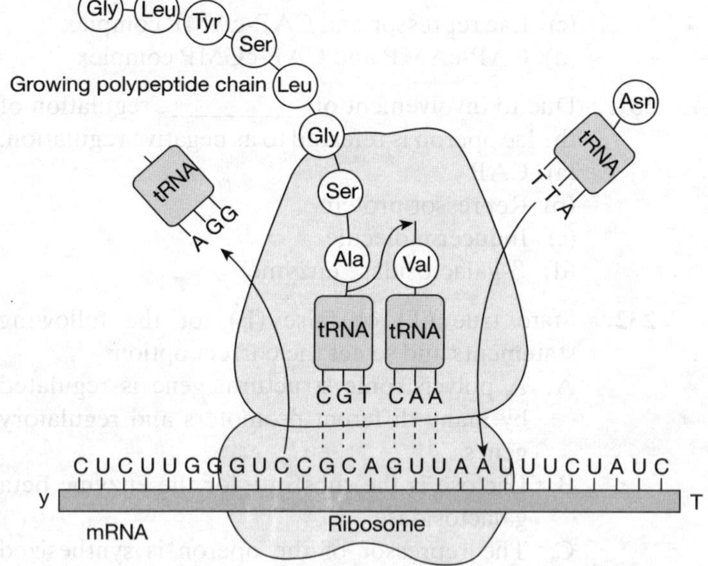

A. Growing polypeptide must have methionine at first position
B. The ribosome acts as a catalyst for the formation of peptide bond
C. The ribosome moves from codon to codon in the 3′ → 5′ direction
D. At the end of the translation process, a release factor binds to the stop codon

(a) Only (A) and (C) are correct
(b) Only (B), (C) and (D) are correct
(c) Only (C) is incorrect
(d) (A), (B), (C) and (D) are correct

215. George Beadle and Edward Tatum in the early 1940s worked on the:
(a) Fruit fly *Drosophila*
(b) Fungus *Neurospora crassa*
(c) Pea *Pisum sativum*
(d) Yeast *Saccharomyces*

216. Beadle and Tatum performed experiments on *Neurospora* by creating mutants, which were not able to synthesize specific substances on minimal media. Such mutants are called:
(a) Phototrophs (b) Auxotrophs
(c) Lethal (d) Sublethal

217. Beadle and Tatum produced nutritional mutant strains of *Neurospora* by:
(a) X-rays (b) UV rays
(c) γ-rays (d) β-rays

Regulation of Gene Expression, The Lac Operon

218. In eukaryotes, expression of gene can be regulated at ________ basic levels:
(a) Three (b) Four
(c) One (d) Two

219. In the lac operon model of gene regulation, the word operon stand for:
(a) Group
(b) Single
(c) Groups of different genes
(d) Central

220. The predominant site for control of gene regulation in Eubacteria is:
(a) Transcription initiation
(b) Processing level
(c) Translational level
(d) All of the aboe

221. Operon concept is applicable for:
(a) All prokaryotes
(b) All prokaryotes and viruses
(c) All prokaryotes and some unicellular eukaryotes
(d) All prokaryotes and eukaryotes

222. All statements are correct for the lac operon, except:
(a) It is an inducible operon system
(b) Switches on in the presence of lactose
(c) Consists of three structural genes
(d) It shows feedback mechanism

223. Jacob and Monod won the Nobel Prize for their work on:
(a) Operon model (b) Structure of gene
(c) Genetic disease (d) Function of gene

224. What is the product of i-gene in the lac operon?
(a) An activate repressor
(b) Aporepressor
(c) Corepressor
(d) Activator

225. Regulatory genes occur:
(a) In front of structural gene
(b) Along with structural gene
(c) In the middle of structural gene
(d) At the end of structural gene

226. The figure below shows the structure of the lac operon with four parts labelled A, B, C and D. Select the correct option in which the parts are identified correctly.

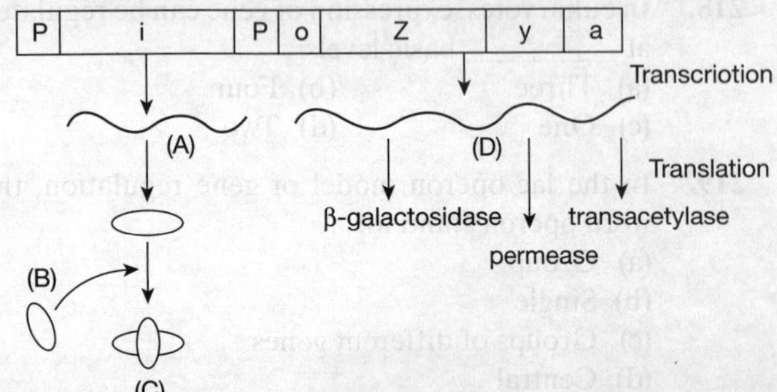

	A	B	C	D
(a)	Repressor mRNA	Inducer	Active repressor	Lac mRNA
(b)	Repressor mRNA	Inducer	In active repressor	Lac mRNA
(c)	Lac mRNA	Repressor	Active inducer	Repressor mRNA
(d)	Lac mRNA	Repressor	Inactive inducer	Active mRNA

227. The lac operon is turned on when allolactose molecules bind to:
(a) mRNA (b) Operator site
(c) Promoter site (d) Repressor protein

228. A very low level of expression of the lac operon has to be present in the cell all the time, otherwise:
(a) Glucose cannot enter the cells
(b) Water cannot enter the cells
(c) Ions cannot enter the cells
(d) Lactose cannot enter the cells

229. According to the Jacob–Monod (lac operon) model of gene regulation, inducer substances in bacterial cells probably:
(a) Combine with operator regions, activating the associated operons
(b) Combines with structural genes stimulating them to synthesize mRNA
(c) Combine with repressor proteins, inactivating them
(d) Combine with promoter regions, activating RNA polymerase

230. Lac operon is regulated by:
(a) Lac repressor only
(b) CAP-cAMP complex only
(c) Lac repressor and CAP-cAMP complex
(d) CAP-cAMP and CAP-cGMP complex

231. Due to involvement of _________ , regulation of the lac operon is referred to as negative regulation:
(a) CAP
(b) Repressor protein
(c) Inducer molecule
(d) β-galactosidase enzyme

232. State true (T) or false (F) for the following statements and select the correct option:
A. A polycistronic structural gene is regulated by many different promoters and regulatory genes
B. Lactose is the substrate for the enzyme beta galactosidase
C. The repressor of the operon is synthesized continuously from the i-gene
D. The development and differentiation of embryo into adult organisms are also a result of the coordinate regulation of expression of several sets of genes

	A	B	C	D
(a)	T	T	F	F
(b)	F	T	T	T
(c)	F	F	T	T
(d)	T	T	F	T

233. The wild type *E.coli* cells are growing in normal medium containing glucose. They are transferred to a medium containing only lactose as sugar. Which of the following changes takes place?
(a) The lac operon is repressed
(b) *E.coli* cells stop dividing
(c) The lac operon is induced
(d) Both (a) and (b)

234. *E.coli* with mutated Z gene of the lac operon cannot grow in medium containing only lactose as the carbon source because:
(a) The lac operon is constitutively active in these cells
(b) They cannot synthesize functional β-galactosidase
(c) In the presence of glucose, bacteria cannot utilise lactose
(d) The bacterium cannot transport lactose from the medium into the cell

235. Some genes that may express themselves in the liver, some in kidney and still others in reproductive tissues are knows as:
(a) Housekeeping genes
(b) Non-constitutive genes
(c) Luxury genes
(d) Both (b) and (c)

236. Transposons discovered by Barbara McClintock are better known as:
(a) Jumping genes (b) Constitutive genes
(c) Artificial genes (d) Homeotic genes

237. Which is a constitutive gene in the lac operon?
(a) lac i (b) lac z
(c) lac a (d) lac y

238. Match Column I and Column II:

Column I	Column II
A. lac-z	(i) Transacetylase
B. lac-y	(ii) β-galactosidase
C. lac-a	(iii) Permease

(a) A – (i), B – (iii), C – (ii)
(b) A – (ii), B – (iii), C – (i)
(c) A – (ii), B – (i), C – (iii)
(d) A – (iii), B – (ii), C – (i)

239. In the lac operon, the i-gene functions as:
(a) Inhibitor (b) Regulator
(c) Inducer (d) Both (a) and (b)

240. Which enzyme will be produced in cells in which there is a nonsense mutation in the lac y gene?
A. β-galactosidase
B. Permease
C. Transacetylase
(a) Only (A) (b) (B) and (C)
(c) Only (C) (d) (A), (B) and (C)

Human Genome Project (HGP)

241. The human genome project was officially started in the year:
(a) 1989 (b) 1990
(c) 2003 (d) 2006

242. The human genome project as megaproject was coordinated by the:
(a) US Department of Energy
(b) National Institute of Health
(c) US Department of Genomes
(d) All except (c)

243. HGP has been called a megaproject due to:
(a) Huge cost estimate to be 9 billion US dollars
(b) Very arge number of base pairs to be identified and sequenced
(c) Requires a large number of scientists, technicians and supporting staff
(d) All of the above

244. HGP was closely associated with the rapid development of new ares in biology is called:
(a) DNA fingerprinting
(b) DNA profiling
(c) Bioinformatics
(d) Gene sequencing

245. ELSI stands for (in reference to HGP):
(a) Ethical legal and social issues
(b) Embedded low software index
(c) Endonuclease ligase surface immunity
(d) Ear lung spleen immunity

246. The genome of which of the following organisms was not sequenced during HGP?
(a) *Caenorhabditis* (b) *Arabidopsis*
(c) Yeast (d) *Paramecium*

247. In which year was HGP completed?
(a) 1993 (b) 2003
(c) 2006 (d) 2013

248. How many genes are found in the human genome?
(a) 18,000 (b) 13,000
(c) 30,000 (d) 1,00,000

249. The sequence of chromosome 1 was completed in:
(a) May 2006 (b) May 2005
(c) April 2006 (d) May 2009

250. The benefits of HGP include:
(a) Better understanding of disease and new ways to diagnose and treat thousands of disorders
(b) Give a better understanding of disorders
(c) Study of interactions between various genes, proteins as well as mechanism of forming tissues organ or tumours
(d) All of the above

251. Select the incorrect match with respect to HGP:
(a) Dystrophin gene – 2.4 million bp
(b) Chromosome 1 – 2968 genes
(c) EST – 1.4 million locations
(d) Human genome – 3164.7 million bp

252. Which of the following is not a salient feature of HGP?
(a) More than 2 per cent of genome codes of proteins
(b) The average gene consist of 3000 bp
(c) Chromosome 1 has most genes
(d) 1.4 million locations have SNPS

253. Read the following statements and select the correct option:
A. Sanger is credited with developing the method for determining amino acid sequence in proteins
B. In HGP, bacteria and yeast were used as host cells
(a) Only (A) is correct
(b) Only (B) is correct
(c) Both (A) and (B) are correct
(d) Both (A) and (B) are incorrect

254. Sequencing the whole set of the genome that contains all the coding and non-coding parts is:
(a) Expression sequence tags
(b) Sequence annotation
(c) PAGE
(d) Microarray

255. Methodology of HGP which includes identification of all the genes that are expressed as RNA is referred to as:
(a) EST (b) RFLP
(c) Bioinformatics (d) Sequence annotation

256. How many locations been identified in the human genome where single base differences occurred?
(a) 1.4 million (b) 14 million
(c) 1.4 billion (d) 3.4 million

257. Select the incorrectly matched pair:
(a) Mega project - HGP
(b) Frederick sanger – Automated DNA sequence
(c) Bioinformatics – Data storage, retrieval and analysis
(d) Sequence annotation – Sequencing of coding sequence only

258. Which of the following is not a salient feature of HGP?
(a) The human genome contains 3164.7 million nucleotide bases
(b) Less than 2% of the genome codes for proteins
(c) The functions are unknown for over 90% of discovered genes
(d) Repeated sequences make up a very large portion of the human genome

259. The average gene consists of ________ bases:
(a) 3000 (b) 30,000
(c) 80,000 (d) 231

260. SMP, which is pronounced "snips", stands for:
(a) Small nuclear protein
(b) Small nicking points
(c) Single nucleotide polymorphism
(d) Simple nucleotide polymorphism

261. The diagram given below represents:

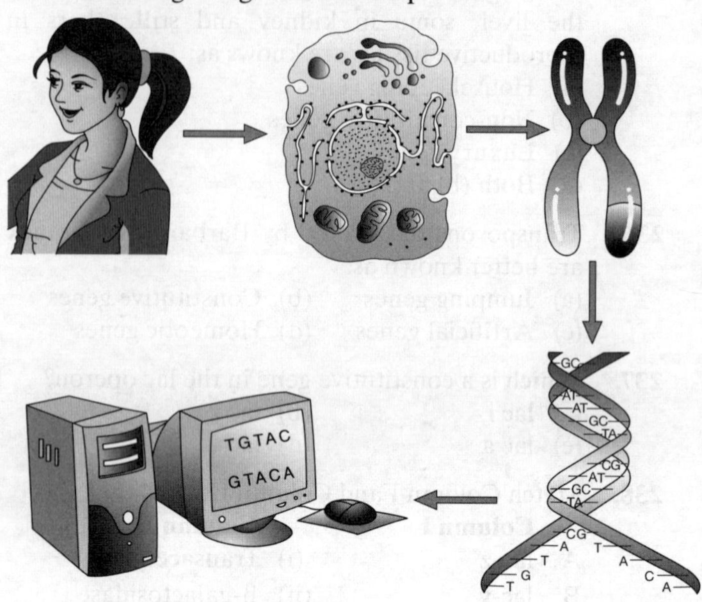

(a) Gel electrophoresis
(b) Polymerase chain reactions
(c) DNA fingerprinting
(d) HGP

262. Frederick Sanger has developed an automated DNA sequence that arranges the DNA fragments on the basis of:
(a) Satellite DNA
(b) Repetitive DNA
(c) Expression sequence tag
(d) Overlapping regions

DNA Fingerprinting

263. DNA fingerprinting technique was discovered by:
(a) A Jeffreys (b) Schleiden
(c) E Southern (d) Edwards and Steptoe

264. There was a parental dispute in a hospital with exchange of newborns to parents both coincidently with similar blood groups. As a biotechnologist, what would you suggest to solve the parental dispute without doubt?
(a) Hybridoma technology
(b) DNA fingerprinting
(c) Western blotting
(d) Chromatography

265. Allelic sequence variations, where more than one variant (allele) at a locus in a human population with a frequency greater than 0.01, are referred to as:
(a) Incomplete dominance

(b) EST
(c) SNP
(d) DNA polymorphism

266. The bulk of DNA forms the major peaks during density gradient centrifugation. The other small peaks are referred to as:
(a) Satellite DNA (b) Non-satellite DNA
(c) Exome DNA (d) Intron DNA

267. Which is not true regarding VNTRs and SSR?
(a) They are tandem repeats
(b) They are excellent genetic markers
(c) They vary greatly from individual to individual
(d) They constitute 10% of the human genome

268. Size of VNTR varies from:
(a) 100 kbs (b) 50–500 kb
(c) 0.1–20 kb (d) 1000 kb

269. If an inheritable mutation is observed in a population at ____A____ frequency, it is referred to as ____B____. The correct option for the words A and B is:

	A	B
(a)	Very low	RNA polymorphism
(b)	High	Frame shift mutation
(c)	High	DNA polymorphism
(d)	Low	Genetic drift

270. Hypervariable region of DNA is formed of:
(a) Minisatellite DNA
(b) Microsatellite DNA
(c) Probes
(d) Both (a) and (b)

271. VNTRs used as markers in DNA fingerprinting are related to which of the following?
(a) Short nucleotide repeats of 1.6 bp
(b) Length as well as position of VNTRs is variable for each person
(c) Considered sequences are usually present which produce homeodomain
(d) A satellite DNA probe that shows very low degree of polymorphism

272. During DNA fingerprinting, DNA fragments are separated by:
(a) Gel electrophoresis
(b) Chromatography
(c) PAGE
(d) Centrifugation

273. When bands of RNA are transferred to a nitrocellulose membrane for identification, the technique is called:
(a) Southern blotting (b) Northern blotting
(c) Western blotting (d) Eastern blotting

274. DNA fingerprinting method is very useful for:
(a) Relationship determination
(b) Forensic studies
(c) Determining population and genetic diversity
(d) All of the above

275. DNA polymorphism is useful in:
(a) DNA fingerprinting
(b) Forensic applications
(c) Genetic mapping
(d) All of the above

276. An inheritable mutation is considered as DNA polymorphism when __________:
(a) It occurs only in a small portion of a population
(b) It occurs in all generations but in low frequency
(c) It is observed in the population in high frequency
(d) It keeps on accumulating generation after generation

277. The VNTR belongs to a class of satellite DNA referred as minisatellites and its size varies from:
(a) 1 to 6 kb (b) 60 to 80 kb
(c) 0.1 to 20 kb (d) 11 to 60 kb

278. Which process is used for amplification or multiplication of DNA for fingerprinting?
(a) PCR
(b) Southern plotting
(c) Agarose gel electrophoresis
(d) Auto radiography

279. DNA fingerprinting requires:
(a) Restriction endonuclease
(b) Taq polymerase
(c) Oligonucleotide primers
(d) All of the above

280. Given below are the different steps followed during DNA fingerprinting:
A. Southern blotting
B. DNA isolation
C. Hybridisation with UNTR probes
D. Restriction digestion
E. Autoradiography
F. Agarose gel electrophoresis
(a) B → A → C → E → F → D
(b) B → D → F → A → C → E
(c) B → D → F → A → E → C
(d) B → E → F → A → E → C

281. Select the incorrect statement with respect to UNTR and SSR:
(a) They are tandem repeats
(b) They vary from chromosome to chromosome in an individual

(c) They vary greatly from individual to individual
(d) They constitute less than 10% of the human genome

282. PCR and RFLP are employed in:
(a) DNA sequencing
(b) Genetic engineering
(c) Study of enzymes
(d) Genetic transformation

283. Select the correct statements for DNA fingerprinting:
A. It is an Elisa-based technique
B. It is a PCR-based technique
C. It is used by forensic scientists
D. It is based on fingerprints of the individual
E. It is a test for paternity
(a) A, B, C (b) B, C, E
(c) A, D E (d) A, C, D

NCERT EXEMPLAR QUESTIONS

1. In a DNA strand, the nucleotides are linked together by:
(a) Glycosidic bonds (b) Phosphodiester bonds
(c) Peptide bonds (d) Hydrogen bonds

2. A nucleoside differs from a nucleotide. It lacks the:
(a) Base (b) Sugar
(c) Phosphate group (d) Hydroxyl group

3. Both deoxyribose and ribose belong to a class of sugars called:
(a) Trioses (b) Hexoses
(c) Pentoses (d) Polysaccharides

4. The fact that a purine base always pairs through hydrogen bonds with a pyrimidine base in the DNA double-helix leads to:
(a) Anti-parallel nature
(b) Semiconservative nature
(c) Uniform width throughout DNA
(d) Uniform length in all DNA

5. The net electric charge on DNA and histones is:
(a) Both positive
(b) Both negative
(c) Negative and positive, respectively
(d) Zero

6. The promoter site and the terminator site for transcription are located at:
(a) 3′ (downstream) end and 5′ (upstream) end, respectively, of the transcription unit
(b) 5′ (upstream) end and 3′ (downstream) end, respectively, of the transcription unit
(c) The 5′ (upstream) end
(d) The 3′ (downstream) end

7. Which of the following statements is the most appropriate for sickle-cell anaemia?
(a) It cannot be treated with iron supplements
(b) It is a molecular disease
(c) It confers resistance to acquiring malaria
(d) All of the above

8. Which of the following is true with respect to AUG?
(a) It codes for methionine only
(b) It is an initiation codon
(c) It codes for methionine in both prokaryotes and eukaryotes
(d) All of the above

9. The first genetic material could be:
(a) Protein (b) Carbohydrates
(c) DNA (d) RNA

10. With regard to mature mRNA in eukaryotes:
(a) Exons and introns do not appear in the mature RNA
(b) Exons appear but introns do not appear in the mature RNA
(c) Introns appear but exons do not appear in the mature RNA
(d) Both exons and introns appear in the mature RNA

11. The human chromosome with the highest and least number of genes in them, are respectively:
(a) Chromosome 21 and Y
(b) Chromosome 1 and X
(c) Chromosome 1 and Y
(d) Chromosome X and Y

12. Who amongst the following scientists had no contribution in the development of the double-helix model for the structure of DNA?
(a) Rosalind Franklin (b) Maurice Wilkins
(c) Erwin Chargaff (d) Meselson and Stahl

13. DNA is a polymer of nucleotides which are linked to each other by 3′-5′ phosphodiester bond. To prevent polymerisation of nucleotides, which of the following modifications would you choose?

(a) Replace purine with pyrimidines
(b) Remove/Replace 3′ OH group in deoxyribose
(c) Remove/Replace 2′ OH group with some other group in deoxyribose
(d) Both 'b' and 'c'

14. Discontinuous synthesis of DNA occurs in one strand, because:
(a) DNA molecule being synthesised is very long
(b) DNA-dependent DNA polymerase catalyses polymerisation only in one direction ($5' \rightarrow 3'$)
(c) It is a more efficient process
(d) DNA ligase joins short stretches of DNA

15. Which of the following steps in transcription is catalysed by RNA polymerase?
(a) Initiation (b) Elongation
(c) Termination (d) All of the above

16. Control of gene expression in prokaryotes takes place at the level of:
(a) DNA replication (b) Transcription
(c) Translation (d) None of the above

17. Which of the following statements is correct about the role of regulatory proteins in transcription in prokaryotes?
(a) They only increase expression
(b) They only decrease expression
(c) They interact with RNA polymerase but do not affect the expression
(d) They can act both as activators and as repressors

18. Which was the last human chromosome to be completely sequenced?
(a) Chromosome 1 (b) Chromosome 11
(c) Chromosome 21 (d) Chromosome X

19. Which of the following are the functions of RNA?
(a) It is a carrier of genetic information from DNA to ribosomes synthesising polypeptides
(b) It carries amino acids to ribosomes
(c) It is a constituent component of ribosomes
(d) All of the above

20. While analysing the DNA of an organism, a total of 5386 nucleotides were found, of which the proportion of different bases were: Adenine = 29%, Guanine = 17%, Cytosine = 32%, Thymine = 17%. Considering Chargaff's rule, it can be concluded that:
(a) It is a double-stranded circular DNA
(b) It is single-stranded DNA
(c) It is a double-stranded linear DNA
(d) No conclusion can be drawn

21. In some viruses, DNA is synthesised by using RNA as template. Such a DNA is called:
(a) A-DNA (b) B-DNA
(c) cDNA (d) rDNA

22. If Meselson and Stahl's experiment is continued for four generations in bacteria, the ratio of N^{15}/N^{15}: N^{15}/N^{14}: N^{14}/N^{14} containing DNA in the fourth generation would be:
(a) 1:1:0 (b) 1:4:0
(c) 0:1:3 (d) 0:1:7

23. If the sequence of nitrogen bases of the coding strand of DNA in a transcription unit is 5′ - A T G A A T G - 3′,the sequence of bases in its RNA transcript would be:
(a) 5′ - A U G A A U G - 3′
(b) 5′ - U A C U U A C - 3′
(c) 5′ - C A U U C A U - 3′
(d) 5′ - G U A A G U A - 3′

24. The RNA polymerase holoenzyme transcribes:
(a) The promoter, structural gene and the terminator region
(b) The promoter and the terminator region
(c) The structural gene and the terminator region
(d) The structural gene only

25. If the base sequence of a codon in mRNA is 5′-AUG-3′, the sequence of tRNA pairing with it must be:
(a) 5′ - UAC - 3′ (b) 5′ - CAU - 3′
(c) 5′ - AUG - 3′ (d) 5′ - GUA - 3′

26. The amino acid attaches to the tRNA at its:
(a) 5′ - end (b) 3′ - end
(c) Anticodon site (d) DHU loop

27. To initiate translation, the mRNA first binds to:
(a) The smaller ribosomal subunit,
(b) The larger ribosomal subunit
(c) The whole ribosome
(d) No such specificity exists

28. In *E.coli,* the lac operon is switched on when:
(a) Lactose is present and it binds to the repressor
(b) Repressor binds to operator
(c) RNA polymerase binds to the operator
(d) Lactose is present and it binds to RNA polymerase

PRACTICE TEST PAPER

1. The backbone of a polypeptide chain is formed of:
(a) Sugar and phosphate
(b) Only phosphate
(c) Sugar and nitrogen base
(d) Only sugar

2. A nucleoside does not contain:
(a) Phosphate (b) Nitrogen base
(c) Pentose sugar (d) Glycosidic bond

3. In the double-helix model of DNA, how far is each base pair from the next?
(a) 0.34 nm (b) 2 nm
(c) 3.4 nm (d) 34 nm

4. Among the following, which has least number of nucleotides in its genome?
(a) ϕX174 bacteriophage
(b) *E.coli*
(c) Lambda phage
(d) Human being

5. RNA acts as genetic material in:
(a) Prokaryotes (b) QB – bacteriophage
(c) TMV (d) Both (b) and (c)

6. Which of the following events (labelled A, B, C and D) is performed by RNA-dependent DNA polymerase?

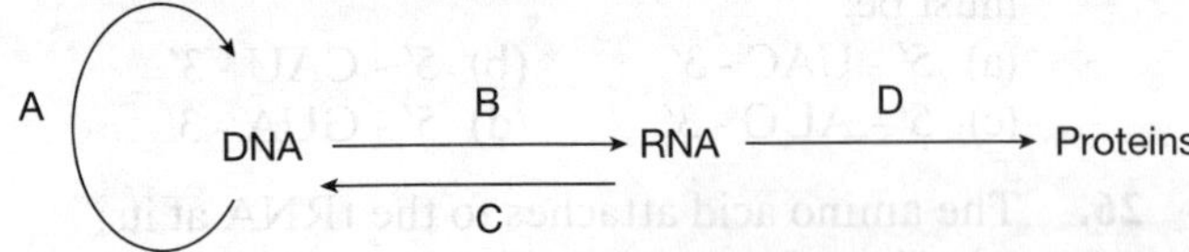

(a) A (b) B
(c) C (d) D

7. Structural gene in a transcription unit is mostly polycistronic in:
(a) *Drosophila* (b) *Neurospora*
(c) *Arabidopsis* (d) *E.coli*

8. The debate between proteins versus DNA as the genetic material was resolved from the experiment of:
(a) Frederick Griffith (b) Hershey and Chase
(c) Watson and Crick (d) Meselson and Stahl

9. DNA is preferred as genetic material over RNA, as RNA lacks:
(a) Free 2′ OH in sugar
(b) Uracil that provides stability
(c) Faster rate of mutation
(d) Thymine that provides stability

10. How many peptide bonds are present in 100 amino acids containing polypeptide chain?
(a) 75 (b) 50
(c) 25 (d) 99

11. Select the correct statement
(a) RNA acts as adapter and catalyst
(b) DNA is preferred for the transmission of genetic information
(c) Presence of thymine confers stability to the helical structure of DNA
(d) RNA is more labile due to absence of OH at the 2nd carbon of ribose sugar

12. Select the correct match:

Column I	Column II
A. UTRs	(i) High degree of polymorphism
B. VNTR	(ii) β-galactosidase
C. ESTs	(iii) Efficient translation
D. Lac z	(iv) Exonic sequence

(a) A – (iii), B – (i), C – (iv), D – (ii)
(b) A – (iii), B – (iv), C – (i), D – (ii)
(c) A – (i), B – (iii), C – (iv), D – (ii)
(d) A – (iv), B – (i), C – (iii), D – (ii)

13. The enzyme required for the post-translational event and which represents the dominance of the RNA world is:
(a) Guanylyl transferase
(b) Sn RNPs
(c) Severo ochoa enzyme
(d) Peptidyl transferase

14. Which of the following codons does not justify the degeneracy rule?
(a) UCG (b) CUG
(c) GGG (d) GAG

15. The lactose operon of *E.coli*:
A. Consists of one regulatory gene
B. Consists of three structural genes
C. Is always regulated negatively
D. Synthesizes lactose from glucose and galactose
(a) (A) and (B) (b) (A) and (C)
(c) (B) and (C) (d) (C) and (D)

16. The DNA-dependent DNA polymerase catalyses polymerization in the ___A___ direction and the replication is continuous on the template strand with polarity ___B___:

	A	B
(a)	$5' \rightarrow 3'$	$5' \rightarrow 3'$
(b)	$3' \rightarrow 5'$	$5' \rightarrow 3'$
(c)	$5' \rightarrow 3'$	$3' \rightarrow 5'$
(d)	$3' \rightarrow 5'$	$3' \rightarrow 5'$

17. Which among the given enzymes is not a ribozyme?
(a) Ribonuclease P (b) Snurp
(c) RNA polymerase (d) Peptidyl transferase

18. All of the following types of rRNAs are synthesized by RNA polymerase I, except:
(a) 28 S (b) 5.8 S
(c) 18 S (d) 5 S

19. A nutritionally wild type of organism, which does not require any additional growth supplement, is known as:
(a) Phenotype (b) Auxotroph
(c) Prototroph (d) Autotroph

20. Read the following statements with respect to human genome project:
A. Less than 2% of the genome codes for protein
B. Repeat sequences make up a very large portion of the human genome
C. Chromosome 1 has the most genes and Y has the fewest
(a) Only (B) is incorrect
(b) Only A is correct
(c) Only (A) and (B) are correct
(d) (A), (B) and (C) are correct

21. Repeated unit of chromatin is/has:
(a) Nucleosome
(b) 200 bases in DNA
(c) H_1 histone protein
(d) All of the above

22. Probe used in DNA fingerprinting is/has:
(a) Microsatellite
(b) Satellite DNA
(c) Large DNA sequence
(d) Radioactively labelled oligonucleotides

23. Which of the following codons does not have any anticodons?
(a) AUG (b) UGG
(c) UGA (d) AGG

24. In the lac operon, nonsense mutation in cistron 'Z' leads to the synthesis of:
(a) β-galactosidase (b) Permease
(c) Transacetylase (d) No enzyme

25. DNA fingerprinting involves identifying differences in some specific regions in the DNA sequence called:
(a) Palindromic DNA (b) Satellite DNA
(c) Repetitive DNA (d) All except (a)

26. In a transcription unit, the promoter is located towards:
(a) 5′ end of coding strand
(b) 3′ end of coding strand
(c) 5′ end of template strand
(d) 3′ end of template strand

27. The functional unit of the DNA molecule that codes for a particular gene product is:
(a) Cistron (b) Intron
(c) Gene (d) Exon

28. The process of transfer of genetic information from a polymer of ribonucleotides to a polymer of amino acids is:
(a) Transcription (b) Replication
(c) Translation (d) Duplication

29. in prokaryotes, peptidyl transferase activity is concerned with:
(a) 28 S - rRNA (b) 23 S -rRNA
(c) 16 - SrRNA (d) 5s-rRNA

30. If *E.coli* completes the process of DNA replication within 18 minutes, the rate of polymerisation of DNA would be approximately:
(a) 4.6×10^6 bp/sec (b) 500 bp/sec
(c) 2000 bp/sec (d) 4000 bp/sec

31. The discontinuously synthesized fragments of DNA are joined by the enzyme:
(a) DNA ligase
(b) DNA-dependent DNA polymerase
(c) Topoisomerase
(d) DNA gyrase

32. Leaset number of genes are present on which of the following human chromosomes?
(a) Chromosome 1 (b) Chromosome X
(c) Chromosome Y (d) Chromosome 21

33. State true (T) or false (F) for the given statements and select the correct option:
A. HGP was closely associated with the development of a new area in biology called bioinformatics
B. HGP was completed in 2001
C. Identification of all genes expressed as RNA is referred to as sequence annotation

	A	B	C
(a)	T	F	F
(b)	T	F	T
(c)	T	T	T
(d)	F	F	T

34. During DNA replication, deoxyribonucleoside triphosphates serve dual purposes which are:
(a) Acting as substrate
(b) Providing energy for polymerisation
(c) Acting as catalyst
(d) All except (c)

35. Find the correct statement with respect to repetitive DNA:
(a) Code for proteins
(b) Show high degree of polymorphism
(c) Form a large portion of human genome
(d) All are correct except (a)

36. Euchromatin is said to be:
(a) Transcriptionally active
(b) Densely packed
(c) Darkly stained
(d) Both (a) and (c)

37. Find the mismatch:
(a) Exons – Coding sequences
(b) Polycistronic structural genes – *Drosophila*
(c) hnRNA – Primary transcript
(d) Topoisomerase – Removes DNA supercoils

38. In *E.coli* during lactose metabolism, the repressor binds to:
(a) Regulator (b) Operator gene
(c) Structural gene (d) Promotor gene

39. Housekeeping genes:
(a) Produce antibiotics
(b) Constantly operate for cellular activity
(c) Form hormones
(d) Control embryonic development

40. Severo ochoa enzyme is also known as:
(a) Kornberg enzyme
(b) RNA-dependent DNA polymerase
(c) Polynucleotide phosphorylase
(d) Polynucleotide polymerase

41. Translation in bacteria:
(a) Can begin before the mRNA is fully transcribed
(b) Cannot take place in the cytoplasm of a bacterial cell
(c) Requires only one RNA polymerase
(d) Occurs after post-transcriptional modifications of the primary transcript

42. 3′ end of the polynucleotide chain has:
(a) A free phosphate moiety at ribose sugar
(b) A free OH group at ribose sugar
(c) A phosphodiester linkage
(d) A free carboxyl group

43. Which of the following is not a function of RNA?
(a) Messenger (b) Catalytic
(c) Adapter (d) Translation

44. Which of the following structures is present in the core particle of a nucleosome?
(a) H_1 histone protein
(b) Octamer of histone protein
(c) 80 bp of DNA
(d) Linker DNA

45. Find the odd one out with respect to the structure of the transcription unit:
(a) Promoter (b) Terminator
(c) mRNA (d) Structural gene

ANSWER KEYS

Exercises

1. (d)	**2.** (b)	**3.** (c)	**4.** (b)	**5.** (a)	**6.** (a)	**7.** (d)	**8.** (c)	**9.** (c)	**10.** (a)
11. (a)	**12.** (d)	**13.** (c)	**14.** (d)	**15.** (c)	**16.** (d)	**17.** (a)	**18.** (a)	**19.** (c)	**20.** (b)
21. (d)	**22.** (a)	**23.** (c)	**24.** (a)	**25.** (b)	**26.** (b)	**27.** (c)	**28.** (a)	**29.** (a)	**30.** (c)
31. (c)	**32.** (b)	**33.** (a)	**34.** (c)	**35.** (a)	**36.** (b)	**37.** (c)	**38.** (b)	**39.** (a)	**40.** (a)
41. (c)	**42.** (c)	**43.** (d)	**44.** (c)	**45.** (c)	**46.** (d)	**47.** (a)	**48.** (c)	**49.** (b)	**50.** (d)
51. (b)	**52.** (b)	**53.** (d)	**54.** (c)	**55.** (a)	**56.** (c)	**57.** (c)	**58.** (b)	**59.** (a)	**60.** (d)
61. (b)	**62.** (a)	**63.** (b)	**64.** (b)	**65.** (d)	**66.** (c)	**67.** (c)	**68.** (a)	**69.** (b)	**70.** (b)
71. (c)	**72.** (a)	**73.** (b)	**74.** (a)	**75.** (d)	**76.** (d)	**77.** (c)	**78.** (d)	**79.** (a)	**80.** (a)
81. (c)	**82.** (c)	**83.** (b)	**84.** (d)	**85.** (d)	**86.** (b)	**87.** (d)	**88.** (c)	**89.** (b)	**90.** (b)
91. (b)	**92.** (b)	**93.** (a)	**94.** (c)	**95.** (c)	**96.** (a)	**97.** (a)	**98.** (c)	**99.** (b)	**100.** (d)

101. (a) **102.** (d) **103.** (c) **104.** (b) **105.** (d) **106.** (d) **107.** (a) **108.** (a) **109.** (a) **110.** (d)
111. (c) **112.** (b) **113.** (a) **114.** (a) **115.** (a) **116.** (a) **117.** (b) **118.** (c) **119.** (b) **120.** (a)
121. (c) **122.** (b) **123.** (c) **124.** (d) **125.** (b) **126.** (a) **127.** (a) **128.** (c) **129.** (a) **130.** (d)
131. (a) **132.** (b) **133.** (a) **134.** (a) **135.** (c) **136.** (d) **137.** (b) **138.** (c) **139.** (a) **140.** (c)
141. (d) **142.** (b) **143.** (b) **144.** (c) **145.** (a) **146.** (d) **147.** (a) **148.** (d) **149.** (d) **150.** (d)
151. (c) **152.** (a) **153.** (d) **154.** (a) **155.** (d) **156.** (b) **157.** (d) **158.** (a) **159.** (b) **160.** (b)
161. (a) **162.** (b) **163.** (c) **164.** (d) **165.** (d) **166.** (b) **167.** (b) **168.** (a) **169.** (c) **170.** (d)
171. (a) **172.** (c) **173.** (b) **174.** (c) **175.** (b) **176.** (c) **177.** (b) **178.** (a) **179.** (a) **180.** (b)
181. (a) **182.** (d) **183.** (b) **184.** (c) **185.** (c) **186.** (b) **187.** (c) **188.** (c) **189.** (c) **190.** (a)
191. (a) **192.** (c) **193.** (a) **194.** (b) **195.** (c) **196.** (c) **197.** (b) **198.** (a) **199.** (c) **200.** (c)
201. (a) **202.** (b) **203.** (a) **204.** (c) **205.** (b) **206.** (a) **207.** (b) **208.** (b) **209.** (a) **210.** (b)
211. (b) **212.** (a) **213.** (a) **214.** (c) **215.** (b) **216.** (b) **217.** (a) **218.** (b) **219.** (c) **220.** (a)
221. (a) **222.** (d) **223.** (a) **224.** (a) **225.** (a) **226.** (b) **227.** (d) **228.** (d) **229.** (c) **230.** (c)
231. (b) **232.** (b) **233.** (c) **234.** (b) **235.** (d) **236.** (a) **237.** (a) **238.** (b) **239.** (d) **240.** (a)
241. (b) **242.** (d) **243.** (d) **244.** (c) **245.** (a) **246.** (d) **247.** (b) **248.** (c) **249.** (a) **250.** (d)
251. (d) **252.** (a) **253.** (c) **254.** (b) **255.** (a) **256.** (a) **257.** (d) **258.** (c) **259.** (a) **260.** (c)
261. (d) **262.** (d) **263.** (a) **264.** (b) **265.** (d) **266.** (a) **267.** (d) **268.** (c) **269.** (c) **270.** (d)
271. (b) **272.** (a) **273.** (b) **274.** (d) **275.** (d) **276.** (c) **277.** (a) **278.** (a) **279.** (d) **280.** (b)
281. (d) **282.** (b) **283.** (b)

NCERT Exemplar Questions

1. (b) **2.** (c) **3.** (c) **4.** (c) **5.** (c) **6.** (b) **7.** (d) **8.** (d) **9.** (d) **10.** (b)
11. (c) **12.** (d) **13.** (b) **14.** (b) **15.** (d) **16.** (b) **17.** (d) **18.** (a) **19.** (d) **20.** (b)
21. (c) **22.** (d) **23.** (a) **24.** (d) **25.** (b) **26.** (b) **27.** (a) **28.** (a)

Practice Test Paper

1. (a) **2.** (a) **3.** (a) **4.** (a) **5.** (d) **6.** (c) **7.** (d) **8.** (b) **9.** (d) **10.** (d)
11. (a) **12.** (a) **13.** (b) **14.** (a) **15.** (a) **16.** (c) **17.** (c) **18.** (d) **19.** (c) **20.** (d)
21. (a) **22.** (d) **23.** (c) **24.** (d) **25.** (d) **26.** (a) **27.** (a) **28.** (c) **29.** (b) **30.** (c)
31. (a) **32.** (c) **33.** (a) **34.** (d) **35.** (d) **36.** (a) **37.** (b) **38.** (b) **39.** (b) **40.** (c)
41. (a) **42.** (b) **43.** (d) **44.** (b) **45.** (c)

SOLUTIONS

DNA, Structure of Polynucleotide Chain, Packaging of DNA Helix

1. Human genome has 3.3×10^9 bp.

2. Friedrich Miescher isolated nuclei acids for the first time from pus cells and called them nuclein. Richard Altmann later called these nuclein nucleic acids.

3. Miescher

4. The length of DNA is usually defined as the number of nucleotides or a pair of nucleotides referred to as base pairs (bp) in it. This is characteristic for an organism.

5. Chargaff, along with his colleagues, performed base composition studies and put forward certain generalisations about double-stranded DNA, called Chargaff's Rule.

6.
- In a double-stranded DNA, the amount of purine nucleotides is equal to the amount of pyrimidine nucleotides. A + G = T + C
- Base ratio $\frac{A+G}{T+C} = 1$, this value is constant for all species.
- Base ratio $\frac{A+T}{C+G}$ is specific for a species.

7. The DNA should have an amount of guanine equal to cytosine and an amount of adenine equal to thymine.

8. In the ribose of RNA, unlike DNA, every nucleotide residue has an additional OH group at the 2[1] position.

9. Two nucleotides are linked through the 3′–5′ phosphodiester linkage to form a dinucleotide.

10. According to the Chargaff Rule, equimolar concentration of A = T and G = C.
$C = G \rightarrow 18 + 18 = 36\%$
Thus, A = T amount is 64%, with 32% A and 32% T.

11. A nitrogenous base is linked to pentose sugar through N-glycosidic linkage to form a nucleoside. Purine nucleosides have 1′-9 glycosidic linkages while pyrimidine nucleosides have 1′-1 linkage.

12. A phosphate group is linked to the 5′-OH of a nucleoside through phosphoester linkages; a corresponding nucleotide is formed.

13. The bases of two strands are paired through hydrogen bonds, forming base pairs. Adenine forms two hydrogen bonds with thymine and guanine forms three hydrogen bonds with cytosine.

14. DNA is acidic due to phosphoric acid.

15. Variable part of DNA molecule is nitrogen base.

16. Prokaryotic cells do not have a well-defined nucleus; it is found in the cytoplasm in the super coiled stage. The coils are maintained by non-histonic basic proteins called polyamines. The packaged structure of double-stranded circular DNA is called genophore or nucleoid.

17. Nucleosome core is made up of four types of histone proteins. H_2A, H_2B, H_3 and H_4. H_1 protein is not a part of core of nucleosome.

18. A – 3.4 nm, B – 0.34 nm, C – 2 nm

19. Sequence of nitrogenous base on a DNA strand is not uniform in all DNA molecules.

20. In a polynucleotide chain, Number of phosphodiester bonds = Number of nucleotides –1.

21. In bacteria, the DNA in a nucleoid is organised in large loops held by proteins.

22. A – DNA, B – Histone octamer, C – H_1 protein

23. Pneumococcus

24. Four histone proteins (H_2A, H_2B, H_3 and H_4) occur in pairs to produce a histone octamer or nu-body.

25. Total number of nucleotides = 100. Number of phosphodiester bonds = 98. Number of N-glycosidic linkages = 100.

26. Distance between two consecutive base pairs is 3.4 Å.
Length of DNA with 23 bp is $= 23 \times 3.4 = 78.2$ Å

27. 11 base pairs per turn are generally present in a DNA.

28. Total number of nucleotides is 400. Nucleotide = Nitrogenous base = Sugar = Phosphate.
Number of phosphate = 400. Number of N-glycosidic linkage = 400.

29. Base pairing

30. About 200 bp (400 nucleotides) of DNA is wrapped around the positively charged histone octamer to form a structure of nucleosome.

31. Non-histone chromosomal proteins

32. Heterochromatin is darkly stained, densely packed and transcriptionally inactive chromatin.

33. 6.6×10^9 bp

34. A – Histone octamer, B – Nucleosome, C – Euchromatin

35. Option (a) is correct.

36. 200 bp

37. Wilkins and Franklin. In 1950–1953, Rosalind Franklin working at the lab of Morris Wilkins obtained improved samples of X-ray data from more purified samples of DNA.

38. 1953

39. For the work on DNA structure, Watson, Crick and Wilkins were awarded the Nobel Prize in 1962.

40. Only (B) and (C) are correct. DNA consists of two polynucleotide chains. The backbone is constituted of sugar phosphate and the bases project inside. Purine nucleosides have 1′–9 glycosidic linkage while pyrimidine nucleosides have 1′–1 glycosidic linkage.

41. DNA less with $G \equiv C$ than A = T has low melting areas and is denatured more easily.

42. G:C ratio

43. Hydrogen bonds

44. C-value is the total amount of DNA in the genome (haploid content of DNA). C-value paradox is the lack of correlation between genome size and organism complexity. The C-value of an organism increases according to increasing complexity, but some organisms like salamanders have higher C-value than humans; hence the paradox.

45. The bases in two strands are paired through hydrogen bonds.

46. All the statements are correct.

47. Option (a) is correct.

48. The plane of one base pair stacks over the other, causing hydrophobic and dipole interactions between stacked base pairs in a double helix. In addition to hydrogen bonds, this confers stability to the helical structure of DNA.

49. The genetic information of DNA is encoded in a sequence of nitrogenous bases.

50. In a nucleoside, the nitrogenous base is attached to the 1st carbon of the ribose sugar.

51. In a DNA helix, both the polynucleotide chains have anti-parallel polarity, that is, one chain has polarity of $5' \rightarrow 3'$ and the other has $3' \rightarrow 5'$ polarity. Anti-parallel nature arises due to the feasibility of H bonds between complementary nitrogenous bases in DNA.

52. The nucleosomes in chromatin give a beads-on-string appearance under the electron microscope.

53. Nucleosome contains histone octamer and approximately two rounds of linear ds DNA.

54. Histones are a set of positively charged basic proteins.

55. Lysines and arginines

56. Histones are organizsed to form a unit of eight molecules, called histone octamer or nu body.

57. Equal to number of base pairs divided by 200

58. Option (b) is correct.

59. Option (a) is correct.

60. Oligonucleotides

61. Adenylic acid is a nucleotide.

62. In DNA, phosphate group forms a bridge between OH groups of two adjacent nucleotides.

63. Option (b) is correct.

The Search for Genetic Material (Transforming Principle, The Genetic Material is DNA, Properties of Genetic Material, RNA World)

64. F Griffith conducted transformation experiments with *Streptococcus pneumoniae*

65. *Diplococcus pneumoniae*

66. The biochemical characterisation of transforming principle was carried out by Avery, Macleod and Mccarty. They identified the biochemical nature of transforming substances. They proved that this substance is DNA.

67. DNase inhibits the transformation process.

68. Protein

69. Hershey and Chase conducted experiments on bacteriophage to prove that DNA is the genetic material.

70. Hershey and Chase

71. Option (c) is correct.

72. Infection → Blending → Centrifugation

73. S^{35} and P^{32}

74. Central dogma of molecular biology explains one way of unidirectional flow of information from DNA to RNA and RNA to polypeptide. It was proposed by Francis Crick.

Replication ↻ DNA —Transcription→ mRNA —Translation→ Protein

75. RNA being a catalyst is reactive and hence unstable because of the presence of 2′OH of ribose sugar, mutation at faster rate and the presence of uracil.

76. Presence of thymine (5-methyl uracil) in the place of uracil confers additional stability to DNA.

77. All the statements are correct.

78. 5-methyl uracil

79. DNA and RNA differ by nitrogen bases and sugars.

80. RNA acts as genetic material in the QB bacteriophage.

81. Francis Crick

82. DNA acts as a template for the synthesis of both DNA and RNA.

83. 23S rRNA only

84. Both (A) and (B) are correct.

85. Temin and Baltimore independently discovered reverse transcription in some viruses. These viruses produce an enzyme reverse transcriptase which can synthesize DNA over an RNA template.
RNA → DNA → RNA → Protein

86. In eukaryotes, the dominance of RNA world is represented by the process of splicing. Splicing is the process of removal of introns and joining of exons in a defined order. Introns are removed by Sn RNA and protein complex.

87. Option (d) is correct.

88. It should provide scope for slow changes (mutation) that are required for evolution.

89. Temin and Baltimore

90. Option (b) is correct.

91. Some RNA called ribozyme has catalytic activity. For example, ribonuclease P, Sn RNA, peptidyl transferase (23-s rRNA in prokaryotes and 28s rRNA in eukaryotes).

92. Reverse transcriptase (RNA-dependent DNA polymerase)

93. A – RNA, B – RNA

94. (B), (C) and (D) are correct.

95. C – DNA is complementary ssDNA produced from the mRNA template during the reverse transcription process.

Replication (The Experimental Proof, The Machinery and the Enzyme)

96. Replication

97. DNA

98. After completion of DNA replication, each DNA molecule would have one parental and one newly synthesized strand. This is called semiconservative mode of DNA replication.

99. Watson and Crick

100. A heavy isotope of nitrogen, N^{15}.

101. The two strands of the DNA molecule of a first-generation bacteria have different density and do not resemble the parent DNA (hybrid DNA with intermediate density).

102. DNA replication is a semiconservative, semi-discontinuous and bidirectional process.

103. Both (A) and (B) are correct.

104. Semiconservative mode

105. *Vicia faba*

106. CsCl gradient

107. DNA replication is discontinuous in the form of short Okazaki fragments on the template strand with polarity $5' \rightarrow 3'$. DNA replication occurs in the $5' \rightarrow 3'$ direction.

108. DNA polymerase I is called Kornberg enzyme and was discovered by Arthur Kornberg.

109. Only (A) and (B) are correct. In bacteria, the main polymerising enzyme is DNA polymerase III.

110. Eukaryotes have multiple ori sites.

111. Taylor

112. $5' \rightarrow 3'$

113. Leading, lagging

114. Due to unbinding, super coiling is developed at the end opposite to the replicating fork. This tension is released by the enzyme topoisomerase.

115. Helicase enzyme

116. In prokaryotes, DNA gyrase has topoisomerase activity.

117. Okazaki fragments are joined by the enzyme DNA ligase (molecular glu).

118. Only B is incorrect.

119. 100 hybrid and 100 light DNA molecules

120. During the synthesis of new strands, deoxyribonucleotides are added to the free 3′ OH of the previous nucleotide. Due to the absence of the OH group at the 3′ end of the nucleotide, no additional nucleotide would be added to a growing strand containing that nucleotide.

121. Two terminal phosphates in deoxyribonucleotide triphosphate are high-energy phosphates, the same as in the case of ATP.

122. DNA polymerase enzyme in bacteria has the ability to polymerise some 2000 bp per second.

123. Lagging strand.

124. DNA polymerase I enzyme is also known as the DNA repair enzyme because it separates RNA primer from DNA and also fills the gap.

Transcription (Transcription Unit and the Gene, Types of RNA, The Process of Transcription)

125. Transcription

126. A – Promoter, B – Template strand, C – Terminator

127. (A) and (B) are correct. The fully processed hnRNA is called mRNA and it does not contain an intervening sequence. In bacteria, many times translation can begin well before the mRNA is fully transcribed.

128. Sigma factor performs correct promoter binding to initiate the transcription process.

129. Activity

130. The promoter and terminator flank the structural gene in a transcription unit.

131. A transcription unit in DNA is defined primarily by the three regions in the DNA: (i) promoter, (ii) structural gene and (iii) terminator.

132. Both (A) and (B) are correct for prokaryotic organisms like *E. coli*.

133. Option (a) is correct.

134. With the help of the σ factor, RNA polymerase enzyme attaches to a specific site of DNA called the promoter site.

135. UTRs (untranslated regions) in mRNA include 5′ cap (5′ untranslated region) 3′ poly A tail (3′ untranslated region). Though they are not translated, they are required for efficient translation process.

136. Three statements (A, B and E) are correct for RNA polymerase enzyme.

137. mRNA is the longest RNA. According to size, mRNA > rRNA > tRNA.

138. In prokaryotes, only one type of RNA polymerase enzyme is found which can transcribe all types of RNA: mRNA, rRNA, tRNA.

139. In eukaryotes, the precursor of mRNA is hnRNA.

140. hnRNA

141. RNA polymerase III transcribes tRNA, scRNA, snRNA and 5s-rRNA.

142. At the 5′ end of hnRNA (primary transcript), 7-methyl guanosine triphosphate is added by guanyl transferase activity. This process is called capping.

143. mRNA is approximately 5% of the total RNA in the cell.

144. Proteins

145. Eukaryotic DNA contains both exons and introns. When it is transcribed, it forms hnRNA, which has both exon and introns, but introns are removed by the process of splicing.

146. rRNA is approximately 80% of the total RNA of the cell. Nucleolus is the site of rRNA synthesis.

147. One gene contains one cistron.

148. mRNa template is transcribed from DNA.

149. Option (d) is correct.

150. The three RNA types can be differentiated on the basis of their size, sedimentation behaviour and genetic function.

151. Nucleoside triphosphate acts as substrate and polymerase in a template-dependent manner.

152. A structural gene in a transcription unit is polycistronic in prokaryotes or bacteria. Polycistronic genes synthesize different proteins or polypeptides.

153. The mRNA of eukaryotes is a monocistronic gene which carries information of one type of polypeptide or protein.

154. A is false. Capping takes place at the 5′ end of the primary transcript.

155. Transcription factor

156. In eukaryotes, a cistron is a split gene of exons and introns.

157. Post-transcriptional processing of hnRNA occurs in the nucleus, and in prokaryotes, mRNA does not require any processing to become active.

158. A – Capping, B – Introns, C – Exons, D – Polyadenylation

Genetic Code (Mutations and Genetic Code, t-RNA, The Adapter Molecule)

159. Genetic code determines the sequence of amino acids in a protein.

160. George Gamow coined the term genetic code.

161. Marshall W Nirenberg and Matthaei used a synthetic polyURNA and deciphered the code by translating this as polyphenylalanine.

162. Genetic code translate the language of RNA into that of proteins.

163. F Crick

164. Severo Ochoa enzyme was helpful in polymerising RNA with defined sequence in a template-independent manner.

165. Some amino acids are coded by more than one codon, hence the code is degenerate.

166. There are four codons having all the three bases the same in 64 triplet codons. These are UUU(phe), CCC(pro), AAA(cys) and GGG(gly).

167. UAC – GUG

168. UGU and GUG

169. Ochoa

170. Insertion or deletion of one or two bases changes the reading frame from the point of insertion or deletion. Such mutations are referred to as frame shift mutations.

171. Wobble hypothesis was proposed by FH Crick. According to this hypothesis, a change in the nitrogenous base at the third position of a codon does not normally cause any change in the expression of the codon because the codon is usually read by the first two nitrogenous bases.

172. Wobbling helps one tRNA to read more than one codon and thus provides economy in the number of tRNA molecules at the time of protein synthesis.

173. Degeneracy of genetic code

174. $3^3 = 9$

175. Tryptophan has only one codon, UGG.

176. Terminator codons (UAA, UAG, UGA) do not code for any amino acid. If either of these three codons come into mRNA, then protein synthesis terminates.

177. All the tRNA molecules commonly have unpaired – CCA at the 3′ end. This acts as the amino acid binding site of tRNA.

178. The 3D structure of tRNA is an inverted L-shape. This is the actual structure of tRNA.

179. Clover-leaf model of tRNA shows a two-dimensional structure.

180. During the translation process, tRNA carries amino acid to the ribosome.

181. tRNA is also called soluble RNA since it is soluble in 1 m NaCl solution.

182. In anticodon loop, three bases act as anticodon for a particular triplet codon present on mRNA.

183. Degeneracy of codon

184. Crick

185. Genetic codes are triplet, universal, degenerate and non-ambiguous. Non-ambiguous means single codon codes for only one amino acid.

186. Four statements (A, B, D and E) are correct. These codons are read in the 5′ → 3′ direction on mRNA.

187. Seth Wright observed some short-legged (Ancon) variety in a population of long-legged sheep.

188. Frame shift mutation leads to change in all amino acids in the structure of the protein. So a new protein is formed which is completely different from the original protein.

189. Addition or deletion of one or two bases

190. Polypeptide of 24 amino acid

191. Non-sense mutation arises when a codon is changed into a chain terminating codon (UAA, UAG, UGA) resulting in the production of an incomplete polypeptide.

192. Silent mutation is the change in codon that does not change the amino acid coded for; for example, UCA (serine) → UCU (serine). Silent mutation occurs due to degeneracy of genetic code.

193. t-RNA is also called adapter molecule.

194. CUG is an ambiguous codon as it normally codes for valine, but at start position, it codes for methionine.

195. A – Ser, B – Tyr

Translation

196. Translation

197. Ribosomes

198. A translational unit in mRNA is flanked by the start codon at the 5′ end and the stop codon at the 3′ end.

199. The order and sequence of amino acids for a polypeptide chain is defined by the sequence of codons in mRNA.

200. P-site and A-site

201. A free tRNA molecule can combine with one specific amino acid only.

202. Peptide bond formation is catalyzed by the enzyme peptidyl transferase (a type of ribozyme); 23 srRNA in prokaryotes and 28 srRNA in eukaryotes are found in the layer subunit of a ribosome.

203. t-RNA

204. All the statements are correct.

205. R-group

206. Two

207. Ribosome moves along mRNA in the 5′→3′ direction. This is called translocation.

208. Termination codons (UAA, UAG, UGA)

209. Correct sequence of code transfer during polypeptide formation is DNA, mRNA, tRNA and amino acids.

210. Transfer of amino acid to the 3′ end of tRNA is called amino acylation of tRNA on charging of tRNA.

211. Seven amino acids remain unchanged because each codon is made up of three adjacent nitrogen bases.

212. UAC

213. In the first stage of initiation of translation, a free 30 S subunit of ribosome interacts with an mRNA molecule and the initiation factor.

214. Only (C) is incorrect.

215. Beadle and Tatum worked on the fungus *Neurospora crassa* and stated the one gene one enzyme hypothesis.

216. An organism that is unable to synthesize a particular cellular metabolite, such as an amino acid, is called auxotroph.

217. Beadle and Tatum produced nutritional mutants by performing x-rays treatment on the cells.

Regulation of Gene Expression, The Lac Operon

218. In eukaryotes, the expression of a gene can be regulated at four basic levels: transcriptional, processing, transport of mRNA from nucleus to cytoplasm and translational.

219. Operon means group of different genes

220. In prokaryotes, control of the rate of transcriptional initiation is the predominant site for the control of gene expression.

221. All prokaryotes.

222. Option (d) is correct.

223. Jacob and Monod proposed a scheme for induction and repression of enzyme synthesis, popularly known as the operon model. For their excellent work, they were awarded the Nobel Prize in 1965.

224. The repressor protein (tetramer protein) is synthesized by the activity of the regulator gene (i gene).

225. Regulatory genes occur in front of the structural gene.

226. A – Repressor mRNA, B – Inducer, C – Inactive repressor, D – Lac mRNA

227. In the presence of an inducer (lactose or allolactose), the repressor protein is inactivated by interaction with the inducer. This allows the RNA polymerase enzyme to bind to the promoter region.

228. Lactose cannot enter the cells.

229. Option (c) is correct.

230. Lac operon is regulated by lac-repressor and CAP-cAMP complex. They act as negative and positive controls, respectively.

231. Repressor protein

232. Only A is false. A polycistronic gene is regulated by one promoter gene.

233. The lac operon is induced as follows: Inducer (lactose) + Repressor → Switched on.

234. Mutated z gene cannot synthesize functional β-galactosidase, which is responsible for hydrolysis of lactose into galactose and glucose.

235. Non-constitutive genes or luxury genes cannot always express themselves in a cell. They are switched on or off according to the requirement of cellular activities.

236. Jumping genes

237. In the lac operon, the i gene is expressed all the time, which is why it is a constitutive gene that is functional always.

238. Lac Z – β-galactosidase, Lac Y – Permease, Lac a – Transacetylase

239. The i gene functions as inhibitor/regulator.

240. Only β-galactosidase

Human Genome Project (HGP)

241. A very ambitious project of sequencing the human genome was launched in the year 1990. It was a 13-year project and completed in 2003.

242. Human Genome Project was a mega project coordinated by the US Department of Energy and the National Institute of Health. The Welcome Trust of UK also joined the project as a major partner. Additional contributions came from Japan, France, Germany, China and others.

243. Option (d) is correct.

244. The science of bioinformatics developed during the period of HGP.

245. Ethical legal and social issues

246. *Paramecium*

247. 2003

248. The total number of genes is estimated at 30,000 in the human genome.

249. The sequence of chromosome 1 was completed in May 2006.

250. Option (d) is correct.

251. The human genome contains 3164.7 million nucleotide bases.

252. Less than 2% of the genome codes for proteins.

253. Both (A) and (B) are correct. The commonly used hosts were bacteria and yeast and vectors were called as BAC (bacterial artificial chromosome) and YAC (yeast artificial chromosome).

254. Sequence annotation

255. Expression sequence tags (ESTs)

256. Scientist have identified about 1.4 million locations where single-base DNA differences occur in humans. This is known as SNPs-single nucleotide polymorphism pronounced snips.

257. Option (d) is correct.

258. The functions are unknown for over 50% of discovered genes.

259. The average gene consist of 3000 bases.

260. Single nucleotide polymorphism

261. HGP

262. Overlapping regions

DNA Fingerprinting

263. A Jeffreys

264. DNA fingerprinting resolves paternity and maternity disputes.

265. DNA polymorphism

266. Satellite DNA

267. Option (d) is correct.

268. Size of UNTRs varies from 0.1 to 20 kb.

269. A – High, B – DNA polymorphism

270. Hyper variability region of DNA is formed of mini satellite and micro satellite DNA.

271. Length as well as position of VNTRs is variable for each person.

272. DNA fragments are separated by agarose gel electrophoresis.

273. Northern blotting

274. Option (d) is correct.

275. Option (c) is correct.

276. Option (c) is correct.

277. Size of mini satellite varies from 1 to 6 kb.

278. PCR

279. Option (d) is correct.

280. DNA isolation → Restriction digestion → Agarose gel electrophoresis → Southern blotting → Hybridisation with VNTR probs → Autoradiography

281. Option (d) is correct.

282. Genetic engineering

283. (B), (C) and (E) are correct.

7 Evolution

EXERCISES

Origin of Life

1. Mark the incorrect statement:
   (a) According to Oparin, the first forms of life could have come from pre-existing, non-living, organic molecules
   (b) SL Miller created an electric discharge in a closed chamber containing $CH_4 \cdot H_2$ and oxygen at 800°C
   (c) Earth was formed around 4.5 billion years ago
   (d) There was no atmosphere on primitive Earth

2. Which of the following theories believed that life came out of decaying and rotting matter like straw, mud, etc.?
   (a) Theory of Panspermia
   (b) Theory of Biogenesis
   (c) Theory of Spontaneous Generation
   (d) Big Bang Theory

3. Oparin of ________ and Haldane of ________ believed that the formation of life was preceded by chemical evolution:
   (a) England, Holland
   (b) Russia, Holland
   (c) Russia, England
   (d) England, Russia

4. SL Miller, a/an ________ scientist, created similar conditions as proposed by Oparin and Haldane in the laboratory and provided experimental proof of their theory:
   (a) Russian (b) English
   (c) Polish (d) American

5. Early Greek thinkers thought that the unit of life called spores were transferred to different planets including the Earth from outer space. It is true according to:
   (a) Theory of Special Creation
   (b) Theory of Panspermia
   (c) Theory of Spontaneous Generation
   (d) Theory of Catastrophism

6. Which of the following is the correct sequence?
   (a) Chemoheterotrophs – Chemoautotrophs – Photoautotrophs
   (b) Chemoautotrophs – Chemoheterotrophs – Photoautotrophs
   (c) Anaerobic photoautotrophs – Chemoautotrophs – Aerobic photoautotrophs
   (d) Chemoautotrophs – Aerobic photoautotrophs – Anaerobic photoautotrophs

7. Find the incorrect statement:
   (a) The conditions on primitive Earth were high temperature, volcanic storms and reducing atmosphere
   (b) Pasteur through his swan-neck flask experiment disproved the theory of abiogenesis
   (c) There was no oxygen on primitive Earth
   (d) Miller by careful experimentation demonstrated that life comes only from pre-existing life

8. Which of the following did not exist on primitive Earth in free form just before the origin of life?
   (a) CO_2 (b) NH_3
   (c) CH_4 (d) O_2

9. Select the incorrect pair:
   (a) Theory of extraterrestrial origin – Panspermia
   (b) Haldane – Hot dilute soup
   (c) Theory of abiogenesis – Proposed by Louis Pasteur
   (d) Coacervates – Oparin

10. Miller made the first successful simulation experiment in 1953 to assess the validity of the claim for:
    (a) Life originated from pre-existing life
    (b) Biogenesis occurred first, but abiogenesis ever since

(c) Origin of organic molecules in primeval Earth conditions
(d) Hot dilute soup was the region where formation of various chemical elements occurred

11. Which of the following groups of organisms have the ability to synthesise organic food from inorganic raw materials and also carry out photolysis of water?
(a) Chemoautotrophs
(b) Chemoheterotrophs
(c) Photoautotrophs; anoxygenic
(d) Photoautotrophs; oxygenic

12. SL Miller created an electric discharge in a closed flask and observed the formation of:
(a) Fats (b) Amino acids
(c) Nucleic acid (d) Polysaccharides

13. Mark the incorrect statement:
(a) The first non-cellular forms of life could have originated 3 billion years ago
(b) The first cellular forms of life did not originate till about 2000 million years ago
(c) Analysis of meteorite content revealed the presence of simple organic compounds as synthesized by Miller in his experiment
(d) Pasteur showed that in pre-sterilised flasks, life came from killed yeast even if it was not kept open to air

14. Which of the following theories regarding the origin of life is more or less accepted by most scientists?
(a) Theory of Panspermia
(b) Theory of Chemical Origin
(c) Theory of Catastrophism
(d) Theory of Spontaneous Generation

15. Mark the incorrect statement:
(a) When we see stars, we are apparently peeping into the past
(b) The universe is almost 20 billion years old
(c) Stellar distances are measured in light years
(d) Life appeared 1500 million years after the formation of the Earth

16. Which of the following describes "abiogenesis"?
(a) Origin of prokaryotes
(b) Formation of life from pre-existing life
(c) Origin of life from non-living matter
(d) Vegetative propagation in plants

17. Which of the following is incorrect with respect to connotations of the Theory of Special Creation?
(a) Earth is about 40,000 years old
(b) All the living organisms that we see today were created as such
(c) Diversity was always the same since creation and will be the same in the future
(d) Life was created by the supernatural powers of God

18. The spontaneous generation theory was dismissed by:
(a) Aristotle (b) Louis Pasteur
(c) Arrhenius (d) Thales

19. Read the following statements and choose the correct option:
I: When we look at stars on a clear night sky, we are, in a way, looking back in time
II: When we see objects in our immediate surroundings, we are looking at light emitted millions of years ago
(a) Both statements are correct
(b) Both statements are incorrect
(c) Only statement I is correct
(d) Only statement II is correct

20. Following are two statements regarding the origin of life:
A. The earliest living organisms that appeared on Earth were non-green and presumably anaerobes
B. The first autotrophic organisms were the chemoautotrophs that never released oxygen
(a) Both (A) and (B) are false
(b) (A) is correct but (B) is false
(c) (A) is false (B) is correct
(d) Both (A) and (B) are correct

Evidence of Evolution, Theories of Evolution

21. Fossils provide which type of evidence of evolution?
(a) Embryological
(b) Biogeographical
(c) Palaeontological
(d) Morphological

22. Animals called ________ evolved into the first amphibians. Fill in the blank with the correct option:
(a) Jawless fishes (b) Chimaera
(c) Lobe fin fish (d) Elasmobranchs

23. Tendrils of *Cucurbita* and thorns of *Bougainvillea* are:
(a) Homologous organs that evolved due to convergent evolution
(b) Homologous organs that evolved due to divergent evolution

(c) Analogous organs that evolved due to convergent evolution
(d) Analogous organs that evolved due to divergent evolution

24. Animal husbandry and plant breeding programmes are examples of:
(a) Natural selection
(b) Artificial selection
(c) Disruptive selection
(d) Both (a) and (b)

25. ______ used the term "saltation" to describe the main cause of evolution:
(a) Von Baer (b) Thomas Malthus
(c) Hugo de Vries (d) Ernst Haeckel

26. Which of the following represents discontinuous distribution of closely related species?
(a) Lung fish (b) Pigeons
(c) Rabbits (d) Humans

27. Darwin's Theory of Pangenesis was rejected by:
(a) Theory of Panspermia
(b) Mutation Theory
(c) Theory of Continuity of Germplasm
(d) Theory of Inheritance of Acquired Characters

28. Which of the following is correct with respect to evolutionary theories?
(a) Hugo de Vries' variations are directional
(b) Darwinian variations are directionless
(c) Theory of Inheritance of Acquired Characters was given by Hugo de Vries
(d) Fitness is the end result of the ability to adapt and be selected by nature

29. Sauropsids gave rise to the following animals, except:
(a) Turtles (b) Lizards
(c) Snakes (d) Mammals

30. Mark the odd one out with respect to marsupial mammals:
(a) Numbat (b) Koala
(c) Lemur (d) Tasmanian wolf

31. "Survival of the fittest" phrase was first used by:
(a) Darwin (b) Ernst Haeckel
(c) Lamarck (d) Herbert Spencer

32. Which of the following is not an example of convergent evolution?
(a) Flippers of penguins and dolphin
(b) Brain of vertebrates
(c) Sweet potato and potato
(d) Wings of birds and insects

33. Which of the following is incorrect with respect to Darwinism?
(a) Branching descent and natural selection are two key concepts
(b) Variations are gradual
(c) All the acquired characters are passed on to the next generation
(d) It is based on survival of the fittest

34. Which of the following examples does not show an analogy?
(a) Eyes of octopus and mammals
(b) Sting of honey bee and scorpion
(c) Mouth parts of mosquito and cockroach
(d) Leaf tendril of *Pisum sativum* and stem tendril of *Passiflora*

35. Select the incorrect statement:
(a) Dinosaurs suddenly disappeared from Earth around 65 mya
(b) *Archaeopteryx* is the missing link between reptiles and aves
(c) Success of marsupials can be attributed to continental separation
(d) Analogous organs are a result of divergent evolution

36. Variations caused by mutation, as proposed by Hugo de Vries, are:
(a) Random and directional
(b) Small and directional
(c) Random and directionless
(d) Small and directionless

37. The similarity of bone structure in the forelimbs of many vertebrates is an example of:
(a) Homology
(b) Analogy
(c) Convergent evolution
(d) Atavism

38. Following are two statements regarding Darwinian theory:
A. The rate of appearance of new forms is linked to the life cycle or the lifespan
B. In microbes, new species would evolve in millions of years but the same process appears sooner in a fish or fowl

Which of the statements is correct?
(a) (A) is correct but (B) is incorrect
(b) (A) is incorrect but (B) is correct
(c) Both statements are correct
(d) Both statements are incorrect

39. Choose the odd one out with respect to vestigial organs in humans:
(a) Third molar teeth
(b) Vermiform appendix
(c) Ear pinna
(d) Plica semilunaris

40. Identify the incorrect statement:
(a) Darwin's finches represent adaptive radiation
(b) Seed-eating finches were the ancestral finches from which the other finches evolved
(c) Australian marsupials evolved due to artificial selection
(d) Darwin went on a voyage on *HMS Beagle*

41. Variations proposed by Hugo de Vries are fundamentally different from those of Darwin as:
(a) These are continuous variations
(b) They can take place in any direction
(c) They cannot bring sudden change in life forms
(d) They are small and directional

42. Which of the following is an incorrect statement?
(a) Evolution is not a directed process in the sense of determinism but is a stochastic process
(b) Study of fossils in different sedimentary layers indicates the geological period in which they existed
(c) Lichens can grow in areas which are polluted and so are used as industrial pollution indicator
(d) Comparative anatomy and morphology show similarities and differences among the organisms of today and those that existed years ago

43. Some marsupials of Australia resemble placental mammals as they faced similar environmental pressure. Which of the following combinations does not show phenotypic convergence?

	Placental mammal	Australian marsupial
(a)	Anteater	Numbat
(b)	Flying squirrel	Flying phalanger
(c)	Bobcat	Tasmanian wolf
(d)	Lemur	Spotted cuscus

44. The *Rhynia* type plant lineage was ancestral to most groups of the following land plants, except:
(a) Ferns
(b) Conifers
(c) Cycads
(d) Herbaceous lycopods

45. Identify the naturalist who worked in the Malay Archipelago and came to similar conclusions as Darwin, around the same time:
(a) Alfred Wallace (b) Lamarck
(c) Hugo de Vries (d) Gregor Mendel

46. In a collection of moths made in the 1850s, before industrialisation set in, it was observed that they were:
(a) All melanised moths
(b) All white-winged moths
(c) More white-winged moths than melanised moths
(d) More melanised moths than white-winged moths

47. Choose an example of evolution by anthropogenic action:
(a) Evolution of finches in the Galapagos Islands
(b) Evolution of marsupials in Australia
(c) Evolution of antibiotic-resistant microbes
(d) Evolution of horse

48. Identify the correct statement:
(a) Wing of birds and insects are homologous
(b) Mesozoic era is the "Age of Pisces"
(c) Natural selection is a process in which individuals that have certain heritable characteristics survive and reproduce at higher rate than other individuals
(d) Jawless fish evolved around 700 mya

49. The first mammals were like:
(a) Cat (b) Dog
(c) Shrew (d) Rabbit

50. Some of the land reptiles went back to the water and evolved into fish-like reptiles, called ichthyosaurs. This was about:
(a) 100 mya (b) 65 mya
(c) 350 mya (d) 200 mya

51. How many of the following structures are vestigial in humans?
Nictitating membrane, Caudal vertebrae, Ear pinna, Wisdom teeth, Vermiform appendix, Nipples in males, Scalp muscles
(a) Four (b) Five
(c) Six (d) Seven

52. Which one can be considered as phylogenetically a more closer relative of mammals?
(a) Dinosaurs (b) Thecodonts
(c) Pelycosaurs (d) Therapsids

53. Which of the following reptiles does not belong to Sauropsida?
(a) Snakes (b) Turtles
(c) Dinosaurs (d) Pelycosaurs

54. Which of the following sequences was proposed by Darwin for organic evolution?
A. Natural selection
B. Overproduction

C. Appearance of variations
D. Struggle for existence
(a) (A) → (B) → (D) → (C)
(b) (B) → (D) → (C) → (A)
(c) (B) → (A) → (C) → (D)
(d) (B) → (C) → (D) → (A)

55. Darwin's theory of natural selection is not based on the concept of:
(a) Branching descent
(b) Natural selection
(c) Doctrine of appetency
(d) Struggle for existence

56. Which of the following animals is the connecting link between Annelida and Arthropoda?
(a) *Neopilina* (b) *Peripatus*
(c) Platypus (d) *Protopterus*

57. Which of the following animals did not evolve from thecodont reptiles?
(a) Dinosaurs (b) Crocodiles
(c) Birds (d) Snakes

58. Lamarck's theory was discarded by Weismann, who gave:
(a) Theory of Germplasm
(b) Theory of Pangenesis
(c) Theory of Panspermia
(d) Theory of Natural Selection

59. Psilophyton gave rise to the following set of plants, except:
(a) *Ginkgo*
(b) Sphenopsida
(c) Progymnosperms
(d) Bryophytes

60. The term 'positive checks' was used by Malthus for the following factors, except:
(a) Epidemics (b) Floods
(c) Earthquakes (d) Mutations

61. Recapitulation theory provides ________ in favour of evolution:
(a) Anatomical evidence
(b) Taxonomical evidence
(c) Physiological evidence
(d) Embryological evidence

62. The humming bird, woodpecker and hawk are examples of:
(a) Convergent evolution
(b) Parallel evolution
(c) Adaptive radiation
(d) Sibling species

63. Which of the following is an incorrect statement?
(a) *Archaeopteryx* illustrates palaeontological evidence in favour of organic evolution
(b) Haeckel's theory of recapitulation means that the life history of an animal reflects its evolutionary history
(c) Excessive use of herbicides and pesticides has resulted in the selection of resistant varieties in a much smaller time scale
(d) Darwin observed on the Galapagos Islands that from the original insectivorous finches, many other forms with altered beaks arose, enabling them to become seed-eating

64. DDT, when first introduced, was very effective in destroying mosquitoes and other insects. However, within a few years, most insects developed resistance to it. This does not support the concept of:
(a) Evolution by anthropogenic action
(b) Natural selection
(c) Pre-adaptive nature of mutations
(d) Allopatric speciation

65. Similarities in biomolecules like DNA, cytochromes, insulin, blood, proteins, etc. in humans and apes is an example of:
(a) Serial homology
(b) Molecular homology
(c) Structural homology
(d) Phylogenetic homology

66. Which of the following does not support Lamarckism?
(a) Limbless condition of snakes
(b) Flightlessness of ostrich
(c) Loss of eyes in the case of salamander
(d) Constantly beating heart

67. According to the modern concept of evolution, the basic unit of evolution is:
(a) Species (b) Population
(c) Individual (d) Family

68. Which one of the following is not likely to disappear in future generations of humans as per Lamarck's view?
(a) Ear muscles
(b) Vermiform appendix
(c) Ear ossicles
(d) Wisdom teeth

69. Select the incorrect statement:
(a) French naturalist Lamarck has said that evolution of life forms had occurred but was driven by the use and disuse of organs

(b) According to Darwin, variations which are heritable and which make resource utilisation better for a few (better adapted to the habitat) will enable only those to reproduce and leave more progeny
(c) Analogous organs are a result of convergent evolution
(d) Hugo de Vries concluded that existing living forms share similarities to varying degrees not only among themselves but also with forms that existed millions of years ago

70. "Age of Amphibians" is:
(a) Devonian (b) Silurian
(c) Carboniferous (d) Ordovician

71. The strongest evidence for change over a long period of time comes from:
(a) Embryo studies
(b) Biogeography
(c) Analogous organs
(d) Paleontological evidence

72. The most accurate method of dating of fossils is:
(a) Uranium – Lead method
(b) Radioactive – Carbon dating
(c) Potassium – Argon method
(d) Electron spin resonance method

73. Phylogeny means:
(a) Study of fossils
(b) Molecular homology
(c) Developmental history
(d) Evolutionary history

74. Which of the following is an incorrect statement?
(a) In 1938, a fish caught in South Africa happened to be a coelacanth which was thought to be extinct
(b) Different aged rock sediments contain fossils of different life forms that probably died during the formation of the particular sediment
(c) By 500 mya, invertebrates were formed
(d) None of the above

75. *Triceratops* and *Pteranodon* were:
(a) Extinct birds
(b) Extinct reptiles
(c) Extinct amphibians
(d) Extinct mammals

76. The half-life of radioactive carbon (C^{14}) is ______:
(a) 10,000 years (b) 5730 years
(c) 70,000 years (d) 5 billion years

77. Read the following statements. Which of the following are correct?
(i) *Pteranodon* had patagium for flying
(ii) Fossilised faecal matter of animals is called coprolite
(iii) According to Darwin, evolution is a jerky and discontinuous process
(iv) When more than one adaptive radiation appears to have occurred in an isolated geographical area (representing different habitats), one can call this divergent evolution
(a) (i) and (ii) (b) (ii) and (iii)
(c) (iii) and (iv) (d) (i) and (iv)

78. Which of the following is not embryological evidence of evolution?
(a) Presence of filamentous protonema stage in the life cycle of bryophytes
(b) Presence of fish-like tadpole in the development of frog
(c) Presence of tooth buds and gill clefts in bird embryo
(d) Similarities in the eyes of humans and octopus

79. Select the incorrect statement from the following:
(a) Older fossils are found in deeper layers in sedimentary rock than recent fossils
(b) Mesozoic era was dominated by dinosaurs, toothed birds and giant gymnosperms
(c) The book "*Philosophie Zoologique*" was written by Lamarck
(d) Fitness according to Hugo de Vries refers to reproductive fitness

80. Which of the plants can grow in soil rich in selenium?
(a) *Agrostis tenuis*
(b) *Impatiens balsamina*
(c) *Oenothera lamarckiana*
(d) *Astragalus* and *Haplopappus*

81. Mark the odd one out with respect to mutation:
(a) Directionless
(b) Gradual and accumulate
(c) Cause speciation
(d) Single-step large variation

82. Read the following statements. Which of the following are incorrect?
(i) According to Darwin, there has been gradual evolution of life forms
(ii) Comparative anatomy and morphology show similarities and differences among the organisms of today and those that existed millions of years ago

(iii) Before industrialisation set in, tree trunks were dark due to industrial smoke and soot
(iv) Mole (placental mammal) shows convergent evolution with marsupial mouse (marsupial mammal)
(a) (i) and (ii) (b) (iii) and (iv)
(c) (ii) and (iv) (d) (i) and (iv)

83. The following illustration exhibits:

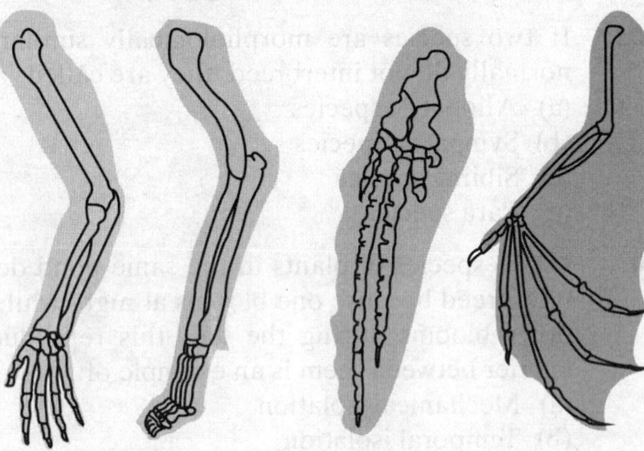

(a) Analogous organs
(b) Homologous organs
(c) Divergent evolution
(d) Both (b) and (c)

84. The following diagram exhibits:

(a) Homologous organs
(b) Analogous organs
(c) Vestigial organs
(d) Convergent evolution

85. Flying phalanger, a marsupial mammal that evolved in Australia, resembles the placental flying squirrel in their ability to glide through air. These two distantly related groups of mammals show:
(a) Divergent evolution
(b) Convergent evolution
(c) Coevolution
(d) Retrogressive evolution

Population Genetics, Hardy–Weinberg Principle

86. If nature selects more individuals with mean character value, which kind of selection is said to be operating?
(a) Directional (b) Disruptive
(c) Stabilising (d) Progressive

87. Industrial melanism (natural selection of peppered moth) in England is an example of ___I___ selection, in which ___II___. Fill in the blanks with the correct options:

	I	II
(a)	Disruptive	Two peaks are formed
(b)	Directional	Peak shifts in one direction
(c)	Stabilising	Peak becomes higher and narrower
(d)	Directional	Two peaks are formed

88. In which of the following isolating mechanisms can two species living in different habitats not mate with each other?
(a) Mechanical isolation
(b) Temporal isolation
(c) Ecological isolation
(d) Behavioural isolation

89. Which of the following factors will not cause change in allele frequency in a population?
(a) Gene migration
(b) Genetic drift
(c) Random mating
(d) Natural selection

90. Which of the following is incorrect with respect to sympatric speciation?
(a) New species evolve alongside their parent population
(b) The isolation barrier is physical
(c) It occurs from a segment within a population
(d) It can occur due to polyploidy

91. The allelic frequency of recessive allele is 0.4. Find out the number of heterozygous individuals in a population of 500:
(a) 80 (b) 120
(c) 240 (d) 280

92. Which of the following is incorrect with respect to premating factors/barriers causing reproductive isolation to hybridisation?
(a) Temporal isolation
(b) Mechanical isolation
(c) Geographical isolation
(d) Hybrid sterility

93. Horse and donkey, when allowed to mate, produce a hybrid. This is an example of:
(a) Hybrid breakdown
(b) Hybrid sterility
(c) Interspecific hybridisation
(d) Both (b) and (C)

94. Hardy–Weinberg equation is used to check:
(a) The average lifespan of a population
(b) Size of population
(c) Whether evolution is occurring in a population or not
(d) More than one option is correct

95. Species can be best described as:
(a) Group of individuals that resemble each other morphologically
(b) Sexually interbreeding group of individuals sharing a common gene pool
(c) Individuals sharing different gene pools
(d) Group of organisms living in different geographical areas

96. In a population of 200 individuals, 98 exhibit recessive phenotype. What percentage of the population is heterozygous?
(a) 9% (b) 3%
(c) 7% (d) 42%

97. The newborns of unusually low and unusually high body weight have higher mortality rates than newborns of average weight. This is an example of:
(a) Disruptive selection
(b) Directional selection
(c) Diversifying selection
(d) Stabilising selection

98. Directional selection can be best defined as:
(a) The least common type of selection
(b) The type of selection which moves the mean phenotype towards one phenotype extreme
(c) The type of selection seen in animal husbandry, during artificial selection
(d) Both (b) and (c) are correct

99. Select the incorrect statement:
(a) Tigon is a fertile hybrid between captive tiger and lioness
(b) Darwin's finches on the Galapagos Islands are an example of adaptive radiation
(c) Genetic drift is also called Sewall–Wright effect
(d) Allopatric species are formed without geographical isolation from the parent population

100. In a population, new alleles arise due to:
(a) Genetic drift (b) Natural selection
(c) Mutation (d) Random mating

101. In the expression, $p^2+2pq+q^2$, used to explain the Hardy–Weinberg equilibrium, the frequency of heterozygous individuals is represented by:
(a) p^2 (b) q^2
(c) 2pq (d) p^2+q^2

102. If two species are morphologically similar but normally do not interbreed, they are called
(a) Allopatric species
(b) Sympatric species
(c) Sibling species
(d) Para species

103. If two species of plants in the same pond do not interbreed because one blooms at night while the other blooms during the day, this reproductive barrier between them is an example of:
(a) Mechanical isolation
(b) Temporal isolation
(c) Geographical isolation
(d) Ecological isolation

104. Mark the incorrect statement:
(a) The effects of genetic drift are most apparent in a small population
(b) The occurrence of large and small birds and the absence of medium-sized birds is an example of disruptive selection
(c) All the genes and their alleles found in an interbreeding population are part of the allele gene pool
(d) Genetic drift helps to maintain genetic equilibrium or the Hardy–Weinberg equilibrium

105. Change in allele frequency in a small population by chance is called:
(a) Gene flow (b) Gene migration
(c) Genetic drift (d) Recombination

106. ________ is a process in which heritable variations enabling better survival are enabled to reproduce and leave a greater number of progeny:
(a) Mutation (b) Gene flow
(c) Natural selection (d) Recombination

107. Identify the incorrect statement:
(a) According to the Hardy–Weinberg principle, the sum total of the allelic frequencies is 1
(b) Disturbance in genetic equilibrium does not result in evolution
(c) When migration of a section of population to another place and population occurs, gene

frequencies change in the original as well as in the new population
(d) Microbial experiments show that pre-existing advantageous mutations when selected will result in observation of new phenotypes

108. Allopatric speciation is caused by:
(a) Polyploidy
(b) Genetic drift
(c) Reproductive isolation without geographical isolation
(d) Reproductive isolation due to geographical isolation

109. If gene migration happens multiple times, it is called:
(a) Gene flow (b) Genetic drift
(c) Founder's effect (d) Natural selection

110. Which of the following is a hybrid produced by mating two different species?
(a) Horse (b) Mare
(c) Donkey (d) Hinny

Origin and Evolution of Humans

111. Read the following statements and choose the correct option:
I: The skull of a baby chimpanzee is more like an adult human skull than that of an adult chimpanzee
II: The skull of an adult chimpanzee is the same as that of an adult human
(a) Both statements are correct
(b) Both statements are incorrect
(c) Only Statement I is correct
(d) Only Statement II is correct

112. Identify the incorrect statement with respect to *Homo habilis*:
(a) Its cranial capacity was 650–800 cc
(b) They probably did not eat meat
(c) This was the first human-like being, the hominid
(d) Its fossils were discovered in Java

113. In recent years, DNA sequences of mitochondrial DNA and Y chromosomes were considered significant to study and understand human evolution because:
(a) They are only present in humans
(b) They are small in size and easy to study
(c) They are uniparental in inheritance and do not take part in recombination
(d) They can be obtained from any living or dead humans

114. Arrange the following hominids according to their increasing cranial capacities:
(a) *Australopithecus* → *Homo habilis* → *Homo erectus* → *Homo sapiens*
(b) *Homo habilis* → *Australopithecus* → *Homo sapiens* → *Homo erectus*
(c) *Australopithecus* → *Homo erectus* → *Homo habilis* → *Homo sapiens*
(d) *Australopithecus* → *Homo sapiens* → *Homo habilis* → *Homo erectus*

115. Identify human fossils having the following features:
A. Used hides to protect their body
B. They buried their dead
C. Cranial capacity 1400 cc
(a) Java man (b) Neanderthal man
(c) *Australopithecus* (d) Peking man

116. Identify the first prehistoric humans to use fire for hunting, defence and cooking:
(a) *Dryopithecus* (b) *Australopithecus*
(c) *Homo erectus* (d) Neanderthal man

117. Which of the following is a direct ancestor of *Homo sapiens*?
(a) *Dryopithecus* (b) *Australopithecus*
(c) *Homo habilis* (d) *Homo erectus*

118. Common ancestry of great apes and humans can be shown by:
(a) Similar banding pattern of chromosomes
(b) Similar blood groups
(c) Similar types of blood proteins
(d) All of the above

119. *Dryopithecus* and *Ramapithecus* existed about:
(a) 50 mya (b) 15 mya
(c) 2 mya (d) 7 mya

120. Select the incorrect statement:
(a) *Dryopithecus* and *Ramapithecus* were hairy and walked like gorillas and chimpanzees
(b) Seven mya, Australopithecines probably lived in the East African grasslands
(c) *Homo erectus* had a large brain around 900 cc
(d) Australopithecines hunted with stone weapons but essentially ate fruit

121. Pre-historic cave art developed around ______ years ago:
(a) 10,000 (b) 18,000
(c) 34,000 (d) 50,000

122. Which of the following is an incorrect statement?
(a) Fossils discovered in Java in 1891 revealed *Homo erectus*
(b) *Ramapithecus* was more ape-like while *Dryopithecus* was more human-like

(c) Few fossils of human-like bones have been discovered in Ethiopia and Tanzania
(d) About 3–4 mya, humans like primates walked in eastern Africa

123. The fossil of *Australopithecus africanus* was named:
(a) Fossil Lucy (b) Taung baby
(c) Peking man (d) Java man

124. Which of the following is the most significant aspect of human evolution?
(a) Opposable thumb
(b) Absence of tail
(c) Increased brain size
(d) Erect posture

125. Identify the true (T) /false (F) statements and choose the correct option:
I. Neanderthal man with a brain size of 1400 cc lived in near-east and central Asia between 100,000–40,000 years ago
II. *Homo erectus* used hides to protect their body and they buried their dead
III. During the Ice Age, around 75,000–10,000 years ago, modern *Homo sapiens* arose
IV. Agriculture began around 50,000 years ago and human settlements started

	I	II	III	IV
(a)	T	T	F	F
(b)	T	F	T	F
(c)	F	T	F	T
(d)	T	F	F	T

NCERT EXEMPLAR QUESTIONS

1. Which of the following is used as an atmospheric pollution indicator?
(a) Lepidoptera (b) Lichens
(c) *Lycopersicon* (d) *Lycopodium*

2. The Theory of Spontaneous Generation stated that:
(a) Life arose from living forms only
(b) Life can arise from both living and non-living forms
(c) Life can arise from non-living things only
(d) Life arises spontaneously, neither from living nor from the non-living

3. Animal husbandry and plant breeding programmes are the examples of:
(a) Reverse evolution
(b) Artificial selection
(c) Mutation
(d) Natural selection

4. Palaentological evidences for evolution refer to the:
(a) Development of embryo
(b) Homologous organs
(c) Fossils
(d) Analogous organs

5. The bones of forelimbs of whale, bat, cheetah and humans are similar in structure, because:
(a) One organism has given rise to another
(b) They share a common ancestor
(c) They perform the same function
(d) The have biochemical similarities

6. Analogous organs arise due to:
(a) Divergent evolution
(b) Artificial selection
(c) Genetic drift
(d) Convergent evolution

7. $(p + q)^2 = p^2 + 2pq + q^2 = 1$ represents an equation used in:
(a) Population genetics
(b) Mendelian genetics
(c) Biometrics
(d) Molecular genetics

8. Appearance of antibiotic-resistant bacteria is an example of:
(a) Adaptive radiation
(b) Transduction
(c) Pre-existing variation in the population
(d) Divergent evolution

9. Evolution of life shows that life forms had a trend of moving from:
(a) Land to water
(b) Dry land to wet land
(c) Fresh water to sea water
(d) Water to land

10. Viviparity is considered to be more evolved because:
(a) The young ones are left on their own
(b) The young ones are protected by a thick shell

(c) The young ones are protected inside the mother's body and are looked after once they are born, leading to better chances of survival
(d) The embryo takes a long time to develop

11. Fossils are generally found in:
(a) Sedimentary rocks
(b) Igneous rocks
(c) Metamorphic rocks
(d) Any type of rock

12. For the MN-blood group system, the frequencies of M and N alleles are 0.7 and 0.3, respectively. The expected frequency of MN-blood group bearing organisms is likely to be:
(a) 42% (b) 49%
(c) 9% (d) 58%

13. Which type of selection explains industrial melanism observed in the moth *Biston bitularia*?
(a) Stabilising (b) Directional
(c) Disruptive (d) Artificial

14. The most accepted line of descent in human evolution is:
(a) *Australopithecus* → *Ramapithecus* → *Homo sapiens* → *Homo habilis*
(b) *Homo erectus* → *Homo habilis* → *Homo sapiens*
(c) *Ramapithecus* → *Homo habilis* → *Homo erectus* → *Homo sapiens*
(d) *Australopithecus* → *Ramapithecus* → *Homo erectus* → *Homo habilis* → *Homo sapiens*

15. Which of the following is an example of the connecting link between pisces and amphibians?
(a) Lobe fish (b) Dodo bird
(c) Seaweed (d) Chimpanzee

16. Match the scientists listed under Column I with ideas listed Column II:

Column I	Column II
A. Darwin	(i) Abiogenesis
B. Oparin	(ii) Use and disuse of organs
C. Lamarck	(iii) Continental drift theory
D. Wagner	(iv) Evolution by natural selection

(a) A – (i), B – (iv), C – (ii), D – (iii)
(b) A – (iv), B – (i), C – (ii), D – (iii)
(c) A – (ii), B – (iv), C – (iii), D – (i)
(d) A – (iv), B – (iii), C – (ii), D – (i)

17. In 1953, SL Miller created primitive Earth conditions in the laboratory and gave experimental evidence for the origin of the first form of life from pre-existing non-living organic molecules. The primitive earth conditions created include:
(a) Low temperature, volcanic storms, atmosphere rich in oxygen
(b) Low temperature, volcanic storms, reducing atmosphere
(c) High temperature, volcanic storms, non-reducing atmosphere
(d) High temperature, volcanic storms, reducing atmosphere containing CH_4, NH_3, etc.

18. Variations during mutations of meiotic recombinations are:
(a) Random and directionless
(b) Random and directional
(c) Small and directional
(d) Random, small and directional

PRACTICE TEST PAPER

1. Which of the following incorrectly matches hominids and their corresponding brain size:
(a) *Homo habilis* → 650–800 cc
(b) *Homo erectus* → 900 cc
(c) *Homo sapiens neanderthalensis* → 1400 cc
(d) *Homo sapiens sapiens* → 1200 cc

2. Analogous structures are the result of:
(a) Convergent evolution
(b) Divergent evolution
(c) Stabilising selection
(d) Shared ancestry

3. A population will not exist in the Hardy–Weinberg equilibrium if:
(a) The population size is large
(b) Mating is random
(c) Mutations occur in the population
(d) There is no migration

4. Genetic drift occurs in:
(a) Large isolated populations
(b) Small isolated populations
(c) Slow reproductive populations
(d) Non-reproductive populations

5. Variations caused by mutations as proposed by Hugo de Vries are:
(a) Random and directional
(b) Random and directionless
(c) Small and directional
(d) Small and directionless

6. *Neopilina* is a connecting link between:
(a) Annelids and molluscs
(b) Annelids and arthropods
(c) Mollusca and echinoderms
(d) Non-chordates and chordates

7. Evolution of different species in a given area, starting from a point and spreading to other geographical areas, is called:
(a) Natural selection
(b) Convergent evolution
(c) Adaptive radiation
(d) Gene migration

8. New species formed after geographical isolation, resulting in reproductive barriers with the parent population, are called:
(a) Allopatric species (b) Sympatric species
(c) Polytypic species (d) Sibling species

9. One of the important consequences of geographical isolation is:
(a) Increased gene flow
(b) No change in isolated fauna
(c) Inhibition of natural selection
(d) Speciation through reproductive isolation

10. Around ______ mya, dinosaurs suddenly became extinct:
(a) 35 (b) 65
(c) 90 (d) 200

11. Which of the following is not a living fossil?
(a) Sphenodon (b) *Archaeopteryx*
(c) *Limulus* (d) *Latimeria*

12. The concept of chemical evolution is based on:
(a) Spontaneous origin of life
(b) Extraterrestrial origin of life in the universe
(c) Possible origin of life by combination of chemicals under anaerobic conditions
(d) Creation of life due to supernatural powers

13. Which of the following phenomena support Darwin's concept of natural selection in organic evolution?
(a) Development of transgenic animals
(b) Production of Dolly the sheep by cloning
(c) Prevalence of antibiotic-resistant microbes
(d) Development of organs from stem cells for organ transplantation

14. Which of the following characters in birds show reptilian ancestry?
(a) Four-chambered heart
(b) Calcareous shell of egg
(c) Scales on their hind limbs
(d) Special chambers like crop and gizzard in their digestive tract

15. What was the most significant trend in the evolution of modern humans (*Homo sapiens*) from their ancestors?
(a) Upright posture
(b) Increasing cranial capacity
(c) Binocular vision
(d) Shortening of jaws

16. Identify the incorrect statement:
(a) Vermiform appendix is a vestigial organ
(b) SL Miller provided evidence for the Oparin–Haldane hypothesis in 1953
(c) Louis Pasteur stated the Theory of Spontaneous Generation of life due to abiogenesis
(d) Weismann proposed the Theory of Continuity of Germplasm

17. Which of the following is an example of homologous organs?
(a) Sweet potato and potato
(b) Wings of birds and insects
(c) Thorns of *Bougainvillea* and tendril of *Cucurbita*
(d) Gills of prawn and lungs of humans

18. In a population of 400 individuals, frequency of recessive allele is 40%. Find out which of these represents the total number of individuals with dominant phenotype:
(a) 144 (b) 242
(c) 192 (d) 336

19. Artificial selection to obtain cows yielding higher milk output represents:
(a) Stabilising selection, as it stabilises this character in the population
(b) Directional selection, as it pushes the mean of character in one direction
(c) Disruptive selection, as it splits the population into two, one yielding higher output and the other yielding lower output
(d) Stabilising followed by disruptive selection, as it stabilises the population to produce higher yielding cows

20. The first fossil human to use fire was:
(a) *Australopithecus* (b) *Homo erectus*
(c) *Dryopithecus* (d) *Ramapithecus*

21. The biggest land reptile/dinosaurs with fearsome dagger-like teeth was:
(a) Triceratops (b) Stegosaurus
(c) Tyrannosaurus (d) Brachiosaurus

22. Which of the following is an incorrect statement?
(a) Agriculture began around 10,000 years ago
(b) *Homo habilis* ate meat
(c) *Dryopithecus* and *Ramapithecus* existed 15 million years ago
(d) Neanderthal man lived in Asia between 100, 000 and 40,000 years ago

23. Darwin's Theory of Natural Selection is not based on the concept of:
(a) Branching descent
(b) Survival of the fittest
(c) Use and disuse
(d) Struggle for existence

24. The presence of gill slits in the embryo stages of all vertebrates supports the:
(a) Theory of Germplasm
(b) Theory of Panspermia
(c) Theory of Pangenesis
(d) Biogenetic law

25. Identify an example of evolution by anthropogenic action:
(a) Evolution of marsupials in Australia
(b) Evolution of antibiotic-resistant microbes
(c) Evolution of finches on the Galapagos Islands
(d) Evolution of birds from reptiles

26. Who, among the following, was a naturalist working in the Malay Archipelago and who came to similar conclusions as Darwin?
(a) Thomas Malthus (b) Lamarck
(c) Alfred Wallace (d) Gregor Mendel

27. The first cellular form of life originated around:
(a) 2000 mya (b) 200 mya
(c) 500 mya (d) 4 bya

28. Which among the following evolved from synapsids?
(a) Turtles (b) Snakes
(c) Crocodiles (d) Pelycosaurs

29. Which of the following is an example of heterozygote selection?
(a) Marsupials in Australia
(b) Sickle-cell anaemia
(c) Lung fishes
(d) Darwin's finches

30. Identify the incorrect statement:
(a) Lichens are indicators of pollution-free environment
(b) Study of fossils in different sedimentary layers indicates the geological period in which they existed
(c) Evolution is a directed process in the sense of determinism, and not a stochastic process
(d) Vertebrate hearts and brains are example of homologous organs

31. Which of the following is an incorrect statement?
(a) Analogous organs perform the same functions though they differ in their origin
(b) Louis Pasteur demonstrated that life comes from pre-existing life
(c) Presence of tail in human baby is an example of atavism
(d) The theory of inheritance of acquired characters was given by Hugo de Vries

32. Fossilised faecal matter of animals is called:
(a) Petrified fossils (b) Moulds
(c) Coprolites (d) Casts

33. Mesozoic era is the:
(a) Age of mammals (b) Age of reptiles
(c) Age of pisces (d) Age of amphibians

34. The recapitulation theory was given by:
(a) Darwin (b) Lamarck
(c) Haeckel (d) Hooker

35. Populations are called sympatric when:
(a) Two populations live together and interbreed to produce sterile offspring
(b) Two populations are physically isolated by natural barriers
(c) Two populations share the same environment but cannot interbreed
(d) Two populations are isolated but occasionally come together to interbreed

36. In a population of 1000 individuals, 360 belong to genotype "AA", 480 to "Aa" and the remaining 160 to "aa". Based on this data, the frequency of allele A in the population is:
(a) 0.4 (b) 0.6
(c) 0.24 (d) 0.16

37. Which of the following is the most primitive ancestor of humans?
(a) *Australopithecus*
(b) *Homo erectus*
(c) *Homo neanderthalensis*
(d) *Ramapithecus*

38. According to the Theory of Spontaneous Generation:
(a) Life came from pre-existing life
(b) Life originated in outer space

(c) Life originated from decaying and rotting matter like straw, mud, etc.
(d) Life came from both living and non-living matter

39. Miller performed experiments to prove the abiogenic molecular evolution of life. Which molecule was not present in Miller's experiment?
(a) Oxygen (b) Water
(c) Methane (d) Ammonia

40. Darwin went on a voyage on a ship named <u>I</u> during <u>II</u>:

	I	II
(a)	*INS Vikrant*	1841–44
(b)	*HMS Beagle*	1831–36
(c)	*HVS Soyale*	1831–34
(d)	*JBS Royale*	1859–64

41. The ancestors of modern-day frogs and salamanders are:
(a) *Amphioxus* (b) *Ichthyophis*
(c) Jawless fish (d) Coelacanth

42. Which of the following is an incorrect match:
(a) Thomas Malthus – Studies on population
(b) Charles Darwin – Branching descent
(c) Hugo de Vries – Saltation
(d) Lamarck – Natural selection

43. Who wrote the famous book *On the Origin of Species*?
(a) Lamarck (b) Darwin
(c) Weismann (d) David Hooker

44. Darwin's Theory of Natural Selection could not explain:
(a) Struggle for existence
(b) Survival of the fittest
(c) Arrival of the fittest
(d) Reproductive fitness

45. Which of the following is the correct sequence of events in the origin of life:
I – Formation of protobionts
II – Synthesis of organic monomers
III – Synthesis of organic polymers
IV – Formation of DNA-based genetic systems
(a) I, III, IV, II (b) II, III, I, IV
(c) II, III, IV, I (d) II, I, III, IV

ANSWER KEYS

Exercises

1. (b) **2.** (c) **3.** (c) **4.** (d) **5.** (b) **6.** (a) **7.** (d) **8.** (d) **9.** (c) **10.** (c)
11. (d) **12.** (b) **13.** (d) **14.** (b) **15.** (d) **16.** (c) **17.** (a) **18.** (b) **19.** (c) **20.** (d)
21. (c) **22.** (c) **23.** (b) **24.** (b) **25.** (c) **26.** (a) **27.** (c) **28.** (d) **29.** (d) **30.** (c)
31. (d) **32.** (b) **33.** (c) **34.** (c) **35.** (d) **36.** (c) **37.** (a) **38.** (a) **39.** (c) **40.** (c)
41. (b) **42.** (c) **43.** (c) **44.** (d) **45.** (a) **46.** (c) **47.** (c) **48.** (c) **49.** (c) **50.** (d)
51. (c) **52.** (d) **53.** (d) **54.** (b) **55.** (c) **56.** (b) **57.** (d) **58.** (a) **59.** (d) **60.** (d)
61. (d) **62.** (c) **63.** (d) **64.** (d) **65.** (b) **66.** (d) **67.** (b) **68.** (c) **69.** (d) **70.** (c)
71. (d) **72.** (d) **73.** (d) **74.** (d) **75.** (b) **76.** (b) **77.** (a) **78.** (d) **79.** (d) **80.** (d)
81. (b) **82.** (b) **83.** (d) **84.** (a) **85.** (b) **86.** (c) **87.** (b) **88.** (c) **89.** (c) **90.** (b)
91. (c) **92.** (d) **93.** (d) **94.** (c) **95.** (b) **96.** (d) **97.** (d) **98.** (d) **99.** (d) **100.** (c)
101. (c) **102.** (c) **103.** (b) **104.** (d) **105.** (c) **106.** (c) **107.** (b) **108.** (d) **109.** (a) **110.** (d)
111. (c) **112.** (d) **113.** (c) **114.** (a) **115.** (b) **116.** (c) **117.** (d) **118.** (d) **119.** (b) **120.** (b)
121. (b) **122.** (b) **123.** (b) **124.** (c) **125.** (b)

NCERT Exemplar Questions

1. (b) **2.** (c) **3.** (b) **4.** (c) **5.** (b) **6.** (d) **7.** (a) **8.** (c) **9.** (d) **10.** (c)
11. (a) **12.** (a) **13.** (b) **14.** (c) **15.** (a) **16.** (b) **17.** (d) **18.** (a)

Practice Test Paper

1. (d)	**2.** (a)	**3.** (c)	**4.** (b)	**5.** (b)	**6.** (a)	**7.** (c)	**8.** (a)	**9.** (d)	**10.** (b)
11. (b)	**12.** (c)	**13.** (c)	**14.** (c)	**15.** (b)	**16.** (c)	**17.** (c)	**18.** (d)	**19.** (b)	**20.** (b)
21. (c)	**22.** (b)	**23.** (c)	**24.** (d)	**25.** (b)	**26.** (c)	**27.** (a)	**28.** (d)	**29.** (b)	**30.** (c)
31. (d)	**32.** (c)	**33.** (b)	**34.** (c)	**35.** (c)	**36.** (b)	**37.** (d)	**38.** (c)	**39.** (a)	**40.** (b)
41. (d)	**42.** (d)	**43.** (b)	**44.** (c)	**45.** (b)					

SOLUTIONS

Origin of Life

1. In 1953, SL Miller, an American scientist, replicated the conditions proposed by Oparin–Haldane in the laboratory. He created an electric discharge in a closed flask containing CH_4, H_2, NH_3 and water vapour at 800°C. He observed the formation of amino acids.
2. According to the Theory of Spontaneous Generation/Abiogenesis, life came out of decaying and rotting matter like straw, mud, etc.
3. Oparin of Russia and Haldane of England proposed that the first forms of life could have come from pre-existing non-living organic molecules (RNA, protein, etc.) and that the formation of life was preceded by chemical evolution or the formation of diverse organic molecules from inorganic constituents.
4. SL Miller, an American scientist, created the conditions proposed by Oparin–Haldane in a laboratory.
5. Early Greek thinkers thought the unit of life called "spores" were transferred to different planets including Earth. This was called Theory of Panspermia/extra-terrestrial origin of life.
6. The first living organisms on Earth were anaerobic chemoheterotrophs. Later, due to exhaustion of chemicals, organisms turned into chemoautotrophs. Photoautotrophs developed much later.
7. Louis Pasteur, by careful experimentation, demonstrated that life comes only from pre-existing life. He showed that in pre-sterilised flasks, life did not come from 'killed yeast', while in another flask open to air, new living organisms arose from 'killed yeast'. Spontaneous generation theory was dismissed once and for all.
8. Oxygen was not present in free form in the atmosphere of primitive Earth. It was, therefore, called a reducing environment.
9. Louis Pasteur advocated the Theory of Biogenesis. He experimentally disproved the Theory of Abiogenesis/Spontaneous Generation.
10. Miller created similar conditions on a laboratory scale to experimentally prove the Oparin–Haldane theory of the origin of organic molecules in primeval Earth conditions.
11. Oxygenic photoautotrophs are organisms that have the ability to synthesise organic food from inorganic raw materials and also carry out photolysis of water.
12. SL Miller created an electric discharge in a closed flask and observed the formation of amino acids.
13. Louis Pasteur demonstrated that life comes only from pre-existing life. He showed that in pre-sterilised flasks, life did not arise from 'killed yeast', while in another flask open to air, new living organisms arose from 'killed yeast'.
14. The theory of the chemical origin of life is more or less accepted by most scientists.
15. Life appeared 500 million years after the formation of the Earth; that is, almost four billion years ago.
16. According to the Theory of Abiogenesis, life occurred from non-living matter. It is also called the Theory of Spontaneous Generation.
17. Conventional religious literature tells about the theory of special creation, according to which the Earth is 4000 years old.
18. The spontaneous generation theory/theory of abiogenesis was dismissed by Louis Pasteur.

19. When we look at stars in a clear night sky, we are, in a way, looking back in time. Stellar distances are measured in light years. What we see today is an object whose emitted light began its journey millions of years ago and from trillions of kilometres away, reaching our eyes now. However, when we see objects in our immediate surroundings, we see them instantly and hence in the present time. Therefore, when we see stars, we are peeping into the past.

20. Option (d) is correct.

Evidence of Evolution, Theories of Evolution

21. Fossils provide palaeontological evidences of evolution. Fossils are the remains of plants, animals, fungi, bacteria and single-celled living things that have been replaced by rock material or impressions of organisms preserved in rock.

22. In 1938, a fish caught in South Africa happened to be a coelacanth which was thought to be extinct. These animals called lobe fins evolved into the first amphibians that lived on both land and water. There are no specimens of them left with us. However, these were the ancestors of modern-day frogs and salamanders.

23. Tendrils of *Cucurbita* and thorns of *Bougainvillea* are homologous organs that evolved due to divergent evolution.

24. Animal husbandry and plant bleeding programmes are examples of artificial selection.

25. Hugo de Vries used the term saltation (single–step large mutation) and believed that mutations caused evolution and not the minor variations (heritable) that Darwin talked about.

26. Lung fish are examples of discontinuous distribution of closely related species. They are found in Africa (*Protopterus*), South America (*Lepidosiren*) and Australia (*Neoceratodus*).

27. Darwin's Theory of Pangenesis was disproved by August Weismann's Theory of Germplasm. According to Weismann, germplasm is a continuous stream from generation to generation while the somatoplasm is formed anew in every generation and is discontinuous. Therefore, only germplasm is responsible for the inheritance of variations and not "pangenes", as proposed by Darwin.

28. Mutations are random and directionless, while Darwinian variations are small and directional. Evolution for Darwin was gradual while de Vries believed mutation caused speciation and hence called it saltation. The theory of inheritance of acquired characters was given by a French naturalist, Lamarck.

29. Sauropsids did not give rise to mammals. Mammals originated from synapsids. Synapsids gave rise to pelycosaurs, which then formed therapsids. Therapsids were mammal-like reptiles from which mammals evolved.

30. Option (c) is correct.

31. The phrase "survival of the fittest" was first used by Herbert Spencer.

32. Homology indicates common ancestry. Vertebrate hearts or brains are examples of homologous organs. Homologous organs suggest divergent evolution, while analogy refers to a situation that is exactly opposite.

33. The inheritance of acquired characters was proposed by a French naturalist, Lamarck. He said that evolution of life forms occurred but was driven by use and disuse of organs. He gave the examples of giraffes who, in an attempt to forage leaves on tall trees, had to adapt by elongation of their necks. As they passed on this acquired character of elongated neck to succeeding generations, giraffes, slowly, over the years came to acquire long necks.

34. Mouth parts of insects like mosquito and cockroach are homologous organs. They are derived from the same internal structures but are modified according to their feeding habits.

35. Homology is based on divergent evolution whereas analogy refers to a situation that is exactly opposite. Wings of butterfly and of birds look alike. They are not anatomically similar structures though they perform similar functions. Hence, analogous structures are a result of convergent evolution; that is, different structures evolving for the same function and hence having similarity.

36. The variations caused by mutation, as proposed by Hugo de Vries, are random and directionless.

37. Whales, bats, cheetah and humans share similarities in the pattern of the forelimb. Though these forelimbs perform different functions in these animals, they have similar anatomical structures; all of them have a humerus, radius, ulna, carpals, metacarpals and phalanges in their forelimbs. Hence, in these animals, the same structure developed along different directions due to adaptations to different needs. This is divergent evolution and these structures are homologous.

38. The rate of appearance of new forms is linked to the life cycle or the lifespan. Microbes that divide fast have the ability to multiply and become millions of individuals within hours. However, for new species to be formed in fish or fowl, it would take millions of years as the lifespans of these animals are in years.

39. The ear pinna is not a vestigial organ as it collects sound waves and directs them towards the ear drum (tympanum).

40. Australian marsupials have evolved due to adaptive radiation. A number of marsupials, each different from the other, evolved from ancestral stock, but all within the Australian island continent.

41. Hugo de Vries based on his work on the evening primrose and brought forth the idea of mutations – large differences arising suddenly in a population. He believed that it is mutation which causes evolution and not the minor variations (heritable) that Darwin talked about. Mutations are random and directionless while Darwinian variations are small and directional.

42. Lichens can be used as industrial pollution indicator. They will not grow in areas that are polluted.

43. Option (c) is correct.

44. Option (d) is correct.

45. Alfred Wallace, a naturalist who worked in the Malay Archipelago, had also come to similar conclusions as Darwin and popularised natural selection as a mechanism of evolution.

46. In a collection of moths made in the 1850s, before industrialisation set in, it was observed that there were more white-winged moths on trees than dark-winged or melanised moths. However, in the collection from the same area, but after industrialisation, in the 1920s, there were more dark-winged moths in the same area and the proportion was reversed.

47. Excessive use of herbicides and pesticides has only resulted in the selection of resistant varieties in a much smaller time scale. This is also true for microbes against which we employ antibiotics or drugs against eukaryotic organisms/cells. Hence, resistant organisms/cells are appearing in a time scale of months or years and not centuries. These are examples of evolution by anthropogenic action.

49. The first mammals were like shrews.

50. Some of the land reptiles went back into the water to evolve into fish-like reptiles, about 200 mya (example, ichthyosaurs).

51. Nictitating membrane (plica semilunaris), caudal vertebrae, wisdom teeth, vermiform appendix, nipples in males and scale muscles are all vestigial structures. Ear pinna is not vestigial as it collects sound waves.

52. Therapsids were "mammal-like reptiles" and are ancestors to mammals, including humans. Therapsids flourished from the early Permian to late Triassic periods.

53. Dinosaurs, turtle and snakes have descended from Sauropsida. Pelycosaurs are descendants of Synapsida.

54. Option (b) is correct.

55. "Doctrine of desires" or appetency was proposed by Lamarck, according to which new structures or organs can be formed by an organism according to its needs.

56. *Peripatus* is considered a connecting link between annelids and arthropods as it has characters of both the phyla.

57. Dinosaurs, crocodiles and birds are descendants of thecodonts. Snakes have directly descended from sauropsids.

58. Lamarck's Theory of Inheritance of Acquired Characters was discarded by August Weismann's Theory of Germplasm.

59. Option (d) is correct.

60. According to Malthus, positive check is any event or circumstance that shortens the human lifespan; for example, war, plague, famine, flood, earthquake or epidemic.

61. The theory of recapitulation, also called biogenetic law or embryological parallelism – often expressed using Ernst Haeckel's phrase "ontogeny recapitulates phylogeny"– is a historical hypothesis that the development of the embryo of an animal, from fertilisation to gestation or hatching (ontogeny), goes through stages resembling or representing successive adult stages in the evolution of the animal's remote ancestors (phylogeny).

62. The hummingbird, woodpecker and hawk are examples of adaptive radiation, since they show the development of different feeding habits, beaks, claws, etc. in different birds according to their habitat.

63. Darwin observed that from the original seed-bearing features in the finches found on the Galapagos islands, many other forms with altered beaks arose, enabling them to become insectivorous and vegetarian finches.

64. Allopatric speciation is a mode of speciation that occurs when the biological populations of the same species become isolated from each other to an extent that prevents or interferes with gene flow. Various geographic changes can arise, such as movement of continent, and the formation of mountains, islands, bodies of water or glaciers. These factors can substantially alter a region's geography, resulting in the separation of a species population into isolated subpopulations.

65. Molecular homology is an important concept in evolutionary biology, used to test the relationships between modern taxa, and to examine the evolutionary processes driving evolution at a molecular level; for example, similarities in biomolecules like DNA, cytochromes, insulin, blood proteins, etc. in humans and apes.

66. According to Lamarck, the evolution of life forms had occurred but was driven by the use and disuse of organs. Snakes lost their limbs due to disuse. Similarly, the wings of flightless birds like ostrich and eyes of cave salamanders degenerated due to disuse.

67. According to the modern synthetic theory of evolution, the basic unit of evolution is population.

68. The auricular muscles, vermiform appendix and wisdom teeth are examples of vestigial structures and may thus disappear due to Lamarck's concept of evolution; that is, the use and disuse theory.

69. According to Darwin, the existing living forms share similarities to varying degrees not only among themselves but also with forms that existed millions of years ago.

70. Carboniferous period is called the "age of amphibians".

71. The palaeontological evidence (fossils) is the strongest evidence for change over a long period of time.

72. Electron spin resonance is the most accurate method of dating of fossils.

73. Phylogeny refers to the evolutionary history of a kind of organism.

74. Option (d) is correct.

75. *Triceratops* and *Pteranodon* were extinct reptiles. *Triceratops* had a three-horned face and was herbivorous. *Pteranodon* is a genus of pterosaur that included some of the largest known flying reptiles, with wingspans of over 7 metres.

76. The half-life of radioactive carbon (C^{14}) is around 5730 years. Carbon dating is a method for determining the age of an object/fossil containing organic material by using the properties of radiocarbon, a radioactive isotope of carbon.

77. According to Darwin, evolution is a gradual process, while Hugo de Vries believed mutations caused speciation and hence called it saltation. When more than one adaptive radiation appeared to have occurred in an isolated geographical area (representing different habitats), one can call this convergent evolution.

78. Eyes of human and octopus are examples of analogous organs.

79. Fitness, according to Darwin, refers ultimately and only to reproductive fitness. Hence, those who are more fit in an environment, leave more progeny than others. These, therefore, are more likely to survive and hence are selected by nature. He called it natural selection and implied it as a mechanism of evolution.

80. Plants like *Astragalus* and *Haplopappus* can grow in soil rich in selenium. *Agrostis tenuis* is a grass found near lead mines while *Impatiens balsamina* is found near zinc mines. Thus, these are indicator organisms that help in locating minerals and their mines.

81. Mutations are not gradual, rather they are single-step large discontinuous variations or saltation.

82. Before industrialisation set in, thick growth of almost white-coloured lichen covered the trees – in that background, the white-winged moths survived but the dark-coloured moths were picked out by predators. Mole (placental mammal) shows convergent evolution with marsupial mole (Australian marsupial).

83. The forelimbs of whales, bats, cheetah and humans share similarities in the pattern of bones of the forelimbs. Though these forelimbs perform different functions in these animals, they have similar anatomical structure – all of them have humerus, radius, ulna, carpals, metacarpals and phalanges in their forelimbs. Hence, in these animals, the same structure developed along different directions due to adaptations to different needs. This is divergent evolution and these structures are homologous.

84. The given diagram exhibits the thorn of *Bougainvillea* and tendril of *Cucurbita*, and are examples of homologous organs.

85. Marsupial flying phalanger and placental flying squirrel show convergent evolution.

Population Genetics, Hardy–Weinberg Principle

86. If nature selects more individuals with mean character value, the stabilising type of natural selection is said to be in operation.

87. Industrial melanism (natural selection of peppered moth) in England is an example of directional selection, in which the peak shifts in one direction.

88. Ecological isolation refers to the isolation mechanism in which two species living in different habitats cannot mate with each other.

89. Random mating does not cause change in allele frequency in a population, and helps to maintain the Hardy–Weinberg equilibrium.

90. Sympatric speciation is the evolution of new species from a surviving ancestral species while both continue to inhabit the same geographical region. In sympatric speciation, there is no geographical constraint to interbreeding.

91. The frequency of recessive allele (q) is 0.4, and therefore the frequency of dominant allele (p) is 0.6. Thus, in a population of 500, the number of heterozygotes (2pq) is 240.

92. If hybrids fail to reproduce, it is called hybrid sterility. This is an example of post-mating factor/barrier causing reproductive isolation.

93. Offspring produced by mating horse and donkey is an example of interspecific hybridisation. These hybrids are sterile.

94. Disturbance in genetic equilibrium, or Hardy–Weinberg equilibrium, which is change in allele frequency in a population, would be interpreted as resulting in evolution. On the contrary, if the Hardy–Weinberg equilibrium is maintained, the population would not undergo any evolution.

95. Species can be best described as sexually interbreeding groups of individuals.

96. Option (d) is correct.

97. If mortality is high among newborns of unusually low or unusually high body weight, it suggests a stabilising selection.

98. Directional selection is one in which more individuals acquire value other than the mean character value. It is a type of selection seen in animal husbandry, during artificial selection.

99. Allopatric speciation is a mode of speciation that occurs when biological populations of the same species become isolated from each other to an extent that prevents or interferes with gene flow. Various geographic changes can arise, such as the movement of continents and the formation of mountains, islands, bodies of water or glaciers.

100. In a population, new alleles arise due to mutations.

101. In the expression given by Hardy–Weinberg, the frequency of heterozygous individuals is represented by 2pq.

102. Sibling species are species which look alike, but which cannot breed with each other. The classic case is *Drosophila persimilis* and *Drosophila pseudoobscura*. They are almost identical, but if flies from one species are mated with flies from the other species, they do not interbreed.

103. If flowers bloom at different times, they show temporal isolation.

104. Genetic drift refers to the change in allele frequency brought about by chance. It therefore causes change in the Hardy–Weinberg equilibrium.

105. Change in allele frequency in a small population by chance is called genetic drift.

106. Natural selection is a process in which heritable variations enabling better survival are enabled to reproduce and leave greater number of progeny.

107. Disturbance in genetic equilibrium or Hardy–Weinberg equilibrium, which is change of frequency of alleles in a population, would be interpreted as resulting in evolution.

108. Allopatric speciation is a mode of speciation that occurs when biological populations of the same species become isolated from each other geographically and prevent or interfere with gene flow between them.

109. Gene migration occurs when migration of a section of population of another place and population occurs, gene frequencies change in the original as well as in the new population, new genes/alleles are added to the new population and these are lost from the old population. There would be gene flow if gene migration happens multiple times.

110. Hinny refers to the offspring produced by mating a male horse and a female donkey.

Origin and Evolution of Humans

111. Option (c) is correct.

112. Fossils discovered in Java revealed *Homo erectus*, which existed 1.5 mya.

113. DNA sequence of mitochondrial DNA and Y chromosomes were considered significant to study and understand human evolution because they are uniparental in inheritance and do not take part in recombination.

114. Option (a) is correct.

115. The Neanderthal man with a brain size of 1400 cc lived in near-east and central Asia between 100,000 and 40,000 years ago. They used hides to protect their body and they buried their dead.

116. *Homo erectus* (Java man) was the first pre-historic human to use fire for hunting, defence and cooking.

117. *Homo erectus* is the direct ancestor of *Homo sapiens*.

118. The common ancestry of great apes and humans can be shown by similar banding pattern of chromosomes, similar blood groups and similar type of blood proteins.

119. About 15 mya, primates called *Dryopithecus* and *Ramapithecus* existed. They were hairy and walked like gorillas and chimpanzees. *Ramapithecus* was more human-like while *Dryopithecus* was more ape-like.

120. Two mya, Australopithecines probably lived in the East African grasslands.

121. Pre-historic cave art developed about 18,000 years ago.

122. *Ramapithecus* was more human-like while *Dryopithecus* was more ape-like.

123. The fossil of *Australopithecus africanus* was discovered by Raymond Dart in the Taung Valley of Africa. The fossil was a skull of a young child and was called the Taung baby.

124. Option (c) is correct.

125. Neanderthal man used hides to protect the body and they buried their dead. Agriculture developed around 10,000 years ago and human settlements began.

Human Health and Diseases

EXERCISES

Common Diseases in Humans

1. Which of the following is incorrect with respect to 'health'?
   (a) It is defined as a stage of complete physical, mental and social well-being
   (b) It brings prosperity and increases productivity
   (c) It increases longevity of people
   (d) It increases infant and maternal mortality

2. The 'good humour' hypothesis of health was disproved by:
   (a) Hippocrates (b) William Harvey
   (c) Aristotle (d) Empedocles

3. Identify the incorrect statement with respect to typhoid:
   (a) It is caused by the pathogenic bacterium *Salmonella typhi*
   (b) The pathogen generally infects through droplets while coughing and sneezing
   (c) Sustained high fever (39° to 40°C), weakness, stomach pain, constipation, headache and loss of appetite are some of the common symptoms of the disease
   (d) Intestinal perforation and death may occur in severe cases

4. Which of the following is/are responsible for the disease pneumonia?
   (a) *Streptococcus pneumoniae*
   (b) *Haemophilus influenzae*
   (c) *Vibrio cholerae*
   (d) Both (a) and (b)

5. Identify the odd one out with respect to bacterial diseases in humans:
   (a) Diphtheria (b) Plague
   (c) Typhoid (d) Malaria

6. Read the following statements. Which of the following is incorrect?
   (a) Rhinoviruses cause some of the most infectious human ailments like common cold
   (b) In patients with pneumonia, the alveoli are filled with fluid, leading to severe problems in respiration
   (c) Cholera can be confirmed by the Widal test
   (d) A healthy person acquires pneumonia by inhaling droplets/aerosols released by infected persons

7. The malignant tertian malaria is caused by:
   (a) *Plasmodium vivax*
   (b) *Plasmodium malariae*
   (c) *Plasmodium falciparum*
   (d) *Plasmodium ovale*

8. Humans become infected with malaria through _________, by the bite of _________:
   (a) Sporozoites, female *Culex*
   (b) Trophozoites, female *Anopheles*
   (c) Sporozoites, female *Anopheles*
   (d) Gametocytes, female *Aedes*

9. Identify the incorrect match:
   (a) Tetanus – Lock jaw
   (b) Typhoid – Enteric fever
   (c) Poliomyelitis – Infantile paralysis
   (d) Malaria – Black death

10. In the *Plasmodium* life cycle, fertilisation and development take place in:
    (a) Salivary glands of mosquito
    (b) Human intestine
    (c) Human liver
    (d) Mosquito's intestine

11. Which of the following is a non-infectious disease?
    (a) Pneumonia (b) Plague
    (c) Dengue fever (d) Cancer

12. Which of the following is incorrect with respect to amoebiasis?
(a) *Entamoeba histolytica* is a protozoan parasite in the small intestine which causes amoebic dysentery
(b) Symptoms of this disease include constipation, abdominal pain, cramps and stool with excess mucus and blood clots
(c) Houseflies act as mechanical carriers and serve to transmit the parasite from the faeces of infected persons to food and food products
(d) Drinking water and food contaminated by faecal matter is the main source of infection

13. Which one of the following is not responsible for ringworm infection in humans?
(a) *Microsporum* (b) *Trichophyton*
(c) *Epidermophyton* (d) *Corynebacterium*

14. Ringworms are generally acquired:
(a) From soil
(b) Using towels or clothes of infected person
(c) Sharing comb of infected individual
(d) All of the above

15. Elephantiasis is caused by:
(a) *Ascaris* (b) *Wuchereria*
(c) *Enterobius* (d) *Trichinella*

16. Read the following statements. Which of the following are incorrect?
(i) Appearance of dry scaly lesions on various parts of the body such as skin, nails and scalp are the main symptoms of ringworms.
(ii) Filariasis is spread by the bite of the male *Culex*.
(iii) A person acquires *Ascaris* infection through contaminated water, vegetables fruit, etc.
(iv) In the life cycle of *Plasmodium*, the female mosquito takes up sporozoites with blood meal.
(a) (i) and (iii) (b) (i) and (iii)
(c) (iii) and (iv) (d) (ii) and (iv)

17. The symptoms of which of the following diseases include internal bleeding, muscular pain, fever, anemia and blockage of the intestinal passage?
(a) Filariasis (b) Ascariasis
(c) Amoebiasis (d) Malaria

18. Identify the incorrect statement:
(a) Blood circulation was discovered by William Harvey
(b) Fish like *Gambusia* feed on mosquito larvae and are used for biological control of malaria
(c) Mary Mallon was a typhoid carrier who continued to spread disease for several years through the food she prepared
(d) Pneumonia infects the nose and respiratory passage, but not the lungs

19. All of the following are helminth diseases, except:
(a) Ascariasis (b) Taeniasis
(c) Enterobiasis (d) Amoebiasis

20. Which of the following is not a vehicle-borne disease?
(a) Amoebiasis (b) Typhoid
(c) Ringworms (d) Ascariasis

21. Proper disposal of waste and excreta, periodic cleaning and disinfection of water reservoirs, pools, cesspools and tanks are useful for preventing diseases like:
(a) Typhoid and ascariasis
(b) Amoebiasis and ascariasis
(c) Typhoid and amoebiasis
(d) All of the above

22. Which of the following diseases is caused by a protozoan?
(a) Syphilis (b) Influenza
(c) Blastomycosis (d) Babesiosis

23. 'Typhoid Mary' is the nickname of:
(a) Mary Clinton (b) Mary Mallon
(c) Mary Meister (d) Mary Pasteur

24. Which of the following is/are useful for maintaining good health?
(a) Awareness about diseases
(b) Personal and public hygiene
(c) Preventing close contact with infected persons
(d) All of the above

25. Select the incorrect statement:
(a) *Salmonella typhi* causes enteric fever
(b) Parasites like bacteria, viruses, fungi and protozoans are pathogenic as they harm hosts
(c) Symptoms of amoebiasis include fever, chills, cough and headache
(d) Among non-infectious diseases, cancer is a major cause of death

26. Which of the following is incorrect for common cold?
(a) It is characterised by nasal congestion and discharge, sore throat, hoarseness, cough and headache
(b) It usually lasts 3–7 days
(c) Infection may be transmitted through droplets from coughing and sneezing by an infected person
(d) In severe cases, the lips and finger nails may turn grey to bluish in colour

27. In patients with malaria, chills and high fever recurring every three to four days occurs due to rupture of ___A___ and release of toxic substance ___B___. Fill in the blanks with the correct options:

	A	B
(a)	WBCs	Interferon
(b)	RBCs	Haemozoin
(c)	Lymphocytes	Haemozoin
(d)	RBCs	Cytokine

28. Identify the incorrect statement:
(a) Kala azar is caused by *Leishmania*
(b) Measures for personal hygiene include keeping the body clean, consumption of clean drinking water, food, vegetables, etc.
(c) Ringworm infections thrive in skin folds of groin and toes
(d) In the life cycle of *Plasmodium*, the parasite reproduces sexually in liver cells

29. Elephantiasis is caused by a member of:
(a) Arthropoda (b) Annelida
(c) Platyhelminthes (d) Aschelminthes

30. Ronald Ross received the Nobel Prize for Physiology or Medicine for his work on the transmission of:
(a) Dengue fever (b) Malaria
(c) Amoebiasis (d) Pneumonia

31. Inflammation of lymphatic vessels of the lower limbs and genital organs is seen in:
(a) Ascariasis (b) Amoebiasis
(c) Filariasis (d) Ringworm disease

32. Ascariasis:
(a) Is caused by a nematode parasite
(b) Spreads through contaminated food and water
(c) Spreads by the bite of the female mosquito
(d) More than one option is correct

33. *Aedes* is a vector of:
(a) Malaria and dengue fever
(b) Filariasis and malaria
(c) Dengue and chikungunya
(d) Leprosy and amoebiasis

34. Avoiding stagnation of water in and around residential areas, regular cleaning of household coolers and use of mosquito nets is useful in preventing:
(a) Ascariasis and filariasis
(b) Typhoid and pneumonia
(c) Amoebiasis and common cold
(d) Dengue fever and chikungunya

35. Which of the following is a causative agent of plague?
(a) *Yersinia pestis*
(b) *Bordetella pertussis*
(c) *Streptococcus pneumoniae*
(d) *Staphylococcus aureus*

36. Motile zygote of *Plasmodium* occurs in:
(a) Human RBCs
(b) Human liver
(c) Gut of female *Anopheles*
(d) Salivary glands of *Anopheles*

37. Athlete's foot is caused by:
(a) *Tinea pedis* (b) *Tinea capitis*
(c) *Tinea barbae* (d) Retrovirus

38. Benign tertian malaria is caused by:
(a) *Plasmodium vivax*
(b) *Plasmodium falciparum*
(c) *Plasmodium ovale*
(d) *Plasmodium malariae*

39. Sandfly is the vector for:
(a) Sleeping sickness (b) Kala azar
(c) Malaria (d) Dysentery

40. Which of the following is a pair of viral diseases?
(a) Ringworm, AIDS
(b) Common cold, AIDS
(c) Dysentery, Tuberculosis
(d) Leprosy, Syphilis

Immunity

41. Which of the following is not a physiological barrier of innate immunity?
(a) Acid in stomach
(b) Saliva in mouth
(c) Tears from eyes
(d) Mucus coating of respiratory lining

42. Interferons:
(a) Are cytokine barriers
(b) Are secreted by virus-infected cells
(c) Protect non-infected cells from viral infections
(d) All are correct

43. Which of the following is incorrect with respect to innate immunity?
(a) Is present at the time of birth
(b) Is called inborn immunity
(c) Is pathogen specific
(d) Is a non-specific type of defence

44. The cellular barrier(s) in innate immunity are:
(a) PMNL (neutrophils)

(b) Monocytes
(c) Natural killer cells
(d) All of the above

45. The primary lymphoid organs include:
(a) Spleen and thymus
(b) Lymph node and bone narrow
(c) Bone narrow and thymus
(d) Peyer's patches and appendix

46. The heavy and light chains of an antibody are connected by:
(a) Glycosidic bonds
(b) Disulphide bonds
(c) Phosphoester bonds
(d) Hydrogen bonds

47. The antigen binding site on the antibody comprises:
(a) The variable region of light and heavy chains
(b) The constant region of light and heavy chains
(c) The variable region of light chain and constant region of heavy chain
(d) The variable region of heavy chain and constant region of light chain

48. The first antibody to appear in serum following stimulation by antigen is:
(a) IgM (b) IgG
(c) IgD (d) IgE

49. DPT vaccine is effective in humans against:
(a) Diphtheria, polio and typhoid
(b) Diabetes, pertussis and typhoid
(c) Diphtheria, pertussis and tetanus
(d) Diabetes, pertussis and tetanus

50. Passive immunity is:
(a) Achieved through vaccination
(b) Acquired after recovering from disease
(c) Obtained by receiving ready-made antibodies
(d) Acquired by receiving antibiotics

51. The secretory immunoglobulin present in the colostrum of the mother is:
(a) IgG (b) IgM
(c) IgA (d) IgD

52. Histamine, serotonin and heparin are secreted by:
(a) Lymphocytes (b) Monocytes
(c) Neutrophils (d) Basophils

53. Identify the incorrect statement:
(a) Kupffer cells are phagocytic cells of the liver
(b) Natural killer cells are examples of macrophages
(c) Neutrophils are called PMNL
(d) Monocytes and neutrophils are phagocytic leucocytes of blood

54. Which of the following is related to humoral immunity?
(a) Cytotoxic T-lymphocytes
(b) B-lymphocytes
(c) Monocytes
(d) Macrophages

55. Which of the following immunoglobulin is found as a pentamer?
(a) IgG (b) IgA
(c) IgM (d) IgD

56. Select the incorrect statement:
(a) Immunosuppressants are prescribed to patients who have received organ transplants
(b) B-lymphocytes are responsible for rejection of grafts
(c) Antibody has two heavy and two light chains
(d) Peyer's patches are masses of lymphoid tissue in the wall of the ileum

57. Immunity that develops in the foetus after receiving antibodies from the mother's blood through the placenta is:
(a) Naturally acquired active immunity
(b) Naturally acquired passive immunity
(c) Artificially acquired passive immunity
(d) Artificially acquired active immunity

58. Which of the following is an autoimmune disease?
(a) Muscular dystrophy
(b) Rheumatoid arthritis
(c) Osteoarthritis
(d) Gouty arthritis

59. Which of the following is a correct statement?
(a) The yellowish fluid colostrum has abundant IgE antibodies
(b) IgA antibodies are produced in an allergic reaction
(c) B-lymphocytes mediate cell-mediated immunity
(d) Spleen is a secondary lymphoid organ

60. Natural killer (NK) cells are examples of:
(a) Physical barrier of specific immunity
(b) Physiological barrier of innate immunity
(c) Cellular barrier of innate immunity
(d) Cytokine barrier of specific immunity

61. Immunoglobulins are:
(a) Glycolipids (b) Glycoproteins
(c) Steroids (d) Only sugars

62. Anti-venom injection contains preformed antibodies, while polio drops that are administered orally contain:
(a) Activated pathogens

(b) Attenuated pathogens
(c) Killed pathogens
(d) Gamma globulins

63. The letter 'T' in T-lymphocyte refers to:
(a) Thymus (b) Thyroid
(c) Tonsil (d) Thalamus

64. MALT (mucosa-associated lymphoid tissue) constitutes about ________ per cent of the lymphoid tissue in the human body:
(a) 70 (b) 50
(c) 25 (d) 10

65. If you suspect major deficiency of antibodies in a person, to which of the following would you look for confirmatory evidence?
(a) Serum albumins (b) Fibrinogen
(c) Serum globulins (d) Haemocytes

66. If a person has abundant interferons in blood, this patient is suffering from:
(a) Tetanus (b) Malaria
(c) Diphtheria (d) Measles

67. Which of the following is an incorrect statement?
(a) Epitope or antigenic determinant is the part of the antigen to which the antibody binds
(b) Anti-tetanus serum and anti-venom are examples of passive immunity
(c) IgE is produced in response to hypersensitivity reactions
(d) Passive immunity lasts longer than active immunity and also has immunological memory that is absent in active immunity

68. Allergy is caused due to release of chemicals like ________ and ________:
(a) Histamine, adrenaline
(b) Heparin, anti-histamine
(c) Histamine, serotonin
(d) Serotonin, anti-histamine

69. Which of the following is an incorrect statement with respect to vaccination?
(a) The principle of vaccination is based on the property of "memory" of the immune system
(b) In vaccination, inactivated/weakened pathogens are introduced into the body
(c) Vaccination involves injection of preformed antibodies against pathogens
(d) Vaccines generate memory B and T-cells that recognise the pathogens quickly on subsequent encounter with the pathogen

70. If a person meets with a road accident, which of the following is administered?
(a) Anti-histamines
(b) Anti-venom
(c) Anti-tetanus serum
(d) Tetanus toxoid

71. Which of the following processes stimulates antigen recognition by phagocytes?
(a) Neutralisation (b) Opsonisation
(c) Phagocytosis (d) Agglutination

72. Deficiency of the enzyme adenosine deaminase causes:
(a) Allergy
(b) Hypersensitivity
(c) Autoimmune diseases
(d) Immunodeficiency

73. Mucosa-associated lymphoid tissue (MALT) is found in all, except:
(a) Respiratory tract (b) Digestive tract
(c) Urogenital tract (d) Heart

74. Select the incorrect statement with respect to secondary immune response:
(a) It occurs due to memory cells
(b) It is called anamnestic response
(c) It occurs upon first exposure to the pathogen
(d) It is also called booster response

75. Cell-mediated immunity (CMI) is involved in:
(a) Killing virus infected cells
(b) Killing tumour cells
(c) Graft rejection
(d) All of the above

76. The second most abundant antibody constituting about 10% of the total serum immunoglobulins is:
(a) IgM (b) IgG
(c) IgA (d) IgD

77. Which of the following vaccines is prepared from the live attenuated (weakened) organism?
(a) Oral polio vaccine
(b) Typhoid vaccine
(c) Injectable polio vaccine
(d) Diphtheria vaccine

78. Which of the following cells can be included under antigen presenting cells (APCs)?
(a) Macrophage (b) B-lymphocytes
(c) Dendritic cells (d) All of the above

79. Which of the following is an incorrect statement?
(a) Mary Mallon was nicknamed Typhoid Mary as she was a carrier of typhoid
(b) Louis Pasteur developed vaccines against chicken cholera, rabies and anthrax

(c) The alphabet "R" in the vaccine MMR stands for Rubeola
(d) Haptens are substances that are incapable of inducing antibody formation by themselves, but can induce antibody formation by combining with large protein molecules

80. All of the following are a part of innate immunity, except:
(a) Interferons (b) Natural killer cells
(c) Macrophages (d) Cytotoxic T-cells

81. Hepatitis B vaccine is:
(a) Prepared from transgenic *Escherichia coli*
(b) Prepared from transgenic yeast
(c) Prepared from cultured virus
(d) Prepared from bacteria causing Hepatitis B

82. Free antibodies have which of the following sets of functions?
(a) Opsonisation, agglutination, phagocytosis
(b) Agglutination, opsonisation, neutralisation
(c) Opsonisation only
(d) Secretion of perforin proteins

83. Select the incorrect statement:
(a) Peyer's patches are called abdominal tonsils
(b) The most abundant antibodies in blood are the smallest and can cross the placenta
(c) B- and T-lymphocytes form the cellular barrier of innate immunity
(d) Injection of tetanus toxoid (TT) vaccination is an example of active immunity

84. One of the drawbacks of active immunity is that:
(a) It is not long lasting
(b) It is harmful
(c) It is very fast and can destroy the body's cells
(d) It is slow and takes time to form antibodies

85. Paratope is:
(a) Antigenic determinant site of the antigen
(b) Antigen binding site of antibody
(c) Region of the antigen at which antibody combines
(d) None of the above

86. ________ predominantly increases during helminthic infection:
(a) IgA (b) IgE
(c) IgD (d) IgG

87. Read the following statements.
(i) Innate immunity is specific immunity
(ii) Some viral diseases can be prevented by the use of vaccines
(iii) Disease causing viruses cannot be killed by antibiotics
(iv) Oral rehydration therapy is administered to patients suffering from cholera
(v) Malaria and amoebiasis are caused by pathogenic bacteria

Which of the above statements are incorrect?
(a) (i) and (ii) (b) (iii) and (iv)
(c) (i) and (v) (d) (ii) and (v)

88. Which of the following is not related to hyperactivity of the immune system?
(a) Urticaria (b) Hay fever
(c) Anaphylaxis (d) AIDS

89. The largest antibody is:
(a) Pentameric with 10 paratopes
(b) The first antibody to be produced in primary immune response
(c) Both (a) and (b)
(d) Dimeric in nature

90. Select the incorrect statement:
(a) Cholera, typhoid and Hepatitis A are spread by the faeco-oral route
(b) Anti-venin injected in a person suffering from snake bite is a collection of preformed antibodies produced in a heterologous host
(c) Opsonisation refers to attachment of antibodies to pathogens to make them susceptible to phagocytosis by macrophages
(d) HIV that causes AIDS first starts destroying B-lymphocytes

AIDS, Cancer, Drugs and Alcohol Abuse

91. AIDS was first reported in:
(a) 1991 (b) 1981
(c) 1974 (d) 2001

92. People who are at high risk of HIV infection are:
(a) Those who have multiple sexual partners
(b) Drug addicts who take drugs intravenously
(c) Individuals who require repeated blood transfusions
(d) All of the above

93. Select the incorrect statement:
(a) HIV is a member of a group of viruses called retrovirus
(b) Transmission of HIV may occur by sexual contact with an infected person
(c) HIV/AIDS is not spread by mere cough or physical contact

(d) There is no time lag between the infection and appearance of AIDS symptoms

94. In the human body, HIV infects primarily:
(a) Macrophages and B-lymphocytes
(b) Helper T-lymphocytes and macrophages
(c) B-lymphocytes and helper T-lymphocytes
(d) Cytotoxic T-lymphocytes and mast cells

95. Metastasis is the most feared property of:
(a) Benign tumours (b) Malignant tumours
(c) Both (a) and (b) (d) Crown gall tumours

96. Which of the following is an incorrect statement?
(a) Benign tumours remain confined to their original location
(b) The cells of malignant tumours grow very rapidly and invade the surrounding normal tissues
(c) Cancer cells divide rapidly and starve normal cells by competing for vital nutrients
(d) Cancer cells show the property of contact inhibition

97. ________ uses X-rays to generate a three-dimensional image of the internals of an object:
(a) Magnetic resonance imaging (MRI)
(b) Ultrasonography
(c) Computed tomography (CT)
(d) Positron emission tomography (PET)

98. World AIDS day is observed every year on:
(a) 4th February (b) 1st December
(c) 11th July (d) 6th March

99. The organisation of the Indian government that spreads awareness about AIDS is:
(a) ICAR (b) CDRI
(c) NDDB (d) NACO

100. Migration of cancer cells from the site of origin to other parts of the body, forming secondary tumours, is called:
(a) Metagenesis (b) Metastasis
(c) Metamorphosis (d) Metaphor

101. Which of the following cells are called HIV factory?
(a) Neutrophils (b) Macrophages
(c) Mast cells (d) Basophils

102. Which of the following diagnostic techniques is used for screening patients for breast cancer?
(a) PAP smear
(b) Mammography
(c) Bone marrow examination
(d) Ultrasonography

103. Which of the following can produce hallucinations when consumed in high doses and interferes with the transport of dopamine?
(a) Morphine (b) Cocaine
(c) Hashish (d) Heroin

104. The opioid receptors are present in:
(a) Central nervous system (CNS)
(b) Gastrointestinal tract (GIT)
(c) Both (a) and (b)
(d) Lungs

105. Which of the following non-ionising radiations causes DNA damage, leading to neoplastic transformation?
(a) UV rays (b) X rays
(c) Gamma rays (d) Alpha rays

106. Which of the following does not bind with opioid receptors?
(a) Morphine (b) Heroin
(c) Codeine (d) Psilocybin

107. ________ is an analgesic drug and used for relieving intense surgical pain:
(a) Cocaine (b) Barbiturate
(c) Morphine (d) Amphetamine

108. Which of the following is incorrect with respect to heroin?
(a) It is commonly called smack
(b) Chemically, it is diacetylmorphine
(c) It is a white, odourless, bitter crystalline compound
(d) It is obtained from the inflorescence of the plant *Cannabis sativa*

109. Select the incorrect statement with respect to cocaine:
(a) It is obtained from the plant *Erythroxylum coca*
(b) It is commonly called coke or crack and is usually snorted
(c) It produces a sense of euphoria
(d) It has depressant action on the central nervous system

110. Identify the incorrect statement:
(a) Opioids are obtained from the latex of the poppy plant *Papaver somniferum*
(b) Heroin is a depressant and slows down body functions
(c) These days cannabinoids are being abused by some sportspersons
(d) The flower tops, leaves and resin of the cannabis plant are used in various combinations to produce marijuana

111. Smoking reduces:
(a) Carbon monoxide content in blood
(b) Haembound oxygen in blood
(c) Blood pressure
(d) Heart rate

112. Select the incorrect statement:
(a) Morphine is a sedative and a painkiller
(b) Sarcomas are cancers of mesodermal origin
(c) Smoking is associated with increased incidence of cancers of the lung, urinary bladder and throat
(d) Withdrawal symptoms are not observed if regular dose of drugs/alcohol is abruptly discontinued

113. Match Column I with Column II and choose the correct option:

Column I	Column II
A. Cocaine	(i) Marijuana
B. Benzodiazepines	(ii) Crack
C. Cannabinoids	(iii) Smack
D. Opioids	(iv) Tranquiliser

(a) A – (i), B – (iii), C – (ii), D – (iv)
(b) A – (ii), B – (iv), C – (i), D – (iii)
(c) A – (iii), B – (i), C – (ii), D – (iv)
(d) A – (i), B – (iv), C – (ii), D – (iii)

114. Read the following statements. Identify the incorrect one with respect to the source plant of the diagram given below:

(a) The chemicals yielded by this plant interact with cannabinoid receptors present principally in the brain
(b) The flower tops, leaves and resin of this plant are used in combination to produce marijuana, hashish, charas and ganja
(c) Generally taken by inhalation and oral ingestion, these are known for their side effects on the cardiovascular system of the body
(d) None of the above

115. Identify the plant and its corresponding category in the diagram given below:

(a) *Cannabis sativa*: Hallucinogen
(b) *Datura*: Hallucinogen
(c) Opium: Depressant
(d) *Erythroxylum coca*: Stimulant

116. Choose the correct option with respect to the drug containing the molecule given below:

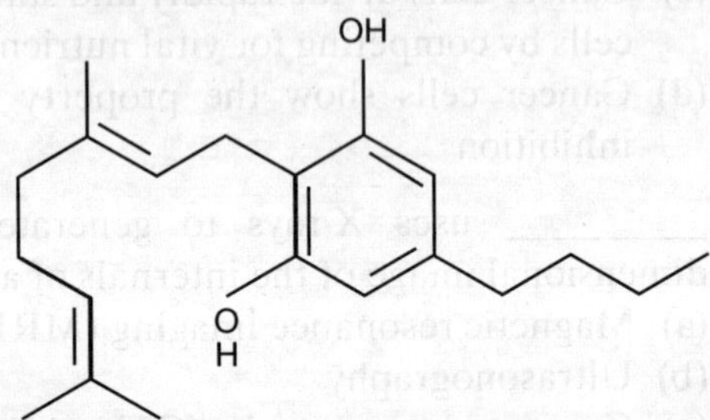

(a) Morphine (b) Cocaine
(c) Marijuana (d) Amphetamine

117. Identify the diagram given below in figures A and B:

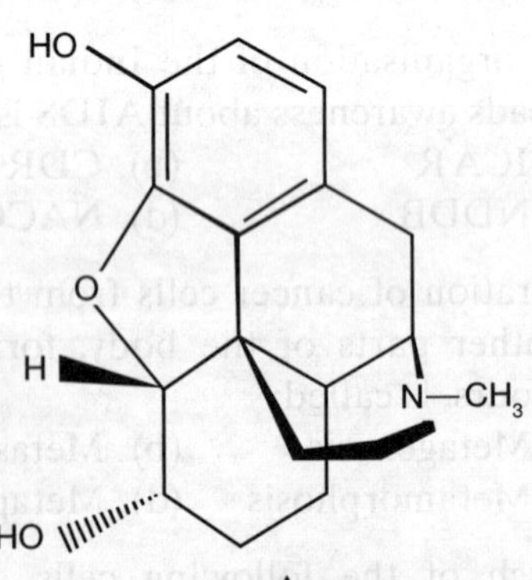

(a) A – Morphine, B – *Datura*
(b) A – Cannabinoid, B – Opium poppy
(c) A – Morphine, B – Opium poppy
(d) A – Morphine, B – *Cannabis sativa*

118. Select the incorrect statement:
(a) Tobacco contains a large number of chemical substances including nicotine, an alkaloid
(b) Nicotine simulates the adrenal gland to release adrenaline and nor-adrenaline into blood circulation
(c) Tobacco chewing is associated with increased risk of cancer of the oral cavity
(d) Smoking reduces the incidence of bronchitis, emphysema and gastric ulcer

119. Read the following statements.
(i) Those who take drugs intravenously are less likely to acquire serious infections like AIDS and Hepatitis B
(ii) The chronic use of drugs and alcohol damages the nervous system and liver (cirrhosis)
(iii) The side-effects of the use of anabolic steroids in females include masculinisation, mood swings, depression, abnormal menstrual cycles, enlargement of clitoris and deepening of voice
(iv) Habits such as smoking, taking drugs or alcohol are most likely to be started during adult life and not during young age or adolescence

Which of the above statements are incorrect?
(a) (i) and (ii) (b) (ii) and (iii)
(c) (iii) and (iv) (d) (i) and (iv)

120. Fatty liver syndrome is due to excessive intake of:
(a) Morphine (b) Tobacco
(c) Alcohol (d) Barbiturates

121. At which stage of HIV infection does one usually show symptoms of AIDS?
(a) When the viral DNA is produced by reverse transcriptase
(b) When the infected retrovirus enters the host cells
(c) When HIV damages a large number of helper T-lymphocytes
(d) Within two weeks of sexual contact with an infected person

122. Which one of the following statements is correct?
(a) Benign tumours show the property of metastasis
(b) Heroin accelerates body functions
(c) Patients who have undergone surgery are given cannabinoids to relieve pain
(d) Cocaine has a potent stimulating action on the central nervous system, producing a sense of euphoria and increased energy

123. Carcinoma refers to:
(a) Benign tumour of the connective tissue
(b) Malignant tumour of the bone
(c) Malignant tumour of the glial cells
(d) Malignant tumour of the skin or mucous membrane

124. Select the incorrect statement:
(a) Plants with hallucinogenic properties are *Atropa belladonna* and *Datura*
(b) Patients with cancer are given biological response modifiers such as α-interferon, which activates their immune system and helps in destroying the tumour
(c) Chemical carcinogens present in tobacco smoke have been identified as a major cause of lung cancer
(d) LSD (lysergic acid diethylamide) is the most powerful hallucinogen extracted from *Papaver somniferum*

125. State whether true (T)/false (F) and choose the correct option:
I. Addiction is a psychological attachment to certain effects – such as euphoria and a temporary feeling of wellbeing – associated with drugs and alcohol
II. Dependence is the tendency of the body to manifest a characteristic and unpleasant withdrawal syndrome if regular dose of drugs/alcohol is abruptly discontinued
III. With the repeated use of drugs/alcohol, the tolerance level of the receptors in our body reduce; as a result, receptors respond to lower doses of the drugs/alcohol
IV. Immediate adverse effects of drugs and alcohol abuse are manifested in the form of reckless behaviour, vandalism and violence

	I	II	III	IV
(a)	T	T	F	F
(b)	T	F	F	T
(c)	T	T	F	T
(d)	F	T	F	T

NCERT EXEMPLAR QUESTIONS

1. The term 'Health' is defined in many ways. The most accurate definition would be:
   (a) Health is the state of body and mind in a balanced condition
   (b) Health is the reflection of a smiling face
   (c) Health is a state of complete physical, mental and social well-being
   (d) Health is the symbol of economic prosperity

2. The organisms which cause diseases in plants and animals are called:
   (a) Pathogens (b) Vectors
   (c) Insects (d) Worms

3. The clinical test that is used for diagnosis of typhoid is:
   (a) ELISA (b) ESR
   (c) PCR (d) Widal

4. Diseases are broadly grouped into infectious and non-infectious diseases. In the list given below, identify the infectious diseases.
   (i) Cancer
   (ii) Influenza
   (iii) Allergy
   (iv) Smallpox
   (a) (i) and (ii) (b) (ii) and (iii)
   (c) (iii) and (iv) (d) (ii) and (iv)

5. The sporozoites that cause infection when a female *Anopheles* mosquito bites a person are formed in:
   (a) Liver of the person
   (b) RBCs of mosquito
   (c) Salivary glands of mosquito
   (d) Gut of mosquito

6. The disease chikungunya is transmitted by:
   (a) House fly
   (b) *Aedes* mosquito
   (c) Cockroach
   (d) Female *Anopheles*

7. Many diseases can be diagnosed by observing the symptoms in the patient. Which group of symptoms are indicative of pneumonia?
   (a) Difficulty in respiration, fever, chills, cough, headache
   (b) Constipation, abdominal pain, cramps, blood clots
   (c) Nasal congestion and discharge, cough, constipation, headache
   (d) High fever, weakness, stomach pain, loss of appetite and constipation

8. Cancer causing genes are called:
   (a) Structural genes (b) Expressor genes
   (c) Oncogenes (d) Regulatory genes

9. In malignant tumors, the cells proliferate, grow rapidly and move to other parts of the body to form new tumors. This stage of disease is called:
   (a) Metagenesis (b) Metastasis
   (c) Teratogenesis (d) Mitosis

10. When an apparently healthy person is diagnosed as unhealthy by a psychiatrist, the reason could be that:
    (a) The patient was not efficient at his work
    (b) The patient was not economically prosperous
    (c) The patient shows behavioural and social maladjustment
    (d) He does not take interest in sports

11. Which of the following are the reason(s) for rheumatoid arthritis? Choose the correct option.
    (i) The ability to differentiate pathogens or foreign molecules from self cells increases
    (ii) Body attacks self cells
    (iii) Fewer antibodies are produced in the body
    (iv) The ability to differentiate pathogens or foreign molecules from self cells is lost
    (a) (i) and (ii) (b) (ii) and (iv)
    (c) (iii) and (iv) (d) (i) and (iii)

12. AIDS is caused by HIV. Among the following, which one is not a mode of transmission of HIV?
    (a) Transfusion of contaminated blood
    (b) Sharing the infected needles
    (c) Shaking hands with infected persons
    (d) Sexual contact with infected persons

13. 'Smack' is a drug obtained from the:
    (a) Latex of *Papaver somniferum*
    (b) Leaves of *Cannabis sativa*
    (c) Flowers of *Datura*
    (d) Fruits of *Erythroxylum coca*

14. The substance produced by a cell in viral infection that can protect other cells from further infection is:
    (a) Serotonin (b) Colostrum
    (c) Interferon (d) Histamine

15. Transplantation of tissues/organs to save certain patients often fails due to rejection of such tissues/organs by the patient. Which type of immune response is responsible for such rejections?
    (a) Auto-immune response

(b) Humoral immune response
(c) Physiological immune response
(d) Cell-mediated immune response

16. Antibodies present in colostrum which protect the new born from certain diseases is of
(a) IgG type (b) IgA type
(c) IgD type (d) IgE type

17. Tobacco consumption is known to stimulate secretion of adrenaline and nor-adrenaline. The component causing this could be:
(a) Nicotine (b) Tannic acid
(c) Curamin (d) Catechin

18. Anti-venom against snake poison contains:
(a) Antigens
(b) Antigen-antibody complexes
(c) Antibodies
(d) Enzymes

19. Which of the following is not a lymphoid tissue?
(a) Spleen (b) Tonsils
(c) Pancreas (d) Thymus

20. Which of the following glands is large sized at birth but reduces in size with ageing?
(a) Pineal (b) Pituitary
(c) Thymus (d) Thyroid

21. Haemozoin is a:
(a) Precursor of hemoglobin
(b) Toxin released from *Streptococcus* infected cells
(c) Toxin released from *Plasmodium* infected cells
(d) Toxin released from *Haemophilus* infected cells

22. Which of the following is not the causal organism for ringworm?
(a) *Microsporum* (b) *Trichophyton*
(c) *Epidermophyton* (d) *Macrosporum*

23. A person with sickle cell anemia is
(a) More prone to malaria
(b) More prone to typhoid
(c) Less prone to malaria
(d) Less prone to typhoid

PRACTICE TEST PAPER

1. Which of the following is not related to ringworm infection?
(a) *Microsporum* (b) *Trichophyton*
(c) *Epidermophyton* (d) Taeniasis

2. Which set of diseases cannot be included under bacterial diseases?
(a) Cholera, Plague
(b) Leprosy, Tetanus
(c) Diphtheria, Tuberculosis
(d) Measles, Rubella

3. Which of the following is a viral disease in which the pathogen infects the nose and upper respiratory passage, but not the lungs?
(a) Pneumonia (b) Common cold
(c) Diphtheria (d) Tuberculosis

4. Widal test is used for the diagnosis of:
(a) Cholera (b) Tetanus
(c) Typhoid (d) Plague

5. In patients suffering from malaria, high-grade fever and chills are caused due to release of:
(a) Sporozoite (b) Haemozoin
(c) Gametocyte (d) Haemoglobin

6. Which of the following is an incorrect statement?
(a) Diabetes mellitus is a non-infectious disease
(b) Malaria is spread by the bite of the female *Anopheles*
(c) Mumps is a viral infection of the parotid glands
(d) Amoebiasis is caused by *Amoeba proteus*

7. Symptoms of which of the following diseases include internal bleeding, muscular pain, fever, anaemia and blockage of the intestinal passage?
(a) Filariasis (b) Ascariasis
(c) Cholera (d) Typhoid

8. Mark the incorrect set with respect to communicable diseases:
(a) AIDS, typhoid
(b) Chicken pox, mumps
(c) Measles, rubella
(d) Asthma, haemophilia

9. Swelling of body parts like limbs occurs in elephantiasis due to:
(a) Heart failure
(b) Renal failure
(c) Protein deficiency causing oedema
(d) Blockage of lymphatic circulation by the filarial worm

10. Select the incorrect match:
(a) Pneumonia – *Streptococcus pneumoniae*
(b) Typhoid – *Salmonella typhi*
(c) Common cold – Rhinovirus
(d) Diphtheria – *Haemophilus influenzae*

11. Which of the following is a source for production of the Hepatitis B vaccine?
(a) *Drosophila* (b) Goat's liver
(c) Yeast (d) Pig's pancreas

12. Which of the following are not the constituents of innate immunity?
(a) Skin, mucus coating of gut
(b) Interferons, cytokines
(c) Neutrophils, macrophages
(d) B-lymphocytes, T-lymphocytes

13. All of the following drugs are used to reduce the symptoms of allergy, except:
(a) Steroids (b) Morphine
(c) Adrenaline (d) Anti-histamines

14. If a person meets with a road accident, which of the following is administered?
(a) Anti-venom (b) Tetanus toxoid
(c) Plasma cells (d) Anti-tetanus serum

15. Which of the following is not a pair of secondary lymphoid organs?
(a) Tonsil and lymph nodes
(b) Spleen and appendix
(c) Bone narrow and thymus
(d) MALT and Peyer's patches

16. In which of the following diseases does the body fail to distinguish self-antigens from foreign antigens and starts killing its own cells?
(a) Cancer
(b) Communicable disease
(c) Autoimmune diseases
(d) Immunodeficiency diseases

17. In which lymphoid organ do the immature lymphocytes differentiate into antigen-sensitive lymphocytes?
(a) Spleen (b) Thymus
(c) Tonsil (d) Appendix

18. T-lymphocytes mediate:
(a) Humoral immunity
(b) Antibody-mediated immunity
(c) Cell-mediated immunity
(d) All of the above

19. The principle of vaccination is:
(a) Providing passive immunity
(b) Providing preformed antibodies
(c) Exposure to virulent pathogens
(d) Feeding of immunological memory

20. The yellowish fluid colostrum secreted by the mother during the initial days of lactation has which of the following antibodies in abundance?
(a) IgM (b) IgG
(c) IgA (d) IgE

21. Which of the following is the most abundant class of immunoglobulins constituting nearly 80% of the total antibodies?
(a) IgA (b) IgG
(c) IgD (d) IgM

22. Polymorphonuclear leucocytes (PMNL) are included in:
(a) Cytokine barrier
(b) Cellular barrier
(c) Physiological barrier
(d) Inflammatory barrier

23. Secondary immune response is also called:
(a) Cellular response
(b) Specific response
(c) Anamnestic response
(d) Primary immune response

24. Which of the following is an incorrect statement with respect to the spleen?
(a) Spleen is a large reservoir of erythrocytes
(b) Spleen is a large bean-shaped organ which mainly contains lymphocytes and phagocytes
(c) It acts as primary lymphoid organ
(d) It acts as a filter of blood, by trapping blood-borne microorganisms

25. Cell-mediated immunity (CMI) is involved in:
(a) Killing virus-infected cells
(b) Killing of tumour cells
(c) Rejection of foreign tissue obtained by transplant
(d) All of the above

26. Select the incorrect option with respect to examples of physiological barriers of immunity:
(a) Acid in stomach
(b) Tears
(c) Saliva in mouth
(d) Mucus coating of epithelium

27. All of the following drugs have clinical uses, except:
(a) Morphine (b) Barbiturates
(c) Amphetamine (d) Heroin

28. The side effects of the use of anabolic steroids in males do not include:

(a) Mood swings and depression
(b) Reduction in the size of testicles
(c) Excess hair growth on face and body
(d) Breast enlargement

29. Which of the following can produce hallucinations when consumed in high doses and interferes with the transport of dopamine?
(a) Morphine (b) Cocaine
(c) Heroin (d) Barbiturate

30. Mark the odd one out with respect to examples of opioids:
(a) Morphine (b) Heroin
(c) Codeine (d) Charas

31. HIV infects which of the following cells in our body?
(a) Helper T-cells (b) Cytotoxic T-cells
(c) Eosinophils (d) B-lymphocytes

32. Tumours are caused due to:
(a) Loss of contact inhibition
(b) Failure in regulation of cell division
(c) Uncontrolled proliferation of cells
(d) All of the above

33. HIV is called retrovirus because:
(a) It has DNA as genetic material
(b) It has RNA as genetic material
(c) It suppresses the immunity of the body
(d) There is time lag between infection and manifestation of symptoms

34. Multiple sclerosis belongs to a group of diseases called:
(a) Hypersensitivity
(b) Autoimmune diseases
(c) Lifestyle diseases
(d) Immunodeficiency diseases

35. The side effects of chemotherapy is/are:
(a) Hair loss
(b) Anaemia
(c) Bone marrow depression
(d) All of the above

36. The organisation of the Indian government that spreads awareness about AIDS is:
(a) NACO (b) NDDB
(c) NDRI (d) ICAR

37. Cancer cells are more easily damaged by radiation than normal cells because they are:
(a) Non-dividing
(b) Mutated
(c) Undergoing rapid division
(d) Different in structure

38. Diacetylmorphine is a semi-synthetic opiate and is several times more potent than morphine. It is also called:
(a) Codeine (b) Pethidine
(c) Heroin (d) Methadone

39. Which of the following is not a property of innate immunity?
(a) It is also called non-specific immunity
(b) It is also called inborn immunity
(c) It occurs due to memory cells
(d) Skin acts as physical barrier of this immunity

40. Which of the following components does not participate in innate immunity?
(a) Macrophages
(b) Neutrophils
(c) Natural killer cells
(d) B-lymphocytes

41. Interferons are used for the treatment of:
(a) Viral disease (b) Cancer
(c) Bacterial disease (d) Both (a) and (b)

42. Among non-infectious diseases, the major cause of death is:
(a) Diabetes (b) Cancer
(c) Mumps (d) Hypertension

43. Sustained high fever, weakness, stomach pain, constipation, headache and loss of appetite are some of the common symptoms of:
(a) Rabies (b) Typhoid
(c) Cholera (d) Measles

44. Tetanus is also called:
(a) Gangrene (b) Lockjaw
(c) Shingles (d) German measles

45. Which of the following is an incorrect statement?
(a) Tuberculosis is also called Koch disease
(b) Filariasis is caused by *Wuchereria bancrofti*
(c) Edward Jenner is called Father of Immunology
(d) Cholera is called enteric fever

ANSWER KEYS

Exercises

1. (d) **2.** (b) **3.** (b) **4.** (d) **5.** (d) **6.** (c) **7.** (c) **8.** (c) **9.** (d) **10.** (d)
11. (d) **12.** (a) **13.** (d) **14.** (d) **15.** (b) **16.** (d) **17.** (b) **18.** (d) **19.** (d) **20.** (c)
21. (d) **22.** (d) **23.** (b) **24.** (d) **25.** (c) **26.** (d) **27.** (b) **28.** (d) **29.** (d) **30.** (b)
31. (c) **32.** (d) **33.** (c) **34.** (d) **35.** (a) **36.** (c) **37.** (a) **38.** (a) **39.** (b) **40.** (b)
41. (d) **42.** (d) **43.** (c) **44.** (d) **45.** (c) **46.** (b) **47.** (a) **48.** (a) **49.** (c) **50.** (c)
51. (c) **52.** (d) **53.** (b) **54.** (b) **55.** (c) **56.** (b) **57.** (b) **58.** (b) **59.** (d) **60.** (c)
61. (b) **62.** (b) **63.** (a) **64.** (b) **65.** (c) **66.** (d) **67.** (d) **68.** (c) **69.** (c) **70.** (c)
71. (b) **72.** (d) **73.** (d) **74.** (c) **75.** (d) **76.** (c) **77.** (a) **78.** (d) **79.** (c) **80.** (d)
81. (b) **82.** (b) **83.** (c) **84.** (d) **85.** (b) **86.** (b) **87.** (c) **88.** (d) **89.** (c) **90.** (d)
91. (b) 92. (d) 93. (d) 94. (b) 95. (b) 96. (d) 97. (c) 98. (b) 99. (d) 100. (b)
101. (b) **102.** (b) **103.** (b) **104.** (c) **105.** (a) **106.** (d) **107.** (c) **108.** (d) **109.** (d) **110.** (d)
111. (b) **112.** (d) **113.** (b) **114.** (d) **115.** (b) **116.** (c) **117.** (c) **118.** (d) **119.** (d) **120.** (c)
121. (c) **122.** (d) **123.** (d) **124.** (d) **125.** (c)

NCERT Exemplar Questions

1. (c) **2.** (a) **3.** (d) **4.** (d) **5.** (d) **6.** (b) **7.** (a) **8.** (c) **9.** (b) **10.** (c)
11. (b) **12.** (c) **13.** (a) **14.** (c) **15.** (d) **16.** (b) **17.** (a) **18.** (c) **19.** (c) **20.** (c)
21. (c) **22.** (d) **23.** (c)

Practice Test Paper

1. (d) **2.** (d) **3.** (b) **4.** (c) **5.** (b) **6.** (d) **7.** (b) **8.** (d) **9.** (d) **10.** (d)
11. (c) **12.** (d) **13.** (b) **14.** (d) **15.** (c) **16.** (c) **17.** (b) **18.** (c) **19.** (d) **20.** (c)
21. (b) **22.** (b) **23.** (c) **24.** (c) **25.** (d) **26.** (d) **27.** (d) **28.** (c) **29.** (b) **30.** (d)
31. (a) **32.** (d) **33.** (b) **34.** (b) **35.** (d) **36.** (a) **37.** (c) **38.** (c) **39.** (c) **40.** (d)
41. (d) **42.** (b) **43.** (b) **44.** (b) **45.** (d)

SOLUTIONS

Common Diseases in Humans

1. In a healthy society, infant and maternal mortality is low. Health increases longevity of people.
2. The discovery of blood circulation by William Harvey using experimental methods and the demonstration of normal body temperature in persons with black bile using a thermometer disproved the 'good humour' hypothesis of health.
3. Typhoid is caused by *Salmonella typhi,* which generally enters the small intestine through food and water contaminated with them and migrates to other organs through blood.
4. Bacteria like *Streptococcus pneumoniae* and *Haemophilus influenzae* are responsible for the disease pneumonia in humans which infects the alveoli (air-filled sacs) of the lungs.
5. Malaria is caused by a protozoan of the genus *Plasmodium*. It is spread by the bite of the female *Anopheles* mosquito.
6. Typhoid fever is confirmed by the Widal test.
7. Malignant tertian malaria is caused by *Plasmodium falciparum*.
8. Humans become infected with malaria through sporozoites (infectious form), by the bite of the female *Anopheles.*
9. Plague is commonly called black death.
10. In the *Plasmodium* life cycle, fertilisation and development takes place in the mosquito's intestine.
11. Cancer is an example of a non-infectious disease.
12. *Entamoeba histolytica* is a protozoan parasite in the large intestine of humans, which causes amoebiasis/amoebic dysentery.
13. *Corynebacterium* causes diphtheria in humans. Fungi belonging to genera *Microsporum*, *Trichophyton* and *Epidermophyton* are responsible for ringworms, which is one of the most common infectious diseases in humans.
14. Ringworms are generally acquired from soil or by using towels, clothes or even the comb of infected individuals.
15. *Wuchereria bancrofti* is the filarial worm that causes a slowly developing chronic inflammation of the organs in which they live for many years, usually the lymphatic vessels of the lower limbs. The disease is called elephantiasis or filariasis.
16. Filariasis is spread by the bite of the female *Culex* mosquito. In the life cycle of *Plasmodium*, the female *Anopheles* mosquito acquires gametocytes upon biting an infected person. These gametocytes enter the mosquito's body and undergo further development.
17. Symptoms of ascariasis include internal bleeding, muscular pain, fever, anaemia and blockage of intestinal passage.
18. Pneumonia is caused by bacterial pathogens like *Streptococcus pneumoniae* and *Haemophilus influenzae*, which infect the alveoli (air-filled sacs) of the lungs.
19. Amoebiasis is a protozoan disease of the large intestine caused by *Entamoeba histolytica*.
20. Amoebiasis, typhoid and ascariasis are spread by consuming contaminated food and water carrying the infectious forms of the pathogens.
21. Public hygiene includes proper disposal of waste and excreta, periodic cleaning and disinfection of water reservoirs, pools, cesspools and tanks, and observing standard practices of hygiene in public catering. These measures are particularly essential where the infectious agents are transmitted through food and water such as typhoid, amoebiasis and ascariasis.
22. Babesiosis is caused by a protozoan *Babesia bigemina.*
23. 'Typhoid Mary' is the nickname of Mary Mallon, who was a cook by profession and was a typhoid carrier who continued to spread

typhoid for several years through the food she prepared.

24. Option (d) is correct.

25. Symptoms of amoebiasis include constipation, abdominal pain and cramps, stool with excess mucus and blood clots.

26. The common cold is characterised by nasal congestion and discharge, sore throat, hoarseness, cough, headache, tiredness, etc. which usually last for 3–7 days. In patients with pneumonia, the lips and finger nails may turn grey to bluish in colour in severe cases.

27. In patients with malaria, chills and high fever recurring every three to four days occurs due to rupture of RBCs and release of toxic substance haemozoin.

28. In the life cycle of *Plasmodium,* the parasite initially multiplies asexually in the liver cells and then attacks the red blood cells (RBCs), resulting in their rupture.

29. Elephantiasis is caused by *Wuchereria bancrofti*, a member of Aschelminthes.

30. Sir Ronald Ross was a British medical doctor who received the Nobel Prize for Physiology or Medicine in 1902 for his work on the transmission of malaria. His discovery of the malarial parasite in the gastrointestinal tract of the mosquito in 1897 proved that malaria was transmitted by the female *Anopheles* mosquitoes.

31. In patients with filariasis, inflammation of the lymphatic vessels of the lower limbs and genital organs is seen.

32. *Ascaris*, the common roundworm, is a nematode parasite that causes ascariasis. The eggs of the parasite are excreted along with the faeces of infected persons which contaminate soil, water, plants, etc. A healthly person acquires this infection through contaminated water, vegetables, fruits, etc.

33. *Aedes* mosquito is the vector of dengue fever and chikungunya.

34. For diseases such as dengue fever, malaria, chikungunya and filariasis that are transmitted through insect vectors, the most important measure is to control or eliminate the vectors and their breeding places. This can be achieved by avoiding stagnation of water in and around residential areas, regular cleaning of household coolers, use of mosquito nets, introducing fishes like *Gambusia* in ponds that feed on mosquito larvae, and spraying of insecticides in ditches, drainage areas and swamps, etc.

35. Plague is caused by the bacterium *Yersinia pestis/Pasteurella pestis*. It is spread by the bite of the rat flea (*Xenopsylla cheopis*).

36. The fertilisation of gametes and thus the motile zygote of *Plasmodium* occurs in the gut of the female *Anopheles* mosquito.

37. Athlete's foot is caused by *Tinea pedis* (ringworms). Ringworm of the scalp is caused by *Tinea capitis*, while that of face and neck is caused by *Tinea barbae*.

38. Benign tertian malaria is caused by *Plasmodium vivax*.

39. Kala azar is caused by a flagellate protozoan *Leishmania donovani*. It is spread by the bite of the sandfly (*Phlebotomus*).

40. Common cold and AIDS are diseases caused by viruses.

Immunity

41. Mucus coating of the epithelium lining the respiratory, gastrointestinal and urogenital tracts help in trapping microbes entering our body and constitute physical barriers of innate immunity.

42. Virus-infected cells secrete proteins called interferons which protect non-infected cells from further viral infections and constitute a cytokine barrier of innate immunity.

43. Innate immunity in a non-specific type of defence, that is present at the time of birth.

44. Cellular barriers of innate immunity include certain types of leukocytes (WBC) of our body like polymorpho-nuclear leukocytes (PMNL-neutrophils) and monocytes and natural killer (type of lymphocytes) in blood as well as macrophages in tissues.

45. The primary lymphoid organs are the bone marrow and thymus, where immature lymphocytes differentiate into antigen-sensitive lymphocytes.

46. The heavy and light chains of antibodies are connected by disulphide bonds.

47. Antigen binding on the antibody comprises the variable regions of light and heavy chains.

48. IgM is the first antibody to appear in serum following stimulation by antigen.

49. DPT vaccine is effective in humans against diphtheria, pertussis and tetanus.

50. Passive immunity is the transfer of immunity in the form of ready-made antibodies. It can occur naturally, when maternal antibodies are transferred to the foetus through the placenta, and it can also be induced artificially when high levels of antibodies specific to a pathogen or toxin are transferred to non-immune persons through blood products that contain antibodies. This is called immunoglobulin therapy or antiserum therapy.

51. Colostrum is rich in IgA.

52. Histamine, serotonin and heparin are secreted by basophils.

53. Natural killer (NK) cells are a type of lymphocyte and a component of the innate immune system. NK cells play a major role in host rejection of both tumours and virus-infected cells.

54. B-lymphocytes are a type of white blood cell. They function in the humoral immunity component of the adaptive immune system by secreting antibodies.

55. IgM is the largest immunoglobulin and is the first antibody to appear in response to initial exposure to an antigen. IgM is mostly a pentamer or a polymer of five monomers.

56. T-lymphocytes are central to the process of transplant rejection.

57. Naturally acquired passive immunity is obtained by the foetus from the mother in the form of IgG across the placenta.

58. Rheumatoid arthritis is an autoimmune disease that causes joint pain and damage throughout the body. It occurs when the immune system mistakenly attacks the body's own tissues and causes joint stiffness and tender, warm and swollen joints.

59. The yellowish fluid colostrum has abundant IgA antibodies. IgE antibodies are produced in allergic reactions. T-lymphocytes mediate cell-mediated immunity (CMI).

60. Natural killer (NK) cells are part of the cellular barrier of innate immunity.

61. Immunoglobulins, also known as antibodies, are glycoprotein molecules produced by plasma cells. They act as a critical part of the immune response by specifically recognising and binding to particular antigens, such as bacteria or viruses, and aiding in their destruction.

62. Oral polio drops contain live attenuated poliovirus strains of each of the three serotypes, selected by their ability to mimic the immune response following infection with wild polioviruses, but with a significantly reduced incidence of spreading to the central nervous system.

63. The letter 'T' in T-lymphocytes refers to thymus. The thymus is a lobed organ located near the heart and beneath the breastbone (sternum). The thymus is quite large at birth but keeps reducing with age and by the time puberty is attained, it reduces to a very small size.

64. There is lymphoid tissue located within the lining of the major tracts (respiratory, digestive and urogenital tracts) called mucosa-associated lymphoid tissue (MALT). It constitutes about 50 per cent of the lymphoid tissue in the human body.

65. Antibodies are glycoproteins belonging to the immunoglobulin superfamily. They constitute most of the gamma globulin fraction of blood proteins.

66. Interferons are proteins produced by virus-infected cells to protect un-infected cells from further viral infection. Measles or rubeola is a viral infection that starts in the respiratory system.

67. Active immunity lasts longer than passive immunity and also has immunological memory. B- and T-memory cells are generated in the

body upon the development of active immunity to produce highly intensified secondary or anamnestic response upon subsequent encounter with the same pathogen.

68. Allergy is caused due to release of histamine and serotonin.

69. In vaccination, a preparation of antigenic proteins of the pathogen or inactivated/weakened pathogen are introduced into the body. The antibodies produced in the body against these antigens would neutralise the pathogenic agents during actual infection.

70. Anti-tetanus serum (ATS), also known as tetanus antitoxin, is a medication made of antibodies against the tetanus toxin. It is used to prevent tetanus in those who have a wound like in a road accident, and are at high risk of developing disease.

71. An opsonin is any molecule that enhances phagocytosis by marking an antigen for an immune response. Opsonin, in ancient Greece, referred to the delicious side-dish of any meal. Opsonisation is a term that refers to an immune process where particles such as bacteria are targeted for destruction by an immune cell known as a phagocyte. The process of opsonisation is a means of identifying the invading particle to the phagocyte.

72. Adenosine deaminase (ADA) deficiency is an inherited disorder that damages the immune system and causes severe combined immunodeficiency (SCID). People with SCID lack virtually all immune protection from bacteria, viruses and fungi.

73. Mucosal-associated lymphoid tissue (MALT) is a lymphoid tissue located within the lining of the major tracts (respiratory, digestive and urogenital tracts).

74. When our body encounters a pathogen for the first time, it produces a response called primary response, which is low intensity. Subsequent encounters with the same pathogen elicit a highly intensified secondary or anamnestic response.

75. Cell-mediated immunity (CMI) is involved in killing virus-infected cells, killing tumour cells and is also responsible for graft rejection.

76. The most abundant antibody in our body is IgG. IgA is the second most abundant antibody, constituting 10% of the total antibodies in the body.

77. Oral polio vaccine (OPV) consists of a mixture of live attenuated poliovirus strains of each of the three serotypes, selected for their ability to mimic the immune response following infection with wild polioviruses, but with a significantly reduced incidence of spreading to the central nervous system.

78. Antigen presenting cells (APCs) are a heterogeneousgroupofimmunecellsthatmediate the cellular immune response by processing and presenting antigens for recognition by certain lymphocytes such as T-helper cells. Classic APCs include macrophages, dendritic cells and B-lymphocytes.

79. The vaccine "MMR" is given for immunisation against measles, mumps and rubella (German measles).

80. Cytotoxic T-cells are a component of specific immunity. Interferons are a part of cytokine barriers, while NK cells and macrophages are part of the cellular barrier of innate/non-specific immunity.

81. Hepatitis B vaccine is prepared from transgenic yeast. The gene for Hepatitis B surface antigen is introduced in yeast. Such recombinant yeast produces these antigens to provide immunity.

82. Free antibodies have functions like agglutination, opsonisation and neutralisation.

83. Certain types of leucocytes (WBC) of our body like polymorphonuclear leucocytes (PMNL)/neutrophils and monocytes and natural killer (NK) cells in the blood as well as macrophages in tissue can phagocytose and destroy microbes.

84. Active immunity is slow and it takes time to produce antibodies against pathogens. This immunity can occur naturally when a microbe or other antigen is received by a person who has not yet come into contact with the microbe and has no pre-made antibodies for defence.

85. A paratope, also called an antigen binding site, is a part of an antibody which recognises and binds to an antigen.

86. IgE is predominantly increased during helminthic infection.

87. Innate immunity is a non-specific type of defence, that is present at the time of birth. Malaria and amoebiasis are caused by protozoan pathogens.

88. AIDS is caused due to T-helper cell depletion causing poor immunity in patients due to HIV infection.

89. IgM is the largest immunoglobulin that exists as a pentamer with 10 paratopes. It is also the first antibody to be produced in primary immune response.

90. HIV attacks a specific type of immune cell called CD-4/helper T-cells, and uses the cells to make more of the viruses. HIV destroys CD-4 cells by using their replication machinery to create new copies of the virus. This ultimately causes the CD-4 cells to swell and burst.

AIDS, Cancer, Drugs and Alcohol Abuse

91. AIDS was first reported in 1981 by research groups led by Gallo and Luc Montagnier.

92. People who are at high risk of HIV infection include individuals who have multiple sexual partners, drug addicts, who take drugs intravenously, individuals who require repeated blood transfusions and children born to HIV-infected mothers.

93. There is always a time lag between the infection and appearance of AIDS symptoms. This period may vary from a few months to many years (usually 5–10 years).

94. In the human body, HIV infects primarily helper T-cells and macrophages that have CD-4 antigens on their surface.

95. Metastasis is a property of malignant tumours, in which the cancer cells break away from the main tumour and enter the bloodstream or lymphatic system and spread to distant locations in the body.

96. Normal cells show a property called contact inhibition by virtue of which contact with other cells inhibits their uncontrolled growth. Cancer cells appears to have lost this property.

97. Computed tomography used X rays to generate a three-dimensional image of the internals of the object.

98. World AIDS Day is observed on 1st December.

99. National AIDS Control Organisation (NACO) and the other non-governmental organisations (NGOs) are working towards educating people about AIDS.

100. Metastasis refers to migration of cancer cells from the site of origin to other body parts, forming secondary tumours.

101. After entering the body of a person, HIV enters the macrophages where the RNA genome of the virus replicates to form viral DNA with the help of the enzyme reverse transcriptase. The viral DNA is then incorporated into the host cell's DNA and directs the infected cells to produce virus particles. The macrophages continue to produce viruses and in this way acts like an HIV factory.

102. A mammogram is an X-ray picture of the breast used to look for early signs of breast cancer.

103. Cocaine interferes with the transport of the neurotransmitter dopamine. Excessive dosage of cocaine causes hallucinations.

104. Opioids are drugs that bind to specific opioid receptors present in our central nervous system and gastrointestinal tract.

105. UV rays are non-ionising radiation that causes DNA damage, leading to neoplastic transformation.

106. Morphine, heroin and codeine are opioid drugs. Psilocybin is a hallucinogenic drug obtained from *Psilocybin mexicana* (magic mushroom).

107. Morphine is a pain medication of the opiate family, obtained from the latex of the poppy plant *Papaver somniferum*.

108. Heroin, commonly called smack, is chemically diacetylmorphine. This is obtained by acetylation of morphine, which is extracted from the latex of the poppy plant *Papaver somniferum*.

109. Cocaine has potent stimulating action on the central nervous system, producing a sense of euphoria and increased energy.

110. The flower tops, leaves and resin of the cannabis plant are used in various combinations to produce marijuana, hashish, charas and ganja.

111. Smoking increases the carbon monoxide (CO) content in blood and reduces the concentration of haemoglobin oxygen.

112. Dependence is the tendency of the body to manifest a characteristic and unpleasant withdrawal syndrome if regular doses of the drugs/alcohol is abruptly discontinued. This is characterised by anxiety, shakiness, nausea and sweating which may be relieved when use is resumed again. In some cases, withdrawal symptom can be severe and even life threatening.

113. Option (b) is correct.

114. Option (d) is correct.

115. Option (b) is correct.

116. Option (c) is correct.

117. Option (c) is correct.

118. Smoking is associated with increased incidence of cancers of the lung, urinary bladder and throat, bronchitis, emphysema, coronary heart disease, gastric ulcer, etc.

119. Intravenous drug abusers are more likely to acquire serious infections like AIDS and Hepatitis B. The viruses that are responsible for these diseases are transferred from one person to another by shared infected needles and syringes. Curiosity, need for adventure and excitement and experimentation, constitute common causes, which motivate youngsters towards smoking, drug abuse or alcohol consumption. So, these habits are more likely to be taken up during adolescence than in adulthood.

120. Fatty liver syndrome is due to excessive intake of alcohol. This is the earliest stage of liver damage in alcoholics. With continued intake of alcohol, alcoholic hepatitis and liver cirrhosis are seen in these patients.

121. HIV enters the helper T-lymphocytes, replicates and produces progeny viruses. The progeny viruses released into blood attack other helper T-lymphocytes. This is repeated, leading to progressive decrease in the number of helper T-lymphocytes, precipitating symptoms of AIDS.

122. Malignant tumours show the property of metastasis. Heroin is a depressant and slows down body functions. Patients who have undergone surgery are given opioids like morphine to relieve pain.

123. Carcinoma is a category of a type of cancer that develops from epithelial cells. Specifically, a carcinoma is a cancer that begins in a tissue that lines the inner or outer surfaces of the body and that arises from cells originating in the endodermal, mesodermal or ectodermal germ layers during embryogenesis.

124. Lysergic acid diethylamide (LSD) is a powerful hallucinogen obtained from the ergot fungus, *Claviceps purpurea*, present on the rye plant.

125. With repeated use of drugs/alcohol, the tolerance level of the receptors present in our body increases. Consequently, the receptors respond only to higher doses of drugs or alcohol, leading to greater intake and addiction.

Strategies for Enhancement in Food Production

EXERCISES

Plant Breeding

1. The branch of biology that deals with the development of plant varieties is:
(a) Plant breeding (b) Eugenics
(c) Agrology (d) Horticulture

2. Green Revolution in India occurred during:
(a) 1960s (b) 1970s
(c) 1980s (d) 1950s

3. Green Revolution in India led to the increased production of higher yielding, disease-resistant varieties of:
(a) Wheat (b) Rice
(c) Pulses (d) All except (c)

4. The recorded evidence of plant breeding dates back to:
(a) 9000–11,000 years ago
(b) 900–1100 years ago
(c) 7000–13,000 years ago
(d) 14,000–20,000 years ago

5. Who is known as the Father of the Green Revolution in India?
(a) NF Borlaug (b) MS Swaminathan
(c) P Maheshwari (d) AK Singh

6. In plant breeding programmes, the entire collection of (plants/seeds) having diverse alleles for all genes in a given crop is called:
(a) Selection of superior recombinants
(b) Germplasm collection
(c) Evaluation and selection of parent
(d) Selection of superior traits

7. Classical plant breeding involves:
(a) Artificial selection only
(b) Hybridisation of heterozygous varieties
(c) Hybridisation of pure lines followed by artificial selection
(d) Utilisation of molecular genetic tools.

8. If we were to list the traits or characters that breeders have tried to incorporate into crop plants, the first preference would be:
(a) Resistance to plant pathogens
(b) Increased tolerance to insect pests
(c) Increased crop yield and improved quality
(d) Increased tolerance to environmental stress

9. Which of the following traits cannot be seen in plants developed by plant breeding techniques?
(a) Increased tolerance to salinity
(b) Resistance to pathogen and pest
(c) Increased yield and nutrient quality
(d) Decreased tolerance to environment stress

10. Which of the following events of plant breeding is a very time consuming and tedious process?
(a) Germplasm collection
(b) Evaluation and selection of parents
(c) Cross-hybridisation
(d) Selection and testing of superior recombinants

11. When a cross is made between two species of the same genus, the cross is known as:
(a) Intraspecific hybridisation
(b) Interspecific hybridisation
(c) Intergeneric hybridisation
(d) Intervarietal hybridisation

12. Superiority of hybrid over parent is:
(a) Hybrid vigour
(b) Heterosis
(c) Hybridised progeny
(d) All except (c)

13. Desired improved varieties of economically useful crops are raised by:
(a) Migration (b) Biofertiliser
(c) Hybridisation (d) Natural selection

14. Green Revolution in India was possible due to:
(a) Better irrigation
(b) Chemical fertiliser and pesticide facilities

(c) Intensive cultivation
(d) All of the above

15. Concept of crop scheduling and crop cafeteria was developed by:
(a) NE Borlaug (b) AK Singh
(c) P Maheshwari (d) MS Swaminathan

16. Oldest method of crop improvement used by farmers in cross-pollinated crop is:
(a) Mass selection (b) Pure line selection
(c) Clonal selection (d) Cross hybridisation

17. Which of the following is the crucial step in the success of plant breeding programmes?
(a) Collection of variability
(b) Evaluation and selection of parents
(c) Selection and testing of superior recombinants
(d) Testing release and commercialisation of new cultivars

18. Which is the most useful method of selection to obtain the desired characters in homozygous form?
(a) Mass selection (b) Clonal collection
(c) Artificial selection (d) Pure line selection

19. The new selected lines are cultivars emulated for their yield and other agronomic traits. This evaluation is carried out by growing these:
A. In the research field and recording their performance with low fertiliser and water-deficient soil
B. In the farmer's field for at least three growing seasons at different locations in the country, representing all agronomic zones
(a) Only (A) is correct
(b) Only (B) is correct
(c) Both (A) and (B) are correct
(d) Both (A) and (B) are incorrect

20. Norman Borlaug, known as the Father of the Green Revolution, developed new cultivating varieties of:
(a) Paddy (b) Rice
(c) Wheat (d) Sugarcane

21. The improved variety of wheat in the Green Revolution developed by Norman Borlaug was
(a) Tall (b) Semi-dwarf
(c) Thick-stemmed (d) Frost-resistant

22. India's wheat yield revolution in the 1960s was possible primarily because of:
(a) Mutations leading to reduction in plant height
(b) Increased chlorophyll content
(c) Use of hybrid seeds
(d) Mutation of quantitative traits

23. Improved rice variety of IR-8 has been introduced in India from:
(a) Taiwan (b) Japan
(c) Philippines (d) China

24. New varieties of plants are produced by:
(a) Selection of hybridisation
(b) Mutation and selection
(c) Introduction and mutation
(d) Selection and introduction

25. Agriculture contributes about ________ of India's GDP and gives employment ________ of the population:
(a) 15%, 30% (b) 33%, 62%
(c) 62%. 33% (d) 62%, 70%

26. Several hybrid varieties of millets are produced and made resistant to water stress. They may include:
A. *Zea mays*
B. Bajara
C. Sorghum
(a) Only (A) (b) Only (B) and (C)
(c) Only (B) (d) (A), (B) and (C)

27. Scented basmati rice is the contribution of:
(a) Borlaug (b) BP Paul
(c) MS Swaminathan (d) AK Singh

28. Jaya and Ratna developed for the Green Revolution in India are varieties of:
(a) Bajara (b) Rice
(c) Wheat (d) Maize

29. Semi-dwarf rice variety IR-8 was developed in:
(a) Taiwan (b) Philippines
(c) India (d) China

30. Sonalika and Kalyansona are:
(a) High yielding and disease-resistant wheat varieties
(b) Varities of rice
(c) Wheat varieties developed by mutation breeding
(d) More than one option is correct

31. *Saccharum barberi* was crossed with *S. officinarum* resulting in the formation of sugarcane varieties which possess:
(a) Thick stem (b) High sugar content
(c) High yield (d) All of the above

32. *Saccharum officinarum* is different from *S. barberi*:
(a) Due to better adaptability in north India
(b) Due to presence of thin stem
(c) Presence of high sugar content
(d) More than one option is correct

Plant Breeding for Disease Resistance, for Developing Resistance to Insects and Pests and for Improved Food Quality, Biofortification

33. Resistance to yellow mosaic virus in *Abelmoschus esculentus* was transferred from a wild species and resulted in a new variety called:
(a) Parbhani kranti (b) Pusa gaurav
(c) Pusa sadabahar (d) Pusa komal

34. Agriculture lost due to disease is about:
(a) 5% (b) 10%
(c) 20–30% (d) Less than 5%

35. All of the given plant diseases are caused by fungi, except:
(a) Brown rust of wheat
(b) Black rot of crucifers
(c) Late blight of potato
(d) Red rot of sugarcane

36. Which of the following varieties is resistant to the tobacco mosaic virus and leaf curl:
(a) Pusa swarnim (b) Pusa komal
(c) Pusa sawani (d) Pusa sadabahar

37. Parbhani kranti, a variety of bhindi, is resistant to:
(a) Bacterial blight (b) Yellow mosaic virus
(c) Black rot (d) Leaf curl

38. Find the correct match with respect to crop variety for disease resistance:

Column I	Column II
A. Himgiri	(i) White rust
B. Karan rai	(ii) Bacterial blight
C. Pusa snowball K-1	(iii) Hill bunt
D. Pusa komal	(iv) Black rot

(a) A – (iii), B – (i), C – (iv), D – (ii)
(b) A – (iii), B – (iv), C – (i), D – (ii)
(c) A – (iv), B – (i), C – (iii), D – (ii)
(d) A – (ii), B – (i), C – (iv), D – (iii)

39. Breeding for disease resistance requires:
(a) Disease test
(b) A good source of resistance
(c) Planned hybridisation
(d) All of the above

40. Plants can be made disease resistant through:
(a) Colchicine treatment
(b) X-ray treatment
(c) Breeding wild relatives
(d) Hormone treatment

41. Which of the following is a disease-resistant variety of *Brassica* developed against the disease white rust?
(a) Pusa sadabahar (b) Pusa swarnim
(c) Pusa gaurav (d) Pusa shubhra

42. Insect resistance is due to which of the following characteristics in the host crop plant?
(a) Morphological (b) Physiological
(c) Biochemical (d) All of the above

43. The conventional breeding methods for disease resistance involve the following steps:
A. Hybridisation of selected parents
B. Testing and release of new varieties
C. Securing germplasm from disease-resistant sources
D. Selection and evaluation of hybrids
Arrange the above steps in sequential order:
(a) (C) → (A) → (B) → (D)
(b) (B) → (A) → (C) → (D)
(c) (B) → (C) → (A) → (D)
(d) (C) → (A) → (D) → (B)

44. 'Pusa sawani' is an improved variety of ___A___, which is resistant to ___B___:

	A	B
(a)	Bhindi	Shoot and fruit borer
(b)	Bhindi	Yellow mosaic virus
(c)	Rapeseed	Aphids
(d)	Flat bean	Jassids

45. Which mutagen was responsible for the Green Revolution in India?
(a) X-rays (b) HNO_3
(c) γ radiation (d) UV rays

46. In mung bean, resistance to yellow mosaic virus and powdery mildew was induced by:
(a) Mutation breeding
(b) Hybridisation with wild relatives
(c) Mass selection
(d) Pure line selection

47. The scientific process by which crop plants are enriched with certain desirable nutrients is called:
(a) Plant breeding (b) Biofortification
(c) Bio-prospecting (d) Bio-remediation

48. Biofortification is used to deal with the problem of 'hidden hunger', which is:
(a) To increase the quality of vitamins
(b) To enhance the N_2 fixing ability in certain plants
(c) The most practical means to improve public health

(d) A breeding practice to increase production of cereal crops

49. Biofortification can be achieved through:
(a) Single-cell proteins
(b) Breeding practices
(c) Disease-resistant varieties
(d) All of the above

50. During biofortification, breeding for improved nutritional quality is undertaken with the objective of improving all, except:
(a) Protein content and quality
(b) Oil content and quality
(c) Vitamin content
(d) Mineral and micronutrient quality

51. Maize hybrids have been developed for higher amount of:
(a) Methionine (b) Lysine
(c) Leucine (d) Cysteine

52. Shakti, Ratan and Protina are three important lysine-rich varieties of:
(a) Rice (b) Pulses
(c) Wheat (d) Maize

53. Atlas-66 is rich in:
(a) Minerals
(b) Lysine and tryptophan
(c) Vitamins
(d) Protein

54. Vitamin A–rich vegetables crops released by IARI are:
(a) Spinach and bathua
(b) Better gourd, bathua, mustard and tomato
(c) Carrots, spinach and pumpkin
(d) Broad bean, *Lablab*, French and garden peas

55. IARI, New Delhi has developed biofortified spinach and bathua, which is rich in:
(a) Protein and vitamins
(b) Iron and calcium
(c) Amino acid and iron
(d) Protein and calcium

56. Which variety of flat bean shows resistance against jassids, aphids and fruit borer?
(a) Pusa sem-2 (b) Pusa sem-3
(c) Pusa A-4 (d) All except (c)

57. Pusa shubhra is a disease-resistant variety of:
(a) Cauliflower (b) Cow pea
(c) *Brassica* (d) Chilli

58. The plant whose ancestry has become obscure and which cannot survive in nature without human help is:
(a) Wheat (b) Maize
(c) Pisum (d) Barley

59. Fill in the blanks correctly and select the correct options:
A. In 2000, maize hybrids had twice the amount of amino acids ____**A**____ and ____**B**____ compared to existing maize hybrids.
B. Atlas-66 is a protein-rich variety of ____**C**____.

	A	B	C
(a)	Lysine	Tryptophan	Wheat
(b)	Lysine	Arginine	Rice
(c)	Lysine	Tryptophan	Barley
(d)	Methionine	Cysteine	Wheat

60. Resistance of the host plant to a disease causing pathogen is determined by:
(a) Host genotype
(b) Environmental conditions
(c) Pathogen genotype
(d) All of the above

61. Hairy leaves in cotton shows resistance to:
(a) Bollworms (b) Jassids
(c) Aphids (d) Stem sawfly

62. Correlate the following with respect to morphological characters that help to develop resistance against insects in plants:
Cotton : Hairy leaves : Wheat : ____________
(a) Solid stem (b) Thin stem
(c) Hollow stem (d) Low N_2 content

63. Find the odd one out with respect to characteristics that help maize to develop resistance against stem borers:
(a) Low nitrogen content
(b) Low sugar content
(c) High aspartic acid content
(d) High sugar content

64. Smooth leaves and nectar-less cotton varieties do not attract:
(a) Jassids (b) Aphids
(c) Bollworms (d) All of the above

65. Phenomenon of heterosis was studied in detail for the first time in:
(a) Maize (b) Sugarcane
(c) Wheat (d) Cotton

66. How can hybrid vigour be eroded?
(a) By repeated selfing
(b) By repeated crossing
(c) By repeated selection
(d) By mutation

Single-cell Protein, Tissue Culture, Green Manure, Energy Crops, Petroleum Plants

67. A single-cell protein refers to:
(a) A specific polypeptide extracted from the pure culture of a single type of cell
(b) Sources of mixed proteins extracted from pure or mixed culture of organisms or cells
(c) Protein extracted from a single cell
(d) A specific protein extracted from a single cell

68. Select the incorrect statement with respect to single-cell proteins:
(a) The biomass is obtained from unicellular microorganisms only
(b) It provides a protein-rich supplement
(c) It helps to minimise environmental pollution
(d) SCP has to be processed before use

69. All are used a source of SCP, except:
(a) *Spirulina* (b) *Methylophilus*
(c) Mushroom (d) *Chlamydomonas*

70. 250 g of a microorganism like *Methylophilus methylotrophus* produces 25 tonnes of protein per day. This is because of:
(a) High quality of proteins present in them
(b) High rate of biomass production
(c) Culturing bacteria in nutrient-rich culture media
(d) High rate of protein synthesis

71. The technique of obtaining a large number of plantlets by tissue culture method is called:
(a) Micropropagation (b) Macropropagation
(c) Plantlet culture (d) Organ culture

72. The technique of plant tissue culture was started by:
(a) Haberlandt
(b) Guba and Maheshwari
(c) Carlson et al.
(d) Alexis Carroll

73. The piece of sterile plant tissue to be used for tissue culture under aseptic conditions is:
(a) Inoculant (b) Explant
(c) Callus (d) Somaclone

74. Explant is required to be disinfected before placing in the culture medium. It is done by:
(a) Auto cleaning
(b) UV radiation
(c) X rays
(d) Chlorax or hyperchlorite

75. Which of the following is incorrectly matched?
(a) Explant – Excised plant part used for callus formation
(b) Cytokinins – Root initiation in callus
(c) Anther culture – Formation of androgenic haploids
(d) Somatic embryo – Embryo produced from a mass vegetative cell

76. To obtain virus-free healthy plants from a diseased one by tissue culture technique, which plant/parts of the disease plant will be taken?
(a) Apical meristem only
(b) Palisade parenchyma
(c) Both apical and axillary meristem
(d) Epidermal cells

77. Axenic culture refers to:
(a) Culture lacking agar in its nutrient media
(b) Culture of somatic tissue
(c) Culture without contamination
(d) Culture of pollen

78. A technique of micropropagation is:
(a) Somatic embryo genesis
(b) Protoplast fusion
(c) Embryo rescue
(d) Somatic hybridisation

79. Somaclones are obtained by:
(a) Plant breeding (b) Tissue culture
(c) Irradiation (d) Genetic engineering

80. Protoplasts of two different species are fused in:
(a) Micropropagation (b) Clonal propagation
(c) Organography (d) Somatic hybridisation

81. The enzymes required to obtain wall-free/naked protoplasts are:
(a) Cellulase and pectinase
(b) Cellulase and amylase
(c) Pectinase and protease
(d) Amylase and pectinase

82. Protoplast is:
(a) Another name for protoplasm
(b) Protoplasm of animal cell
(c) A cell without cell wall
(d) Cytoplasm without nucleus

83. On culturing the young anther of a plant, a botanist obtains a few diploid plants along with haploid plants. Which of the following might have produced the diploid plants?
(a) Exine of pollen grain
(b) Vegetative cell of pollen
(c) Cell of anther wall
(d) Generative cell of pollen

84. In plant tissue culture, roots can be induced by:
(a) Lower concentration of cytokinin and higher concentration of auxins
(b) Only cytokinin no auxins
(c) No cytokinin and only auxin
(d) Higher concentration of cytokinin and lower concentration of auxin

85. Callus is:
(a) Undifferentiated mass of tissue
(b) Differentiated mass of tissue in culture media
(c) Plant part used for tissue culture purpose
(d) Genetically identical clone developed through tissue culture technique

86. In tissue culture media, the resources of phytohormone is:
(a) Agar (b) Carbon source
(c) N source (d) Coconut milk

87. In vitro clonal propagation in plants in characterised by:
(a) PCR and RAPD
(b) Northern blotting
(c) Electrophoresis and HPLC
(d) Microscopy

88. Tissue culture technique can produce infinite number of new plants from a small parental tissue. The economic importance of the technique is in raising:
(a) Variants through picking up somaclonal variations
(b) Genetically identical population of an elite species
(c) Homozygous diploid plants
(d) Development of new species

89. Sterilisation of tissue culture medium is done by:
(a) Autoclaving of medium at 120° C for 15 minutes
(b) Filtering the medium through a bacteria-proof filter
(c) Mixing the medium with antimicrobial agents
(d) Keeping the medium at -196° C in liquid nitrogen

90. Agitation of liquid tissue culture serves the purpose of:
(a) Aeration
(b) Constant mixing
(c) Breaking cell aggregates
(d) All of the above

91. In plant tissue culture, callus can be induced to form shoots or roots by altering the ratio of:
(a) Auxin and cytokinin
(b) ABA and ethylene
(c) Auxin and gibberellin
(d) Gibberellin and cytokinin

92. Somaclonal variations are those:
(a) Caused by mutagens
(b) Produced during tissue culture
(c) Induced during sexual embryogeny
(d) Caused by gamma radiation

93. Androgenic haploids were produced from anther culture for the first time by:
(a) Bateson and Punnett
(b) Steward
(c) Guha and Maheshwari
(d) Auerbach and Stadler

94. Haploids from anther were first obtained from:
(a) Mustard (b) *Datura*
(c) Tobacco (d) Cotton

95. Embryo rescue method is used:
(a) To obtain homozygous diploids
(b) For multiple shoot production
(c) In interspecific hybridisation
(d) In intraspecific hybridisation

96. Who is known as the Father of Plant Tissue Culture?
(a) Haberlandt (b) Steward
(c) White (d) Skoog

97. Pomato is a somatic hybrid of:
(a) Brinjal and potato
(b) Potato and tomato
(c) Pac and tomato
(d) Potato and sweet potato

98. Which of the following can be used for the cultivation of SCPs like spirulina?
(a) Straw
(b) Sewage
(c) Waste water from potato processing plant
(d) All of the above

99. Which one of the following is being utilised as a source of biodiesel in the Indian countryside?
(a) Beetroot (b) Maize
(c) Sugarcane (d) *Euphorbia*

100. Which one is a source of single-cell proteins?
A. *Spirulina*
B. *Methylophilus*
C. Mushroom
D. *Chlorella*
(a) (A) and (B) only
(b) (A) and (D) only
(c) (A), (B) and (D) only
(d) (A), (B), (C) and (D)

101. The stage at which green manure crops are ploughed in soil to increase its soil fertility is:
(a) Seeding stage
(b) Mature phase
(c) Before flowering and fruiting
(d) All the end of the life cycle

102. The pioneer country in the production of fuel alcohol is:
(a) Brazil (b) Japan
(c) America (d) Iran

103. Recently, the Government of India allowed mixing of alcohol with petrol. What is the amount of alcohol permitted for mixing in petrol?
(a) 2.5% (b) 10–15%
(c) 10% (d) 5%

104. Maximum alcohol will be obtained from:
(a) Wood (b) Sugarcane
(c) Sugar beet (d) Maize

105. 250 g of the bacteria *Methylophilus methylotrophus,* because of its high biomass production, can produce __________ of protein per day:
(a) 25 tonnes (b) 250 g
(c) 25 kg (d) 1.5 kg

106. BGA used in SCP production is:
(a) *Spirulina* (b) *Chlorella*
(c) *Methylophilus* (d) All of the above

Animal Husbandry

107. Hisardale is a new breed of sheep developed in Punjab by:
(a) Inbreeding
(b) Out-crossing
(c) Cross-breeding
(d) Interspecific hybridisation

108. Some of the marine fishes that are eaten include:
(a) *Catla* and rohu
(b) Common carp and calbasu
(c) *Hilsa* and sardines
(d) Mrigal and magur

109. The practice of mating of animals within the same breed, but having no common ancestors on either side of their pedigree up to 4 6 generations, is called
(a) Cross-breeding
(b) Out-crossing
(c) Interspecific hybridisation
(d) Inbreeding

110. The industry devoted to the catching, processing or selling of fish, shellfish or other aquatic animals is called:
(a) Aquaculture (b) Fishery
(c) Apiculture (d) MOET

111. Select the incorrect statement:
(a) More than 70 per cent of the world's livestock population is in India and China
(b) Animal husbandry is the agricultural practice of breeding and raising livestock
(c) The contribution of India and China to the world farm produce is 50 per cent
(d) When breeding is between animals of the same breed, it is called inbreeding

112. Select the incorrect statement with respect to inbreeding:
(a) It increases homozygosity
(b) Inbreeding is necessary if we want to evolve a pure line in any animal
(c) It helps in accumulation of superior genes and elimination of less desirable genes
(d) It is the practice of mating superior males of one breed with superior females of another breed

113. Multiple ovulation embryo transfer (MOET) technology has been demonstrated for all of the following, except:
(a) Cattle (b) Sheep
(c) Mare (d) Turkey

114. Which of the following is a viral disease of poultry birds?
(a) Pullorum (b) Fowl cholera
(c) Newcastle disease (d) Infectious coryza

115. Which of the following is a high milk yielding breed of buffalo?
(a) Gir (b) Murrah
(c) Tharparkar (d) Sahiwal

116. The breed of sheep, originally a native of Spain but widespread all over the world now, which was also used to produce a cross-breed variety by mating it with an Indian sheep is:
(a) Dorset (b) Lincoln
(c) Marino (d) Nali

117. Select the incorrect statement with respect to animal husbandry:
(a) Cross-breeding gives rise to improved varieties of domesticated animals
(b) Rearing of poultry birds for eggs and meat is a part of animal husbandry

(c) Interspecific hybridisation helps to overcome inbreeding depression
(d) MOET is used to increase the herd size of high milk yielding breeds of females and high-quality meat yielding bulls

118. Which of the following fish is not a part of inland culture fishery?
(a) Rohu (b) Mrigal
(c) Magur (d) Pomfret

119. Draught breeds are used:
(a) To obtain milk (b) To plough fields
(c) Both (a) and (b) (d) None of the above

120. ________ is obtained from the skin of shark:
(a) Isinglass (b) Cod oil
(c) Blubber (d) Shagreen

121. Pashmina variety of wool is obtained from:
(a) Rabbit (b) Sheep
(c) Goat (d) Chiru

122. *Nosema*, a protozoan, causes ________ disease of the silk moth.
(a) Flacherie (b) Pebrine
(c) Coccidiosis (d) Muscardine

123. Identify the viral disease of cattle from the following:
(a) Rinderpest (b) Anthrax
(c) Pneumonia (d) Mastitis

124. Read the following statements. Which of the following are correct?
(i) Aseel fowls are used in cock fighting
(ii) Gaddi is a breed of buffalo
(iii) Fowls used for their eggs are called broilers
(iv) Flacherie is a viral disease of the silk moth
(a) (i) and (ii) (b) (ii) and (iii)
(c) (i) and (iv) (d) (ii) and (iv)

125. Enhanced milk production is called:
(a) White revolution (b) Silver revolution
(c) Blue revolution (d) Green revolution

126. For superovulation in MOET, cattle are administered with ________ to include follicular maturation:
(a) Progesterone
(b) Oestrogen
(c) Follicle stimulating hormone (FSH)
(d) Stilbesterol

127. Bees are effective for pollination in:
(a) Apple (b) *Brassica*
(c) Pear (d) All of the above

128. Hisardale is a new breed of sheep developed in Punjab by crossing Bikaneri ewes and:
(a) Lohi rams (b) Merino rams
(c) Nali rams (d) Nellore rams

129. Mark the incorrect statement:
(a) Mule and hinny are examples of interspecific hybridisation
(b) Shahtoosh is obtained from chiru
(c) Worker bees are sterile diploid females
(d) Nellore and Bhakarwal are high milk yielding 'milch' breed of cattle

130. A gelatinous substance obtained from the air bladder of bony fish used in clarification of wines and beer is:
(a) Shagreen (b) Isinglass
(c) Fish silage (d) Ampulla of Lorenzini

131. The practice of keeping more than one type of compatible fish together for utilising all the available area in ponds called:
(a) Inland fishery
(b) Marine fishery
(c) Capture fishery
(d) Composite fish farming

132. Tick fever (Babesiosis) of cattle is caused by:
(a) Fungus (b) Bacteria
(c) Virus (d) Protozoa

133. Reduction in fertility due to continued inbreeding is called inbreeding depression and is overcome by mating the animals with:
(a) Superior animals of different breeds
(b) Unrelated superior animals of the same breed
(c) Related superior animals of the same breed
(d) Superior animals of different species

134. The Nobel Prize for the study of communication methods of honey bees was given to:
(a) Karl Correns (b) Hugo de Vries
(c) Karl von Frisch (d) Darlington

135. Select the correct match:

Column I	Column II
A. Indian bee	(i) *Apis dorsata*
B. Rock bee	(ii) *Apis florea*
C. Little bee	(iii) *Apis mellifera*
D. European bee	(iv) *Apis indica*

(a) A – (iv), B – (i), C – (ii), D – (iii)
(b) A – (iii), B – (i), C – (ii), D – (iv)
(c) A – (ii), B – (i), C – (iv), D – (iii)
(d) A – (i), B – (iv), C – (iii), D – (ii)

136. Artificial selection to obtain cows yielding higher milk output represents:
(a) Stabilising selection as it stabilises this character in the population
(b) Disruptive as it splits the population into two, one yielding higher output and the other lower output
(c) Directional as it pushes the mean of the character in one direction
(d) Stabilising followed by disruptive as it stabilses the population to produce higher yielding cows

137. Protein present in silk fibre is:
(a) Collagen (b) Fibroin
(c) Elastin (d) Casein

138. The scientific name of the moth which produces "tussar silk" is:
(a) *Bombyx mori* (b) *Antheraea mylitta*
(c) *Antheraea assama* (d) *Philosamia ricini*

139. Which one of the following species of bees is used for the commercial production of honey?
(a) *Apis dorsata* (b) *Apis florea*
(c) *Apis mellifera* (d) *Apis indica*

140. From which stage of the silk moth is silk obtained?
(a) Adult (b) Egg
(c) Cocoon (d) Caterpillar

141. Mark the odd one out with respect to economically useful insects:
(a) *Tachardia lacca* (b) *Apis indica*
(c) *Bombyx mori* (d) Termites

142. Holstein-Friesian, Brown-Swiss and Jersey are well-known:
(a) Exotic breeds of cow
(b) Exotic breeds of goat
(c) Exotic breeds of poultry
(d) Animal husbandry scientists

143. Select the correct match:
(a) Sericulture – Fish
(b) Aquaculture – Silk moth
(c) Apiculture – Honey bee
(d) Pisciculture – Cattle

144. In which method of animal breeding are two different species of male and female animals mated?
(a) Cross-breeding
(b) Inbreeding
(c) Out-crossing
(d) Interspecific hybridisation

145. Identify the incorrect statement:
(a) Parthenogenesis is observed in honey bee
(b) Inland fisheries are involved in raising and capturing fish in fresh water
(c) Silk is the product of the salivary gland of the adult moth
(d) Compared to a bull, bullock is docile because of lower level of blood testosterone

146. Mark the incorrect statement with respect to MOET:
(a) FSH-like hormones are injected to induce superovulation
(b) 6–8 eggs are produced instead of a single egg per cycle
(c) The embryos at the 8–32 cell stage are recovered surgically and transferred to surrogate mothers
(d) MOET is used to increase herd size in rabbit, mare, sheep, cattle, etc.

NCERT EXEMPLAR QUESTIONS

1. Sonalika and Kalyan Sona are varieties of:
(a) Wheat (b) Rice
(c) Millet (d) Tobacco

2. Which one of the following is not a fungal disease?
(a) Rust of wheat
(b) Smut of bajra
(c) Black rot of crucifers
(d) Red rot of sugarcane

3. In virus-infected plants, the meristematic tissues in both apical and axillary buds are free of virus because:
(a) The dividing cells are virus resistant
(b) Meristems have antiviral compounds
(c) The cell division of meristems is faster than the rate of viral multiplication
(d) Viruses cannot multiply within meristem cell(s)

4. Several south Indian states raise 2–3 crops of rice annually. The agronomic feature that makes this possible is because of:
(a) Shorter rice plant
(b) Better irrigation facilities

(c) Early yielding rice variety
(d) Disease-resistant rice variety

5. Which one of the following combinations would a sugarcane farmer look for in a sugarcane crop?
(a) Thick stem, long internodes, high sugar content and disease resistance
(b) Thick stem, high sugar content and profuse flowering
(c) Thick stem, short internodes, high sugar content, disease resistance
(d) Thick stem, low sugar content, disease resistance

6. Fungicides and antibiotics are chemicals that:
(a) Enhance yield and disease resistance
(b) Kill pathogenic fungi and bacteria, respectively
(c) Kill all pathogenic microbes
(d) Kill pathogenic bacteria and fungi, respectively

7. Use of certain chemicals and radiation to change the base sequences of genes of crop plants is termed:
(a) Recombinant DNA technology
(b) Transgenic mechanism
(c) Mutation breeding
(d) Gene therapy

8. The scientific process by which crop plants are enriched with certain desirable nutrients is called:
(a) Crop protection (b) Breeding
(c) Biofortification (d) Bio-remediation

9. The term 'totipotency' refers to the capacity of a:
(a) Cell to generate the whole plant
(b) Bud to generate the whole plant
(c) Seed to germinate
(d) Cell to enlarge in size

10. Given below are a few statements regarding somatic hybridisation. Choose the correct statements:
A. Protoplasts of different cells of the same plant are fused
B. Protoplasts from cells of different species can be fused
C. Treatment of cells with cellulase and pectinase is mandatory
D. The hybrid protoplast contains characters of only one parental protoplast
(a) (A) and (C) (b) (A) and (B)
(c) (A) and (D) (d) (B) and (C)

11. An explant is:
(a) Dead plant
(b) Part of the plant
(c) Part of the plant used in tissue culture
(d) Part of the plant that expresses a specific gene

12. The biggest constraint of plant breeding is:
(a) Availability of desirable gene in the crop and its wild relatives
(b) Infrastructure
(c) Trained manpower
(d) Transfer of genes from unrelated sources

13. Lysine and tryptophan are:
(a) Proteins
(b) Non-essential amino acids
(c) Essential amino acids
(d) Aromatic amino acids

14. Micro-propagation is:
(a) Propagation of microbes in vitro
(b) Propagation of plants in vitro
(c) Propagation of cells in vitro
(d) Growing plants on smaller scale

15. Protoplast is:
(a) Another name for protoplasm
(b) An animal cell
(c) A plant cell without a cell wall
(d) A plant cell

16. To isolate the protoplast, one needs:
(a) Pectinase
(b) Cellulase
(c) Both pectinase and cellulase
(d) Chitinase

17. Which one of the following products of apiculture is used in cosmetics and polishes?
(a) Honey (b) Propolis
(c) Wax (d) Royal jelly

18. More than 70 per cent of livestock population is found in:
(a) Denmark (b) India
(c) China (d) India and China

19. The agriculture sector of India employs about:
(a) 50 per cent of the population
(b) 70 per cent of the population
(c) 30 per cent of the population
(d) 60 per cent of the population

20. Thirty-three per cent of India's Gross Domestic Product comes from:
(a) Industry
(b) Agriculture
(c) Export
(d) Small-scale cottage industries

21. A collection of all the alleles of all the genes of a crop plant is called:
(a) Germplasm collection
(b) Protoplasm collection
(c) Herbarium
(d) Somaclonal collection

PRACTICE TEST PAPER

1. Objective of plant breeding is:
(a) Better yield (b) Better quality
(c) Disease resistance (d) All of the above

2. Norman Borlaug is associated with:
(a) White revolution (b) Blue revolution
(c) Green revolution (d) Pink revolution

3. Which of the following is correct with respect to inbreeding?
(a) Useful in cross-pollinated plants and produces ill effects in self-pollinated plants
(b) Useful in self-pollinated plants and produces ill effects in cross-pollinated plants
(c) Useful in both self-pollinated as well as cross-pollinated plants
(d) Produces ill effects in both self-pollinated as well as cross-pollinated plants

4. Which of the following may not be included in plant breeding programmes?
(a) Introduction of resistance against pests
(b) Organic farming and green manuring
(c) Fertiliser responsiveness
(d) Biofortification

5. Jaya and Ratna are high yielding, semi-dwarf varieties of:
(a) Wheat (b) Rice
(c) Sugarcane (d) Millets

6. In India, the Green Revolution occurred during:
(a) 1960s (b) 1950s
(c) 1980s (d) 1990s

7. International Rice Research Institute (IRRI) is located in:
(a) Taiwan (b) Japan
(c) Philippines (d) Mexico

8. A bhindi variety called parbhani kranti is resistant to:
(a) Yellow mosaic virus
(b) Black rust
(c) Black rot
(d) Yellow rust

9. The sugarcane originally grown in north India was:
(a) *Saccharum spontaneum*
(b) *Saccharum barberi*
(c) *Saccharum officinarum*
(d) *Saccharum munja*

10. Crucial step for the success of any plant breeding programme is:
(a) Testing, release and commercialisation of new cultivars
(b) Collection of genetic variability
(c) Cross-hybridisation among selected parents
(d) Selection of superior recombinants

11. "Pusa swarnim" is a disease-resistant variety of:
(a) Sugarcane (b) Cauliflower
(c) Mustard (d) Cowpea

12. Which is not an objective of biofortification?
(a) Improving protein content
(b) Improving oil content
(c) Improving vitamin content
(d) Improving alkaloid content

13. Atlas-66 is a nutritionally improved variety of wheat. It has high:
(a) Protein content (b) Heathier fat content
(c) Iron content (d) Vitamin C content

14. Match Column I with Column II and select the correct option:

Column I	Column II
A. Totipotency	(i) Unorganised mass of cells
B. SCP	(ii) Capacity to generate whole plant from any plant part
C. Explant	(iii) *Spirulina*
D. Callus	(iv) Plant part which is cultured

(a) A – (ii), B – (iv), C – (i), D – (iii)
(b) A – (ii), B – (i), C – (iv), D – (iii)
(c) A – (ii), B – (iii), C – (iv), D – (i)
(d) A – (ii), B – (iii), C – (i), D – (iv)

15. From a virus-infected plant, we can obtain healthy plants by culturing its:
(a) Embryo (b) Shoot apical meristem
(c) Anther wall (d) Differentiated tissues

16. Which technique was used to produce pomato?
(a) Mutation breeding
(b) Protoplast fusion
(c) Somatic hybridisation
(d) Both (b) and (c)

17. The developed maize variety is resistant to the stem-borer insect because of:
(a) Solid stem

(b) Hairy leaves
(c) High aspartic acid, low nitrogen and sugar content
(d) Low aspartic acid, high nitrogen and sugar content

18. Single-cell protein:
(a) Is obtained only from single-cell organisms
(b) Is produced through somatic hybridisation
(c) Is an alternate source of proteins for animals and humans
(d) All except (b)

19. Which of the following is a viral disease of plants?
(a) Mosaic disease of turnip
(b) Black rust of wheat
(c) Late blight of potato
(d) Red rot of sugarcane

20. Isolated protoplasts from two different plant cells can be fused to obtain:
(a) Monoclonal cultures
(b) Somatic hybrids
(c) Pure lines
(d) Hybrid vigour

21. "Hidden hunger" observed in people is usually not because of deficiency of:
(a) Micronutrients (b) Proteins
(c) Vitamins (d) Carbohydrates

24. Improved variety of cow pea against the disease bacterial blight is:
(a) Pusa sadabahar (b) Pusa shubhra
(c) Pusa komal (d) Pusa sawani

23. Pathogen-free clones of plants can be obtained through:
(a) Embryo culture (b) Shoot tip culture
(c) Anther culture (d) Somatic hybridisation

24. Read the following statements regarding somatic hybridisation and select the correct option:
A. Protoplasts of different cells of the same plant are fused.
B. Protoplasts from cells of different species are fused.
C. Treatment of cells with cellulose and pectinase is mandatory.
D. The hybrid protoplast contains characters of only one parental protoplast.
(a) (A) and (C) (b) (A) and (D)
(c) (B) and (C) (d) (B) and (D)

25. Three crops that contribute maximum to global food grain production are:
(a) Wheat, rice and maize
(b) Wheat, rice and barley
(c) Wheat, maize and sorghum
(d) Rice, maize and barley

26. An artificial cereal is:
(a) *Triticale* (b) *Triticum*
(c) *Zea* (d) *Secale*

27. Somaclones are obtained by:
(a) Genetic engineering
(b) Tissue culture
(c) Plant breeding
(d) Irradiation

28. Crop improvement is possible through:
(a) Selection
(b) Introduction
(c) Scientific improvement of cultivated plants
(d) Judicious combination of selection, introduction and hybridisation

29. Genetically improved crop varieties can be developed by:
(a) Somatic hybridisation
(b) Transgenic technology
(c) Somaclonal variations
(d) Both (a) and (b)

30. Greatest threat of genetic diversity in agriculture crops is:
(a) Extensive use of insecticides and pesticides
(b) Extensive mixed cropping
(c) Introduction of high yielding varieties
(d) Extensive use of fertilisers

31. Multiple ovulation embryo transfer (MOET) technology, which uses hypophysis extracts, is a technique of improvement in:
(a) Fishery (b) Cattle herds
(c) Apiculture (d) Sericulture

32. Which breed of fowl has been traditionally used in India for cock fighting?
(a) Kadaknath (b) Aseel
(c) Plymouth rock (d) New Hampshire

33. Angora variety of wool is obtained from which of the following animals?
(a) Kashmiri goat (b) Tibetan antelope
(c) Merino sheep (d) Rabbit

34. Which of the following is prepared from the air bladder of bony fish and is used in the clarification of alcoholic beverages?
(a) Shagreen (b) Isinglass
(c) Fish flour (d) Cod liver

35. Which of the following is known as the "king of wool" for its superior quality?
(a) Angora (b) Pashmina
(c) Shahtoosh (d) Mohair

36. Which of the following cattle disease is also known as "cattle plague"?
(a) Anthrax (b) Rinderpest
(c) Mastitis (d) Pullorum

37. The breeding method which is preferably used in cattle to remove inbreeding depression without causing a large-scale change in the superior characteristics of the breed is:
(a) Inbreeding
(b) Out-crossing
(c) Cross-breeding
(d) Interspecific hybridisation

38. The mountain artillery type of mules are used by the army to transport heavy ammunition in tough mountain ranges. This animal is an example of:
(a) Cross-breeding
(b) Out-crossing
(c) Interspecific hybridisation
(d) Inbreeding

39. Which of the following animals is called "poor man's cow" due to its lower milk yield but also lower resource requirement for rearing?
(a) Sheep (b) *Pantholops*
(c) Goat (d) *Camelus*

40. Which of the following animals is considered as one of the most economic and fast "meat making machines"?
(a) Goat (b) Chicken
(c) Pig (d) Buffalo

41. "Tussar silk" is a type of silk obtained from which of the following types of silk moths?
(a) *Antheraea assama* (b) *Attacus ricini*
(c) *Bombyx mori* (d) *Antheraea roylei*

42. The chicken breeds used only for meat yielding purpose are known as:
(a) Layers (b) Broilers
(c) Jungle fowls (d) Indigenous birds

43. "Karan-Swiss" is a cross-breed developed by the National Dairy Research Institute (NDRI), Karnal by mating:
(a) Sahiwal × Brown-Swiss
(b) Tharparkar × Brown-Swiss
(c) Sahiwal × Holstein-Friesian
(d) Local Kerala cattle × Jersey

44. Mark the odd one out with respect to edible freshwater fish:
(a) *Catla* (b) Rohu
(c) Calbasu (d) Mackerel

45. __________ refers to the mating of more closely related individuals within the same breed for 4–6 generations:
(a) Out-breeding (b) Inbreeding
(c) Out-crossing (d) Cross-breeding

ANSWER KEYS

Exercises

1. (a) 2. (a) 3. (d) 4. (a) 5. (b) 6. (b) 7. (c) 8. (c) 9. (d) 10. (c)
11. (b) 12. (d) 13. (c) 14. (d) 15. (d) 16. (a) 17. (c) 18. (d) 19. (b) 20. (c)
21. (b) 22. (c) 23. (c) 24. (a) 25. (b) 26. (d) 27. (c) 28. (b) 29. (b) 30. (a)
31. (d) 32. (c) 33. (a) 34. (c) 35. (b) 36. (d) 37. (b) 38. (a) 39. (d) 40. (c)
41. (b) 42. (d) 43. (d) 44. (a) 45. (c) 46. (a) 47. (b) 48. (c) 49. (b) 50. (d)
51. (b) 52. (d) 53. (d) 54. (c) 55. (b) 56. (d) 57. (a) 58. (b) 59. (a) 60. (d)
61. (b) 62. (a) 63. (d) 64. (c) 65. (a) 66. (a) 67. (b) 68. (a) 69. (d) 70. (b)
71. (a) 72. (a) 73. (b) 74. (d) 75. (b) 76. (c) 77. (c) 78. (a) 79. (b) 80. (d)
81. (a) 82. (c) 83. (c) 84. (a) 85. (a) 86. (d) 87. (d) 88. (b) 89. (a) 90. (d)
91. (a) 92. (b) 93. (c) 94. (b) 95. (c) 96. (a) 97. (b) 98. (d) 99. (d) 100. (d)
101. (c) 102. (a) 103. (c) 104. (b) 105. (a) 106. (a) 107. (c) 108. (c) 109. (b) 110. (b)
111. (c) 112. (d) 113. (d) 114. (c) 115. (b) 116. (c) 117. (c) 118. (d) 119. (b) 120. (d)
121. (c) 122. (b) 123. (a) 124. (c) 125. (a) 126. (c) 127. (d) 128. (b) 129. (d) 130. (b)
131. (d) 132. (d) 133. (b) 134. (c) 135. (a) 136. (c) 137. (b) 138. (b) 139. (c) 140. (c)
141. (d) 142. (a) 143. (c) 144. (d) 145. (c) 146. (c)

NCERT Exemplar Questions

1. (a) 2. (c) 3. (c) 4. (c) 5. (a) 6. (b) 7. (c) 8. (c) 9. (a) 10. (d)
11. (c) 12. (a) 13. (c) 14. (b) 15. (c) 16. (c) 17. (c) 18. (d) 19. (d) 20. (b)
21. (a)

Practice Test Paper

1. (d) 2. (c) 3. (b) 4. (b) 5. (b) 6. (a) 7. (c) 8. (a) 9. (b) 10. (d)
11. (c) 12. (d) 13. (a) 14. (c) 15. (b) 16. (d) 17. (c) 18. (c) 19. (a) 20. (d)
21. (d) 24. (c) 23. (b) 24. (c) 25. (a) 26. (a) 27. (b) 28. (d) 29. (d) 30. (c)
31. (b) 32. (b) 33. (d) 34. (b) 35. (c) 36. (b) 37. (b) 38. (c) 39. (c) 40. (c)
41. (d) 42. (b) 43. (a) 44. (d) 45. (b)

SOLUTIONS

Plant Breeding

1. Plant breeding is the purposeful manipulation of plant species in order to create desired plant types that are better suited for cultivation, give better yield and which are disease resistant.

2. Green Revolution in India occurred during the 1960s.

3. Green Revolution in India led to increased production of high yielding and disease-resistant varieties of wheat, rice and maize.

4. Conventional plant breeding has been used for thousands of years (9000–11,000 years ago) for the production of better quality crops.

5. MS Swaminathan is known as the Father of the Green Revolution in India.

6. The sum total of all the genes present in a crop and its related species is called germplasm. The entire collection of plants/seeds having all the diverse alleles for all genes in a given crop is called germplasm collection.

7. Classical plant breeding involves crossing of pure lines followed by artificial selection to produce plants with desirable traits of higher yield, nutrition and resistance to diseases.

8. If we were to list the traits that plant breeders have tried to incorporate into crop plants, the first preference would be increased crop yield and improved quality. Increased tolerance to environmental stresses (salinity, extreme, temperature, drought), resistance to pathogens and increased tolerance to insect pests would be on our list too.

9. Decreased tolerance to environmental stress is not a desirable trait.

10. Cross-hybridisation is not only a time consuming and tedious process but the success rate of hybridisation is also very low. One plant in a few hundred or thousands may have the desirable characters.

11. When the parents of two different species of the same genes are crossed to produce a hybrid, it is called interspecific hybridisation.

12. Phenotypic superiority of all hybrids over either of its parents in one or more traits is called heterosis or hybrid vigour. The term heterosis was given by Shull.

13. Hybridisation

14. The Green Revolution in India refers to a period when Indian agriculture was converted io an industrial system due to the adoption of modern methods and technology such as the use of high yielding varieties, tractors, irrigation facilities, pesticides and fertilisers.

15. MS Swaminathan

16. Mass selection is the oldest method of crop improvement.

17. The crucial step in the success of plant breeding programmes is the selection and testing of superior recombinants. This step comprises the selection of those plants that have the desired characters and combination among the progeny of hybrids.

18. Pure line selection

19. Only B is correct. Evaluation is carried out by growing crops in the research field under ideal fertiliser and irrigation conditions.

20. Norman E Borlaug at the International Centre for Wheat and Maize Improvement in Mexico developed the semi-dwarf wheat.

21. Semi-dwarf varieties

22. India's wheat yield revolution in the 1960s was possible primarily because of the use of hybrid seeds.

23. Semi-dwarf varieties of rice were developed from IR-8 (developed at International Rice Research Institute, Philippines).

24. New plant varieties are produced by selection and hybridisation process.

25. India is mainly an agricultural country. Agriculture accounts for approximately 33% of Indian GDP and employs 62% of the population.

26. (A), (B) and (C) are correct.

27. Scented basmati rice is the contribution of MS Swaminathan.

28. India developed high yielding, semi-dwarf rice varieties like Jaya and Ratna.

29. Philippines

30. Sonalika and Kalyansona are high yielding and disease-resistant wheat varieties.

31. The new sugarcane variety formed by crossing two varieties had the following qualities: (i) high yield, (ii) thick stem, (iii) high sugar content and (iv) ability to grow in north India.

32. *S. officinarum* did not grow in north India but had a thicker stem and higher sugar content.

Plant Breeding for Disease Resistance, for Developing Resistance to Insects and Pests and for Improved Food Quality, Biofortification

33. Resistance to yellow mosaic virus was incorporated from a wild species of bhindi. The new resistant variety is called parbhani kranti.

34. Agriculture loss due to disease is about 20–30%, sometimes even the total.

35. Black rot of crucifers is a bacterial disease caused by *Xanthomonas campestris.*

36. Pusa sadabahar is a disease-resistant variety of chilli which is resistant to chilly mosaic virus, tobacco mosaic virus and leaf curl.

37. Yellow mosaic virus

38. Himgiri - Hill bunt, Karan rai - White rust, Pusa snowball K-1 - Black rot, Pusa komal - Bacterial blight

39. Breeding for disease resistance requires screening of germplasm for disease resistance, planned hybridisation, etc.

40. Several wild relatives of different cultivated species have been shown to have certain resistant characters.

41. Pusa swarnim is a disease-resistant variety of *Brassica.*

42. The host crop plant may be resistant to insect pests due to morphological, biochemical or physiological characteristics.

43. $C \rightarrow A \rightarrow D \rightarrow B$

44. A – Bhindi, B – Shoot and fruit borer

45. Gamma radiation

46. In mung bean, resistance to yellow mosaic virus and powdery mildew was introduced by mutations.

47. Biofortification is a method for developing crops with higher levels of vitamins, minerals, proteins and healthier fats to improve public health.

48. Majority of people are unable to buy enough fruits, vegetables, legumes, fish and meat, and thus, suffer from deficiencies or hidden hunger. So, biofortification is the most practical means to improve public health.

49. Biofortification can be achieved through plant breeding practices.

50. Micronutrient and mineral content

51. In 2000, maize hybrids that had twice the amount of lysine and tryptophan were developed as compared to exiting varieties.

52. Shakti, Rattan and Protina are lysine-rich varieties of maize.

53. Atlas-66 is a protein-rich variety of wheat.

54. IARI, New Delhi has developed vitamin A–enriched carrots, pumpkin and spinach.

55. IARI has developed biofortified spinach and bathua, which is rich in iron and calcium.

56. Pusa sem-2 and Pusa sem-3 are improved varieties of flat bean resistant to aphids, jassids and fruit borer.

57. Cauliflower

58. Maize is dependent on human beings for propagation and release of grains from the cob as it remains tightly adhered.

59. A – Lysine, B – Tryptophan, C – Wheat

60. The development of disease in a plant depends on interaction among the following factors: (a) Host genotype, (b) Pathogen genotype, (c) Pathogen genotype, (d) Environmental conditions.

61. Hairy leaves in cotton shows resistance to jassids. Smooth leaves and nectar-less cotton varieties do not attract bollworms.

62. Solid stem in wheat exhibits non-preference by stem sawfly.

63. In maize, high aspartic acid and low nitrogen and sugar content protects them from stem borers.

64. Bollworms

65. Heterosis was studied in detail for the first time in maize.

66. Reduction in hybrid vigour is due to continuous selfing. This is called inbreeding depression.

Single-cell Protein, Tissue Culture, Green Manure, Energy Crops, Petroleum Plants

67. A single-cell protein refers to sources of mixed proteins extracted from pure or mixed cultures of organism or cells.

68. SCP is obtained from unicellular and multicellular microorganisms.

69. *Chlamydomonas* is not a source of SCP.

70. High rate of biomass production

71. The method of growing or producing thousands of plants through tissue culture is called micropropagation.

72. Haberlandt

73. The part of the plant taken for tissue culture is called explant.

74. Explants are treated with specific antimicrobial chemicals, chlorax or hypherchlorite. This is called surface sterilisation.

75. Cytokinin promotes shoot initiation in callus.

76. Meristem (apical and axillary) is the only virus-free part of a virus-infected plant.

77. Axenic culture refers to culture without any contamination.

78. Somatic embryogenesis is a method of micropropagation where a cell or group of cells from somatic tissue forms an embryo. Somatic embryos are useful in clonal propagation of genetically identical plant material.

79. The plants produced from tissue culture are genetically identical to the original plant from which they are grown; so they are called somaclones.

80. The process of fusion of protoplast of somatic cells obtained from different varieties or species of plant is called somatic hybridisation.

81. The cell walls of cells are digested by enzymes like pectinase and cellulose to expose the naked protoplasts.

82. A plant cell without cell wall is called protoplast.

83. Cells of anther wall

84. High auxin and low cytokinin concentration induces root initiation in tissue culture.

85. Callus is an unorganised mass of cells.

86. The growth regulators commonly used in tissue culture are auxins and cytokinin. The source of cytokinin is coconut milk.

87. Clonal propagation refers to the multiplication of genetically identical plants by micropropagation. They are selected using microscopy and culture on a suitable medium where multiplication takes place.

88. Genetically identical population of elite species

89. Autoclave

90. All of the above

91. Auxin and cytokinin

92. Somaclonal variations are produced during tissue culture. Some of these variations are useful and stable. For example, short duration sugarcane, rice resistant to tungro virus and leaf hopper.

93. Androgenic haploids was developed by Guha and Maheshwari in *Datura innoxia*.

94. *Datura*

95. Interspecific hybrids are often sterile because of embryo mortality and seed collapse. In such cases, hybrid embryo is excised in the early stage and cultured through tissue culture.

96. Haberlandt

97. Pomato is a somatic hybrid between potato and tomato. Unfortunately, the pomato did not have all the desired combinations of characteristics for its commercial utilisation.

98. *Spirulina* can be grown on materials like waste water from potato processing plant, straw, manure, sewage, etc.

99. *Euphorbia, Hevea, Jatropha* plants are a source of latex, which contains long-chain liquid hydrocarbons.

100. (A), (B), (C) and (D) are used as sources of SCP.

101. Green manure is prepared from young crop plants by ploughing them back into the soil before flowering and fruiting.

102. Brazil

103. 10%

104. Sugarcane

105. 25 tonnes

106. *Spirulina* (BGA) is used in the production of SCP.

Animal Husbandry

107. Hisardale is a new breed of sheep developed in Punjab by cross-breeding Bikaneri ewes end Merino rams. In this method, superior males of one breed are mated with superior females of another breed. Cross-breeding allows the desirable qualities of two different breeds to be combined.

108. Some of the marine fishes that are eaten include *Hilsa*, sardine, mackerel and pomfret.

109. Out-crossing is the practice of mating of animals within the same breed, but having no common ancestors on either side of their pedigree up to 4–6 generations. The offspring of such mating are known as out-cross.

110. Fishery is the industry devoted to the catching, processing or selling of fish, shellfish or other aquatic animals.

111. It is estimated that more than 70% of the world's livestock population is in India and China, but their contribution to the world farm produce is only 25%.

112. Inbreeding refers to the mating of more closely related individuals within the same breed for 4–6 generations.

113. Multiple ovulation embryo transfer (MOET) technology has been demonstrated for cattle, sheep, rabbits, buffaloes, mares, etc.

114. Newcastle disease (Ranikhet disease) is a viral disease of poultry.

115. Murrah is a high milk-yielding breed of buffalo.

116. Merino is a breed of sheep, native to Spain, which has been used to produce a cross-breed Hisardale by mating it with an Indian sheep.

117. Inbreeding depression is overcome by mating the selected animals with unrelated superior animals of the same breed. Thus, a single out-cross often helps to overcome inbreeding depression.

118. Pomfret is an edible marine fish and thus not a part of inland culture fishery or the cultivation of fish in ponds and tanks (freshwater bodies).

119. Draught breeds of cattle are exclusively meant for pulling carts and ploughing fields. They are well-built. The bulls are used for draught work. The cows are poor milk-yielders.

120. Shagreen is a leather-like substance obtained from the skin of shark.

121. Pashmina variety of wool is obtained from goat.

122. *Nosema bombycis* is a protozoan that causes pebrine disease of the silk moth.

123. Rinderpest is an infectious disease of ruminants, especially cattle, caused by a paramyxovirus. It is characterised by fever, dysentery and inflammation of the mucous membranes.

124. Gaddi is a breed of goat. Fowls used for their eggs are called layers.

125. White revolution aimed at increasing the yield of milk and milk products.

126. For superovulation in MOET, cattle are administered with follicle stimulating hormone (FSH) to induce follicular maturation.

127. Bees are effective for pollination in apple, *Brassica*, pear and sunflower.

128. Hisardale is a new breed of sheep developed in Punjab by crossing Bikaneri ewes and Merino rams.

129. Nellore and Bhakarwal are breeds of sheep.

130. Isinglass is a gelatinous substance obtained from the air bladder of bony fish and used in clarification of wine and beer.

131. Composite fish farming is the practice of keeping more than one type of compatible fish together for utilising all the available area in ponds. Fishes with different food habits are chosen so that they do not compete for food among themselves, for example, *Catla*, rohu and mrigal.

132. Tick fever (Babesiosis) of cattle is caused by a protozoan, *Babesia bigemina*.

133. Inbreeding depression can be overcome by mating the animals with unrelated superior animals of the same breed.

134. Karl von Frisch was awarded the Nobel Prize for the study of communication methods of honey bees.

135. Option (a) is correct.

136. Artificial selection to obtain cows yielding higher milk output represents directional selection as it pushes the mean in one direction.

137. Fibroin protein is present in silk fibre.

138. Tussar silk is produced from the larvae of several species of silkworms belonging to the moths of genus *Antheraea*, including *Antheraea paphia, Antheraea mylitta* and *Antheraea roylei.*

139. *Apis mellifera* (European bee) is commonly used for the commercial production of honey.

140. Silk is obtained from the cocoon stages of the silk moth.

141. Termites/White ants are small, pale, soft-bodied insects that feed on wood and can be highly destructive to trees and timber.

142. Holstein-Friesian, Brown-Swiss and Jersey are well-known exotic breeds of cow.

143. Option (c) is correct.

144. In interspecific hybridisation, two different species of male and female members are mated.

145. Silk is composed mainly of fibroin and is produced by certain insert larvae to form cocoons.

146. In MOET, the embryos at the 8–32 cell stage are recovered non-surgically and transferred to surrogate mothers.

10 Microbes in Human Welfare

EXERCISES

Introduction, Microbes in Household Products, Microbes in Industrial Products (Fermented Beverages, Antibiotics, Chemical Enzymes and Other Bioactive Molecules)

1. Microbes are a diverse group that includes:
   A. Protozoans, bacteria and fungi
   B. Microscopic animal and plant viruses
   C. Viruses, viroids and proteinaceous infectious agents
   (a) Only (A) (b) Only (A) and (B)
   (c) Only (B) and (C) (d) (A), (B) and (C)
2. Microbes are present in:
   (a) Soil, water and air
   (b) Our bodies as parasites
   (c) Geysers, deep in the soil
   (d) All of the above
3. Select the incorrect statement with respect to microorganisms:
   (a) Prions are infectious protein particles
   (b) Bacteria and many fungi can be grown on culture media to form colonies that cannot be seen with the naked eye
   (c) Microbes are present even at sites where no other life forms could possible exist
   (d) Microbes cause disease in animals and plants
4. The given figure is:

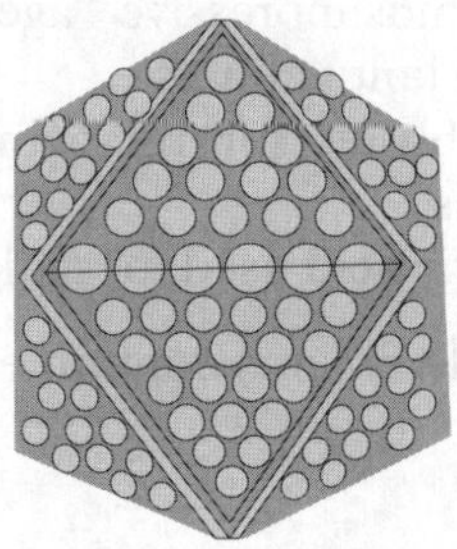

   (a) Adenovirus (b) Bacteriophage
   (c) Fungal colony (d) Tobacco mosaic virus
5. Lactic acid bacteria convert milk into curd and improve its nutritional quality by enhancing vitamin:
   (a) A (b) B_2
   (c) B_{12} (d) D
6. All of the following dairy products are produced by the activity of bacteria, except:
   (a) Curd (b) Buttermilk
   (c) Swiss cheese (d) Roquefort cheese
7. LAB stands for:
   (a) Lactic acid bacteria
   (b) Lactobacillus acidophilus bacteria
   (c) Lactose acetaldehyde utilising bacteria
   (d) Laboratory of biology
8. Microbes produce different types of end products during growth and metabolism. The type of end product depends upon:
   (a) Microbes (b) Substrate
   (c) Medium (d) (a) and (b)
9. Cheese is classified on the basis of:
   (a) Flavour (b) Colour
   (c) Texture (d) All of the above
10. Roquefort cheese is ripened using:
    (a) A type of yeast (b) Fungus
    (c) Bacterium (d) Cyanobacteria
11. Which gas is responsible for the puffed-up appearance of dough?
    (a) CO_2 (b) O_2
    (c) SO_2 (d) NO_2
12. Dosa and idli are preparations of:
    (a) Wheat flour
    (b) Rice
    (c) Rice and black gram
    (d) Wheat and black gram

13. Rennet is employed in:
(a) Synthesis of antibiotics
(b) Synthesis of organic acids
(c) Preparation of cheese
(d) Bread-making

14. Read the following statements:
A. Toddy is prepared by fermenting palm sap
B. Propionibacterium is used in fermentation of cheese
C. Puffed-up appearance of dough is due to production of CO_2
D. LAB produces acid which coagulates and partially digests the milk fat
How many of the given statements are correct?
(a) Three (b) Four
(c) Two (d) One

15. Pasteurisation is:
(a) Heating of liquid to 65°C
(b) Heating of liquid between 65°C and 80°C followed by rapid cooling
(c) Heating of solid to 65°C
(d) Low temperature storage of food product

16. Probiotics are:
(a) Live microbial food supplements
(b) Cancer inducing microbes
(c) New kind of food allergen
(d) Broad spectrum antibiotics

17. Toddy, a traditional drink of some parts of southern India, is made by fermenting:
(a) Barley grains
(b) Sap from coconut
(c) Sap from *Caryota urens*
(d) Fruit juices

18. The most common substrate used in distilleries for the production of ethanol is:
(a) Molasses (b) Corn meal
(c) Soya meal (d) Ground grain

19. Ethanol is commercially produced through a particular species of:
(a) *Aspergillus* (b) *Saccharomyces*
(c) *Clostridium* (d) *Trichoderma*

20. Broad spectrum antibiotics are those that attack:
(a) Pathogens as well as hosts
(b) A wide range of pathogens
(c) Only pathogens
(d) Only hosts

21. Highest number of antibiotics are produced by:
(a) *Bacillus* (b) *Penicillium*
(c) *Streptomyces* (d) *Streptococcus*

22. A bioreactor is:
(a) Fermentation tank
(b) Culture containing radioactive isotope
(c) Culture for synthesis of few chemicals
(d) Hybridoma technology

23. All of the following deadly diseases are treated by antibiotics, except:
(a) Diphtheria (b) Leprosy
(c) Plague (d) Cancer

24. Which of the following is one of the most significant discoveries of the twentieth century that greatly contributed towards the welfare of human society?
(a) Biogas (b) Curd
(c) Antibiotics (d) Citric acid

25. Match the following correctly:

Column I	Column II
A. Butyric acid	(i) *Trichoderma*
B. Acetic acid	(ii) *Monascus purpureus*
C. Cyclosporine	(iii) *Acetobacter aceti*
D. Statins	(iv) *Clostridium butyricum*

(a) A – (iv), B – (i), C – (iii), D – (ii)
(b) A – (iv), B – (iii), C – (i), D – (ii)
(c) A – (iv), B – (iii), C – (ii), D – (i)
(d) A – (iii), B – (iv), C – (ii), D – (i)

26. An enzyme that stimulates germination of barley seeds is:
(a) Invertase (b) *a*-amylase
(c) Lipase (d) Protease

27. Organic acid first produced through fermentation:
(a) Propionic acid (b) Lactic acid
(c) Citric acid (d) Oxalic acid

28. Wine and beer are produced:
(a) Through distillation of barley malt
(b) Through distillation of fruit juices
(c) With or without distillation of molasses
(d) Without distillation of ripe fruit and barley malt

29. *Trichoderma polysporum* is involved in the synthesis of:
(a) Blood cholesterol lowering agent
(b) Immunosuppressive agent used in organ transplant patients
(c) Clot buster for removing clots from blood vessels
(d) Butyric acid used for making rancid butter

30. Modern detergents contain enzyme preparations of:

(a) Thermoacidophiles
(b) Alkaliphiles
(c) Acidophiles
(d) Thermophiles

31. The product of which microorganism has been commercialised for lowering blood cholesterol?
(a) *Trichoderma polysporin*
(b) *Monascus purpureus*
(c) *Saccharomyces cerevisiae*
(d) *Aspergillus niger*

32. A person was admitted to a hospital as he had myocardial infarction. A cardiologist injected him with streptokinase. Why?
(a) It reduces hypertension
(b) It reduces the level of blood cholesterol
(c) It stimulates the heart beat
(d) It acts as clot buster

33. Streptokinase, which is used as a 'clot buster', is obtained from:
(a) *Streptococcus* (b) *Staphylococcus*
(c) *Lactobacillus* (d) *Saccharomyces*

34. Which among these are produced by distillation of fermented broth?
A. Whisky
B. Wine
C. Beer
D. Rum
E. Brandy
(a) (B) and (C) alone
(b) (A) and (B) alone
(c) (A), (D), and (E) alone
(d) (A), (C) and (D) alone

35. The following change is observed due to the addition of hops in beer during fermentation:
(a) Colour
(b) Flavour
(c) Mild antibacterial activity
(d) All of the above

36. Which one of the following processes of alcohol production is not involved in wine production?
(a) Malting (b) Mashing
(c) Fermentation (d) Distillation

37. Beer has an alcoholic content of:
(a) 3–6% (b) 9–12%
(c) 40% (d) 60%

38. Wine and beer are produced directly by fermentation whereas brandy and whisky require both fermentation and distillation. This is because:
(a) Fermentation is inhibited at an alcohol level of 10–13%
(b) Distillation prolongs storage
(c) Distillation improves quality
(d) Distillation purifies the beverage

39. Statin, a bioactive molecule, inhibits the enzyme responsible for the synthesis of:
(a) Cholesterol (b) Cyclosporin A
(c) Vitamin (d) Protein

40. Enzymes used in detergents are:
(a) Amylases (b) Lipases
(c) Proteases (d) Glucoisomerases

41. Interferons are specific immune chemicals secreted by which of the following entities?
(a) Virus (b) Virus-infected cells
(c) Fungus (d) Bacteria

42. Cyclosporin A is a bioactive molecule, which is used in:
(a) Immune resistance
(b) Organ transplantation
(c) Dissolving blood clots
(d) Lowering blood cholesterol

43. Function of statin is based on:
(a) Competitive inhibition
(b) End product inhibition
(c) Feedback inhibition
(d) Allosteric inhibition

Microbes in Sewage Treatment, Microbes in Production of Biogas

44. Which of the following in sewage treatment removes suspended solids?
(a) Primary treatment
(b) Secondary treatment
(c) Biological treatment
(d) Tertiary treatment

45. The primary treatment of sewage water involves:
(a) Sludge digestion
(b) Anaerobic bacterial activity
(c) Sequential filtration and sedimentation
(d) Aerobic bacterial activity

46. Secondary treatment in STP is mainly a:
(a) Physical process
(b) Physio-chemical process
(c) Biological process
(d) Chemical process

47. Flocs formed during secondary treatment are made up of:
(a) Anaerobic bacteria and anaerobic fungal filaments

(b) Aerobic bacteria and anaerobic fungal filaments
(c) Anaerobic bacteria and aerobic fungal filaments
(d) Aerobic bacteria and aerobic fungal filaments

48. BOD is the measure of the presence of ________ in water:
(a) Aerobic microbes (b) Organic matter
(c) Inorganic waste (d) Soil and pebbles

49. Passage of effluents into oxidation tank is for:
(a) Primary treatment
(b) Secondary treatment
(c) Tertiary treatment
(d) Physiochemical treatment

50. In STP, microbes are used in:
A. Primary treatment of sewage
B. Secondary treatment
C. Anaerobic sludge digester
D. Tertiary treatment
(a) (A) and (B) (b) (B) and (D)
(c) (B) and (C) (d) (A) and (D)

51. The stage of treatment that compresses the use of anaerobic sludge digester is:
(a) Primary (b) Secondary
(c) Tertiary (d) Quaternary

52. The domestic sewage in large cities:
A. Has high BOD as it contains both aerobic and anaerobic bacteria
B. Has very high amounts of suspended solids and dissolved inorganic salts
C. Is processed by aerobic and anaerobic bacteria during secondary treatment in STPs
(a) Only (A) is correct
(b) Only (C) is correct
(c) (A) and (B) are correct
(d) (A), (B) and (C) are correct

53. In STPs, the activated sludge is formed in ___A___ and its major part is pumped into ___B___:

	A	B
(a)	Primary settling tank	Aeration tank
(b)	Aeration tank	Tertiary treatment tank
(c)	Aeration tank	Anaerobic sludge digester
(d)	Secondary settling tank	Aerobic sludge digester

54. Physio-chemical process in sewage treatment plant helps to get rid of:
(a) Floating debris (b) Pathogens
(c) Pebbles (d) Flocs

55. Activated sludge is:
(a) Formed after activity of anaerobic microbes in anaerobic sludge digester
(b) Released into running water bodies
(c) Settled anaerobic bacterial flocs after biological treatment
(d) Settled mass of aerobic bacteria fungi

56. Secondary treatment of sewage does not include:
(a) Mechanical agitation and aeration
(b) Floc formation
(c) Activated sludge formation
(d) Reverse osmosis and UV treatment

57. Activated sludge is used as inoculum in:
(a) Anaerobic sludge digester
(b) Aeration tanks
(c) Production of biogas
(d) Tertiary treatment

58. Group of bacteria used in biogas production is:
(a) Eubacteria (b) Organotrophs
(c) Methanogens (d) Thermoacidophiles

59. *Methanobacterium* is not:
(a) Present in rumen of cattle
(b) Helpful in breakdown of cellulose
(c) Found in aerobic conditions
(d) Used for generation of gobar gas

60. Read the following statements with respect to BOD and select the correct option:
A. The BOD test measures the rate of uptake of oxygen by microorganisms in a sample of water
B. BOD is an indirect measure of organic waste present in water
C. If BOD increases, DO of water body decreases
D. Higher the BOD value, lower will be the polluting potential of water
(a) Only (A) and (B) are correct
(b) (A), (B) and (C) are correct
(c) Only (A) and (C) are correct
(d) (A), (B), (C) and (D) are correct

61. The Ganga action plan and Yamuna action plan have been initiated by:
(a) Khadi and Village Industries Commission
(b) The Ministry of Environment and Forests
(c) Indian Agriculture Research Institute
(d) Both (A) and (C)

62. Which of the following is not a component of biogas?
(a) SO_2 (b) H_2
(c) H_2S (d) CH_4

63. Select the incorrect(s) statement with respect to the production of biogas:

A. Biogas producing bacteria are collectively called methanogens
B. Methanogens are present in the rumen of cattle
C. Methanogens help in aerobic breakdown of organic waste in cattle dung to produce biogas
(a) Only (B) (b) Both (A) and (B)
(c) Both (A) and (C) (d) Only (C)

64. The technology of biogas production was developed in India mainly due to the efforts of:
(a) IARI
(b) KVIC
(c) Ministry of Environment and Forests
(d) Both (a) and (b)

65. Organisms called methanogens are most abundant in a:
(a) Hot spring (b) Sulphur rock
(c) Cattle yard (d) Polluted stream

66. In gobar gas, the maximum amount is that of:
(a) Butane (b) Methane
(c) Propane (d) CO_2

67. The given figure is concerned with:

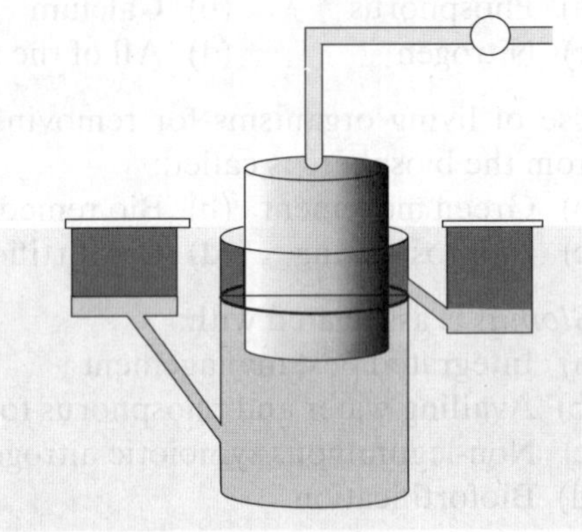

(a) Commercial production of antibiotics
(b) Biogas production
(c) Floating debris removed by primary treatment
(d) Fermentation and production of alcohol

68. During sewage treatment, biogases are produced, which include:
(a) Methane, oxygen, hydrogen sulphide
(b) Hydrogen sulphide, methane, sulphur dioxide
(c) Hydrogen sulphide, nitrogen, methane
(d) Methane, hydrogen sulphide, carbon dioxide

69. Group of bacteria used in biogas production is:
A. Eubacteria
B. Heterotrophs
C. Obligate anaerobes
D. Methanogens
(a) (B) and (D) (b) (C) and (D)
(c) Only (D) (d) (B), (C) and (D)

70. Slurry in biogas plant means:
(a) A fluid form of manure
(b) Dung without methanogens
(c) Waste water after removing organic matter
(d) Methane gas

71. Select the correct statement from the following:
(a) Biogas commonly called gobar gas is pure methane
(b) Activated sludge sediment in settlement tanks of sewage treatment plant is a rich source of aerobic bacteria
(c) Biogas is produced by the activity of aerobic bacteria on animal waste
(d) *Methanobacterium* is an aerobic bacterium found in the rumen of cattle

Microbes as Biocontrol Agents, Microbes as Biofertiliser

72. The ladybird and dragonfly are, respectively, used to get rid of:
(a) Aphids and mosquitoes
(b) Mosquitoes and aphids
(c) Caterpillars and jassids
(d) Aphids and caterpillars

73. A biocontrol agent *Trichoderma* is a:
(a) Virus (b) Fungus
(c) Cyanobacterium (d) Symbiotic bacterium

74. *Trichoderma* has proved a useful microorganism for:
(a) Biological control of soil-borne plant pathogens
(b) Bioremediation of contaminated soil
(c) Reclamation of wasteland
(d) Gene transfer in higher plants

75. Butterfly caterpillars can be controlled by a biocontrol agent like:
(a) VAM
(b) *Streptomyces*
(c) *Bacillus thuringiensis*
(d) Dragonflies

76. The majority of baculoviruses are used as biological control agents because:
(a) They are species-specific
(b) They have no negative impact on non-targets
(c) Beneficial insects are being conserved
(d) All of the above

77. Which of the following statements is not true about baculovirus?
(a) Most of the members used as biocontrol agents belong to the genus *Nucleopolyhedrovirus*
(b) Attack mammals, birds, fish or even non-target insects
(c) Attack insects and other arthropods
(d) Have narrow spectrum insecticidal application

78. Using Bt spores for pest control is:
(a) Biological control
(b) IPM
(c) Concept of sustainable agriculture
(d) All of the above

79. Example(s) of microbial control is/are:
(a) Control of aphids by ladybird beetle
(b) Control of butterfly caterpillars by Bt
(c) Control of mosquitoes by dragonflies
(d) All of the above

80. Sustainable agriculture does not include:
(a) Ecofriendly cropping
(b) Green revolution
(c) IPM
(d) Biological control

81. Bt spores are:
(a) Inert spores
(b) Fungal spores which are used to control butterfly caterpillars
(c) Mixed with water and sprayed on Brassica and other trees
(d) All except (a)

82. Biofertilisers include:
(a) Nitrogen fixing bacteria
(b) Mycorrhiza
(c) Nitrogen fixing cyanobacteria
(d) All of the above

83. Organic farming is raising crops through the use of:
(a) Biofertilisers
(b) Manure
(c) Resistant varieties
(d) All of the above

84. Which of the following is not a biofertiliser?
(a) *Glomus* (b) *Nostoc*
(c) *Penicillium* (d) *Azospirillum*

85. Consider the following statements A to D related to organic farming and select the correct option stating which ones are true (T) and which ones are false (F):
A. It utilises genetically modified crops like Bt cotton
B. It supports the use of only naturally produced inputs like compost
C. It is raising unpolluted crops through the use of bacteria, fungi and cyanobacteria
D. It produces vitamin- and mineral-rich vegetable and crops

	A	B	C	D
(a)	F	T	T	F
(b)	F	T	T	T
(c)	T	F	T	T
(d)	T	T	T	T

86. Mycorrhiza acts as:
(a) Mechanical tissue
(b) Root hair in adverse conditions
(c) Modified root
(d) Organ for vegetative propagation

87. Mycorrhiza is used to:
(a) Obtain nutrients from the soil
(b) Synthesize food
(c) Increase soil fertility
(d) Provide resistance against different regulators

88. Vermicompost is a biofertiliser rich in:
(a) Phosphorus (b) Calcium
(c) Nitrogen (d) All of the above

89. Use of living organisms for removing pollutants from the biosphere is called:
(a) Green movement (b) Bio remediation
(c) Bioprospecting (d) Bio fortification

90. *Glomus* is associated with:
(a) Integrated pest management
(b) Availing water and phosphorus for plants
(c) Non-leguminous symbiotic nitrogen fixation
(d) Biofortification

91. Organic farming works on the principle of:
(a) Eradicating pests from agriculture field
(b) Keeping the pest population under control
(c) The use of fertilisers of biological origin for raising of crops
(d) The use of biological and chemical methods for controlling plant diseases and pests

92. Which of the following is not a function of mycorrhizae?
(a) Enrich soil with phosphorus
(b) Provide tolerance to salinity
(c) Increase plant growth and development
(d) Enhance soil fertility with nitrogen content

93. Which larvicidal fish is used to control the mosquito larvae?
(a) *Gambusia* (b) Electric ray
(c) Dog fish (d) Singhara fish

94. Which of the following is an incorrect match:
(a) *Glomus:* Phosphate absorption
(b) *Rhizobium:* Symbiotic N_2 fixer in root nodule of leguminous plants
(c) *Trichoderma:* Common in root ecosystem
(d) *Thuricide:* Mutant strains of Bt

95. Which of the following insecticides is of plant origin?
(a) Ecdysone (b) Rotenone
(c) Parathion (d) Malathion

96. Consider the following statements:
A. Cyanobacteria are autotrophic microbes widely distributed in aquatic and terrestrial environments
B. *Anabaena*, *Nostoc* and *Oscillatoria* can fix nitrogen only in free-living conditions
C. In a paddy field, cyanobacteria serve as important biofertilisers
D. BGA increases soil fertility by adding organic matter to the soil
The correct statements are:
(a) (A) and (B) only
(b) (B) and (C) only
(c) (A), (C) and (D) only
(d) (C) only

97. Biocontrol of pests is better than chemical control as:
(a) Chemicals do not pollute the environment
(b) Biocontrol predators kill both useful and harmful life forms indiscriminately
(c) Chemicals only affect the target pests
(d) Biocontrol predators do not completely eradicate but keep the target pests at manageable levels

98. *Frankia* is:
(a) Free-living nitrogen fixer
(b) Found in paddy fields
(c) Found in root nodules of non-leguminous plants
(d) Parasitic roots of *Alnus* and *Casuarina*

99. Which of the following is common to *Azospirillum*, *Azotobacter*, *Anabaena*, *Nostoc* and *Oscillatoria*?
(a) Prokaryotic organisms
(b) Nitrogen fixer
(c) Show symbiotic relationship
(d) All except (c)

100. Sustainable agriculture is:
(a) The development of genetically engineered plants to develop resistance against pests
(b) The practice of using mutation and polyploidy as a mode of plant breeding programme
(c) Use of renewable resources which cause minimum pollution and maintain optimum yield levels
(d) Formation of somatic hybrids to assemble the desired traits in one species

NCERT EXEMPLAR QUESTIONS

1. The vitamin whose content increases following the conversion of milk into curd by lactic acid bacteria is:
(a) Vitamin C (b) Vitamin D
(c) Vitamin B_{12} (d) Vitamin E

2. Waste water treatment generates a large quantity of sludge, which can be treated by:
(a) Anaerobic digesters
(b) Floc
(c) Chemicals
(d) Oxidation pond

3. Methanogenic bacteria are not found in:
(a) Rumen of cattle
(b) Gobar gas plant
(c) Bottom of water-logged paddy fields
(d) Activated sludge

4. Match the following list of bacteria and their commercially important products:

Bacterium	Product
A. *Aspergillus niger*	(i) Lactic acid
B. *Acetobacter aceti*	(ii) Butyric acid
C. *Clostridium butylicum*	(iii) Acetic acid
D. *Lactobacillus*	(iv) Citric acid

Choose the correct match:
(a) A – (ii), B – (iii), C – (iv), D – (i)
(b) A – (ii), B – (iv), C – (iii), D – (i)
(c) A – (iv), B – (iii), C – (ii), D – (i)
(d) A – (iv), B – (i), C – (iii), D – (ii)

5. Match the following list of bioactive substances and their roles:

Bioactive substance	Role
A. Statin	(i) Removal of oil stains
B. Cyclosporin A	(ii) Removal of clots from blood vessels
C. Streptokinase	(iii) Lowering of blood cholesterol
D. Lipase	(iv) Immunosuppressive agent

Choose the correct match:
(a) A – (ii), B – (iii), C – (i), D – (iv)
(b) A – (iv), B – (ii), C – (i), D – (iii)
(c) A – (iv), B – (i), C – (ii), D – (iii)
(d) A – (iii), B – (iv), C – (ii), D – (i)

6. The primary treatment of waste water involves the removal of:
(a) Dissolved impurities
(b) Stable particles
(c) Toxic substances
(d) Harmful bacteria

7. BOD of waste water is estimated by measuring the amount of:
(a) Total organic matter
(b) Biodegradable organic matter
(c) Oxygen evolution
(d) Oxygen consumption

8. Which one of the following alcoholic drinks is produced without distillation?
(a) Wine (b) Whisky
(c) Rum (d) Brandy

9. The technology of biogas production from cow dung was developed in India largely due to the efforts of:
(a) Gas Authority of India
(b) Oil and Natural Gas Commission
(c) Indian Agricultural Research Institute and Khadi & Village Industries Commission
(d) Indian Oil Corporation

10. The free-living fungus *Trichoderma* can be used for:
(a) Killing insects
(b) Biological control of plant diseases
(c) Controlling butterfly caterpillars
(d) Producing antibiotics

11. What would happen if oxygen availability to activated sludge flocs is reduced?
(a) It will slow down the rate of degradation of organic matter
(b) The centre of the flocs will become anoxic, which would cause the death of bacteria and eventually the breakage of flocs
(c) Flocs would increase in size as anaerobic bacteria would grow around them
(d) Protozoa would grow in large numbers

12. Mycorrhiza does not help the host plant in:
(a) Enhancing its phosphorus uptake capacity
(b) Increasing its tolerance to drought
(c) Enhancing its resistance to root pathogens
(d) Increasing its resistance to insects

13. Which one of the following is not a nitrogen-fixing organism?
(a) *Anabaena* (b) *Nostoc*
(c) *Azotobacter* (d) *Pseudomonas*

14. Big holes in Swiss cheese are made by:
(a) A machine
(b) A bacterium that produces methane gas
(c) A bacterium producing a large amount of carbon dioxide
(d) A fungus that releases a lot of gas during its metabolic activities

15. The residue left after methane production from cattle dung is:
(a) Burnt
(b) Buried in landfills
(c) Used as manure
(d) Used in civil construction

16. Methanogens do not produce:
(a) Oxygen (b) Methane
(c) Hydrogen sulfide (d) Carbon dioxide

17. Activated sludge should have the ability to settle quickly so that it can:
(a) Be rapidly pumped back from sedimentation tank to aeration tank
(b) Absorb pathogenic bacteria present in waste water while sinking to the bottom of the settling tank
(c) Be discarded and anaerobically digested
(d) Absorb colloidal organic matter

18. Match the items in Column 'A' and Column 'B' and choose the correct answer:

Column I	Column II
A. Ladybird	(i) *Methanobacterium*
B. Mycorrhiza	(ii) *Trichoderma*
C. Biological control	(iii) Aphids
D. Biogas	(iv) *Glomus*

The correct answer is:
(a) A – (ii), B – (iv), C – (iii), D – (i)
(b) A – (iii), B – (iv), C – (ii), D – (i)
(c) A – (iv), B – (i), C – (ii), D – (iii)
(d) A – (iii), B – (ii), C – (i), D – (iv)

PRACTICE TEST PAPER

1. Curd is more nutritious than milk as it contains a number of vitamins, especially:
(a) Vitamin K (b) Vitain D
(c) Vitamin B_{12} (d) Vitamin A

2. The microorganism richest in protein is:
(a) *Spirulina* (b) *Nostoc*
(c) *Morchella* (d) *Chlorella*

3. Broad spectrum antibiotics are those that attack:
(a) Pathogens as well as hosts
(b) A wide range of pathogens
(c) Only pathogens
(d) Only hosts

4. A bio reactor is a:
(a) Fermentation tank
(b) Culture containing radioactive isotopes
(c) Part of sewage treatment plant
(d) Anaerobic sludge digester

5. Which of the following statements is correct regarding microbes in human welfare?
(a) *Saccharomyces cerevisiae* is useful in the production of citric acid
(b) Cyclosporin A is used as blood cholesterol lowering agent
(c) *Aspergillus niger* is used to obtain citric acid
(d) Statins are used as immune suppressive agents

6. During sewage treatment, secondary treatment is a:
(a) Biological process
(b) Physical process only
(c) Physico-chemical process
(d) Chemical process

7. Read the following statements and select the correct option stating which ones are true (T) and which ones are false (F):
A. Roquefort cheese is ripened by growing a bacteria *Propionibacterium shermanii* on it
B. Brewer's yeast is used for fermenting malted cereals and fruit juices
C. LAB improves the nutritional quality of curd during conversion of milk into curd
D. Toddy is prepared by fermenting sap from palm

	A	B	C	D
(a)	F	T	T	F
(b)	F	T	T	T
(c)	T	F	F	T
(d)	T	F	T	F

8. Microbial biocontrol agent which is used to control butterfly caterpillars is:
(a) *Bacillus thuringiensis*
(b) Nucleopolyhedrovirus
(c) Ladybird
(d) Dragonflies

9. Good producer of statins is:
(a) *Monascus* (b) A yeast
(c) *Trichoderma* (d) Both (a) and (b)

10. Cyclosporine A is used as immunosuppressive agent in organ transplant patients. It is produced by a:
(a) Fungus – *Trichoderma*
(b) Yeast – *Monascus*
(c) Bacterium – *Streptococcus*
(d) Bacterium – *Methylophilus*

11. Which of the following is a free-living microbial biocontrol agent for plant pathogens?
(a) *Rhizopus* (b) Ladybird beetle
(c) *Trichoderma* (d) *Glomus*

12. In anaerobic sludge digester, during digestion, bacteria produce a mixture of gases such as:
(a) CH_4, H_2S and CO_2
(b) CH_4, H_2S and N_2
(c) H_2s and CO_2 only
(d) CH_4 only

13. *Azolla* is an aquatic fern used as biofertiliser in rice fields. The N_2 fixing microbe which remains associated with *Azolla* is:
(a) *Rhizobium* (b) *Anabaena*
(c) *Frankia* (d) *Glomus*

14. Full potential of penicillin as an effective antibiotic was established by:
(a) Alexander Fleming
(b) Waksman
(c) Chain and Florey
(d) Beadle and Tatum

15. Read the following statements with respect to BOD and select the correct option:
A. BOD is directly proportional to polluting potential
B. The BOD test measures the rate of uptake of oxygen by microorganisms for degradation of biodegradable and non-biodegradable organic matter
C. BOD is the indirect measure of inorganic matter present in polluted water

(a) (A) and (B) (b) Only (A)
(c) Only (B) (d) (A) and (C)

16. During biological treatment in STP, a mesh-like structure is formed, known as flocs. It is:
(a) Masses of bacteria associated with fungal filaments
(b) Masses of bacteria, zooflagellates and ciliates
(c) Masses of anaerobic bacteria and fungi
(d) Mass of aerobic bacteria only

17. Which of the following is not a biofertiliser?
(a) *Rhizobium* (b) *Glomus*
(c) *Aulosira* (d) Baculovirus

18. Bioactive molecule statin is used:
(a) To remove clots from blood vessels
(b) As blood cholesterol lowering agent
(c) As fungicide
(d) As immunosuppressive agent

19. Select the incorrectly matched pair:
(a) *Azospirillum* – Free-living N_2 fixing bacteria in soil
(b) *Glomus* – Form mycorrhiza
(c) BGA – Reduce alkalinity of soil
(d) *Rhizobium* – Form symbiotic association for N_2 fixation with leguminous and non-leguminous plants

20. Which of the following steps in sewage treatment removes large and small particles through filtration and sedimentation?
(a) Primary treatment
(b) Secondary treatment
(c) Biological treatment
(d) Tertiary treatment

21. Match Column I with Column II and select the correct option:

Column I	Column II
A. Statin	(i) *Trichoderma*
B. Clot buster	(ii) *Aspergillus niger*
C. Cyclosporine A	(iii) *Streptococcus*
D. Citric acid	(iv) *Monascus purpureus*

(a) A – (iv), B – (i), C – (ii), D – (iii)
(b) A – (i), B – (iv), C – (ii), D – (iii)
(c) A – (iv), B – (iii), C – (i), D – (ii)
(d) A – (ii), B – (iii), C – (i), D – (iv)

22. Yeast *Saccharomyces cerevisiae* is commonly known as:
(a) Brewer's yeast (b) Baker's yeast
(c) Both (a) and (b) (d) Jackpot of genetics

23. Which microbial product inhibits activation of T-cells and, therefore, prevents rejection reaction in organ transplantation?
(a) Statin (b) Viridian
(c) Cyclosporin A (d) TPA

24. The primary effluents are passed into:
(a) Primary settling tank
(b) Secondary settling tank
(c) Aeration tank for the action of heterotrophic microbes
(d) A large tank for biological treatment by anaerobic bacteria and fungi

25. Biofertilisers are microorganisms which bring about:
(a) Soil nutrient enrichment
(b) Minimise ecological benefits
(c) Maximise environmental hazards
(d) Pest control

26. Functioning of statin is based on:
(a) Allosteric inhibition
(b) Competitive inhibition
(c) Non-competitive inhibition
(d) Feedback inhibition

27. Which bioinsecticide was first developed on a commercial scale?
(a) Sporeine (b) Quinine
(c) Devine (d) Willigo

28. Biogas production is mainly carried out by:
(a) Thermoacidophiles
(b) Methanogens
(c) Halophiles
(d) Anaerobic bacteria

29. Microbes are useful to humans in diverse ways. Which of the following products is formed by the fermentative activity of *Propionibacterium shermanii*?
(a) Swiss cheese (b) Cyclosporin A
(c) Vitamin B_{12} (d) Citric acid

30. Which is not a part of organic farming?
(a) Recycling of organic waste
(b) Least use of synthetic fertilisers
(c) Use of biofertilisers and bio pesticides
(d) Use of fertiliser responsive crops

31. Primary treatment of waste water involves the removal of:
(a) Dissolved impurities
(b) Floating and suspended solids
(c) Toxic substances
(d) Turbidity and harmful bacteria

32. Rice wine is:
(a) Beer (b) Wine
(c) Cider (d) Sake

33. Activated sludge should have the ability to settle quickly so that it can:
(a) Be rapidly pumped back from sedimentation to the aeration tank
(b) Absorb pathogenic bacteria present in waste water while sinking to the bottom of the settling tank
(c) Be discarded and anaerobically digested
(d) Absorb colloidal organic matter

34. BOD of waste water is estimated by measuring the amount of:
(a) Total organic matter
(b) Oxygen evolution
(c) Biodegradable organic matter
(d) Oxygen consumption

35. Vitamin C was the first vitamin to be produced by a fermentation process using:
(a) *Penicillium* (b) *E. coli*
(c) *Yersinia pestis* (d) *Acetobacter*

36. The most common substrate used in distilleries for the production of ethanol is:
(a) Molasses (b) Corn meal
(c) Soya meal (d) Potato

37. Nucleopolyhedrovirus is:
A. Narrow spectrum insecticide
B. Harmful to non-target insects
C. Used as biocontrol agent
(a) Only (A) (b) (B) and (C) only
(c) Only (A) and (C) (d) (A), (B) and (C)

38. Consider the following statements:
A. Major component of biogas is methane (50–70%) which is highly inflammable
B. Formation of biogas is a completely anaerobic process
(a) Only (A) is correct
(b) Only (B) is correct
(c) Both (A) and (B) are incorrect
(d) Both (A) and (B) are correct

39. Which of the following microbes is a proteinaceous infection agent?
(a) Fungi (b) Prions
(c) Bacteria (d) Protozoa

40. The microbe used in the control of oil spills:
(a) *Pseudomonas putida*
(b) *Trichoderma*
(c) *Bacillus thuringiensis*
(d) *Thiobacillus*

41. Which gas is responsible for the puffed-up appearance of dough?
(a) CO_2 (b) O_2
(c) SO_2 (d) NO_2

42. *Azolla* is used as biofertiliser as it has:
(a) *Rhizobium*
(b) Cyanobacteria
(c) Mycorrhiza
(d) Large quantity of humus

43. The commercial extraction of penicillin was performed by:
(a) Fleming (b) Chain and Florey
(c) Waksman (d) Koch

44. Absence of oxygen in biogas plant will have:
(a) Positive effect
(b) Negative effect
(c) Initial positive then negative effect
(d) Initial negative then positive effect

45. Conversion of sugar into alcohol during fermentation is due to the direct action of:
(a) Temperature
(b) Zymase
(c) Microorganism
(d) Concentration of sugar solution

ANSWER KEYS

Exercises

1. (d)	**2.** (d)	**3.** (b)	**4.** (a)	**5.** (c)	**6.** (d)	**7.** (a)	**8.** (d)	**9.** (d)	**10.** (b)
11. (a)	**12.** (c)	**13.** (c)	**14.** (a)	**15.** (b)	**16.** (a)	**17.** (c)	**18.** (a)	**19.** (b)	**20.** (b)
21. (c)	**22.** (a)	**23.** (d)	**24.** (c)	**25.** (b)	**26.** (b)	**27.** (b)	**28.** (d)	**29.** (b)	**30.** (b)
31. (b)	**32.** (d)	**33.** (a)	**34.** (c)	**35.** (d)	**36.** (d)	**37.** (a)	**38.** (a)	**39.** (a)	**40.** (b)
41. (b)	**42.** (b)	**43.** (a)	**44.** (a)	**45.** (c)	**46.** (c)	**47.** (d)	**48.** (b)	**49.** (b)	**50.** (c)
51. (b)	**52.** (b)	**53.** (c)	**54.** (b)	**55.** (d)	**56.** (d)	**57.** (b)	**58.** (c)	**59.** (c)	**60.** (b)
61. (b)	**62.** (d)	**63.** (d)	**64.** (d)	**65.** (c)	**66.** (b)	**67.** (b)	**68.** (d)	**69.** (b)	**70.** (c)
71. (b)	**72.** (a)	**73.** (b)	**74.** (a)	**75.** (c)	**76.** (d)	**77.** (b)	**78.** (d)	**79.** (b)	**80.** (b)
81. (c)	**82.** (d)	**83.** (d)	**84.** (c)	**85.** (a)	**86.** (b)	**87.** (a)	**88.** (d)	**89.** (b)	**90.** (b)
91. (c)	**92.** (d)	**93.** (a)	**94.** (d)	**95.** (b)	**96.** (c)	**97.** (d)	**98.** (c)	**99.** (d)	**100.** (c)

NCERT Exemplar Questions

1. (c)	**2.** (a)	**3.** (d)	**4.** (c)	**5.** (d)	**6.** (b)	**7.** (d)	**8.** (a)	**9.** (c)	**10.** (b)
11. (b)	**12.** (d)	**13.** (d)	**14.** (c)	**15.** (c)	**16.** (a)	**17.** (a)	**18.** (b)		

Practice Test Paper

1. (c)	**2.** (a)	**3.** (b)	**4.** (a)	**5.** (c)	**6.** (a)	**7.** (b)	**8.** (a)	**9.** (d)	**10.** (a)
11. (c)	**12.** (a)	**13.** (b)	**14.** (c)	**15.** (b)	**16.** (a)	**17.** (d)	**18.** (b)	**19.** (d)	**20.** (a)
21. (c)	**22.** (c)	**23.** (c)	**24.** (c)	**25.** (a)	**26.** (b)	**27.** (a)	**28.** (b)	**29.** (a)	**30.** (d)
31. (b)	**32.** (d)	**33.** (a)	**34.** (d)	**35.** (d)	**36.** (a)	**37.** (c)	**38.** (d)	**39.** (b)	**40.** (a)
41. (a)	**42.** (b)	**43.** (b)	**44.** (a)	**45.** (b)					

SOLUTIONS

Introduction, Microbes in Household Products, Microbes in Industrial Products (Fermented Beverages, Antibiotics, Chemical Enzymes and Other Bioactive Molecules)

1. Microbes are of various varieties and include protozoa, bacteria, fungi, microscopic animal and plant viruses, viroids and prions.

2. Microbes are found everywhere: in soil, water, air and inside the bodies of living organisms. They can be found in thermal vents, deep in soil, under snow as well as in acidic environments.

3. Bacterial colonies can be seen with the naked eye.

4. Adenovirus, which causes respiratory infections

5. LAB increases the quantity of vitamin B_{12}, thus increasing the nutrient quality of milk.

6. Roquefort cheese is ripened by the fungi *Penicillium roqueforti.*

7. LAB stands for lactic acid bacteria.

8. The type of end product depends upon substrate and fermentative microbes.

9. Over 1000 different cheeses are available and each has its own characteristic taste, texture and flavour.

10. Roquefort cheese is ripened by the fungi *Penicillium roqueforti.*

11. Puffed-up appearance of dough is due to production of CO_2 during the fermentation process.

12. Dosa and idli are preparations of rice and black gram.

13. Rennet is employed in the preparation of cheese.

14. Three statements (I, II, and III) are correct. During growth, LAB produces acids that coagulate and partially digest the milk protein.

15. Pasteurisation is heating of liquid to between 65°C and 80°C followed by rapid cooling.

16. Probiotics are live microbial food supplements that may be able to help prevent and treat some illnesses. Promoting a healthy digestive tract and a healthy immune system are their most widely studied benefits at this time.

17. Toddy is a traditional drink of southern India. It is made by fermentation of sap from the palm tree *Caryota urens* by naturally occurring yeast.

18. Molasses are the most common substrate for alcohol production.

19. Yeast (*Saccharomyces cerevisiae*) is used for commercial production of ethanol.

20. Broad spectrum antibiotics are those that attack a wide range of pathogens.

21. More than 100 antibiotics are produced by different species of *Streptomyces.*

22. Large-scale production of various compounds in industries is carried out in very large vessels called fermenters.

23. Diseases cured by antibiotics include plague, whooping cough, diphtheria and leprosy.

24. Antibiotics produced by microbes are considered as one of the most significant discoveries of the twentieth century and have contributed to the welfare of humans. Antibiotics are chemical substances that are produced by some microorganisms and kill or retard the growth of other disease causing microorganisms.

25. Butyric acid – *Clostridium butyricum,* Acetic acid – *Acetobacter aceti,* Cyclosporin – *Trichoderma,* Statins – *Monascus purpureus*

26. *a*-amylase stimulates germination of barley seeds.

27. Organic acid first produced through fermentation process is lactic acid.

28. Wine and beer are produced without distillation process; they are formed by the fermentation fruit juices and barley malt with *Saccharomyces cerevisiae.*

29. Cyclosporin A is a bioactive molecule used as an immunosuppressive agent in organ

transplantation. It is produced by the fungus *Trichoderma polysporin*.

30. The enzymes used in detergents can perform the task in the presence of anionic and non-anionic detergents, soaps and oxidants at a pH of 8–10.

31. Statins are commercially used as blood cholesterol lowering agents. They are produced by the fermentative activity of the yeast *Monascus purpureus*.

32. Streptokinase is used to dissolve blood clots (clot buster) of the patients suffering from myocardial infarction.

33. Streptokinase is produced by *Streptococcus* bacteria and modified by genetic engineering.

34. Wine and beer are produced without distillation, while whisky, rum and brandy are produced by distillation process.

35. Hops are dried petals of the plant *Humulus lupulus*. They are used primarily as a bittering, flavouring and stability agent in beer; they also show mild antibacterial activity.

36. Distillation

37. Beer has 3–8% alcohol content.

38. Fermentation process is inhibited at an alcohol level of 10–13 %. Distilled beverages have high alcoholic content and are collectively called hard liquor.

39. Statins are used as agents that lower the blood cholesterol level. Inhibition of HMC CoA reductase by statins prevents cholesterol synthesis.

40. Lipase is used in detergents to remove stains from the laundry.

41. Interferons are a group of signalling proteins secreted by host cells in response to virus infection.

42. Cyclosporin A is used as immune suppressive agent in organ transplantation patients.

43. Functioning of statin is based on competitive inhibition. Its mechanism of action is to inhibit the enzyme responsible for the synthesis of cholesterol.

Microbes in Sewage Treatment, Microbes in Production of Biogas

44. Primary treatment involves physical removal of small and large particles from sewage.

45. In primary treatment, the floating objects (like polythene bags, plastics) are removed by sequential filtration and the grit (sand and small pebbles) is removed by sedimentation in a settling tank.

46. Secondary treatment is a biological process carried out by heterotrophic bacteria naturally present in the sewage.

47. Flocs are masses of bacteria associated with fungal filaments to form the mesh-like structure.

48. BOD refers to the amount of oxygen that would be consumed if all the organic matter in one litre of water were oxidised by bacteria. Hence, BOD is a measure of dissolved organic matter present in the waste water.

49. Primary effluents are passed into a large aeration tank with constant mechanical agitation and air supply.

50. In STP, microbes are used in secondary treatment and in anaerobic sludge digester. In the digesters, anaerobic microbes digest the bacteria and fungi in the sludge and produce a mixture of gases such as methane, hydrogen, sulphide, CO_2 which form biogas.

51. Secondary treatment

52. Only (C) is correct. Domestic sewage has a high BOD value as it contains dissolved organic matter.

53. A – Aeration tank, B – Anaerobic sludge digester.
After secondary treatment in the aeration tank, the bacterial flocs settle and the sediment is called activated sludge. A part of the activated sludge is used as an inoculum which is pumped back into the aeration tank and the remaining part is passed into large tanks called anaerobic sludge digester.

54. Tertiary treatment is physico-chemical treatment. It is used to remove turbidity, pesticides, pathogenic microorganisms, etc.

55. After secondary treatment, the effluent of the aeration tank is then passed into the settling tank and bacterial flocs are allowed to sediment. This sediment is called activated sludge.

56. Reverse osmosis and UV treatment are part of tertiary treatment.

57. A small part of the activated sludge is used as an inoculum in the aeration tank.

58. Bacteria which grow anaerobically on a cellulose material produce methane in large amounts with CO_2 and H_2. These bacteria are called methanogens.

59. Methanogens are commonly found in anaerobic conditions.

60. (A), (B) and (C) are correct. The BOD test measures the rate of uptake of oxygen by microorganisms in a sample of water and thus indirectly measure the organic matter present in the water. The greater the BOD of waste water, the more the polluting potential.

61. Ganga action plan and Yamuna action plan have been initiated by the Ministry of Environment and Forests, under which a large number of STPs will be built to treat the sewage before their discharge in the rivers to reduce their pollution.

62. Major component of biogas is methane. Other gases are CO_2, H_2, H_2S, etc.

63. Only (C) is incorrect. Methanogens grow anaerobically on a cellulosic material to produce methane in large amounts.

64. IARI and KVIC developed the technology of biogas production in India.

65. Cattle yard

66. Gobar gas is a mixture of gases containing mostlymethane produced by microbial activity.

67. Biogas production

68. During sewage treatment, the anaerobic microbes digest the activated sludge and produce a mixture of gases such as methane, hydrogen sulphide and carbon dioxide.

69. (C) and (D) are correct. Methanogens grow anaerobically on a cellulosic material to produce methane.

70. Slurry is the waste water after removing the organic matter.

71. After secondary treatment, bacterial flocs (mass of aerobic bacteria and fungi) settle and the sediment is called activated sludge.

Microbes as Biocontrol Agents, Microbes as Biofertiliser

72. Ladybird and dragonfly are used to get rid of aphids and mosquitoes.

73. *Trichoderma* species are free-living fungi present in root ecosystems where they act against several plant pathogens.

74. Biological control of soil-borne plant pathogens.

75. Microbial biocontrol agents, such as bacteria. *Bacillus thuringiensis* (Bt) controls butterfly caterpillars. They are available as dry spores in sachets.

76. Baculoviruses are pathogens that attack insects and other arthropods. They are species-specific and narrow spectrum insecticides. They do not harm plants, mammals, birds, fishes and other non-target insects.

77. No negative impact on plants, mammals, fishes, birds and on other insects.

78. IPM is the practice of pest control through biological or natural methods and using chemical pesticides only when it is essential. Sustainable pest management is otherwise known as integrated pest management.

79. Bt is a microbial biocontrol agent that can be introduced to control butterfly caterpillars.

80. Sustainable agriculture does not include Green Revolution.

81. Dried spores of Bt are mixed with water and sprayed on plants such as *Brassica* and fruit trees.

82. Biofertilisers are the microorganisms which enrich the nutrient (nitrogen and phosphorus) quality of the soil. Bacteria, fungi and cyanobacteria are the three main sources of biofertilisers.

83. Organic farming is raising of crops through the use of biofertilisers that provide optimum nutrients to host plants.

84. Penicillium is not used as biofertiliser.

85. (A) and (D) are false.

86. Mycorrhiza is a symbiotic association between fungal hyphae and roots of higher plants. They act as root hairs and absorb phosphorus from the soil and transport it to other parts of the plant.

87. Mycorrhiza is used to obtaining nutrients, especially phosphorous, from the soil.

88. Vermicompost is a biofertiliser rich in phosphorus, nitrogen, calcium, etc.

89. Bioremediation is a type of waste management technique which involves the use of organisms to remove or utilise the pollutants from a polluted area.

90. Many members of the genus *Glomus* form mycorrhiza which avail water and phosphorus from the soil and pass it to the plant.

91. Organic farmers use a holistic approach and keep pests at manageable levels, by a complex system of checks and balances within the ecosystem instead of their complete eradication. They use fertilisers which are biological in origin.

92. Fungal hyphae absorb phosphorous from soil and pass it to the plants. Plants having mycorrhizal associations also show resistance to root-borne pathogens, tolerance to salinity and drought and overall increase in plant growth and development.

93. *Gambusia* fish is used for biological control of mosquitoes because it eats mosquito larvae.

94. In the pest control form, Bt is known as thuricide. *Bacillus thuringiensis* is a naturally occurring bacterium found in soil throughout world.

95. Rotenone is used as a broad spectrum insecticide which is derived from the roots of *Derris elliptica*.

96. (A), (C) and (D) are correct. Cyanobacteria (*Nostoc anabaena*) are autotrophic microbes widely distributed in aquatic and terrestrial ecosystems and fix atmospheric N_2 in free-living as well as symbiotic conditions.

97. The use of biocontrol measures reduces our dependence on toxic chemicals and pesticides. Biocontrol predators do not completely eradicate but keep target pests at manageable levels by a complex system of checks and balances within a living and vibrant ecosystem.

98. *Frankia* make symbiotic associations with root modules of non-leguminous plants, such as *Casuarina, Alnus*.

99. All of the given organisms are prokaryotic nitrogen fixers.

100. Sustainable agriculture is the use of renewable resources which causes minimum pollution and maintains the optimum yield levels.

11 Biotechnology – Principles and Processes

EXERCISES

Tools of Recombinant DNA Technology

1. Which of the following enzymes is called molecular scissors?
(a) Ligases
(b) Polymerases
(c) Restriction endonuclease
(d) Alkaline phosphatase

2. In which year were the two enzymes responsible for restricting the growth of bacteriophage in *Escherichia coli* isolated?
(a) 1972 (b) 1963
(c) 1977 (d) 1984

3. 'R' in EcoRI stands for:
(a) Genus
(b) Species
(c) Strain for bacterium
(d) Sequence of isolation

4. Identify the correct statement with respect to exonucleases:
(a) They remove nucleotides from the ends of DNA
(b) They join nucleotides at palindromic sequences
(c) They remove nucleotides from palindromic sequences
(d) They join nucleotides at the 5′ end of DNA

5. The part of the plasmid responsible for initiating replication is:
(a) Palindromic sequence
(b) Selectable marker
(c) Cloning sequence
(d) 'ori'

6. EFB stands for:
(a) English Federation of Biotechnology
(b) European Federation of Biotechnology
(c) English Frontier of Biotechnology
(d) European Frontier of Biology

7. Which of the following is the recognition sequence of EcoRI?
(a) 5′GAATTC3′ 3′CTTAAG5′ (b) 5′CCCGGG3′ 3′GGGCCC5′
(c) 5′GGATCC3′ 3′CCTAGG5′ (d) 5′AGCT3′ 3′TCGA5′

8. The ends of DNA are called 'sticky' due to the presence of:
(a) Paired bases (b) Unpaired bases
(c) Phosphate groups (d) Calcium ions

9. The first restriction endonuclease discovered was:
(a) EcoRI (b) BamHI
(c) HindII (d) Pvu I

10. Construction of the first recombinant DNA was carried out using the native plasmid of:
(a) *Escherichia coli*
(b) *Salmonella typhimurium*
(c) *Bacillus thuringiensis*
(d) *Agrobacterium tumefaciens*

11. The function of restriction endonuclease is to:
(a) Join DNA fragments
(b) Break phosphodiester bonds at random sites
(c) Facilitate crossing over
(d) Digest DNA at palindromic sites

12. A technique which involves altering the chemistry of genetic material to introduce it into the host organism is best defined as:
(a) DNA fingerprinting
(b) Genetic engineering
(c) Bioprocess engineering
(d) Cloning

13. Which of the following is a disadvantage of the traditional hybridisation procedure?

(a) Elimination of both desirable and undesirable genes
(b) Preservation of genetic information
(c) Inheritance of undesirable genes along with desirable genes
(d) Recombination of only desirable genes

14. _________ had developed a method of removing plasmids from cells and reinserting them in other cells:
(a) Herbert Boyer (b) Stanley Cohen
(c) Werner Arber (d) Hamilton Smith

15. Maintenance of sterile (microbial contamination-free) environment in chemical engineering process to enable growth of only desirable cells is called:
(a) Genetic engineering
(b) Bioprocess engineering
(c) Traditional hybridisation
(d) Transcription

16. Cloning is a means of:
(a) Fragmenting DNA
(b) Isolating DNA
(c) Preserving genotype
(d) Separating DNA fragments by electrophoresis

17. HindII recognizes a specific base sequence on DNA strands, which is called:
(a) Selectable marker
(b) Origin of replication
(c) Palindromic sequence
(d) Transcription unit

18. The bond digested by EcoRI at the palindromic site is a:
(a) Hydrogen bond (b) Phosphodiester bond
(c) Peptide bond (d) Glycosidic bond

19. In genetic engineering, DNA fragments are joined with the help of:
(a) Exonuclease (b) Endonuclease
(c) Ligase (d) Polymerase

20. Which of the following is the correct statement with respect to plasmids?
(a) It is found only in eukaryotic cells
(b) It is a part of chromosomal DNA
(c) It contains vital genes necessary for cell division
(d) It is used as a vector for gene transfer

21. The enzyme restriction endonuclease is used in recombinant DNA technology and obtained from:
(a) Yeast cells (b) Bacteriophages
(c) Bacterial cells (d) Eukaryotic cells

22. Stanley Cohen and Herbert Boyer isolated an antibiotic resistance gene by cutting a piece of DNA in the year:
(a) 1963 (b) 1977
(c) 1972 (d) 1984

23. Plasmids are used as vectors for gene cloning as they are capable of:
(a) Replicating outside the cells in artificial medium
(b) Self-replicating in bacterial cells
(c) Replicating only with chromosomal DNA
(d) Digesting bacteriophage DNA

24. Which of the following is a source of EcoRI?
(a) *Escherichia coli* RX 17
(b) *Escherichia coli* RY 13
(c) *Entamoeba coli* RY 13
(d) *Escherichia coli* RW 23

25. Identify the incorrect statement:
(a) Genetic material of an organism can be fragmented by nuclease to obtain the gene of interest
(b) The term 'vector' in recombinant DNA technology refers to enzymes that join DNA fragments
(c) Alien DNA must be attached to 'ori' of the vector genome during genetic engineering
(d) In recombinant DNA technology, human genes are often transferred into prokaryotes during cloning

26. During gene cloning, 'gene taxi' is a term used for:
(a) Plasmid (b) Bacterium
(c) Protozoa (d) Fungus

27. Restriction enzymes were discovered by:
(a) Kohler and Milstein
(b) Nirenberg and khorana
(c) Arber, Nathans and Smith
(d) Temin and Baltimore

28. Plasmid is a:
(a) Messenger RNA
(b) Single-stranded DNA
(c) Chromosomal DNA
(d) Double-stranded circular DNA

29. In recombinant DNA technology, the term vector is used for:
(a) Palindromic sequence of DNA
(b) Molecular probe used for identification of gene
(c) Restriction endonucleases
(d) Plasmid used to transfer DNA into a living cell

30. Identify the incorrect statement with respect to restriction endonucleases:
(a) They are used as tool for recombinant DNA technology
(b) They are synthesized by bacteria as part of their defense mechanism
(c) They inspect the length of DNA sequence and cut at a specific site
(d) 230 restriction endonucleases have been isolated from 900 strains of bacteria

31. _________ is often referred to as the "Father of Genetic Engineering":
(a) Kary Mullis (b) Paul Berg
(c) Temin (d) Alec Jeffrey

32. In genetic engineering, recombinant DNA means:
(a) DNA with a piece of RNA
(b) DNA with a piece of foreign DNA
(c) Circular single-stranded DNA
(d) DNA of retrovirus

33. _________ prevents the re-joining of vector DNA fragments once they are digested by restriction enzymes:
(a) DNA ligase (b) Alkaline phosphatase
(c) Exonuclease (d) DNA polymerase

34. Identify the incorrect statement with respect to plasmids:
(a) They are present in one or several copies
(b) They are part of chromosomal DNA
(c) They are formed of circular double-stranded DNA
(d) They can be transferred from one cell to another and can form multiple copies

35. Which of the following is an incorrect statement?
(a) Restriction endonucleases are formed in bacteria to digest bacteriophage DNA
(b) Shuttle vectors are active in both prokaryotic and eukaryotic cells
(c) In genetic engineering, probe is a radioactively labelled double-stranded DNA
(d) DNA ligase catalyses the formation of phosphodiester bonds between two DNA fragments

36. The recombinant DNA fragments are directly injected into the nucleus of an animal cell by a method known as:
(a) Biolistics (b) Microinjection
(c) Gene gun (d) Transformation

37. Read the following statements and choose the correct option:
I: *Agrobacterium tumefaciens* is a pathogen of several dicot plants
II: *Agrobacterium tumefaciens* is able to transform tumorous cells into normal plant cells using 'T-DNA'
(a) Both statements are correct
(b) Both statements are incorrect
(c) Only I is correct
(d) Only II is correct

38. Select the incorrect statement:
(a) DNA is a hydrophilic molecule
(b) DNA can easily pass through cell membranes
(c) The bacterial cells must be made competent to take up DNA
(d) Treating with divalent cations improves the efficiency with which DNA enters the bacteria

39. In pBR322, the gene tet^R has the recognition site for:
(a) Pvu II (b) Pvu I
(c) Pst I (d) SalI

40. Select the odd one out with respect to the features of cloning vector:
(a) Selectable marker
(b) Origin of replication
(c) Unique restriction site
(d) Preferably large size

41. In a method knows as _________, suitable for plants, cells are bombarded with high velocity microparticles of gold or tungsten coated with DNA:
(a) Gene gun (b) Disarmed vectors
(c) Biolistics (d) Both (a) and (c)

42. In ethidium bromide-stained gel exposed to UV light, bands of DNA would appear bright:
(a) Orange (b) Green
(c) Blue (d) Pink

43. Agarose is a natural polymer extracted from:
(a) Corals (b) Seaweed
(c) Oysters (d) Shell fish

44. In agarose gel electrophoresis, DNA fragments separate according to their:
(a) Charge (b) Size
(c) pH (d) Size to charge ratio

45. Specific concentration of _________ increases the efficiency of DNA for entering the bacterial cell wall:
(a) K^+ (b) Na^+
(c) Ca^{2+} (d) Cl^-

46. Insertion of alien DNA at which site of pBR322 will still provide ampicillin and tetracycline resistance to recombinant host cells?
(a) amp^R (b) tet^R
(c) BamHI site (d) Replication of plasmid

47. Which of the following bacteria is considered a natural genetic engineer?
(a) *Entamoeba coli*
(b) *Escherichia coli*
(c) *Agrobacterium tumefaciens*
(d) *Haemophilus influenzae*

48. If the desired gene segment is inserted at the Pvu I site in pBR322, the resulting plasmid will confer resistance to:
(a) Ampicillin (b) Tetracycline
(c) Streptomycin (d) Kanamycin

49. The vector requires a ________, which helps in identifying and eliminating non-transformants and selectively permitting the growth of transformants:
(a) Origin of replication
(b) Selectable marker
(c) Cloning sites
(d) Replication of plasmid

50. In 'blue-white' selection of plasmids with the β-galactosidase gene, colonies of non-recombinants will produce colonies of ________ colour:
(a) Blue (b) White
(c) No (d) Orange

51. Which of the following vectors is used to carry large fragments of foreign DNA up to 1 Mb (10^6)?
(a) Plasmid
(b) Cosmid
(c) Bacterial artificial chromosome (BAC)
(d) Yeast artificial chromosome (YAC)

Processes of Recombinant DNA Technology

52. Which enzyme would be used for isolation of genetic material from fungal cells?
(a) Cellulase (b) Lysozyme
(c) Chitinase (d) Methylase

53. The primers used in PCR technique should be:
(a) Polypeptide in nature
(b) Tagged with radioisotope
(c) Complimentary to the 5′-end sequence of the DNA segment to be amplified
(d) Complimentary to the 3′-end sequence of the DNA segment to be amplified

54. Bioreactors are vessels used:
(a) In PCR technique
(b) For converting raw materials biologically into products
(c) For separation of DNA fragments based on their size
(d) For detection of mutations in genetic diseases

55. The PCR technique is used for:
(a) In vitro synthesis of RNA
(b) In vitro synthesis of DNA
(c) In vivo synthesis of DNA
(d) In vivo synthesis of RNA

56. Sparged tank bioreactor differs from simple stirred-tank bioreactor in having:
(a) Temperature controlling system
(b) pH controlling system
(c) Sampling ports
(d) Sparged sterile air bubbles

57. Bioreactors provide optimum growth conditions like:
A. Vitamins
B. Substrate
C. Oxygen
D. Temperature
(a) (A) and (C) only (b) (B) and (D) only
(c) (A) and (D) only (d) (A), (B), (C) and (D)

58. During PCR, 1 billion copies of DNA are made at the end of ________ cycles. Select the option that fills the blank correctly:
(a) 10 (b) 20
(c) 30 (d) 50

59. Which of the following is the correct sequence of three temperature-dependent steps of PCR?
(a) Extension → Denaturation → Annealing
(b) Denaturation → Annealing → Extension
(c) Annealing → Denaturation → Extension
(d) Denaturation → Extension → Annealing

60. Which of the following chemical substances is used for precipitation of DNA?
(a) Ampicillin (b) Chilled ethanol
(c) Ethidium bromide (d) Tetracycline

61. Thermostable enzymes 'Taq' and 'pfu' isolated from thermophilic bacteria are:
(a) Restriction endonucleases
(b) RNA polymerases
(c) DNA polymerases
(d) Methylases

62. Melting of DNA at 94°C in PCR technique is due to breakdown of:
(a) Phosphodiester bonds

(b) Hydrogen bonds
(c) Glycosidic bonds
(d) Disulphide bonds

63. Downstream processing does not involve:
(a) Separation (b) Purification
(c) Preservation (d) Expression

64. PCR technique was discovered by:
(a) Kary Mullis
(b) Alec Jeffreys
(c) Temin and Baltimore
(d) Khorana

65. The optimum temperature for the polymerisation step in PCR is:
(a) 94°C (b) 72°C
(c) 60°C (d) 110°C

66. The application of PCR technique is:
(a) To harvest stem cells
(b) To amplify specific DNA sequences
(c) To replicate RNA sequences
(d) To form the desired proteins in bioreactors

67. Stirrer in stirred-tank bioreactor is used for:
(a) Increasing availability of oxygen in the entire vessel
(b) Maintaining temperature
(c) Adding preservatives
(d) Adding substrates

68. The blotting technique used for separation of RNA is called:
(a) Southern blotting (b) Northern blotting
(c) Western blotting (d) Eastern blotting

69. __________ is not used while extracting DNA from an organism:
(a) Ribonuclease (b) Deoxyribonuclease
(c) Cellulase (d) Protease

70. Which of the following steps is catalysed by Taq polymerase in a PCR reaction?
(a) Denaturation of template DNA
(b) Annealing of primers to template DNA
(c) Extension of primer end on the template DNA
(d) All of the above

71. Read the following statements and choose the correct option:
I: In a continuous culture system, the fresh medium is added from one side and the used growth medium is drained out from the other side
II: Batch fermentation is an example of continuous culture
(a) Both statements are correct
(b) Both statements are incorrect
(c) Only I is correct
(d) Only II is correct

72. Which of the following is incorrect with respect to DNA fingerprinting?
(a) It is used in forensic science
(b) It is used for settling paternity disputes
(c) It is a PCR-based technique
(d) It is based on the fingerprint of the individual

73. Biolistics is suitable for:
(a) DNA fingerprinting
(b) Disarming pathogen vectors
(c) Transformation of plant cells
(d) Constructing rDNA by joining with vectors

74. Identify the incorrect statement:
(a) Downstream processing relates to the stages of industrial fermentation during which the concerned product is separated and purified
(b) Downstream processing and quality control testing vary from product to product
(c) Some products require formation with suitable preservatives
(d) Strict quality control testing of each product is not required

75. Gel electrophoresis is used for:
(a) Isolating DNA molecules
(b) Fragmentation of DNA
(c) Separation of DNA fragments according to their size
(d) Ligation of DNA fragments

76. If a protein encoding gene is expressed in a heterologous host, it is called:
(a) Recombinant protein
(b) Denatured protein
(c) Purified protein
(d) Selective protein

77. Select the incorrect statement:
(a) Elution means cutting and extraction of DNA bands from agarose gel
(b) Agarose gel extracted from seaweed is used in PCR amplification
(c) PCR and restriction fragment length polymorphism are the methods of genetic fingerprinting
(d) In batch fermentation, the conditions set up are not changed from outside once fermentation starts

NCERT EXEMPLAR QUESTIONS

1. Rising of dough is due to:
(a) Multiplication of yeast
(b) Production of CO_2
(c) Emulsification
(d) Hydrolysis of wheat flour starch into sugars

2. Which of the following enzymes catalyse the removal of nucleotides from the ends of DNA?
(a) Endonuclease (b) Exonuclease
(c) DNA ligase (d) HindII

3. The transfer of genetic material from one bacterium to another through the mediation of a viral vector is termed as:
(a) Transduction (b) Conjugation
(c) Transformation (d) Translation

4. Which of the given statements is correct in the context of visualising DNA molecules separated by agarose gel electrophoresis?
(a) DNA can be seen in visible light
(b) DNA can be seen without staining in visible light
(c) Ethidium bromide stained DNA can be seen in visible light
(d) Ethidium bromide stained DNA can be seen under exposure to UV light

5. 'Restriction' in restriction enzyme refers to:
(a) Cleaving of phosphodiester bond in DNA by the enzyme
(b) Cutting of DNA at specific position only
(c) Prevention of the multiplication of bacteriophage by the host bacteria
(d) All of the above

6. Which of the following is not required in the preparation of a recombinant DNA molecule?
(a) Restriction endonuclease
(b) DNA ligase
(c) DNA fragments
(d) *E.coli*

7. In agarose gel electrophoresis, DNA molecules are separated on the basis of their:
(a) Charge only
(b) Size only
(c) Charge to size ratio
(d) All of the above

8. The most important feature in a plasmid to serve as a vector in gene cloning experiment is:
(a) Origin of replication (ori)
(b) Presence of a selectable marker
(c) Presence of sites for restriction endonuclease
(d) Its size

9. While isolating DNA from bacteria, which of the following enzymes is not required?
(a) Lysozyme (b) Ribonuclease
(c) Deoxyribonuclease (d) Protease

10. Which of the following contributed in popularising the PCR (polymerase chain reactions) technique?
(a) Easy availability of DNA template
(b) Availability of synthetic primers
(c) Availability of cheap deoxyribonucleotides
(d) Availability of 'thermostable' DNA polymerase

11. An antibiotic resistance gene in a vector usually helps in the selection of:
(a) Competent bacterial cells
(b) Transformed bacterial cells
(c) Recombinant bacterial cells
(d) None of the above

12. Significance of 'heat shock' method in bacterial transformation is to facilitate:
(a) Binding of DNA to the cell wall
(b) Uptake of DNA through membrane transport proteins
(c) Uptake of DNA through transient pores in the bacterial cell wall
(d) Expression of antibiotic resistance gene

13. The role of DNA ligase in the construction of a recombinant DNA molecule is:
(a) Formation of phosphodiester bond between two DNA fragments
(b) Formation of hydrogen bonds between sticky ends of DNA fragments
(c) Ligation of all purine and pyrimidine bases
(d) None of the above

14. Which of the following bacteria is not a source of restriction endonuclease?
(a) *Haemophilus influenzae*
(b) *Escherichia coli*
(c) *Entamoeba coli*
(d) *Bacillus amyloliquefaciens*

15. Which of the following steps are catalysed by Taq DNA polymerase in a PCR reaction?
(a) Denaturation of template DNA
(b) Annealing of primers to template DNA

(c) Extension of primer end on the template DNA
(d) All of the above

16. A bacterial cell was transformed with a recombinant DNA molecule that was generated using a human gene. However, the transformed cells did not produce the desired protein. Reasons could be:
(a) Human gene may have intron which bacteria cannot process
(b) Amino acid codons for humans and bacteria are different
(c) Human protein is formed but degraded by bacteria
(d) All of the above

17. Which of the following should be chosen for best yield if one were to produce a recombinant protein in large amounts?
(a) Laboratory flask of largest capacity
(b) A stirred-tank bioreactor without in-lets and out-lets
(c) A continuous culture system
(d) Any of the above

18. Who among the following was awarded the Nobel Prize for the development of PCR technique?
(a) Herbert Boyer (b) Hargovind Khurana
(c) Kary Mullis (d) Arthur Kornberg

19. Which of the following statements does not hold true for restriction enzyme?
(a) It recognises a palindromic nucleotide sequence
(b) It is an endonuclease
(c) It is isolated from viruses
(d) It can produce the same kind of sticky ends in different DNA molecules

PRACTICE TEST PAPER

1. Which of the following is a molecular scissor?
(a) Pvu I (b) Unwindase
(c) Methylase (d) Reverse transcriptase

2. In recombinant DNA technology, the term 'vector' refers to:
(a) Enzyme that prevents attack of restriction enzymes
(b) Disease carrier
(c) Secondary host of pathogen
(d) Cosmid that transfers DNA into a living cell

3. In order to insert alien DNA at the site of the ampicillin resistance gene, the restriction endonuclease used can be:
(a) BamHI (b) SalI
(c) Pvu II (d) Pst I

4. The role of ethidium bromide in gel electrophoresis:
(a) It removes the gel associated with DNA strands
(b) It induces a negative charge on DNA strands
(c) It makes DNA strands visible as orange-coloured strips
(d) It helps in separation of DNA strands on the basis of charge and mass

5. There is a restriction endonuclease called HindII. What does the 'in' part stand for?
(a) Inducer (b) Inactive
(c) Influenzae (d) Insulin

6. Restriction endonucleases:
(a) Digest DNA of only bacteriophages
(b) Hydrolyse internal phosphodiester bonds in polynucleotide chains
(c) Remove nucleotides from the 5′ and 3′ ends of DNA
(d) Can digest DNA at any site non-specifically

7. Human proteins can be produced in bacteria by genetic engineering because:
(a) The mechanism of gene regulation is identical in humans and bacteria
(b) Bacterial cells can carry out splicing of RNA
(c) The genetic code is universal
(d) The human chromosome can replicate in bacterial cells

8. In recombinant DNA technology (RDT), chilled ethanol is used for precipitation of:
(a) RNA (b) DNA
(c) Proteins (d) Lipids

9. Plasmids are used as cloning vectors because of all of the following traits, except:
(a) Small size, making it easy to manipulate them after isolation
(b) Easy to transfer from cell to cell by transformation
(c) Dependent on origin of replication of the host
(d) By attaching a polylinker, it becomes easy to allow insertion of the desired DNA

10. If restriction endonuclease enzyme cuts the dsDNA away from centre of the palindromic sequence, it produces ssDNA stretches at both the cut ends. These stretches are called:
(a) Blunt ends (b) Flush ends
(c) Sticky ends (d) Selectable marker

11. GAATTC is the recognition sequence for restriction endonuclease ___**A**___ and it cuts the nucleotide chain between ___**B**___ carrying nucleotides. Select the option to fill blanks A and B correctly:

	A	B
(a)	HindII	A and T
(b)	SalI	G and A
(c)	EcoRI	G and A
(d)	Pvu I	G and T

12. Which of the following is incorrect with respect to pBR322?
(a) It possesses genes for ampicillin resistance
(b) It does not have recognition sites for restriction enzyme Alu I
(c) It has restriction sites for BamHI and SalI in the streptomycin resistance gene
(d) It has a restriction site for the restriction enzyme HindIII

13. Which of the following techniques is used to obtain large amounts of DNA from fossils to study evolution?
(a) ELISA (b) Gel electrophoresis
(c) PCR (d) Widal

14. Identify the incorrect statement:
(a) Restriction endonucleases are called molecular scissors
(b) During gel electrophoresis, DNA strands are stained bright orange using ethidium bromide
(c) pBR322 was the first artificially constructed plasmid
(d) In PCR technique, the DNA strands separate during denaturation at 72°C

15. Identify the incorrect statement:
(a) HindII was the first restriction endonuclease to be discovered
(b) In 1963, two enzymes responsible for restricting the growth of bacteriophage in bacteria were discovered
(c) The convention of naming restriction enzymes is that the first letter of the name comes from the species of the source
(d) The restriction enzyme cuts each of the two strands of DNA at specific points in their sugar-phosphate backbones

16. Select the incorrect statement:
(a) Restriction endonuclease recognizes a specific palindromic nucleotide sequence in DNA
(b) The palindrome in DNA is a sequence of base pairs that reads the same on the two strands even if the orientation of reading is not kept the same
(c) Restriction enzymes belong to a larger class of enzymes called nucleases
(d) Exonucleases remove nucleotides from the ends of the DNA

17. The Ti-plasmid of *Agrobacterium* will be unable to form a crown gall if:
(a) The host plant is dicot
(b) T-DNA in the Ti-plasmid has been inactivated
(c) The host plant is injured
(d) Tumour cells of the plant produce the chemicals required by the pathogen

18. If the transformed bacterial cells are selected by blue/white screening, the reporter enzyme/protein in this case is:
(a) amp^R (b) tet^R
(c) α-galactosidase (d) β-galactosidase

19. Cosmids carry inserts with a maximum length of:
(a) 23 kb (b) 45 kb
(c) 300 kb (d) 900 kb

20. Plasmids and bacteriophage have:
(a) Ability to replicate within bacterial cells as directed by chromosomal DNA
(b) Ability to replicate within bacterial cells independent of the control of chromosomal DNA
(c) Ability to deliver alien piece of DNA into chromosomal DNA
(d) Very low number per cell

21. The electroporation method of gene transfer:
(a) Uses cellulose to digest the bacterial cell wall
(b) Temporarily increases the pore size of membranes to allow entry of DNA
(c) Digests DNA into smaller fragments to facilitate its entry into cells
(d) Allows entry of DNA using heat shock of 98°C

22. Insertion of prokaryotic DNA into eukaryotic cell without human intervention is:
(a) Seen only in bacteriophages
(b) Never seen
(c) Naturally observed in nature
(d) Not possible due to cellular defense in eukaryotes

23. An ideal vector is one:
(a) That links with the chromosomal DNA of the host
(b) That lacks selectable marker genes
(c) That induces host DNA to replicate
(d) That is easy to isolate and to purify

24. Choose the correct option to arrange the steps of gel electrophoresis in the proper sequence:
I. Application of ethidium bromide
II. Separation of DNA strands on the basis of their size
III. Fragmentation of DNA by restriction endonuclease
IV. Exposure of gel plate with UV rays
(a) I, III, IV, II (b) III, II, I, IV
(c) III, I, II, IV (d) III, I, II, IV

25. DNA is isolated from bacterial cells using the enzyme:
(a) Ligase (b) Lysozyme
(c) Chitinase (d) Cellulase

26. Identify the technique in which the plant cell is bombarded with microparticles of gold or tungsten coated with recombinant DNA to transform the host cell:
(a) Spooling (b) Biolistics
(c) Microinjection (d) RNAi

27. Identify the incorrect match:
(a) rop – Codes for proteins involved in the replication of plasmid
(b) ori – Origin of replication
(c) Cla I site – Restriction site on pBR322
(d) Pvu I – Selectable marker on the plasmid of *Proteus vulgaris*

28. Which of the following can be used as a cloning vector in eukaryotic animal cells?
(a) Phagemid
(b) Plasmid
(c) Disarmed retroviruses
(d) Bacteriophage

29. Primer used during DNA polymerisation is:
(a) DNA polymerase enzyme
(b) Glycolipid
(c) Polypeptide that is complementary to regions of DNA
(d) Oligonucleotides synthesized chemically that are complementary to some regions of DNA

30. Plasmid used in recombinant DNA technology is:
(a) ssRNA
(b) Chromosomal DNA that replicates autonomously
(c) Extrachromosomal DNA that can replicate autonomously
(d) ssDNA

31. A procedure through which a piece of DNA is introduced in a host bacterium is known as:
(a) Transcription (b) Translation
(c) Transformation (d) Transfection

32. Under the electric field, separated DNA fragments in gel electrophoresis move towards:
(a) Cathode
(b) Anode
(c) Either cathode or anode
(d) Loading wells

33. Competent host cells are forced to take up recombinant DNA by briefly placing them at:
(a) 100°C (b) 42°C
(c) 80°C (d) 150°C

34. The method of cutting and extracting separated bands of DNA from the agarose gel is called:
(a) Spooling (b) Elution
(c) Extension (d) Extraction

35. Which of the following is incorrect with respect to the plasmid?
(a) Circular DNA
(b) Linear DNA
(c) Present in bacteria and some yeast cells
(d) Extra-chromosomal self-replicating DNA

36. Which of the following is incorrect with respect to PCR?
(a) Denaturation, annealing and extension of primers occur at the same temperature
(b) Thermostable DNA polymerases are used
(c) It is used for early diagnosis of pathogens
(d) It is used to detect mutations in cancer patients

37. In a stirred tank bioreactor, the stirrer facilitates:
(a) Maintenance of required pH
(b) Removal of waste
(c) Even mixing and oxygen availability
(d) Temperature homeostasis in the reactor

38. Which of the following cloning vectors is most commonly used in plant genetic engineering?
(a) Disarmed retroviruses
(b) Disarmed Ti-plasmid
(c) Bacterial artificial chromosome (BAC)
(d) pBR322

39. Which of the following sequences of cloning vectors is responsible for controlling the copy number of the linked DNA?

(a) rop (b) ori
(c) amp^R (d) tet^R

40. Read the following statements and choose the correct option:

I: In continuous culture system, the used medium is drained out from one side while fresh medium is added from the other to maintain the cells in their physiologically most active log/exponential phase

II: Bioreactors are used for processing small-volume cultures and cannot yield appreciable quantities of products

(a) Both statements are correct
(b) Both statements are incorrect
(c) Only I is correct
(d) Only II is correct

41. Select the incorrect process with respect to recombinant DNA technology:

(a) Isolation of the genetic material
(b) Always digesting desired DNA by restriction exonuclease
(c) Insertion of recombinant DNA into the host cell
(d) Obtaining the foreign gene product using bioreactors

42. Which of the following is required by the cloning vector for identifying and eliminating non-transformants and selectively permitting the growth of transformants?

(a) Origin of replication
(b) Cloning sites
(c) Selectable marker
(d) Both (a) and (b)

43. ________ are used for joining DNA fragments having the same kind of 'sticky ends' to form recombinant DNA:

(a) DNA ligase
(b) DNA polymerase
(c) Restriction endonuclease
(d) RNA polymerase

44. Which of the following is correct with respect to shuttle vectors?

(a) They can replicate in both *Escherichia coli* and eukaryotic cell
(b) They have two types of origin of replication and selectable marker genes, one for eukaryotic cell and other for *E. coli*
(c) The examples are yeast episomal plasmid (YEp) and modified Ti-plasmid
(d) All are correct

45. Batch fermentation:

(a) Is a continuous culture system
(b) Maintains the cells in their physiologically most active log/exponential phase by draining out used medium from one side and adding fresh medium from the other
(c) Is a type of closed system
(d) Both (a) and (b)

ANSWER KEYS

Exercises

1. (c) **2.** (b) **3.** (c) **4.** (a) **5.** (d) **6.** (b) **7.** (a) **8.** (b) **9.** (c) **10.** (b)
11. (d) **12.** (b) **13.** (c) **14.** (b) **15.** (b) **16.** (c) **17.** (c) **18.** (b) **19.** (c) **20.** (d)
21. (c) **22.** (c) **23.** (b) **24.** (b) **25.** (b) **26.** (a) **27.** (c) **28.** (d) **29.** (d) **30.** (d)
31. (b) **32.** (b) **33.** (b) **34.** (b) **35.** (c) **36.** (b) **37.** (c) **38.** (b) **39.** (d) **40.** (d)
41. (d) **42.** (a) **43.** (b) **44.** (b) **45.** (c) **46.** (d) **47.** (c) **48.** (b) **49.** (b) **50.** (a)
51. (d) **52.** (c) **53.** (d) **54.** (b) **55.** (b) **56.** (d) **57.** (d) **58.** (c) **59.** (b) **60.** (b)
61. (c) **62.** (b) **63.** (d) **64.** (a) **65.** (b) **66.** (b) **67.** (a) **68.** (b) **69.** (b) **70.** (c)
71. (c) **72.** (d) **73.** (c) **74.** (d) **75.** (c) **76.** (a) **77.** (b)

NCERT Exemplar Questions

1. (b) **2.** (b) **3.** (a) **4.** (d) **5.** (c) **6.** (d) **7.** (b) **8.** (a) **9.** (c) **10.** (d)
11. (b) **12.** (c) **13.** (a) **14.** (c) **15.** (c) **16.** (a) **17.** (c) **18.** (c) **19.** (c)

Practice Test Paper

1. (a) **2.** (d) **3.** (d) **4.** (c) **5.** (c) **6.** (b) **7.** (c) **8.** (b) **9.** (c) **10.** (c)
11. (c) **12.** (c) **13.** (c) **14.** (d) **15.** (c) **16.** (b) **17.** (b) **18.** (d) **19.** (b) **20.** (b)
21. (b) **22.** (c) **23.** (d) **24.** (b) **25.** (b) **26.** (b) **27.** (d) **28.** (c) **29.** (d) **30.** (c)
31. (c) **32.** (b) **33.** (b) **34.** (b) **35.** (b) **36.** (a) **37.** (c) **38.** (b) **39.** (b) **40.** (c)
41. (b) **42.** (c) **43.** (a) **44.** (d) **45.** (c)

SOLUTIONS

Tools of Recombinant DNA Technology

1. Restriction endonucleases can cut DNA at specific locations and are called molecular scissors.

2. In the year 1963, the two enzymes responsible for restricting the growth of bacteriophage in *Escherichia coli* were isolated. One of these added methyl groups to DNA, while the other, called restriction endonuclease, cut the DNA.

3. The letter 'R' in EcoRI is derived from the name of the strain, as it is obtained from *Escherichia coli* RY13.

4. Exonucleases remove nucleotides from the ends of DNA.

5. Origin of replication (ori) is a sequence from where replication starts, and any piece of DNA when linked to this sequence can be made to replicate within the host cells. This sequence is also responsible for controlling the copy number of the linked DNA. So, if one wants to recover many copies of the target DNA, it should be cloned in a vector whose origin supports a high copy number.

6. EFB stands for European Federation of Biotechnology.

7. Option (a) is correct.

8. Restriction enzymes cut the strand of DNA a little away from the centre of the palindrome sites, but between the same two bases on the opposite strands. This leaves single-stranded portions at the ends. There are overhanging stretches called sticky ends on each strand.

9. HindII was the first restriction endonuclease to be discovered.

10. The construction of the first recombinant DNA emerged from the possibility of linking a gene encoding antibiotic resistance with a native plasmid (autonomously replicating circular extra-chromosomal DNA) of *Salmonella typhimurium*.

11. Each restriction endonuclease functions by inspecting the length of a DNA sequence. Once it finds its specific recognition sequence, it will bind to the DNA and cut each of the two strands of the double helix at specific points in their sugar-phosphate backbones. Each restriction endonuclease recognizes a specific palindromic nucleotide sequence in the DNA.

12. Genetic engineering refers to the techniques that alter the chemistry of genetic material (DNA and RNA) to introduce these into the host organisms and thus change the phenotype of the host organism.

13. The major disadvantage of traditional hybridisation is that undesirable genes are inherited along with desirable genes.

14. Stanley Cohen had been studying small ringlets of DNA called plasmids, which float about freely in the replicate independently from the coding strand of DNA. Cohen had developed a method of removing these plasmids from the cell and then reinserting them in other cells.

15. Bioprocess engineering refers to the maintenance of a sterile (microbial contamination-free) environment in the chemical engineering process to enable growth of only desirable genes.

16. The ability to multiply a specific gene, for example, antibiotic resistance gene, is called gene cloning.

17. HindII recognises a specific palindromic nucleotide sequence in the DNA.

18. The restriction endonuclease enzymes, like EcoRI, inspect the length of the DNA sequence, and on finding a specific recognition sequence, cut each of the two strands of the double helix at specific points to digest the phosphodiester bond/sugar-phosphate backbone.

19. The enzyme DNA ligase joins the DNA fragments in the genetic engineering process.

20. Plasmids are used as vectors for gene transfer. Some plasmids may have only one to two copies per cell, whereas others may have 15–100 copies per cell.

21. Enzyme restriction endonucleases are used in recombinant DNA technology and obtained from bacteria, where they restrict the growth of bacteriophages.

22. Stanley Cohen and Herbert Boyer isolated an antibiotic resistance gene by cutting a piece of DNA in the year 1972.

23. Plasmids are autonomously replicating circular extra-chromosomal DNA and are therefore used as vectors for gene cloning.

24. EcoRI is a restriction endonuclease enzyme obtained from *Escherichia coli* RY13.

25. The term 'vector' in recombinant DNA technology refers to plasmids or bacteriophages that are used to deliver desirable genes into the host cells. Vectors used at present are engineered in such way that they help easy linking of foreign DNA and selection of recombinants from non-recombinants.

26. During gene cloning, the term 'gene taxi' is used for vectors like plasmid.

27. Restriction enzymes were discovered by Arber, Nathans and Smith.

28. Plasmid is a genetic structure in a cell that can replicate independently of the chromosomes, typically a small circular DNA strand in the cytoplasm of the bacterium or protozoan.

29. In recombinant DNA technology, the term vector is used for a small piece of DNA that can be stably maintained in an organism, and into which foreign DNA fragment can be inserted for cloning purposes. Plasmids are autonomously replicating circular extra-chromosomal DNA. They are standard cloning vectors and most commonly used. Most plasmids may be used to clone DNA inserts of up to 15 kb in size.

30. Besides HindII, we know of more than 900 restriction enzymes that have been isolated from over 230 strains of bacteria, each of which recognize different recognition sequences.

31. Paul Berg is often referred to as "Father of Genetic Engineering".

32. Recombinant DNA molecules are DNA molecules formed by laboratory methods of genetic recombination to bring together genetic material from multiple sources, creating sequences that would not otherwise be found in the genome.

33. Alkaline phosphatase prevents the re-joining of vector DNA fragments once they are digested by restriction enzymes.

34. Plasmids are extra-chromosomal DNA and replicate autonomously or independently of chromosomal DNA.

35. In genetic engineering, probe is a single-stranded DNA to RNA, tagged with a radioactive molecule and is allowed to hybridise to its complementary DNA in a clone of cells followed by detection using autoradiography.

36. In a method known as microinjection, recombinant DNA is directly injected into the nucleus of an animal cell.

37. *Agrobacterium tumefaciens,* a pathogen of several dicot plants, is able to deliver a piece of DNA known as 'T-DNA' to transform normal plant cells into a tumour and direct those tumour cells to produce the chemicals required by the pathogen.

38. DNA is a hydrophilic molecule; it cannot pass through cell membranes.

39. In pBR322, the tetracycline resistance gene (tet^R) has recognition sites for BamHI and SalI.

40. The cloning vector should preferably have a small size, because the large-sized vectors generally break down during the purification process.

41. Gene gun or biolistics is a method suitable for plants, where the cells are bombarded with high velocity micro-particles of gold or tungsten.

42. The DNA fragments separated after electrophoresis can be visualised only after staining the DNA with a compound known as ethidium bromide followed by exposure to UV radiation. Bright orange colour bands of DNA are observed upon exposure to UV light.

43. Agarose is a natural polymer extracted from seaweed and used as a matrix to separate DNA fragments in gel electrophoresis.

44. In gel electrophoresis, the DNA fragments separate (resolve) according to their size through sieving effect provided by the agarose gel. Hence, the smaller the DNA fragments, the farther they move.

45. In order to force bacteria to take up the plasmid, the bacterial cells must first be made 'competent' to take up DNA. This can be done by treating them with a specific concentration of a divalent cation such as calcium which increases the efficiency with which DNA enters the bacterium through pores in its cell wall.

46. Insertion of alien DNA at the replication of the plasmid (rop) gene will still provide resistance to ampicillin and tetracycline.

47. *Agrobacterium tumefaciens,* a pathogen of several dicot plants, is able to deliver a piece of DNA known as T-DNA to transform normal plant cells into tumour cells and direct these tumour cells to produce the chemicals required by the pathogen. The tumour inducing (Ti) plasmid of *Agrobacterium tumefaciens* has now been modified into a cloning vector which is no more pathogenic to the plants but is still able to use the mechanisms to deliver genes of interest into a variety of plants.

48. If the desired gene segment is inserted at the PvuI site in pBR322, the resulting plasmid will confer resistance to tetracycline but will lose ampicillin resistance.

49. The vector requires a selectable marker, which helps in identifying and eliminating non-transformants and selectively permitting the growth of transformants. Normally, the genes encoding resistance to antibiotics such as ampicillin, kanamycin, tetracycline or chloramphenicol, are considered useful selectable marker for *E. coli*.

50. In 'blue-white' selection of plasmids with the β-galactosidase gene, the colonies of non-recombinants will produce blue-coloured colonies in the present of chromogenic substrate. Presence of insert results in insertional inactivation of the β-galactosidase and the colonies do not produce any colour, and are identified as recombinant colonies.

51. Yeast artificial chromosome (YAC) is used to carry large fragments of foreign DNA of up to 1 Mb.

Processes of Recombinant DNA Technology

52. The enzyme chitinase help in digesting the fungal cell wall for isolating its genetic material.

53. Short RNA primers are used in PCR technique that are complimentary to the 3′-end sequence of the DNA segment to be amplified.

54. Bioreactors are vessels of large volume (100–1000 litres) used to culture and produce products in large quantities. Thus, they are vessels in which raw materials are biologically converted into specific products, individual enzymes, etc., using microbial plant, animal or human cells. A bioreactor provides the optimal conditions for achieving the desired product by providing optimum growth conditions (temperature, pH substrate, salts, vitamins, oxygen).

55. The polymerase chain reaction (PCR) technique is used for in vitro synthesis of DNA. Thus, it is used for amplification of genes (or DNA) of interest using two sets of primers (small chemically synthesized oligonucleotides that are complementary to the regions of DNA).

56. Sparged tank bioreactor differs from simple stirred tank bioreactor in having sparged sterile air bubbles.

57. A bioreactor provides the optimal conditions for achieving the desired product by providing optimum growth conditions like temperature, pH, substrate, salts, vitamins and oxygen.

58. During PCR, 1 billion copies of DNA are made at the end of 30 cycles.

59. Option (b) is correct.

60. During isolation of genetic material, purified DNA ultimately precipitates out after the addition of chilled ethanol.

61. Thermostable enzymes 'Taq' and 'Pfu' are DNA polymerases obtained from thermophilic bacteria *Thermus aquaticus* and *Pyrococcus furiosus*. These thermostable DNA polymerases remain active during high temperature–induced denaturation of double-stranded DNA.

62. Melting of DNA at 94°C in PCR technique is due to breakdown of hydrogen bonds, to separate the two strands of DNA.

63. After completion of biosynthetic stage, the product has to be subjected to a series of processes before it is ready for marketing as a finished product. The processes include separation and purification, which are collectively referred to as downstream processing.

64. PCR technique was discovered by Kary Mullis.

65. The optimum temperature for polymerisation step of PCR is 72°C.

66. PCR technique is used to make millions of copies of a target piece of DNA. It is an indispensable tool in modern molecular biology and has transformed scientific research and diagnostic medicine. Thus, it allows scientists to take a very small sample of DNA and amplify it to a large enough amount to study in detail.

67. The stirrer in the stirred tank bioreactor facilitates even mixing and oxygen availability throughout the bioreactor.

68. The northern blot, or RNA blot, is a technique used in molecular biology research to study gene expression by detection of RNA in a sample. Northern blotting involves the use of electrophoresis to separate RNA samples by size and detection with hybridisation probe complementary to a part of or the entire target sequence. The term 'northern blot' actually refers specifically to the capillary transfer of RNA from the electrophoresis gel to the blotting membrane.

69. The enzyme deoxyribonuclease is not used while extracting DNA from an organism, as it will digest DNA.

70. Taq polymerase is a thermostable DNA polymerase obtained from *Thermus aquaticus.* The enzyme extends the primers using the nucleotides provided in the reaction and the genomic DNA as template.

71. Batch fermentation is what is described as a 'closed system', whereby the substrate and producing microorganism are added to the system at time zero and not removed until fermentation is complete.

72. DNA fingerprinting is the process of determining an individual's DNA characteristics. DNA analysis is intended to identify a species rather than an individual and is called DNA barcoding. DNA profiling is a forensic technique in criminal investigations, comparing criminal suspect profiles to DNA evidence so as to assess the likelihood of their involvement in the crime. It is also used in parentage testing, to establish immigration eligibility and in genealogical and medical research.

73. Biolistics or gene gun is suitable for plants, and cells are bombarded with high velocity microparticles of gold or tungsten coated with DNA.

74. In downstream processing, strict quality control testing for each product is required.

75. Gel electrophoresis is used for separation of DNA fragments according to their size. Since DNA fragments are negatively charged, they can be separated by forcing them to move towards the anode under an electric field through a matrix like agarose.

76. If any protein encoding gene is expressed in a heterologous host, it is called recombinant protein.

77. Agarose gel extracted from seaweed is used as a matrix in gel electrophoresis. The DNA fragments separate (resolve) according to their size through the sieving effect provided by the agarose gel.

12 Biotechnology and Its Applications

EXERCISES

1. The Green Revolution succeeded in tripling the food supply by:
   (a) Better management practices
   (b) Use of agrochemicals
   (c) Use of transgenic crops only
   (d) Both (a) and (b)

2. Which of the following is not a property of genetically modified organisms (GMO)?
   (a) It reduced reliance on chemical pesticides
   (b) It helped to reduce post-harvest losses
   (c) It made crops more tolerant to abiotic stresses (cold, drought, salt, heat)
   (d) It reduced the efficiency of mineral usage by plants

3. Select the incorrect statement with respect to Bt crops:
   (a) Bt toxin is produced by a bacterium called *Bacillus thuringiensis*
   (b) Bt crops are resistant to pests
   (c) Bt toxin gene has been cloned from bacteria and has been expressed in plants to provide resistance to insects without the need for insecticides
   (d) Bt crops have increased the use of pesticides for protection against plant pests

4. Which of the following is incorrect with respect to the Bt toxin?
   (a) It exists as an inactive protoxin
   (b) It is converted into an active form of toxin due to the acidic pH of the gut, which solubilises the crystals
   (c) The activated toxin binds to the surface of midgut epithelial cells and creates pores
   (d) Both (a) and (c)

5. The proteins encoded by gene ________ controls the corn borer:
   (a) cryIAc (b) cryIIAb
   (c) cryIAb (d) Both (a) and (b)

6. How many amino acids are present in insulin?
   (a) 29 (b) 21
   (c) 30 (d) 51

7. Select the incorrect statement:
   (a) Insulin in synthesized as a pro-hormone which contains an extra stretch called C-peptide
   (b) Insulin consists of two short polypeptide chains: chain A and chain B, that are linked together by phosphoester bonds
   (c) Insulin used for diabetes was earlier extracted from the pancreas of slaughtered cattle and pigs
   (d) Genetically engineered insulin is now available for human use

8. ________ is an American company that prepared two DNA sequences corresponding to chains A and B of insulin:
   (a) Calgene (b) Eli Lilly
   (c) Panacea Biotech (d) Gene Corp

9. The first genetically modified plant commercially released in India was:
   (a) Golden rice (b) Bt cotton
   (c) Bt tomato (d) Bt brinjal

10. The technique of DNA fingerprinting was initially developed by:
    (a) Ian Wilmut (b) Jacque Monod
    (c) Alec Jeffreys (d) Hargobind Khorana

11. Some of the characteristics of Bt cotton are:
    (a) Long fibre and resistance to aphids
    (b) Medium yield, long fibre and resistance to beetle pests
    (c) High yield and production of toxic protein crystals which kill dipteran pests
    (d) High yield and resistance to bollworms

12. The thermostable enzymes 'Taq' and 'Pfu', isolated from thermophilic bacteria, are:
    (a) RNA polymerases

(b) DNA ligases
(c) Restriction endonucleases
(d) DNA polymerases

13. A transgenic food crop which may help in solving the problem of night blindness in developing countries is:
(a) Flavr Savr tomatoes
(b) Bt soyabean
(c) Starlink maize
(d) Golden rice

14. The first clinical gene therapy was given for treating:
(a) Diabetes mellitus
(b) Rheumatoid arthritis
(c) Alzheimer's disease
(d) Adenosine deaminase deficiency

15. Tobacco plant resistant to a nematode was developed by the introduction of DNA that produced:
(a) Both sense and anti-sense RNA
(b) A particular hormone
(c) A toxic protein
(d) Enzymes for killing nematode

16. In *Bacillus thuringiensis,* the bacillus itself is not killed by the toxic protein crystals produced by it because Bt toxin:
(a) Protein is not produced in the bacteria
(b) Cannot cause any harm to the bacillus
(c) Protein is produced in very small amounts in the bacillus
(d) Exists as inactive toxin

17. Which of the following techniques is used to make numerous copies of a specific segment of DNA quickly and accurately?
(a) Translation
(b) Transcription
(c) Polymerase chain reaction
(d) Gel electrophoresis

18. Bt brinjal is an example of a transgenic crop. In this, Bt refers to:
(a) *Bacillus tuberculosis*
(b) Biotechnology
(c) *Bacillus thuringiensis*
(d) *Bordetella thuringiensis*

19. Consumption of which one of the following foods can prevent the kind of blindness associated with vitamin A deficiency?
(a) Flavr Savr tomato (b) Bt brinjal
(c) Canola (d) Golden rice

20. *Bacillus thuringiensis* is used to control:
(a) Bacterial pathogens
(b) Fungal pathogens
(c) Nematodes
(d) Insect pests

21. *Bacillus thuringiensis* forms protein crystals, which contain insecticidal protein. This protein:
(a) Is activated by the acid pH of the foregut of the insect pest
(b) Does not kill the carrier bacterium which is itself resistant to the toxin
(c) Is produced in active form only
(d) Binds with epithelial cells of the midgut of the insect pest and ultimately kills it

22. Use of bioresources by multinational companies and organisations without authorisation from the concerned country and its people is called:
(a) Biodegradation (b) Bioexploitation
(c) Biopiracy (d) Bio-infringement

23. Which part of the tobacco plant is infected by *Meloidogyne incognita*?
(a) Leaf (b) Stem
(c) Root (d) Flower

24. In India, the organisation responsible for assessing the safely of introducing genetically modified organisms for public use is:
(a) Indian Council of Medical Research (ICMR)
(b) Research Committee on Genetic Manipulation (RCGM)
(c) Genetic Engineering Approval Committee (GEAC)
(d) Council for Scientific and Industrial Research (CSIR)

25. Which of the following recent techniques is used for separating fragments of DNA?
(a) Eastern blotting (b) Northern blotting
(c) Southern blotting (d) Western blotting

26. A transgenic sheep 'Tracy' has yielded ________ for the treatment of emphysema:
(a) Platelet-derived growth factor (PDGF)
(b) a-1-antitrypsin
(c) Interleukins
(d) Interferons

27. In ____**I**____, the first transgenic cow ____**II**____, produced ____**III**____ enriched milk. Fill in the blanks with the correct options:

	I	II	III
(a)	1983	ANDi	a-lactalbumin
(b)	1997	Rosie	a-lactalbumin
(c)	1981	Dolly	Globulin
(d)	1994	Molly	Fibrinogen

28. Select the incorrect statement:
(a) Bt toxin gene cryIAC controls the cotton bollworm
(b) Human insulin is being commercially produced from transgenic species of *Entamoeba coli*
(c) A transgenic monkey ANDi has the gene for green fluorescent protein (GFP)
(d) Golden rice is rich in vitamin A

29. The techniques used for early diagnosis is/are:
(a) Polymerase chain reaction (PCR)
(b) Recombinant DNA technology
(c) Enzyme Linked Immunosorbent Assay (ELISA)
(d) All of the above

30. The vaccine for __________ has been developed using recombinant DNA technology:
(a) Tetanus (b) Polio
(c) Hepatitis B (d) Diphtheria

31. __________ was developed by AM Chakrabarty and is used for clearing oil spills:
(a) *Arthrobacter oxydans*
(b) *Staphylococcus equorum*
(c) *Pseudomonas putida*
(d) *Nitrosomonas*

32. How many recombinant therapeutics have been approved for human use in the world?
(a) 12 (b) 30
(c) 42 (d) 27

33. Which of the following is an incorrect statement?
(a) The bacterium *Bacillus thuringiensis* is widely used to develop biopesticides, or pest-resistant plants
(b) Green Revolution quadrupled the food supply, which was sufficient to feed the growing human population
(c) Bioremediation is the use of microorganism metabolism to remove pollutants
(d) Transgenic animals are designed to increase our understanding of how genes contribute to the development of diseases

34. Transgenic mice are being used to test the safety of the __________ vaccine:
(a) Influenza (b) Polio
(c) Rabies (d) Typhoid

35. Infestation of beetles is prevented by Bt toxin. These insects belong to the order:
(a) Diptera (b) Coleoptera
(c) Lepidoptera (d) Hymenoptera

36. __________ is used as a vector for introducing adenosine deaminase (ADA) cDNA into the cells of patients receiving gene therapy:
(a) Reovirus (b) *Agrobacterium*
(c) Retrovirus (d) *Bacillus thuringiensis*

37. A transgenic plant __________ is used as a source of the anticoagulant hirudin:
(a) Bt brinjal
(b) *Brassica napus*
(c) *Bacillus napus*
(d) *Meloidogyne incognita*

38. Select the incorrect statements:
(a) Insulin can be orally administered to diabetic patients
(b) Porcine or bovine insulin can cause allergic reactions in diabetic patients
(c) Conventional methods of diagnosis like serum and urine analysis are very useful in the early diagnosis of disease
(d) Both (a) and (c)

39. Over 95% of all existing transgenic animals are:
(a) Pigs (b) Mice
(c) Fowls (d) Cows

40. Transgenic models of animals exist for human disease like:
(a) Cystic fibrosis
(b) Alzheimer's disease
(c) Rheumatoid arthritis
(d) All of the above

41. Deficiency of which of the following enzymes causes severe combined immune deficiency (SCID)?
(a) Alcohol dehydrogenase
(b) Adenosine deaminase
(c) Glucose-6-phosphate dehydrogenase
(d) Pyruvate dehydrogenase

42. Which of the following was issued as a bioweapon?
(a) *Bacillus anthracis* (b) *Bacillus thuringiensis*
(c) *Bacillus subtilis* (d) *Clostridium tetani*

43. Which of the following describes anti-sense technology?
(a) Production of somaclonal variants in tissue culture
(b) A cell displaying a foreign antigen used for the synthesis of antigens
(c) RNA polymerase producing DNA
(d) When a piece of RNA that is complimentary in sequence is used to stop the expression of a specific gene

44. Which of the following is correct with respect to transgenic crops?
(a) Crops grown in artificial medium after hybridisation in the field
(b) Crops produced by a somatic embryo in artificial medium
(c) Crops produced after protoplast fusion in artificial medium
(d) Crops generated by introducing foreign DNA into a cell and regenerating a plant from that cell

45. Which of the following is the main objective for the production of herbicide-resistant GM crops?
(a) Reduce herbicide accumulation in food articles for health and safety
(b) Encourage eco-friendly herbicides
(c) Eliminate weeds from the field without the use of manual labour
(d) Eliminate weeds from the field without the use of herbicides

46. Polyethylene glycol method is used for:
(a) Gene transfer without vector
(b) Energy production from sewage
(c) Biodiesel production
(d) Seedless fruit production

47. The expression of which of the following genes has been blocked in the Flavr Savr variety of transgenic tomato?
(a) Cellulase (b) Polygalacturonase
(c) Chitinase (d) Methylase

48. How many documented varieties of basmati rice are grown in India?
(a) 12 (b) 30
(c) 27 (d) 42

49. The genes for the synthesis of β-carotene was obtained from ________ to be inserted into rice for producing transgenic golden rice:
(a) *Oryza sativa*
(b) Daffodil
(c) *Narcissus pseudonarcissus*
(d) Both (b) and (c)

50. RNAi was first discovered in 1998 by Andrew Fire and Craig Mello in a nematode worm:
(a) *Ascaris lumbricoides*
(b) *Meloidogyne incognita*
(c) *Caenorhabditis elegans*
(d) *Enterobius vermicularis*

51. A patent for "use of turmeric in wound healing" was granted by the US patent and trademark office, though turmeric has been used in India for centuries. This is an example of:
(a) Bioplant (b) Biopiracy
(c) Bioweapon (d) Bioremediation

52. Identify the incorrect statement:
(a) In 1997, the first transgenic cow Rosie was developed
(b) Dolly was the first transgenic sheep to be cloned
(c) *Monascus purpureus* is a yeast used commercially in the production of cholesterol lowering statins
(d) Father of Green Revolution is Norman E Borlaug

53. Which of the following cannot be patented?
(a) Cell lines
(b) Strain of microorganisms
(c) Genetically modified organisms
(d) Wind energy

54. Gene therapy is a technique to:
(a) Detect genetic disease
(b) Treat infectious disease
(c) Replace a normal functional gene with a faulty gene
(d) Replace a faulty gene with a normal functional gene

55. Which of the following is incorrect regarding the plant *Pentadiplandra brazzeana*?
(a) It is found in West Africa
(b) It is 2000 times sweeter than sugar
(c) It is a low-calorie sweetener
(d) Local people in Africa have patented the protein and are using it commercially

56. Select the incorrect statement:
(a) Transgenic animals are being created for the treatment of phenylketonuria (PKU) and cystic fibrosis
(b) Rosie, the first transgenic cow, produced human protein–enriched milk (2.4 grams per litre)
(c) ELISA is based on the principle of antigen–antibody interaction
(d) Introduction of functional adenosine deaminase (ADA) cDNA (using a retroviral vector) in the lymphocytes is the permanent cure for ADA deficiency

57. Which of the following is an incorrect statement?
(a) The Indian parliament has recently cleared the second amendment of the Indian Patents Bill
(b) In 1997, a British company obtained rights on basmati rice through the UK patent and trademark office

(c) MS Swaminathan is called the "Father of Green Revolution" in India
(d) ADA deficiency cannot be permanently cured by enzyme replacement therapy or by bone narrow transplantation

58. In hybridoma technology:
(a) B cells are fused with T cells
(b) B cells are fused with plasma cells
(c) B cells are fused with myeloma cells
(d) T cells are fused with myeloma cells

59. Select the correct statement:
(a) Superbugs were developed by Anand Mohan Chakrabarty
(b) For RNAi, nematode-specific genes were introduced into the host plant using retroviruses
(c) C-peptide is a part of mature insulin and is added during maturation
(d) Recombinant DNA technology has not been able to make any impact in the area of healthcare

60. The genetically modified (GM) brinjal in India has been developed for:
(a) Insect resistance
(b) Enhancing shelf-life
(c) Drought resistance
(d) Enhancing mineral content

NCERT EXEMPLAR QUESTIONS

1. Bt cotton is not:
(a) A GM plant
(b) Insect resistant
(c) A bacterial gene expressing system
(d) Resistant to all pesticides

2. C-peptide of human insulin is:
(a) A part of mature insulin molecule
(b) Responsible for formation of disulphide bridges
(c) Removed during maturation of pro-insulin to insulin
(d) Responsible for its biological activity

3. GEAC stands for:
(a) Genome Engineering Action Committee
(b) Ground Environment Action Committee
(c) Genetic Engineering Approval Committee
(d) Genetic and Environment Approval committee

4. α-1 antitrypsin is:
(a) An antacid
(b) An enzyme
(c) Used to treat arthritis
(d) Used to treat emphysema

5. A probe which is a molecule used to locate homologous sequences in a mixture of DNA or RNA molecules could be:
(a) ssRNA
(b) ssDNA
(c) Either ssRNA or ssDNA
(d) Can be ssDNA but not ssRNA

6. Choose the correct option regarding retrovirus:
(a) An RNA virus that synthesises DNA during infection
(b) A DNA virus that synthesises RNA during infection
(c) An ssDNA virus
(d) A dsRNA virus

7. The site of production of ADA in the body is:
(a) Erythrocytes (b) Lymphocytes
(c) Blood plasma (d) Osteocytes

8. A protoxin is:
(a) A primitive toxin
(b) A denatured toxin
(c) Toxin produced by protozoa
(d) Inactive toxin

9. Pathophysiology is the:
(a) Study of physiology of pathogen
(b) Study of normal physiology of host
(c) Study of altered physiology of host
(d) None of the above

10. The trigger for activation of toxin of *Bacillus thuringiensis* is:
(a) Acidic pH of stomach
(b) High temperature
(c) Alkaline pH of gut
(d) Mechanical action in the insect gut

11. Golden rice is:
(a) A variety of rice grown along the yellow river in China
(b) Long stored rice having yellow colour tint

(c) A transgenic rice having gene for β-carotene
(d) Wild variety of rice with yellow coloured grains

12. In RNAi, genes are silenced using:
(a) ss DNA (b) ds DNA
(c) ds RNA (d) ss RNA

13. The first clinical gene therapy was done for the treatment of:
(a) AIDS
(b) Cancer
(c) Cystic fibrosis
(d) SCID (Severe Combined Immuno Deficiency resulting form deficiency of ADA)

14. ADA is an enzyme which is deficient in a genetic disorder SCID. What is the full form of ADA?
(a) Adenosine deoxyaminase
(b) Adenosine deaminase
(c) Aspartate deaminase
(d) Arginine deaminase

15. Silencing of a gene could be achieved through the use of:
(a) RNAi only
(b) Antisense RNA only
(c) Both RNAi and antisense RNA
(d) None of the above

PRACTICE TEST PAPER

1. Abiotic stresses of plants include all, except:
(a) Heat (b) Pest
(c) Cold (d) Soil pH

2. RNAi has been used in the development of tobacco plants resistant to:
(a) Corn borer (b) Bollworms
(c) Nematodes (d) Viruses

3. Maximum number of existing transgenic animals are:
(a) Monkeys (b) Mice
(c) Guinea pig (d) Sheep

4. Crystals of Bt toxin do not kill the bacteria themselves because:
(a) Bacteria have an enzyme which neutralises the toxin
(b) Bacteria are resistant to the toxin
(c) Toxin is stored in inactive form
(d) Toxin is less toxic in bacterial organelles

5. Which of the following Bt crops is being grown in India by farmers?
(a) Maize (b) Cotton
(c) Brinjal (d) Potato

6. Which of the following is known as 'Flavr Savr'?
(a) Herbicide-resistant crop
(b) Transgenic tomato
(c) Transgenic rice
(d) Transgenic mice

7. Genetically modified (GM) crops can be produced by:
(a) Cross-breeding
(b) Somatic hybridisation
(c) Micropropagation
(d) Recombinant DNA technology

8. RNA interference involves:
(a) Synthesis of mRNA from DNA
(b) Synthesis of cDNA from RNA by reverse transcription
(c) Splicing of primary transcript
(d) Silencing of specific mRNA due to complementary RNA

9. Two bacteria most useful in genetic engineering are:
(a) *Aspergillus* and *Agrobacterium*
(b) *Escherichia* and *Agrobacterium*
(c) *Saccharomyces* and *Azotobacter*
(d) *Agrobacterium* and *Rhizopus*

10. Mobile genetic elements are also called:
(a) Transposons (b) Transformants
(c) Transgenic (d) Transmembrane

11. Which of the following is not a benefit of transgenic animals?
(a) Study of disease
(b) Testing of vaccines
(c) Formation of biological products
(d) Study of lineage

12. An American company obtained patent rights on basmati rice in the year:
(a) 1972 (b) 1990
(c) 1997 (d) 1992

13. When an abnormal gene is replaced by a normal gene for therapeutic purposes, the technique involved is called:

(a) Mutation (b) Cloning
(c) Gene therapy (d) RNAi

14. ADA deficiency can be permanently cured by:
(a) Enzyme replacement therapy
(b) Bone marrow transplantation
(c) Transgenic lymphocytes with cDNA for adenosine deaminase
(d) Introduction of gene producing ADA into cells at early embryo stage

15. Read the following statements and choose the correct option:
I: Transgenic animals are used for carrying out toxicity/safety testing
II: Transgenic animals carry genes which makes them more sensitive to toxic substances than non-transgenic animals
(a) Both statements are correct
(b) Both statements are incorrect
(c) Only I is correct
(d) Only II is correct

16. Identify the incorrect statement:
(a) Insulin is synthesized as a prohormone
(b) Pro-hormone form of insulin contains C-peptide
(c) Insulin used for diabetes was earlier extracted from the pancreas of slaughtered cattle and pigs
(d) Insulin from animal sources is readily accepted without any complication or allergic reaction

17. Biopiracy is:
(a) Taking decisions regarding the validity of GM research
(b) Patenting bioresources of others with authorisation
(c) Exploitation of biological resources without proper authorisation
(d) Analysing the safety of introducing GM organisms for public services

18. Early detection of diseases is not possible using:
(a) Polymerase chain reaction (PCR)
(b) Recombinant DNA technology
(c) Enzyme linked immuno-sorbent assay (ELISA)
(d) Serum and urine analysis

19. Mature form of the hormone insulin consists of how many polypeptide chains?
(a) 2 (b) 3
(c) 4 (d) 5

20. All of the following are killed by strains of *Bacillus thuringiensis*, except:
(a) Beetles
(b) Tobacco budworm and armyworm
(c) Roundworm
(d) Flies and mosquitoes

21. The Green Revolution succeeded in increasing food supply by all of the following ways, except:
(a) Use of improved crop varieties
(b) Use of better management practices
(c) Use of transgenic crops
(d) Use of fertilisers and pesticides

22. Genetically engineered plants are generated in the laboratory by altering their genetic make-up. This is done by adding one or more genes to a plant's genome by:
(a) Fusing liposomes to intact plant cells
(b) Biolistic method or *Agrobacterium tumefaciens* mediated transformation
(c) DNA injection or heat shock method
(d) *Bacillus thuringiensis* mediated transformation

23. The first transgenic cow, Rosie, produced human protein–enriched milk containing:
(a) 4.8 grams per litre
(b) 2.4 grams per litre
(c) 7.2 grams per litres
(d) 2.4 milligrams per litre

24. India has an estimated ________ varieties of rice, with the richest diversity in the world:
(a) 27 (b) 200,000
(c) 30,000 (d) 5400

25. Transgenic animals are used to treat emphysema by producing:
(a) Alpha-lactalbumin
(b) α-1-antitrypsin
(c) Streptokinase
(d) Interferons

26. RNA interference is essential for the:
(a) Cell differentiation
(b) Cell proliferation
(c) Cellular defense
(d) Micropropagation

27. Protein encoded by the gene cryIAb controls the infestation of which of the following insects?
(a) Cotton bollworm (b) Corn borer
(c) *Aedes* mosquito (d) *Anopheles* mosquito

28. Insect-tolerant gene from *Bacillus thuringiensis* is introduced using the Ti-plasmid of:
(a) *Haemophilus influenzae*
(b) *Escherichia coli*
(c) *Agrobacterium tumefaciens*
(d) *Arabidopsis thaliana*

29. Read the following statements and choose the correct option:

I: *Agrobacterium tumefaciens* is the causative agent of crown gall disease of dicots
II: *Agrobacterium tumefaciens* causes infection by entering the plant through wounds and injuries
(a) Both statements are correct
(b) Both statements are incorrect
(c) Only I is correct
(d) Only II is correct

30. A transgenic food crop which may help in solving the problem of night blindness in developing countries is:
(a) Bt soyabean (b) Flavr Savr tomatoes
(c) Golden rice (d) Starlink maize

31. A protein encoding gene expressed in a heterologous host will produce a protein product, called:
(a) Native protein
(b) Recombinant protein
(c) Non-recombinant protein
(d) Restriction enzyme

32. The first human hormone produced by recombinant DNA technology is:
(a) Insulin (b) Growth hormone
(c) Thyroxine (d) Estradiol

33. The first clinical gene therapy was given for treating:
(a) Diabetes mellitus
(b) Rheumatoid arthritis
(c) Adenosine deaminase deficiency
(d) Dwarfism

34. Bt toxin gene:
(a) Has been cloned from bacteria
(b) Has been expressed in plants
(c) Has created a bio-pesticide
(d) All are correct

35. Which of the following can be used as a bioweapon?
(a) *Treponema pallidum*
(b) *Bacillus anthracis*
(c) *Clostridium tetani*
(d) *Mycobacterium tuberculosis*

36. Monoclonal antibodies are produced by using ________ cells:
(a) Hybridoma (b) Prokaryote
(c) Yeast (d) Multinucleate

37. The 51 amino acids of insulin are arranged in:
(a) Two polypeptides having 20 and 31 amino acids
(b) Two polypeptides having 21 and 30 amino acids
(c) Two polypeptides having 25 and 26 amino acids
(d) Single polypeptide

38. In 'Flavr Savr' tomato, the transgene inactivates the enzyme:
(a) Cellulase (b) Polygalacturonase
(c) Lipase (d) Nuclease

39. Transgenic yeast has been used to produce the vaccine for:
(a) Chicken pox (b) Hepatitis B
(c) Plague (d) Cholera

40. *Bacillus thuringiensis* strains have been used for designing novel:
(a) Biofertilisers
(b) Bio-pesticide
(c) Boo-mineralisation process
(d) Bio-metallurgical techniques

41. Which of the following is incorrect with respect to the uses of genetically modified (GM) plants?
(a) Increased reliance on chemical pesticides
(b) Have reduced post-harvest losses
(c) Have enhanced nutritional value of food
(d) Have made crops more tolerant to abiotic stresses

42. Transgenic animals are extensively used for all of the following procedures, except:
(a) Obtaining biological products like alpha-lactalbumin
(b) Study of diseases like cancer and cystic fibrosis
(c) Vaccine safety testing
(d) Bioremediation

43. Probe is:
(a) Single-stranded DNA
(b) Single-stranded RNA
(c) Tagged with radioactive molecule
(d) All of the above

44. Which of the following is incorrect with respect to the ELISA technique?
(a) It is based on the principle of antigen–antibody interaction
(b) ELISA can detect antigens of infections pathogens
(c) It can detect antibodies synthesized against the pathogen
(d) It involves the use of radio-labelled antibodies

45. Transgenic mice are being used to test the safety of the polio vaccine. If successful and found to be reliable, they could replace the use of:
(a) Guinea pigs (b) Monkeys
(c) Pigs (d) Rabbit

ANSWER KEYS

Exercises

1. (d)	**2.** (d)	**3.** (d)	**4.** (b)	**5.** (c)	**6.** (d)	**7.** (b)	**8.** (b)	**9.** (b)	**10.** (c)
11. (d)	**12.** (d)	**13.** (d)	**14.** (d)	**15.** (a)	**16.** (d)	**17.** (c)	**18.** (c)	**19.** (d)	**20.** (d)
21. (d)	**22.** (c)	**23.** (c)	**24.** (c)	**25.** (c)	**26.** (b)	**27.** (b)	**28.** (b)	**29.** (d)	**30.** (c)
31. (c)	**32.** (b)	**33.** (b)	**34.** (b)	**35.** (b)	**36.** (c)	**37.** (b)	**38.** (d)	**39.** (b)	**40.** (d)
41. (b)	**42.** (a)	**43.** (d)	**44.** (d)	**45.** (c)	**46.** (a)	**47.** (b)	**48.** (c)	**49.** (d)	**50.** (c)
51. (b)	**52.** (b)	**53.** (d)	**54.** (d)	**55.** (d)	**56.** (d)	**57.** (b)	**58.** (c)	**59.** (a)	**60.** (a)

NCERT Exemplar Questions

1. (d)	**2.** (c)	**3.** (c)	**4.** (d)	**5.** (c)	**6.** (a)	**7.** (b)	**8.** (d)	**9.** (c)	**10.** (c)
11. (c)	**12.** (c)	**13.** (d)	**14.** (b)	**15.** (c)					

Practice Test Paper

1. (b)	**2.** (c)	**3.** (b)	**4.** (c)	**5.** (b)	**6.** (b)	**7.** (d)	**8.** (d)	**9.** (b)	**10.** (a)
11. (d)	**12.** (c)	**13.** (c)	**14.** (d)	**15.** (a)	**16.** (d)	**17.** (c)	**18.** (d)	**19.** (a)	**20.** (c)
21. (c)	**22.** (b)	**23.** (b)	**24.** (b)	**25.** (b)	**26.** (c)	**27.** (b)	**28.** (c)	**29.** (a)	**30.** (c)
31. (b)	**32.** (a)	**33.** (c)	**34.** (d)	**35.** (b)	**36.** (a)	**37.** (b)	**38.** (b)	**39.** (b)	**40.** (b)
41. (a)	**42.** (d)	**43.** (d)	**44.** (d)	**45.** (b)					

SOLUTIONS

1. Green Revolution increased yields due to improved crop varieties, use of better management practices and use of agrochemicals (fertilisers and pesticides).

2. Genetically modified crops increase the efficiency of mineral usage by plants to prevent early exhaustion of the fertility of soil.

3. The Bt toxin gene has been cloned from bacteria and been expressed in plants to provide resistance to insects without the need for insecticides, in effect creating a bio-pesticide.

4. The Bt toxin protein exists as inactive protoxins, but once an insect ingests the inactive toxin, it is converted into the active form of the toxin due to the alkaline pH of the gut which solubilises the crystals.

5. The proteins encoded by the genes cryIAc and cryIIAb control the cotton bollworms, while that of cryIAb controls the corn borer.

6. Insulin has a total 51 amino acids, chain A consists of 21 amino acids and chain B has 30 amino acids.

7. Insulin consists of two short polypeptides, chains A and B that are linked by disulphide bonds.

8. In 1983, Eli Lilly, an American company, prepared two DNA sequences corresponding to chains A and B of human insulin and introduced them in plasmids of *E. coli* to produce insulin chains.

9. Bt cotton was the first genetically modified plant commercially released in India.

10. The technique of DNA fingerprinting was developed by Alec Jeffreys.

11. Bt cotton has high yield and resistance to bollworms.

12. 'Taq' polymerase and 'Pfu' polymerase are DNA polymerase enzymes obtained from the thermostable bacteria *Thermus aquaticus* and *Pyrococcus furiosus*, respectively.

13. Golden rice is a variety of rice produced through genetic engineering to biosynthesize beta-carotene, a precursor of vitamin A. It will therefore help in solving the problem of night blindness in developing nations.

14. The first clinical gene therapy was given in 1990 to a four-year-old girl with adenosine deaminase (ADA) deficiency.

15. Using RNA interference (RNAi), tobacco plants resistant to a nematode (*Meloidogyne incognita*) have been developed by the introduction of DNA that produces both sense and antisense RNA in the host cell. These two RNAs are complementary to each other and form a double-stranded dsRNA that initiated RNAi, and silences the specific mRNA of the nematode. The consequence is that the parasite cannot survive in a transgenic host expressing the specific interfering RNA.

16. In the case of *Bacillus thuringiensis*, the bacillus itself is not killed by the toxic protein crystals as it is released as a protoxin (inactive toxin).

17. Polymerase chain reaction (PCR) technique is used to make numerous copies of a specific segment of DNA quickly and accurately.

18. 'Bt' in Bt brinjal refers to *Bacillus thuringiensis*.

19. Golden rice can prevent the night blindness associated with Vitamin A deficiency.

20. Some strains of *Bacillus thuringiensis* produce proteins that kill certain insects such as lepidopterans (tobacco budworm, armyworm), coleopterans (beetles) and dipterans (flies, mosquitoes). *Bacillus thuringiensis* forms protein crystals during a particular phase of its growth and these crystals contain a toxic insecticidal protein.

21. The activated toxin of *Bacillus thuringiensis* binds to the surface of midgut epithelial cells and creates pores that cause cell swelling and lysis, eventually causing death of the insect.

22. Biopiracy refers to the use of bioresources by multinational companies and organisations without authorisation from the concerned country or with proper compensation.

23. A nematode *Meloidogyne incognita* infects the root of tobacco plants and causes great reduction in yield.

24. The Indian government has set up organisations such as GEAC (Genetic Engineering Approval Committee), which will make decisions regarding the validity of GM research and the safety of introducing GM organisms for public services.

25. Southern blot is a method used in molecular biology for the detection of a specific DNA sequence in DNA samples. Southern blotting combines transfer of electrophoresis-separated DNA fragments to a filter membrane and subsequent fragment detection by probe hybridisation.

26. A transgenic sheep 'Tracy' has yielded α-1-antitrypsin for the treatment of emphysema.

27. In 1997, the first transgenic cow 'Rosie' produced α-lactalbumin-enriched milk.

28. Eli Lilly, an American company, prepared two DNA sequences corresponding to the A and B chains of human insulin and introduced them in plasmids to *Escherichia coli* to produce insulin chains.

29. Recombinant DNA technology, polymerase chain reaction (PCR) and enzyme-linked immuno-sorbent assay (ELISA) are some of the techniques used for early diagnosis.

30. The vaccine for Hepatitis B was developed in transgenic yeast using recombinant DNA technology.

31. *Pseudomonas putida* is the first patented organism in the world. It was discovered by Ananda Mohan Chakrabarty, who discovered its diverse metabolism, including its ability to degrade organic solvents such as toluene. This ability has been put to use in bioremediation, or the use of microorganisms to degrade environmental pollutants and oil- spills.

32. At present, about 30 recombinant therapeutics have been approved for human use the world over.

33. The Green Revolution succeeded in tripling the food supply but it was not enough to feed the growing human population.

34. Transgenic mice are being used to test the safety of the polio vaccine. If successful and found to be reliable, they could replace the use of monkeys to test the safety of batches of the vaccine.

35. Infestation of beetles is prevented by the Bt toxin, which belongs to the order coleoptera.

36. As the first step towards gene therapy, lymphocytes from the blood of the patient are grown in culture outside the body. Using a retrovirus vector, a functional adenosine deaminase cDNA is then introduced into these lymphocytes, which are subsequently returned to the patient.

37. A transgenic plant *Brassica napus* is used as a source of the anticoagulant hirudin.

38. Insulin cannot be orally administered to diabetes patients as it is a polypeptide hormone and digested by enzymes present in the gut. Early detection of diseases is not possible using conventional methods of diagnosis like serum and urine analysis.

39. Over 95% of all existing transgenic animals are mice.

40. Many transgenic animals are designed to increase our understanding of how genes contribute to the development of diseases. Today, transgenic models exist for many human diseases such as cancer, cystic fibrosis, rheumatoid arthritis and Alzheimer's disease.

41. Deficiency of the enzyme adenosine deaminase (ADA) causes Severe Combined Immuno Deficiency (SCID).

42. Spores of *Bacillus anthracis* are used as bioweapon in dry form.

43. Anti-sense technology refers to the use of a piece of RNA that is complimentary in sequence to stop the expression of a specific gene. Thus, it involves silencing of a specific mRNA due to the complementary dsRNA molecule that binds to and prevents translation of the mRNA.

44. Transgenic crops are generated by introducing foreign DNA into a cell and regenerating a plant from that cell.

45. The main objective of producing herbicide-resistant GM crops is to eliminate weeds from the field without the use of manual labour.

46. Polyethylene glycol is used for gene transfer without vector as it helps in somatic hybridisation.

47. In the Flavr Savr variety of transgenic tomato, the expression of the gene for the enzyme

polygalacturonase is blocked. This enzyme is known to digest the middle lamella and induce softening and ripening of fruits.

48. Twenty-seven documented varieties of basmati rice are grown in India.

49. In transgenic golden rice, the gene for the synthesis of β-carotene was obtained from daffodil/*Narcissus pseudonarcissus.*

50. RNAi was first discovered in 1998 by Andrew Fire and Craig Mello in a nematode, *Caenorhabditis elegans.*

51. Though turmeric has been used in India for centuries, a patent for the "use of turmeric in wound healing" was granted by the US Patent and Trademark Office. This is an example of biopiracy.

52. Dolly was the first sheep to be cloned. Polly and Molly were the first transgenic sheep to be cloned.

53. Biopatents are awarded for cell lines, strains of microorganisms and genetically modified organisms.

54. Gene therapy is the correction of genetic defect by delivering a normal gene into the individual or embryo to take over the function of and compensate for the non-functional gene.

55. A classic example of biopiracy is the patenting of the low-calorie sweet protein brazzein obtained from a West African plant, *Pentadiplandra brazzeana,* which is approximately 2000 times as sweet as sugar. In addition, brazzein is a low-calorie sweetener. But the protein brazzein was patented in the USA. Subsequently, the gene encoding brazzein was also isolated, sequenced and patented in the USA.

56. Introduction of functional adenosine deaminase cDNA (using retroviral vector) into lymphocytes is not a permanent cure for ADA deficiency because these cells are not immortal and the patient requires periodic infusion of such genetically engineered lymphocytes.

57. In 1997, an American company acquired patent rights on basmati rice through the US Patent and Trademark Office. This allowed the company to sell a 'new' variety of basmati in the USA and abroad. This 'new' variety of basmati was derived from the Indian farmer's variety.

58. Hybridoma technology is a method for producing a large number of identical antibodies. In this method, antibody producing B lymphocytes are fused with immortal cancer cells or myeloma cells to produce a hybrid cell line called hybridoma, which has both the antibody producing ability of the B cell and the longevity and reproductivity of the myeloma. The production of monoclonal antibodies by this method was invented by Cesar Milstein and Georges Kohler in 1975.

59. For RNAi, nematode-specific genes were introduced into the host plants using *Agrobacterium* vectors. The C-peptide is part of the immature/pro-hormone form of insulin in which it is released. This C-peptide is not present in mature insulin and is released during maturation. Recombinant DNA technology has made an immense impact in the area of healthcare by mass production of safe and more effective therapeutic drugs.

60. Genetically modified (GM) brinjal in India has been developed for insect resistance. Bt brinjal has been developed to provide resistance against lepidopteron insects, in particular, the brinjal fruit and shoot borer.

13 Organism and Population

EXERCISES

Introduction, Organism and its Environment, Major Abiotic Factors: Temperature, Water, Light, Soil, Responses to Abiotic Factors, Adaptations

1. The study of the interrelationship between living organisms and their environment is called:
(a) Ecology (b) Phytogeology
(c) Phytogeography (d) Zoogeography

2. Ecology is basically concerned with four levels of biological organisation. Which of the following is the correct representation?
(a) Population, community, biome, biosphere
(b) Organism, community, biome, biosphere
(c) Organism, population, community, biome
(d) Species, ecosystem, landscape, biome

3. In the given figure, identify the grassland and coniferous forest, respectively, from the markings A–F and select the correct option:

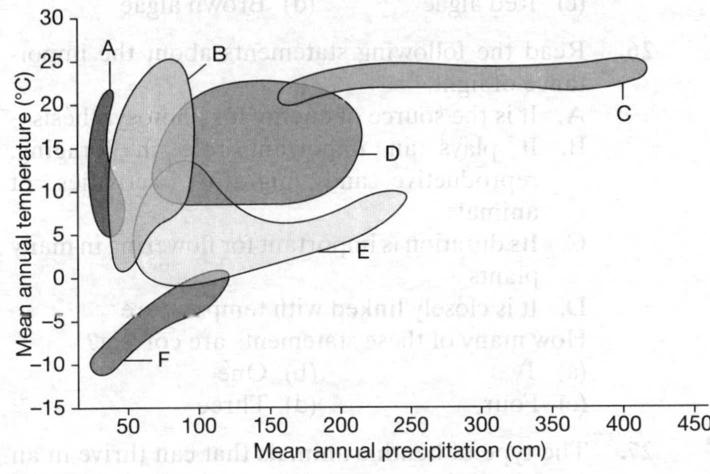

(a) A and B (b) B and D
(c) B and E (d) C and F

4. Nature and extent of biomes are decided by all, except:
(a) Climatic factors (b) Topographic factors
(c) Edaphic factors (d) Types of fauna

5. Which among the following is not an abiotic factor?
(a) Light (b) Population
(c) Rainfall (d) Soil type

6. Maximum mean annual rainfall is found in:
(a) Coniferous forest (b) Tropical rain forest
(c) Temperate forest (d) Grassland

7. Which of the following is a mainly treeless biome?
(a) Tropical rain forest (b) Grassland
(c) Coniferous forest (d) Desert

8. Heavy rainfall throughout the year results in:
(a) Scrub forest
(b) Deciduous forest
(c) Luxuriant evergreen forest
(d) Xerophytic forest

9. In India, the temperate evergreen type of vegetation is found mostly in:
(a) Western Ghats and Assam
(b) Eastern and Western Himalayas at less than 3,500 metres or in the higher slopes of the Himalayas
(c) Western Himalayas above 3,500 metres in altitude
(d) Rajasthan and Punjab

10. Ecologically, the most relevant environmental factor is:
(a) Temperature (b) Soil
(c) Water (d) Light

11. Read the following statements carefully:
A. Mango trees do not grow in temperate countries
B. Tuna fish are rarely found beyond tropical latitudes in the oceans
C. Snow leopards are not found in Kerala forests
D. Temperature does not affect the enzyme kinetics of organisms
E. Most mammals are eurythermal
How many of these statements are correct?
(a) Two (b) Three
(c) Four (d) Five

12. Temperature affects organisms by affecting their:
(i) Enzyme kinetics
(ii) Basal metabolism
(iii) Nutrient requirement
(iv) Water requirement
(a) (i) and (iii) (b) (ii) and (iii)
(c) (i) and (ii) (d) (iii) and (iv)

13. Select the incorrect statement:
(a) More than 70% of the world's freshwater is contained in polar ice
(b) Salt concentration for inland water measured as PPT is 5
(c) Euryhaline organisms tolerate a wide range of salinity
(d) The productivity and distribution of plants is not dependent on water

14. Succulent xerophytes and deep-rooted shrubs are found in:
(a) Tropical rain forest
(b) Grassland
(c) Desert
(d) Arctic and alpine tundra

15. Vegetation and soil type of an area is mainly determined by:
(a) Light and humidity
(b) Rainfall and light
(c) Temperature and rainfall
(d) Humidity and wind

16. The mango tree does not and cannot grow in temperate countries like Canada and Germany. Which abiotic factor is responsible for this?
(a) Soil type (b) Water
(c) Temperature (d) Rainfall

17. Among the following characters, which does not characterise a tropical rain forest?
(a) Maximum biodiversity
(b) Stratification
(c) Presence of lianas and epiphytes
(d) Deciduous trees

18. Stage of temporary suspension of development under unfavourable conditions can be observed in:
(a) Phytoplanktons (b) Zooplanktons
(c) Snails (d) Fishes

19. The salt concentration (ppt) of hyper-saline lagoons is:
(a) 30–35 (b) >100
(c) Less than 5 (d) >50

20. The salt concentration (ppt) of the sea is:
(a) >100 (b) 5
(c) 30–35 (d) <100

21. An organism is called stenohaline when it tolerates:
(a) A wide range of salinity
(b) A narrow range of salinity
(c) All the salt concentration
(d) High temperature

22. The best soil for health and vigorous growth of most plants is:
(a) Sand soil (b) Loam soil
(c) Clay soil (d) Gravel soil

23. The foraging, reproductive and migratory activities of organisms are primarily dependent upon:
(a) Light (b) Temperature
(c) Water (d) Soil

24. A behavioural strategy of adaptation called echolocation is found in:
(a) Bats (b) Praying mantis
(c) Deer (d) Bear

25. The algae that absorbs mostly green wavelength and is found at the greatest depth in oceans is:
(a) Blue-green algae (b) Green algae
(c) Red algae (d) Brown algae

26. Read the following statements about the importance of light.
A. It is the source of energy for photosynthesis
B. It plays an important role in foraging, reproductive and migratory activities of animals
C. Its duration is important for flowering in many plants
D. It is closely linked with temperature
How many of these statements are correct?
(a) Two (b) One
(c) Four (d) Three

27. The type of benthic animals that can thrive in an aquatic environment is determined by:

(a) Sediment characteristics
(b) Soil grain size
(c) Weathering process
(d) Soil composition

28. Small animals are rarely found in:
(a) Desert (b) Polar region
(c) Water (d) Air

29. Regarding temperature and osmotic concentration, nearly all plants and 99% of animals are:
(a) Regulators (b) Partial regulators
(c) Conformers (d) Escapers in time

30. Organism are able to maintain homeostasis by:
(a) Physical means
(b) Behavioural means
(c) Physiological means
(d) All of the above

31. Some organisms are able to maintain homeostasis by physiological means (sometimes behavioural also), which ensures:
(a) Constant body temperature
(b) Constant osmotic concentration
(c) Maintenance of physiological conditions
(d) Both (a) and (b)

32. The given graph represents how three different living organisms (X, Y and Z) cope with external environmental conditions. Study the graph and select the correct option regarding XYZ:

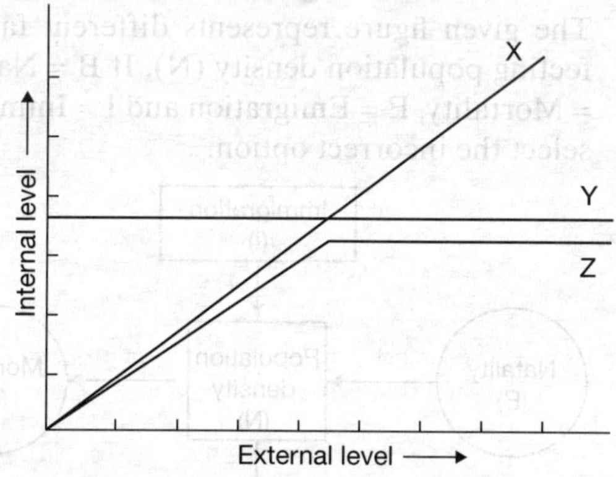

(a) X could be a bird (b) Y could be a mammal
(c) Z could be bird (d) X could be a mammal

33. Organisms whose body temperature changes with ambient temperature are:
(a) Mammals (b) Birds
(c) Nearly all plants (d) Both (a) and (b)

34. Bears escape in time during winter by a process called:
(a) Aestivation (b) Hibernation
(c) Diapause (d) Eluviation

35. Read the following statements and select the incorrect ones:
A. Birds and mammals maintain homeostasis by physiological and behavioural means
B. Majority of animals and nearly all plants are conformers
C. The small animals have smaller surface area relative to their volume
D. The conformers are able to maintain their body temperature inspite of changes in ambient temperature
(a) (A) and (C) (b) (B) and (D)
(c) (A) and (B) (d) (C) and (D)

36. The famous Keoladeo National Park is located in:
(a) Nagpur (b) Bharatpur
(c) Sitapur (d) Raipur

37. If the stressful external conditions are localised or remain only for a short duration, the organism has two alternatives:
(a) Migrate and regulate
(b) Migrate and suspend
(c) Suspend and conform
(d) Suspend and regulate

38. Identify the mismatched pair:
(a) Hibernation – Snail
(b) Diapause – Zooplankton
(c) Aestivation – Fish
(d) Migrate – Siberian crane

39. Select the correct combination of true (T) and false (F) for the following statements:
A. Many fishes thrive in the Antarctic waters where temperature is always below zero
B. Desert lizards have a marvelous physiological ability to survive the scorching heat of the desert
C. Under unfavourable conditions, many zooplankton species go into aestivation
D. Thermoregulation is an energetically expensive process

	A	B	C	D
(a)	T	T	F	F
(b)	T	F	F	T
(c)	F	T	T	F
(d)	F	T	F	T

40. Which of the following is incorrect with respect to adaptations of xerophytes:
(a) Presence of CAM pathway
(b) Presence of thick cuticle on leaf surfaces
(c) Presence of sunken stomata
(d) Presence of poorly developed root system

41. Read the following physiological adaptations.
A. Increase in RBC production
B. Decreases binding affinity of haemoglobin
C. Decrease in breathing rate
Which of these adaptations is/are useful to overcome altitude sickness?
(a) Only (A) (b) Only (A) and (B)
(c) Only (B) and (C) (d) (A), (B) and (C)

42. Which statement is correct about Allen's Rule?
(a) Aquatic mammals have blubbers as insulators
(b) Mammals of humid and warmer regions have more melanin in their skin
(c) Bears undergo hibernation during winter
(d) Mammals of colder climates have shorter ears and limbs

43. The reason for altitude sickness is:
(a) High atmospheric pressure
(b) Low atmospheric pressure
(c) High temperature
(d) Low temperature

44. Aquatic mammals like seals reduce loss of body heat in polar seas because of the presence of:
(a) Auto freezing proteins
(b) High atmospheric pressure
(c) Thicker layer of fat
(d) Branched-chain lipids in cell membrane

45. Some species have evolved the ability to regulate, but only over a limited range of environmental conditions, beyond which they simply conform. Such individuals are known as:
(a) Partial regulators
(b) Conformers
(c) Regulators
(d) Cold-blooded animals

Populations, Population Growth, Growth Models, Exponential Growth, Logistic Growth, Life History Variation

46. Natality refers to:
(a) Number of individuals leaving the habitat
(b) Birth rate
(c) Death rate
(d) Number of individuals entering the habitat

47. Population ecology links ecology to:
(a) Individuals and population
(b) Population and the environment
(c) Natural selection and ecology
(d) Population genetics and evolution

48. The factor that does not determine the population size is:
(a) Mortality (b) Emigration
(c) Immigration (d) Migration

49. While studying exponential growth, the intrinsic rate of natural increase helps us to assess:
(a) Birth rate
(b) Death rate
(c) Availability of land and resources
(d) Impact of biotic and abiotic factors on population growth

50. A parameter of habitat which determines its carrying capacity is:
(a) Mortality
(b) Natality
(c) Environmental resistance
(d) Emigration

51. Tiger census in our national parks is often based upon:
(a) Relative densities (b) Biomass
(c) Faecal pellets (d) Per cent cover

52. Emigration is:
(a) Outward movement of some individuals to return after some time
(b) Temporary inward movement of some individuals
(c) Permanent outward movement of some individuals from a population
(d) Permanent inward movement of some individuals into a population

53. The given figure represents different factors affecting population density (N). If B = Natality, D = Mortality, E = Emigration and I = Immigration, select the incorrect option:

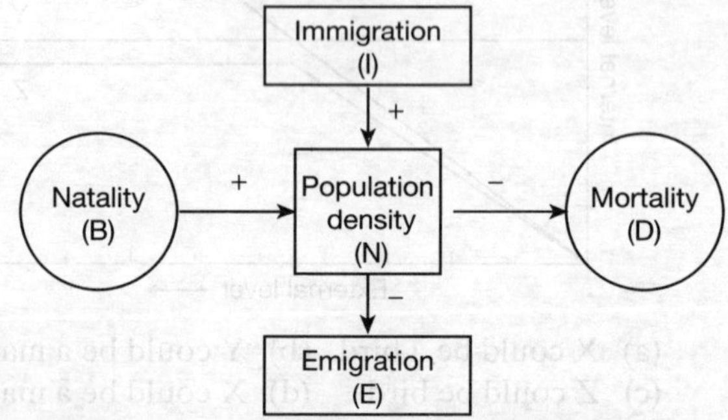

(a) B and D are most the influential factors under normal conditions, while I and E become important in special conditions
(b) In a new habitat just being colonised, I becomes more important than B
(c) B and I cause positive changes in N
(d) I is generally equal to E

54. Exponential growth:
(a) Occurs under unlimited resources

(b) Shows sigmoid curve
(c) Shows asymptote at carrying capacity
(d) Is the realistic demonstration of growth of most organisms

55. The influence of environmental resistance over the biotic potential is denoted by:
(a) $\left(\frac{1-K}{N}\right)$ (b) $\frac{(K-N)}{K}$
(c) N/K (d) $\frac{1-N}{K}$

56. Biotic potential is represented by the symbol:
(a) r (b) N_o
(c) K (d) N_t

57. In an area, if there are 200 *Parthenium* plants but only a huge banyan tree with a large canopy, the population density is measured in terms of:
(a) Biomass or per cent cover
(b) Indirect count
(c) Relative densities
(d) Total number

58. When in a population, pre-reproductive individuals are followed by a large number of reproductive individuals, the population is said to be ________ and its age pyramid would be ________:
(a) Declining, triangular
(b) Declining, urn-shaped
(c) Stable, urn-shaped
(d) Expanding, bell-shaped

59. Which statement is correct for a bell-shaped pyramid?
(a) Low percentage of pre-reproductive individuals
(b) Stable population
(c) Very high proportion of pre-reproductive individuals
(d) Population shows decline in growth

60. J-shaped growth can be observed for:
(a) Insect population (b) Algal bloom
(c) Both of these (d) None of these

61. When resources are unlimited:
A. The population grows to express a J-shaped curve
B. Carrying capacity has no role in population growth
C. Population growth is called Verhulst–Pearl logistic growth
(a) Only (A) is correct
(b) (B) and (C) are correct
(c) (A) and (B) are correct
(d) (A), (B) and (C) are correct

62. rN represents:
(a) Carrying capacity
(b) Environmental resistance
(c) Exponential growth
(d) Logistic growth

63. Asymptote stage indicates ________ population:
(a) Stabilised (b) Increasing
(c) Decreasing (d) Unstable

64. In nature, a given habitat has the resources to support a maximum, beyond which no further growth is possible. This limit known as:
(a) Environmental resistance
(b) Vital index
(c) Carrying capacity
(d) None of the above

65. In the Verhulst–Pearl logistic growth model:
(a) Population does not reach beyond carrying capacity
(b) Population shows sigmoid curve
(c) Environment resistance is effective from the beginning
(d) All of the above

66. Verhulst–Pearl population growth is described by the equation:
(a) $\frac{dN}{dt} = rn$ (b) $Nt = N_0e^{rt}$
(c) $\frac{dN}{dt} = rN\left(\frac{K-N}{K}\right)$ (d) $\frac{dN}{dt} = rn\left(\frac{N-K}{N}\right)$

67. Match the following:

Column I	Column II
A. Breeding once in a life	(i) Mammals
B. Breeding several times in life	(ii) Oysters
C. Large number of small offspring	(iii) Most birds
D. Small number of large offspring	(iv) Pacific salmon fish

(a) A – (iv), B – (ii), C – (iii), D – (i)
(b) A – (iv), B – (iii), C – (ii), D – (i)
(c) A – (iii), B – (iv), C – (ii), D – (i)
(d) A – (ii), B – (iii), C – (iv), D – (i)

68. Ecologists suggest that the life history trait of organisms has evolved in relation to the constraints imposed by:
(a) Abiotic component of the habitat
(b) Biotic component of the habitat
(c) Both abiotic and biotic components of the habitat
(d) None of the above

69. If age distribution is plotted for a population, the resulting structure is known as:
(a) Growth model (b) Age pyramid
(c) Eltonian pyramid (d) Ecological pyramid

70. Genotypically adapted population is called:
(a) Ecotype (b) Biotype
(c) Ecotone (d) Ecoline

Population Interactions, Competition, Parasitism, Commensalism, Mutualism

71. In which of the following interactions is species A harmed (–) while species B is benefitted (+)?
(a) Competition (b) Parasitism
(c) Amensalism (d) Commensalism

72. Commensalism is a:
(a) +, 0 interaction (b) +, + interaction
(c) +, – interaction (d) –, 0 interaction

73. Which of the following interactions is related to the mechanism of population control?
(a) Competition (b) Predation
(c) Parasitism (d) Neutral interaction

74. A. +, + B. –, 0
The interactions (A) and (B) between species are called:

	A	B
(a)	Protocooperation	Commensalism
(b)	Protocooperation	Predation
(c)	Mutualism	Parasitism
(d)	Mutualism	Amensalism

75. How many insects are known to be phytophagous?
(a) Nearly 25% (b) Nearly 50%
(c) Nearly 35% (d) Nearly 70%

76. In which population is the interaction a "give and take" relationship?
(a) *Cuscuta*–Hedge plant
(b) Mango tree–Orchid
(c) Fungus–*Pinus* roots
(d) Sparrow–Seed

77. According to their lifestyle, parasites have evolved all the following adaptations, except:
(a) Loss of unnecessary sense organs
(b) Presence of suckers
(c) High reproductive capacity
(d) Well-developed digestive system

78. In brood parasitism:
(a) Cuckoo lays its eggs in the nest of crow
(b) Crow lays its eggs in the nest of cuckoo
(c) The eggs of parasitic birds never resemble the host's egg in size and colour
(d) The host bird detects the foreign eggs and expels them from the nest

79. The wasp pollinates fig inflorescence while searching for suitable egg-laying sites. In return for the favour of pollination, the fig offers the wasp some of its developing seeds as food for the developing wasp larvae. This population interaction belongs to:
(a) Mutualism (b) Amensalism
(c) Commensalism (d) Parasitism

80. Choosing different times for feeding and different foraging patterns can avoid competition in:
A. Closely related species found in different habitats
B. Two species competing for the same resources
C. Species having similar niche and sharing the same habitat
D. Two species having different niches in the same habitat
(a) A, B (b) B, C
(c) C, D (d) D, A

81. Select the statement which explains the term commensalism:
(a) One organism is benefitted, the other is unaffected
(b) Organism feeds on living or dead organic matter
(c) Animals and detritivores feed on organic remains
(d) Organism feeds upon other living organisms

82. Gause's experiment on *Paramecium* is associated with the phenomenon of:
(a) Competition release
(b) Competitive exclusion
(c) Resource partitioning
(d) Competitive coexistence

83. Find the correct match with respect to an example of a type of population interaction:
(a) Mycorrhiza – Protocooperation
(b) Ticks and dog – Predation
(c) Mango tree and orchid – Commensalism
(d) Monarch butterfly and birds – Competition

84. How many of the following are correctly matched?

Population interactions	Examples
A. Mutualism	Fig and fig wasp
B. Commensalism	Hermit crab and sea anemone
C. Competition	Goats and Abingdon tortoise

(a) Three (b) Two
(c) Four (d) One

85. *Paramecium aurelia*, when kept in a water beaker along with *P. caudatum*, will kill *P. caudatum*. This represents:
(a) Competitive exclusion
(b) Co-existence
(c) Resource partitioning
(d) Predation

86. Species that face competition might evolve a mechanism of changing the feeding time or foraging pattern, showing:
(a) Competitive release
(b) Co-existence
(c) Resource partitioning
(d) Both (b) and (c)

87. MacArthur found that closely related species of warblers living on the same tree show:
(a) Co-evolution (b) Competitive exclusion
(c) Co-existence (d) Competitive release

88. Fitness of one species (measured in terms of intrinsic rate of increase) is significantly lower in the presence of another species during the interaction between:
(a) Barnacles and whale
(b) Abingdon tortoise and goats
(c) *Ophrys* and bee
(d) Fig and fig wasp

89. Gauss's 'Competitive Exclusion Principle' is counteracted by which of the following principles?
(a) Connell's Elegant Field Experiment
(b) Resource Partitioning by MacArthur
(c) Natural Selection Theory of Darwin
(d) Species Area Relationship of Alexander Von Humboldt

90. In how many population interactions mentioned below are both the species benefitted?
Parasitism, Mutualism, Amensalism, Commensalism, Protocooperation, Predation, Competition
(a) Two (b) Three
(c) One (d) Four

91. Select the odd one out with respect to population interaction:
(a) Clown fish and sea anemone
(b) Barnacle and whale
(c) Smother crop and weed interaction
(d) Mango and orchid tree

92. Read the following statements and select the correct option:
A. Parasitism is a relationship between two organisms where one organism depends for the whole of its life on the body of the other organism and gets nourishment and shelter from the second organism
B. Female mosquitoes are considered as parasites as they need our blood for reproduction
(a) Only (A) is correct
(b) Only (B) is correct
(c) Both (A) and (B) are correct
(d) Both (A) and (B) are incorrect

93. Which of the following cannot be used by prey for defence against predator?
(a) Cardiac glycoside (b) Strychnine
(c) Nectar (d) Nicotine

94. Which of the following is a means of removal of competition?
(a) Behaviour diversification
(b) Choosing different times for feeding
(c) Habitat diversification
(d) All of the above

95. During interaction between orchid and mango tree, which is benefitted?
(a) Mango tree (b) Orchid
(c) Both (d) Neither (a) or (b)

96. The close association of cattle egret and grazing cattle is an example of:
(a) Amensalism (b) Commensalism
(c) Parasitism (d) Predation

97. Select the incorrect statement for predation:
(a) Predation is commonly illustrated by the herbivore-carnivore interaction
(b) Predators keep prey population under control
(c) It maintains species diversity in a community
(d) Reduction in prey population may increase the population of the predator

98. Monarch butterfly is highly distasteful to its predator birds because of:
(a) Cardiac glycosides (b) Sinigrin
(c) Nicotine (d) Lectins

99. Competition is most severe between two:
(a) Closely related species growing in different habitat
(b) Closely related species growing in the same habitat
(c) Distantly related species growing in the same habitat
(d) Distantly related species growing in different niches

100. Which of the following is/are an example of co-evolution?
(a) Orchid and bee (b) *Yucca* and *Pronuba*
(c) Wasp and fig (d) All of the above

NCERT EXEMPLAR QUESTIONS

1. Autecology is the:
(a) Relation of heterogeneous populations to its environment
(b) Relation of an individual to its environment
(c) Relation of a community to its environment
(d) Relation of a biome to its environment

2. Ecotone is:
(a) A polluted area
(b) The bottom of a lake
(c) A zone of transition between two communities
(d) A zone of developing community

3. Biosphere is:
(a) A component in the ecosystem
(b) Composed of the plants present in the soil
(c) Life in outer space
(d) Composed of all living organisms present on earth which interact with the physical environment

4. Ecological niche is:
(a) The surface area of the ocean
(b) An ecologically adapted zone
(c) The physical position and functional role of a species within the community
(d) Formed of all plants and animals living at the bottom of a lake

5. According to Allen's Rule, mammals from colder climates have:
(a) Shorter ears and longer limbs
(b) Longer ears and shorter limbs
(c) Longer ears and longer limbs
(d) Shorter ears and shorter limbs

6. Salt concentration (salinity) of the sea measured in parts per thousand is:
(a) 10–15 (b) 30–70
(c) 0–5 (d) 30–35

7. Formation of tropical forests needs a mean annual temperature and mean annual precipitation of:
(a) 18–25°C and 150–400 cm
(b) 5–15°C and 50–100 cm
(c) 30–50°C and 100–150 cm
(d) 5–15°C and 100–200 cm

8. Which of the following forest plants controls light conditions on the ground?
(a) Lianas and climbers
(b) Shrubs
(c) Tall trees
(d) Herbs

9. What will happen to a well-growing herbaceous plant in the forest if it is transplanted outside the forest in a park?
(a) It will grow normally
(b) It will grow well because it is planted in the same locality
(c) It may not survive because of change in its microclimate
(d) It grows very well because the plant receives more sunlight

10. If a population of 50 *Paramecium* present in a pool increases to 150 after an hour, what would be the growth rate of the population?
(a) 50 per hour (b) 200 per hour
(c) 5 per hour (d) 100 per hour

11. What would be the per cent growth or birth rate per individual per hour for the same population mentioned in the previous question (Question 10)?
(a) 100 (b) 200
(c) 50 (d) 150

12. A population has more young individuals compared to older individuals. What would be the status of the population after some years?
(a) It will decline
(b) It will stabilise
(c) It will increase
(d) It will first decline and then stabilise

13. What parameters are used for tiger census in our country's national parks and sanctuaries?
(a) Pug marks only
(b) Pug marks and faecal pellets
(c) Faecal pellets only
(d) Actual head counts

14. Which of the following would necessarily decrease the density of a population in a given habitat?
(a) Natality > mortality
(b) Immigration > emigration
(c) Mortality and emigration
(d) Natality and immigration

15. A protozoan reproduces by binary fission. What will be the number of protozoans in its population after six generations?

(a) 128 (b) 24
(c) 64 (d) 32

16. In 2005, for each of the 14 million people present in a country, 0.028 were born and 0.008 died during the year. Using exponential equation, the number of people present in 2015 is predicted as:
(a) 25 million (b) 17 million
(c) 20 million (d) 18 million

17. Amensalism is an association between two species where:
(a) One species is harmed and the other is benefitted
(b) One species is harmed and the other is unaffected
(c) One species is benefitted and the other is unaffected
(d) Both the species are harmed

18. Lichens are association of:
(a) Bacteria and fungus
(b) Alga and bacterium
(c) Fungus and alga
(d) Fungus and virus

19. Which of the following is a partial root parasite?
(a) Sandalwood (b) Mistletoe
(c) *Orobanche* (d) *Ganoderma*

20. Which one of the following organisms reproduces sexually only once in its lifetime?
(a) Banana (b) Mango
(c) Tomato (d) Eucalyptus

PRACTICE TEST PAPER

1. A vast majority of organisms are restricted to ______ range of temperatures and are called ______:
(a) Wide, eurythermal
(b) Narrow, stenothermal
(c) Narrow, eurythermal
(d) Wide, stenothermal

2. Under unfavourable conditions, many zooplankton species in lakes and ponds enter:
(a) Diapause (b) Hibernation
(c) Aestivation (d) Migration

3. An interaction favourable to both populations, but not obligatory to each other, is:
(a) Protocooperation (b) Mutualism
(c) Commensalism (d) Parasitic

4. Ratio between mortality and natality is called:
(a) Population ratio (b) Vital index
(c) Density coefficient (d) Census ratio

5. Resemblance of an organism to another for protection and hiding is:
(a) Camouflage (b) Mimicry
(c) Predation (d) Adaptation

6. In an exponential bacterial culture, the number of cells/ml is plotted on a half-log graph. The graph is:
(a) Sigmoid
(b) Hyperbola
(c) Ascending straight line
(d) Descending straight line

7. Which of the following is correct for the specific interaction shown in the graph?

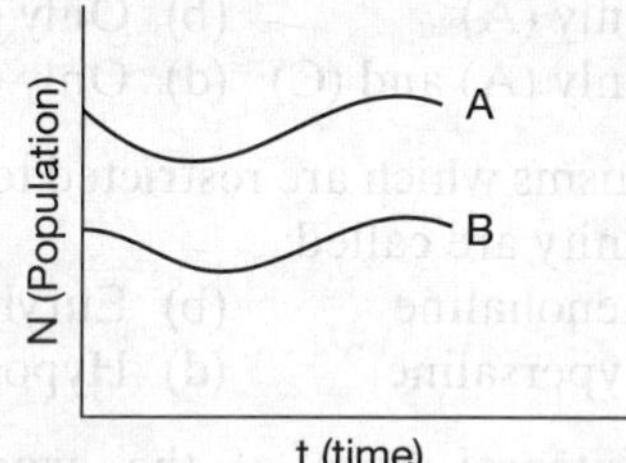

(a) Commensalism (b) Mutualism
(c) Parasitism (d) Competition

8. In which population interaction are both the species detrimentally affected?
(a) Mutualism (b) Commensalism
(c) Competition (d) Predation

9. Kangaroo rat shows ______ adaptation to meet its water requirements:
(a) Morphological (b) Anatomical
(c) Physiological (d) Cryptic

10. Savannas are:
(a) Tropical rain forest
(b) Dense forest with close canopy
(c) Desert
(d) Grassland with scattered trees

11. A fertile agricultural soil appears deep-coloured at the surface as compared to soil one metre down. The reason for the colour of the top soil is:
(a) More moisture

(b) Rich in organic matter
(c) Rich in iron, calcium, magnesium
(d) Recent formation

12. In a population showing Verhulst–Pearl logistic growth, the deceleration phase begins when $\left[\frac{dN}{dt} = rN\frac{(K-N)}{K}\right]$:
(a) N is exactly equal to one
(b) r is equal to zero
(c) N is nearly equal to K
(d) $\frac{K-N}{K}$ is equal to one

13. What type of growth curve can you expect for cells in tissue culture?
(a) Bell-shaped (b) J-shaped
(c) S-shaped (d) Straight line

14. Which of the following statements is true about regulators?
A. Their body temperature changes with ambient temperature
B. They are able to maintain constant osmotic concentration in aquatic conditions
C. An overwhelming majority of animals and all flowering plants are regulators
(a) Only (A) (b) Only (B)
(c) Only (A) and (C) (d) Only (B) and (C)

15. Organisms which are restricted to a narrow range of salinity are called:
(a) Stenohaline (b) Euryhaline
(c) Hypersaline (d) Hyposaline

16. The integral form of the exponential growth equation is:
(a) $\frac{dN}{dt} = rN$ (b) $Nt = N_0 e^{rt}$
(c) $\frac{dN}{dt} = (b-d)N$ (d) $\frac{dN}{dt} = \left(1 - \frac{N}{K}\right)$

17. Ecological niche of an organism represents:
A. The range of conditions that it can tolerate
B. The resources which it utilises
C. Its functional role in the ecosystem
(a) Only (A) (b) Only (C)
(c) Only (B) and (C) (d) (A), (B) and (C)

18. The interdependent evolution of flowering plants and pollinating insects is known as:
(a) Mutualism (b) Coevolution
(c) Commensalism (d) Cooperation

19. Two opposite forces operate in the growth and development of every population. One of them has the ability to reproduce at a given rate. The opposing force is:
(a) Mortality
(b) Fecundity
(c) Biotic potential
(d) Environmental resistance

20. Monarch butterfly escapes from predators by:
(a) Four smell
(b) Bitter taste
(c) Colour combination
(d) Rough skin

21. Biotic potential refers to:
(a) Natural increase of population under optimum conditions
(b) Potential of organisms in a biome
(c) Number of organisms in a biome
(d) Number of organisms in a population

22. Select the incorrect option with respect to the role of predators in an ecosystem:
(a) Transfer of energy across the trophic level
(b) Maintain species diversity in a community
(c) Non-biological method of pest control
(d) Keep prey population under control

23. Few species have evolved adaptations to avoid unfavourable conditions in time. Choose the odd one out with respect to this:
(a) Aestivation (b) Hibernation
(c) Diapause (d) Migration

24. What is represented by the given pyramid of age?

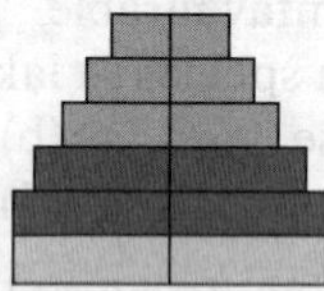

(a) A declining population
(b) A stable population
(c) A expanding population
(d) A growing population

25. Abingdon tortoise and goats in the Galapagos Islands are examples of:
(a) Commensalism (b) Competition
(c) Amensalism (d) Protocooperation

26. Crow and cuckoo interaction is an example of:
(a) Predation (b) Amensalism
(c) Brood parasitism (d) Commensalism

27. In logistic growth, a plot of population density (N) in relation to time (t) results in a sigmoid curve, which finally shows an asymptote, when:
(a) Intrinsic rate of natural increase is zero

(b) Carrying capacity = Population density
(c) Carrying capacity > Population density
(d) Carrying capacity < population density

28. The principle of competitive exclusion was given by:
(a) C Darwin (b) GF Gauss
(c) MacArthur (d) Verhulst and Pearl

29. Select the correct statement for r-selected species:
(a) Large number of progeny with small size
(b) Large number of progeny with large size
(c) Small number of progeny with small size
(d) Small number of progeny with large size

30. An association of individuals of different species living in the same habitat and having functional interactions is:
(a) Ecosystem (b) Population
(c) Ecological niche (d) Biotic community

31. An insect population showed explosive increase in its population in a short time during the rainy season. At the end of the season, the population declined abruptly. What would be the most appropriate reason?
(a) Environmental resistance becomes effective suddenly or resources may become depleted
(b) The population of its predators increases suddenly
(c) Population growth curve is sigmoid
(d) All food plants die suddenly at the end of the rainy season

32. An orchid resembling the female of an insect so as to be able to be pollinated is due to the phenomenon of:
(a) Pseudo pollination
(b) Pseudocopulation
(c) Mimicry
(d) Camouflage

33. Annual migration does not occur in the case of:
(a) Arctic tern (b) Salmon
(c) Siberian crane (d) Salamander

34. Population dynamics is related to:
(a) Increase in population
(b) Decrease in population
(c) Change in population
(d) All of the above

35. Natality is:
(a) Birth rate (b) Death rate
(c) Net increase (d) Net decrease

36. The largest amount of freshwater on our planet is in:
(a) Lakes and streams (b) Rivers
(c) Underground (d) Polar ice and glaciers

37. Species found exclusively in ecotone are called:
(a) Edge species (b) Sibling species
(c) Cryptic species (d) Allopatric species

38. Shortening of ears, limbs and other extremities of mammals so that heat loss can be minimised is associated with:
(a) Allen's Rule (b) Bergmann Rule
(c) Jordan's Rule (d) Rensch's Rule

39. Next to temperature, water is the most important factor influencing the life of organisms. Which of the following water characteristics is/are an influencing factor?
(a) pH (b) Salinity
(c) Turbidity (d) All of the above

40. Plants that produce characteristic pneumatophores and show vivipary belong to:
(a) Halophytes (b) Psammophytes
(c) Hydrophytes (d) Mesophytes

41. Select the option that is different from others while showing mutualism:
(a) Lichen
(b) Mycorrhizae
(c) Crocodile and plover
(d) Coralloid roots of cycas and BGA

42. Grazing is an example of:
(a) Protocooperation (b) Predation
(c) Parasitism (d) Amensalism

43. Find the odd one out with respect to biological organisation:
(a) Biome (b) Community
(c) Species (d) Population

44. A J-shaped growth curve corresponds to:
(a) Exponential growth
(b) High biotic potential
(c) No environmental resistance
(d) All of the above

45. Interaction of two different organisms in which one receives benefit without loss of the other is:
(a) Parasitism (b) Scavenging
(c) Symbiosis (d) Commensalism

ANSWER KEYS

Exercises

1. (a) **2.** (c) **3.** (c) **4.** (d) **5.** (b) **6.** (b) **7.** (b) **8.** (c) **9.** (b) **10.** (a)
11. (c) **12.** (c) **13.** (d) **14.** (b) **15.** (c) **16.** (c) **17.** (d) **18.** (b) **19.** (b) **20.** (c)
21. (b) **22.** (b) **23.** (a) **24.** (a) **25.** (c) **26.** (c) **27.** (a) **28.** (b) **29.** (c) **30.** (d)
31. (d) **32.** (b) **33.** (c) **34.** (b) **35.** (d) **36.** (b) **37.** (b) **38.** (a) **39.** (b) **40.** (d)
41. (b) **42.** (d) **43.** (b) **44.** (c) **45.** (a) **46.** (b) **47.** (d) **48.** (d) **49.** (d) **50.** (c)
51. (c) **52.** (c) **53.** (d) **54.** (a) **55.** (b) **56.** (a) **57.** (a) **58.** (b) **59.** (b) **60.** (c)
61. (c) **62.** (c) **63.** (a) **64.** (c) **65.** (d) **66.** (c) **67.** (b) **68.** (c) **69.** (b) **70.** (a)
71. (b) **72.** (a) **73.** (b) **74.** (d) **75.** (a) **76.** (c) **77.** (d) **78.** (a) **79.** (a) **80.** (b)
81. (a) **82.** (b) **83.** (c) **84.** (a) **85.** (a) **86.** (d) **87.** (c) **88.** (b) **89.** (b) **90.** (a)
91. (c) **92.** (a) **93.** (c) **94.** (d) **95.** (b) **96.** (b) **97.** (d) **98.** (a) **99.** (b) **100.** (d)

NCERT Exemplar Questions

1. (b) **2.** (c) **3.** (d) **4.** (c) **5.** (d) **6.** (d) **7.** (a) **8.** (b) **9.** (c) **10.** (d)
11. (b) **12.** (c) **13.** (b) **14.** (c) **15.** (c) **16.** (b) **17.** (b) **18.** (c) **19.** (a) **20.** (c)

Practice Test Paper

1. (b) **2.** (a) **3.** (a) **4.** (b) **5.** (b) **6.** (c) **7.** (b) **8.** (c) **9.** (c) **10.** (d)
11. (b) **12.** (c) **13.** (b) **14.** (b) **15.** (a) **16.** (b) **17.** (d) **18.** (b) **19.** (d) **20.** (b)
21. (a) **22.** (c) **23.** (d) **24.** (b) **25.** (b) **26.** (c) **27.** (b) **28.** (b) **29.** (a) **30.** (d)
31. (a) **32.** (b) **33.** (d) **34.** (d) **35.** (a) **36.** (d) **37.** (a) **38.** (a) **39.** (d) **40.** (d)
41. (c) **42.** (b) **43.** (c) **44.** (d) **45.** (d)

SOLUTIONS

Introduction, Organism and its Environment, Major Abiotic Factors: Temperature, Water, Light, Soil, Responses to Abiotic Factors, Adaptations

1. The study of the interrelationship between living organisms and their environment is called ecology.
2. Ecology is basically concerned with four levels of biological organisation. The correct representation is organism, population, community and biome.
3. A – Desert, B – Grassland, C – Tropical rain forest, D – Temperate forest, E – Coniferous forest, F – Tundra
4. Nature and extent of biomes are decided by environmental factors like climate factors, topographic factors and edaphic factors.
5. Population is not an abiotic factor.
6. Maximum mean annual rainfall is found in tropical rain forest, 2000–3500 mm.
7. Grasslands are treeless biomes.
8. Heavy rainfall throughout the year results in luxuriant evergreen forest.
9. Eastern and Western Himalayas at less than 3500 metres and on the higher slopes of the Himalayas
10. Temperature is the most ecologically relevant environmental factor.
11. Four statements (A, B, C and E) are correct.
12. Temperature significantly affects enzyme kinetics and basal metabolism as well as the activity and other physiological functions of the organism.
13. Salt concentration of inland water is measured as less than 5 ppt.
14. Desert biomes are characterised by the presence of succulent xerophytes and deep-rooted shrubs.
15. Vegetation and soil type of an area are mainly determined by temperature and rainfall.
16. Temperature plays an important role in both latitudinal and altitudinal distribution of organisms. For example, mango, a tropical and subtropical tree, is not found in temperate countries like Canada and Germany.
17. Tropical rain forests are evergreen forests.
18. A stage of suspended development is found in many zooplankton species in lakes and ponds.
19. The salt concentration of hyper-saline lagoon is > 100 ppt.
20. 30–35 ppt
21. Stenohaline are those that are restricted to a narrow range of salinity (example, shark).
22. Loam soil is the best soil for plant growth. It has moderate water-holding capacity, moderate porosity and good fertility. Loam soil contains 20% clay, 40% sand and 40% silt.
23. Many plants are dependent on sunlight to meet their photoperiodic requirements for flowering. Light also affects other processes like growth, reproduction, movement and phenology in plants.
24. Echolocation is the use of sound waves and echoes to determine where objects are in space. Bats use echolocation to navigate and find food in the dark.
25. Phycoerythrin pigment of red algae absorbs mostly green wavelength, so red algae extend to the greatest depth in water.
26. All four statements are correct.
27. In the aquatic environment, the sediment characteristics often determine the type of benthic animals that can thrive there.

28. Small animals have a larger surface area relative to their volume. They tend to lose body heat very fast when it is cold outside. Therefore, they have to spend much energy in generating body heat through metabolism. This is the main reason why small animals are not found in the polar regions.

29. 99% of animals and nearly all plants cannot maintain a constant internal environment. They are simply conformers.

30. Physical, physiological and behavioural means

31. Organisms maintain homeostasis, which ensures constant body temperature (thermoregulation) and constant osmotic concentration (osmoregulation).

32. X represents conformers (99% of animals and nearly all plants), Y represents regulators (all birds, mammals and a few vertebrates and invertebrates), Z represents partial regulators

33. Nearly all plants

34. Bear escapes in time during winter by a process called hibernation.

35. (C) and (D) are incorrect. The small animals have larger surface area relative to their volume. Conformers cannot maintain their body temperature. Their body temperature changes with ambient temperature.

36. The famous Keoladeo National Park is located in Bharatpur (Rajasthan).

37. Migrate and suspend

38. Hibernation (winter sleep) – Bear

39. (B) and (C) are false. The desert lizard lacks the physiological ability to cope with extreme temperature but manages body temperature by behavioural means. A stage of suspended development is found in many zooplankton species.

40. Xerophytic plants are characterised by the presence of a well-developed root system.

41. Increase in RBC production, decreased binding capacity of haemoglobin and increased breathing rate

42. Mammals from colder climates generally have shorter ears and limbs (extremities) to minimise heat loss. This is called as Allen's Rule.

43. At high altitude, the body does not receive enough oxygen due to low atmospheric pressure.

44. A thick layer of fat (blubber) is found in aquatic mammals like seals below their skin. This fat acts as insulator and reduces loss of body heat.

45. Partial regulation

Populations, Population Growth, Growth Models, Exponential Growth, Logistic Growth, Life History Variation

46. Natality refers to birth rate.

47. Population ecology links ecology to population genetics and evolution.

48. In migration, an organism can move away temporarily from the stressful habitat to a more hospitable area and return when the stressful period is over.

49. The value of r is an important parameter to assess the impact of environmental factors on population growth.

50. The sum of environmental factors that limits the population size is called environmental resistance.

51. Population size measurement can also be carried out indirectly without actually counting or seeing the organism. For example, the tiger census in national parks and tiger reserves in India is often based on pugmark and faecal pellets.

52. Emigration is the permanent outward movement of some individuals from a population.

53. I is generally not equal to E.

54. Exponential growth occurs when resources in the habitat are unlimited.

55. The influence of environmental resistance over the biotic potential is denoted by

$$\left(\frac{K-N}{K}\right).$$

56. Biotic potential is represented by the symbol r.

57. In an area, if there are 200 *Parthenium* plants but only a single huge banyan tree with a large

canopy, stating that the population density of banyan is low relative to that of *Parthenium* amounts to underestimating the enormous role of the banyan in that community. In this case, the population density is measured in terms of biomass or per cent cover.

58. Declining, urn-shaped

59. In the bell-shaped pyramid, population is said to be mature or stable.

60. J-shaped growth can be obtained for insect population and algae bloom.

61. (A) and (B) are correct. Logistic growth is called the Verhulst–Pearl logistic growth.

62. rN represents exponential growth.

63. Asymptote stage indicates a stabilised population.

64. The sum of environmental factors that limits population use is called environmental resistance.

65. All the statements are correct.

66. $\frac{dN}{dt} = rN\left(\frac{K-N}{K}\right)$

67. A – (iv), B – (iii), C – (ii), D – (i)

68. Both abiotic and biotic components of the habitat

69. Age pyramid

70. A genotypically adapted population is called ecotype.

Population Interactions, Competition, Parasitism, Commensalism, Mutualism

71. In parasitism, only one species benefits (parasite) and the interaction is detrimental to the other species (host).

72. Commensalism is a +, 0 interaction. In this interaction, one species is benefitted and the other is neither harmed nor benefitted.

73. Predators keep prey population under control.

74. A – Mutualism, B – Amensalism

75. Nearly 25% of all insects are known as phytophagous.

76. Fungus and *Pinus* roots show mutualism (give and take relationship). Fungi absorbs essential nutrients from the soil, while the plant in turn provides energy yielding carbohydrates to the fungi.

77. Loss of digestive system

78. In brood parasitism, the cuckoo lays its eggs in the nest of crows.

79. Mutualism

80. (B) and (C) are correct. The species facing competition might evolve a mechanism that promotes coexistence rather than exclusion.

81. One organism is benefitted and the other is unaffected.

82. Gauss gave the Law of Competitive Exclusion. It states that two closely related species competing for the same resources cannot co-exist indefinitely and the competitively inferior one will be eventually eliminated.

83. Mycorrhiza – Mutualism, Ticks and dog – Parasitism, Mango tree and orchid – Commensalism, Monarch butterfly and bird – Competition

84. All are correctly matched pairs.

85. Competitive exclusion

86. Co-existence and resource portioning

87. Five closely related species of warblers avoid competition by changing their foraging pattern.

88. Introduction of goats resulted in exclusion of Abingdon tortoise from the Galapagos Islands because goats are better browsers.

89. Resource Partitioning of MacArthur

90. In mutualism and protocooperation, both the species are benefitted.

91. Interaction between smoother crop and weeds shows amensalism.

92. Only A is correct. Female mosquito is not considered a parasite.

93. Nectar

94. Behaviour diversification, choosing different timed for feeding, habitat diversification

95. Orchid growing on plants like mango (host) are benefitted in the form of shelter, but the host neither derives any apparent benefit nor is it harmed.

96. Commensalism

97. Option (d) is correct.

98. Monarch butterfly is highly distasteful to its predator birds because of cardiac glycosides. This chemical is acquired by the monarch butterfly from a poisonous weed during its caterpillar stage.

99. Intra-specific competition is more acute because all organisms of the species have similar requirements for food, space, light, water, shelter, mate, etc.

100. Plant and animal interactions often involve co-evolution of mutualists.

14 Ecosystem

EXERCISES

Introduction, Structure and Function, Productivity, Decomposition

1. The correct definition of ecosystem is:
   (a) A community of organisms interacting with one another
   (b) The abiotic component of an area
   (c) The part of the earth and its atmosphere which is inhabited by living organisms
   (d) A community of organisms together with the environment in which they live

2. Which of the following is not correct for ecosystem?
   (a) The term ecosystem was given by AG Tansley
   (b) It is a self-regulatory and self-sustaining unit
   (c) It cannot maintain resilience
   (d) Regular input of energy is essential to maintain homeostasis

3. The importance of ecosystem lies in:
   (a) Flow of energy (b) Cycling of nutrients
   (c) Productivity (d) All of the above

4. An ecosystem does not normally alter because it is in a state of:
   (a) Homeostasis (b) Imbalance
   (c) Deficient light (d) Deficient components

5. Which of the following could not be considered as ecosystem?
   (a) A small pond
   (b) All the fish in a coral reef
   (c) Agriculture field
   (d) A pool of dung in a pasture

6. A pond is:
   (a) A biome
   (b) A natural ecosystem
   (c) An artificial ecosystem
   (d) A community of plants only

7. Which of the following is not an abiotic component of an ecosystem?
   (a) Edaphic factors (b) Saprotrophs
   (c) Climatic factors (d) Topographic factors

8. The structural component of the ecosystem includes:
   (a) Species composition
   (b) Stratification
   (c) Nutrient cycling
   (d) All except (c)

9. Which is an artificial ecosystem?
   (a) Herbarium (b) Tissue culture
   (c) Forest (d) Aquarium

10. Biotic component of an ecosystem includes:
    (a) Producers, consumers and decomposers
    (b) Producers and consumers only
    (c) Producers only
    (d) Consumers and decomposers only

11. Which is not a functional unit of an ecosystem?
    (a) Productivity (b) Decomposition
    (c) Stratification (d) Energy flow

12. Which of the following statements are correct?
    A. Ecosystem forms a self-sustaining or functional unit of the living world
    B. Entire biosphere is regarded as global ecosystem
    C. Anthropogenic ecosystem has high diversity and little productivity
    D. Ecosystem is normally a closed system
    (a) A and B only (b) A, C and D
    (c) A, B and C (d) A and D only

13. Which of the following characteristics are not true for artificial ecosystems?
    A. Simple food chain
    B. High productivity
    C. High species diversity
    D. Possess self-regulatory mechanisms

E. Little cycling of nutrients
(a) Only C and D (b) Only B, C and E
(c) Only A, C and D (d) All except E

14. The driving force for an ecosystem is:
(a) Biomass (b) Producers
(c) Decomposers (d) Solar energy

15. Ecosystem is:
(a) Always open
(b) Always closed
(c) Both open and closed depending upon community
(d) Both open and closed depending upon biomass

16. State true (T) or false (F) for the given statements regarding the biotic components of the ecosystem and select the correct option:
A. Producers are also known as transducers
B. Primary carnivores are also known as key industry animals
C. Top carnivores are not eaten by other animals
D. Bacteria, fungi and flagellates are decomposers of pond ecosystem and abundant at the bottom of the pond

	A	B	C	D
(a)	T	F	T	F
(b)	T	F	T	T
(c)	F	T	F	T
(d)	F	F	T	F

17. Stratification means vertical distribution of:
(a) Individuals of different species in temperate needle-like forest
(b) Individuals of the same species
(c) Producers, consumers and decomposers in the same species
(d) Trees, shrubs and herbs

18. Stratification is more common in:
(a) Tropical rain forest (b) Deciduous forest
(c) Temperate forest (d) Tropical savannah

19. The amount of biomass produced per unit area over a time period by plants during photosynthesis is referred to as:
(a) Primary production
(b) Secondary production
(c) Primary productivity
(d) Secondary productivity

20. The amount of biomass or organic matter produced per unit area over a time period by plants during photosynthesis is expressed in terms of:
(a) gm^{-2} (b) $K\ cal\ m^{-2}$
(c) $(K\ cal\ m^{-2})\ yr^{-1}$ (d) Both (a) and (b)

21. Which ecosystem has the maximum biomass?
(a) Lake ecosystem (b) Forest ecosystem
(c) Pond ecosystem (d) Grassland ecosystem

22. In an ecosystem, the rate of production of organic matter during photosynthesis is termed:
(a) Gross primary productivity
(b) Net productivity
(c) Net primary productivity
(d) Secondary productivity

23. Which of the following is correct about GPP and NPP in ecosystems?
(a) NPP = GPP – Plant respiration
(b) NPP = GPP + Plant respiration
(c) NPP = GPP – Animal respiration
(d) NPP = GPP + Animal respiration

24. Secondary productivity:
A. 10% higher than primary productivity
B. Is the available biomass for consumption by herbivores and decomposers
C. Is the rate of formation of new organic matter by consumers
Which of the statement(s) given above is/are correct?
(a) A, B and C (b) A and B
(c) C only (d) B only

25. Which of the following ecosystems is the most productive in terms of net primary production?
(a) Desert (b) Tropical rain forest
(c) Ocean (d) Estuary

26. The annual net primary productivity of the whole biosphere is approximately 170 billion tons of organic matter. Of this, despite occupying about 70% of the surface, the productivity of the oceans is only 55 billion tons. What is the reason behind the low productivity of oceans?
(a) Little light penetration in depth
(b) Nitrogen is limiting
(c) High availability of nitrogen and CO_2
(d) (a) and (b)

27. Storage of energy at the consumer's level is:
(a) Gross primary productivity
(b) Secondary productivity
(c) Net primary productivity
(d) Primary productivity

28. Which ecosystem has the highest gross primary productivity?

(a) Rain forest (b) Coral reefs
(c) Mangroves (d) Grassland

29. Which nutrient is most likely to limit primary production in terrestrial ecosystems?
(a) Carbon (b) Sulphur
(c) Phosphorus (d) Nitrogen

30. Productivity in terrestrial ecosystem is affected by:
(a) Temperature
(b) Light intensity
(c) Availability of nutrients and water
(d) All of the above

31. Breakdown of detritus into smaller particles by the earthworm is a process called:
(a) Humification (b) Fragmentation
(c) Mineralisation (d) Catabolism

32. Select the odd one out with respect to the steps of the decomposition process:
(a) Pedogenesis (b) Fragmentation
(c) Leaching (d) Catabolism

33. The most stable ecosystem is:
(a) Forest (b) Mountain
(c) Desert (d) Ocean

34. 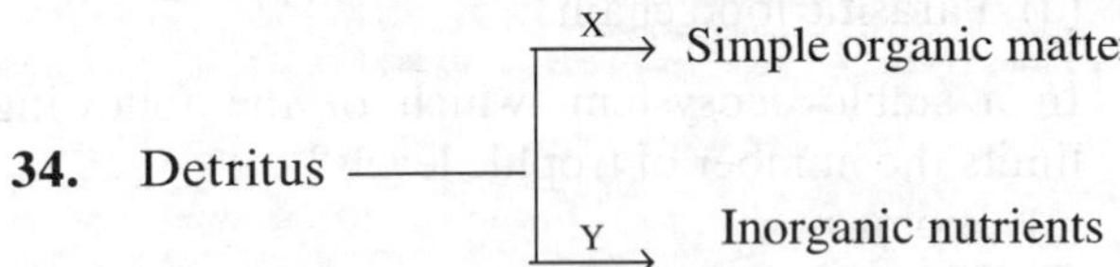

In the above flow chart, Y denotes:
(a) Fragmentation (b) Leaching
(c) Catabolism (d) Mineralisation

35. In which of the following processes of decomposition is there no direct role for living organisms?
(a) Fragmentation of detritus
(b) Leaching
(c) Mineralisation
(d) Humification

36. Consider the following statements A to D related to the decomposition process and select the correct option having two incorrect statements:
A. Microbial activity is very high in acidic soil and detritivores are abundant
B. Warm and moist environment inhibits the decomposition process, resulting in increase of organic matter
C. Reduced moisture will slow down the decomposition process
D. Excessive moisture impedes the decomposition process

(a) (A) and (D) (b) (A) and (B)
(c) (B) and (D) (d) (B) and (C)

37. The phenomenon of incorporation of nutrients in decomposers and detritivores is called:
(a) Humification
(b) Leaching
(c) Nutrient immobilisation
(d) Eluviation

38. In the pond ecosystem, decomposers are especially abundant:
(a) At the surface of the pond
(b) At the bottom of the pond
(c) At the edges of the pond
(d) All of the above

39. Decomposition rate is slow if detritus is rich in:
(a) Nitrogen (b) Lignin and chitin
(c) Humus (d) Simple sugars

40. Which of the following factors generally does not influence the process of decomposition of organic matter in soil?
(a) Chemical nature of detritus
(b) Soil aeration and temperature
(c) Humidity and soil pH
(d) Climatic conditions like light and wind current

41. Humus:
A. Is a dark-coloured amorphous compound
B. Is more or less decomposed organic matter
C. Is slightly acidic in nature
D. Is not easily attacked by microbes
E. Increases the water holding capacity of soil but decreases aeration in clay soil

How many of the above statements are correct?
(a) Two (b) Three
(c) Four (d) Five

Energy Flow, Ecological Pyramids

42. What per cent of PAR is captured for GPP?
(a) 1–5% (b) 2–10%
(c) 0.8–4% (d) 50%

43. Read the following statements (A–D) and select the option with all correct statements:
A. Of the total incident solar radiation, less than 50% is useful for photosynthesis
B. Plants utilise only 1–5% of PAR in the synthesis of organic matter
C. NPP is 0.8–4% of incident radiation
D. The sun is the only source of energy for all ecosystems on earth, except for the deep sea hydrothermal ecosystem

(a) (A) and (D) (b) (A) and (B)
(c) (A), (C) and (D) (d) (A), (B), (C) and (D)

44. The wavelength of PAR is:
(a) 400–700 nm
(b) More than UV radiation
(c) Less than UV rays
(d) Both (a) and (b)

45. The transfer of energy in a food chain is:
(a) Unidirectional (b) Multidirectional
(c) Bidirectional (d) Irreversible

46. The 10% law of energy transfer in food chain was given by:
(a) Stanley (b) Tansley
(c) Weismann (d) Lindeman

47. Trophic level in ecosystems are formed by:
(a) Only bacteria
(b) Only herbivores
(c) Organisms linked in the food chain
(d) Only plants

48. Mr. Gaurav is eating curd. For his food intake in a food chain, he should be considered as occupying?
(a) First trophic level
(b) Second trophic level
(c) Third trophic level
(d) Fourth trophic level

49. A food chain comprises:
(a) Producers, herbivores and carnivores
(b) Producers, consumers and decomposers
(c) Producers and primary consumers
(d) Producers, carnivores and decomposers

50. Which one occurs at the same trophic level?
(a) Crow and cow (b) Snake and earthworm
(c) Deer and bee (d) Tiger and wild bear

51. In which of the following is there no difference?
(a) T_1 and herbivores
(b) Primary consumer and herbivores
(c) Primary carnivore and T_2
(d) Secondary consumer and T_2

52. A food chain begins with:
(a) Photosynthetic organisms
(b) Consumers
(c) Herbivores
(d) Decomposers

53. Which is false about the food chain?
(a) Grazing food chain is a major conduit of energy for the aquatic food chain
(b) In a terrestrial ecosystem, a large fraction of energy flows through the detritus food chain
(c) Primary consumers belong to the first trophic level
(d) Detritus food chain begins with dead organic matter

54. Which organism occupies more than one trophic level in the same ecosystem at the same time?
(a) Sparrow (b) Goat
(c) Frog (d) Lion

55. The frog that feeds on an insect is a:
(a) Primary consumer
(b) Secondary carnivore
(c) Primary carnivore
(d) Key industry animal

56. Which of the following is the most diverse in a food chain?
(a) Herbivores (b) Producers
(c) Decomposers (d) Carnivores

57. The type of food chain in which the energy-rich organic matter produced by producers is decomposed by microbes and converted into an energy-rich compound is called:
(a) Detritus food chain
(b) Grazing food chain
(c) Auxiliary food chain
(d) Parasitic food chain

58. In a stable ecosystem, which of the following limits the number of trophic levels?
(a) Biomass
(b) The number of nutrients
(c) Availability of nutrients
(d) Presence of contaminant that increases in concentration along the food chain

59. Concept of ecological pyramids was proposed by:
(a) Odum (b) Reiter
(c) Elton (d) Tansley

60. Read the following statements about food chains and energy flow.
A. A single organism can feed at several trophic levels
B. The lower the trophic level at which an organism feeds, the more energy is available
C. Detritivores feed at all trophic levels, except the producer level
D. Food webs include two or more food chains
How many of the above statements are correct?
(a) Two (b) One
(c) Three (d) Four

61. When a peacock eats a snake which eat insects thriving on green plants, the peacock is:

(a) Top carnivore (b) Primary carnivore
(c) Final decomposer (d) Secondary consumer

62. The trophic level that converts plant matter into animal matter is:
(a) T_1 (b) T_2
(c) T_3 (d) T_4

63. Which of the following is a key industry animal?
(a) Cow (b) Tiger
(c) Snake (d) Frog

64. Food chains differ from food webs in that:
A. Food chains better represent the entire community
B. In a food chain, one organism can hold more than one position
C. Food webs represent the complex interactions among food chains
D. In a food web, the flow of energy is very difficult to calculate
(a) A and C (b) B and D
(c) C and D (d) B, C and D

65. Flow of energy declines as it passes from lower to higher trophic level. This is explained by:
(a) First law of thermodynamics
(b) Second law of thermodynamics
(c) Newton's second law
(d) Newton's third law

66. Which of the following is not used for the construction of ecological pyramids?
(a) Dry weight
(b) Number of individuals
(c) Rate of energy flow
(d) Fresh weight

67. Detritus food chain begins with:
(a) Primary producers
(b) Primary consumers
(c) Dead organic matter
(d) Secondary consumers

68. Earthworm is a:
(a) Herbivore
(b) Secondary consumer
(c) Tertiary consumer
(d) Detritivore

69. Most animals that live in deep oceanic waters are:
(a) Tertiary consumers
(b) Detritivores
(c) Primary consumers
(d) Secondary consumers

70. Read the following statements and select the correct option:
A. Populations of top-level predators are generally smaller than populations of primary consumers
B. The biomass of producers in an ecosystem is generally higher than the biomass of primary consumers
C. Only a small portion of the energy captured by producers is transferred to consumers
(a) Only (A) is correct
(b) Only (B) is correct
(c) Only (B) and (C) are correct
(d) (A), (B) and (C) are correct

71. Pyramid of numbers in a grassland ecosystem is:
(a) Spindle shaped (b) Upright
(c) Urn shaped (d) Inverted

72. The ecological pyramid given below:

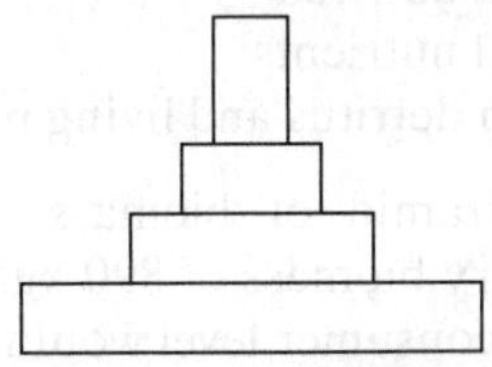

A. May be a pyramid of the energy of a pond ecosystem
B. May be the pyramid of biomass in an aquatic ecosystem
C. Assumes a complex food chain
D. May be a pyramid of numbers in a grassland ecosystem
(a) (A) and (B) (b) (A) and (D)
(c) (B) and (D) (d) (B) and (C)

73. Which of the following pyramids cannot be inverted?
(a) An ideal pyramid of energy
(b) Pyramid of biomass
(c) Pyramid of number
(d) All of the above

74. Which of the following is a common feature of DFC and GFC?
(a) Major conduit for energy flow in aquatic ecosystem
(b) Size of organism commonly increases at higher trophic level
(c) Always begins with producers
(d) Source of energy is the sun

75. The amount of nutrients such as carbon, nitrogen, phosphorus, calcium, etc., present in the soil at any given time is referred to as the:
(a) Standing crop (b) Standing state
(c) Standing quality (d) Both (b) and (c)

76. If 20 J of energy is trapped at producer level, how much energy will be available to a peacock as food in the following chain: Plant → Mice → Snake → Peacock
(a) 0.002 J (b) 0.2 J
(c) 0.0002 J (d) 0.02 J

77. Food web refers to:
(a) Transfer of energy from one trophic level to the next
(b) Unidirectional energy flow
(c) Capturing solar energy by autotrophs
(d) Connected feeding patterns in a biotic community

78. In an ecosystem, standing crop at any time consists of:
(a) Total living matter
(b) Total detritus
(c) Total nutrients
(d) Both detritus and living matter

79. In a pyramid of biomass, primary producers have a dry biomass of 890 kg/m^2. The biomass at tertiary consumer level would be:
(a) 37 kg/m^2 (b) 11 kg/m^2
(c) 5 kg/m^2 (d) 1.5 kg/m^2

80. Loss of energy from one trophic level to the next higher level is:
(a) 30% (b) 40%
(c) 60% (d) 90%

81. In an ecosystem, all the pyramids that are made up of number, energy and biomass:
A. Are upright
B. Saprophytes are not given any place
C. Do not accommodate a food web
(a) Only (B) (b) (B) and (C)
(c) (A) and (B) (d) (A), (B) and (C)

Ecological Succession, Nutrient Cycling, Ecosystem Services

82. Ecological succession is:
(a) Series of biotic communities that appear gradually in a barren area
(b) Gradual, convergent, directional and continuous process
(c) Orderly process of community change till stability
(d) All of the above

83. Who coined the term ecological succession?
(a) Hodges (b) Odum
(c) King (d) Hult

84. Ecological succession is:
(a) Directional but unpredictable
(b) Directionless but predictable
(c) Directional and predictable
(d) Directionless and unpredictable

85. Ecological succession is a:
(a) Long-term process
(b) Very fast process
(c) Process leading to the development of a population
(d) Migration

86. In biological succession, ecesis is:
(a) Establishment of a plant in a new place
(b) A condition of equilibrium
(c) Establishment of climax community
(d) Invasion of a number of plant species

87. The pioneer community of primary succession on the rocks is:
(a) Lichen (b) Moss
(c) Annual grass (d) Perennial grass

88. Intermediate community between pioneer and climax communities is called:
(a) Biotic community
(b) Seral community
(c) Temporary community
(d) Ecosere

89. All succession, whether taking place in water or on land, proceeds to a similar climax community, that is:
(a) Hydrosere (b) Xeric
(c) Mesic (d) Halosere

90. Which of the given areas are the sites of primary succession?
A. Newly cooled lava
B. Abandoned farmland
C. Cut forest
D. Bare rock
E. Flooded lands
F. Newly created pond
(a) A, B, D, F (b) A, D, E, F
(c) B, C, E (d) A, D, F

91. A primary succession starts with lichens. Which of the following lichens are responsible for biological weathering of rocks in the initial stages?
(a) Foliose (b) Fruticose
(c) Crustose (d) All of the above

92. Read the following statements with respect to secondary succession:
A. Occurs in the area where no living organism ever existed

B. Shows difficulty in establishment for the pioneer community
C. Takes a very long time to reach climax
D. Occurs in areas which already have some soil or sediment

How many of the above statement(s) is/are correct?
(a) Two (b) One
(c) Four (d) Three

93. The climax community remains stable:
(a) Even when environmental conditions are changing
(b) As long as the environment remains unchanged
(c) As long as heterotrophic members remain dominating
(d) Even when saprophytes are completely absent

94. Select the odd one out with respect to changes in ecosystem characteristics that occur during secondary succession:
(a) Species diversity increases
(b) Niche becomes more specific
(c) Decrease in humus content of soil
(d) Aquatic to dry condition to mesic condition

95. Select the correct sequence of stages in hydrarch succession:
(a) Phytoplankton stage → Submerged plant stage → Submerged free-floating stage → Marsh meadow stage → Reed swamp stage → Scrub stage → Forest stage
(b) Phytoplankton stage→ Submerged plant stage → Submerged free-floating stage → Reed swamp stage → Marsh meadow stage → Scrub stage → Forest stage
(c) Phytoplankton stage → Submerged free-floating stage → Submerged plant stage → Marsh meadow stage → Reed swamp stage → Scrub stage → Forest stage
(d) Phytoplankton stage → Submerged free-floating stage → Submerged plant stage → Reed swamp stage → Marsh meadow stage → Scrub stage → Forest stage

96. In the reed swamp stage during succession of pond succession, what is meant by reed?
(a) Rooted emergent (b) Free emergent
(c) Submerged floaters(d) Fixed submerged

97. The circulation or cycling of elements in an ecosystem is known as:
(a) Geological cycling
(b) Geochemical cycling
(c) Biogeochemical cycling
(d) Chemical cycling

98. Biogeochemical cycle with gaseous phase:
(a) Carbon (b) Sodium
(c) Phosphorus (d) Magnesium

99. Which one is a sedimentary cycle?
(a) Oxygen cycle (b) Nitrogen cycle
(c) Phosphorus cycle (d) Carbon cycle

100. Crystalline rocks are natural sources of the biogenetic element:
(a) Calcium (b) Phosphorus
(c) Magnesium (d) Sulphur

101. Which is incorrect regarding gaseous cycles?
(a) Exchange of nutrients occurs in vapour form
(b) Biogeochemical reservoir is non-mineral
(c) Exemplified by carbon cycle
(d) Reservoir pool is lithosphere

102. About 71% of global carbon is found in:
(a) Forests (b) Grassland
(c) Agroecosystem (d) Oceans

103. Role of bacteria in carbon cycle is:
(a) Photosynthesis
(b) Chemosynthesis
(c) Breakdown of organic compounds
(d) Assimilation of nitrogen compounds

104. Carbon constitutes 43% of the dry weight of organisms and is next only to water if we look at the total quantity. At global carbon, we find that total dissolved oceanic carbon is:
(a) 71% (b) 4 x 10^3 kg
(c) 1% (d) 20%

105. Which of the following statements is incorrect for the cycle given below:

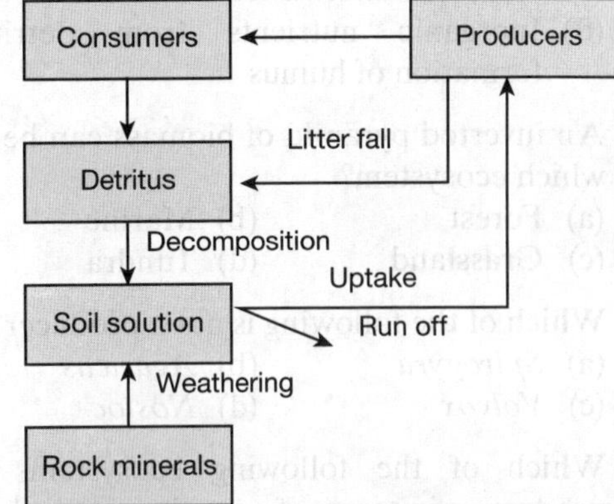

(a) There is no respiratory release in the atmosphere
(b) Reservoir is rock or the earth's crust
(c) Great exchanges between organism and environment
(d) Atmospheric inputs through rainfall are much smaller

106. Annual fixation of carbon through photosynthesis in biosphere is:
(a) 4×10^3 kg (b) 4×10^{13} kg
(c) 4×10^{30} kg (d) 4×10 kg

107. The valuable practical services that helps to preserve ecosystems which are performed by nature are called ________:
(a) Greenhouse effect
(b) Biological control
(c) Biosphere balancing
(d) Ecosystem services

108. According to Robert Costanza, 50% of the total cost of ecosystem services goes to:
(a) Climate regulation
(b) Soil formation
(c) Recreation
(d) Nutrient cycling

109. Robert Costanza and his colleagues have put the value of ecosystem services at 33 trillion US dollars. It is 6% for:
A. Soil formation
B. Climate regulation
C. Habitat for wildlife
D. Nutrient cycling
(a) (B) and (C) (b) (B) and (D)
(c) (C) and (D) (d) (A) and (B)

110. Of the total cost of various ecosystem services, nutrient cycling accounts for:
(a) 5% (b) 25%
(c) 10% (d) 50%

NCERT EXEMPLAR QUESTIONS

1. Decomposers like fungi and bacteria are:
(i) Autotrophs
(ii) Heterotrophs
(iii) Saprotrophs
(iv) Chemo-autotrophs
(a) (i) and (iii) (b) (i) and (iv)
(c) (ii) and (iii) (d) (i) and (ii)

2. The process of mineralisation by microorganisms helps in the release of:
(a) Inorganic nutrients from humus
(b) Both organic and inorganic nutrients from detritus
(c) Organic nutrients from humus
(d) Inorganic nutrients from detritus and formation of humus

3. An inverted pyramid of biomass can be found in which ecosystem?
(a) Forest (b) Marine
(c) Grassland (d) Tundra

4. Which of the following is not a producer?
(a) *Spirogyra* (b) *Agaricus*
(c) *Volvox* (d) *Nostoc*

5. Which of the following ecosystems is most productive in terms of net primary production?
(a) Deserts (b) Tropical rain forests
(c) Oceans (d) Estuaries

6. Pyramid of numbers is:
(a) Always upright
(b) Always inverted
(c) Either upright or inverted
(d) Neither upright nor inverted

7. Approximately how much of the solar energy that falls on the leaves of a plant is converted to chemical energy by photosynthesis?
(a) Less than 1% (b) 2–10%
(c) 30% (d) 50%

8. Among the following, where do you think the process of decomposition would be the fastest?
(a) Tropical rain forest
(b) Antarctic
(c) Dry arid region
(d) Alpine region

9. How much of the net primary productivity of a terrestrial ecosystem is eaten and digested by herbivores?
(a) 1% (b) 10%
(c) 40% (d) 90%

10. During the process of ecological succession, the changes that take place in communities are:
(a) Orderly and sequential
(b) Random
(c) Very quick
(d) Not influenced by the physical environment

11. Climax community is in a state of:
(a) Non-equilibrium (b) Equilibrium
(c) Disorder (d) Constant change

12. Among the following bio-geo-chemical cycles, which one does not have losses due to respiration?

(a) Phosphorus (b) Nitrogen
(c) Sulphur (d) All of the above

13. The sequence of communities of primary succession in water is:
(a) Phytoplankton, sedges, free-floating hydrophytes, rooted hydrophytes, grasses and trees
(b) Phytoplankton, free-floating hydrophytes, rooted hydrophytes, sedges, grasses and trees
(c) Free-floating hydrophytes, sedges, phytoplankton, rooted hydrophytes, grasses and trees
(d) Phytoplankton, rooted submerged hydrophytes, floating hydrophytes, reed swamp, sedges, meadow and trees

14. The reservoir for the gaseous type of bio-geochemical cycle exists in:
(a) Stratosphere (b) Atmosphere
(c) Ionosphere (d) Lithosphere

15. If the carbon atoms fixed by producers have already passed through three species, the trophic level of the last species would be:
(a) Scavenger
(b) Tertiary producer
(c) Tertiary consumer
(d) Secondary consumer

16. Which of the following types of ecosystems is expected in an area where evaporation exceeds precipitation, and mean annual rainfall is below 100 mm?
(a) Grassland (b) Shrubby forest
(c) Desert (d) Mangrove

17. The zone at the edge of a lake or ocean which is alternatively exposed to air and immersed in water is called:
(a) Pelagic zone (b) Benthic zone
(c) Lentic one (d) Littoral zone

18. Edaphic factor refers to:
(a) Water (b) Soil
(c) Relative humidity (d) Altitude

19. Which of the following is an ecosystem service provided by a natural ecosystem?
(a) Cycling of nutrients
(b) Prevention of soil erosion
(c) Pollutant absorption and reduction of the threat of global warming
(d) All of the above

PRACTICE TEST PAPER

1. Which of the following is not a functional component of the ecosystem?
(a) Energy flow (b) Decomposition
(c) Productivity (d) Species composition

2. Driving force of ecosystem is:
(a) Producers (b) Key industry animals
(c) Solar energy (d) Microorganisms

3. Bacteria and fungi enzymes degrade detritus into simpler inorganic substances. This process is called:
(a) Humification (b) Catabolism
(c) Mineralisation (d) Immobilisation

4. Community characteristic due to which organisms can grow to different heights is:
(a) Energy flow (b) Stratification
(c) Decomposition (d) Community diversity

5. Minimum components needed for an ecosystem to survive are:
(a) Producer and decomposers
(b) Primary consumer and decomposers
(c) Producers and primary consumers
(d) Producers and primary carnivores

6. Find the odd one out with respect to ecosystem functions:
(a) Nutrient cycling (b) Energy flow
(c) Decomposition (d) Stratification

7. Total amount of living organic matter present in a particular area at a particular time in an ecosystem is known as:
(a) Productivity (b) Standing crop
(c) Standing state (d) Biotic potential

8. The ecological pyramid of numbers for the grazing food chain of a grassland ecosystem is:
(a) Straight (b) Inverted
(c) Bell-shaped (d) Spindle-shaped

9. Which of the following groups of organisms belong to the second trophic level?
(a) Grasses, grasshopper, wolf
(b) Zooplankton, grasshopper, cow
(c) Phytoplankton, birds, fishes
(d) Trees, wolf, birds

10. Transfer of energy from organism to organism in a natural community establishes:
(a) Food chains (b) Biological control
(c) Natural barriers (d) All of the above

11. Food chain that has least trophic level is:
(a) Parasitic food chain
(b) Detritus food chain
(c) Grazing food chain
(d) Predatory food chain

12. Ecological pyramid does not accommodate:
(a) Food chain (b) Biomass
(c) Energy (d) Decomposer

13. Identify the following statements as true (T) or false (F) and select the option accordingly:
A. Net primary productivity is biomass available for consumption to heterotrophs
B. Secondary productivity is defined as the rate of formation of new organic matter by heterotrophs
C. The annual net primary productivity of the ocean is greater than that of land
D. Warm and moist environment favours decomposition

	A	B	C	D
(a)	T	T	F	T
(b)	T	T	F	F
(c)	F	F	T	T
(d)	T	F	F	T

14. All succession, whether it takes place in water or on land, proceeds to which climax community?
(a) Hydric (b) Xeric
(c) Mesic (d) Saline

15. What per cent of carbon is contained in the atmosphere out of total global carbon?
(a) 75% (b) 1%
(c) 30% (d) 50%

16. Limitations of ecological pyramids are:
A. It does not take into account the same species belonging to two or more trophic levels
B. It assumes a simple food chain
C. It does not accommodate food webs
D. Saprophytes are not given any place
(a) (A) and (B) only
(b) (B) and (D) only
(c) (A), (C) and (D) only
(d) (A), (B), (C) and (D)

17. What type of ecological succession would operate after a volcanic eruption and forest fire?
(a) Primary
(b) Primary and secondary, respectively
(c) Secondary and primary, respectively
(d) Secondary

18. In which of the following conditions does biomass degrade at a faster rate?
(a) Nitrogen rich content in detritus
(b) Anaerobic condition
(c) Low temperature
(d) High temperature and low moisture

19. Which of the following ecosystems has the highest gross primary productivity?
(a) Grassland (b) Tropical rain forest
(c) Desert (d) Deep ocean

20. Pyramid of energy is:
(a) Always upright (b) Upright or inverted
(c) Always inverted (d) Spindle shaped

21. Succession begins with invasion of a bare lifeless area by pioneers (a) which is later succeeded by bigger plants and ultimately a stable community (b) is formed. Choose the correct option for (a) and (b) in Lithosere.
(a) Phytoplanktons, trees
(b) Mosses, Grasses
(c) Lichens, trees
(d) Sedges, Grasses

22. Read the following statements and select the correct option
A: Pyramid of Biomass is inverted for aquatic ecosystem
B: Ecological pyramids consider simple food chains
(a) Only (A) is correct
(b) Only (B) is correct
(c) Both (A) and (B) are incorrect
(d) Both (A) and (B) are correct

23. Secondary succession
(a) Occurs in area which never had any vegetation
(b) Is faster than primary succession
(c) Does not follow any sequential steps
(d) Never predictable and is always slow

24. The process of degradation of humus by some microbes and release of inorganic nutrients is known as
(a) Mineralisation (b) Fragmentation
(c) Humification (d) Leaching

25. Which of the following contribute to the carbon cycle?
(a) Photosynthesis (b) Fossil fuel combustion
(c) Respiration (d) All of the above

26. A food chain that starts from plants and goes from smaller to larger animals is:
(a) Predator food chain
(b) Saprophytic food chain
(c) Detritus food chain
(d) Parasitic food chain

27. Tiger lies at the apex of the food chain because:
(a) Tiger has maximum biomass
(b) Tiger feeds on a number of herbivores which feed on a number of plants
(c) Tiger has many enemies
(d) Tiger is omnivorous

28. Seaweed belongs to the trophic level:
(a) Primary consumer (b) Decomposer
(c) Primary producer (d) Secondary consumers

29. Rate of conversion of light energy into chemical energy of organic molecules in an ecosystem is called:
(a) Net secondary productivity
(b) Net primary productivity
(c) Gross primary productivity
(d) Gross secondary productivity

30. Who has calculated the value of different ecosystem services?
(a) R Costanza (b) Elton
(c) AV Humboldt (d) David Tilman

31. The pyramid that cannot be inverted in a stable ecosystem is the pyramid of:
(a) Energy (b) Number
(c) Biomass (d) Both (b) and (c)

32. Which of the following words is related to *Homo sapiens*?
(a) Herbivore (b) Carnivore
(c) Autotroph (d) Omnivore

33. In a forest ecosystem, the pyramid of number is:
(a) Upright (b) Inverted
(c) Spindle shaped (d) Any of these

34. Top of ecological pyramid is occupied by:
(a) Herbivores (b) Carnivore
(c) Decomposers (d) Secondary consumer

35. The first fish that feeds upon planktonic forms is:
(a) Primary consumer (b) Carnivore
(c) Decomposer (d) Secondary consumer

36. Every ecosystem must have a continuous external source of:
(a) Energy (b) Oxygen
(c) Living organism (d) Bacteria

37. Mark the correct statement with reference to the phosphorus cycle:
(a) Inorganic phosphate is lost by leaching
(b) Ocean phosphates are lost by sedimentation
(c) Soluble phosphates are lost by erosion
(d) Soil has plenty of dissolved phosphate

38. The 'to eat and be eaten' relationship is called:
(a) Food chain (b) Food web
(c) Symbiosis (d) Phagocytosis

39. Trophic levels are formed by:
(a) Only plants
(b) Only animals
(c) Only carnivores
(d) Organisms linked in food chains

40. Energy flow and energy transformations in living systems strictly conform to the:
(a) Law of limiting factors
(b) Leibig law of minimum
(c) Law of thermodynamics
(d) Biogenetic low

41. In hydrosere, sedge meadow stage replaces:
(a) Submerged stage (b) Floating stage
(c) Scrub stage (d) Reed swamp stage

42. Choose the odd one with respect to the trophic level:
(a) Zooplanktons (b) Tadpole
(c) Grasshopper (d) Phytoplanktons

43. GFC are the major conduit for energy flow in:
(a) Aquatic ecosystem
(b) Agriculture ecosystem
(c) Grassland ecosystem
(d) Forest ecosystem

44. The biomass available for consumption by herbivores and decomposers is:
(a) Primary productivity
(b) Secondary productivity
(c) GPP
(d) NPP

45. Most animals that live in deep oceanic waters are:
(a) Tertiary consumers
(b) Detritivores
(c) Primary consumers
(d) Secondary consumers

ANSWER KEYS

Exercises

1. (d) **2.** (c) **3.** (d) **4.** (a) **5.** (b) **6.** (b) **7.** (b) **8.** (d) **9.** (d) **10.** (a)
11. (c) **12.** (a) **13.** (a) **14.** (d) **15.** (a) **16.** (b) **17.** (d) **18.** (a) **19.** (a) **20.** (d)
21. (b) **22.** (a) **23.** (a) **24.** (c) **25.** (b) **26.** (d) **27.** (b) **28.** (b) **29.** (c) **30.** (d)
31. (b) **32.** (a) **33.** (d) **34.** (d) **35.** (b) **36.** (b) **37.** (c) **38.** (b) **39.** (b) **40.** (d)
41. (c) **42.** (b) **43.** (c) **44.** (d) **45.** (a) **46.** (d) **47.** (c) **48.** (c) **49.** (a) **50.** (c)
51. (b) **52.** (a) **53.** (c) **54.** (a) **55.** (c) **56.** (c) **57.** (a) **58.** (c) **59.** (c) **60.** (c)
61. (a) **62.** (b) **63.** (a) **64.** (c) **65.** (b) **66.** (d) **67.** (c) **68.** (d) **69.** (b) **70.** (d)
71. (b) **72.** (b) **73.** (a) **74.** (b) **75.** (d) **76.** (d) **77.** (d) **78.** (a) **79.** (d) **80.** (d)
81. (b) **82.** (d) **83.** (d) **84.** (c) **85.** (a) **86.** (a) **87.** (a) **88.** (b) **89.** (c) **90.** (d)
91. (c) **92.** (b) **93.** (b) **94.** (c) **95.** (b) **96.** (a) **97.** (c) **98.** (a) **99.** (c) **100.** (b)
101. (d) **102.** (d) **103.** (c) **104.** (a) **105.** (c) **106.** (b) **107.** (d) **108.** (b) **109.** (a) **110.** (c)

NCERT Exemplar Questions

1. (c) **2.** (a) **3.** (b) **4.** (b) **5.** (b) **6.** (c) **7.** (b) **8.** (a) **9.** (b) **10.** (a)
11. (b) **12.** (d) **13.** (d) **14.** (b) **15.** (c) **16.** (c) **17.** (d) **18.** (b) **19.** (d)

Practice Test Paper

1. (d) **2.** (c) **3.** (b) **4.** (b) **5.** (a) **6.** (d) **7.** (b) **8.** (a) **9.** (b) **10.** (a)
11. (a) **12.** (d) **13.** (a) **14.** (c) **15.** (c) **16.** (d) **17.** (b) **18.** (a) **19.** (b) **20.** (a)
21. (c) **22.** (d) **23.** (b) **24.** (a) **25.** (d) **26.** (a) **27.** (b) **28.** (c) **29.** (c) **30.** (a)
31. (a) **32.** (d) **33.** (d) **34.** (b) **35.** (a) **36.** (a) **37.** (b) **38.** (a) **39.** (d) **40.** (c)
41. (d) **42.** (d) **43.** (a) **44.** (d) **45.** (b)

SOLUTIONS

Introduction, Structure and Function, Productivity, Decomposition

1. An ecosystem is the basic functional ecological unit in which living organisms interact among themselves and with their surrounding physical environment.
2. Ecosystem can maintain resilience.
3. The importance of ecosystem lies in the flow of energy, cycling of nutrients, productivity and decomposition.
4. Ecosystem homeostasis is all about equilibrium. So, an ecosystem in equilibrium is said to be in a relatively stable state.
5. All the fish in a coral reef
6. A pond is a natural ecosystem because it develops in nature without human support or interference.
7. Decomposers are biotic components of the ecosystem and they are saprotrophs.
8. Nutrient cycling is a functional aspect of the ecosystem.
9. Artificial ecosystems are crop field and aquarium. These ecosystems do not possess self-regulatory mechanism.
10. Producer, consumer and decomposer
11. Stratification is a structural unit of the ecosystem. Stratification is vertical distribution of different species occupying different levels. For example, in a forest ecosystem, trees occupy the top vertical strata of the forest, shrubs occupy the second layer, and herbs and grasses occupy the bottom layer.
12. Only (A) and (B) are correct. Anthropogenic (artificial) ecosystems have little diversity and high productivity. Any ecosystem is an example of an open system. Energy can enter the system in the form of sunlight and leave in the form of heat. In an open system, both matter and energy are exchanged between the system and its surrounding environment.
13. (C) and (D) are not true for artificial ecosystem. These ecosystems have little biodiversity and do not possess self-regulatory mechanism.
14. The driving force of an ecosystem is solar energy.
15. An ecosystem is always open.
16. Only B is false. Primary consumers are herbivores. They directly feed on producers. They are also called key industry animals because they convert plant matter into animal matter.
17. Stratification means vertical distribution of trees, shrubs and herbs in a forest ecosystem.
18. Stratification is more common in tropical rain forests.
19. The amount of biomass or organic matter produced per unit area over a time period in plants during photosynthesis is called primary production. It is expressed in terms of weight (gm^{-2}) or energy ($Kcal\ m^{-2}$).
20. Primary production is gm^{-2} or $Kcal\ m^{-2}$ while primary productivity is expressed as $(KCal\,m^{-2})yr^{-1}$ or $(gm^{-2})yr^{-1}$. The rate of biomass production per unit area over a time period by plants during photosynthesis is called productivity.
21. Forest ecosystem has the maximum biomass.
22. GPP is the rate of production of biomass by producers during photosynthesis per unit time and area.
23. NPP = GPP – Plant respiration. NPP is the biomass available for the consumption by heterotrophs.
24. The rate of formation of new organic matter by consumers is called secondary productivity.
25. The most productive ecosystems are coral reefs, tropical rain forests and sugar cane fields.
26. In deep marine habitats, light decreases with depth and nitrogen is the most limiting nutrient.
27. Secondary productivity

28. Coral reefs

29. Phosphorus is considered the dominant limiting nutrient in terrestrial ecosystems, while in the aquatic ecosystem, nitrogen is the most limiting mineral nutrient.

30. Productivity in terrestrial ecosystems is affected by (i) Photosynthetic capacity of producers, (ii) Sunlight, (iii) Temperature, (iv) Soil moisture and (v) Availability of nutrients.

31. The process of breakdown of detritus into smaller particles is called fragmentation and it is carried out by detritivores like earthworm and termite.

32. (i) Steps in decomposition; (ii) Fragmentation; (iii) Leaching; (iv) Catabolism; (v) Humification; (vi) Mineralisation. The process of soil formation is called pedogenesis.

33. Oceans are the most stable ecosystems. Other terrestrial ecosystems undergo changes but oceans remain stable for a long duration of time.

34. The enzymatic process by which degraded detritus is converted into simple organic matter is called humification. The mineralization process of release of inorganic substances is by degradation of humans by microbes.

35. The process by which a part of the water-soluble substances present in fragmented detritus go down into soil horizons and are precipitated as unavailable salts. Leaching has no direct role in living organisms.

36. (A) and (B) are incorrect. Most microbial processes inducing the decomposition of organic matter and cycling of nutrients are reduced in acidic soil because growth and reproduction of soil microbes are greatly reduced. Warm and moist environment favours the decomposition process. Temperature and soil moisture are the most importance climatic factors that regulate the decomposition process.

37. The phenomenon of incorporation of nutrients in living microbes is called nutrient immobilisation.

38. Fungi, bacteria and flagellates are decomposers of the pond ecosystem and they are abundant at the bottom of the pond.

39. The decomposition rate is slow if detritus is rich in lignin and chitin. The decomposition rate is higher when detritus is rich in nitrogen and water-soluble substances like sugars.

40. Option (d) is correct.

41. Four statements (a, b, c and d) are correct. Increasing the amount of humus in clay soil can help improve aeration, reduce water holding capacity and increase nutrient content. Humus would also reduce the density of clay soil through separation of its particles and allow air circulation.

Energy Flow, Ecological Pyramids

42. Photosynthetic active radiation (PAR) accounts for less than 50% of the total incident solar radiation. Plants absorb only 2–10% of PAR and only this amount of energy sustains the entire living world.

43. (A), (C) and (D) are correct. Plant utilise only 1–5% of incident solar radiation.

44. The wavelength of PAR is 400–700 nm (more than UV radiation).

45. The energy flow in an ecosystem is always unidirectional.

46. Ten per cent law of energy transfer was proposed by Lindeman in 1942.

47. The trophic level of an organism is the position it occupies in a food chain.

48. The first trophic level is occupied by the plants (producers). Second trophic level is occupied by cows which feeds on plants. The third trophic level is occupied by Mr. Gaurav who feeds on the product of cows, that is, curd.

Plants → Cow (curd) → Humans

T_1 T_2 T_3

49. A food chain comprises producers, herbivores and carnivores. As the decomposers (microbes like bacteria and fungi) decompose every organism at each trophic level, it is possible to place the decomposers at the specific tropic level, because they are related with each trophic level. That is why decomposers are not considered in the food chain.

50. Deer and bee occupy the same trophic level.

51. Herbivores are primary consumers.

52. A food chain begins with a photosynthetic organism or producer.

53. Primary consumers belong to the second trophic level.

Primary producers → Primary consumers →
First trophic level Second trophic level
Secondary consumers → Tertiary consumers
Third trophic level Fourth trophic level

54. Sparrow is a primary consumer when it eats seeds, fruit, etc. and a secondary consumer when it eats insects or worms.

55. Primary carnivore
Plant producer → Insect → Frog
Producer Herbivore Primary carnivore

56. Decomposers are most diverse because they decompose every organism at each trophic level.

57. Detritus food chain

58. Availability of nutrients limits the number of trophic levels in a stable ecosystem.

59. Concept of ecological pyramids was proposed by Elton. The relation between producers and consumers in an ecosystem can be graphically represented in the form of a pyramid called ecological pyramid. The common parameter used in preparing ecological pyramids are the number of individuals, biomass and energy at different trophic levels.

60. Three statements (a, b and d) are correct. Detritivores are animals which feed on detritus. For example, termites, earthworm, etc.

61. Peacock is the top carnivore. The carnivores that are not eaten by others are called top carnivores.

62. Herbivores convert plant matter into animal matter, so they constitute the second trophic level (T_2).

63. Herbivores (Cow) act as key industry animals because they convert plant matter into animal matter.

64. C and D are correct. In a food chain, organisms hold only one position while the food web better represents the entire community.

65. The energy lost at every trophic level in the form of heat follows the second law of thermodynamics.

66. Fresh weight is not used for the construction of ecological pyramids. Fresh weight of organisms and their body parts comprises the water content along with the actual dry weight. Fresh weight deviates with respect to the metabolism of different organisms taken under observation.

67. Detritus food chain (DFC) begins with dead organic matter or detritus.

68. Earthworm is a detritivore because it feeds on dead and decayed organic matter.

69. Most animals that live in oceanic waters are called benthos. They are scavengers or detritivores. These organisms include crustaceans, polychaetes, etc.

70. (A), (B) and (C) are correct.

71. In a grassland ecosystem, with successive trophic level, the number of individuals decreases; therefore, the pyramid of numbers is upright.

72. (A) and (D) are correct. Pyramid of biomass in an aquatic ecosystem is always inverted as the biomass of fishes is greater than that of phytoplanktons. The pyramid assumes a simple food chain and does not accommodate a food web.

73. The pyramid of energy is always upright because the flow of energy is unidirectional, from producer to consumer level.

74. In DFC and GFC, the size of organisms commonly increases at higher tropic level. GFC is a major conduit of energy flow in aquatic ecosystems while in terrestrial ecosystems, a much larger fraction of energy flows through DFC.

75. The amount of all the inorganic nutrients present in an ecosystem per unit area at a given time is called standing stage or standing quality.

76. Each trophic level transfers 10% of energy to the next trophic level.
Plant → Mice → Snake → Peacock
20 J 2 J 0.2 J 0.02 J

77. A number of food chains interconnected with each other and forming a web-like pattern is called food web.

78. The amount of living material present in different trophic levels at a given time is called standing crop. It is expressed as the number or biomass of organisms per unit area.

79. Total biomass of producers in a specific area is more than that of herbivores and it gradually decreases at each successive trophic level. It is least in top carnivores.

80. 90%

81. (A), (B) and (C) are correct.

Ecological Succession, Nutrient Cycling, Ecosystem Services

82. The sequential gradual and predictable changes in species composition in an area are called succession or ecological succession. It is a gradual, convergent and directional process. The community that is in near equilibrium with the environment is called a climax community.

83. Hult coined the term ecological succession.

84. The gradual, directional and fairly practicable change in the species composition of a given area is called ecological succession.

85. Succession occurred over millions of years and it takes a very long time to reach climax.

86. Successful germination of propagules and its establishment in a bare area is known as ecesis.

87. The species that invade a bare area are called pioneer species. Lichens are the pioneer species on a bare area during primary succession on rocks.

88. The transitional community between pioneer and climax communities is called seral community.

89. All succession, whether taking place in water or on land, proceeds to a similar climax community that is mesic.

90. (A), (D) and (F) are correct. Primary succession begins in areas where no living organisms ever existed. Therefore, the establishment of a community is very slow. For example, newly cooled lava, bare rock, newly created pond or reservoir.

91. The pioneer lichens on such habitats are usually crustose lichens.

92. Only one statement (A) is correct. Secondary succession begins in areas where natural biotic communities have been destroyed. For example, abandoned farm land, burred or cut forests. Pioneer communities are established with comparative ease. Since soil is available, it is a faster process.

93. The climax community remains stable as long as the environment remains unchanged.

94. During succession, human content in the soil increases.

95. Option (b) is correct.

96. In the reed swamp stage, reed means rooted emergent.

97. The movement of nutrient elements through various components (abiotic and biotic) of an ecosystem is called nutrient cycling or biogeochemical cycle.

98. Carbon cycle is a gaseous cycle. Its reservoir is the atmosphere and carbon occurs as gas or vapour.

99. Phosphorous cycle is a sedimentary cycle and its reservoir is the earth's crust.

100. The natural reservoir of phosphorous is rock, which contains phosphorous in the form of phosphate.

101. In the gaseous cycle, the reservoir pool is the atmosphere or hydrosphere.

102. Carbon constitutes 49% of the dry weight of an organism. 71% of carbon is found dissolved in oceans which is responsible for its regulation in atmosphere.

103. Bacteria and other microbes also contribute to the CO_2 pool by decomposition of dead organic matter

104. 71% of the carbon is found in oceans. It is estimated that 4×10^{13} kg of carbons is fixed annually in the biosphere through photosynthesis.

105. Atmospheric inputs of phosphorous though rainfall are much smaller than the carbon cycle and no respiratory release of phosphorous takes place in the atmosphere.

106. 4×10^{13} kg carbon is fixed through photosynthesis annually.

107. The products of the ecosystem process are called ecosystem services.

108. Formation of soil accounts for about 50% of the total cost of various ecosystem services.

109. Climate regulation and habitat for wildlife costs about 6% each.

110. Contribution of nutrient cycling is 10%.

Biodiversity and Conservation

EXERCISES

Biodiversity (How Many Species Are There on Earth and How Many in India, Pattern of Biodiversity, Latitudinal Gradient, Species–Area Relationship)

1. _________ popularised the term biodiversity to describe combined diversity at all levels of biological organisation:
(a) Edward Wilson
(b) David Tilman
(c) Alexander Von Humboldt
(d) Robert Costanza

2. The genetic variation shown by the medicinal pant *Rauwolfia vomitoria* growing in different Himalayan ranges might be termed _________:
(a) Allelic variation
(b) Ability to form subspecies
(c) Potency and concentration of the active chemical reserpine that the plant produces
(d) Ability to adapt to environmental conditions

3. The variety of indigenous cows is an example of:
(a) Species diversity (b) Genetic diversity
(c) Global diversity (d) Ecological diversity

4. India has more than _________ genetically different strains of mango:
(a) 100 (b) 50,000
(c) 1000 (d) 1,500

5. Occurrence of several hundred varieties of mango in our country with different shapes, colours and flavours explains:
(a) Genetic diversity (b) Species diversity
(c) Ecological diversity(d) Global diversity

6. Maximum diversity, called taxonomic diversity, occurs when species of taxonomically:
(a) Different groups occur in almost equal abundance
(b) Different groups occur in different proportions
(c) Same groups occur in almost equal abundance
(d) Same groups occur in different proportions

7. In our country, _________ different strains of rice are found due to _________:
(a) 1000, species diversity
(b) 50,000, genetic diversity
(c) 1000, genetic diversity
(d) 50,000, species diversity

8. Biologists performed a statistical comparison of _________species from temperate and tropical areas to estimate the number of species on earth:
(a) Amphibians (b) Fishes
(c) Insects (d) Fungi

9. Biodiversity that is based on species richness and species evenness is:
(a) Genetic diversity (b) Species diversity
(c) β diversity (d) Regional diversity

10. A very large number of amphibian species are endemic to:
(a) Northeast
(b) Western Ghats
(c) Northwest Himalayas
(d) Andaman and Nicobar islands

11. Which of the following types of diversity enables a population to adapt to the environment to help in formation of ecotype and to respond to natural selection?
(a) Genetic (b) Species
(c) Community (d) Ecological

12. The diversity of communities along the environmental gradient is called:

(a) Alpha diversity (b) Beta diversity
(c) Gamma diversity (d) Omega diversity

13. A table of species diversity in different areas is given below:

↓	Taxonomic group					
	I	II	III	IV	V	
A	5	5	–	–	15	Number of individuals
B	10	4	3	2	–	
C	5	4	4	5	6	
D	8	–	4	3	9	

Identify the most diverse area:
(a) A (b) D
(c) B (d) C

14. It is hard to believe that there are more than 2,00,000 species of ants, 3,00,000 species of beetles, ___A___ species of fish and nearly ___B___ species of orchids:

	A	B
(a)	28,000	20,000
(b)	20,000	28,000
(c)	50,000	1,000
(d)	1,000	50,000

15. According to the IUCN (2004), the total number of plant and animal species described so far is slightly more than:
(a) 1.5 million (b) 1.5 billion
(c) 7 million (d) 7 billion

16. According to Robert May, global species diversity is about:
(a) 1.5 million (b) 7 million
(c) 15 million (d) 11.4 million

17. Select the correct option with respect to India for area covered (A) and global diversity (B):

	A	B
(a)	8.1%	2.4%
(b)	2.4%	8.1%
(c)	1.7%	8.1%
(d)	1.5%	5.1%

18. The number of fungi species in the world is more than the combined total of the species of:
(a) Fishes + Amphibians
(b) Amphibians + Reptiles
(c) Fishes + Amphibians + Reptiles
(d) Fishes + Amphibians + Reptiles + Mammals

19. Among vertebrates, the most species-rich taxonomic group is:
(a) Fishes (b) Insects
(c) Mammals (d) Birds

20. Biologists are not sure how many prokaryotic species there may be. The problem is that:
(a) Microbes are microscopic
(b) Conventional taxonomic methods are not suitable for identifying microbial species
(c) Many microbial species are simply not culturable
(d) More than one option is correct

21. David Tilman performed a long-term ecosystem experiment using outdoor plots. Select the correct option:
A. Plots with more species showed lower year-to-year variation in total biomass
B. Plots with fewer species showed lower year-to-year variation in total biomass
C. Increased diversity contributed to higher productivity
D. Plots with more species showed greater year-to-year variation in total biomass
(a) (A) and (C) (b) (A) and (D)
(c) (B) and (C) (d) (A), (C) and (D)

22. High species diversity is essential for:
A. High productivity
B. Stability
C. Resilience
D. Ecosystem health
(a) Only (A) and (B)
(b) Only (B) and (D)
(c) Only (A), (B) and (D)
(d) (A), (B), (C), (D)

23. The Rivet Popper Hypothesis was proposed by:
(a) Paul Ehrlich (b) Robert May
(c) Mayr (d) Von Humboldt

24. According to the Rivet Popper Hypothesis, in an aeroplane, all the parts are joined together using thousands of rivets. The aeroplane and rivets stand for:
(a) Habitat and organism
(b) Ecosystem and species
(c) Biosphere and ecosystem
(d) Ecosystem and key species

25. According to the analogy used by Paul Ehrlich, loss of rivets on the wings of an aeroplane can be related to:
(a) Mass extinction of species from the ecosystem
(b) Loss of habitat
(c) Loss of keystone species that drive the major ecosystem functions
(d) Loss of non-functioning producers in the ecosystem

26. Sample plot with maximum biodiversity is:
(a) Parrot – 8, Beetle – 16, Crow – 18, Deer – 8

(b) Pigeon – 8, Crow – 12, Lizard – 10
(c) Elephant – 4, Insect – 4, Lizard – 4, Pigeon – 4
(d) Lion – 8, Aphid – 15, Deer – 20

27. Species diversity decreases from lower to higher altitudes on mountains. This is due to:
(a) Increase in temperature
(b) Decrease in temperature
(c) Greater seasonal variability
(d) Both (b) and (c)

28. The pattern of biodiversity is affected by:
(a) Latitudinal gradient
(b) Species–area relationship
(c) Both of the above
(d) None of the above

29. Who observed that within a region, species richness increased with increasing explored area but only up to a limit:
(a) Paul Ehrlich (b) David Tilman
(c) A Von Humboldt (d) Edward Wilson

30. Given below is a representation of the extent of global diversity of invertebrates. What groups do the four labels (A – D) represent, respectively?

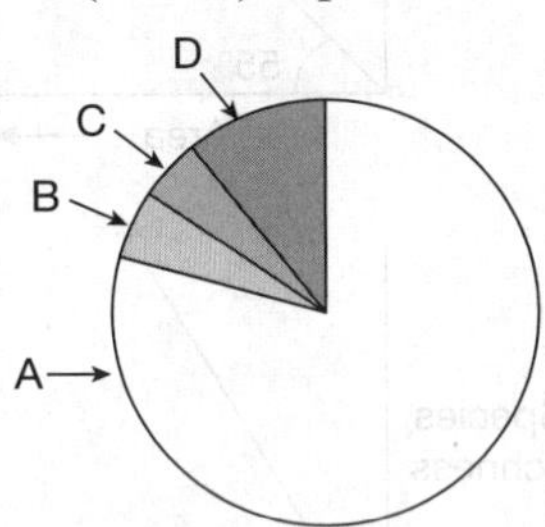

	A	B	C	D
(a)	Insects	Molluscs	Crustaceans	Other animal groups
(b)	Insects	Crustaceans	Molluscs	Other animal groups
(c)	Molluscs	Other animal groups	Crustaceans	Insects
(d)	Crustaceans	Insects	Other animal groups	Molluscs

31. Read the following statements and select the correct option:
A: More than 70% of all the species recorded are animals, while plants comprise no more than 22% of the total
B: Among animals, insects are the most species-rich taxonomic group, making up more than 70% of the total
(a) Only (A) is correct
(b) Only (B) is correct
(c) Both (A) and (B) are correct
(d) Both (A) and (B) are incorrect

32. The given pie diagram represents the proportionate number of species of major taxa of vertebrates. Identify the groups A, B and C:

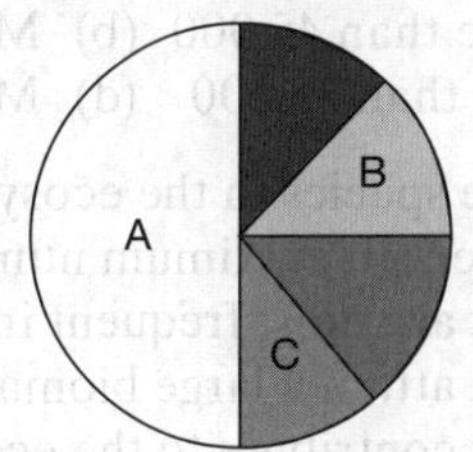

	A	B	C
(a)	Fishes	Birds	Reptiles
(b)	Fishes	Birds	Amphibians
(c)	Birds	Mammals	Fishes
(d)	Reptiles	Birds	Mammals

33. Identify the groups of organisms marked A and B in the given pie diagram, representing the proportionate number of species of major taxa of plants:

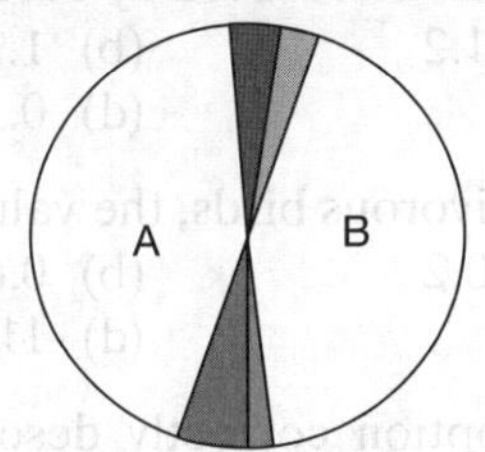

	A	B
(a)	Fungi	Angiosperm
(b)	Angiosperms	Fungi
(c)	Fungi	Lichens
(d)	Angiosperms	Algae

34. Pattern of biodiversity depends upon:
(a) Latitudinal gradient
(b) Altitudinal gradient
(c) Species–area relationship
(d) All of the above

35. In the species–area relationship, on a logarithmic scale, the relationship is:
(a) Rectangular hyperbola
(b) Rectangular parabola
(c) Straight line
(d) Sigmoid

36. According to May's global estimates, only 22% of the total species have been recorded so far. If this

proportion is applied to India's diversity figure, how many species are yet to be discovered and described?
(a) 3 lakh plant and animal species
(b) 3 lakh plant species and 1 lakh animal species
(c) 1 lakh plant species and 3 lakh animal species
(d) Almost 2 lakh plant species and double the number of animal species

37. How many animal species have been recorded from India?
(a) More than 45,000 (b) More than 20,000
(c) Less than 45,000 (d) More than 90,000

38. Keystone species in the ecosystem are those:
(a) Present in maximum number
(b) That are most frequent in a community
(c) That attain a large biomass
(d) That contribute to the ecosystem's properties

39. In the equation, $\log S = \log C + Z \log A$, what does Z represent?
(a) Species richness
(b) Area
(c) Regression coefficient
(d) Y intercept

40. Regardless of taxonomic group region, what is the value of Z, discovered by ecologists?
(a) 0.6–1.2 (b) 1.15
(c) 1.2 (d) 0.1–0.2

41. For frugivorous birds, the value of Z suggested is:
(a) 0.1–0.2 (b) 0.6–1.2
(c) 1.15 (d) 11.5

42. Which option correctly describes the equations for curves A and B in the given graph of a species–area relationship?

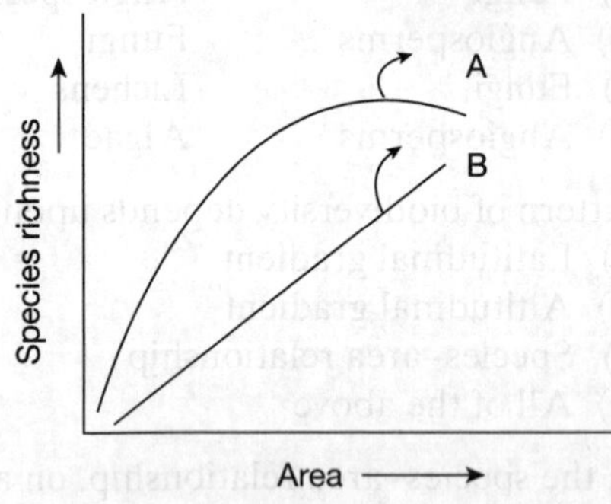

	A	B
(a)	$S = CA^2$	$\log S = \log C + Z \log A$
(b)	$\log S = \log C + Z \log A$	$S = CA^2$
(c)	$\log C = \log S + Z \log A$	$S = CA^2$
(d)	$S = CA^2$	$\log C = \log S + Z \log A$

43. More species in a community tends towards greater stability than communities with fewer species. This statement is supported by:
(a) David Tilman (b) Humboldt
(c) Paul Ehrlich (d) Both (a) and (b)

44. Which of the following curves represents the highest value of regression coefficient and species richness?

(a)

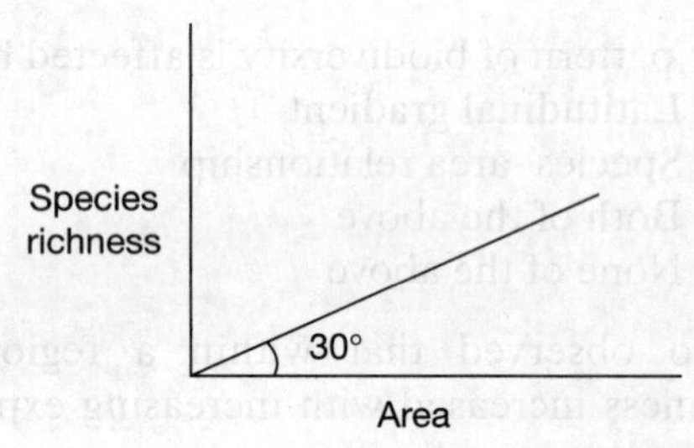

(b)

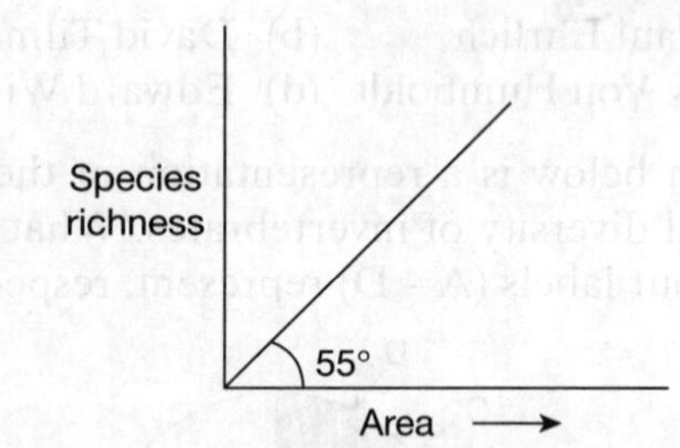

(c)

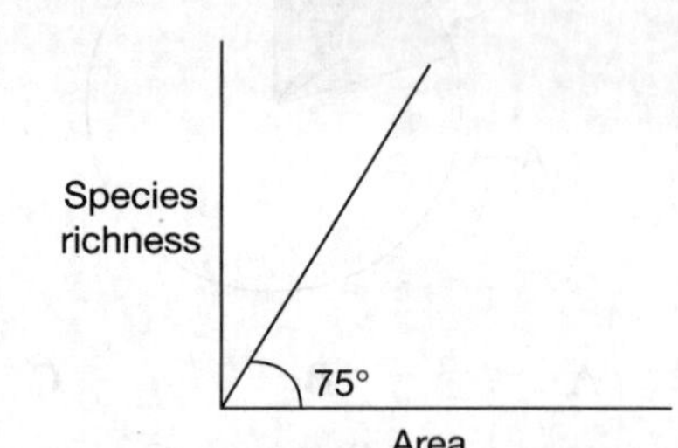

(d)

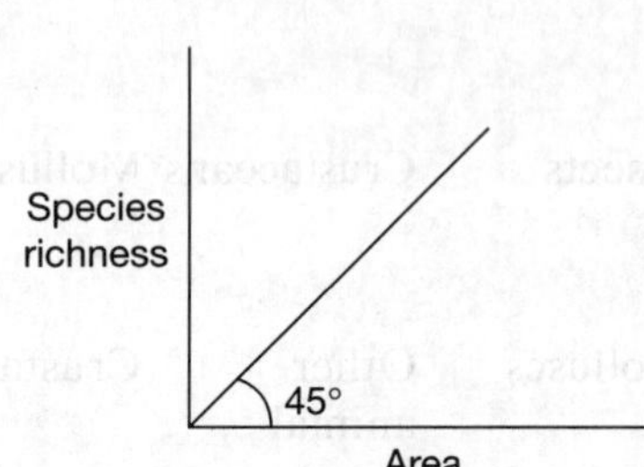

45. The species–area relationship is used by ecologists to:
(a) Determine the population density of a species in a certain habitat
(b) Examine how human populations are growing
(c) Estimate the number of species extinctions resulting from habitat destruction
(d) Determine how much area is required for a species

46. Speciation is generally a function of:
(a) Area (b) Time
(c) Volume (d) Both (a) and (b)

47. The tropics have higher biological diversity because:
(a) Lower humidity and temperature
(b) They have low pest pressure
(c) They have smaller seasonal variations but an unpredictable environment
(d) They had more evolutionary time for species diversification

48. The equator has up to ________ times as much biodiversity as the mid-west of USA:
(a) 2 (b) 10
(c) 4 (d) 20

49. Identify the following statements as true (T) or false (F) and select the option accordingly:
A. Biodiversity shows latitudinal gradient
B. Tropics are rich in biodiversity
C. There are 8 mega diversity regions in the world
D. Plant diversity is greater than animal diversity

	A	B	C	D
(a)	T	T	F	F
(b)	T	T	F	T
(c)	T	F	T	T
(d)	F	T	F	T

50. Biodiversity increases from:
A. Poles to equator
B. Equator to poles
C. Lower to higher altitudes
D. Higher to lower altitudes
(a) (A) and (C) (b) (B) and (C)
(c) (A) and (D) (d) (B) and (D)

Importance of Species (Diversity in the Ecosystem, Loss of Biodiversity, Conservation of Biodiversity)

51. IUCN Red List (2004) extinction of 784 species includes:
(a) 335 vertebrates, 360 invertebrates and 89 plants
(b) 337 vertebrates, 362 invertebrates and 88 plants
(c) 338 vertebrates, 359 invertebrates and 87 plants
(d) 340 vertebrates, 357 invertebrates and 87 plants

52. Percentage of angiosperms of all the threatened species is:
(a) 51% (b) 42%
(c) 28% (d) 18%

53. Number of plant species estimated to be present in India is:
(a) 40,000 (b) 45,000
(c) 58,000 (d) 80,000

54. A population characteristic of a species susceptible to extinction is:
A. Large body size
B. Small population size and low reproductive rate
C. Feeding at high trophic level
D. Fixed migratory roots and habitat
(a) Only (A) and (C) (b) (A), (B), (C)
(c) Only (C) (d) (A), (B), (C) and (D)

55. Species endangered due to low reproduction rate is:
(a) Giant panda (b) Lion
(c) Bald eagle (d) Island species

56. A threatened species is:
(a) Endangered (b) Rare
(c) Vulnerable (d) All of the above

57. The Red List contains data or information on:
(a) All economically important plants
(b) Plants whose products are in international trade
(c) Threatened species
(d) Marine vertebrates only

58. The giant panda is the official symbol of the WWF (World Wild Fund for Nature). In which country is this animal found?
(a) China (b) India
(c) Myanmar (d) New Zealand

59. International Union for Conservation of Nature (IUCN) was founded by:
(a) USA (b) UNESCO
(c) European Union (d) Great Britain

60. IUCN has its headquarters in:
(a) North America (b) South America
(c) Switzerland (d) Rome

61. The organisation responsible for maintaining the Red Data Book is:
(a) IUCN (b) WWF
(c) WWE (d) IBWN

62. All the biodiversity hotspots of the world occupy an area of:

(a) Less than 2% (b) 12%
(c) 5% (d) 9%

63. The Amazon rain forest is being cut and cleared for cultivating __________ or for conversion to grassland for raising beef cattle:
(a) Soya beans (b) Potato
(c) Cotton (d) Rice

64. IUCN stands for:
(a) Indian Union for Conservation of Nature
(b) International Union for Conservation of Nature
(c) Indian Union for Chemical Nomenclature
(d) International Union for Conservation of Nutrients

65. In India, the Red List of plant species is prepared by:
(a) Botanical Survey of India
(b) Forest Department of India
(c) Geological Survey of India
(d) Census Department of India

66. Most of the endangered species are victims of:
(a) Acid rain
(b) Competition with introduced species
(c) Habitat destruction
(d) Hunting by humans

67. Which of the following faces the maximum threat of extinction?
(a) Birds (b) Amphibians
(c) Mammals (d) Gymnosperms

68. How many species are presently facing the threat of extinction?
(a) 1000 (b) 7840
(c) 15,500 (d) 1500

69. What percentage of bird species are facing the worldwide threat of extinction?
(a) 12% (b) 23%
(c) 32% (d) 31%

70. Match Column I and Column II and select the correct option:

Column I (Extinct species)	Column II (Place where they belong)
A. Thylacine	(i) Mauritius
B. Dodo	(ii) Africa
C. Steller's sea cow	(iii) Australia
D. Quagga	(iv) Russia

(a) A – (iii), B – (iv), C – (i), D – (ii)
(b) A – (iii), B – (i), C – (iv), D – (ii)
(c) A – (ii), B – (iv), C – (i), D – (iii)
(d) A – (iv), B – (iii), C – (ii), D – (i)

71. The loss of 2000 species of native birds from the tropical Pacific islands was due to:
(a) Extreme environmental conditions
(b) Alien species invasion
(c) Human colonisation
(d) Epidemic of bird flu

72. The last 20 years alone have witnessed the disappearance of:
(a) 787 species (b) 27 species
(c) 127 species (d) 87 species

73. The IUCN Red List (2004) documents the extinction of how many species in the last 500 years?
(a) 784 (b) 359
(c) 84 (d) 2000

74. Some examples of recent extinctions include the following three subspecies of tiger:
(a) Dodo, Bali and Caspian
(b) Dodo, Quagga and Bali
(c) Bali, Javan and Caspian
(d) Thylacine, Quagga and Bali

75. Presently, __________% of all gymnosperm species in the world is facing the threat of extinction:
(a) 31 (b) 12
(c) 23 (d) 32

76. Exploring molecular-, genetic- and species-level diversity for products of economic importance like medicines is called:
(a) Biopiracy (b) Bioprospecting
(c) Bioprocessing (d) Biomagnification

77. More than 25% of drugs are derived from plants. What is the benefit of the study of these plants?
(a) Ethical value (b) Narrowly utilitarian
(c) Broadly utilitarian (d) Aesthetic value

78. The Amazon forest is estimated to produce through photosynthesis __________ of the total O_2 in the earth's atmosphere:
(a) 10% (b) 20%
(c) 30% (d) 50%

79. The narrowly utilitarian arguments for conserving biodiversity are all of the following, except:
(a) Humans derive countless direct economic benefits from nature
(b) Construction material, industrial products
(c) Products of medicinal importance
(d) Pollination and soil formation

80. Broadly utilitarian argument for conserving biodiversity relates to the:

(a) Ecosystem services that nature provides
(b) Aesthetic pleasures we derive from nature
(c) Direct economic benefits
(d) All except (c)

81. Bioprospecting is related to:
(a) Narrowly utilitarian
(b) Broadly utilitarian
(c) Ethical
(d) Both (b) and (c)

82. Biodiversity Act of India was passed by parliament in:
(a) 1992 (b) 2002
(c) 2004 (d) 2012

83. Which animal has become extinct in India?
(a) Snow leopard (b) Hippopotamus
(c) Wolf (d) Cheetah

84. Mass extinction of species as a result of human activity represents depletion of biodiversity, called:
(a) Background extinction
(b) Sixth extinction
(c) Rapid extinction
(d) Secondary extinction

85. The term "The Evil Quartet" is related to:
(a) Four major causes of forest loss
(b) Four major causes of population explosion
(c) Four major causes of pollution in the Ganga river
(d) Four major causes of biodiversity loss

86. In recent years, the number of species driven to extinction has increased dramatically. Which of the following is not a reason for this?
(a) Over-exploitation
(b) Habitat destruction
(c) Natural parasites
(d) Introduction of alien species

87. Many marine fish populations around the world are extensively harvested, endangering the continued existence of some commercially important species. This is an example of:
(a) Habitat destruction
(b) Over-exploitation
(c) Alien species invasion
(d) Co-extinction

88. Decrease in the biological wealth of plants is mostly due to:
(a) Climate change (b) Natural calamities
(c) Human activities (d) Volcanic eruption

89. In the last 500 years, we have lost so many species, such as Steller's sea cow and passenger pigeon, because of:
(a) Habitat loss and fragmentation
(b) Over-exploitation
(c) Alien species invasion
(d) Co-extinction

90. Extinction of more than 200 species of cichlid fish in Lake Victoria in East Africa was due to:
(a) Co-evolution (b) Habitat destruction
(c) Over-exploitation (d) Alien species invasion

91. The exotic species which was introduced in India is:
(a) *Lantana*
(b) *Eicchornia*
(c) *Parthenium*
(d) More than one option is correct

92. Which of the following fishes is an exotic species introduced in India for aquaculture?
(a) Dog fish (b) Shark
(c) *Clarias gariepinus* (d) Coloured fish

93. Which among the following can be considered an example of co-extinction?
A. Obligatory associated plant and animal species
B. Plant pollinator mutualism
C. Aquaculturing of *Clarias* with indigenous catfish
(a) Only (A) and (B) (b) (A) and (C)
(c) Only (A) (d) (A), (B) and (C)

94. The term used for conservation of ecosystems and natural habitats and the maintenance and recovery of viable populations of species in their natural habitat is:
(a) Core conservation
(b) Ex-situ conservation
(c) In-situ conservation
(d) Off-site conservation

95. Hot spot of biodiversity means:
(a) Areas of the earth that contain entire communities in a particular area
(b) Species serves as proxy for entire communities in a particular area
(c) Species in a particular niche/area
(d) Species diversity in a particular area

96. To designate priority areas for in-situ conservation, Norman Myers developed the 'hot spots' concept in:

(a) 1975 (b) 1988
(c) 1972 (d) 1999

97. Number of biodiversity hot spots in the world is:
(a) 52 (b) 25
(c) 34 (d) 14

98. Number of hot spots in our country is:
(a) 25 (b) 3
(c) 14 (d) 34

99. Number of national parks, biosphere reserves and wildlife sanctuaries that are currently operating in India at present:
(a) 90, 14, 448 (b) 90, 25, 448
(c) 90, 34, 448 (d) 89, 14, 338

100. A particular area exhibits the following key features:
A. Reserved for the betterment of wildlife, both flora and fauna
B. Private ownership is not allowed
C. Grazing, cultivation, forestry is not permitted
After careful analysis of the condition, you should consider that area as a:
(a) Botanical garden (b) National park
(c) Wildlife sanctuary (d) Biosphere reserve

101. Which of the following is considered a hot spot of biodiversity in India?
(a) Aravalli hills (b) Western Ghats
(c) Eastern Ghats (d) Indo-Gangetic plains

102. Sacred groves are unique and useful because:
(a) It is a in-situ strategy of conservation
(b) Promotes alien invasion
(c) It is the last refuge for a large number of rare plants
(d) Both (a) and (c)

103. An endemic species is:
(a) One found in many different geographic areas
(b) One found naturally and in one geographic area
(c) One found only in forests
(d) One that has been introduced to a new geographic area

104. Project Tiger, a programme to maintain a viable population of tigers in the country and to chalk out areas for their habitat, was launched in the year:
(a) 1975 (b) 1973
(c) 1974 (d) 1971

105. Tiger is not a resident in which of the following national parks?
(a) Jim Corbett (b) Ranthambore
(c) Sundarbans (d) Gir

106. Which of the following national parks is home to the famous musk deer or hangul?
(a) Keibul Lamjao National Park, Manipur
(b) Bandhavgarh National Park, Madhya Pradesh
(c) Eaglenest Wildlife Sanctuary, Arunachal Pradesh
(d) Dachigam National Park, Jammu and Kashmir

107. Which is the national aquatic animal of India?
(a) Blue whale (b) Seahorse
(c) Gangetic shark (d) River dolphin

108. Manas National Park in Assam is popular for its project:
(a) Elephant (b) Lion
(c) Snow leopard (d) Black buck

109. Which of the following is not an ex-situ conservation?
(a) Botanical garden (b) Zoological park
(c) Biosphere reserve (d) Cryopreservation

110. Convention on biodiversity came into force on:
(a) 29 December 1993 (b) 6 June 1992
(c) 4 October 1993 (d) 3 October 1994

111. Fill in the blanks and select the correct option:
(i) Wildlife Act was enacted in India in ____A____.
(ii) MAB programme of UNESCO was launched in ____B____.

	A	B
(a)	1972	1971
(b)	1972	1975
(c)	1971	1972
(d)	1986	1975

112. A sacred lake is:
(a) Dal Lake
(b) Khecheopalri Lake of Sikkim
(c) Surajkund Lake
(d) Chilka Lake

113. The jungle in Rudyard Kipling's *The Jungle Book* describes which part of the Indian forest?
(a) Central Indian forest near Satpura range
(b) Uttarakhand forest
(c) Himalayan forest in Himachal
(d) Nilgiri jungles

114. How many of the following approaches are used for ex-situ conservation?
(i) Seed banks
(ii) Gene banks
(iii) Tissue culture
(iv) Arboreta
(v) Cryopreservation

(vi) Home gardens
(a) Three (b) Six
(c) Four (d) Five

115. Refer to the given statements representing different zones of biosphere reserves:
A. Limited human activity is allowed for research and educational purposes
B. Legally protected and completely undisturbed from human interference
C. Active co-operation occurs between reserve management and local people for activities like cropping, forestry, settlement and recreation

Choose the correct answer:

	A	B	C
(a)	Core zone	Buffer zone	Manipulation zone
(b)	Buffer zone	Core zone	Transition zone
(c)	Buffer zone	Transition zone	Natural zone
(d)	Transition zone	Buffer zone	Manipulation zone

116. Endangered or threatened animals and plants are taken out of their natural habitat and given special care and protection in:
(a) Zoological parks and botanical gardens
(b) Biosphere reserves
(c) National parks
(d) Wildlife sanctuaries

117. The ex-situ conservation of biodiversity does not include:
(a) Botanical gardens, zoos
(b) Gene, pollen, seed bank
(c) Tissue culture and cryopreservation methods
(d) Protected areas as national parks

118. Conservation hot spots are best described as:
(a) Areas where a large number of endemic species are disappearing rapidly
(b) Areas where people are particularly active supporters of biological diversity
(c) Islands that are experiencing high rates of extinction
(d) Areas where natural species are being replaced by alien species

119. Of the following organisms, which has the highest conservation priority?
(a) A plant found on North America and in Europe
(b) A plant endemic to New Zealand
(c) A plant found in different geographical regions
(d) A plant found worldwide

120. Read the following statements with respect to hot spots:
A. Currently, 34 hot spots are recognised with an area less than 2% of the total land area
B. Three of the hot spots — Western Ghats and Sri Lanka, Indo-Burma and the Himalayas — cover our country's exceptionally high biodiversity regions
C. Regions with high level of species and low degree of endemism
(a) Only (A) is correct
(b) Only (B) is correct
(c) Only (C) is incorrect
(d) (A), (B) and (C) are incorrect

121. Sacred groves are especially useful in:
(a) Generating environmental awareness
(b) Religious purposes
(c) Year-round flow of water in rivers
(d) Conserving rare and threatened species

122. World Biodiversity Day is celebrated annually on:
(a) 22nd May (b) 16th September
(c) 5th June (d) 29th December

123. Periyar Wildlife Sanctuary in Kerala is famous for:
(a) Elephant (b) Water bird
(c) Panther (d) Migratory birds

124. Select the incorrect match:
(a) Lungs of the plant: Amazon rain forest
(b) Alien species: *Parthenium*
(c) Recent extinctions: Dodo
(d) Cryopreservation: In-situ conservation

125. Proper and strict protection of all the biodiversity hot spots could reduce the on-going mass extinction by almost:
(a) 10% (b) 15%
(c) 30% (d) 20%

126. Among the ecosystems mentioned below, where can one find maximum biodiversity?
(a) Mangroves (b) Desert
(c) Alpine meadows (d) Coral reefs

127. Which of the following pairs of geographical areas show maximum biodiversity in our country?
(a) Sundarbans and Rann of Kutch
(b) Eastern Himalayas and Western Ghats
(c) Eastern Ghats and West Bengal
(d) Kerala and Punjab

128. Preservation of genetic resources is carried out in field gene banks:
(a) At low temperature
(b) At the temperature of liquid nitrogen
(c) Under controlled environmental conditions
(d) Under normal growing conditions

129. Which of the following is the best method of germplasm conservation?
(a) Herbarium (b) Botanical garden
(c) Seed bank (d) Zoological bank

130. The objective of Ramsar Convention was:
(a) Forest conservation
(b) Wildlife conservation
(c) Wetland conservation
(d) Biodiversity conservation

131. 'Silent Valley' is tropical evergreen forest located in:
(a) Kerala (b) Karnataka
(c) Maharashtra (d) Orissa

132. Which one of the following was not an objective of the convention on biological diversity?
(a) Conservation of biodiversity
(b) Sustainable utilisation of its benefits
(c) Equitable use of genetic resources
(d) Exploitation of threatened species

133. World Summit on Sustainable Development was held in:
(a) Johannesburg in 2002
(b) Rio de Janeiro in 1992
(c) New York in 2002
(d) Canada in 1987

134. Gene bank is a collection of:
(a) Frozen germplasm (b) Spores
(c) Seeds (d) All of the above

135. First national park of India is:
(a) Kanha NP (b) Periyar NP
(c) Corbett NP (d) Bandipur NP

136. Venue and year of Earth Summit on conservation of biodiversity was:
(a) South Africa, 2002
(b) Rio de Janeiro, 1992
(c) Johannesburg, 2004
(d) Ramsar, 2004

NCERT EXEMPLAR QUESTIONS

1. Which of the following countries has the highest biodiversity?
(a) Brazil (b) South Africa
(c) Russia (d) India

2. Which of the following is not a cause of loss of biodiversity?
(a) Destruction of habitat
(b) Invasion by alien species
(c) Keeping animals in zoological parks
(d) Over-exploitation of natural resources

3. Which of the following is not an invasive alien species in the Indian context?
(a) *Lantana* (b) *Cynodon*
(c) *Parthenium* (d) *Eichhornia*

4. Where among the following will you find the pitcher plant?
(a) Rain forest of North-East India
(b) Sunderbans
(c) Thar Desert
(d) Western Ghats

5. Which one of the following is not a major characteristic feature of biodiversity hot spots?
(a) Large number of species
(b) Abundance of endemic species
(c) Mostly located in the tropics
(d) Mostly located in the polar regions

6. Match the animals given in Column I with their location in Column II:

	Column I	Column II
A.	Dodo	(i) Africa
B.	Quagga	(ii) Russia
C.	Thylacine	(iii) Mauritius
D.	Stellar's sea cow	(iv) Australia

Choose the correct match from the following:
(a) A – (i), B – (iii), C – (ii), D – (iv)
(b) A – (iv), B – (iii), C – (i), D – (ii)
(c) A – (iii), B – (i), C – (ii), D – (iv)
(d) A – (iii), B – (i), C – (iv), D – (ii)

7. What is common to the following plants: *Nepenthes, Psilotum, Rauwolfia* and *Aconitum*?
(a) All are ornamental plants
(b) All are phylogenic link species
(c) All are prone to over-exploitation
(d) All are exclusively present in the eastern Himalayas

8. The one-horned rhinoceros is specific to which of the following sanctuaries?
(a) Bhitar Kanika (b) Bandipur
(c) Kaziranga (d) Corbett

9. Amongst the animal groups given below, which one appears to be more vulnerable to extinction?
(a) Insects (b) Mammals
(c) Amphibians (d) Reptiles

10. Which one of the following is an endangered plant species of India?
(a) *Rauwolfia serpentina*
(b) *Santalum album* (Sandal wood)
(c) *Cycas beddonei*
(d) All of the above

11. What is common to *Lantana, Eichhornia* and African catfish?
(a) All are endangered species in India
(b) All are keystone species
(c) All are mammals found in India
(d) All the species are neither threatened nor indigenous species of India

12. The extinction of passenger pigeon was due to:
(a) Increased number of predatory birds
(b) Over-exploitation by humans
(c) Non-availability of food
(d) Bird flu virus infection

13. Which of the following statements is correct?
(a) *Parthenium* is an endemic species of our country
(b) African catfish is not a threat to indigenous catfishes
(c) Steller's sea cow is an extinct animal
(d) *Lantana* is popularly known as carrot grass

14. Among the ecosystems mentioned below, where can one find maximum biodiversity?
(a) Mangroves (b) Desert
(c) Coral reefs (d) Alpine meadows

15. Which of the following forests is known as the 'lungs of planet Earth'?
(a) Taiga forest
(b) Tundra forest
(c) Amazon rain forest
(d) Rain forests of North-East India

16. The active chemical drug reserpine is obtained from:
(a) *Datura* (b) *Rauwolfia*
(c) *Atropa* (d) *Papaver*

17. Which of the following groups exhibit more species diversity?
(a) Gymnosperms (b) Algae
(c) Bryophytes (d) Fungi

18. Which of the regions mentioned below exhibit less seasonal variation?
(a) Tropics (b) Temperate zones
(c) Alpines (d) Both (a) and (b)

19. The historic convention on Biological Diversity held in Rio de Janeiro in 1992 is known as:
(a) CITES Convention
(b) The Earth Summit
(c) G-16 Summit
(d) MAB Programme

20. What is common to the techniques (i) in vitro fertilisation, (ii) cryo preservation and (iii) tissue culture?
(a) All are in-situ conservation methods
(b) All are ex-situ conservation methods
(c) All require ultra-modern equipment and large space
(d) All are methods of conservation of extinct organisms

PRACTICE TEST PAPER

1. Variety of species within a region is called:
(a) Genetic diversity (b) Community diversity
(c) Species diversity (d) Ecosystem diversity

2. Among vertebrates, maximum diversity is of:
(a) Fishes (b) Birds
(c) Amphibians (d) Reptiles

3. Read the following statements and select the correct option:

A. Biodiversity increases when we move from high to low latitude

B. Biodiversity is minimum in the arctic region and maximum in tropical areas

(a) Only (A) is correct
(b) Only (B) is correct
(c) Both (A) and (B) are correct
(d) Both (A) and (B) are incorrect

4. According to the Rivet Popper Hypothesis, the key species are considered as:
(a) Aeroplane
(b) All rivets of the aeroplane
(c) Rivets on wing
(d) Wings

5. Identify the odd one out with respect to ex-situ conservation strategies for organisms:
(a) Botanical garden (b) Seed bank
(c) Aquaria (d) Wildlife sanctuary

6. Which of the following statements are correct?
A. Passenger pigeon is extinct due to over-exploitation
B. Earth Summit was held in 1992 at Rio de Janeiro
C. World Summit was held at Johannesburg in 2002
D. Sacred groves are meant for in-situ conservation
(a) Only (B) and (C)
(b) Only (A), (B) and (C)
(c) Only (A) and (B)
(d) (A), (B), (C) and (D)

7. Which of the following pairs of geographical areas shows maximum biodiversity in our country?
(a) Sundarbans and Rann of Kutch
(b) Eastern Ghats and Best Bengal
(c) Eastern Himalaya and Western Ghats
(d) Kerala and Punjab

8. Causes of biodiversity loss can be:
A. Habitat loss of a species
B. Over-exploitation of a species
C. Alien species invasion
(a) (A) only (b) (A) and (B) only
(c) (B) and (C) (d) (A), (B) and (C)

9. All of the following are direct economic uses or narrow utilitarian services of biodiversity, except:
(a) Food
(b) Fibre
(c) Industrial product
(d) Oxygen

10. A traditional strategy for the protection of biodiversity in India is:
(a) Ex-situ conservation
(b) Wildlife safari
(c) Biosphere reserve
(d) Sacred forests and lakes

11. Agenda 21 is related to:
(a) Oil pollution
(b) Wetland conservation
(c) Sustainable development
(d) Biodiversity conservation

12. How many biodiversity hot spots are present in India?
(a) One (b) Two
(c) Three (d) Four

13. Which of the following protected areas is meant for conservation of the lion?
(a) Kaziranga National Park
(b) Keoladeo National Park
(c) Gir National Park
(d) Kanha National Park

14. Which of the following is not a recently extinct species?
(a) Dodo (b) Kangaroo
(c) Steller's sea cow (d) Quagga

15. The part of the biosphere that is strictly prohibited and protected from any external interference is called:
(a) Core zone (b) Buffer zone
(c) Transition zone (d) (a) and (b)

16. Match the following columns and choose the correct option:

	Column I	Column II
A.	Dodo	(i) Africa
B.	Quagga	(ii) Russia
C.	Thylacine	(iii) Mauritius
D.	Steller's sea cow	(iv) Australia

(a) A – (iii), B – (i), C – (iv), D – (ii)
(b) A – (ii), B – (i), C – (iv), D – (iii)
(c) A – (iii), B – (iv), C – (i), D – (ii)
(d) A – (iv), B – (iii), C – (ii), D – (i)

17. Which of the following countries has the highest biodiversity?
(a) Brazil (b) South Africa
(c) Russia (d) India

18. Read the following statements and select the correct option:
A. Red List has eight categories of species
B. Taxon facing extremely high risk of extinction in the immediate future is called endangered
C. A taxon which has not been assessed is known as Not Evaluated
D. A taxon is vulnerable when it is not critically endangered or endangered but facing a high risk of extinction in the wild in the near future
The correct statements are:
(a) (A) and (B) (b) (B) and (D)
(c) (A), (B) and (C) (d) (A), (C) and (D)

19. Identify the incorrectly matched pair:

	Organism	**Reason for extinction/threat**
(a)	Dodo	Habitat loss and fragmentation
(b)	Cichlid fish	Nile perch
(c)	Passenger pigeon	Over-exploitation
(d)	Indigenous catfish in our rivers	*Clarias gariepinus*

20. Among the animal groups given below, which one has the highest percentage of endangered species?
(a) Insects (b) Mammals
(c) Amphibians (d) Reptiles

21. In a national park, protection is provided to:
(a) Flora and fauna (b) Entire ecosystem
(c) Flora only (d) Fauna only

22. Western Ghats has a greater number of amphibian species than Eastern Ghats. What kind of diversity does it represent?
(a) Species diversity
(b) Genetic diversity
(c) Ecological diversity
(d) Community diversity

23. What is common to cryopreservation, in vitro fertilisation and tissue culture?
(a) All are in-situ conservation methods
(b) All are ex-situ conservation methods
(c) All require ultra-modern equipment
(d) All are methods of conservation of extinct organisations

24. MAB (Man and Biosphere) programme was started by:
(a) UNEP (b) UNCED
(c) UNESCO (d) IUCN

25. A stable biological community with high species diversity:
(i) Should not show too much variation in productivity from year to year
(ii) Must be resistant to occasional disturbances that are natural in origin or which result from human activity
(iii) Shows no resistance to invasion by alien species
(a) (i) only (b) (ii) and (iii)
(c) (i) and (ii) (d) (i), (ii) and (iii)

26. Increased diversity contributing to higher productivity was the idea of:
(a) Robert May (b) David Tilman
(c) Edward Wilson (d) AV Humboldt

27. Anthropogenic extinction is called:
(a) Third mass extinction
(b) Fourth mass extinction
(c) Sixth mass extinction
(d) Seventh mass extinction

28. Biosphere reserve differs from national parks and wildlife sanctuaries because in the former:
(a) Human beings are not allowed to enter
(b) People are an integral part of the ecosystem
(c) Plants are paid greater attention than animals
(d) Living organisms are brought in from all over the world and preserved

29. Select the correct match of bird species and country:
(a) Columbia – 2000 (b) India – 1200
(c) New York – 56 (d) Greenland – 105

30. Loss of biodiversity in a region, in general, may lead to:
(a) Increase in plant production
(b) Higher resistance to environmental perturbations
(c) Increased variability in water use
(d) Stable plant productivity

31. Which of the following is not a part of the "evil quartet"?
(a) Habitat loss and fragmentation
(b) Alien species invasion
(c) Over-exploitation
(d) Co-evolution

32. Ex-situ conservation methods include protective maintenance of threatened species in:
(a) Botanical gardens and zoological parks
(b) Biosphere reserve and seed bank
(c) Hot spots and cryopreservation
(d) National parks and zoological parks

33. Tropical environments, unlike temperate ones, are less seasonal, relatively more constant and predictable. Such constant environments promote:
(a) Deforestation
(b) Mass extinction
(c) Over-exploitation
(d) Niche specialisation and speciation

34. Which of the following are the last refuges for a large number of rare and threatened plants in Meghalaya?
(a) Sacred groves (b) Botanical gardens
(c) Wildlife safari park (d) Sanctuaries

35. Read the following statement carefully: "Amazon forest is estimated to produce, through photosynthesis, 20% of the total oxygen in the earth's atmosphere".

This is aspect for conserving biodiversity is:
(a) Narrowly utilitarian
(b) Broadly utilitarian
(c) Economic aspect
(d) Ethical

36. Pattern of biodiversity depends up on:
(a) Latitudinal gradient
(b) Altitudinal gradient
(c) Species–area relationship
(d) All of the above

37. In the species–area relationship, on a logarithmic scale, the relationship is:
(a) Rectangular hyperbola
(b) Straight line
(c) Rectangular parabola
(d) Sigmoid

38. Differences of alleles, entire genes and chromosomal structure of a species refers to its:
(a) Species diversity
(b) Genetic diversity
(c) Community diversity
(d) β diversity

39. India has ___A___ national parks, ___B___ biosphere reserves and ___C___ wildlife sanctuaries.
Complete the statement by choosing the correct options for A, B and C:

	A	B	C
(a)	90	14	448
(b)	75	16	440
(c)	14	90	448
(d)	448	14	90

40. The most dramatic examples of habitat loss come from tropical rain forests. Once covering more than 14% of the earth's land surface, they now cover no more than __________:
(a) 5% (b) 6%
(c) 10% (d) 13%

41. According to ecologists, if the present trends continue, nearly half the species on earth might be wiped out within how many years?
(a) 100 (b) 1000
(c) 50 (d) 500

42. Main cause of extinction of species from tropical areas is:
(a) Afforestation (b) Deforestation
(c) Pollution (d) Soil erosion

43. Species endangered due to low reproductive rate is:
(a) Giant panda (b) Lion
(c) Bald eagle (d) Island species

44. Which of the following has maximum genetic diversity in India?
(a) Tea (b) Teak
(c) Wheat (d) Mango

45. The objective of the Ramsar Convention was:
(a) Forest conservation
(b) Wildlife conservation
(c) Wetland conservation
(d) Biodiversity conservation

ANSWER KEYS

Exercises

1. (a)	2. (c)	3. (b)	4. (c)	5. (a)	6. (a)	7. (b)	8. (c)	9. (b)	10. (b)
11. (a)	12. (c)	13. (d)	14. (a)	15. (a)	16. (b)	17. (b)	18. (d)	19. (a)	20. (d)
21. (a)	22. (d)	23. (a)	24. (b)	25. (c)	26. (c)	27. (d)	28. (c)	29. (c)	30. (a)
31. (c)	32. (b)	33. (a)	34. (d)	35. (c)	36. (c)	37. (d)	38. (d)	39. (c)	40. (d)
41. (c)	42. (a)	43. (a)	44. (c)	45. (c)	46. (d)	47. (d)	48. (b)	49. (a)	50. (c)
51. (c)	52. (a)	53. (b)	54. (d)	55. (a)	56. (d)	57. (c)	58. (a)	59. (b)	60. (c)
61. (a)	62. (a)	63. (a)	64. (b)	65. (a)	66. (c)	67. (b)	68. (c)	69. (a)	70. (b)
71. (c)	72. (b)	73. (a)	74. (c)	75. (a)	76. (b)	77. (b)	78. (b)	79. (d)	80. (d)
81. (a)	82. (b)	83. (d)	84. (b)	85. (d)	86. (c)	87. (b)	88. (c)	89. (b)	90. (d)
91. (d)	92. (c)	93. (a)	94. (c)	95. (a)	96. (b)	97. (c)	98. (b)	99. (a)	100. (b)
101. (b)	102. (d)	103. (b)	104. (b)	105. (d)	106. (d)	107. (d)	108. (a)	109. (c)	110. (a)
111. (a)	112. (b)	113. (a)	114. (b)	115. (b)	116. (a)	117. (d)	118. (a)	119. (b)	120. (c)
121. (d)	122. (a)	123. (a)	124. (d)	125. (c)	126. (d)	127. (b)	128. (d)	129. (c)	130. (c)
131. (a)	132. (d)	133. (a)	134. (d)	135. (c)	136. (b)				

NCERT Exemplar Questions

1. (a)	2. (c)	3. (b)	4. (a)	5. (d)	6. (d)	7. (c)	8. (c)	9. (c)	10. (d)
11. (d)	12. (b)	13. (c)	14. (c)	15. (c)	16. (b)	17. (d)	18. (a)	19. (b)	20. (b)

Practice Test Paper

1. (c)	2. (a)	3. (c)	4. (c)	5. (d)	6. (d)	7. (c)	8. (d)	9. (d)	10. (d)
11. (c)	12. (c)	13. (c)	14. (b)	15. (a)	16. (a)	17. (a)	18. (d)	19. (a)	20. (c)
21. (b)	22. (a)	23. (b)	24. (c)	25. (c)	26. (b)	27. (c)	28. (b)	29. (b)	30. (c)
31. (d)	32. (a)	33. (d)	34. (a)	35. (b)	36. (d)	37. (b)	38. (b)	39. (a)	40. (b)
41. (a)	42. (b)	43. (a)	44. (d)	45. (c)					

SOLUTIONS

Biodiversity (How Many Species Are There on Earth and How Many in India, Pattern of Biodiversity, Latitudinal Gradient, Species–Area Relationship)

1. Edward Wilson
2. The genetic variation shown by the medicinal plant *Rauwolfia vomitoria*, growing in different Himalayan ranges, might be in terms of potency and concentration of the active chemical reserpine that the plant produces.
3. Genetic diversity
4. 1000 genetically different varieties of mango are found in India.
5. Genetic diversity
6. Maximum taxonomic diversity occurs where species of taxonomically different groups occur in almost equal abundance because species diversity is a product of species richness and species evenness.
7. 50,000 genetic diversity
8. Insects
9. Species diversity is based on species richness and species evenness. Species richness is the number of species present within a unit area, while species evenness is the proportionate number of individuals of different species.
10. The Western Ghats has greater amphibian species diversity.
11. Genetic diversity within a species increases with environmental variability, which results in the formation of ecotypes. Therefore, it provides the raw material for adaptation and evolution of new life forms (speciation).
12. Gamma diversity
13. C is the most diverse area due to a high level of species richness and species evenness.
14. A – 28,000, B – 20,000
15. 1.5 million
16. According to Robert May, global species diversity is about 7 million.
17. India has only 2.4% of the world's land area and 8.1% of the global species diversity.
18. The number of fungi species (72,000) in the world is more than the combined total of the species of fishes (28,000), amphibians (4780), reptiles (7150) and mammals (4650).
19. Among vertebrates, fishes are the most species-rich taxonomic group.
20. (B) and (C) are correct.
21. (A) and (C) are correct. A higher number of species increases the stability of a community. Plots with more species showed lower year-to-year variation in total biomass.
22. (A), (B), (C) and (D) are correct.
23. Paul Ehrlich
24. Aeroplane – Ecosystem, Rivets – Species
25. Rivets on the wing represent keystone species.
26. Species richness and species evenness
27. Species diversity declines with increasing distance from the base of mountains. This is due to decrease in temperature and greater seasonal variability.
28. Pattern of biodiversity is affected by latitudinal gradient and species–area relationship. As we move from low to high latitude, the biodiversity decreases. Alexander Von Humboldt found that within a region, species richness increased with increased explored area but only up to a limit.
29. A Von Humboldt
30. A – Insects, B – Molluscs, C – Crustaceans, D – Other animal groups
31. Both (A) and (B) are correct.
32. A – Fishes, B – Birds, C – Amphibians
33. A – Fungi, B – Angiosperms
34. Option (d) is correct.
35. Straight line

36. 1 lakh plant species and 3 lakh animal species

37. There are nearly 45,000 species of plants and twice as many animal species.

38. A species whose presence and role within an ecosystem has a disproportionate effect on other organisms within the system

39. Z represents the slope of the line or the regression coefficient.

40. The value of Z lies in the range 0.1 to 0.2.

41. For frugivorous birds, the value of Z is 1.15.

42. $A - S = CA^2$, $B - \log S = \log C + Z \log A$

43. David Tilman and Humboldt

44. The greater the slope, the higher the value of the regression coefficient and species richness

45. Option (c) is correct.

46. Speciation is generally a function of area and time.

47. Temperate regions have been subjected to frequent glaciations in the past, but tropical regions remained undisturbed. Therefore, tropics had longer evolutionary time for species diversification. Tropics have greater solar energy exposure, which contributes to higher productivity and greater diversity.

48. A forest in a tropical region like Ecuador has 10 times more species of vascular plants as compared to a forest of equal area in a temperate region like the midwest of the USA.

49. (C) and (D) are false. There are 12 mega diversity regions in the world. The number of animal species is more than 70%, plants accounts for nearly 22% of the total.

50. Biodiversity increases from (i) Poles to equator, (ii) Higher to lower altitude

Importance of Species (Diversity in the Ecosystem, Loss of Biodiversity, Conservation of Biodiversity)

51. According to the IUCN report in 2004, in 500 years, 784 species (338 vertebrates, 359 invertebrates and 87 plants) will become extinct.

52. Option (a) is correct.

53. 45,000 plant species

54. Species more susceptible to extinction have the following population characteristics: (i) Large body size, like rhinoceros, lion; (ii) Small population size and low reproductive rate, like in giant panda, blue whale; (iii) High trophic level in the food chain, like bald eagle, Bengal tiger; (iv) Fixed habitat and migratory routes, like whooping crane, blue whale.

55. Giant panda

56. Threatened species are those that are liable to become extinct if they are not provided proper habitat, food and protection so that they can realise their full biotic potential.

57. IUCN maintains a Red Data Book, which is a catalogue of threatened plants and animals facing risk of extinction.

58. In the wild, giant pandas are only found in the remote, mountainous regions of central China.

59. IUCN is an international organisation working in the field of nature conservation and sustainable use of natural resources. IUCN was established on 5 October, 1948 by UNESCO.

60. IUCN has its headquarters in Switzerland.

61. IUCN maintains the Red Data Book.

62. Biodiversity hot spots cover less than 2% of the land surface with about 20% of the human population.

63. The Amazon rain forest harbouring millions of species is being cut and cleared for cultivating soya beans or for conversion to grassland for raising beef cattle.

64. IUCN stands for International Union for Conservation of Nature.

65. Botanical Survey of India

66. Most of the endangered species are victims of habitat loss and fragmentation.

67. Presently, some 15,500 species worldwide are facing the threat of extinction. They include 12% of all bird species, 23% of all mammal species, 31% of all gymnosperm species and 32% of all amphibian species. Thus, amphibians face the maximum threat of extinction.

68. 15,500 species

69. 12% of all bird species

70. Thylacine – Australia, Dodo – Mauritius, Steller's sea cow – Russia, Quagga – Africa

71. Colonisation of tropical Pacific islands by humans has caused the extinction of more than 2000 species of nature birds.

72. In the last 20 years, 27 species have become extinct.

73. The IUCN Red List (2004) documents the extinction of 784 species in the last 500 years.

74. Bali, Javan, Caspian

75. 31% of all gymnosperm species

76. Exploring molecular-, genetic- and species-level diversity for products of economic importance like medicines is called bioprospecting.

77. Narrowly utilitarian (direct or economic uses)

78. Amazon rain forest is estimated to contribute to 20% of total oxygen in the atmosphere on Earth.

79. Pollination and soil formation are ecosystem services that Nature provides. They are related to broadly utilitarian aspects.

80. Broadly utilitarian argument for conserving biodiversity related to (i) Ecosystem services, (ii) Aesthetic pleasures.

81. Bioprospecting is related to the narrowly utilitarian argument for conserving biodiversity.

82. Biodiversity Act of India was passed by parliament in 2002.

83. Cheetah

84. Anthropogenic (caused by humans) extinction is causing a sixth mass extinction. The current extinction rates are different from the previous episodes as they are estimated to be 100 to 1000 times faster than those in the pre-human period. If the present trends continue, nearly all the species on earth might be wiped out within the next 100 years.

85. The term "The Evil Quartet" is related to four major causes of biodiversity loss: (1) Habitat loss and fragmentation, (2) Over-exploitation, (3) Alien species invasion and (4) Co-extinctions.

86. Natural parasites are not a cause of extinction of species.

87. Over-exploitation

88. Human activities

89. When a biological system is over-exploited by humans for natural resources, its results in the degradation and extinction of the resources. Passenger pigeon, dodo and Steller's sea cow have become extinct due to over-exploitation.

90. Nile perch (alien species), a large predator fresh, when introduced in Lake Victoria, caused the extinction of an ecologically unique species of cichlid fish in the lake.

91. *Lantana, Eichhornia* and *Parthenium* all are exotic or alien species, which were introduced in India.

92. Introduction of African catfish (*Clarias gariepinus*) for aquaculture purpose is posing a threat to the indigenous catfishes of Indian rivers.

93. (A) and (B) are correct.

94. Option (c) is correct. In-situ conservation approach involves protection of species in their natural habitat.

95. Hot spots of biodiversity are regions of high level of species richness with high degree of endemism.

96. The term biodiversity hot spot was coined by Norman Myers in 1988.

97. Initially, 25 hot spots were identified globally, but now the number is 34.

98. India has three hot spots: (1) Western Ghats and Sri Lanka; (2) Indo-Burma; (3) Himalayas.

99. 90 national parks, 14 biosphere reserves, 448 wildlife sanctuaries

100. National park

101. Western Ghats

102. Sacred grooves are forest patches set aside for worship. All the trees and wildlife within are given total protection by tribal people.

103. Endemic species are confined to a particular region and not found anywhere else.

104. Tiger project was started in 1973.

105. Gir National Park in Junagadh, Gujarat is famous for the lion.

106. Dachigam National Park, Jammu and Kashmir

107. River dolphin is the national aquatic animal of India.

108. Elephant

109. Biosphere reserve is an example of in-situ conservation.

110. Earth Summit at Rio de Janeiro (1992), Brazil promoted the Convention on Biological Diversity (CBD), which was signed by 152 nations. Its recommendations came into effect on 29 December, 1993.

111. A – 1972, B – 1971

112. A sacred lake is the Khecheopalri Lake of Sikkim.

113. *The Jungle Book* (1894) is a collection of stories by English author Rudyard Kipling. The stories are from central Indian forests near the Satpura range.

114. Ex-situ conservation approach involves placing threatened animals and plants in special care units for their protection. Ex-situ conservation approach includes seed bank, gene bank, tissue culture, arboreta, cryopreservation and home gardens.

115. A. Buffer zone, B. Core zone, C. Transition zone

116. Ex-situ conservation approach (Zoological park and botanical garden)

117. National Park

118. Conservation hot spots are areas where a large number of endemic species are disappearing rapidly.

119. A plant endemic to New Zealand

120. Only (C) is incorrect.

121. Large number of rare and threatened plants can be found in sacred groves.

122. World Biodiversity Day is celebrated annually on 22nd May.

123. Periyar Wildlife sanctuary in Kerala is famous for elephant.

124. Cryopreservation comes under ex-situ conservation approach.

125. Proper and strict protection of all the biodiversity hot spots could reduce mass extinction by almost 30%.

126. Coral reefs

127. Eastern Himalaya and Western Ghats

128. Preservation of genetic resource is carried out in field gene banks under normal growing conditions.

129. Seed bank

130. The international convention that has been formed to decide the base for the identification of wetlands is known as the Ramsar Convention. It has been named after a city in Iran where this convention was signed in 1971.

131. Silent Valley is tropical evergreen forest located in Kerala.

132. Exploitation of threatened species is not an objective of the Convention on Biological Diversity.

133. The World Summit on sustainable development was held in Johannesburg, South Africa, in 2002, in which 190 countries pledged to reduce the current rate of biodiversity loss at global, regional and local levels by 2010.

134. Gene bank is a collection of frozen germplasm, spores, seeds, etc.

135. Corbett National Park was the first national park established in India.

136. The Earth Summit was held in Rio de Janeiro in 1992.

16 Environmental Issues

EXERCISES

Air Pollution and its Control, Controlling Vehicular Air Pollution – A Case Study of Delhi

1. Act formulated in 1986 was:
   (a) The Environmental (Protection) ACT
   (b) The Water (Prevention and Control of Pollution) Act
   (c) The Air (Prevention and Control of Pollution) Act
   (d) The Insecticide Act
2. A non-biodegradable pollutant is:
   (a) Newsprint (b) Green leaves
   (c) DDT (d) Cow dung
3. Which of the following is not a cause of natural pollution?
   (a) Particulate matter by volcanos
   (b) Landslides and forest fires
   (c) Marsh gas and UV rays
   (d) Thermal power plants
4. Select the incorrectly matched pair with respect to pollutants:
   (a) Biodegradable pollutant – Domestic sewage
   (b) Non-biodegradable pollutant – Plastic material
   (c) Secondary pollutant – PAN
   (d) Quantitative pollutant – Pesticides
5. A secondary pollutant is:
   (a) DDT (b) SO_2
   (c) PAN (d) CO
6. Domestic waste is:
   (a) Not a pollutant
   (b) Biodegradable
   (c) Non-biodegradable
   (d) Air pollutant
7. According to the Central Pollution Control Board (CPCB), which particulate size in diameter (in micrometres) of air pollutants is responsible for the greatest harm to human health?
   (a) 10 or less (b) 5.2–2.5
   (c) 2.5 or less (d) 10 or more
8. ________ are used in electrostatic precipitators:
   (a) Electrodes (b) Costly metals
   (c) Absorbers (d) Scrubber
9. The given figures represent two devices, A and B, used to control air pollution. Identify them and select the correct answer:

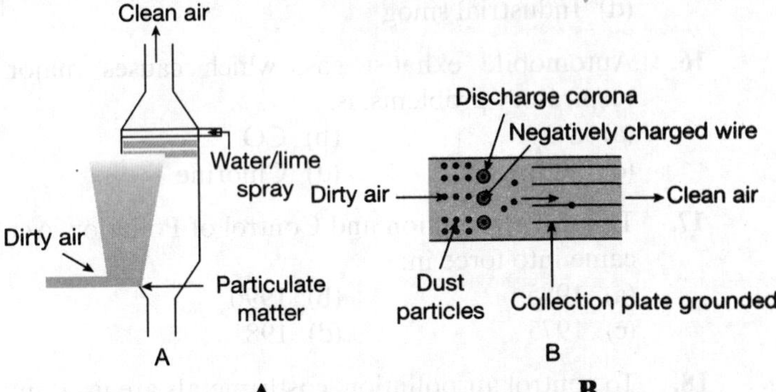

	A	B
(a)	Electrostatic precipitator	Scrubber
(b)	Scrubber	Electrostatic precipitator
(c)	Scrubber	Cyclone filter
(d)	Cyclone filter	Scrubber

10. Electrostatic precipitators are employed to remove particulate pollutants of the size of:
    (a) 5–20 μm (b) 20–50 μm
    (c) 50 mm and larger (d) 0.5–5.0 mm
11. Which one is the most widely used for the removal of over 99% of the particulate matter present in exhausts from thermal power plants?
    (a) Scrubber

(b) Catalytic converter
(c) Electrostatic precipitator
(d) Micro filter

12. The scrubber is used mainly to remove:
(a) Particulate matter from thermal power plants
(b) SO_2 from industrial effluent
(c) CO and unburnt hydrocarbon from automobile exhausts
(d) Dust and mist released from industries

13. CNG is better than diesel because:
(a) It is cheaper
(b) It burns more efficiently
(c) It cannot be adulterated
(d) All of the above

14. How does SO_2 affect plants?
(a) It inhibits ETS in plants
(b) It damages the membrane system
(c) It causes chloroses and necrosis
(d) More than one option is correct

15. Nitrogen oxides formed during emission from automobiles and power plants are a source of fine air particles which lead to:
(a) Photochemical smog
(b) Dry acid deposition
(c) Wet acid deposition
(d) Industrial smog

16. Automobile exhaust gas, which causes major respiratory problems, is:
(a) SO_2 (b) CO
(c) NO_2 (d) Chlorine

17. The Air Prevention and Control of Pollution Act came into force in:
(a) 1985 (b) 1990
(c) 1975 (d) 1981

18. To control air pollution, costly metals are used in:
(a) Electrostatic precipitators
(b) Scrubbers
(c) Catalytic converters
(d) Incinerators

19. In vehicles, catalytic converters are used:
(a) To increase the mileage of vehicles
(b) To convert SO_2 into sulphates
(c) To increase the efficiency of lead mixed petrol
(d) To convert unburnt hydrocarbons into CO_2 and water vapour

20. Catalytic converters convert carbon monoxide and nitric oxide into:
(a) CO_2 and nitrogen gas
(b) Carbon, hydrogen and oxygen
(c) Hydrocarbons and nitrogen gas
(d) CO_2 and ammonia

21. SO_2 pollution is indicated by the destruction of:
(a) Grasses (b) Lichens
(c) Herbs (d) Mosses

22. Acid rain is due to:
(a) Water pollution
(b) Air pollution
(c) Automobile pollution
(d) Pesticide pollution

23. Noise was recognised as an air pollutant through the amendment of:
(a) Environment Protection Act
(b) Air Prevention and Control of Pollution Act
(c) Noise Control and Pollution Act
(d) Insecticide Act

24. The Taj Mahal of Agra is affected by:
(a) SO_2 (b) O_2
(c) O_3 (d) NO_2

25. Rain is called acid rain when its pH is below:
(a) 7 (b) 6.5
(c) 6 (d) 5.65

26. Green muffler is related to pollution of:
(a) Air (b) Noise
(c) Soil (d) Water

27. Maximum permissible noise as per Noise Pollution Rules 2000 is:
(a) 75 dB (b) 65 dB
(c) 55 dB (d) 45 dB

28. Lead is considered as primarily:
(a) Soil pollutant (b) Water pollutant
(c) Noise pollutant (d) Air pollutant

29. dB is the standard abbreviation used for the quantitative expression of:
(a) The dominant bacillus in a culture
(b) A certain pesticide
(c) The density of bacteria in a medium
(d) The unit of sound intensity

30. The toxic effect of CO is due to its greater affinity for haemoglobin as compared to oxygen by:
(a) 20 times (b) 100 times
(c) 200 times (d) 2 times

31. Increased asthmatic attacks in certain seasons are related to:
(a) Inhalation of seasonal pollen
(b) Eating of seasonal vegetables
(c) Low temperature
(d) Wet and dry environment

32. Photochemical smog formed in congested metropolitan cities mainly consists of:
(a) Ozone, peroxyacetyl nitrate and NO_X
(b) Smoke, peroxyacetyl nitrate and SO_2
(c) Hydrocarbons, SO_2 and CO_2
(d) Hydrocarbons, ozone and SO_2

33. The pollution in a city like Delhi may be controlled to a great extent:
(a) By wide roads and factories away from the city
(b) Use of catalytic converters in vehicles
(c) Application of stringent pollution norms for vehicles
(d) All of the above

34. All are correct with respect to classical smog, except:
(a) Occurs at low temperature and contains H_2S and SO_2
(b) Also called London smog
(c) It has mainly O_3, PAN and NO_X
(d) Secondary pollutant has no role

35. Read the following statements and select the correct option:
A. Greatest harm to human health is caused by particulate size 2.5 μm or less
B. Motor vehicles equipped with catalytic converters should not use unleaded petrol because lead in petrol inactivates the catalysts
C. Euro III norms stipulate that sulphur be controlled at 350 ppm in diesel and 150 ppm in petrol
(a) Only A is correct
(b) Only (A) and (B) are correct
(c) Only (B) and (C) are correct
(d) (A), (B) and (C) are correct

Water Pollution and its Control, Domestic Sewage, Industrial Effluents, Eutrophication, Case Study of Integrated Waste Water Treatment

36. ________% of impurities in domestic sewage is in the form of suspended solids, colloidal material and dissolved materials:
(a) 0.1% (b) 0.01%
(c) 1% (d) 5%

37. Water (Prevention and Control of Pollution) Act was passed by the Government of India in:
(a) 1981 (b) 1987
(c) 1974 (d) 1980

38. Natural ageing of lake by biological enrichment of its water is called:
(a) Water logging (b) Bio magnification
(c) Eutrophication (d) Biodegradation

39. Cultural or accelerated eutrophication is most often caused by input of:
(a) PCBs
(b) Nitrates and phosphates
(c) Radioactive waste
(d) Sediments

40. In clean water, the concentration of BOD is ____A____ and DO is ____B____:

	A	B
(a)	Low	High
(b)	High	Low
(c)	Low	Low
(d)	High	High

41. Water is often treated with chlorine to:
(a) Increase oxygen content
(b) Remove hardness
(c) Kill germs
(d) Remove suspended particles

42. Biochemical oxygen demand (BOD) in river water:
(a) Increases when sewage is mixed with river water
(b) Remains unchanged when algal bloom occurs
(c) Has no relationship with concentration of oxygen in water
(d) Gives a measure of salmonella in the water

43. The algal bloom:
A. Is so-called due to the large amount of nutrients in the water bodies
B. Imparts a distinct colour to the water bodies
C. Causes fish mortality and deterioration of water quality
(a) Only (A) and (B) are correct
(b) Only (C) is correct
(c) Only (A) and (C) are correct
(d) (A), (B), and (C) are correct

44. Which of the following plant species is considered the world's most problematic aquatic weed?
(a) *Lautana* (b) *Eichhornia*
(c) *Parthenium* (d) Carrot grass

45. When thermal waste water mixes with river water:
(a) Small fish will die after drinking the river water
(b) The growth of plants and fish in hot areas is enhanced
(c) The number of organisms sensitive to high temperature is reduced or eliminated

(d) The increased microbial activity uses up dissolved oxygen

46. What is true for label A in the given figure?

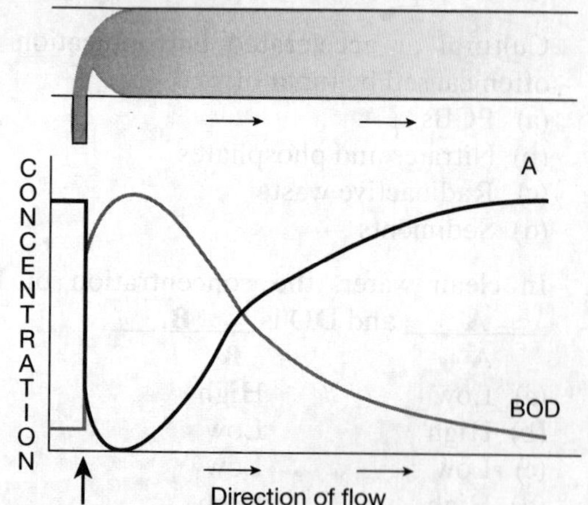

(a) There is a sharp decline in its value downstream from the point of sewage discharge
(b) It leads to rapid fish mortality
(c) Its value of dissolved oxygen increases
(d) It is highest in polluted water bodies

47. Presence of *E. coli* in water indicates:
(a) Water is clear
(b) Water is polluted with inorganic fertilisers
(c) Faecal pollution
(d) Industrial waste pollution

48. Blue body syndrome is caused by:
(a) CO
(b) Fluoride in drinking water
(c) Nitrate
(d) Mercury

49. Which of the following is absent in polluted water?
(a) *Hydrilla* (b) Larva of stone fly
(c) Water hyacinth (d) BGA

50. Match Column I and Column I:

Column I	Column II
A. Mercury	(i) Black foot disease
B. Cadmium	(ii) Methemoglobinemia
C. Arsenic	(iii) Minamata disease
D. Nitrate	(iv) Itai-itai

(a) A – (iii), B – (iv), C – (i), D – (ii)
(b) A – (ii), B – (iv), C – (i), D – (iii)
(c) A – (iv), B – (iii), C – (i), D – (ii)
(d) A – (iv), B – (i), C – (iii), D – (ii)

51. MIC is concerned with:
(a) Minamata disease (b) Photochemical smog
(c) Bhopal gas tragedy (d) Radioactive fall out

52. Fluoride pollution initially affects:
(a) Kidneys (b) Hair
(c) Brain (d) Teeth

53. A water body has high BOD, indicating that the water is:
(a) Being aerated
(b) Being contaminated with sewage
(c) Receiving minerals
(d) Atrophic

54. Entry of sewage in water causes a spurt in the growth of algae but kills fish due to:
(a) Decrease in nutrients
(b) Reduction in light
(c) Depletion of oxygen
(d) All of the above

55. Use of pesticides is problematic as:
(a) Mosquitoes have become resistant to DDT
(b) Kills silkworms
(c) Their residues persist in water and environment
(d) Deforms the gills of some fishes

56. Detergents are water pollutants because they contain:
(a) Sulphates (b) Phosphates
(c) Nitrates (d) Carbonates

57. The waste water industries may contain toxic heavy metals having a density of more than:
(a) 5 g/cm^3 (b) 10 g/cm^3
(c) 2 g/cm^3 (d) 15 g/cm^3

58. Eutrophication of water bodies leading to killing of fish is mainly due to non-availability of:
(a) Oxygen (b) Light
(c) Food (d) Essential nutrients

59. The concentration of DDT is maximum in the breast muscles of birds that eat:
(a) Sea fish (b) Sea weeds
(c) Flesh (d) All of the above

60. Which harmful item was discussed in Rachel Carson's book *Silent Spring* on damage to wildlife?
(a) DDT (b) CO_2
(c) CFC (d) PCB

61. Biomagnification refers to:
(a) Rapid growth due to excessive intake of nutrients
(b) Increase in population size
(c) Decrease in population size
(d) Increase in concentration of non-degradable pollutants as they pass through the food chain

62. DDT residues are rapidly passed through the food chain, causing biomagnification, because DDT is:
(a) Water soluble
(b) Liposoluble
(c) Moderately toxic
(d) Non-toxi uatic animals

63. High concentration of DDT in birds disturbs the metabolism of:
(a) Sodium and potassium
(b) Iron
(c) Calcium
(d) Phosphorus

64. Drawback of DDT as pesticide is that it:
(a) Becomes ineffective after some time
(b) Is less effective than others
(c) Is not easily/rapidly degraded in nature
(d) Has high cost

65. Lead concentration in blood is considered alarming if it is:
(a) 10 μg /100 ml (b) 20 μg /100 ml
(c) 30 μg /100 ml (d) 46 μg /100 ml

66. The given figure represents the biomagnification of DDT in the aquatic food chain. The concentration of DDT increases with each trophic level as:

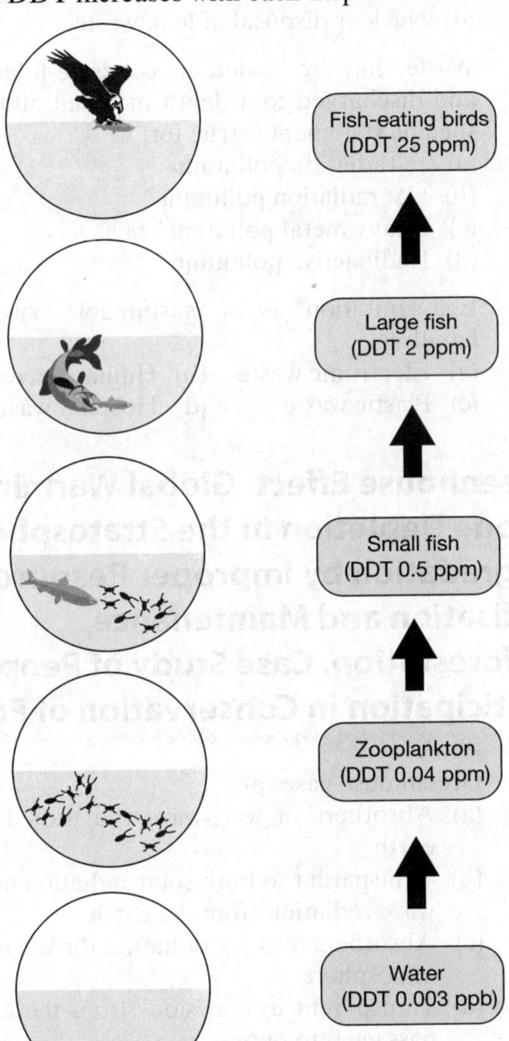

(a) DDT is a non-biodegradable pesticide
(b) It becomes accumulated in fat deposit tissues
(c) It cannot be metabolised and broken down or excreted out
(d) All of the above

67. An integrated waste water treatment process which was initiated in Arcata, involves cleaning in two stages. The first stage involves:
(a) Physical treatment only
(b) Conventional sedimentation, filtering and chlorine treatment
(c) Biological treatment
(d) Secondary treatment similar to STP

68. Ecosan toilets:
(a) Are non-hygienic, efficient and cost effective
(b) Require a lot of water
(c) Create a lot of sewage
(d) Reduce the need for chemical fertiliser

69. FOAM is a group of citizens responsible for the integrated process of:
(a) Reducing eutrophication
(b) Sewage and water treatment
(c) Radioactive waste disposal
(d) Organic farming

70. Measuring biochemical oxygen demand (BOD) is a method used for:
(a) Measuring the activity of *Saccharomyces* in producing curd on a commercial scale
(b) Working out the efficiency of RBCs in their capacity to carry oxygen
(c) Estimating the amount of organic matter in sewage water
(d) Working out the efficiency of oil-driven automobile engines

Solid Waste, Case Study of Remedy for Plastic Waste, Agrochemicals and their Effects, Case Study of Organic Farming, Radioactive Waste

71. Reduction of soil fertility due to loss of the top fertile layer is called:
(a) Negative pollution
(b) Positive pollution
(c) Landscape pollution
(d) Third pollution

72. All are true for negative soil pollution, except:
(a) Soil erosion
(b) Insecticide and pesticide

(c) Deforestation
(d) Fault irrigation

73. Third pollution is:
(a) Pollution caused by the addition of an undesirable substance in air, water, soil or land
(b) Deterioration in the quality of air, water, soil, etc. due to the removal or reduction in the quality of an important or vital ingredient
(c) Ground water pollution due to seepage of minerals, toxic chemicals and sewage
(d) Landscape pollution caused by throwing of rubbish, waste and garbage on land

74. Soil fertility is depleted due to:
(a) Mulching
(b) Terracing
(c) Intensive agriculture
(d) Contour formation

75. Who found the ideal solution to the ever-increasing problem of plastic waste?
(a) Ramesh Chandra Dagar
(b) Amrita Devi
(c) Ahmed Khan
(d) Anand Mohan Chakrabarty

76. The single most serious obstacle to using nuclear power is:
(a) Ensuring safe operation
(b) Safe disposal of waste
(c) High cost of operation
(d) Securing plutonium waste

77. The 'polyblend' is a/an:
(a) Recycled/Modified plastic used for laying roads
(b) Electronic waste buried in landfills
(c) Plastic film waste used to make disinfectants
(d) Fine powder of plastic waste used to make plastic bags

78. Select the correct statement from the following:
(a) Sanitary landfills are open dumps
(b) Landfills cause underground water pollution
(c) All solid waste generated by us is divided into two categories: biodegradable and non-biodegradable
(d) Irreparable computers and other electronic goods are called chemical weed

79. Select the odd one out with respect to integrated organic farming:
(a) Zero waste procedure
(b) Minimum utilisation of resources
(c) Extremely economical
(d) Sustainable venture

80. Combustion of solid waste in the presence of oxygen is called:
(a) Incineration (b) Pyrolysis
(c) Burning (d) Both (b) and (c)

81. The use of incinerators is crucial to the disposal of:
(a) E-waste (b) Municipal solid waste
(c) Hospital waste (d) Both (a) and (b)

82. Which type of serious problem arises from the use of nuclear energy?
(a) Accidental leakage
(b) Safe disposal of nuclear waste
(c) Depletion of ozone layer
(d) Both (a) and (b)

83. The Chernobyl disaster in Ukraine was caused by:
(a) Accidental leakage of nuclear reactor
(b) Radioactive fall out
(c) Nuclear test
(d) Nuclear disposal of leak waste

84. Waste may be sealed in concrete-filled drums and discharged to a depth of about 500 m. This specific statement is true for:
(a) γ-radiation pollutant
(b) UV radiation pollutant
(c) Heavy metal pollutant
(d) Radioactive pollutant

85. Eco-sanitation is a sustainable system for handling:
(a) Electronic waste (b) Human excrete
(c) Plastic waste (d) Hospital waste

Greenhouse Effect, Global Warming, Ozone Depletion in the Stratosphere, Degradation by Improper Resource Utilisation and Maintenance, Deforestation, Case Study of People Participation in Conservation of Forests

86. Greenhouse gases are:
(a) Absorbers of long-wave radiation from the earth
(b) Transparent to both solar radiation and long-wave radiation from the earth
(c) Absorbers of solar radiation for warming the atmosphere
(d) Transparent to emissions from the earth for passage into outer space

87. In the absence of the greenhouse gases, the temperature of the earth's surface would fall to:

(a) 0°C (b) 18°C
(c) -18°C (d) -15°C

88. Which of the following pairs of gases are the major cause of greenhouse effect?
(a) CO_2 and O_3 (b) CO_2 and CO
(c) CFCs and SO_2 (d) CO_2 and N_2O

89. The most effective greenhouse gas is:
(a) CFC (b) CO_2
(c) Methane (d) NOX

90. Match the following columns with respect to the relative contribution of greenhouse gases in global warming:

Column I	**Column II**
A. CFCs	(i) 60%
B. N_2O	(ii) 14%
C. CO_2	(iii) 6%
D. CH_4	(iv) 20%

(a) A – (ii), B – (iii), C – (i), D – (iv)
(b) A – (iii), B – (ii), C – (i), D – (iv)
(c) A – (iv), B – (iii), C – (i), D – (ii)
(d) A – (ii), B – (iv), C – (i), D – (iii)

91. Maximum greenhouse gases are released by which of the following countries?
(a) India (b) France
(c) USA (d) Britain

92. Combined relative contribution of N_2O and CH_4 gases to total global warming is:
(a) 14% (b) 20%
(c) 34% (d) 26%

93. Which of the following is not related to global warming?
(a) More extreme weather conditions
(b) Melting of polar ice caps
(c) Decrease in sea level
(d) Cooling of stratosphere

94. Carbon dioxide fertilisation effect is:
(a) Warming effect of CO_2
(b) Photosynthetic enhancement of elevated CO_2 level
(c) Both summer and winter rainfall at higher latitude
(d) Poleward shifting of temperate zone

95. We can control global warming by:
A. Cutting down use of fossil fuel
B. Improving efficiency of energy use
C. Reducing deforestation
D. Slowing down the growth of human population
(a) (A) and (C) only
(b) (B) and (C) only
(c) (A), (C) and (D) only
(d) (A), (B), (C) and (D)

96. Good ozone is found in the:
(a) Ionosphere (b) Mesosphere
(c) Troposphere (d) Stratosphere

97. A chemical weed in the troposphere and protectant in the stratosphere is:
(a) CH_4 (b) O_3
(c) CFC (d) NO_2

98. Increase in the rate of skin cancer and mutation in organisms can be due to:
(a) Thinning of ozone layer
(b) CO_2 fertilisation effect
(c) Secondary pollutants
(d) High fluoride concentration in drinking water

99. Every year between late August and early October, the ozone hole is observed over:
(a) Pacific region (b) Antarctic region
(c) Atlantic region (d) Arctic region

100. Identify the figure given below, which is related to:

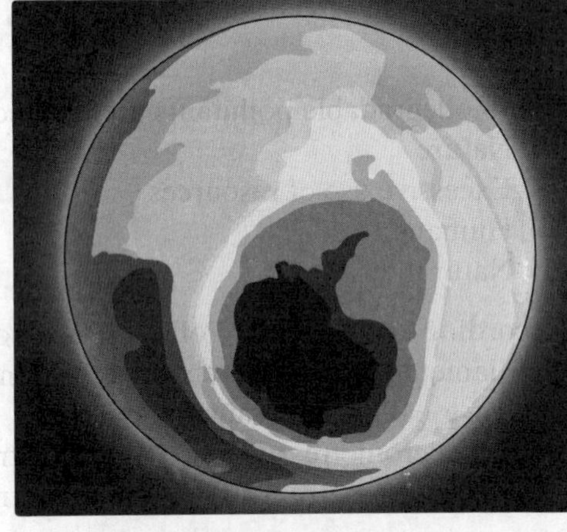

(a) Greenhouse effect (b) Ozone hole
(c) El Nino effect (d) Global warming

101. Jhum cultivation is related to:
(a) Chipko movement
(b) Slash and burn agriculture
(c) Joint forest management
(d) More than one option is correct

102. Amrita Devi Bishnoi Wildlife Protection Award for showing extraordinary courage and dedication in protecting wildlife is given to:
(a) Individuals
(b) Communities from rural areas
(c) NGOs
(d) More than one option is correct

103. Who among the following is related to the Chipko movement?
(a) Amrita Devi Bishnoi
(b) Ramesh Chandra Dagar
(c) Sunder Lal Bahuguna
(d) Ahmad Khan

104. Which of the following is not associated with maintenance and conservation of forests?
(a) Joint forest management
(b) Chipko movement
(c) Van Mahotsava
(d) Jhum cultivation

105. Which of the following conferences had obtained a commitment from different countries for reducing overall greenhouse gas emission at a level of 5% below the 1990 level by 2008–2012?
(a) Kyoto protocol, 1987
(b) Earth summit, Rio de Janeiro 1992
(c) Montreal protocol 1987
(d) Helsinki declaration 1989

106. Government of India has introduced a concept to work closely with local communities for the protection and management of forests called:
(a) Jhum cultivation
(b) Chipko movement
(c) Appiko movement
(d) Joint forest management

107. World Environment Day is celebrated on:
(a) 22 December (b) 1 May
(c) 5 June (d) 6 February

108. Montreal protocol was connected with:
(a) Phasing out ODS
(b) Replacing CFCs with chlorine and bromine
(c) Reduction in CFCs
(d) Both (b) and (c)

109. Kyoto protocol was endorsed at:
(a) CoP-6 (b) CoP-4
(c) CoP-3 (d) CoP-5

NCERT EXEMPLAR QUESTIONS

1. Non-biodegradable pollutants are created by:
(a) Nature
(b) Excessive use of resources
(c) Humans
(d) Natural disasters

2. According to the Central Pollution Control Board, the diameter of particles that are responsible for causing great harm to human health is:
(a) 2.5 micrometre (b) 5.0 micrometre
(c) 10.0 micrometre (d) 7.5 micrometre

3. The material generally used for soundproofing of rooms like recording studio and auditorium is:
(a) Cotton (b) Coir
(c) Wood (d) Styrofoam

4. Compressed Natural Gas (CNG) is:
(a) Propane (b) Methane
(c) Ethane (d) Butane

5. World's most problematic aquatic weed is:
(a) *Azolla* (b) *Wolffia*
(c) *Eichhornia* (d) *Trapa*

6. Which of the following exhibits biomagnification?
(a) SO_2 (b) Mercury
(c) DDT (d) Both (b) and (c)

7. The expanded form of DDT is:
(a) Dichloro diphenyl trichloroethane
(b) Dichloro diethyl trichloroethane
(c) Dichloro dipyridyl trichloroethane
(d) Dichloro diphenyl tetrachloroacetate

8. Which of the following materials takes the longest time for biodegradation?
(a) Cotton (b) Paper
(c) Bone (d) Jute

9. Choose the incorrect statement:
(a) The Montreal protocol is associated with the control of emission of ozone depleting substances
(b) Methane and carbon dioxide are greenhouse gases
(c) Dobson units are used to measure the oxygen content of air
(d) Use of incinerators is crucial to the disposal of hospital waste

10. Among the following, which one causes maximum indoor chemical pollution?
(a) Burning coal
(b) Burning cooking gas
(c) Burning mosquito coil
(d) Room spray

11. The green scum seen in fresh water bodies is:
(a) Blue green algae (b) Red algae
(c) Green algae (d) Both (a) and (c)

12. The loudness of a sound that a person can withstand without discomfort is about:
(a) 150 dB (b) 215 dB
(c) 30 dB (d) 80 dB

13. The major source of noise pollution worldwide is due to:
(a) Office equipment
(b) Transport system
(c) Sugar, textile and paper industries
(d) Oil refineries and thermal power plants

14. Match the following and choose the correct option:

	Column I	Column II
A.	Environment Protection Act	(i) 1974
B.	Air Prevention & Control of Pollution Act	(ii) 1987
C.	Water Act	(iii) 1986
D.	Amendment of Air Act to include noise as an air pollutant	(iv) 1981

The correct matches are:
(a) A – (iii), B – (iv), C – (i), D – (ii)
(b) A – (i), B – (iii), C – (ii), D – (iv)
(c) A – (iv), B – (i), C – (ii), D – (iii)
(d) A – (iii), B – (iv), C – (ii), D – (i)

15. Catalytic converters are fitted into automobiles to reduce emission of harmful gases. Catalytic converters change unburnt hydrocarbons into:
(a) Carbon dioxide and water
(b) Carbon monoxide
(c) Methane
(d) Carbon dioxide and methane

16. Why is it necessary to remove sulphur from petroleum products?
(a) To reduce the emission of sulphur dioxide in exhaust fumes
(b) To increase efficiency of automobiles engines
(c) To use sulphur removed from petroleum for commercial purposes
(d) To increase the lifespan of engine silencers

17. Which one of the following impurities is easiest to remove from waste water?
(a) Bacteria (b) Colloids
(c) Dissolved solids (d) Suspended solids

18. Which one of the following diseases is not caused due to contamination of water?
(a) Hepatitis B (b) Jaundice
(c) Cholera (d) Typhoid

19. Nuisance growth of aquatic plants and bloom-forming algae in natural waters is generally due to high concentrations of:
(a) Carbon (b) Sulphur
(c) Calcium (d) Phosphorus

20. Algal blooms impart a distinct colour to water due to:
(a) Their pigments
(b) Excretion of coloured substances
(c) Formation of coloured chemicals in water facilitated by physiological degradation of algae
(d) Absorption of light by algal cell wall

21. Match the items in Column I and Column II and choose the correct option:

	Column I	Column II
A.	UV	(i) Biomagnification
B.	Biodegradable Organic matter	(ii) Eutrophication
C.	DDT	(iii) Snow blindness
D.	Phosphates	(iv) BOD

The correct match is:
(a) A – (ii), B – (i), C – (iv), D – (iii)
(b) A – (iii), B – (ii), C – (iv), D – (i)
(c) A – (iii), B – (iv), C – (i), D – (ii)
(d) A – (iii), B – (i), C – (iv), D – (ii)

22. In your textbook, you came across the "Three Mile Island" and Chernobyl disasters associated with accidental leakage of radioactive wastes. In India, we had the Bhopal gas tragedy. It is associated with which of the following?
(a) CO_2 (b) Methyl isocyanate
(c) CFC (d) Methyl cyanate

PRACTICE TEST PAPER

1. Most effective device to remove particulate matter from the exhaust release in thermal power plants is:
(a) Scrubber
(b) Catalytic converter
(c) Electrostatic precipitator
(d) Pyrolysis

2. To safeguard our water resources, the Water (Prevention and Control of Pollution) Act came into force in:
(a) 1971 (b) 1974
(c) 1981 (d) 1987

3. The Government of India, through a new auto fuel policy, has laid out a roadmap to cut down vehicular pollution in Indian cities. The most stringent norms for fuels means:
(a) Steadily reducing the sulphur content in petrol
(b) Steadily reducing the aromatic content in petrol
(c) Steadily reducing the sulphur and aromatic content in petrol and diesel
(d) Steadily reducing the particulated matter in petrol and diesel

4. Which of the following is the most dangerous metal pollutant of automobile exhausts?
(a) Cadmium (b) Copper
(c) Mercury (d) Lead

5. Industrial waste water is rich in:
(a) Heavy metals
(b) Dissolved organic waste
(c) Non-biodegradable waste
(d) More than one option is correct

6. Which pollutant can be removed by spraying water or lime in scrubbers?
(a) SO_2
(b) Faecal matter in sewage
(c) N_2O
(d) Particular matter

7. Chlorofluorocarbons are air polluting agents which are produced by:
(a) Diesel trucks (b) Jet planes
(c) Rice fields (d) Cell phones

8. Which metal is used as catalytic converter in vehicles?
(a) Platinum (b) Palladium
(c) Rhodium (d) All of the above

9. Which of the following is a secondary pollutant?
(a) SO_2 (b) CO
(c) NO_2 (d) O_3

10. In a lake polluted with pesticides, the highest level of pesticides will be found in:
(a) Fishes (b) Hydrophytes
(c) Fish-eating birds (d) Planktons

11. Mark the following statements as true (T) or false (F) and select the correct option:
A. Lichens can be used as industrial pollution indicators
B. Bad ozone is found in the troposphere
C. Eutrophication occurs due to nutrient enrichment in lakes
D. Biological oxygen demand (BOD) is a measure of industrial waste poured into water bodies

	A	B	C	D
(a)	T	T	T	F
(b)	T	F	F	T
(c)	F	T	T	F
(d)	F	T	T	T

12. How much of impurities make fresh water unfit for humans?
(a) 50% (b) 10%
(c) 0.1% (d) 1%

13. The UN conference of parties on climate change in the year 2014 was held at:
(a) Paris (b) Doha
(c) Lima (d) Katowice

14. Release of thermal waste water:
(a) Reduces the number of high temperature-sensitive organisms
(b) May enhance the growth of plants in extremely cold areas
(c) May decrease the growth of fish in colder areas
(d) Both (a) and (b) are correct

15. Match the following columns with respect to the relative contribution of greenhouse gases in global warming:

Column I	Column II
A. CO_2	(i) 20%
B. CH_4	(ii) 6%
C. CFC	(iii) 60%
D. N_2O	(iv) 14%

(a) A – (iii), B – (i), C – (iv), D – (ii)
(b) A – (iii), B – (ii), C – (iv), D – (i)
(c) A – (ii), B – (iii), C – (iv), D – (i)
(d) A – (i), B – (iv), C – (ii), D – (iii)

16. The accumulation of toxic or non-biodegradable chemicals in the food chain is:
(a) Biomagnification (b) Eutrophication
(c) Smog (d) Algal bloom

17. Gases like CO_2, CFC, and N_2O are responsible for:
(a) Global warming (b) Deforestation
(c) Ozone depletion (d) Eutrophication

18. Joint forest management was started by the Government of India in:
(a) 1984 (b) 1980
(c) 1986 (d) 1987

19. Which of the following about highly sewage-polluted water is true?
(a) High DO and BOD
(b) High DO and Less BOD
(c) Low DO and BOD
(d) Low DO and high BOD

20. Good ozone and bad ozone are formed, respectively, in:
(a) Troposphere and stratosphere
(b) Stratosphere and troposphere
(c) Stratosphere and mesosphere
(d) Troposphere and mesosphere

21. Pollution from animal excreta and organic waste from kitchens can be most profitably minimised by:
(a) Storing them in underground storage tanks
(b) Using them for producing biogas
(c) Dumping them in rivers
(d) Using them directly as biofertiliser

22. DDT residues are rapidly passed through the food chain, causing biomagnification because DDT is:
(a) Water soluble
(b) Moderately toxic
(c) Non-toxic to aquatic animals
(d) Lipid soluble

23. Accelerated eutrophication occurs due to:
(a) Increase in amount of dissolve oxygen
(b) Increase in concentration of DDT and heavy metals in water
(c) Disposal of waste rich in nitrates and phosphates
(d) Unsafe disposal of radioactive waste

24. Compressed natural gas (CNG) is:
(a) Propane (b) Methane
(c) Ethane (d) Butane

25. Read the following statements and select the correct option:
A. DDT causes thinning of egg shells and their premature breaking by disturbing calcium metabolism
B. El Nino is a climatic change which causes deleterious environmental changes
C. Incomplete combustion of fossil fuels in automobiles release 80% of CO_2
(a) Only (A) is correct
(b) (A) and (C) are correct
(c) (A) and (B) are correct
(d) (A), (B) and (C) are correct

26. Kyoto protocol is to:
(a) Mitigate climate change
(b) Check depletion of ozone layer
(c) Check soil erosion
(d) Preserve water resources

27. Why is ozone known as "chemical weed"?
(a) Because it is formed by chemical reactions
(b) Because it is harmful as well as useful
(c) Because it is harmful, just like weeds, to humans
(d) Ozone is not designated as chemical weed

28. Blue baby syndrome is caused by:
(a) Cadmium pollution
(b) Mercury poisoning
(c) Chronic exposure to arsenic
(d) Excessive nitrate in drinking water

29. In Bhopal gas tragedy, the gas released was:
(a) Methyl isocyanate (b) Ethyl isocyanate
(c) Sodium isocyanate (d) Potassium isocyanate

30. In India, the Air Prevention and Control of Pollution Act came into force in ____**A**____ but was amended in ____**B**____ to include ____**C**____ as an air pollutant:

	A	B	C
(a)	1980	1987	Radioactive
(b)	1981	1987	Noise
(c)	1974	1986	Noise
(d)	1981	1987	Soil

31. Slash and burn agriculture is associated with:
(a) Deforestation
(b) Jhum cultivation
(c) Shifting cultivation
(d) All of the above

32. Which of the following is not an influence of UV-B radiation on health?
(a) Ageing of skin (b) Snow blindness
(c) Skin cancer (d) Depigmentation

33. The unique idea of integrated organic farming was executed by:
(a) Ramesh Chandra Dagar
(b) Ahmed Khan
(c) Amrita Devi
(d) Sunder Lal Bahuguna

34. E-waste generated in developed countries is used by developing countries for the recovery of:
(a) Gold (b) Nickel
(c) Copper (d) All of the above

35. Pollutants from human activities like effluents from industries and homes can radically accelerate the ageing of lakes, which is known as:
(a) Rising eutrophication
(b) Cultural eutrophication
(c) Accelerated eutrophication
(d) All except (a)

36. Greenhouse flux is:
(a) Downward flux of long-wave radiation by greenhouse gases
(b) Cyclical zero waste procedure where waste products from one process are cycled as nutrients for another process
(c) Increase in average temperate of the globe
(d) Enhancement in bitumen's water repellant properties

37. High concentration of DDT in birds disturbs the metabolism of:
(a) Magnesium (b) Iron
(c) Calcium (d) Phosphorus

38. A dental disease is characterised by the mottling of teeth due to the presence of a certain chemical element in drinking water. What is that element?
(a) Boron (b) Chlorine
(c) Fluorine (d) Mercury

39. Biologists celebrate 5th June as:
(a) World Population Day
(b) World Environment Day
(c) World Ozone Day
(d) World Biodiversity Day

40. If there were no CO_2 in the earth's atmosphere, the temperature of earth's surroundings would be:
(a) Higher than the present
(b) Lower than the present
(c) The same
(d) Dependent on the amount of oxygen in the atmosphere

41. Maximum threat to the survival of life on earth is from:
(a) Deforestation and desertification
(b) Increase in urbanisation
(c) Air pollution
(d) Increase in radioactivity

42. In domestic sewage, impurities in the form of suspended solids, colloidal materials and dissolved materials are about:
(a) 0.5 ppm (b) 5.0 ppm
(c) 15 ppm (d) 25.0 ppm

43. A disease caused by eating fish contaminated by industrial waste containing mercury compounds is:
(a) Black foot disease (b) Minamata disease
(c) Hashimoto disease (d) Osteosclerosis

44. Most important causative pollutant of soil may be:
(a) Plastics (b) Iron junks
(c) Detergents (d) Glass junks

45. The sound level which is considered harmful:
(a) Above 40 dB (b) Above 60 dB
(c) Above 80 dB (d) Above 120 dB

ANSWER KEYS

Exercises

1. (a)	**2.** (c)	**3.** (d)	**4.** (d)	**5.** (c)	**6.** (b)	**7.** (c)	**8.** (a)	**9.** (b)	**10.** (a)
11. (c)	**12.** (b)	**13.** (d)	**14.** (d)	**15.** (a)	**16.** (b)	**17.** (d)	**18.** (c)	**19.** (d)	**20.** (a)
21. (b)	**22.** (b)	**23.** (b)	**24.** (a)	**25.** (d)	**26.** (b)	**27.** (a)	**28.** (d)	**29.** (d)	**30.** (c)
31. (a)	**32.** (a)	**33.** (d)	**34.** (c)	**35.** (d)	**36.** (a)	**37.** (c)	**38.** (c)	**39.** (b)	**40.** (a)
41. (c)	**42.** (a)	**43.** (d)	**44.** (b)	**45.** (c)	**46.** (c)	**47.** (c)	**48.** (c)	**49.** (b)	**50.** (a)
51. (c)	**52.** (d)	**53.** (b)	**54.** (c)	**55.** (c)	**56.** (b)	**57.** (a)	**58.** (a)	**59.** (a)	**60.** (a)
61. (d)	**62.** (b)	**63.** (c)	**64.** (c)	**65.** (c)	**66.** (d)	**67.** (b)	**68.** (d)	**69.** (b)	**70.** (c)

71. (a)	**72.** (b)	**73.** (d)	**74.** (c)	**75.** (c)	**76.** (b)	**77.** (a)	**78.** (b)	**79.** (b)	**80.** (a)
81. (c)	**82.** (d)	**83.** (a)	**84.** (d)	**85.** (b)	**86.** (a)	**87.** (c)	**88.** (d)	**89.** (b)	**90.** (a)
91. (c)	**92.** (d)	**93.** (c)	**94.** (b)	**95.** (d)	**96.** (d)	**97.** (b)	**98.** (a)	**99.** (b)	**100.** (b)
101. (b)	**102.** (d)	**103.** (c)	**104.** (d)	**105.** (a)	**106.** (d)	**107.** (c)	**108.** (a)	**109.** (c)	

NCERT Exemplar Questions

1. (c)	**2.** (a)	**3.** (d)	**4.** (b)	**5.** (c)	**6.** (d)	**7.** (a)	**8.** (c)	**9.** (c)	**10.** (a)
11. (d)	**12.** (d)	**13.** (b)	**14.** (a)	**15.** (a)	**16.** (a)	**17.** (d)	**18.** (a)	**19.** (d)	**20.** (a)
21. (c)	**22.** (b)								

Practice Test Paper

1. (c)	**2.** (b)	**3.** (c)	**4.** (d)	**5.** (d)	**6.** (a)	**7.** (b)	**8.** (d)	**9.** (d)	**10.** (c)
11. (a)	**12.** (c)	**13.** (c)	**14.** (c)	**15.** (a)	**16.** (a)	**17.** (a)	**18.** (b)	**19.** (d)	**20.** (b)
21. (b)	**22.** (d)	**23.** (c)	**24.** (b)	**25.** (c)	**26.** (a)	**27.** (c)	**28.** (d)	**29.** (a)	**30.** (b)
31. (d)	**32.** (d)	**33.** (a)	**34.** (d)	**35.** (d)	**36.** (a)	**37.** (c)	**38.** (c)	**39.** (b)	**40.** (b)
41. (d)	**42.** (d)	**43.** (b)	**44.** (a)	**45.** (c)					

SOLUTIONS

1. The Government of India passed the Environment (Protection) Act in 1986 to protect and improve the quality of the environment.
2. DDT is a non-biodegradable pollutant. Non-biodegradable pollutants are not degraded and often get biologically magnified.
3. Thermal power plant
4. Quantitative pollutants become pollutants only when their concentration reaches beyond a critical value in the environment. For example, CO, CO_2, NOX, etc.
5. Reaction between two or more primary pollutants gives rise to secondary pollutants; for example, PAN, ozone.
6. Domestic waste is a biodegradable pollutant and easily decomposed by a natural process.
7. According to CPCB, the particulate size 2.5 μm or less in diameter is responsible for the greatest harm to human health.
8. Electrostatic precipitator has an electrode wire that is maintained at several thousand volts which produces a corona that releases electrons.
9. A – Scrubber, B – Electrostatic precipitator Scrubbers are used to remove gases like SO_2 from industrial exhausts, while the electro static precipitator is an electrical device used to remove particulate matter present in the exhaust of thermal power plants.
10. 5–20 μm
11. More than 99% of particulate matter can be removed by the electrostatic precipitator. It has electrode wires which are provided with an electric current of several thousand volts, which produce a corona that releases electrons. Electrons attach to dust particles and give them a negative charge. Collecting plates are grounded so that they attract the charged dust particles.
12. The scrubber is used to remove SO_2 from industrial effluents. The exhaust is passed through a slurry of water and crushed limestone ($CaCO_3$). The calcium in limestone combines chemically with the sulphur to produce $CaSO_4$, which is separately collected.
13. Advantage of CNG over diesel or petrol: (i) It is cheaper; (ii) It burns more efficiently without leaving any unburnt remnant; (iii) It cannot be siphoned off by thieves and adulterated like petrol or diesel.
14. SO_2 inhibits ETS in plants damaging the membrane system and is responsible for phaeophytization in lichens.

15. Photochemical smog is a mixture of air pollutants that have been chemically altered into further noxious compounds by exposure to sunlight. The main components of photochemical smog are nitrogen oxides, volatile organic compounds, ozone and PAN.

16. Carbon monoxide produces carboxy haemoglobin, which is responsible for the oxygen carrying capacity of blood.

17. The Air Prevention and Control of Pollution Act came into force in 1981.

18. Catalytic converters have expensive metals like platinum-palladium and rhodium as catalysts.

19. In vehicles, catalytic converters are used (i) to convert unburnt hydrocarbons into CO_2 and water vapour; (ii) to covert nitrogen oxides into free nitrogen; (iii) to convert carbon monoxide into carbon dioxide.

20. CO_2 and nitrogen gas, respectively

21. Lichens are sensitive to atmospheric pollution, especially SO_2. If the air is very badly polluted with SO_2, there may be no lichens present. So, lichens are widely used as bio-indicators of SO_2 pollution.

22. Acid rain is a result of air pollution. Some gases, especially nitrogen oxide and SO_2, react with tiny droplets of water in clouds to form sulphuric and nitric acids. The rain from these clouds then falls as very weak acid, which is why it is known as acid rain.

23. In 1987, an important amendment to the Air Act 1981 was made and noise was recognised as an air pollutant.

24. The Taj Mahal of Agra is affected by SO_2.

25. Acid rain has a pH below 5.65.

26. Large green plants are planted in high noise pollution zones because they have the capacity to absorb sound waves. These green plants which are responsible for checking noise pollution are called green mufflers.

27. Any value more than 80 dB causes noise pollution.

28. Lead is an elemental heavy metal found naturally in the environment as well as in manufactured products. Lead can be released directly into the air as suspended particles.

29. Noise is measured by a sound meter and is expressed in a unit called decibel (dB).

30. Carbon monoxide has 200 times more affinity than oxygen for haemoglobin.

31. Pollen grains is one of the most common triggers of seasonal allergies. Pollen allergy is also known as seasonal allergic rhinitis.

32. Photochemical smog has mainly O_3, PAN and NOX.

33. All the statements are correct.

34. Classical smog occurs in a cool, humid climate. Its components include smoke, fog and SO_2. It is reducing in nature. It lacks secondary pollutants like PAN, ozone, etc.

35. (A), (B) and (C) are correct.

Water Pollution and its Control, Domestic Sewage, Industrial Effluents, Eutrophication, Case Study of Integrated Waste Water Treatment

36. A mere 0.1% of impurities makes domestic sewage unfit for human use.

37. The Government of India passed the Water (Prevention and Control of Pollution) Act 1974 to safeguard our water resources.

38. Eutrophication is the natural ageing of a lake by biological enrichment of its water.

39. The accelerated ageing of lakes due to sewage and agricultural and industrial wastes is called cultural or accelerated eutrophication.

40. In clean water, the concentration of BOD is low and DO is high. Heavily polluted water has very low DO content.

41. Water is often treated with chlorine to kill germs.

42. The amount of oxygen required for microbial breakdown of biodegradable organic matter is called BOD. BOD in river water increases when sewage gets mixed with it.

43. (A), (B) and (C) are correct. Domestic sewage contains nutrients like nitrogen and phosphorus which favour the excessive growth of planktonic

algae, called algal bloom. This imparts a distinct colour to water bodies. Algal bloom causes fish mortality and deterioration of water quality.

44. *Eichhornia crassipes* (Water hyacinth) is the world's most problematic aquatic weed. It grows abundantly in eutrophic water bodies and imbalances the water ecosystem.

45. Thermal waste water eliminates or reduces the number of organisms sensitive to high temperature and may enhance the growth of plants and fish in extremely cold areas.

46. A denotes dissolved oxygen.

47. Presence of *E. coli* indicates pollution by faecal matter.

48. The most common cause of blue baby syndrome is water contaminated with nitrates. After a baby drinks nitrate-rich water, the body converts the nitrates into nitrites. These nitrites bind to the haemoglobin in the body, forming methemoglobin, which is unable to carry oxygen. It damages the respiratory and vascular systems and sometimes causes suffocation.

49. Larva of stone fly

50. Mercury – Minamata disease, Cadmium – Itai-Itai, Arsenic – Black foot disease, Nitrate – Methemoglobinemia

51. MIC (Methyl isocyanate) is concerned with the Bhopal gas tragedy. On the night of 2–3 December, 1984, the Union Carbide pesticide plant released approximately 40 tonnes of toxic methyl isocyanate gas.

52. Exposure to high concentrations of fluoride is the reason for a serious disease called fluorosis. It is categorised as skeletal and dental fluorosis. Dental fluorosis is a major adverse effect due to fluoride contamination in water.

53. High BOD value indicates that the water is being contaminated with sewage.

54. Depletion of oxygen

55. Use of pesticides is problematic as their residue persists in water and environment aquatic microorganisms absorb them in fats and oil. Fish feeding on these plankton further concentrate these pesticides in their tissues (biological magnification).

56. Detergents are the major source of phosphate pollution in water bodies.

57. Toxic heavy metals having density of more than 5 g/cm^3

58. It is due to non-availability of oxygen.

59. DDT gets accumulated in the adipose tissue of the organism and shows biological magnification in the aquatic food chain. The concentration of DDT increases at successive trophic levels and is ultimately the highest in fish-eating birds.

60. The main theme of *Silent Spring* is the destruction of the delicate balance of nature by the wholesale use of insecticides (DDT).

61. Biological magnification is defined as increase in the concentration of non-biodegradable pollutants as they pass through the food chain.

62. DDT cannot be metabolised or excreted; therefore it gets accumulated in an organism in the fat deposit tissues as it is liposoluble.

63. DDT disturbs calcium metabolism in birds, which causes thinning of egg shell and their premature breaking, eventually causing decline in bird populations.

64. DDT is a non-biodegradable pesticide.

65. Lead concentration in blood is considered alarming if it is 30 µg /100 ml.

66. All the statements are correct.

67. The cleaning occurs in two stages: (i) The conventional sedimentation filtration and chlorine treatment was given. (ii) Appropriate plants algae, fungi and bacteria were grown in marshland through which water was flowed. They neutralise, absorb and assimilate the pollutants and purify the water naturally.

68. Eco-sanitation is a practical, hygienic and efficient method of waste disposal. It is cost effective, in which human excreta is recycled into natural fertiliser to replace the chemical fertiliser.

69. FOAM (Friends of Arcata Marsh) is a citizens group responsible for the integrated process of sewage and water treatment.

70. Measuring BOD is a method used for estimating the amount of organic matter in sewage water.

71. Reduction of soil fertility due to loss of the top fertile layer is called negative soil pollution.

72. Negative soil pollution is due to intensive agriculture, faulty irrigation, soil erosion, deforestation, etc. Addition of insecticide, pesticides and other chemicals causes positive soil pollution.

73. Third pollution is also called landscape pollution, which is caused by throwing rubbish, waste and garbage over land and results in the conversion of fertile land into barren areas.

74. Soil fertility is depleted due to intensive agriculture.

75. Ahmed Khan found the ideal solution for the ever-increasing problem of plastic waste.

76. Safe disposal of nuclear waste is the major problem of radioactive waste.

77. Polyblend is a fine powder of recycled and modified plastic. This power is mixed with bitumen and used to lay roads.

78. Landfills cause underground water pollution. Solid waste is divided into three categories, biodegradable, non-biodegradable and recyclable. Irreparable computers and other electronic goods are called e-waste.

79. Integrated organic farming is maximum utilisation of resources.

80. Incineration is the controlled aerobic combustion of solid waste at a temperature of 850°C–1000°C.

81. The use of incinerators is crucial to the disposal of hospital waste.

82. Two serious problems arise from the use of nuclear energy: (1) accidental leakage, (2) safe disposal of nuclear waste.

83. Chernobyl disaster in Ukraine was caused by accidental leakage of nuclear reactor.

84. Radioactive pollutants (nuclear waste) should be pretreated and stored in shielded containers and then buried about 500 m deep below the earth's surface.

85. Eco-sanitation is a sustainable system for handling human excreta.

86. Option (a) is correct.

87. Without greenhouse effect, the average temperature on the earth's surface would have been a chilly -18°C rather than the present average of 15°C.

88. CO_2 and N_2O. Other greenhouse gases are methane and CFCs.

89. The most effective greenhouse gas is CO_2.

90. CFCs 14%, N_2O 6%, CO_2 60%, CH_4 20%

91. USA and China are the world's largest contributing countries to CO_2 emissions.

92. N_2O - 6%, CH_4 - 20%, total = 26%

93. Rise in temperature will lead to increased melting of polar ice caps, which will cause rise in sea level and many coastal areas will be submerged.

94. Increase in CO_2 concentration in the atmosphere increases productivity of C_3 plants and decreases rate of transpiration due to partial closure of stomata.

95. (A), (B), (C) are correct.

96. Good ozone is formed in the stratosphere and absorbs harmful UV radiations from the sun.

97. Ozone acts as chemical weed in the troposphere.

98. Thinning of ozone layer causes skin ageing, skin cell damage and skin cancers.

99. Antarctic region

100. Ozone hole

101. Jhum cultivation or slash and burn agriculture practiced in the north-eastern states of India has contributed to deforestation.

102. Option (d) is correct.

103. Chipko movement was started in Garhwal in 1974 by Sunder Lal Bahuguna to prevent cutting down of trees.

104. Jhum cultivation is related to deforestation.

105. Kyoto protocol (1987)

106. Joint forest management

107. World Environment Day is celebrated on 5 June every year.

108. An international treaty, the Montreal protocol, was signed at Montreal, Canada in 1987 to protect atmospheric ozone by limiting the production of ozone depleting substances (ODS).

109. Kyoto protocol was endorsed at CoP-3.